Composers' Intentions?

Composers' Intentions?
Lost Traditions of Musical Performance

Andrew Parrott

THE BOYDELL PRESS

© Andrew Parrott 2015

All Rights Reserved. Except as permitted under current legislation no part of this work may be photocopied, stored in a retrieval system, published, performed in public, adapted, broadcast, transmitted, recorded or reproduced in any form or by any means, without the prior permission of the copyright owner

The right of Andrew Parrott to be identified as the author of this work has been asserted in accordance with sections 77 and 78 of the Copyright, Designs and Patents Act 1988

First published 2015
The Boydell Press, Woodbridge

ISBN 978 1 78327 032 3

The Boydell Press is an imprint of Boydell & Brewer Ltd
PO Box 9, Woodbridge, Suffolk IP12 3DF, UK
and of Boydell & Brewer Inc.
668 Mount Hope Ave, Rochester, NY 14620–2731, USA

website: www.boydellandbrewer.com

A catalogue record for this book is available from the British Library

The publisher has no responsibility for the continued existence or accuracy of URLs for external or third-party internet websites referred to in this book, and does not guarantee that any content on such websites is, or will remain, accurate or appropriate

This publication is printed on acid-free paper

Designed and typeset in Adobe Warnock Pro
by David Roberts, Pershore, Worcestershire

Contents

List of Illustrations   *vii*
Preface   *ix*

INTRODUCTION

1 Composers' Intentions, Performers' Responsibilities   *1*

VOCAL SCORING

2 A Brief Anatomy of Choirs   *16*
3 Falsetto Beliefs: The 'Countertenor' Cross-Examined   *46*
4 Falsetto and the French: 'Une toute autre marche'   *122*

MONTEVERDI

5 Transposition in Monteverdi's Vespers of 1610   *146*
6 Monteverdi's Vespers of 1610 Revisited   *194*
7 Monteverdi: Onwards and Downwards   *205*
8 High Clefs and Down-to-Earth Transposition: A Brief Defence of Monteverdi   *228*

PURCELL

9 Performing Purcell   *237*

J. S. BACH

10 How Many Singers?   *287*
11 Vocal Ripienists and J. S. Bach's Mass in B minor   *290*
12 Bach's Chorus: The Leipzig Line   *328*

MISSING MUSIC

13 J. S. Bach's *Trauer-Music* for Prince Leopold: Clarification and Reconstruction   *347*

MISCELLANEOUS

14 Performing Machaut's Mass on Record   *361*
15 'Grett and solompne singing':
    Instruments in English Church Music before the Civil War   *368*
16 Monteverdi's *L'Orfeo*   *381*
17 Purcell's *Dido & Aeneas* on Record   *385*
18 'Hail! bright Cecilia' (Purcell at 350)   *391*

Selected Recordings   *397*
Further Writings   *398*
Index   *399*

Illustrations

2.1 Woodcut from Arnolt Schlick, *Spiegel der Orgelmacher und Organisten* (Mainz/Speyer, 1511), showing a straight cornett, organ and singers (three boys and two men); London, British Library MS Hirsch I.546 © The British Library Board — 21

2.2 (*top*) 'View of the ORCHESTRA and Performers in Westminster Abbey' (drawing by E. F. Burney, engraving by J. Collyer); (*bottom*) 'Plan of the Orchestra and Disposition of the Band'; both from Charles Burney, *An Account of the Musical Performances ... in Commemoration of Handel* (London, 1785) — 43

3.1 The Guidonian Hand, from Lorenzo Penna, *Li primi albori musicali* (Bologna, 1672), 9 — 50

3.2 Detail from a miniature by Robinet Testard, from *Des Eschez amoureux et des echez d'amours*, F-Pn MS fr. 143 (*c.* 1500), fol. 66. Bibliothèque nationale de France — 65

3.3 H. Battre, *Gaude virgo mater Christi*, I-TRmp 87, fols. 262v–263 © Castello del Buonconsiglio, Trento, Italy — 70–1

3.4 Title-page from Andrea Antico, *Canzoni nove* (Rome, 1510). Universitätsbibliothek Basel, Sign. kk II 32 — 113

5.1 Two-manual harpsichord by Joannes Ruckers, 1638 (Russell Collection, University of Edinburgh) — 157

5.2 Simone Verovio, *Diletto spirituale* (Rome, 1586), for voices, keyboard and lute; London, British Library, MS K.8.d.8, fol. 19 © The British Library Board — 162–3

7.1 'Modi tutti da sonar il cornetto', from Aurelio Virgiliano, *Il dolcimelo* (MS, *c.* 1590), [105] — 208

8.1 The Gospel organ (1596) by Baldassarre Malamini in the Basilica di San Petronio, Bologna, showing its three split keys: $D\#/E\flat$, $G\#/A\flat$ and $d\#/e\flat$. Photograph by Mario Berardi, ©Fondazione Carisbo, Bologna — 232

9.1 [?Henry Purcell], 'Rules for Graces', in *The Harpsichord Master* (London, 1697) — 242

12.1 Fold-out illustration from Christian Siegismund Georgi, *Wittenbergische Jubel-Geschichte* (Wittenberg, 1756); London, British Library MS 9930, fol. 34(1) © The British Library Board — 340–1

12.2 Detail from C. S. Georgi, *Wittenbergische Jubel-Geschichte*, showing the musical ensemble — 342

13.1 Title-page of the libretto [by Picander] of J. S. Bach's *Trauer-Music* for Prince Leopold [1729]. Landeshauptarchiv Sachsen-Anhalt, Abteilung Dessau   348

15.1 Details from the case of a chamber organ by Christianus Smith (1643) (Photograph by John Mander)   371

The author and publishers are grateful to all the institutions and individuals listed for permission to reproduce the materials in which they hold copyright. Every effort has been made to trace the copyright holders; apologies are offered for any omission, and the publishers will be pleased to add any necessary acknowledgement in subsequent editions.

Preface

To what extent can the performance intentions of long-dead composers be reliably known, and how integral to their compositions might such intentions have been? The experience of planning and directing musical performances has never ceased to confront me with awkward musical questions of this kind, from my earliest efforts (as a first-year undergraduate in 1967) to my present work. And, since vocal music was central to most earlier periods of music-making, it is natural that many of those difficult questions should concern vocal practices. Do we even fully understand what a 'choir' might have been? Has falsetto singing really been around since the Middle Ages, and what exactly was the French *haute-contre*? What does high-clef notation imply, not least in the case of Monteverdi's 1610 Magnificat (*a7*)? Were Purcell's countertenors 'countertenors' in today's sense? If much of Bach's choral writing was designed for one voice per part, how was this supposed to work in practice? Complex issues of this nature, issues directly affecting perceptions of music we may think we know well, form the common thread running through these collected essays.

For the most part my researches have been driven by a performer's simple aspiration: to understand as fully as possible how composers of the more distant past intended their written works to function in performance. The intimate workings of those contemporary performances are, of course, lost for all time. Of certain underlying principles, however, there is plenty to be learned: not so much matters of style – the often barely definable characteristics of musical delivery – but rather those fundamental *pre*-performance factors that determine not only a composition's intended medium (the performing body) but also the multifarious conventions by which that composition is tacitly expected to operate.

The essays that together form this book were written over many years: some are from as long ago as 1977, others as recent as the present decade. After a brief introductory essay, they are arranged here in six thematic groups.

INTRODUCTION

The short article that forms Chapter 1, and from which the present book derives its title, was written to celebrate the 40th anniversary of *Early Music* in 2013, and is now supplied with fuller notes. It is a belated contribution to one of the furthest-reaching musical debates of the late 20th century – albeit a debate whose scholarly legacy may not extend much further than the so-called scare quotes now placed around the word 'authenticity'.

VOCAL SCORING

A full-length history of 'the choir' has yet to be written, but Chapter 2 offers a partial and highly condensed account, commissioned to open *The Cambridge Companion to Choral Music*. The essay draws attention to critical factors defining and differentiating some of the diverse musical bodies encompassed by the single word 'choir' prior to the emergence of the secular and amateur choirs that now predominate.

Chapter 3 addresses the uncertain pedigree of today's countertenor – an issue that has exercised me from the outset. In numerous talks I have attempted to convey how the disparate fragments of evidence may reasonably be pieced together to form a very different picture from the generally accepted one. Key findings – presented in published form for the first time in 2015 – are here supplemented by eight appendices.

One of the many occasions on which I put forward some of my ideas on falsetto singing was a 2002 Basel conference on early vocal practices. Faced with then having to organize the material for publication, however, I switched to the far more straightforward but equally necessary task of defining the 18th-century *haute-contre* – and in so doing became aware of just how valuable French sources could also be for the light they shed on the nature of the corresponding Italian *tenore*. The resulting essay is here published as Chapter 4.

MONTEVERDI

Brought together for the first time, the four essays forming Chapters 5–8 constitute an extensive survey of a single issue – albeit one with ramifications well beyond the particular work and period on which they focus. Certain puzzling discrepancies of vocal tessitura in Monteverdi's 1610 Vespers music had first struck me as a student singer. In due course I reached the conclusion that the composer's exceptional *high*-clef notation, like that of earlier repertories, must have implied a relatively *low* sounding pitch level – and thus, for instruments, the necessity of downward transposition. At a BBC Promenade performance in 1977 I therefore presented both the psalm *Lauda Jerusalem* and the Magnificat *a7* a 4th lower than the remaining items.

By 1984, and with the imminent release of a recording, it was clear that the reasoning behind these transpositions needed to be set out in full. The resultant account, Chapter 5, examines theoretical writings, performance instructions, instrumental transposition practices, discrepancies within and between musical sources, and in particular the 1610 Magnificat *a7*.

An opportunity to amplify my earlier conclusions, while at the same time answering a broad objection to them, arose with a London University conference in 1993 to mark the 350th anniversary of Monteverdi's death. The paper, which is printed here as Chapter 6, also briefly addresses questions of pitch standard and of the liturgical place of the *Sonata sopra Sancta Maria*.

A more specific challenge emerged in 2003, a full quarter of a century after the ideas had first been publicly aired. While acknowledging the principle of downward transposition, Roger Bowers now proposed a narrower interval: ↓2nd, rather than ↓4th. Chapter 7 reprints my prompt reply, introducing more than 20 fresh instances of the expected (wider) transposition, and demonstrating that the smaller interval was clearly reserved for *standard*-clef notation.

Chapter 8 is a short critique (2012) of further thoughts from Bowers. I include a table of no fewer than '100 documented cases of the explicit link between high-clef notation and transposition ↓4th (and ↓5th)'. Together with abundant evidence of significantly lower vocal scoring than is expected today, this might reasonably be thought to settle the matter.

PURCELL

1995 saw the 300th anniversary of Henry Purcell's death. In my youth the Purcell–Handel celebrations of 1959 had given me a memorable introduction to the music of both composers, but in the interim the revival of 'period' instruments had effected a transformation in performance styles. Despite many undeniable advances, however, it seemed to me that the distinctive character of Purcell's own music was at risk of being masked by an all-purpose Handelian manner of performance. My contribution to *The Purcell Companion* (1995) therefore sought to gather together as much detailed information as possible about musical performance in late 17th-century England, from the nature of keyboard instruments and temperaments to matters of continuo practice, pitch and vibrato – and, of course, voices in general and the 'countertenor' in particular. In order to extend the usefulness of this survey, a list of more recent literature has now been added.

J. S. BACH

One of the longest-running musical controversies of recent times has been the issue of Bach's choir: were there several singers per part, or just one? Here I have resisted the temptation to retrace my early steps in that discussion, and have chosen instead to present three diverse items which complement and supplement *The Essential Bach Choir* (2000), the full-length study I completed just in time for the 250th anniversary of Bach's death.

Specifically designed as a layman's guide to the 'debate', Chapter 10 provides a very brief overview. It picks up the story in 2000, and stands here as a general introduction to the later and decidedly more substantial contribution presented in Chapter 11. This gives a systematic examination of each of the Mass in B minor's 16⁺ choruses in the light of traditional 18th-century concertist/ripienist practice, so as to leave the reader better placed to assess whether or not this 'great' work carries any indications of vocal forces that are exceptionally 'great' (numerically) in Bach's terms. Originally a paper for a Belfast symposium in 2007 ('Understanding Bach's B-minor Mass'), the chapter includes an appendix which both reviews key arguments and introduces some 20 new items of evidence.

A further Bach conference (at Leuven in 2008, and in honour of Sigiswald Kuijken) was the stimulus for the essay in Chapter 12, which sums up the divergent thinking at the heart of this 30-year-old 'debate'. Abiding misconceptions on the part of influential Bach scholars are demonstrated in case studies dealing with 'new' parts to BWV23 and a fresh record of contemporary singer/instrumentalist ratios.

MISSING MUSIC

Unlike most other items in the present collection, Chapter 13's study of an extended lost work by J. S. Bach has little to do with issues of performance practice; rather it is concerned with the shape and content of the composition itself. More specifically, it not only explores how Bach intended the four parts of his *Trauer-music* to serve the elaborate funeral ceremonies for Prince Leopold, but also identifies possible music for the one truly 'missing' chorus.

MISCELLANEOUS

In this handful of shorter items previous themes recur in the context of particular major works – by Machaut (Chapter 14), Monteverdi (Chapter 16) and Purcell (Chapters 17 and 18). (Each of the works in question has been recorded by the Taverner Choir, Consort & Players at one time or another; see the list of 'Selected Recordings' at the end of this volume.) The one exception, Chapter 15, looks at the occasional use of wind – and stringed? – instruments in Anglican church music of the decades immediately before and after 1600. To this 1978 article, which was based on an even earlier broadcast for BBC Radio 3, I have added a postscript in the wake of a Cambridge conference (2013) on the English verse anthem.

To all those friends and colleagues, scholars, performers, librarians, editors and others who contributed in various ways to the preparation of the individual essays I renew my thanks; I am also grateful to the original publishers for granting permission for the essays to be reprinted here. For their assistance with putting together the present volume I am indebted, in particular, to Marianne Fisher, Hugh Griffith, Michael Middeke, Pippa Thynne and Emily Van Evera.

Andrew Parrott
January 2015

1

Composers' Intentions, Performers' Responsibilities

> ... how can a piece of music have the effect its author has sought to achieve if it is not also set up and performed in accordance with the wishes of the same and in conformity with his intentions?
>
> (J. A. Scheibe, 1740)[1]

WHEN the first issue of *Early Music* appeared in 1973, its intended readership of 'listeners, performers and instrument makers ... scholars and students' may well have shared at least one broad understanding:[2] that the recent ground-swell of interest in 'pre-Classical' music had been due in no small measure to the efforts of performers (and instrument builders) in learning and adopting earlier practices. Or, to put it another way: that the exploration of earlier performance styles and conventions was not merely of academic value but had opened up something of practical significance, with the capacity to breathe new life into forgotten repertories and familiar masterpieces, and to illuminate what composers themselves may have intended with their music.

By the early 1980s this surge of enthusiastic activity had met with vociferous opposition from certain quarters. The attempt to identify and then emulate the sort of performance a composer may have intended was a naïve and anti-musical goal, neither achievable nor desirable, a fool's errand and a recipe for soulless music-making. A new orthodoxy duly emerged (and still prevails), which runs roughly as follows. Since the musical intentions of long-dead composers remain largely unknowable and may in any case be deemed no longer 'relevant', those who nevertheless choose to perform their music bear no real responsibilities toward its composers, only toward themselves and today's audiences: the performer's job (as Richard Taruskin has put it) is simply 'to discover ... how we really like it'.[3]

First appeared in *Early Music* 41/1 (2013), 37–43.

---

[1] '... wie kann ein musikalisches Stücke diejenige Wirkung thun, welche der Verfasser desselben zu erreichen gesuchet hat, wenn es nicht auch nach dem Sinne desselben, und seinen Absichten gemäß, bestellet und aufgeführet wird?'; Johann Adolph Scheibe, *Der Critische Musikus* (Hamburg, 1740), 709–10. Scheibe is remembered as a writer of musical criticism but was also both a composer and a *Capellmeister*.

[2] John M. Thomson, *Early Music* 1/3 (1973), 129.

[3] Richard Taruskin, 'The Pastness of the Present', in *Authenticity and Early Music*, ed. N. Kenyon (1988), 203.

Amongst the myriad questions that immediately arise are these:

- how unknowable are a composer's intentions?
- in what sense is the notion of a composition separable from the sort(s) of performance envisaged for it by its composer?
- why do we bother with the works of composers whose musical intentions are in large part believed to be no longer relevant?
- given that individual taste varies, does discovering 'how we really like it' mean tailoring a composer's work to satisfy any and every taste, or merely popular taste?
- is it unreasonable of today's audiences to expect that specialist performers (of any repertory), before determining their own performance intentions, will have seriously examined those of the composer whose work they use?
- what views on such matters did earlier composers and their fellow performers hold?

Only the last of these questions will be addressed here, not least because the opinions of early writers have so rarely been canvassed; in *Authenticity and Early Music* (1988), for example, none appears in any of its seven contributions (though both Schoenberg and Stravinsky are liberally quoted).[4] It should come as no surprise, however, to learn that the vital but intricate nature of the relationship between composer and performer has long exercised musicians. Johann Mattheson, a man of vast experience in both capacities, concluded his encyclopedic survey of the art of a Director of Music (*Der vollkommene Capellmeister*) with these words:

> someone who has never discovered what the writer of a piece himself might dearly want will scarcely be able to represent it well; instead he will often deprive the thing of its true vigour and charm, to such an extent that the author, should he himself be among the listeners, would probably hardly recognize his own work.
>
> (Mattheson, 1739)[5]

---

[4] *Authenticity and Early Music*, ed. Kenyon (1988).

[5] '… wer nie erfahren hat, wie es der Verfasser selber gerne haben mögte, wird es schwerlich gut heraus bringen, sondern dem Dinge die wahre Krafft und Anmuth offt dergestalt benehmen, daß der Autor, wenn ers selber mit anhören sollte, sein eigenes Werck kaum kennen dürffte'; Johann Mattheson, *Der vollkommene Capellmeister* (Hamburg, 1739), 484.

THE WRITTEN WORK

COMPOSERS, naturally enough, have always tended to be protective of what they have written –

> I have made a song at your request ... I beg that you deign to hear it, and be acquainted with the thing just as it is, without adding or taking away
>
> (Guillaume de Machaut, c. 1363)[6]

– and particularly so when, with 'copies passing from hand to hand', even the safe transmission of an accurate musical text could not be guaranteed:

> a smal oversight committed by the first writer, by the second will bee made worse, which will give occasion to the third to alter much both in the wordes and notes, according as shall seeme best to his owne judgement, though (God knowes) it will be far enough from the meaning of the author ...
>
> (Morley, 1597)[7]

One way around this particular problem was to go into print, as Schütz chose to do on discovering

> just how many such compositions of mine were being carelessly and imperfectly copied and spread around from time to time (as is then often the case), even ending up in the hands of eminent *Musici*.
>
> (Schütz, 1647)[8]

A reliable musical text clearly mattered to its composer, but how much detailed guidance for the performer can any such source be expected to convey?

> All composers who wish their work to be executed as well as possible must seize every opportunity to achieve this end. In general they must therefore explain themselves in their notation with such clarity that they can be understood at every single point.
>
> (C. P. E. Bach, 1762)[9]

---

[6] '... iay fait un chant a vostre commandement ... Si vous suppli que vous le daigniez oir et savoir la chose einsi comme elle est faite sanz mettre ne oster'; Guillaume de Machaut, letter to Peronnelle D'Armentières [Reims, c. 1363]; D. Leech-Wilkinson, 'Le Voir Dit and La Messe de Nostre Dame: Aspects of Genre and Style in Late Works of Machaut', *Plainsong and Medieval Music* 2 (1993), 50.

[7] Thomas Morley, *A Plaine and Easie Introduction to Practicall Musicke* (London, 1597), 151.

[8] '... wie viel Stücken solcher meiner Composition (wie dann zu geschehen gepfleget) unfleißig und mangelhafft abgeschrieben/ hinn und wieder außgestreuet/ und fürnehmen Musicis auch in die Hände gerathen weren'; Heinrich Schütz, *Symphoniae sacrae* ii (Dresden, 1647), preface.

[9] 'Jeder Componist, welcher wünschet, daß seine Arbeit so gut als möglich ausgeführet werde, muß auch alle Mittel ergreifen, diesen Endzweck zu

Bach is here referring to the figuring of a bass part, and in this respect his ideal (of harmonic completeness) is perfectly attainable, but other areas of notation rarely prove so obliging, even at a quite rudimentary level. 'Since I cannot be present myself', wrote Haydn in a letter despatched with the score of his *Applausus* cantata (1768) to a monastery in Lower Austria, 'I have found that one or two explanations are needed': in accompanied recitatives the orchestra's cadences are to be delayed, 'even though the contrary is often shown in the score', and with certain appoggiaturas one of the written notes is always to be 'left out entirely'.[10]

Clarification of notational ambiguities of this sort and the faithful reproduction of a written composition (in one form or another) have long been major scholarly preoccupations, yet the large corner of the composer's mind that concerned itself with the final *performed* composition has commonly been assumed to lie almost exclusively beyond the reach of scholarship. Although the importance of tempo, for example, is generally acknowledged (since it plays such a readily identifiable role in defining musical character), only the most approximate tempo can be safely inferred from a time signature, a dance metre, a sung text or even a special instruction. Machaut could therefore do little more than ask for his song to be sung 'in goodly long measure',[11] and Haydn for some of his allegros be taken 'a bit more briskly than is otherwise customary'.[12] In even less specific terms Nicolas Lebègue merely hoped

> that all those who will do me the honour of playing these pieces may wish to play them according to my intention, that is to say ... with the proper tempo for each piece ...
>
> (Lebègue, 1676)[13]

This notational deficiency almost certainly contributed to the poor reception of Lully's compositions when they were first performed outside

---

erlangen. Er muß sich also überhaupt in der Schreibart so deutlich erklären, daß er an einem jeden Orte verstanden werden könne'; C. P. E. Bach, *Versuch über die wahre Art das Clavier zu spielen* ii (Berlin, 1762), 300.

[10] '*Weilen Ich bey diesen Applaus nicht selbst zu gegen seyn kan, habe ein und andere Ercklärungen vor nöthig gefunden*'; Joseph Haydn, *Applausus*, ed. H. C. Robbins Landon (*c.* 1969), preface.

[11] '*... de bien longue mesure*'; Leech-Wilkinson, '*Le Voir Dit*', 50.

[12] '*... ist mir lieber, wan ein und anders Allegro etwas schärffer wie sonst gewähnlich Tractiret wird*'; Haydn, *Applausus*, ed. Robbins Landon, preface.

[13] '*Je souhaiterois fort que tous ceux qui me feront l'honneur de toucher ces pieces voulussent les joüer selon mon intention, c'est à dire ... avec le mouvement propre pour chaque piece*'; Nicolas Lebègue, *Les Pièces d'orgue* (Paris, 1676), preface. Lebègue's most frequent indications are *gayement* and *gravement*, which (like *allegro* and *grave*) strictly denote character rather than speed.

France, 'robbed of their correct tempi and graces'.[14] The problem was (and is) a recurrent one:

> a Presto is often turned into an Allegretto and an Adagio into an Andante, which truly does a very great disservice to the composer, who cannot always be present.
>
> (Quantz, 1752)[15]

> However much trouble and care a good composer may take for an accurate performance of his piece, all his trouble to specify the tempo precisely and correctly will be in vain unless he himself is present each time at the performance of his piece of music; for, if his piece is performed in his absence by others, he cannot so easily rely on its being performed in the proper tempo that he had in mind.
>
> (Scheibe, 1773)[16]

FROM NOTATION TO PERFORMANCE

WHILE the eventual arrival of the metronome mitigated this particular problem, tempo – in terms of performance style – is but the tip of the iceberg. The Jesuit mathematician Louis Bertrand Castel hints at a much broader underlying conundrum:

> Musicians are never happy with the way people perform their works. Why then have they not put their meaning [*esprit*] into the notation?
>
> (Castel, 1735)[17]

To this the short answer is that a composer's 'meaning' necessarily extends far beyond the written composition and into the real or imagined

---

[14] Georg Muffat, *Florilegium Primum* (Augsburg, 1695), preface.

[15] 'Man weis, daß ... öfters aus einem Presto ein Allegretto, und aus einem Adagio ein Andante gemachet wird: welches doch dem Componisten, welcher nicht allezeit zugegen seyn kann, zum größten Nachtheile gereichet'; Johann Joachim Quantz, *Versuch einer Anweisung die Flöte traversiere zu spielen* (Berlin, 1752), 267–8.

[16] 'So viel Mühe und Vorsorge auch ein guter Componist für die Richtigkeit der Aufführung seines Stückes trägt, so wird er doch, um die Bewegung genau und richtig zu bestimmen, alle seine Mühe umsonst anwenden, wenn er nicht jedesmal selbst bey der Aufführung seiner Musikstücke gegenwärtig ist; denn, wird sein Stück in seiner Abwesenheit von andern aufgeführet: so kann er sich nicht so leicht darauf verlassen, daß es in der rechten Bewegung, die er in Gedanken gehabt hat, aufgeführet wird'; Johann Adolph Scheibe, *Ueber die Musikalische Composition* i (Leipzig, 1773), 299.

[17] 'Les Musiciens ne sont jamais contens de la maniere dont on execute leurs ouvrages: que n'ont-ils donc mis leur esprit dans la note?'; 'Suite & Cinquème Partie de Nouvelles Experiences d'Optique & d'Acoustique', *Mémoires pour l'histoire des sciences et des beaux-arts* (the so-called 'Journal de Trévoux' 35) (Paris, 1735), art. cxiii (November 1735), 2365–6.

performance idiom within which it was conceived, and which not even the most thorough musical notation can ever adequately convey. François Couperin (*le grand*) made this analogy:

> there is a great distance from Grammar to Declamation; there is also an infinite one between Notation and good playing-style.
>
> (Couperin, 1717)[18]

From the composer's perspective, performance style – broadly defined – was inseparable from the written work, and was vital to it. 'In music', declared J. S. Bach's friend Johann Abraham Birnbaum (a teacher of rhetoric at Leipzig University), 'everything depends on execution':

> a piece acknowledged to be composed with the most beautiful harmony and melody certainly cannot please the ear if those who are to execute it are neither able nor willing to discharge their obligations.
>
> (Birnbaum, 1738)[19]

The performer's contribution was critical but inevitably double-edged, since (in the words of Walter Porter) 'the Ignorant judge frequently by the Performance, not by the Composition'.[20] In a plea on behalf of his *Psalmes, Songs, and Sonnets* Byrd eloquently expresses the precariousness of the composer's position:

> Onely this I desire; that you will be but as carefull to heare them well expressed as I have been both in the Composing and correcting of them. Otherwise the best Song that ever was made will seeme harsh and unpleasant, for that the well expressing of them ... is the life of our labours ...
>
> (William Byrd, 1611)[21]

---

[18] '*Comme il y a une grande distance de la Grammaire, à la Déclamation; il y en a aussi une infinie entre la Tablature, et la façon de bien-joüer*'; François Couperin, *L'Art de toucher le clavecin* (Paris, 2/1717), preface.

[19] '*Es kommt ohne dem in der Music alles auf die execution an. ... Hingegen kann ein stück aus dessen composition man die schönste harmonie und melodie ersehen kann, alsdenn freylich dem gehör nicht gefallen, wenn die, so es executieren sollen ihre schuldigkeit weder beobachten können, noch wollen*'; Johann Abraham Birnbaum, *Unpartheyische Anmerckungen* [Leipzig, 1738], 20; *Bach-Dokumente* ii (1969), 302 (no. 409).

[20] Walter Porter, *Motetts of Two Voyces* (London, 1657), preface.

[21] William Byrd, *Psalmes, Songs, and Sonnets* (London, 1611), preface.

ORNAMENTATION

THE symbiotic relationship between composer and performer was always delicately balanced, and not least in the matter of unwritten ornamentation. Before the 19th century composers generally expected professional performers to know how and when to embellish their compositions – and when not to:

> While Josquin was living in Cambrai, when someone singing his music wanted to use embellishments and ornaments which he himself had not composed, he went into the choir and with everyone listening launched a fierce attack on the man, and then said: 'You ass, what are you adding an ornament for? If that's what I'd wanted, I'd have put it in myself. If you want to make changes in pieces that have been properly composed, write your own music, but kindly leave mine alone.'
>
> (Manlius, 1562)[22]

Contrapuntal writing was at particular risk from those who ornamented too elaborately:

> on occasion composers have avoided the opportunity to have some of their pieces sung, not wishing to hand them over and have them sung by singers like this; for the sole reason that they liked to hear them with plain and simple ornaments, so they could hear the artistic devices that they had used in weaving and constructing them.
>
> (Zacconi, 1592)[23]

In order not only to caution against excessive ornamentation, but also to influence its general nature, Giovanni Paolo Cima appended a courteous note to his *Concerti ecclesiastici*:

---

[22] 'Josquinus, vivens Cameraci, cum quidam vellet ei in suo cantu adhibere colores seu coloraturas, quas ipse non composuerat, ingressus est chorum, et acriter increpavit illum, omnibus audientibus, addens: Tu asine, quare addis coloraturam? Si mihi ea placuisset, inseruissem ipse. Si tu velis corrigere cantilenas recte compositas, facias tibi proprium cantum, sinas mihi meum incorrectum'; Johannes Manlius, *Locorum communium collectanea* (Basel, 1562), 542; R. Wegman, '"And Josquin laughed ...": Josquin and the Composer's Anecdote in the 16th Century', *Journal of Musicology* 17/3 (1999), 322. (For assistance with this and various other translations I am greatly indebted to Hugh Griffith.)

[23] '... io ho trouato alle volte i Compositori hauer fuggito l'occasione di far cantar alcune cose loro: per non farle cantare, & darle in mano à simili Cantori: non per altro solo perche haueano a piacere di sentirle con gli accenti schietti, & semplici: accioche s'udißero gli artificij con che le haueano tessute, & fatte'; Lodovico Zacconi, *Prattica di musica* i (Venice, 1592), fol. 64v (bk 1, ch. 66).

> I pray you, most gracious Sirs ... grant me the favour of singing them as they stand, in the most affecting way possible. Yet if the gentle singers should prefer to make some addition to them, could they kindly do this only with *accenti* and *trilli*.
>
> (G. P. Cima, 1610)[24]

Giovanni Maria Bononcini was rather more forthright:

> today there are some who have so little understanding of this art that whether singing or playing, they always want to be altering pieces – or rather mutilating them – with their erratic and ill-judged whims of bow or voice, however much care and attention has gone into the composition. As a result, authors have reached the point where they have to beg these singers and players to content themselves with rendering the works plainly and simply, exactly as they stand.
>
> (Bononcini, 1672)[25]

In Italian and Italianate music it nevertheless remained true that

> a great deal is left to the discretion and ability of the player. ... certain passages are purposely fashioned to be very plain and dry, in order to allow the performer the freedom to vary them more than once, according to his understanding and pleasure, so as always to surprise the listeners with new inventions.
>
> (Quantz, 1752)[26]

And under favourable circumstances the composer's trust in a performer could, of course, yield handsome dividends. On hearing Faustina Bordoni at a Venetian theatre in 1721 a German visitor reported that she

---

[24] '*Pregovi Gentilissimi Signori ... mi facciate gratia di cantarli come stanno, con quello maggiore affetto, che sia possibile. Et se pure alli leggiadri cantanti piacesse d'accrescerli qualche cosa; per cortesia lo faccino solo ne gli accenti, e trilli*'; Giovanni Paolo Cima, *Concerti ecclesiastici* (Milan, 1610), 'Alli benigni lettori'.

[25] '*... oggidi sono alcuni così poco intelligenti di quest'arte che ò cantando, ò sonando vogliono sempre co' loro sregolati & indiscreti capricci d'arco, ò di Voce, alterare, anzi deformare le Composizioni (quantunque fatte con tutto studio e applicazione) in modo che gli autori sono arrivati à dover pregare gli medesimi Cantanti e Sonatori, acciò si contentino di dire e di fare le cose schiettamente e puramente come per appunto stanno*'; Giovanni Maria Bononcini, *Sonate da chiesa a due violini*, op. 6 (Venice, 1672), preface.

[26] '*Bey der Musik nach italiänischem Geschmacke aber, wird vieles der Willkühr und Fähigkeit dessen der spielet, überlassen. ... [gewisse] Gänge, welche in der letztern mit Fleiß sehr simpel und trocken gesetzet werden, um dem Ausführer die Freyheit zu lassen, sie nach seiner Einsicht und Gefallen mehr als einmal verändern zu können, um die Zuhörer immer durch neue Erfindungen zu überraschen*'; Quantz, *Versuch*, 94 (ch. 10, §13).

indeed always sang the first part of an aria initially as the composer had written it, but when she repeated it at the da capo she did all kinds of *doublements* and *maniere* without losing the slightest precision with the accompaniment; in this way a composer finds his arias far more beautiful and pleasing in the throats of those that sing them than in his own original conception.

(Nemeitz, 1726)[27]

French ornamentation of the same period followed a different path:

pieces in French taste are mostly both characterized and fashioned with appoggiaturas and trills in such a way that one can do almost nothing more than what the composer has written.

(Quantz, 1752)[28]

Lully and his musicians each knew exactly where the other stood on the issue:

the instrumentalists scarcely dared to decorate anything. He would no more have tolerated this from them than he tolerated it from his singers. He thought it absolutely wrong that they should claim to know more about it than he did, and add ornaments to their written part.

(Le Cerf de la Viéville, 1705)[29]

The fastidiously expressed ornaments we find in Couperin's works clearly constituted an integral and inviolable part of the composition, despite which

I am always surprised, after the trouble I went to to indicate the appropriate ornaments for my pieces (which I have very clearly

---

[27] '[ich habe] die berühmte Faustinam gehöret, welche den vordersten Theil von einer Aria zwar allemahl erstlich so, wie sie der Componist gesetzt hatte, weg sang, wenn es aber da Capo kam, und sie solchen repetirte, so thate sie allehand doublements und manieren, ohne das geringste von der acuratesse des accompagnemens zu verlieren, hinzu; so, dass ein Componist selbsten seine Arien in der Kähle derjenigen, die sie hervor singen, zuweilen viel schöner und angenehmer findet, als in seiner eigenen Idée selbsten'; Johann Christian Nemeitz, *Nachlese besonderer Nachrichten von Italien* (Leipzig, 1726), 426.

[28] 'Denn die Stücke im französischen Geschmacke sind meistentheils charakterisiret, auch mit Vorschlägen und Trillern so gesetzet, daß fast nichts mehr, als was der Componist geschrieben hat, angebracht werden kann'; Quantz, *Versuch*, 94 (ch. 10, §13).

[29] '... sur tout les instrumens ne s'avisoient gueres de rien broder. Il ne leur auroit pas plus souffert, qu'il le souffroit aux Chanteuses. Il ne trouvoit point bon qu'ils prétendissent en sçavoir plus que lui, & ajoûter des notes d'agrément à leur tablature'; Jean-Laurent Le Cerf de la Viéville, *Comparaison de la musique italienne et de la musique françoise* ii (Brussels, 1705), 227.

explained elsewhere in a special method book known by the title *L'Art de toucher le clavecin*), to hear of people who have learned them but do not treat them as binding. This is an unpardonable oversight, the more so because it is absolutely not a matter of personal choice to put in whatever ornaments one wishes. I declare therefore that my pieces should be performed as I have marked them, and that they will never make a definite impression on people of true taste so long as players do not observe to the letter all that I have marked, without adding or removing anything.

(Couperin, 1722)[30]

REPRESENTING THE COMPOSER

With no more effective means at their disposal of influencing how others might present their music, composers persisted in supplementing their published music with practical instructions or advice. Fearing 'unjustified opprobrium' from unmonitored performances of his Italian-style compositions, Schütz recommended that

> those of us Germans who are not familiar with or practised in the proper tempo of this modern music and the black notes and the constant broad violin bow-stroke ... should not be ashamed to seek instruction from those experienced in this style nor balk at private practice before venturing to use any of these pieces in public. Otherwise they and the author himself – through no fault of his – may perhaps be met with unexpected ridicule instead of due thanks.

(Schütz, 1647)[31]

---

[30] '*Je suis toujours surpris, apres les soins que je me suis donné pour marquer les agrémens qui conviennent à mes Piéces, (dont j'ay donné, à part, une explication assés intelligible dans une* Méthode *particuliere, connüe sous le titre de* L'art de toucher le Clavecin*) d'entendre des personnes qui les ont aprises sans s'y assujétir. C'est une négligence qui n'est pas pardonnable, d'autant qu'il n'est point arbitraire d'y mettre tels agrémens qu'on veut. Je déclare donc que mes piéces doivent être exécutées comme je les ay marquées, et qu'elles ne feront jamais une certaine impression sur les personnes qui ont le goût vray, tant qu'on n'observera pas à la lettre tout ce que j'y ay marqué, sans augmentation ni diminution*'; François Couperin, *Pieces de clavecin* iii (Paris, 1722), preface.

[31] '*Also ist ...| bevorab aber [an] die jenigen| welchen der rechtmässige Tact über vorgedachte heutige Music| und die schwartzen Noten| so wohl auch der stäte ausgedehnete musicalische Strich auff dem Violin| bey uns Deutschen| nicht bekand noch in übung ist| ... mein freundliches bitten| sie wollen| ehe und zuvor sie sich unterstehen| eines oder das andere dieser Stücken| offentlich zu gebrauchen| sich nicht schämen| deswegen zuvor eines Unterrichts| bey solcher Manier Erfahrnen zu erholen| auch an der Privat übung keinen Verdruß zu schöpffen| damit im wiedrigen nicht etwa ihnen| und dem Autori*

Worrying more perhaps that his new cantata might receive a generally sub-standard performance, Haydn proposed 'at least three or four rehearsals of the whole work' and issued a firm reminder of the composer's stake in all this by urging everyone in his absence 'to be as diligent as possible, in order to further my reputation as well as their own'.[32]

The farther afield a composition travelled, the less control the composer had over its fate – and the greater the risk of a compromised reputation. Performers, for their part, nevertheless seem – at least in principle – to have respected the primacy of the composer, a figure who, however remote, was often both their near contemporary and a revered fellow executant. The performing musician was to 'shake off self-love' and strive to do

> as the author does, without altering or adding anything of his own (which if he does, he will disoblige them and be esteemed a vain man, as if he had more wit than those whose production he is glad to borrow).
>
> (Burwell Lute Tutor, c. 1670)[33]

Such respect for a composer was in no way believed to restrict executants to mere 'mechanical' rendition of the written notes:

> The performer of a piece must seek to enter into the principal and subsidiary passions that he is to express. ... In this manner alone will he satisfy the intentions of the composer and the ideas he has formed in writing the piece.
>
> (Quantz, 1752)[34]

Indeed, the very function of the performer's 'Musical Expression' was (in Charles Avison's view)

> to do a Composition Justice, by playing it in a *Taste* and *Stile* so exactly corresponding with the Intention of the Composer, as to preserve and illustrate *all* the Beauties of his Work.
>
> (Avison, 1753)[35]

---

selbsten/ wieder seine Schuld/ vor gehörigen Danck/ ein unverhoffter Spott zuwachsen möge'; Schütz, *Symphoniae sacrae* ii, preface.

[32] '*Verhoffe ich wenigstens von den gantzen werckh 3 oder 4 Proben*'; '*Bitte jeden besonders von denen Herrn Musicis um meine und ihre eigene Ehre zu befördern Ihren möglichsten Fleiß anzuwenden*'; Haydn, *Applausus*, ed. Robbins Landon, preface.

[33] The Burwell Lute Tutor (MS c. 1670), fol. 40v; facsimile ed. R. Spencer and L. Hewitt (1974).

[34] '*Der Ausführer eines Stückes muß sich selbst in die Haupt- und Nebenleidenschaften, die er ausdrücken soll, zu versetzen suchen. ... Auf diese Art nur wird er den Absichten des Componisten, und den Vorstellungen so sich dieser bey Verfertigung des Stückes gemacht hat, eine Gnüge leisten*'; Quantz, *Versuch*, 107 (ch. 11, §15).

[35] Charles Avison, *An Essay on Musical Expression* (London, 2/1753), 41.

In short, commentators from various traditions seem to have been in broad agreement that

> A musical work, if it is to have its proper effect, must be performed with and in the same sentiment with which the composer has set it or which he has sought to express and which it should thus, as it were, inspire; otherwise it would be something of a miracle if it were to move the listeners fully.
>
> (Scheibe, 1773)[36]

DISCERNING THE COMPOSER'S MEANING

Living up to this ideal was another matter entirely, one that clearly demanded a set of very special qualities, as a succession of mid-18th-century authorities acknowledged:

> keen discernment is necessary in order to hit upon the real sense and meaning of unfamiliar thoughts.
>
> (Mattheson, 1739)[37]

> a director may belong to any class of practical musician so long as he evinces all the qualities mentioned [previously]; he will then always be capable of performing a piece according to the author's intention.
>
> (Scheibe, 1740)[38]

> A *musicus* ... must have the greatest sensibility and the most auspicious power of divination if he is to execute correctly every piece that is set before him.
>
> (Marpurg, 1750)[39]

---

[36] 'Ein Musikstück muß mit und in derselben Empfindung, mit welcher es der Componist gesetzt, oder die er auszudrücken gesuchet hat, und die es also gleichsam beseelen soll, aufgeführet werden, wenn es seine Würkung thun soll; sonst würde es gleichsam einem Wunderwerke ähnlich seyn, wenn es die Zuhörer vollkommen rühren sollte'; Scheibe, *Ueber die Musikalische Composition* i, 299.

[37] '... eine scharffe Urtheils-Krafft dazu erfordert werde, fremder Gedancken Sinn und Meinung recht zu treffen'; Mattheson, *Der vollkommene Capellmeister*, 484 (pt 3, ch. 26, §34).

[38] '... ein director mag nun unter diese oder jene Classe praktischer Musikanten gehören, wenn er nur alle angeführte Eigenschaften beweist: so wird er allemal geschickt seyn, ein Stück nach dem Sinne des Verfassers aufzuführen'; Scheibe, *Der Critische Musikus*, 712.

[39] 'Ein Musicus muß also die größte Empfindlichkeit und die glücklichste Errathungskraft haben, wenn er jedes ihm vorgelegtes Stück recht executiren soll'; Friedrich Wilhelm Marpurg, *Critscher Musicus* (Berlin, 1750), 216.

The highest level of knowledge required of a director is that he have a perfect understanding of how to play all types of composition in accordance with their taste, affect, purpose and correct tempo.

(Quantz, 1752)[40]

For his part, Jean-Jacques Rousseau regarded these skills as attributes of musical taste, declaring 'it is taste which makes the performer catch the ideas of the composer'.[41] Just how subtle such a process could be is tellingly demonstrated by Gluck in a catalogue he gives of certain tiny details of performance which might subvert a composer's larger intentions:

> It takes almost nothing, a mere change in the manner of expression, for my aria in *Orfeo*, '*Che farò senza Euridice*', to turn into a puppet dance. A note more or less sustained, an overlooked emphasis in timing or singing, a misplaced appoggiatura, a trill, a *passaggio*, a run – each can ruin a whole scene in an opera of this kind; yet these have no effect on a work of the usual sort, except perhaps to make it more beautiful. The presence of the composer, therefore, in the performance of this type of music is, so to speak, as necessary as the presence of the sun in the works of nature. He is absolutely its soul, its life, and without him everything remains in confusion and darkness.
>
> (Gluck, 1770)[42]

In Mattheson's opinion the matter was clear: directing one's own music – even, in his case, on a memorable occasion when none other than Handel was already installed at the harpsichord – was 'something which without question every author can do better than anyone else'.[43]

---

[40] '*Der höchste Grad, der von einem Anführer erfoderlichen Wissenschaft, ist: daß er eine vollkommene Einsicht habe, alle Arten der Composition nach ihrem Geschmacke, Affecte, Absicht und rechtem Zeitmaaße zu spielen*'; Quantz, *Versuch*, 179 (ch. 17, sec. 1, §4).

[41] '... *c'est le Goût qui fait saisir à l'Exécutant les idées du Compositeur*'; Jean-Jacques Rousseau, *Dictionnaire de musique* (Paris, 1768), 236.

[42] '*Non ci vuol nulla, per che la mia Aria nell'Orfeo:* Che farò senza Euridice, *mutando solamente qualche cosa nella maniera dell'espressione, diventi un saltarello da Burattini. Una nota più o meno tenuta, un rinforzo trascurato di tempo, o di voce, un appoggiatura fuor di luogo, un trillo, un passagio, una volata, può rovinare tutta una scena in un Opera simile; e non fa nulla o non fa che abbellire un'opera delle solite. La presenza perciò del compositore nell'esecuzione di questa specie di musica è, per modo di dire, tanto necessaria, quanto la presenza del Sole nell'opere della natura. Egli n'é assolutamente l'anima, e la vita, e senza di lui tutto resta nella confuonsie* [sic]*, e nelle tenebre*'; Christoph Willibald Gluck, *Paride ed Elena* (Vienna, 1770), preface (dated 30 October).

[43] '... *welches doch unstreitig ein jeder Verfasser besser, als ein andrer, thun kann*'; Johann Mattheson, *Grundlage einer Ehren-Pforte* (Hamburg, 1740), 95.

TWO principal arguments have commonly been advanced to demonstrate that today's musicians need feel no responsibility to follow an early composer's performance intentions: (1) any such intentions are clearly impossible to establish with certainty, and (2) attempts to realize them are in any case pointless, as 'our ears have changed'. ('Try as we might, we cannot disown our ears, accustomed as they are to modern pitch and modern instrumental and vocal sounds'.)[44]

In practice, of course, we have always been at liberty to treat compositions of earlier periods in whatever fashion we please. Yet if we choose to respect the notated form of such music, we might reasonably expect to learn still more about its essential nature from the performance idiom within which it was conceived, which its written form presupposes and which composers themselves evidently considered an intrinsic facet of their work. Only thus may we hope (in the words of Avison already quoted) 'to do a Composition Justice, by playing it in a *Taste* and *Stile* so exactly corresponding with the Intention of the Composer, as to preserve and illustrate *all* the Beauties of his Work'.

The question then remains: how much can we really know? Less than one may wish but rather more than is sometimes acknowledged; nowhere near enough to replicate a specific performance but sufficient to enrich and even transcend previous understanding; perhaps (with luck and application) more than is currently known. Precise knowledge of un-notatable subtleties on the micro-level of Gluck's 'mere change in the manner of expression' will always remain elusive, yet exactly the same surely holds true for all composed music from before the age of recorded sound. The particular barrier between us and the music of our more distant ancestors lies elsewhere; the musical languages of, say, Monteverdi and Wagner differ not merely in compositional terms but in a whole host of underlying performance premises (from instrumental and vocal scoring to tuning systems and pitch levels) for which musical 'instinct' alone is no substitute. And, in contrast to the minutiae of expressive delivery, these are all areas where research really can provide clear answers.

Consider the cornett, an instrument all but obsolete by the mid-18th century and subsequently viewed as 'entirely superseded'.[45] From tentative beginnings in the 1950s its rehabilitation on very precise historical principles and through collaborative efforts in building, researching and playing has been an undoubted triumph, transforming our perceptions of expressive music-making from Lassus to Biber – and at the same time evidently speaking to today's listeners with ease and directness.[46] A development of this sort neatly undermines the oft-repeated argument that

---

[44] Frederick Neumann, *New Essays on Performance Practice* (1989), 30.

[45] Percy A. Scholes, *The Oxford Companion to Music* (9/1955), 254.

[46] Sceptics may choose to account for any such turn of events by claiming historically informed performance to be 'in essence a modernist phenomenon'. See *Rethinking Music*, ed. N. Cook and M. Everist (1999), 12.

'The meaning of a composition can be revealed ... most effectively in the musical language that is most familiar, hence most readily understood and assimilated by today's listener'.[47] (Frederick Neumann [d. 1994], some 25 years on, would doubtless have been horrified to find so many of today's listeners thoroughly acclimatized to period performance and its various languages.)

The undeniable 'sea change in our listening habits', as Nicholas Kenyon has described it, has not been achieved overnight.[48] It is the result of a steady accumulation of knowledge and experience stretching back well over 40 years and driven by sheer musical curiosity and a healthy pragmatism. Behind all this lies a commonsense belief that the more thoroughly the musical practices of the past are understood the more immediate its music is likely to become. Those pleas from composers for their performance intentions to be heeded are no less relevant today than when their works were new.

[47] Neumann, *New Essays*, 29.
[48] *Authenticity and Early Music*, ed. Kenyon, 1.

2

A Brief Anatomy of Choirs

JOSQUIN des Prez, Tallis, Victoria, Monteverdi, Charpentier, Bach – the great choral composers of the past may be presumed to have understood the inner workings of their choirs comprehensively well; most had received a choirboy's education and virtually all spent a lifetime amongst their chosen singers. But to what extent do we share their understanding? Was Dufay's body of singers little different from that which Handel knew some 300 years later? Has 'the choir' somehow managed to remain essentially one and the same thing through the ages to our own time? Though much transcribed, discussed and performed, music written for choirs in earlier centuries generally reaches us through a filter of more recent choral expectations, with unfamiliar features disregarded, overlooked, or misconstrued. Thus, while close attention is routinely paid to specific works and their composers, and to compositional genres and choral institutions, the focus here will instead be on the very nature of those diverse musical bodies we call choirs.

Since for much of the period under consideration choral performance was nurtured almost single-handedly by the Church, it will suffice to define a 'choir' provisionally as 'An organized body of singers performing or leading in the musical parts of a church service.'[1] This has the merit of making no attempt to prescribe *how* such a body is musically organized (whether for unison singing, or for music requiring just three solo voices or a multiplicity of voices intermixed with instruments), and it therefore encourages us not to concentrate unduly on familiar aspects of 'choral' performance as we now understand it.

IMPROVISED POLYPHONY

THE bedrock of the Church's music-making was plainchant, much of it sung from memory,[2] and an evolutionary link between solo or unison chant and later composed choral polyphony lies in the hidden (and little explored) world of extempore chant-based singing. This could take many

---

First appeared as 'A Brief Anatomy of Choirs, *c.* 1470–1770', in *The Cambridge Companion to Choral Music*, ed. A. de Quadros (2012), 7–26.

---

[1] *The New Shorter Oxford English Dictionary* (1993), 'Choir'.

[2] At Notre Dame in Paris (1313) 'no persons are to receive a payment for Matins unless they have demonstrated to us that they know by heart the antiphoner and the psalter which have customarily been sung by memory'; Craig Wright, *Music and Ceremony at Notre Dame of Paris, 500–1550* (1989), 326.

forms (variously named), from simple note-against-note affairs to the intricate counterpoint of highly skilled singers;[3] by the mid-15th century English clerical singers were practising at least three such techniques – faburden, descant and 'counter'.[4] Different techniques tended to attach themselves to different portions of the liturgy: at the Church of Our Lady in Antwerp (1506), the Alleluia and Sequence were to be performed in *discant*, the Communion with *contrapuncte*, and the Introit 'without singing upon the book'.[5] Though not required in this instance, the technique of singing 'upon the book' (*super librum*) is perhaps particularly relevant to the story of the choir. Its underlying principle, according to Tinctoris in 1477, was that

> when two, three, four or more people sing together upon the book, they are not subject to one another. In fact, it is enough for each of them to accord with the tenor in regard to the rule and ordering of consonances.[6]

Was something of this sort what Thomas Morley (1597) had in mind?

> As for singing uppon a plainsong, it hath byn in times past in England (as every man knoweth) and is at this day in other places, the greatest part of the usuall musicke which in any churches is sung. Which indeed causeth me to marvel how men acquainted with musicke, can delight to heare such confusion as of force must bee amongste so many singing *extempore*.[7]

We may well share Morley's scepticism (and a Neapolitan writer likened the results to 'music made by cicadas'),[8] yet Banchieri (1614) assures us that 'In Rome in the Chapel of Our Lord, in the Santa Casa di Loreto and in countless other chapels' such extempore singing (*contrapunto alla mente*) was 'most tasteful' to hear:

---

[3] Adrian Petit Coclico singles out 'the Belgians, Picards and French, for whom this is almost part of their nature, so that they take the palm of victory from the rest. Thus they alone are kept in the chapels of the Pope, the Emperor, the King of France and certain other rulers'; *Compendium musices* (Nuremberg, 1552), sig. B iv v.

[4] See Frank Ll. Harrison, *Music in Medieval Britain* (1963), 178, 187 etc.

[5] Rob C. Wegman, 'From Maker to Composer: Improvisation and Musical Authorship in the Low Countries, 1450–1500', *Journal of the American Musicological Society* 49 (1996), 424.

[6] Johannes Tinctoris, *Liber de arte contrapuncti* (1477), bk 2, ch. 20. See also P. Canguilhem, 'Singing upon the Book according to Vicente Lusitano', *Early Music History* 30 (2011), 55–103.

[7] Thomas Morley, *A Plaine and Easie Introduction to Practicall Musicke* (London, 1597), 'Annotations Upon the Second Part' (to '*Pag. 70 vers. 29*').

[8] Scipione Cerreto, *Della prattica musica vocale et strumentale* (Naples, 1601), 272.

> It is a general principle that, with as many as a 100 different voices singing in consonance over a bass, all are in harmony, and those wicked 5ths, octaves, oddities and clashes are all graces which create the true effect of improvised counterpoint ...[9]

Although small numbers of skilled singers are likely to have produced more consistently 'correct' results, this particular method of improvising over chant seems to have been capable of accommodating more than a mere handful of solo voices:[10] in mid-18th-century France there were still churches where 'almost everything is sung according to *chant sur le livre* [upon the book]', perhaps by 'thirty or so musicians ... all at the same time; some according to the rules and others completely at random'.[11]

Extempore traditions of one sort or another were clearly a major part of choral practice far and wide.[12] From St Mark's, Venice, at the end of Monteverdi's tenure as *maestro di cappella*, it was reported that 'ordinarily they sing from the large book, and in the *cantus firmi* they improvise counterpoint'.[13] And, as a Dutch traveller observed at the basilica well over a century earlier, in 1525, the elaborate liturgy of a major feast day demanded that the choir's duties were variously distributed amongst the singers present:

> Outside the sanctuary there is a beautiful round large high *stuel* [tribune/pulpit], decoratively hung with red velvet cloth of gold,

---

[9] Adriano Banchieri, *Cartella musicale* (Venice, 1614), 230.

[10] Much earlier, Elias Salomo (1274) had cautioned that even for straightforward parallel organum 'the number [of singers] cannot and should not be more than four, without leading to the disruption and debasement of the whole piece that is being sung'; *Scientia artis musicae*, ch. 30, in Martin Gerbert, *Scriptores ecclesiastici* iii (St Blasien, 1784), 58. A late 15th-century theorist, however, seems to have larger numbers in mind: 'with many singing *ad librum*, as they call it, the *tenorist*'s expression of the text is sufficient for all'; [Matthaeus Herben], *Herbeni Traiectensis De natura cantus* (c. 1496), 58, in E. Rice, *Music and Ritual at Charlemagne's Marienkirche in Aachen* (2009), 213.

[11] Henri Madin, *Traité de contrepoint simple ou chant sur le livre* (Paris, 1742), 1 (preface), 7. See Jean Prim, '*Chant sur le livre* in French Churches in the 18th Century', *Journal of the American Musicological Society* 14 (1961), 37–49, and *Louis-Joseph Marchand Henry Madin Traités du contrepoint simple*, ed. J.-P. C. Montagnier (2004).

[12] The extent of these traditions may illuminate other matters: the significance of chant notated on tablets and walls, the importance of the *tenorista* (see Wegman, 'From Maker to Composer', 445–6), the proliferation of counterpoint books, the fame achieved *as singers* by musicians we know better as 'composers', and, not least, the improvisatory nature of much composed music.

[13] Giacomo Razzi, 1643, in a letter to Carissimi (a potential successor to Monteverdi) outlining musical practices at St Mark's; Thomas D. Culley, *Jesuits and Music* (1970), 332.

where the *discanters* stand and sing. And those who psalmodize sit on both sides of the choir, on the one side plainsong, on the other side *contrapunt* or *fabridon* (whichever name you prefer); these three [groups] each await their time to sing, up to the end of the Mass ...[14]

This alerts us to two recurrent difficulties in establishing the size and nature of earlier choirs. Just as the institutional strength of a choir will not reflect any extra singers brought in on a temporary or occasional basis, so too does it fail to take account of absences, rota systems, the function or importance of an event, and – not least – such divisions of labour within a service as have just been noted. As for depictions and documentary tallies of singers, it is exceptional to be certain whether composed or improvised polyphony or even simple chant is being sung.

These questions arise with a source that may otherwise appear to be a key guide to the performance of composed choral polyphony at the Burgundian court in the time of Busnoys. New ordinances for the court chapel drawn up in 1469 specify that

> for *chant du livre* there shall be at least six high voices, three tenors, three *basses-contre* and two *moiens* ['means'] without including the four chaplains for High Mass or the *sommeliers* who, whenever they are not occupied at the altar or in some other reasonable way, will be obliged to serve with the above-mentioned.[15]

First, by proceeding to ensure 'that the service be always provided with two tenors and two *contres*',[16] the ordinances remind us that this institutional complement (or 'pool') of singers will not have been expected on all occasions. Second, '*chant* du *livre*' may well be no more than a synonym for '*chant* sur le *livre*',[17] an improvisatory technique both suited to fluid numbers of singers and requiring a good spread of voice ranges – a technique, moreover, used 'when they sing each day in the chapels of princes' and notably by 'those from across the Alps, especially the French'.[18]

---

[14] Jan Goverts, in 'Bedevaart nach Jerusalem', ed. C. J. Gonnet, in *Bijdragen voor geschiedenis van het bisdom Haarlem* 11 (1882), 39. Cf. the practice at St Mark's, Venice, in 1564, cited below.

[15] Oxford, Bodleian Library, MS Hatton 13, fol. 13r–v. Cf. David Fallows, 'Specific Information on the Ensembles for Composed Polyphony, 1400–1474', in *Studies in the Performance of Late Mediaeval Music*, ed. S. Borman (1983), 149 (cf. 110).

[16] Fallows, 'Specific Information', 154 (cf. 114).

[17] The most likely term for 'composed' polyphony would have been '*chose faite*'. See Wegman, 'From Maker to Composer', 441 (especially n. 95).

[18] Nicolò Burzio, *Musices opusculum* (Bologna, 1487), bk. 2, ch. 6, 50, 44.

COMPOSED POLYPHONY

WITH the music of Dufay we are on slightly firmer ground. In his lengthy will, drawn up at Cambrai in 1474, the composer requests that on his deathbed – 'time permitting' – two pieces of music be heard: first a chant hymn sung softly (*submissa voce*)[19] by eight Cathedral men, then his own *Ave regina celorum*[20] sung by the (four to six) 'altar boys, together with their master and two companions'.[21] (For a similar grouping see Illus. 2.1.) Instead, as time did not permit, both items were apparently given in the Cathedral the day after his death, together with Dufay's own (lost) Requiem,[22] for which he had specified '12 of the more competent vicars, both great and lesser' (about half of the total).[23] Dufay's will also provides for a mass of his to be sung on a separate occasion by 'the master of the boys and several of the more competent members of the choir', the allocated funds allowing for exactly nine singers.[24] It is worth noting that the precise location for this, and almost certainly for the Requiem, was not the choir of the Cathedral but one of its chapels.[25] Indeed, the (private) chapel, whether part of a church or an independent structure, arguably counted as 'the most important place for music-making in the late Middle Ages', perhaps explaining why the chaplains of a princely chapel, whose

---

[19] *Submissa voce*: literally, 'with a subdued voice'. In the executors' account of the will *submissa voce* is rendered in French as *en fausset*, leading to the mistaken view that falsetto singing is indicated here. Rather, it is *en fausset* that at this period means 'softly', and not *submissa voce* that means 'in falsetto'. Cf. Fallows, 'Specific Information', 126.

[20] Undoubtedly the late setting (*a4*) of *Ave regina celorum*, copied at Cambrai in 1464–5.

[21] Fallows, 'Specific Information', 120–1.

[22] '... for three voices, mournful, sad and very exquisite', according to the chronicler of a performance in Brussels in 1501; William F. Prizer, 'Music and Ceremonial in the Low Countries: Philip the Fair and the Order of the Golden Fleece', *Early Music History* 5 (1985), 133.

[23] Craig Wright, 'Performance Practices at the Cathedral of Cambrai, 1475–1550', *The Musical Quarterly* 64 (1978), 303 (cf. 296). Cf. David Fallows, *Dufay* (1982), 79, inc. n. 25. Under a separate foundation Dufay's Requiem was also sung annually at Cambrai from 1517 to 1521, this time by 'the master of the choirboys with four or five companions chosen at his discretion'; Wright, 'Performance Practices', 303.

[24] The work in question is the mass for St Anthony of Padua (*a3*); Fallows, 'Specific Information', 117–20.

[25] The mass was to be sung 'on the day of St Anthony of Padua in that chapel'; Fallows, 'Specific Information', 118. Dufay left a manuscript containing his Requiem to the Cathedral's chapel of St Stephen, where he was to be buried; Reinhard Strohm, *The Rise of European Music 1380–1500* (1993), 287. *Ave regina celorum* was evidently sung in the chapel of St Étienne; Wright, 'Performance Practices', 305.

Illus. 2.1 Woodcut from Arnolt Schlick, *Spiegel der Orgelmacher und Organisten* (Mainz/Speyer, 1511), showing a straight cornett, organ and singers (three boys and two men); London, British Library MS Hirsch I.546

duties were many and varied, frequently outnumbered the singing body of a great cathedral.[26]

Substantially larger vocal forces than those specified by Dufay were certainly heard from time to time, but only in exceptional circumstances. In 1475, for example, at a Sforza wedding Mass in Pesaro two *capelle* sang 'now one, now the other, and there were about 16 singers per *capella*'.[27] A century later Lassus annotated the alto, tenor, and bass parts of a 12-voice mass by Brumel with the names of 33 men – including himself as 'Cantor'[28] – and for the Medici's extravagant 1589 *intermedi* a madrigal

---

[26] Strohm, *European Music*, 273 and 280–1. Under Ercole I d'Este, the Ferrarese court chapel between 1471 and 1505 frequently comprised over 20 singers; L. Lockwood, *Music in Ferrara, 1400–1505* (1984), 150.

[27] David Fallows, 'The Performing Ensembles in Josquin's Sacred Music', *Tijdschrift van de Vereniging voor Nederlandse Muziekgeschiedenis* 35 (1985), 33, 56.

[28] Antoine Brumel, *Missa Et ecce terrae motus est. Corpus Mensurabilis Musicae 5: Antonii Brumel Opera Omnia* iii, ed. B. Hudson (1970), ix–x. Lassus presumably performed the work at Munich between 1568 and 1570, when according to Michael Praetorius the court *Kapelle* boasted an unparalleled 16 choirboys plus 5 or 6 castratos, 13 altos, 15 tenors and 12 basses; *Syntagma musicum* ii (Wolfenbüttel, 1618), 17.

*a*30 was sung in seven choirs by 60 voices, with opulent instrumental support.[29] By contrast, the musical establishment at Florence Cathedral in 1478 comprised just four boys, their master and four other adult singers.[30] Ensembles of this nature were evidently something of a norm:

- Venetian ambassadors traveling through the Tyrol in 1492 enjoyed 'the singing of five boys and three masters';[31]
- as 'song master' at St Donatian's in Bruges (1499–1500), Obrecht was 'obliged to bring with him to each Salve, besides his children [choirboys], four companion singers from the church, and those who sing best';[32]
- Jean de Saint Gille's testament (1500) promises a *pour-boire* to six named singers and 'several' of the boys at Rouen, who were 'to sing the Mass for the Departed that I have composed'.[33]

Some of these boys may have been the equivalents of today's 11- or 12-year-olds, but the more complex polyphony of the period reminds us that boys' voices were commonly not changing until 16 or even later.[34] Northern Europe led the way in training young singers, and in France (1517–18)

> there is not a cathedral or major church where they do not have polyphony constantly and more than one mass sung every day; each one is supplied with six or eight little boy clerics who learn singing and serve in the choir, tonsured like little monks and receiving food and clothing.[35]

Institutionally these choirboys were often independent of their adult counterparts – Cambrai's boys served as acolytes and sang at their own lectern near the high altar[36] – and the collaboration of men and boys in

---

[29] Howard M. Brown, *Sixteenth-Century Instrumentation: The Music for the Florentine Intermedii* (1973), 129.

[30] Albert Seay, 'The 15th-Century Cappella at Santa Maria del Fiore in Florence', *Journal of the American Musicological Society* 11 (1958), 49.

[31] Hans Joachim Moser, *Paul Hofhaimer: ein Lied- und Orgelmeister des deutschen Humanismus* (1929), 14

[32] Rob C. Wegman, *Born for the Muses: The Life and Masses of Jacob Obrecht* (1994), 373 (and 305).

[33] Rob C. Wegman, 'The Testament of Jean de Saint Gille (†1501)', *Revue de Musicologie* 95 (2009), 18, 28.

[34] In the 1470s the Sforza court requested from Venice 'a boy of 14 or 15 who can sing Venetian songs, has a good voice, and some theoretical knowledge of music, who can play lute well, and sing with and without lute'; Strohm, *European Music*, 544.

[35] Antonio de Beatis (1517), in Ludwig Pastor, *Die Reise des Kardinals Luigi d'Aragona* (1905), 165.

[36] Wright, 'Performance Practices', 306.

elaborate composed polyphony marked a significant development in the 15th century.[37]

Interest in this new wider choral range may in turn have driven the cultivation of another type of high voice: that of the adult falsettist (better known as today's 'countertenor'). To Pietro Aaron (1516) a *cantus* part was now one to be sung by either a boy's voice or a man's 'feigned' voice (*'cum puerili voce, vel ficta'*).[38] In the absence of earlier hard evidence,[39] we may conjecture that the increasing value of keeping boys singing for as long as possible led to an adolescent 'falsetto' technique[40] which some then retained and developed into adulthood as falsettist sopranos. (In Germany it may have been quite usual for boys to move from soprano to alto before settling into a lower range.)[41] Revealingly, non-child sopranos, many of them described as youths, were often taken on only for 'as long as their voices shall last' (and sometimes 'placed in the house of the choirboys'),[42] or given a one-year contract specifically 'in case ... the singer should lose his voice'.[43] In one instance, a soprano who signed such a contract in Florence shortly before Christmas 1481 received a 'farewell gift' just 11 days later.[44]

The need for dependable high voices could, of course, be satisfied in another way – by castratos, who as a musical force seem to have emerged in Spain only a little later. At Burgos Cathedral a castrated boy 'who has a

---

[37] For a handful of works from the earlier part of the 15th century juxtaposing boys and men, see Fallows, 'Specific Information', 122–5.

[38] Pietro Aaron, *Libri tres de institutione harmonica* (Bologna, 1516), fol. 52. For works with parts specifically labelled *puer* or *pueri* ('boy/s') by Battre, Bourgois, Regis, Isaac, Obrecht, and Ockeghem, see Fallows, 'Specific Information', 122–3, and Fallows, 'The Performing Ensembles', 44–5.

[39] The belief that falsetto singing was widespread long before the 16th century is now almost universal. Its foundations, however, are various questionable assumptions about terminology (including *falsus*, *fictus*, and their cognates; see n. 19), about sounding pitch in relation to notation (see text, below) and about interrelated historical issues of age, maturity and status in young male singers.

[40] In 1536 the chapter of Cambrai encouraged the master of the choirboys to 'teach the boys of the choir to sing *submisse* or, as they say in French, in falsetto'; Wright, 'Performance Practices', 309. It may be that this represents a connection, some 60 years after Dufay's death, between soft singing and falsetto in the now familiar sense (cf. n. 19).

[41] According to Joachim Burmeister the soprano voice was suited to boys and females, the alto to youths (*ætati juvenili*), tenor and bass to men; *Musica poetica* (Rostock, 1606), 11.

[42] Wright, 'Performance Practices', 309.

[43] Frank A. D'Accone, 'The Singers of San Giovanni in Florence during the 15th Century', *Journal of the American Musicological Society* 13 (1960), 332.

[44] D'Accone, 'The Singers of San Giovanni'.

good voice' was noted as early as 1506,⁴⁵ and by the 1560s Spanish castratos could be found in Italy at the court of Ferrara, in the papal chapel, and at St Mark's, Venice.⁴⁶ (Homegrown Italian castratos eventually displaced these Spaniards in Italy.)⁴⁷

RANGES, CLEFS, AND VOCAL SCORING

ONLY slowly did the 'voice' labels of polyphonic music (*cantus, contratenor* and so on) begin to attach themselves not just to parts but to distinct vocal ranges and thence to particular categories of singer. In practice, the 'key' to vocal scoring – widely assumed today to have been a distinctly casual affair – was the humble clef,⁴⁸ which mapped out an individual core range (of up to 11 notes) and fixed its relationship to others; see Ex. 2.1. A composer, having chosen a mode and vocal scoring, worked from a corresponding set of clefs, always aware that

> you must not suffer any part to goe without the compasse of his rules [= lines], except one note at the most above or below, without it be upon an extremity for the ditties [= words'] sake or in notes taken for *Diapasons* in the base.
>
> (Morley, 1597)⁴⁹

The clef configuration C1 C3 C4 F4, for example, can thus identify and broadly define the four principal vocal ranges of later Renaissance music: *cantus, altus, tenor,* and *bassus* (*CATB*). Confusingly enough, however, these very same voices could also be expressed by a different set of clefs and consequently at different written pitch levels.⁵⁰ The motet *Absalon, fili mi* (variously attributed to Josquin and Pierre de la Rue) – an extreme example perhaps – survives in 'contradictory' sources, the earliest one lying exceptionally low (C3 C4 F4 F5), others a surprising 9th higher

---

⁴⁵ José López-Calo, *La música en la Catedral de Burgos* iii (1996), 43

⁴⁶ Giuseppe Gerbino, 'The Quest for the Soprano Voice: Castrati in Renaissance Italy', *Studi musicali* 33 (2004), 343, 320; Giulio M. Ongaro, 'La composizione del coro e dei gruppi strumentali a San Marco dalla fine del Quattrocento al primo Seicento', in *Architettura e musica nella Venezia del Rinascimento*, ed. D. Howard and L. Moretti (2006), 106 etc.

⁴⁷ See Gerbino, 'The Quest'.

⁴⁸ Modern editions which fail to report a work's original clefs withhold critical information and feed the misconception that vocal scoring and choice of pitch were on the whole rather arbitrary affairs.

⁴⁹ Thomas Morley, *A Plaine and Easie Introduction*, 166. See also Nicola Vicentino, *L'antica musica ridotta alla modern prattica* (Rome, 1555), bk 4, ch. 17; trans. M. M. Maniates as *Ancient Music Adapted to Modern Practice* (1996), 250.

⁵⁰ For an explanation of the modal background to this convention, see Patrizio Barbieri, '*Chiavette* and Modal Transposition in Italian Practice (*c.* 1500–1837)', *Recercare* 3 (1991), 17–25.

Ex. 2.1 The implied range of a five-line stave and the most commonly used clefs

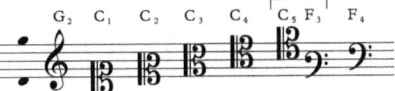

Ex. 2.2 (a) Original notation; (b) Notation as generally transcribed today

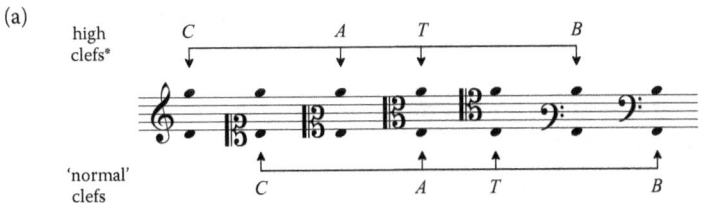

* Only the most common configuration of high clefs is given here.

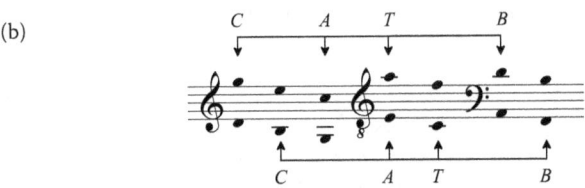

(G1 G2 C2 C3).[51] In fact, only the clefs and key signatures have changed; the notes themselves occupy identical positions on each stave, divergent pitch names being (as Cerone puts it in 1613) 'of no concern to the singer, who is concerned only to sound his notes correctly, observing the intervals of tones and semitones'.[52] Musical notation, in other words, deals in *relative* pitches – and is frustratingly reticent about their absolute *sounding* pitch.

What may appear to be a bewildering array of clef configurations employed by Renaissance composers is perhaps best viewed as a series of purely notational permutations of a limited number of reasonably standard vocal ranges. By the end of the 16th century most choral music was in practice notated either in 'high' clefs (later dubbed *chiavette*) or in a set that had steadily become more 'normal'; see Ex. 2.2. As it happens, two thirds of Palestrina's considerable output is notated in high clefs, giving us the misleading impression that it was intended to *sound* distinctly higher than the remainder (in 'normal' clefs), simply because that is how it *looks*

---

[51] See Fallows, 'Performing Ensembles', 52–3.

[52] Pietro Cerone, *El melopeo y maestro* (Naples, 1613), 494. In terms of solmization the exceptional demands of the lower two-flat notation, symbolically plumbing the depths of the gamut, simply disappear in the higher version. It has also been argued the work may originally have been clefless; P. Urquhart, 'Another Impolitic Observation on *Absalon, fili mi*', *Journal of Musicology* 21 (2004), 364–8 (see also 347–8, 361, 362).

to us – a view that would surely have amused Palestrina's singers, just as theirs may baffle us.

Apparent discrepancies of this sort naturally became real issues whenever instruments were involved, and consequently the art of transposition was viewed by Zarlino (1558) as 'useful and highly necessary both to every skilled organist involved with choral performance and similarly to other instrumentalists'.[53] Thus, while all high-clef items in a book of Palestrina motets reissued in 1608 are found transposed downwards in its newly added organ part,[54] all 37 in a similar collection by G. P. Anerio (1613) bear instructions such as *'alla quarta bassa'* ('to the 4th below').[55] The necessary procedures are set out by Praetorius in 1619 in the clearest possible terms:

> Every vocal piece in high clefs, i.e. where the bass is written in C4 or C3, or F3, must be transposed when it is put into tablature or score for players of the organ, lute and all other foundation instruments, as follows: if it has a flat, down a 4th ..., but if it has no flat, down a 5th ...[56]

Ex. 2.3 compares core ranges of 'normal' and transposed high clefs (↓4th). *Primary* transposition of this sort – almost always obligatory – is not to be confused with any smaller *secondary* adjustment designed to suit specific circumstances: to deal with differing instrumental pitch standards and/or to accommodate particular voices. In both cases the abiding principle was that instruments should defer to voices, rather than the opposite. Hence,

> organists are always (or at least usually) compelled to play lower than the written key in order to accommodate the singers. This is what is done at St Mark's in Venice ...[57]

High- (and low-) clef notation, considered the worst 'among the many abuses which are traditionally current in music',[58] eventually died out, but

---

[53] Gioseffo Zarlino, *Le istitutioni harmoniche* (Venice, 1558), bk 4, ch. 17, 319. The intriguing case of Monteverdi's high-clef 1610 Magnificat *a7* is explored in Andrew Parrott, 'Transposition in Monteverdi's Vespers of 1610', *Early Music* 12/4 (1984), 490–516 (reprinted in this volume, Ch. 5).

[54] Rinaldo Alessandrini, 'Performance Practice in the seconda prattica Madrigal', *Early Music* 27/4 (1999), 636.

[55] James Armstrong, '*The Antiphonae, seu Sacrae Cantiones* (1613) of Giovanni Francesco Anerio: A Liturgical Study', *Analecta musicologica* 14 (1974), 89–150.

[56] Praetorius, *Syntagma musicum* iii (Wolfenbüttel, 1618), 80–1. See Parrott, 'Transposition', 491–4.

[57] Giovanni Battista Morsolino (1582); Guido Pannain, in *La musica in Cremona nella seconda metà del secolo 16*, ed. G. Cesari (1939), xvi.

[58] Banchieri, *Cartella*, 88.

Ex. 2.3 Relative ranges with high clefs transposed ↓4th

as late as 1657 Schütz could still publish a work with the vocal parts in one key (using high clefs) and that of the organ in another (a 4th lower).⁵⁹

VOICE-TYPES

To compound the difficulties of understanding these notational conventions, known pitch standards could vary enormously, anywhere from roughly a tone below today's a' = 440 to a tone above (as, respectively, with many late 17th-century French woodwind instruments and Buxtehude's organs in Lübeck)[60] – and from the 15th century and earlier there is virtually no reliable information. It is therefore critical to recognize that *cantus, altus, tenor* and *bassus* are not necessarily direct equivalents of today's SATB classifications. A particular cause of misunderstanding is the view that 'Falsetto singing has been the most common source of alto voices in all-male choirs throughout the history of Western music'.[61] Wherever they are known to have been employed in the 16th century, falsetto (and castrato) voices were associated not with alto parts but only with soprano parts – which in turn lie significantly lower than those of later periods.[62] As for the (non-falsetto) alto voice, it corresponds to our (high) tenor and formed a pair with a slightly lower 'middling' tenor, generally considered the 'ordinary' voice.[63] Palestrina's voices, for example, are distributed as shown in Table 2.1.

---

[59] Parrott, 'Transposition', 497.
[60] See Bruce Haynes, *A History of Performing Pitch* (2002), 369 and 142.
[61] 'Contratenor altus' in *The New Grove Dictionary of Music and Musicians*, ed. S. Sadie (2/2001). For my more recent discussion of the issues addressed in this section, see Chapter 3 of this volume.
[62] In 1639 André Maugars noted in Rome 'a great number of *castrati* for the *dessus* and for the *haut-contre*'; 'Response …', in *Studies in Music*, ed. R. Grey (1901), 226. At the papal chapel, however, Antimo Liberati still objected in 1662/3 to the suggestion of assigning castratos to alto parts; Gerbino, 'The Quest', 313. (A change did eventually take place there after 1687; 'Chorus', *New Grove 2*, 770.) By 1649 all the altos (and sopranos) at St Mark's, Venice, were castratos, according to H. H. von Oeÿnhausen (see n. 142).
[63] See, for example, Philibert Jambe de Fer, *Épitome musical* (Lyon, 1556), 51–2. The mid-18th-century French *haute-contre* was still this adult male

Table 2.1 Sixteenth-century vocal scoring – Italy and elsewhere

Part	Person		Today's nomenclature
cantus	boy; man (falsettist, castrato)		*treble, countertenor, castrato
altus	man – high	⎫	1st tenor
tenor	man – middle	⎬ 'changed voices'	2nd tenor/baritone
bassus	man – low	⎭	bass

* Neither 'treble' nor 'countertenor' adequately evokes the part's intermediate 'mezzo soprano' range.

Table 2.2 Sixteenth-century vocal scoring – England

Part	Singer
triplex/treble	boy (high)
medius/mean	boy (low)
contratenor/countertenor	1st tenor
tenor/tenor	2nd tenor/baritone
bassus/bass	bass

English vocal scoring, especially in the earlier part of the 16th century, differs significantly from this in often employing not four but five basic ranges (Table 2.2). The lower three of these voices correspond to those of Palestrina and are 'changed voices' covering the two octaves or so above a bass's lowest note, but where Palestrina has just a *cantus* above them, English music often has two distinct upper voices: 'treble' and 'mean'.[64] Not only is there a total absence of documentary evidence for falsetto singing in 16th-century England (unlike Italy, for example), but also, English organ pitch – no higher than a semitone or so above today's $a' = 440$[65] – all but rules out today's countertenor for *contratenor* parts.[66]

non-falsettist, quite distinct in manner from the lighter Italian tenor who now freely incorporated a falsetto or 'head' voice to extend his range upwards; see Andrew Parrott, 'Falsetto and the French: "Une toute autre marche"', *Basler Jahrbuch für historische Musikpraxis* 26 (2002), 129–48 (reprinted in this volume, Ch. 4). For a brief discussion of the English countertenor in the late 17th century, see Andrew Parrott, 'Performing Purcell', in *The Purcell Companion*, ed. M. Burden (1995), 417–24 (reprinted in this volume, Ch. 9).

[64] An occasional lower part for a boy (*secundus puer*) also occurs in, for example, the music of Obrecht and Ockeghem; Fallows, 'Specific Information', 44–6.

[65] See Andrew Johnstone, '"As it was in the beginning": Organ and Choir Pitch in Early Anglican Church Music', *Early Music* 31/4 (2003), 506–26. Cf. David Wulstan, *Tudor Music* (1985), 200–2, where the author argues for a pitch 'perhaps between a tone and a minor third' higher than today's pitch.

[66] For a contrary view see Wulstan, *Tudor Music*, 242–4.

Moreover, though the 'mean' part may appear well suited to today's countertenor,[67] the associated voice was 'higher than mens voyces'.[68] It is only ever documented as belonging to boys: the Earl of Northumberland's 'Childeryn of the chapell', for example, comprised 'ij Tribills and iij Meanys' (*c.* 1505),[69] while Salisbury Cathedral specified 'eight choristers having good commendable voyces for trebles and meanes' (1580).[70]

INSTRUMENTS

BY the mid 1400s the organ had become well established as a church instrument, but only later did other instruments slowly gain admission on any regular basis. While scattered references to 'trumpets' and other wind instruments often relate to the Mass (sometimes specifically to the Elevation), there is little to suggest their direct involvement with liturgical singing on any frequent or systematic basis before 1500.[71] But in that very year we read of masses being sung (at John the Steadfast's wedding in Torgau) 'with the help of the organ, 3 trombones and a cornett, [and] likewise four crumhorns with the *positif*'.[72] Did these instrumental groups merely play, for example, at the Gradual and *Ite missa est* (as the organ might otherwise have done, and as trombones evidently did at Innsbruck three years later),[73] or were they used to bolster the vocal forces in polyphonic settings of the Kyrie, Gloria, and so on? The same questions are raised by recurrent reports (1501–6) citing Augustein Schubinger, an Imperial cornettist in the retinue of Philip the Fair, playing at Mass.[74]

---

[67] For an argument that in England the lower boy's voice was merely 'a substitute for the adult alto' (in the modern sense) for the singing of mean parts – an undocumented occurrence – see Roger Bowers, 'The Vocal Scoring, Choral Balance and Performing Pitch of Latin Church Polyphony in England, *c.* 1390–1559', *Journal of the Royal Musical Association* 112 (1987), 67–8; and Roger Bowers, 'To Chorus from Quartet: The Performing Resource for English Church Polyphony, *c.* 1390–1559', in *English Choral Practice, 1400– 1650*, ed. J. Morehen (1995), 38–9.

[68] London, British Library, MS Royal 18. B. XIX (early 17th c.), fol. 8v; Peter Le Huray, *Music and the Reformation in England, 1549–1660* (1967), 121.

[69] Bowers, 'Latin Church Polyphony', 58, 71–2.

[70] Betty Matthews, 'Some Early Organists and their Agreements', *The Organ* 51 (1972), 150.

[71] Fallows, 'Specific Information', 127. Instruments at this period seem generally to have been confined to the nave; Strohm, *European Music*, 272–3.

[72] Adolf Aber, *Die Pflege der Musik unter den Wettinern und wettinischen Ernestinern* (1921), 82.

[73] Georges Van Doorslaer, 'La Chapelle musicale de Philippe le Beau', *Revue Belge d'archéologie et d'histoire de l'art* 4 (1934), 52.

[74] Keith Polk, 'Augustein Schubinger and the Zinck: Innovation in Performance Practice', *Historic Brass Society Journal* 1 (1989), 84–7. See also Van Doorslaer, 'La Chapelle musicale', 50–1.

The matter is at least partly settled, however, by a woodcut of Maximilian I's *Hofkapelle*, showing a trombonist and a cornettist (almost certainly Schubinger) reading from the same choirbook as a dozen or more singers. England's court singers perhaps first encountered this type of mixed ensemble a little later, at the Field of the Cloth of Gold (1520), when their French counterparts were joined in a Credo by trombones and '*fiffres*'.[75] For Erasmus (1519) these instrumental intruders contributed to the objectionably 'elaborate and theatrical' nature of church music,[76] whereas Vasari's reaction to hearing 'a multitude of trombones, cornetts and voices' perform a Gloria at a Florentine ceremony in 1535 was to proclaim that 'the earth seemed gladdened'.[77]

Instrumental participation of this kind was clearly intended to enhance the pomp and ceremony of grand occasions, but there could also be a more general practical purpose:

> Cornetts and trombones have been invented and introduced into musical ensembles more from the need for soprano and basses, or rather I should say to add body and sheer noise ... than for any good or desirable effect that they may create.
>
> (V. Galilei, 1581)[78]

More specifically,

> singers with sufficiently deep bass voices are extremely rare, which is why the *Basson*, sackbut and serpent are used, in the same way that the cornett is employed to stand in for treble voices, which are usually not good.
>
> (Mersenne, 1636)[79]

---

[75] Jehan La Caille (1520), in Dom Bernard de Montfaucon, *Les Monumens de la Monarchie Françoise* iv (Paris, 1732), 178; Wright, *Notre Dame*, 227, 364. These *fiffres* were most probably the cornetts mentioned in two contemporary Italian accounts; see *Calendar of State Papers ... Venice* iii: *1520–1526*, ed. R. Brown (1869), 29, 75.

[76] Erasmus, 'Annotations on the New Testament' (1519), in *Opera omnia* vi (Leiden, 1705), col. 731

[77] Karl Frey, *Der literarische Nachlass Giorgio Vasaris* (1923), 40–1.

[78] Vincenzo Galilei, *Dialogo della musica antica e della moderna* (Florence, 1581), 142.

[79] Marin Mersenne, *Harmonie Universelle* iii (Paris, 1636), bk 5, prop. xxiv. 16th-century Spanish cathedrals similarly favoured the *bajón* or dulcian (Pamplona from at least 1530), presumably for its clarity and definition at the lower end of the bass range. To a 1615 memorandum proposing that from the Capilla Real 'two singers of each voice, cornett, *bajón* and an organist would be enough' to attend a royal wedding in Burgos, Philip III replied that 'as far as singers are concerned, four or six could go with cornett and *bajón*'. The shawms and *flautas* of minstrel bands attached to certain cathedrals were distinctly less well suited to the task of supporting voices. At least initially these groups seem to have worked independently of the vocal choirs,

At the reopening of England's Chapel Royal in 1660, cornetts were accordingly drafted in to help 'supply the superiour Parts' of the music, 'there being not one Lad, for all that time, capable of Singing his Part readily',[80] while a full century later the bassoon was proving 'in great Request in many Country Churches ... as most of the Bass Notes may be played on it, in the Octave below the Bass Voices'.[81] As Roger North put it in 1676, 'nothing can so well reconcile the upper parts in a Quire, as the cornet (being well sounded) doth'.[82] With their distinctly vocal colour, range and flexibility (of tuning and volume), cornetts and trombones integrated themselves into vocal choirs to the extent that in the late 1580s one singer at a Roman church was able on occasion to send a trombonist to deputize for him,[83] while elsewhere the permanent membership of a courtly chapel included 'two basses, one is a *trombone*'.[84]

Stringed instruments were slower to find a place in church music-making – and slower in England than elsewhere: in 1636 it was noted that 'in our Chyrch-solemnities onely the Winde-instruments (whose Notes ar constant) bee in use'.[85] (The viol consorts associated with English verse anthems of the period belong to the world of domestic performance and are undocumented in church sources.)[86] In Rome, however, the upstart violin had clearly made its entry by 1595, when a *maestro di cappella* might be expected to present 'two vespers and a mass for three choirs all together [*con unite voci*], with members of the Papal Chapel and instruments, namely cornetts, trombones, violins and lutes'.[87] Earlier still in Namur,

allowing one of Seville's minstrels (1586) to double as a singer, and another at Palencia (1592) to serve as both '*bajón* in polyphony' and 'treble shawm in the minstrels' *capilla*'. See Robert Stevenson, *La música en la Catedral de Sevilla, 1478–1606* (1985), 75 (doc. 637); and Kenneth Kreitner, 'Minstrels in Spanish Churches, 1400–1600', *Early Music* 20/4 (1992), 536, 539, 546.

[80] Matthew Locke, *The Present Practice of Musick Vindicated* (London, 1673), 19.

[81] John Arnold, *The Compleat Psalmodist* (London, 5/1761), iv (preface).

[82] *Roger North on Music*, ed. J. Wilson (1959), 40.

[83] At the German College, 1589; Graham Dixon, 'The Performance of Palestrina: Some Questions, but Fewer Answers', *Early Music* 22/4 (1994), 670.

[84] Letter from Scipione Gonzaga to Guglielmo Gonzaga (1586); Seishiro Niwa, '"Madama" Margaret of Parma's Patronage of Music', *Early Music* 33/1 (2005), 37 (and 33).

[85] Stringed instruments, we are told, 'ar often out of tun; (which soomtime happeneth in the mids of the Musik, when it is neither good to continue, nor to correct the fault)'; Charles Butler, *The Principles of Musik* (London, 1636), 103.

[86] The reported 'Vialls, and other sweet Instruments' at Exeter Cathedral in 1635 constitute the only exception of which I am aware. See Andrew Parrott, '"Grett and solompne singing": Instruments in English Church Music before the Civil War', *Early Music* 6/2 (1978), 186 (reprinted in this volume, Ch. 15).

[87] Georg Kinsky, 'Schriftstücke aus dem Palestrina-Kreis', in *Festschrift Peter Wagner*, ed. K. Weinmann (1926), 114. In 1586 a violin had been added to the

Marguerite of Valois had attended a Mass 'after the Spanish fashion, with instruments [*musique*], *violons*, and cornetts'.[88]

NEW DIRECTIONS

THE gradual acceptance of instruments besides the organ led church music in new directions. While double-choir writing of the mid-16th century had in essence been entirely vocal (although instruments might double or even replace voices), the polychoral works of Giovanni Gabrieli and others commonly included not only a basso continuo but also additional parts specifically for instruments. The various 'choirs' – perhaps separated vertically as well as horizontally – might thus be:

- purely vocal (some for single voices, others for multiple voices with or without instrumental doubling),
- purely instrumental (whether or not for a single family of instruments), or
- for a particular combination of voices and instruments.

No longer was the compass of each choir restricted to that of human voices:[89] a tenor might supply the top line of a 'low' choir with trombones beneath, or the lowest line of a 'high' choir headed by a cornett or violin. And in many cases the number of choirs could be varied simply by omitting or duplicating certain of them. Thus Viadana's *Salmi a quattro chori* (1612)

> may also be sung by just two choirs, namely Choirs I and II. However, if one wishes to put on a beautiful display with 4 to 8 choirs as the whole world likes to do nowadays, the intended effect will be achieved by doubling Choirs II, III and IV, without any danger of

instrumental resources for *concerti* at S Antonio, Padua; Jesse Ann Owens, 'Il Cinquecento', in *Storia della musica al Santo di Padova*, ed. S. Durante and P. Petrobelli (1990), 67.

[88] In 1577, according to her memoirs; Robert Stevenson, *Spanish Cathedral Music in the Golden Age* (1961), 341. It is not entirely clear how to interpret the description of a 'splendid Mass' at the Imperial Diet of Constance in 1507, sung 'with organ, trombones, trumpets, cornetts and all sorts of stringed instruments playing' (*In Organis, busonen, Trumeten, Zinggen und allerlay sayten spil*); Manfred Schuler, 'Zur Orgelkunst am Hof Kaiser Maximilian I', in *Musik und Tanz zur Zeit Kaiser Maximilian I*, ed. W. Salmen (1992), 123.

[89] In his *Spem in alium a*40, for example, Tallis uses the same five-part vocal scoring in each of eight choirs (G2 C2 C3 C4 F4). Striggio's slightly earlier 40-part *Ecce beatam lucem*, however, adds to three apparently 'vocal' choirs (C1 C3 C4 F4) seven higher ones (G2 C2 C3 F3), which may have accounted for the documented recorders, viols and trombones in a performance at Munich; see Andrew Parrott, 'A Tale of Five Cities Revisited', *Early Music* 9/3 (1981), 342–3.

making an error; for everything depends on Choir I *a5* being sung well.⁹⁰

While the four-part Choir II functions here as 'the *capella*, the very core and foundation of a good musical ensemble' (for which 'there should not be fewer than 16 singers'), the choir on which 'everything depends' – Viadana's 'favoured' first choir – consists of just one singer per part:

> Choir I *a5* stands in the main organ gallery and is the *coro favorito*; it is sung and recited by five good singers.⁹¹

In practice, *ripieno* or *capella* singers rarely needed to be quite as numerous as Viadana suggests: Usper (1627) speaks of 'doubled and tripled voices together with proportionate instruments on each part, as is done in the most famous city of Venice'.⁹²

This new Italian polychoral manner was soon adopted by German composers, notably by Schütz, who explains in his *Psalmen Davids* (1619) that

> the second choir is used as a *capella* and is therefore strong [in numbers], while the first choir, which is the *coro favorito*, is by contrast slender and comprises only four singers.⁹³

And in France the same underlying principles produced the French *grand motet*:

> the *grand choeur*, which is *a5*, is always filled with a number of voices; in the *petits choeurs* the voices are one to a part.⁹⁴

(For Du Mont, sections marked *'omnes'* are 'when there are two people on the same part'.)⁹⁵ This distinction between an élite one-to-a-part vocal choir and a larger – though not necessarily large – body of singers is fundamental to a proper understanding of much 'concerted' vocal music, whether polychoral or otherwise.⁹⁶ The chief protagonists of

---

⁹⁰ Lodovico Viadana, *Salmi a quattro chori* (Venice, 1612), 'Modo di concertare i detti salmi a quattro chori'; *Recent Researches in the Music of the Baroque Era* 86, ed. G. Wielakker (1998), 2.

⁹¹ Wielakker, *Recent Researches*, 2.

⁹² Andrew Parrott, *The Essential Bach Choir* (2000), 31; see also 51–7 for related questions of positioning and copy-sharing, and more on the size of ripieno groups.

⁹³ Heinrich Schütz, *Psalmen Davids* (Dresden, 1619), preface.

⁹⁴ Thomas Gobert (Paris, 1646), in *Musique et musiciens au XVIIe siècle. Correspondance et oeuvre musicales de Constantin Huygens*, ed. W. J. A. Jonckbloet and J. P. N. Land (Leiden, 1882), ccxvii.

⁹⁵ Henri Du Mont, *Cantica sacra* (Paris, 1652), 'Au lecteur'; ed. J. Lionnet (1996), xcii.

⁹⁶ According to Praetorius (1618) the term *concertando* applied 'when one selects from an entire company of musicians the best and most notable

most 17th-century concerted music were these select one-to-a-part vocal ensembles (or 'consorts', as they are now often called); in Praetorius's words, such 'choirs' of *concertato* voices constituted 'the foundation of the whole *concerto*'.[97] Moreover, where there is *capella* writing, it is generally subsidiary and frequently optional;[98] even for a *grand motet* 'it would suffice to have five solo voices'.[99]

One-to-a-part choral singing was, of course, nothing new. A foundation at Chichester Cathedral (c. 1530) had provided for just four adult singers of polyphony, stipulating a combined vocal range for them of 15 or 16 notes.[100] In Venice in 1553, the Cappella Ducale's 17 members could form four separate choirs for employment outside St Mark's,[101] while at the basilica itself in 1564, in an intriguing anticipation of later practice, they sang psalms 'divided into two choirs, namely, four singers in one choir and all the rest in the other'.[102]

In keeping with his earlier small-scale 'ecclesiastical concertos', Viadana's *Lamentationes* (1609) are designed for 'just four good voices' (though without organ), but for different reasons. These highly charged texts called for the particular expressive capability of an ensemble of expert solo voices,[103] and at the papal chapel one-to-a-part singing by select singers is documented in this and other Holy Week music (including Miserere settings such as Allegri's).[104] Different conditions demanded different treatments, and the *Responsoria* from the same publication are expressly to be sung by four or five singers per part, but with the *falsobordone* verse taken by four solo singers.[105] Similar alternations of solo voices and 'full' choir characterize Byrd's *Great*

---

among them'; *Syntagma musicum* iii, 4–5.

[97] Praetorius, *Syntagma musicum* iii, 196.

[98] Concerted music 'can be performed entirely with these parts alone, without the other vocal capellas or instruments'; Praetorius, *Syntagma musicum* iii, 196. See Parrott, *The Essential Bach Choir*, 30.

[99] Sébastien de Brossard on Du Mont's *grands motets*, in his *Catalogue des livres de musique* (MS, 1724), 140; James R. Anthony, *French Baroque Music from Beaujoyeulx to Rameau* (1974), 171.

[100] Harrison, *Medieval Britain*, 181. For a differing interpretation see Bowers, 'Latin Church Polyphony', 50–1.

[101] Jonathan Glixon, 'A Musicians' Union in 16th-century Venice', *Journal of the American Musicological Society* 36 (1983), 392–421.

[102] Bartolomeo Bonifacio, *Rituum ecclesiasticorum ceremoniale*, fol. 18r. Cf. the reported practice of 1525, quoted above.

[103] Viadana stipulates that the voices sing '*con gravità e schietto*' ('solemnly and plainly'); Lodovico Viadana, *Lamentationes* (Venice, 1609), 'Alli virtuosi di musica'.

[104] Jean Lionnet, 'Performance Practice in the Papal Chapel during the 17th Century', *Early Music* 15/1 (1987), 9–11

[105] Viadana, *Lamentationes*, 'Alli virtuosi di musica'.

Service and are all but explicit in the red- and black-ink underlay of the Eton Choirbook (*c.* 1500).[106] In many other repertoires – notably in most 16th-century masses – certain portions of text (Crucifixus, Benedictus etc.) may imply single voices, especially when set in a reduced number of parts.[107]

Certain idioms lent themselves equally to single and multiple voices. In the largely homophonic writing in Cavalieri's *Rappresentatione di Anima, et di Corpo* (1600), variety was evidently also welcome:

> When the choir's music is in four parts, one can, if desired, double them and have now four singing and sometimes all together, provided the platform can accommodate eight.[108]

Doubled voices, however, had at least one clear disadvantage:

> adding *coloraturae* in a choir spoils the result, for when one part is assigned to be sung by several people, it is inevitable that the *coloraturae* will be completely different, and hence both the beauty and the nature of the sound are obscured.
>
> (Finck, 1556)[109]

As a general rule, vocal writing containing wide ranges, extended runs, complex rhythms or chromatic intricacies is most likely to have been intended for single rather than multiple voices. Defining *'da Capella'* in compositional terms, Walther (1732) explains:

> if many voices and instruments are to do one and the same thing accurately together, the composition must also be designed so that this can happen properly. Accordingly one finds that good and experienced masters employ only whole-, half- and quarter-notes in an *alla breve*, but dispose them in sundry ways with such great artistry and skill ...[110]

FROM MONTEVERDI TO BACH

SINGLE- and multiple-voiced choirs continued to coexist and to complement each other, as did new- and old-style repertory (in *stile concertato* and *stile antico*). Thus Monteverdi's famous 1610 publication opens not with the Vespers music but with a rigorously contrapuntal *Missa*

---

[106] See Harrison, *Medieval Britain*, 316.

[107] See Noel O'Regan, 'The Performance of Palestrina: Some Further Observations', *Early Music* 24/1 (1996), 146.

[108] Emilio de' Cavalieri, *Rappresentatione di Anima, et di Corpo* (Rome, 1600), 'Avvertimento'.

[109] Hermann Finck, *Practica musica* (Wittenberg, 1556), bk 5, sig. Ss iv *v*.

[110] Johann Gottfried Walther, *Musicalisches Lexicon* (Leipzig, 1732), 139.

da capella based on a motet already many decades old,[111] and a century later we find amongst Alessandro Scarlatti's diverse church works a *Messa breve a Palestrina*. Even right at the end of our period, Charles Burney, in Florence, could hear vespers music 'all in the old coral style of the 16th century',[112] and, at Milan Cathedral, music from 'about 150 years ago':

> the service they were to sing [was] printed on wood in four parts, separate, cantus–altus–tenor–bassus – out of which after the tone was given by the organist ... they *all* sung, namely 1 boy, 3 castratos, 2 tenors and 2 basses, under the direction of the Maestro di Capella, without the organ.[113]

In Germany, where the motets of Handl, Lassus and their contemporaries formed the staple diet of Lutheran choirs well into the mid-18th century, a printed anthology of such works – *Florilegium Portense* (1603 and 1621) – may still have been in use in Leipzig as late as 1770.[114]

While Monteverdi's *1610 Vespers* gives not the slightest hint of requiring more singers than there are voice parts (*solo/tutti* indications are entirely absent), the sober writing of the Mass is clearly suited to a reasonably 'strong' *capella* of singers (with continuo, and therefore not *a cappella* in the sense of 'without instruments', a meaning which dates from the 19th century). Similarly the traditional Lutheran motet could invite 'wherever possible ... a very strong contingent of singers',[115] in clear contrast to concerted music. 'How many persons are actually needed for a well-appointed musical ensemble?' asks Johann Beer in 1690:

> I say that one can make a fully satisfying harmony with eight persons, namely four vocalists, two violinists, one organist and the director ... For with six parts there is a complete body of sound, and it is not necessary to trouble oneself further with a larger group ...[116]

Mattheson (1728) duly countered by proposing an ensemble of at least 23 persons (plus director), in which Beer's two violins have turned into what we recognize as an 'orchestra'. Yet Mattheson seems content with just the

---

[111] The *Missa da capella ... fatta sopra il motetto In illo tempore del* Gomberti (*a6*), in Claudio Monteverdi, *Missa ... Ac Vespere* (Venice, 1610).

[112] At the church of the Annunciation (7 September 1770); Charles Burney, *Music, Men, and Manners in France and Italy, 1770*, ed. H. E. Poole (1969), 112.

[113] Burney, *Music, Men, and Manners*, 47.

[114] See Parrott, *The Essential Bach Choir*, 21–7.

[115] Johann Adolph Scheibe, *Critischer Musicus* (Leipzig, 1745), 182 (reprinting an article of 1737). See also Parrott, *The Essential Bach Choir*, 29.

[116] Johann Beer, *Musicalische Discurse* (Nuremberg, 1719), 11; H.-J. Schulze, 'Johann Sebastian Bach's Orchestra: Some Unanswered Questions', *Early Music* 17/1 (1989), 13.

four singers.[117] Lutheran composers were particularly keen to expand their instrumental resources (notably with the newer woodwind instruments), but the essential vocal choir of their concerted music remained in effect the solo-voiced *coro favorito* of Praetorius, Schütz *et al.*, with instruments now almost invariably outnumbering voices by at least five to two.[118] (Telemann's 'pool' of singers in Hamburg seems generally to have consisted of seven, alongside 20 or so instrumentalists.)[119] As before, the four or so *concertists* – standing well forward[120] – might be doubled from time to time by an optional vocal *capella* or ripieno group:

> *Capella* is when a separate choir joins in at certain sections for the splendour and strengthening of the *Music*; it must therefore be separately positioned in a place apart from the concertists. With insufficient people, however, these *capella* sections can even be left out, because they are in any case already also sung by the concertists.
>
> (Fuhrmann, 1706)[121]

The sources of J. S. Bach's earliest-known large-scale cantata *Gott ist mein König*, BWV71 (Mühlhausen, 1708), illustrate these principles with exceptional clarity: the ripieno group – explicitly optional (*'se piace'*) – appears in under half of the choral writing.[122] And from the other end of Bach's working life, the ripieno parts added in 1742 to *Dem Gerechten muß das Licht*, BWV195, operate in exactly the same way: concertists remain responsible not only for solo movements but also for each and every chorus, with ripienists occasionally brought in (under certain conditions) simply to add weight.[123] The dozen or more young singers in Bach's élite First Choir at Leipzig may perhaps all have sung in the congregational chorales and traditional motets (directed by the Prefect), but his own extraordinarily 'intricate' concerted music required only the very best

---

[117] Johann Mattheson, *Der musicalische Patriot* (Hamburg, 1728), 64. See Parrott, *The Essential Bach Choir*, 118.

[118] Parrott, *The Essential Bach Choir*, 117–29. See also Andrew Parrott, 'Vocal Ripienists and J. S. Bach's Mass in B Minor', *Eighteenth-Century Music* 7 (2010), 33–4; and A. Parrott, 'Bach's Chorus: The Leipzig Line', *Early Music* 38/2 (2010), 229–31 (both reprinted in this volume, Chs. 11 and 12, respectively).

[119] Parrott, *The Essential Bach Choir*, 118.

[120] For questions of balance and placement, see Parrott, *The Essential Bach Choir*, 131–9.

[121] Martin Heinrich Fuhrmann, *Musicalischer-Trichter* (Frankfurt an der Spree, 1706). See Parrott, *The Essential Bach Choir*, 29–41.

[122] Parrott, *The Essential Bach Choir*, 36, 68, 141–2; Parrott, 'Vocal Ripienists', 12 (also 14–15, 20, 21).

[123] See Parrott, *The Essential Bach Choir*, 70, 72–3, 85–92; concertists and ripienists in general are discussed at 29–41 and Bach's own use of ripienists at 59–92. See also Parrott, 'Vocal Ripienists'.

of them to sing. Consequently Bach was able to have the second violin 'mostly … taken by pupils, and the viola, violoncello and violone always so (for want of more capable persons)',[124] in line with his earlier formal undertaking to 'instruct the boys not only in vocal but also in instrumental music, so that the churches may not be put to unnecessary expense'.[125]

FEMALE VOICES

At the Thomasschule Bach faced specific difficulties caused by 'the admission hitherto of so many unproficient and musically quite untalented boys',[126] but dissatisfaction with boy singers was a widespread occurrence and, as we have seen, the cornett had been frequently employed 'to supplement … trebles, which are not usually good' (Mersenne, 1636). In Glarean's experience (1547), boys were 'frequently unacquainted with the song',[127] while in Banchieri's (1614) they were 'universally in all cities scarcely to be found, and those with little grounding';[128] the better ones, according to Mattheson (1739), tended moreover 'to think so much of themselves that their behaviour is unbearable'.[129] The main problem, of course, was that 'when one has taken great pains to train a boy's voice, it disappears as the voice breaks, which usually happens between the ages of '15 or 20' (Bacilly, 1668)[130] – or at 'about 13' (Banchieri, 1614).[131] For his *concerti ecclesiastici*, Viadana (1602) consequently advised that 'falsettists will make a better effect'[132] – though within a short time castratos had all but ousted that particular species of soprano from Italy.

For the Church the problem rested on the words of St Paul: 'Let your women keep silence in the churches' (1 Corinthians 14:34). Rich traditions and high standards of polyphonic music-making were nevertheless maintained in many all-female convents, often despite stringent restrictions imposed from outside. In musical publications dedicated to nuns, keyboard transpositions are dealt with by both G. P. Cima (1606)

---

[124] Bach's 1730 'Entwurff einer wohlbestallten Kirchen *Music*'; Parrott, *The Essential Bach Choir*, 165, 168.

[125] Parrott, *The Essential Bach Choir*, 13–15.

[126] As at n. 124.

[127] Heinrich Glarean, *Dodecachordon* (Basel, 1547); reprinted as *Dodecachordon*, trans. C. A. Miller (1965) i, 209.

[128] Banchieri, *Cartella*, 18–19.

[129] Johann Mattheson, *Der vollkommene Capellmeister* (Hamburg, 1739), 482.

[130] Bénigne de Bacilly, *Remarques curieuses sur l'art de bien chanter* (Paris, 1668), 80–1.

[131] Banchieri, *Cartella*, 18.

[132] Viadana, *Cento concerti ecclesiastici* (Venice, 1602), 'A' benigni lettori'.

and Penna (1672),[133] suggesting one way of making certain vocal works accessible to female choirs. A double-choir motet by the Modenese nun Sulpitia Cesis (1606) has a different solution: the Tenor of choir I is expressly to be sung up an octave and the Bass not sung but played, as is choir II in its entirety.[134] In music with basso continuo there was an alternative way of tackling vocal bass parts: nuns 'can sing the bass at the octave, which produces an alto part' (Donati, 1623).[135] This did not convince a German visitor to Venice in 1725, who 'took a strong dislike' to one aspect of the 'fugal and contrapuntal' psalm settings as sung by the *figlie* of the Pietà:

> the bass part was sung by a contralto, thereby creating a succession of very clear 5ths and octaves with the continuo bass and with the viola which was beneath the alto part.[136]

To a Frenchman, the Italian female contralto was simply

> not of the same kind as ours: no type of French voice could render their song well. They are female *bas-dessus* voices, lower than any of ours.[137]

Exactly how Vivaldi's SATB writing for the Pietà was performed nevertheless remains somewhat unclear. While several 'tenors' and the occasional 'bass' are documented amongst the *figlie*, a significant amount of Venetian *ospedale* music survives in SSAA format.[138] And when Burney visited in 1771 it seems that music at the Mendicanti was 'never in more than three parts, often only in two', yet very effective.[139] Quite possibly practices varied according both to fashion and to the availability of singers

---

[133] Parrott, 'Transposition', 492, 494.

[134] Parrott, 'Transposition', 507–8.

[135] Ignatio Donati, *Salmi boscarecci* (Venice, 1623), 'Avvertimenti'.

[136] Mattheson, *Critica Musica* ii (Hamburg, 1725), 243. See Michael Talbot, 'Tenors and Basses at the Venetian *Ospedali*', *Acta musicologica* 66 (1994), 123–38; and M. Talbot, 'Sacred Music at the Ospedale della Pietà in Venice in the Time of Handel', *Händel-Jahrbuch* 46 (2000), 125–56. The Pietà was one of four musically active Venetian *ospedali* – not convents – and most of their *figlie di coro* were in fact women rather than girls.

[137] Charles de Brosses, *Lettres familières écrites d'Italie en 1739 et 1740* ii (4/1885), 317– 18. According to Charles Burney, 'many of the girls [at the Venetian *ospedali*] sing in the countertenor as low as A and G, which enables them always to keep below the *soprano* and *mezzo soprano*, to which they sing the base'; *Dr. Burney's Musical Tours in Europe* i: *An Eighteenth-Century Musical Tour in France and Italy*, ed. P. A. Scholes, (1959), 114.

[138] See Joan Whittemore, *Music of the Venetian Ospedali Composers: A Thematic Catalogue* (1995).

[139] Burney, *Dr. Burney's Musical Tours* i, 114.

with exceptionally low voices.[140] (An ingenious practice by Vienna's Ursuline nuns, when no female bass was available, was for a man to sing 'through a window [which opened on] to the musicians' choir'.)[141]

The outstanding quality of Venice's best *ospedale* singers repeatedly attracted the attention of the city's many visitors, causing a German courtier in 1649 to reflect wistfully: 'I have often wished that the sound of such music might spread to the electoral court chapel in Dresden.'[142] As the demand for elaborate concerted music grew, and especially wherever castratos were not an option, one question came increasingly to the fore: 'whether it be allowed to make use of female singers in music-making in church' (Scheibel, 1721). The frequent shortage of good trebles, this theologian declared, was something 'a good female singer could easily supply'; surely it would be 'better if a musically intelligent woman sang devotional arias in church rather than secular and amorous ones at the opera', using 'this their talent primarily for the praise of God'.[143] Whilst acknowledging that this would be 'a vast improvement of chorall musick', Roger North in 1728 conceded that 'both text and morallity are against it'.[144] A proposal in 1762 to admit women as members of the French chapel royal, 'in order not to have to send for more Italians' (i.e. castratos), seems to have been rejected on everything but musical grounds.[145] (As soloists,

---

[140] Four possible approaches involve no rewriting of SATB music otherwise intended for male choirs:
    SATB   all parts sounding at written pitch
    SSAA Tenor and Bass parts up an 8ve
    SAAT Tenor part at pitch but Bass up an 8ve
    SA(T) Bass part (and Tenor) omitted; or Bass part up an 8ve and both Alto and Tenor parts omitted.

[141] Hauschronik ii, Wiener Ursulinen, 265 (16 July 1731); Janet K. Page, '"A lovely and perfect music": Maria Anna von Raschenau and Music at the Viennese Convent of St Jakob auf der Hülben', *Early Music* 38/3 (2010), 411, 421.

[142] Heinrich Herrmann von Oeÿnhausen (travelling in the retinue of the Landgrave of Hesse-Darmstadt); Mary E. Frandsen, *Crossing Confessional Boundaries* (2006), 443.

[143] Gottfried Ephraim Scheibel, *Zufällige Gedancken von der Kirchen-Music* (Frankfurt and Leipzig, 1721), 59–61. On witnessing 'two or three' women amongst the singers at St Gudula's, Brussels, Burney commented: 'If the practice were to become general, of admitting women to sing the *soprano* part in the cathedrals, it would, in Italy, be a service to mankind, and in the rest of Europe render church music infinitely more pleasing and perfect' (1773); *Dr. Burney's Musical Tours* ii, 20–1.

[144] Wilson, *Roger North*, 271.

[145] '... one can only reflect on the modicum of service one would have had from them, because of their monthly indispositions, their confinements, the perpetual indolence and natural caprice of women: really there was no common sense in the idea. Thanks be to God, it has not come to pass'; Lionel Sawkins, 'For and Against the Order of Nature: Who Sang the Soprano?' *Early Music* 15/3 (1987), 316.

however, female singers had long been accepted there; Lalande's two daughters are known to have taken part in *grands motets* around 1700.)[146]

Away from close ecclesiastical scrutiny, the use of 'female quiristers' alongside males may have been quietly pioneered in private chapels. An English Jesuit priest gives us a tantalizing hint of clandestine worship in the 1580s at the home of a musical Catholic gentleman: not only were there 'choristers, male and female, members of his household', but also 'Mr. Byrd, the very famous English musician and organist, was among the company.'[147] A century later, various musically skilled chambermaids in the employ of Mlle de Guise sang the upper parts in her household ensemble (with Charpentier as singer and composer in residence), for both secular and chapel music.[148] By 1717 at least one German court had followed suit: at Württemberg the 10 people needed for 'a complete and well-set-up' church ensemble included four female sopranos (the younger two designated as 'Ripieno' singers).[149]

Introducing female singers into Germany's municipal churches may have been more of a challenge: 'Initially it was required that I should at all costs position them so that nobody got to see them; but ultimately people could not hear or see them enough.'[150] These early experiences of Mattheson's in Hamburg *c.* 1715 evidently supported his later view that women were 'absolutely indispensable' in a *Kapelle*.[151] Defining a 'complete choir ... for use both in the theatre and in church and chamber', Scheibe in 1737 was equally adamant that 'Of the eight principal singers the sopranos *and altos* should be women, because their voices will be more natural, and of better durability and purity.'[152] Practice varied, of course, but female singers – soprano and alto, younger and older – are documented at the Würzburg court (1746),[153] at Stuttgart's Stiftkirche (from before 1720),[154]

---

[146] This practice can perhaps be traced back to the Medici court, where from *c.* 1600 ecclesiastical propriety was deemed to have been satisfied by having first Vittoria Archilei and then Francesca Caccini contribute to Holy Week services from just outside the body of the church. See, for example, Suzanne G. Cusick, *Francesca Caccini at the Medici Court* (2009), 17, 291–3.

[147] *William Weston: The Autobiography of an Elizabethan*, trans. P. Caraman (1955), 71.

[148] See Patricia Ranum, 'A Sweet Servitude: A Musician's Life at the Court of Mlle de Guise', *Early Music* 15/3 (1987), 347–60.

[149] Samantha Owens, 'Professional Women Musicians in Early 18th-Century Württemberg', *Music & Letters* 82 (2001), 36.

[150] Mattheson, *Der vollkommene Capellmeister*, 482.

[151] Mattheson, *Der vollkommene Capellmeister*, 482.

[152] Scheibe, *Critischer Musicus*, 157 [my italics].

[153] Dieter Kirsch, *Lexikon Würzburger Hofmusiker* (2002), 14–15.

[154] Owens, 'Professional Women Musicians', 43.

and, perhaps most remarkably, at Cologne Cathedral (from as early as 1711 and right through the century).[155]

HANDEL

THE abiding image of 250 choral singers – just six of them female – packed together in Westminster Abbey for the 1784 'Commemoration of Handel' (see Illus. 2.2)[156] raises the question of exactly how large Handel's own choirs may have been. Opportunities to write on the grandest scale arose predominantly in connection with royal or state events, yet the 'Utrecht' Te Deum and Jubilate (1713), given in the vast spaces of St Paul's Cathedral, involved perhaps no more than 20 singers out of an estimated 50 or so performers.[157] It was the coronation of George II in 1727 that gave rise to the 'first Grand Musical performance in the Abbey' and with it some of the most enduring large-scale ceremonial music ever written, not least Handel's setting of *Zadok the Priest*. For the event, the combined Chapel Royal and Abbey choirs reportedly comprised '40 Voices',[158] while instruments – well over 100 of them – again outnumbered singers. Music-making on this scale, however, was exceptional.[159] The clear majority of Handel's Chapel Royal music was designed for St James's Palace and for around 20 singers (with occasional modest orchestral accompaniment), while the musical establishment at Cannons (1717–18), where the Duke of Chandos lived 'en Prince',[160] would

---

[155] Klaus Wolfgang Niemöller, *Kirchenmusik und reichsstafidtische Musikpflege im Köln des 18. Jahrhunderts* (1960), 9, 198 and *passim*.

[156] '... the musicians assembled on this occasion exceeded in abilities, as well as number, those of every band that has been collected in modern times'; Charles Burney, *An Account of the Musical Performances in Westminster Abbey and the Pantheon ... in 1784* (London, 1785), vii. Burney proceeds to report half a dozen or so reported sightings of monster-scale forces – from as far back as 1515 to Jommelli's funeral in 1774, four of them reaching totals of around 300.

[157] Thirteen men and around six boys, the Chapel Royal singers then 'in waiting'; Donald Burrows, *Handel and the English Chapel Royal* (2005), 102–3.

[158] The *Norwich Gazette*, reporting a public rehearsal. The numbers closely match autograph indications in the composer's score of *The King Shall Rejoice*: 'C[anto] 12, H[ughes] et 6, Freem[an] et 6' and so on.

[159] Handel's only other performance on this scale seems to have been of the funeral anthem for Queen Caroline at the Abbey a decade later, reportedly with 'near 80 Vocal Performers' and 100 instrumentalists; *Daily Advertiser*, 19 December 1737, cited in Burrows, *Handel and the English Chapel Royal*, 378.

[160] '... the Musick is made for himself and sung by his own servants'; Sir David Dalrymple (letter), 1718, in Donald Burrows, *Handel* (1994), 80. The local parish church of St Lawrence, Whitchurch, served as a temporary domestic chapel.

A Brief Anatomy of Choirs 43

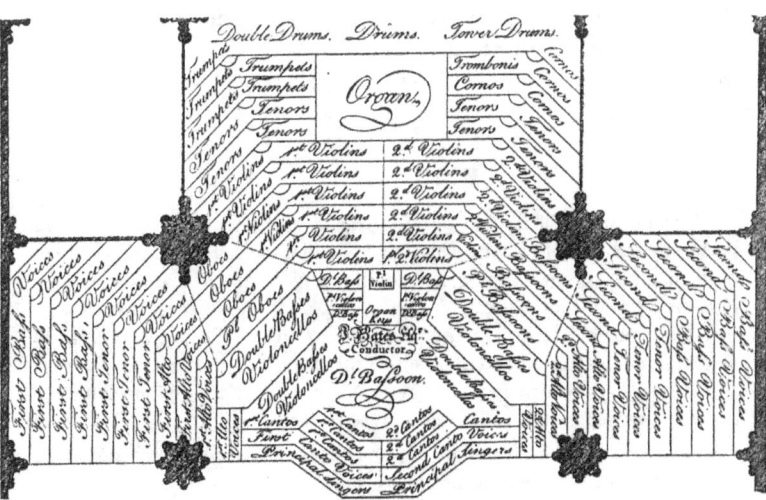

Illus. 2.2 *(top)* 'View of the ORCHESTRA and Performers in Westminster Abbey' (drawing by E. F. Burney, engraving by J. Collyer); *(bottom)* 'Plan of the Orchestra and Disposition of the Band'; both from Charles Burney, *An Account of the Musical Performances ... in Commemoration of Handel* (London, 1785)

have reminded him of many a small German court, with its complement of three to eight voices and eight to ten instruments.

Earlier still the 21-year-old Lutheran had left Hamburg for Italy with operatic ambitions. According to a French traveller, accustomed to the lavish vocal forces of Parisian opera, 'everyone knows that choruses are out of use in Italy, indeed beyond the means of the ordinary Italian opera house'; instead, any choral writing was routinely delivered by the opera's various characters, 'the King, the Clown, the Queen and the Old Woman – all singing together'.[161] Oratorios worked in much the same way; thus, for Handel's *La Resurrezione* (Rome, 1708), which contains two choruses, we find payments to the solo singers and to more than 40 instrumentalists (headed by Corelli) but none for any additional singers.

In Italy's churches, as we have seen, 'Renaissance' polyphony (with or without organ) remained current. Major feasts, however, when extra musicians could be hired,[162] routinely demanded up-to-the-minute *concertato* music – and this is exactly what Handel's three Roman psalm settings of 1707 deliver, each in its own way. The original set of parts to *Laudate pueri* makes it clear that its choral writing was designed for five *concertato* singers (including the starring soprano) with a 'Secondo Coro' of (five?) ripienists, while the concluding double-choir 'Gloria Patri' of *Nisi Dominus*, performed on the same occasion, implies a similar arrangement. In the case of *Dixit Dominus*, however, the consistently challenging vocal writing nowhere suggests a need for vocal reinforcement of its five virtuoso soloists (despite the single appearance of some chant-like writing marked '*cappella*').[163]

A quarter of a century later Handel was turning his attention to the English oratorio. "Tis excessive noisy, a vast number of instruments and voices, who all perform at a time', declared an aristocratic lady on hearing *Deborah* at a London theatre in 1733. Yet, although the orchestra was probably at least 60 strong, singers (including six soloists) were

---

[161] Le Cerf de la Viéville], *Comparaison de la musique italienne, et de la musique françoise*, (Brussels, 2/1705), 71. At one of Handel's London opera performances in 1728, Pierre-Jacques Fougeroux noted that 'the chorus consists of only four voices'; Winton Dean, 'A French Traveller's View of Handel's Operas', *Music & Letters* 55 (1974), 178. In 1741 the castrato Caffarelli was apparently arrested and imprisoned for 'disturbing the other performers' in various ways, which included 'refusing to sing in the ripieno with the others'; Angus Heriot, *The Castrati in Opera* (1956), 144–5.

[162] Even in the 1690s more than half of Rome's 25 ecclesiastical choirs comprised just four or five singers, according to a list drawn up by Padre Martini; 'Musici di Roma nell'anno che il Sig, Gio. Paolo Colonna si portò in Roma' (MS), in Oscar Mischiati, 'Una statistica della musica a Roma nel 1694', *Note d'archivio* ns 1 (1983), 209–27.

[163] In 'De torrente' a chant-like accompaniment to the duetting sopranos is supplied by a 'cappella' of unison tenor and bass voices.

estimated to number no more than 'about twenty-five'.[164] *Messiah* (1742) began its remarkable life in relatively modest circumstances, in Dublin's New Musick Hall, 'a Room of 600 Persons'.[165] All indications are that the work's many choruses were taken by the various soloists (seven of them, male and female) with perhaps half a dozen or so additional singers. Records of subsequent London performances at the Foundling Hospital in the 1750s show payments to five or six vocal soloists, four or six boys and 11 to 13 other adult male singers, together with the conventionally larger complement of instruments (33 or 38 plus continuo).[166] More interesting perhaps than these numbers and ratios is the 'mixed' nature of the resultant choral soprano line: two female 'theater' sopranos (usually Italian) and a few Chapel Royal choirboys, doubled by as many as four oboes. (It should be added that the presence of chorus music in the soloists' books bequeathed by Handel to the Foundling Hospital confirms the expectation of their choral role.)[167]

AFTER Handel's death in 1759, annual performances of *Messiah* at the Foundling Hospital continued for many years – as did the institution's careful book keeping. While orchestral numbers remained much the same, what these later accounts clearly document is a sudden and sharp increase in the number of singers from 1771 onwards, when the number of boys rose to 12 and a considerable body of unpaid chorus singers was added – 26 or more of them.[168] This moment in the emergence of large non-ecclesiastical bodies of amateur singers, male and female in now-familiar SATB formation, is therefore a fitting place to leave the present brief survey.

From Dufay to Handel, composers of earlier choral music knew their choirs intimately – as choirmasters and directors, and frequently as singers themselves. Pitch levels, singer numbers and ratios, voice-types and vocal scoring, conventions of notation and of instrumental participation – rarely do these correspond directly to current practice, yet only exceptionally would any explanation have been required by those for whom the music was carefully crafted. An appreciation of the diverse anatomies of vocal choirs from the first 300 years of modern choral history can only serve to enrich our understanding of the music those composers wrote.

---

[164] Lady Irwin, letter to Lord Carlisle (31 March 1733); Winton Dean, *Handel's Dramatic Oratorios and Masques* (1959), 234.

[165] Donald Burrows, *Handel: Messiah* (1991), 15.

[166] Donald Burrows, 'Lists of Musicians for Performances of Handel's *Messiah* at the Foundling Hospital, 1754–1777', *Royal Musical Association Research Chronicle* 43 (2010), 89–91.

[167] Donald Burrows, 'Handel's Oratorio Performances', in *The Cambridge Companion to Handel*, ed. D. Burrows (1997), 273.

[168] Burrows, 'Lists of Musicians', 97–102.

3

Falsetto Beliefs:
The 'Countertenor' Cross-Examined

Contratenorista est ille qui contratenorem canit.[1]
(Johannes Tinctoris)

TODAY'S 'countertenor' – a man whose singing is exclusively or predominantly in falsetto – is widely seen as the very emblem of early vocal music. Once confined to the Anglican choir-stall, he is now accepted in all manner of vocal ensembles and has achieved international status as a soloist, not least on the world's great operatic stages. Naturally enough, the rise of this new/old voice-type has attracted plenty of comment and speculation *en route*. Yet for the most part the modern countertenor's historical credentials have simply been taken on trust. Indeed, the undoubted complexity of establishing a reliable history for the voice, combined with its unassailable place as a linchpin of the Anglican choir and its evident allure for audiences, have ensured that scholars and performers alike have generally been content not to probe too deeply.

Irrespective of possible conclusions, a root and branch reappraisal of key evidence and of familiar thinking is badly needed. My aim here is therefore to clarify where, when, how and why falsetto singing may have been practised in previous eras. Or more specifically, to dare to ask *whether* any such voice-type was actually cultivated before the 16th century. Although much of the inquiry is necessarily concerned with church vocal ensembles and with early and sparsely documented periods, its consequences for an accurate understanding of 17th- and 18th-century practices, solo as well as choral, are considerable. For if falsetto singing is simply believed to have been an endemic feature of medieval life (as our film-makers evidently suppose), it is all too easy to assume its continued cultivation thereafter.

The issues to be addressed are both numerous and disparate, encompassing familiar and unfamiliar concepts and drawing on a broad range of sources (archival, theoretical, literary and musical). This cross-examination is therefore presented not as a single narrative but as a series of discrete critical case studies. (In order to keep the main text as plain as possible in what is inevitably a complex investigation, useful subsidiary material has been confined to footnotes and Appendices.)

....
First appeared in *Early Music* 43/1 (2015), 79–110.
....

[1] 'A countertenor is one who sings the *contratenor*'; Johannes Tinctoris, *Terminorum musicae diffinitorium* (Treviso, 1495), ch. 3.

LINES OF REASONING

It may be as well to start in relatively familiar territory. In recent decades two related accounts of the 16th- and early 17th-century English 'countertenor' have held sway. Both appear to grow out of a firm belief that falsetto singing was already a long-established feature of church music-making, but they diverge significantly in allocating the falsettist to different voice parts. In one case (associated notably with David Wulstan) it is argued that, as 'mean' parts were intended for boys, the expected falsettist will have been assigned to *contratenor* parts throughout the period. (Support for this scoring, which puts the falsettist in a decidedly lower range than might otherwise be expected, is sought in a reported 'high' organ pitch of a minor 3rd or so above today's $a' = 440$.)[2] Reduced to its bare bones, the more elaborate and extensively argued alternative account (by Roger Bowers)[3] is set out below (left, in italics), alongside an outline of my own very different reading of the same evidence (right):

1 'Modern taste and tradition' divides adult male voices into 'three basic types: bass, tenor and alto.'[4]	1 Men's 'natural' singing voices may be divided into two basic categories (high and low; tenor and bass) but, more realistically, into three (high, middle and low; tenor, baritone and bass). Men's 'falsetto' voices, now usually labelled countertenor or alto, are generally treated separately and as a single category (though unsurprisingly some are higher or lower than others).
2 '... it is clear that something akin to the modern countertenor voice was well known in the Middle Ages.'[5]	2 While the capacity to produce vocal sounds in falsetto is presumably as old as mankind,[6] there is no reliable evidence to suggest that falsetto singing was cultivated as a distinct voice-type in the Middle Ages.

---

[2] David Wulstan, 'The Problem of Pitch in 16th-Century English Vocal Music', *Proceedings of the Royal Musical Association* 93/1 (1967), 98 and 107 n. 9; and David Wulstan, *Tudor Music* (1985), 200–2.

[3] Roger Bowers, various; see below, where Bowers I–III and VI are studies reprinted in Bowers, *English Church Polyphony* (1999).

[4] Bowers II, 13 [= 'To Chorus from Quartet: The Performing Resource for English Church Polyphony, *c.* 1390–1559', in *English Choral Practice, 1400–1650*, ed. J. Morehen (1995)].

[5] Bowers, 'The Performing Pitch of English 15th-Century Church Polyphony', *Early Music* 8/1 (1980), 22.

[6] Also, as *New Grove* helpfully points out, 'There are major elements of this second mode of phonation in the instinctive natural sounds of various animals, for example, the gibbon'; *The New Grove Dictionary of Music and Musicians* viii, ed. S. Sadie (2/2001), 537 ('Falsetto').

3 Since the falsetto voice is 'unlikely to have had anything to contribute to the performance of plainsong', its place must have been in polyphony.[7]	3 Not only is there no obvious place for the falsetto voice in the performance of plainchant, there is no good reason to seek a place for it in early polyphony.
4 As 'boys' voices were not involved in the performance of written polyphony before the mid-15th century, the falsettist's place in the earlier polyphony will have been on the top part.[8]	4 If neither boys' voices nor those of adult falsettists were required for written polyphony before the mid-15th century, the top part will have been intended for a man's high natural voice (our 'tenor').
5 If the top part of early polyphony was intended for the falsetto voice, the music will have been pitched for that voice to sing somewhere in the region of today's $b\flat$–c''.[9]	5 If the top part of early polyphony was intended for a man's high natural voice, the music will have been pitched for that voice to sing somewhere in the region of today's f–g'.
6 As the overall range of early three-part polyphony is almost invariably no more than two octaves (15 notes), pitching it to suit a falsettist on the top part means that no use is made of 'the lower reaches of the adult register, those below about c [at today's pitch]': the bass voice was not used in the performance of polyphony.[10]	6 The overall compass of three-part polyphony almost never exceeds two octaves (15 notes), a range well within the collective span of men's natural voices. Pitching a top part to lie in a suitable 'tenor' range puts the lower parts in an equally suitable 'bass' range (perhaps in the region of today's G–a).
7 Between c. 1450 and c. 1500 a new expanded scoring emerged in England, now spanning three octaves (22 notes) and sometimes more. Of its five core voice parts, the three in the middle (most often in C2 C4 C4 clefs, the lower two sometimes labelled tenor and contratenor) have a 'familiar appearance', suggesting that the earlier three-part scoring has simply acquired two additional parts, one above (for	7 Between c. 1450 and c. 1500 the new expanded scoring that emerged in England spanned three octaves (22 notes) and sometimes more. Notationally the expansion is both upwards and downwards; in other words, both higher and lower written notes are newly pressed into service. However, while these new notes may appear to imply *sounding* pitches that are both higher and lower than those

---

[7] Bowers II, 13.

[8] Bowers I, 178 [= 'The Performing Ensemble for English Church Polyphony, c. 1320–c. 1390', in *Studies in the Performance of Late Mediaeval Music*, ed. S. Boorman (1983)].

[9] Bowers I, 181

[10] Bowers I, 181; Bowers II, 14; and Bowers, 'The Performing Pitch', 22–3. Elsewhere, belief that one of his own hypotheses is 'indisputable' prevents Bowers from comprehending how the bass voice is likely to have fitted into the scheme of things; Bowers, 'False Voices' (reply), *Early Music* 9/1 (1981), 74–5. For what it is worth, the 15th-century English tract recorded in British Library, Lansdowne MS 763 several times specifically addresses the singer of improvised counterpoint who possesses 'a low voice'.

boys) and one below (for the previously excluded basses).[11]

previously used (and thus one new high voice part and one new low one), no such assumption should be made: notation of this period merely defines the intervals between notes and says nothing whatsoever about their absolute pitch. In practice, a lower *notated* pitch level (causing the sounding range of men's natural voices to be *written* lower) allowed not one but two new upper parts (for boys, high and low) to be most efficiently accommodated at the upper end of the traditional 20-note notational gamut (see Illus. 3.1) and with the minimum of additonal notes.

8 In this new scoring the falsettist sings in the same range as before but takes the second highest part – labelled medius or 'mean'.[12] *This part belonged to the adult falsettist. In particular circumstances, however, a boy's voice lower than the treble (although 'not in any way ... a separate voice in its own right') 'was used as a substitute for the adult alto'.*[13]

8 In this new scoring the second highest part – the 'mean' – belonged exclusively to boys. (Nowhere are men recorded as having sung the part, nor do the various references to boys' doing so hint at their being considered mere substitutes for men.)

9 In 1549, with the introduction of the vernacular Book of Common Prayer and in a 'sequence of events [which still] awaits a full elucidation', a 'transition ... was ignited and propelled' that produced a higher sounding pitch (by about a major 2nd or minor 3rd) and turned the 'erstwhile "high-range" tenor ... into falsetto alto'. Contratenor parts were now sung by countertenors as we now know them.[14]

9 Gradual changes of musical fashion through and beyond the 16th century inevitably influenced how composers used the resources at their disposal – men's natural voices and those of boys – but there was no major upheaval either in vocal scoring or in general sounding pitch. Treble and mean parts tended to merge into a single intermediate-range 'mean' part for boys, while the men's contratenor and tenor parts settled into differentiated ranges (for higher- and lower-range tenors, in our terms).

---

[11] Bowers, 'The Performing Pitch', 25; and Bowers II, 23. Cf. '"High" Choirs, "Full" Choirs', below.

[12] Bowers, 'The Performing Pitch', 25; and Bowers II, 24.

[13] Bowers III, 67. See also R. Bowers, 'Chains of (Rehabilitated) Gold', *Early Music Review* 159 (April 2014), 16.

[14] Bowers, 'Chains', 12–13.

50   *Composers' Intentions?*

10 Throughout both the 15th and 16th centuries falsetto singing in England is nowhere explicitly documented: 'it would of course be preferable to have evidence of genuinely contemporary origin; but there seems to be none.'[15]	10 Not only is there no documentation of falsetto singing in England before the 17th century, there is no apparent 'vacancy' for it to fill. There is also good reason to believe that the voice-type was adopted significantly later in England than, for example, in Italy and Germany, perhaps because England had a stronger tradition of boys' singing than the former, and was musically more insular than the latter.

These parallel accounts of one particular segment of the falsettist's possible history raise several significant issues. Matters concerning 16th- and early 17th-century English music will be addressed again later, but before dealing with the critical initial question of whether or not falsetto singing was cultivated in the Middle Ages (see points 2/2 above) I wish to turn to mainland Europe and to the 15th century.

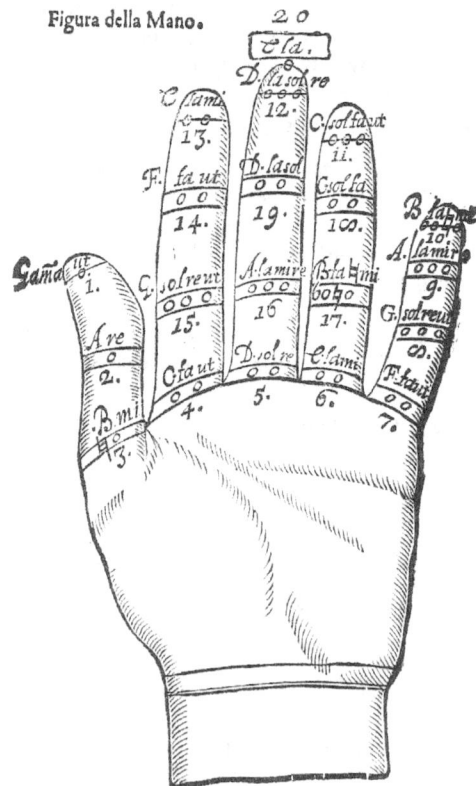

Illus. 3.1 The Guidonian Hand,
from Lorenzo Penna, *Li primi albori musicali* (Bologna, 1672), 9

[15] Bowers, 'False Voices', 74.

DUFAY'S WILL: *FAUSSET*

THE lengthy will drawn up by Guillaume Dufay a few months before his death at Cambrai in 1474 is one of a very small handful of documents that promises truly authoritative help in unravelling some of these issues. Not only does it stem from a major composer (arguably the most famous of his day), it also details the singers required for three distinct and specific musical items. Of these, the first seemingly provides as clear and simple a testimonial for falsetto singing as one could possibly imagine. According to the will's executors, Dufay had requested that, following the administering of the last rites and 'if time permitted', eight men from the cathedral choir were to gather at the dying composer's bedside to sing a hymn 'en fausset' – literally, 'in falsetto'.[16]

The hymn chosen by Dufay – the Palm Sunday processional *Magno salutis gaudio* – is not known to have been set by the composer and in this instance was almost certainly intended to be sung in plainsong.[17] If so, it would undoubtedly have been highly unusual for a single voice-type to be specified, and especially one otherwise understood to have had no place in the performance of chant (see *point 3* above). Equally problematic is the alternative interpretation: a polyphonic work exclusively for falsettists.[18] The apparent riddle, however, arises purely from the French of the executors' account of Dufay's will and is wholly absent from the Latin of the will itself:

> Item *volo et ordino quod postquam ecclesiastica sacramenta michi fuerint ministrata et ad agoniam tendere videbor, si, hora pati possit, sint octo ex sociis ecclesie juxta lectum meum qui, submissa voce cantent hympnum* Magno salutis gaudio ...[19]

Here it is stipulated – appropriately enough – that the eight singers at the composer's bedside sing *submissa voce* ('with lowered voice'), i.e. 'softly'. This expression, both common and evidently unambiguous, is found not only in numerous versions of the medieval Latin church play *Visitatio sepulchri* as a performance direction (e.g., 'with a lowered voice,

---

[16] 'Item *ad cause que le dict deffunct avoit done par son dict testament que se l'eure le pooit souffrier tantost apres qu'il aroit receu son darrain sacrement viii compagnons du coer cantassent en pres lui en fausset le himpne* Magno salutis gaudio'; Alejandro Enrique Planchart, 'Choirboys in Cambrai in the 15th Century', in *Young Choristers, 650–1700*, ed. S. Boynton and E. Rice (2008), 135.

[17] 'Testament de Guillaume Du Fay', in Jules Houdoy, *Histoire artistique de la Cathédrale de Cambrai* (Lille, 1880), 410. But cf. Robert Nosow, *Ritual Meanings in the 15th-Century Motet* (2012), 196.

[18] Would there have been as many as eight 'potential' falsettists at Cambrai?

[19] Houdoy, *Histoire artistique*, 410.

as if speaking into [his] ear'),²⁰ but also in hundreds of contemporary ecclesiastical *ordines* and in diverse musical contexts over the next half millennium and into the 18th century.²¹ For the phrase 'Thou spekest softly' John Stanbridge (1519) gives 'Summisse loqueris',²² and within Dufay's own lifetime the Council of Basel (1435) ruled on 'those who ... say Mass in too low a voice [*nimis basse*]' in the following terms:

> We denounce the improper customs of those who in some churches ... say Mass in so soft a voice [*ita submissa voce*] that it cannot be heard by the bystanders.²³

There can be little doubt that Dufay's chosen wording – 'submissa voce' – was intended straightforwardly to specify that the plainsong hymn be chanted *softly* beside his deathbed. *Exeunt* eight falsettists.

DOES this mean that Dufay's executors simply misunderstood and mistranslated the composer's conventional Latin turn of phrase when they rendered it as 'en fausset' (which could suggest that falsetto seemed a plausible meaning to them)? Or is it we who have misunderstood the vernacular expression?²⁴ (The same equivalence – 'submisse gallice fousset' – crops up in a Cambrai document some 60 years later.)²⁵ The Latin *falsus* ('false') and its various cognates including *fausset/fousset* certainly seem to have acquired more than their fair share of musical connotations: *musica falsa* as used by Elias Salomo in his *Scientia artis*

---

²⁰ '... *submissa voce quasi in aurem dicentes*'; Karl Young, *The Drama of the Medieval Church* (Oxford, 1933), 251.

²¹ Georg Rhau (1520), Bishop Longland (1538), Finck (1556), Zarlino (1558), Dressler (1564), Quitschreiber (1598), Cerone (1612), Calvisius (1612), Praetorius (1613 and 1618), a Venetian ambassador to the French court (1620), Schütz (1636), Butler (1636), Charpentier (c. 1684), Adami (1711) and Beer (1719).

²² John Stanbridge, *Vulgaria* (London, 1519), ed. B. White, Early English Text Society 187 (London, 1932), 17.

²³ Council of Basel, 1435 (*Canonica regula*, VII/9); Don Harrán, *In Defense of Music* (1989), 112–3. 'Saying' Mass may be understood to include singing it; see David Fallows, 'Specific Information on the Ensembles for Composed Polyphony, 1400–1474', *Studies in the Performance of Late Medieval Music*, 130 inc. n. 49.

²⁴ Cf. Craig Wright, 'Performance Practices at the Cathedral of Cambrai, 1475–1550', *The Musical Quarterly* 64/1 (1978), 308 n. 28; Fallows (who nevertheless cautions that both terms might mean 'something else entirely'), 'Specific Information', 126 n. 41; and Rebecca Stewart, 'Voice Types in Josquin's Music', *Tijdschrift van de Vereeniging voor Nederlandse Muziekgeschiedenis* 35 (1985), 123. Planchart seems to allow the term both meanings at the same time: 'it would appear that in the 15th century the normal sound of the falsettists was a soft one'; 'Choirboys in Cambrai', 134–5.

²⁵ Wright, 'Performance Practices', 309.

musicae (1274) has been described as 'a grab bag to cover everything from careless singing or music copying to quite specific elements of notation, mainly those involving chromatic inflections'.[26] Indeed, over the centuries the word 'falsetto' (in one form or another) is known to have applied variously to 'a semitone where it ought not to be' (as with the later term *musica ficta*),[27] to notes 'above *or below*' an instrument's natural range',[28] specifically to violin harmonics,[29] and quite possibly to sub-standard singers.[30] But it is a non-musical source that provides the best contemporary support for interpreting the executors' *en fausset* as 'softly'. Froissart's *Chroniques*, much copied during the 15th century and in print by 1495,[31] describe nocturnal events at Montferrand, where on the town walls one Geronnet awaits news; glimpsing a shadowy figure below,

He began to whistle *en fausset* [?=softly].

Il commença a siffler en fausset.[32]

(A current equivalent might be 'Psst!') Not only is a minimum of sound clearly vital to the circumstances described, any possibility of vocal falsetto being intended is completely ruled out by the inherent voicelessness of whistling or hissing.[33]

---

[26] Joseph Dyer, 'A 13th-Century Choirmaster: The *Scientia Artis Musicae* of Elias Salomon', *The Musical Quarterly* 66/1 (1980), 91.

[27] '... *semitonium ubi non debet esse*'; Philippe de Vitry, *Ars nova* (c. 1320), ch. 14.

[28] Michael Praetorius, *Syntagma musicum* ii (Wolfenbüttel, 1618), 19.

[29] 'A great player on the violin in falset'; Charles Burney, *Memoirs of the Life and Writings of the Abate Metastasio* ii (London, 1796), 174.

[30] In 1598 the Venetian *ospedale delle Zitelle* reportedly classified its 58 singing *figlie* as '*canti, tenori, alti, bassi e falsetti*'; Pier Giuseppe Gillio, *L'attività musicale negli ospedali di Venezia nel settecento* (2006), 102.

[31] Froissart, *Cronicques* (Paris, 1495), printed for Antoine Vérard.

[32] Berlin, Staatsbibliothek – Preußischer Kulturbesitz, MS Rehdiger 3, fol. 293v. (The events described occurred in 1388.) The onomatopoeic verb, which in Paris, Bibliothèque nationale, MS fr. 2650, fol. 262v, for example, is given as *escliffer*, can also mean 'to hiss'.

[33] Where Froissart might perhaps wish convey the idea of falsetto as we now know it, *fausset* is not his chosen word. Setting out to capture a town and castle, seven men disguise themselves as women to join those fetching water from outside the gate at daybreak; when addressed by them the men reply 'a fainte voix' – 'in a feigned voice'/'in a faint voice'; bk 3, ch. 29. Interestingly, while the first references in English to falsetto singing (see below) also use 'to feign' (from the Latin *fingere*), this verb too had earlier been associated with soft singing: 'I Feyne in syngyng/ *Ie chante a basse voyx*. We maye nat synge out we are to nere my lorde/ but lette vs fayne this songe: *Nous nosons pas chanter a playne voyx nous sommes trop pres de monsieur chantons pour tant ceste chancon a basse voyx*.' John Palsgrave, *L'esclaircissement de la langue française* ([London], 1530). When Martin le Franc uses the word 'fainte', however, it is more likely to equate to (*musica*) *ficta*; *Le Champion des dames*

Somewhat removed from Dufay's time and place, *falsetto* as soft singing is found alive and well in the 17th century, both in Italy and on the Iberian peninsula. A Castilian dictionary of 1611 defines 'Cantar en falsete' as

> to sing softly/gently and moderately, as when singing in company or in private [*or* 'in a room or chamber'].
>
> *cantar suave y templadamente, como quando se canta en conversacion, o en camara.*[34]

Thus, according to the Neapolitan Pietro Cerone in 1613, 'The madrigalist does not sing in a full voice, but artistically, in *falsetto* or *sotto voce*',[35] and when in 1614 a boy castrato failed to gain admission to a Roman choir it was explained that, 'although for singing softly, *sotto voce* or *in falsetto* in private, he does very well, nevertheless when he opens out his voice he is not yet satisfactory'.[36] Furthermore, in sacred works by the mid-17th-century Montserrat monk Joan Cererols the terms *veu/vox* ('voice') and *falsete*[37] appear *in all voice parts* simply as dynamic markings (= *forte* and *piano*).[38] (Clearly it would be utterly nonsensical to infer any switching back and forth between natural and falsetto vocal production since all singers, from basses to sopranos, would have to switch exclusively – and pointlessly, unless for comic effect – within their usual singing ranges.)

Naturally, not all cases are quite so instructive. In a late 15th-century Dutch morality play of the wise and foolish virgins the character of Folly is invited to join Waste-of-Time in song, and duly responds:

(c. 1440), see Reinhard Strohm, *The Rise of European Music, 1380–1500* (1993), 127–8.

[34] Sebastián de Covarrubias, *Tesoro de la lengua castellana o española* (Madrid, 1611), fol. 396v.

[35] Pietro Cerone – presumably his *El melopeo y maestro* (Naples, 1613) – cited in Igor Stravinsky, preface to Glenn Watkins, *Gesualdo: The Man and his Music* (2/1991), ix. (I have been unable to locate the original passage.)

[36] '... *se bene per cantare piano, sotto voce o in falsetto in camera fa molto bene, non dimeno à voce spiegata per ancora non puo supplire*'; Thomas D. Culley, *Jesuits and Music* i (1970), 143–4, 320–1 (doc. 146).

[37] '*Cantar en voz, es despedir cada vno la voz natural, sin dissimular, ni fingir nada*' ('To sing *en voz* is to put forth the natural voice, without holding anything back or feigning'); de Covarrubias, *Tesoro de la lengua castellana o española*, fol. 396v.

[38] See, for example, the villancicos *Vivo yo, Si suspiros, ¡Ay qué dolor!, Serrana* and *Serafín*; *Mestres de l'Escolania de Montserrat* iii (Montserrat, 1932). The echoing first choir of the same composer's *Salve Regina a 8 voces con ecos* is marked 'El primer coro en falsete'; *Mestres de l'Escolania de Montserrat* ix (Montserrat, 1981). Similarly, the villancico *Mi Dios, si ofensa te ha hecho mi culpa* by Gracián Babán (Valencia Cathedral's *maestro di capilla* from 1657) uses *falsete* in contradistinction to *fuerte* (strong/loud). Antonio Ezquerro Esteban, 'Músicos del Seiscientos hispánico: Miguel de Aguilar, Sebastián Alfonso, Gracián Babán y Mateo Calvete', *Anuario musicál* 61 (2006), 108–9.

Gladly, but I can only sing *in falsetto*.

Gheerne, maer ken can niet zinghen dan int fosset.[39]

More suggestive, however, are the seemingly elliptical words of a French *'contratenore'*, Jacques (Jachetto) de Marville, in a letter to Francesco Gonzaga in 1500:

I have lost nothing of my singing voice except the *falsetto* – which I never had ...

Io non ho persa ne la voce nel cantare salvo lo falexeto che non havè may ...[40]

Here the veteran singer, recently released from Ferrara, is determinedly seeking re-employment at Mantua. At a time when *da chiesa* and *da camera* singing styles were already frequently differentiated,[41] Jachetto's message to the Marquis could well be that his voice was still in perfect condition but had never been of the softer kind required for intimate and private courtly music-making. (Be that as it may, the letter neatly quashes any lingering notion that a singer of *contratenor* parts at this period might by definition have been a falsettist.)

EARLIER 'FALSE' WORDS

IF 'something akin to the modern countertenor voice' is to be regarded as a serious contender for a place in 15th-century polyphony, it will be helpful to find out exactly how 'well known' it really was in the earlier Middle Ages. Central to this question are four Latin texts from the 12th and 13th centuries in which words derived from *falsus* occur in musical contexts:

    A Cistercian Order statutes (1134)

    B Gilbertine Order statutes (*c.* 1148)

    C *Instituta Patrum* (1210–20), attributed to Ekkehard V of St Gall

    D Roger Bacon, *Opus tertium* (1267–8).

What these texts have in common – beyond being impossible to translate

---

[39] *Het Spel van de V vroede ende van de V dwaeze Maegden*, ed. M. Hoebeke (1959), 117–19 (line 270). See also Rob Wegman, 'From Maker to Composer: Improvisation and Musical Authorship in the Low Countries, 1450–1500', *Journal of the American Musicological Society* 49 (1996), 419.

[40] Lewis Lockwood, *Music in Renaissance Ferrara, 1400–1505* (1984), 167.

[41] See for example Francesco Bagnacavallo, who in 1491 reported to Isabella d'Este her brother's view of a Hungarian singer: *'dice che non ha grande vocce da capella, ma che da camera è suficienti'*; David Fallows, 'The Performing Ensembles in Josquin's Sacred Music', *Tijdschrift van de Vereeniging voor Nederlandse Muziekgeschiedenis* 35 (1985), 64 n. 86. Cf. n. 36 above.

definitively – is the goal of suppressing all 'false' musical practices considered contrary to the principles of religious worship.[42] However, the objects of condemnation in all four sources remain tantalizingly unclear, whether inappropriate vocal production or (more probably) unlicensed melodic or polyphonic embellishment of the chant. And in *B* a puzzling and ungrammatical vernacular word – 'pipeth' – crops up in the middle of the Latin, compounding the problem of pinning down the 'fausetum' with which it may be paired. Relevant passages from these sources are set out in Appendix 1 ('Four Early Sources') with parallel English versions which aim to allow more than one reading.

A few observations may be made on these four key texts:

A The context is surely plainchant, to which falsetto singing is 'unlikely to have had anything to contribute' (see *point 3* above). If instead *falsae voces* is read as meaning unauthorized 'notes' or polyphonic 'voice parts' (as it may well do), the expression cannot simultaneously hint at the falsettists who might now be thought to have had a role in such music.

B The succinct prohibition has two unusual features. First, in being addressed expressly to 'both sexes' of the Gilbertine Order it might well seem to conflict with the interpretation of *fausetum* as a man's falsetto.[43] Second, that strange word 'pipeth' is apparently paired with *fausetum* (to balance the preceding pairing of organum and descant), which may suggest that the two expressions have similar meanings.[44] While Dufay will undoubtedly have expected skilled and sensitive soft singing from

---

[42] In some cases a hindrance to identifying these practices arises not only with the meaning of *falsus* and its derivatives but with that of the innocent-looking *vox* (gen. *vocis*), a noun with at least three distinct musical meanings (often found rubbing shoulders with one another): the *voice* of a singer, a voice *part* in polyphonic music, and a musical *note* or *pitch*.

[43] Bowers points out that 'the Gilbertine canonesses were anyway prohibited from singing the services, except for the psalms'; Bowers, 'False voices', 73. Cf. Heather Josselyn-Cranson, '*Moderate psallendo*: Musical Participation in Worship among Gilbertine Nuns', *Plainsong and Medieval Music* 16/2 (2007), 173–86.

[44] For 'pipeth' Bowers proposes 'instrumental intrusions', while '*fausetum* seems most likely to mean falsetto'; 'False Voices', 73. I would merely add that in this context the modern equivalent of the vernacular word is not necessarily what it has been assumed to be; not 'pipe' but 'peep', a word evoking high-pitched sounds that some might wish to associate with falsetto, but one which connects equally plausibly with *fausetum*'s connotation of soft sound, as in 'not one peep'. In the early 13th-century 'argument' between the Owl and the Nightingale the former taunts the latter with losing his voice after mating: '[*thu*] pipest al so do*th* a mose' ('you peep like a mouse'); *The Owl and the Nightingale*, ed. J. H. G. Grattan and G. F. H. Sykes, Early English Text Society 119 (London, 1935), line 503. Cf. 'meek pipyng wordes'

his cathedral colleagues (see above), *fausset/falsetum* elsewhere could perhaps equally well denote *unduly* soft or 'weak and feeble' chanting on the part of those charged to praise God daily on behalf of others.[45]

C   The Benedictine monk's style is probably too florid to be of much help in the matter at hand, and in any case the critical word he uses is *falsitas* ('falsehood'), not *falsetum*. To take this passage as serious evidence for the falsettist would demand that the other 'voices' be treated equally seriously – for all their chattering, neighing and bleating.

D   David Fallows writes: 'Perhaps the most striking testimony to early falsetto singing is in Hermann Müller's magisterial study of Roger Bacon's comments on music ... where Müller shows that Bacon is discussing falsetto singing as being part of the polyphonic tradition of his time.'[46] In truth, while Müller may well be strong on the polyphonic traditions of the mid-13th century, he never once pauses to question the meaning of Bacon's 'in falseto'.[47]

Conspicuous in these texts are various male–female concepts: *virili voce* (A), *harmoniam virilem* (D), *cantare ... more femineo* (A), *voces foemineas* (C), *voces ... muliebriter dissolutae* (D). The latter and other such expressions have, predictably, been thought to point to falsetto singing, yet, more often than not, what is described as 'effeminate' may not be a voice or a singer but the music itself, or at least some aspect of its character. This vast topic is perhaps most efficiently addressed in the form of a short anthology of extracted writings, from St Ambrose to William Prynne; see Appendix 2 ('Music and Effeminacy'). Against the background of the material presented there, falsetto singing – if and when it may have occurred – would indeed seem more likely than not to have been viewed by our medieval forbears as effeminate. The reverse, however, does not hold: references to effeminate music and singing in the Middle Ages cannot be assumed to imply the falsetto voice.

and 'pipying ypocrisie' in *The Cloud of Unknowing* (early 15th c.), ed. P. Hodgson, Early English Text Society 218 (London, 1944), 101 and 102.

[45] It has been objected that the 'moderation' which these statutes aim to restore 'would certainly seem to have been threatened far more seriously by indulgence in falsetto singing than by a performance that was merely rather meek and over-restrained'; Bowers, 'False Voices'. Cf. Bernard of Clairvaux in Appendix 2, below.

[46] Fallows, 'Specific Information', 126 n. 41.

[47] '*Und wie geht er mit dem Sängerpersonal um! "Sie fälschen", sagt er, "mit ihrem Falsettsingen die männliche heilige Harmonie in knabenhaftem Sichgehenlassen und in weibischer Ausgelassenheit"*'; Hermann Müller, 'Zur Musikauffassung des 13. Jahrhunderts', *Archiv für Musikwissenschaft* 4 (1922), 410.

Before semantic challenges of this sort are (temporarily) put to one side, two further early 13th-century occurrences of 'falsetum' must be mentioned. They are found in a pair of liturgical documents from northern France setting out the Circumcision Offices of Sens and Beauvais Cathedrals. Rubrics in the Sens Office (the slightly earlier of the two) include those accompanying the sung texts *Haec est clara dies* and the ensuing *Salve, festa dies* near the start of First Vespers:

> Four or five [singers] *in falso*, behind the altar. · Two or three *in voce* in front of the altar.
>
> *Quatuor vel quinque in falso, retro altare.* · *Duo vel tres, in voce, ante altare.*[48]

This 'falso' is almost certainly an abbreviated form of the 'falseto' found in the related Beauvais Office (*c.* 1230):

> All psalm antiphons are begun with *falsetum* ...
>
> *Omnes antiphone psalmorum incipiuntur cum falseto ...*[49]

Since at both cathedrals the Feast of the Circumcision (1 January) doubled as the Feast of Fools, these expressions have sometimes been thought to indicate intentional wrong notes or out-of-tune singing (*chanter faux*), or some other form of irregular singing – including a satirical use of falsetto.[50] This, however, is to misunderstand the nature of the Feast, which had been newly developed 'as a dignified alternative to rowdy secular New Year festivities',[51] with the well-known role reversals now properly symbolizing God's deposing of 'the mighty' in favour of 'them of low degree'. A further possibility is suggested both by Froissart's 'en fausset' for 'softly' and by the similarity of *in falso/in voce* to the 17th-century Catalan *falsete/veu* (see above): namely, that *Haec est clara dies* was to be sung quietly for dramatic effect by one group of singers behind the main altar, after which another in front of the altar would sing *Salve, festa dies* in normal full voice ('in voce').

---

[48] *Office de Pierre de Corbeil*, ed. H. Villetard (Paris, 1907), 132–3. For other examples of singing '*post altare*' (in 1215) see Frank A. D'Accone, *The Civic Muse: Music and Musicians in Siena during the Middle Ages and the Renaissance* (1997), 80–3, 85.

[49] London, British Library, MS Egerton 2615, fol. 3.

[50] Cf. *Office de Pierre de Corbeil*, 77–9. A more plausible interpretation is that this *falsetum* was improvised *fauxbourdon*, though *fauxbourdon* and *faburden* did not emerge in written form until much later; ibid., 78; and Max Harris, *Sacred Folly: A New History of the Feast of Fools* (2011), 102. A Dutchman arriving in Oxford in 1357 was astonished at a faburden-like technique 'restricted entirely to 3rds and 6ths, ending on 5ths and octaves', apparently beloved of 'laymen and clerics, young and old'; Johannes Boen, *Musica*, pt 4 §162 (fols. 72v–73r); Wolf Frobenius, *Johannes Boens Musica* (1971), 76.

[51] Harris, *Sacred Folly*, jacket blurb.

Table 3.1 Dufay, *Ave regina celorum* (a4)

	Part	Clef	Written range	Singer(s)	
⎡ ⎡ Cantus	C1	(b) c–f″	boys*	
⎢ 15 ⎨ Contratenor	C3	f–a′	man ⎤
20 ⎢ ⎩ Tenor	C3	(f) g–g′ (a′)	man ⎬ 15
⎣ Bassus	C5	A–d′ (e′)	man ⎦

* Six boys are mentioned at a subsequent point in Dufay's will; Houdoy, *Histoire artistique*, 412. However, 'by 1466/7, some choirboys are referred to as being "beyond the usual number of seven"'; Planchart, 'Choirboys in Cambrai', 129 n. 2.

As the present meaning of 'falsetto' has long been assumed to stretch back at least 900 years, it seems no less reasonable to imagine that a different meaning of the word may have survived for 500 or so.

DUFAY'S WILL: RANGES AND CLEFS

For the second musical item to be sung at his bedside Dufay turns to one of his own polyphonic compositions:

> this hymn being finished the altar boys together with their master and two colleagues ... are to sing my motet *Ave regina celorum* ...
>
> *quo hympno finito pueri altaris, una cum magistro eorum et duobus ex sociis, inibi similiter presentes decantent motetum meum de* Ave regina celorum ...[52]

The work in question is widely agreed to be the unattributed four-part *Ave regina celorum* copied into Cambrai Cathedral's choirbooks a decade earlier.[53] A quite exceptional opportunity thus arises to match a known piece of music to the vocal forces chosen for it by its composer; see Table 3.1, noting the 15-note span of the men's voice parts.

A general presumption for Continental polyphony of Dufay's day is that boys and adult falsettists sang in reasonably similar ranges and in effect held equal claims on most *cantus/superius* parts. Individual cases, one might suppose, would be determined by institutional and liturgical context, as well as by pragmatism and taste. For his *Ave regina celorum* Dufay could accordingly be seen as merely specifying his chosen option: boys' voices

---

[52] Houdoy, *Histoire artisitque*, 410.

[53] Two of the four tropes inserted into the antiphon text could hardly be more personal: *Miserere tui labentis Du Fay,/ Peccatorum ne ruat in ignem fervorum* (Have mercy on your dying Dufay,/ May he not burn in the fire of sinners); *Miserere supplicanti Du Fay/ Sitque in conspectu Dei mors eius speciosa* (Dufay beseeches your mercy,/ May his death be acceptable in the eyes of God).

rather than men's falsetto voices.⁵⁴ Of these putative falsettists, however, there is still no sign.

The example of *Ave regina celorum* nevertheless has more than mere negative significance: it demonstrates the unreliability of a theory touched on earlier (in *point 7* above). According to that proposition, Dufay's lowest voice part would represent the newly introduced bass singer, while 'the very familiar look' of the upper three parts (C1 C3 C3 in this instance) would confirm the continuation of the earlier 15th-century chanson-style vocal layout, 'a pattern involving a single high voice pitched [a 5th] above two lower and equal voices', a *tenor-contratenor* pair.⁵⁵ Consequently, without Dufay's specification of the required singers – included in the will purely for administrative purposes – current scholarship might well have unquestioningly claimed the top part of *Ave regina celorum* not for boys but for the voice that supposedly headed the earlier 'core' scoring: that of the elusive falsettist.⁵⁶

THE third pertinent item in Dufay's will – relating to his Mass for St Anthony of Padua – is not without difficulties of its own. For the saint's feast day the following were to attend:

> the master of the boys and the more able members of the choir, whether they be *vicaires* (*grands* or *petits*) or chaplains, ... who should sing the mass composed by me; for this I assign 30 *solidi*, from which each shall receive 3 *solidi* and 4 *denarii* ...
>
> *magister puerorum et alii quicumque sufficientiores de choro, sive sint magni vicarii seu parvi, vel capellani ... qui missam per me*

---

⁵⁴ Fallows plausibly suggests that 'the written pitches here more or less correspond to their modern equivalents' ('Specific Information', 121), though in practice a semitone or tone below today's pitch might now be considered optimal.

⁵⁵ Bowers II, 5 and 22–5; and Bowers, 'Chains', 10–11. Bowers's theory (brutally summarized in *point 7* above) is formulated as an explanation of developments in late 15th-century English music, but, as he makes clear, the revised pattern of scoring undoubtedly followed 'the model set by the continental secular chanson'. If valid, his proposal should be equally relevant to Continental music of the same period (allowing for other distinctions), and it has certainly been understood in this way; see Fallows, 'Specific Information', 126; and 'Contradistinctions and Contra-Indications', *Early Music* 26/2 (1998), 381 [letter].

⁵⁶ A further illustration of the same point is provided by the Credo of Ockeghem's *Missa Fors seulement* (a5), where the clefs are C1 C2 C4 C4 F4. Here the second part down, in C2, is labelled *Secundus puer* (with the obvious implication that the highest part is also for a 'boy'). Arthur Mendel, 'Pitch in Western Music since 1500: A Re-examination', in *Acta musicologica* 50/1–2 (1978), 69–70.

compositam decantent, quibus assigno xxx solidos, inde quilibet iii solidos iiii denarios ...[57]

As David Fallows has pointed out, these singers – all grown men – were evidently nine in number.[58] Dufay's three-part settings of the Ordinary texts[59] employ between them an overall written compass of 18 notes, wider by a 4th than the comfortable two octaves of men's natural voices. Thus, in the absence of boys' voices, these movements appear to demand falsetto singing for the top part; see Ex. 3.1a. This notational compass is misleading, however, and not merely because its intended sounding pitch is (as usual) unknown, but also because it conflates two distinct sets of ranges; see Exx. 3.1b and 3.1c. While the Kyrie and Gloria are written at one level (in C2 C4 C4 clefs),[60] the Credo, Sanctus and Agnus are written at a higher one (in C1 C3 C3 clefs), tricking us into supposing that because these last three movements *look* higher in their notated form they must also *sound* higher in performance.[61] (Comparable 'inconsistencies' of one sort or another are not uncommon within mass cycles.)[62] While multiple-movement works from more recent centuries tacitly imply a single (fixed) pitch level throughout, to presume the same of their earlier equivalents is unjustified and, as here, unsafe.[63] No given written note in Dufay's Gloria can be assumed to imply the same sounding pitch when it recurs in the Credo.

A brief explanation may be in order. Where modern notation presupposes a fixed sounding pitch and employs multiple key-signatures and accidentals to establish different tonalities, Dufay *et al.* could achieve

---

[57] Houdoy, *Histoire artistique*, 412.

[58] 9 × 3s 4d = 30s; Fallows, 'Specific Information', 118. But cf. Planchart, 'Choir-boys in Cambrai, 138–40.

[59] As for the various Proper movements apparently belonging to Dufay's plenary cycle, 'for the purposes of further examination they are best left aside (though it is easy to integrate them with the rest by transposing them up a 4th)'; Fallows, 'Specific Information', 118–19. Subsequently the same author has commented: 'Having now carefully edited it and attended rehearsals as well as a BBC recording of it, I do not believe Dufay can have composed this cycle'; David Fallows, *Dufay* (2/1988), 310.

[60] More correctly: the top part is *mostly* in C2 but begins in C1.

[61] This way of expressing written compasses also misleadingly incorporates any unique or fleeting departures from the core range, in this case an isolated note a major 3rd below.

[62] See, for example, Roger Bowers, 'Five into Four does Go: The Vocal Scoring of Ockeghem's *Missa L'homme armé*', *Early Music* 31/2 (2003), 262–5. Cf. Ockeghem's *Missa Fors seulement*, in Mendel, 'Pitch in Western Music', 69–70.

[63] See Andrew Parrott, 'Transposition in Monteverdi's Vespers of 1610', *Early Music* 12/4 (1984), 490–516 (reprinted in this volume, Ch. 5), and subsequent writings on the same topic.

all they needed (and with great economy) by means of multiple clefs and a 'floating' pitch level. The intended vocal scoring – apparent to their singers (if not to us) from the configuration of clefs – allowed them to identify an appropriate approximate sounding pitch.[64] This did not amount to a licence to do as they pleased, to choose any pitch, or to adopt a different scoring. Nor did it have anything to do with 'transposition' as understood today. Changes of notation, of key or of fixed pitches are not involved. The principle is a simpler and more flexible one whereby, in most cases, a set of clefs both defines a work's vocal scoring and suggests its likely overall compass, devolving to the performer the task of establishing an exact pitch level, one which would match each of the standard voice-types.

In this particular case, the Kyrie and Gloria, in line with the overwhelming majority of 15th-century three-part vocal polyphony, have a range of only 15 notes, while the subsequent movements stretch upwards occasionally by a mere semitone (and downwards just once for an isolated bass note in the 'Crucifixus'), as shown in Exx. 3.1b and 3.1c. The core 15 notes of each compass lie *notationally* two degrees apart, but when they are aligned *in sound* it becomes clear that – with the exception of that one rogue bass note – Dufay's men will never have needed to exceed a collective 15/16-note compass; see Ex. 3.1d. In other words, all five movements arguably conform to a familiar and perfectly reasonable compass for men's natural voices (our tenors and basses), presumably sounding (in our terms) roughly as in Ex. 3.1e.

Once again, evidence put forward to demonstrate a necessary role for falsetto singing has turned out to be less than convincing. Moreover, all three case studies relating to Dufay, the best-documented composer of his century, have failed to produce a single good reason for believing that falsetto singing played any part in his musical world. Readers familiar with David Fallows's exploratory work on 15th-century performance issues will nevertheless be aware of two further lines of investigation which contribute to a case for the falsettist.[65] Whereas one of these clearly demands special attention (see '*Voces mutatae*' below), the other I believe to be too fragile to contribute anything of substance to the present discussion. Briefly put, Charles the Bold's ordinances for the Burgundian court may reflect the size and composition of his chapel choir in 1469, but without being certain of the repertory to which it relates, the value of the document in establishing whether falsettists were among his singers is

---

[64] To search for *the* performance pitch of early Renaissance polyphony is to approach the issue anachronistically and from the wrong end. For some illuminating examples of how the papal singers went about pitch setting, see Richard Sherr, 'Performance Practice in the Papal Chapel in the 16th Century', *Early Music* 15/4 (1987), 453–6.

[65] In his 'Specific Information' Fallows also deals with the numerical (and acoustical) 'balance' of voices in choirs, performing pitch, the role of instruments and issues relating to the song repertory.

Ex. 3.1 Dufay, Mass for St Anthony of Padua (*a3*); (a) composite compass, (b) Kyrie, Gloria, (c) Credo, Sanctus, Agnus, (d) aligned compasses of (b) and (c) in 'floating' pitch (e) aligned compasses, renotated to reflect approximate sounding pitch in modern terms

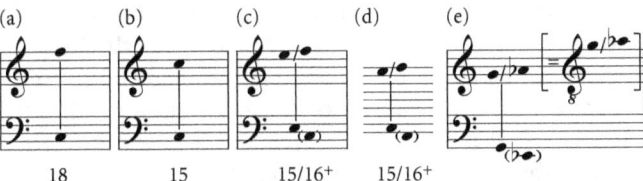

seriously compromised. The source is discussed at length in Appendix 3 ('The Burgundian Court Ordinances of 1469').

'HIGH' CHOIRS, 'FULL' CHOIRS

FROM a 21st-century perspective, high voices – and specifically boys' voices – are easily assumed to have been a *sine qua non* of early church music-making. Yet, although choirboys had long received training in mensural music as well as plainchant, they evidently did not begin to join their adult counterparts in the singing of composed polyphony – at least on any regular basis – until well into the 15th century (see *point 4* above).[66] Their separation was not only institutional but spatial, as at Cambrai Cathedral:

> the choirboys of Cambrai ... comprised an independent polyphonic choir. They were expected to sing antiphons, responds, versicles, Magnificats, motets, and masses. They did not, however, join with the vicars in the antiphonal singing of the psalms at the canonical hours, partly because they did not belong to either the right or the left side of the choir. Rather, they were placed in the sanctuary near the great altar in order to more readily perform their duties as acolytes. When they sang, they grouped around their own lectern and were supplied with their own music books ...[67]

There were thus two distinct kinds of choir at Cambrai, one exclusively adult (such as Dufay specified for his Mass for St Anthony of Padua), the other defined by boys but supported by one or two lower adult voices. This second group – which for convenience I shall refer to as a 'high' choir – operated in

> an apparently stable tradition according to which the choirboys, their master, and possibly one or more of the *petits vicaires* sang a

---

[66] See *Young Choristers*, ed. Boynton and Rice.
[67] Wright, 'Performance Practices', 306. See also Planchart, 'Choirboys in Cambrai'.

polyphonic hymn and a 'motet' at both First and Second Vespers in a number of newly endowed feasts.[68]

In 1445, for example, a motet was to be sung *loco Benedicamus* by the six *pueri altaris*, their master and a *contratenens*.[69] For further documentation of such groups see Appendix 4 ('The "High" Choir'); see also Illus. 3.2.

For as long as these two choirs sang independently of each other and predominantly in music of narrow compass (15 notes or so), there is no reason to suppose that their singing would have sounded at a common pitch level.[70] The boys' formation required no bass voice, while the all-adult group (according to all the evidence thus far presented) did not imply – let alone demand – any voice above the 'natural' range of what we call a tenor.[71]

THE momentous transition from two separate choirs to a single choir (ancestor of the kind that predominates today) took place in the course of the 15th century and still awaits full and thorough investigation. Attention has tended to focus on matters of size (single/multiple voices per part and numerical 'balance' of parts),[72] yet of arguably greater significance is the birth of this 'full' choir – in the sense of a body of singers spanning *a full range* 'from the lowest Note of a Mans Base unto the highest of a Boys Treble'.[73]

---

[68] Planchart, 'Choirboys in Cambrai', 137; see also 142–3. In 1463/4 Simon Meslet was paid for copying music *'pour les enfans de coer teneurs et contres'*; ibid., 132.

[69] The endowment was made by *Magister* Johannes Martini (not the composer). Strohm, *European Music*, 285; cf. Nosow, *Ritual Meanings*, 172, 174, app. C9. The only two works of Dufay's indicating boys (besides *Ave regina celorum*) are *Fulgens iubar ecclesiae Dei* (Cambrai, early or mid-1440s), which has a 16-note range (C1 C3 C3 C4), and *Inclita stella maris* (c. 1430), for which see main text below.

[70] Vocal compositions of limited overall compass continued to be written throughout the 16th century, and from before c. 1560 most of them are for low voices. See Frank Carey, 'Composition for Equal Voices in the 16th Century', *The Journal of Musicology* 9/3 (1991), 300–42. The high and low choirs of later Italian polychoral works may perhaps be seen as incorporating these traditional scorings rather than inventing them.

[71] When men-only choirs today sing this 15-note repertory at 'high'-choir pitch levels, a spurious role is created for the falsettist.

[72] In this context I would seriously question the validity of any definition purporting that 'choral music does not simply arise where there is more than one singer per part, but rather where the music is of such a kind that potentially everyone, even the non-specialist can join in'; Strohm, *European Music*, 283. Cf. Andrew Parrott, 'A Brief Anatomy of Choirs', in *The Cambridge Companion to Choral Music*, ed. A. de Quadros (2012), 7–16 (reprinted in this volume, Ch. 2).

[73] Charles Butler, *The Principles of Musik in Singing and Setting* (London, 1636), 9.

Illus. 3.2 Detail from a miniature by Robinet Testard, from *Des Eschez amoureux et des echez d'amours*, F-Pn MS fr. 143 (c. 1500), fol. 66

The newly available compass constituted an enormous expansion of the tonal space in which composers could work – as much as three octaves instead of just two (22 notes rather than 15) – prompting a parallel surge of interest in writing in four or more parts. This revolution undoubtedly arose hand in hand with the new performing medium, the full choir comprising both boys and the conventional complement of adult male voices. (At Ferrara Duke Ercole I is said to have established two separate choirs in the 1470s, of *adoloscentuli* and of *magiori*, but subsequently to have combined them.)[74] A glance back at the ranges of Dufay's *Ave regina celorum* (Table 3.1, above)[75] will show how the expansion may have been achieved in either of two ways, or in both: by introducing a new part for boys above the conventional range of men's voices, or by adding a bass voice to underpin of the higher choir.

Compositionally it will have mattered little how the new configuration was arrived at, but either way there were consequences for musical notation. The older 15-note repertory fitted comfortably within the traditional 20-note gamut (see point 7 and Illus. 3.1, above) and, more often than not, is found in a more or less central position, occupying

---

[74] '... *facendo de' duo musici chori uni*' (Sabadino degli Arienti, 1497). Lockwood, *Ferrara*, 157–8.

[75] Although probably still unusual, a similiar four-part scoring may perhaps also be inferred from a Cambrai directive of 1457 for a Marian Mass to be sung 'by the master and altar boys with two contratenors' (*per magistrum et pueros altaris cum duobus contratenoribus*); Craig Wright, 'Dufay at Cambrai: Discoveries and Revisions', *Journal of the American Musicological Society* 28/2 (1975), 196. Cathedral payments show that polyphony was still normally sung by the dozen or more *petits vicaires*.

roughly an octave each side of 'middle' *c*. The notation of such music, precisely because it stipulates neither specific voice-types nor fixed sounding pitches, could serve 'high' and 'low' choirs equally well. A single written source might thus be capable of doing double duty, allowing each choir to perform at its own pitch level; an inventory of 1522 from Magdalen College, Oxford, for example, lists music explicitly 'for men only or boys only' (*Unus liber pro hominibus tantum vel pueris tantum*).[76] This notational versatility, I suggest, may explain an otherwise puzzling rubric attached to Dufay's *Inclita stella maris*, a work with three notated voice parts cunningly designed to allow performance variously in two, three or four parts; see Table 3.2. In its three-part manifestation the composition has a 16-note compass equally suitable for a high scoring (headed by boys), and for men only (at a lower sounding pitch and without any need for falsettists). By adding the Contratenor II, however, the overall compass is stretched to 18 notes (including a frequently recurring lowest note), making it too wide for the men-only scoring. Hence Dufay's rubric, explaining that this low *contratenor* part should be used only with the higher scoring, i.e. when boys are assigned to the canonic top part:

> Contratenor II concording with everything: it cannot be sung unless boys say the *Fuga*.
>
> *Secundus contratenor concordans cum omnibus: non potest cantari nisi pueri dicant fugam.*[77]

The relevance of this to the present investigation is that there seems to be no comparably plausible interpretation of Dufay's rubric if falsetto singing enters the equation.

One could speculate further that early collaborations between 'high' and 'low' choirs may have involved delegating to the higher choir self-contained sections of a mass setting, to be sung an octave higher (or even just a 'tonally' compatible 4th or 5th). When these two choirs in effect merged into one, however, the problem inevitably arose of how to reconcile a new expanded notational compass of up to 22 notes with the existing 20-note gamut. In due course – though perhaps not without a certain amount of head-scratching – the limits of the gamut were simply breached. (Adam von Fulda in 1490 specifically credits Dufay with this expansion.)[78] The *Musica practica* (1482) of Bartolomeo Ramos de Pareia, for example, shows

---

[76] Also, as an addition (probably in 1524), 'Item *magnus liber … pro viris tantum vel pueris tantum*'; F. Ll. Harrison, *Music in Medieval Britain* (2/1963), 431.

[77] Cf. Fallows, 'Specific Information', 128–30. For the use of *dicere* as 'to sing' see n. 23 above.

[78] Adam von Fulda, *De musica*, in M. Gerbert, *Scriptores Ecclesiastici* iii (St Blasien, 1784/R1963), 342b & 350a. See also Mendel, 'Pitch in Western Music', 68–9.

Table 3.2 Dufay, *Inclita stella maris* (a2, a3 and a4)

⌈	[*Superius*]	C2	g–d"	texted	⌉
16	*Fuga	[C2]	[g–d"]	[texted]	
⌊	*Contratenor I*	C4	c–f'	–	18
	Contratenor II	F3	A–d'	–	⌋

* an unnotated part in mensural canon with the *Superius*

a three-octave gamut extending from F to f'',[79] and from a similar period come two three-part masses by Tinctoris, one of them notated high, the other exceptionally low and bearing the inscription '... with a *contratenor* outside the [Guidonian] hand, a 5th below [gamma-]ut'.[80]

WHEN Florence Cathedral's first polyphonic choir commenced its duties early in 1478, it clearly experienced teething problems. Alongside a handful of men were four *sovrani* 'drawn in all probability from the choir school established earlier by Pope Eugene',[81] yet within five months these boys were replaced by one Matheus Pauli and their combined salary duly assigned to him. This could easily be viewed as a perfect demonstration of how a single adult falsettist might have been expected to provide a more reliable soprano line than a few ill-prepared boys, yet it is clearly documented elsewhere that Pauli was not a soprano but a *contratenor altus*.[82]

This raises a recurrent problem in identifying possible falsettists: that of determining whether a particular male singer is likely to have been pre- or post-pubertal, boy or man. (The castrato does not begin to confuse the picture further in any significant way until the 16th century.) It has been suggested, for example, that in the first half of the 16th century Cambrai Cathedral employed more than 50 soprano falsettists. Of these, however, 'about a third ... are described as youths (*juvenes*)',[83] while of the six admission documents cited all may be understood as referring in relatively

---

[79] *Musica Practica Bartolomei Rami*, ed. J. Wolf (Leipzig, 1901), 35.

[80] *Missa 3 vocum secundi toni irregularis cum contratenore extra manum in diapenthe sub ut*. Verona, Biblioteca Capitolare, MS.DCCLV, fol. 17v.

[81] Albert Seay, 'The 15th-Century Cappella at Santa Maria del Fiore in Florence', *Journal of the American Musicological Society* 11/1 (1958), 49.

[82] Seay, 'The 15th-Century Cappella', 50. One interpretation might be that the 'high' choir was abandoned in favour of a duly strengthened 'low' choir.

[83] Wright, 'Performance Practices', 308–9, who gives a source but no further details of a first recorded 'adult soprano' in February 1500, and also notes that two priests 'sang successfully as sopranos at Cambrai for many years'. Current concepts of the male youth (*juvenis*) are not easily reconciled with those of the choirboy, but could it be that while puberty is now generally occurring earlier than in most former times, 'youth' has continued to denote a constant age-range? Cf. Appendix 5 ('Boys' Changing Voices').

straightforward fashion to boys with unbroken voices – thus accounting quite naturally for the many who 'were admitted and soon dismissed':

1531 'soprano ... if he changes or loses his voice [*si mutet vel amittat vocem*] he will be dismissed.'

1534 'two sopranos ... as long as their voices shall last [*quamdiu voces eorum durabunt*].'

1535 'soprano ... provisionally committed to the regimen of the choirboys.'

1536 'young soprano ... to be placed in the house of the choirboys.'

1539 'A young soprano ... whose voice has hardly changed [*vix mutate*] ... at half salary.'

1542 'A certain young soprano singer ... as long as his voice shall last [*quamdiu sibi vox ipsa duraverit*].'[84]

The underlying issue with these young singers was scarcely a new one. In 1485, after a very brief spell at Cambrai as master of the choirboys, Jacob Obrecht took the post of succentor at the church of St Donatian in Bruges, bringing with him one Egidius Zelandrinus – only for the singer promptly to lose his soprano voice on arrival.[85] Perhaps even more unfortunate was Ghottifredo di Thilman de Liegio, who in 1481 made the long journey to Italy, signed a one-year contract with the SS Annunziata in Florence and just 11 days later was given a 'farewell gift'. The following year Johannes Hurtault with greater foresight signed a similar contract at the same church but with the proviso that 'in case the said Ianes the singer should lose his voice and should not be able to sing soprano, he is not to be dismissed before [the end of] the said year'.[86]

Is any of these singers, or the *giovane* soprano recruited for Isabella d'Este in 1492,[87] really likely to have been other than a teenage boy? For further samples of historical data relevant to this issue, see Appendix 5

---

[84] Wright, 'Performance Practices', 309. Despite the 1536 reference to singing '*submisse gallice fousset*' (see above), none of these entries mentions falsetto.

[85] '... *et vocem suam supremi cantus ab aliquo tempore amisit*'; Reinhard Strohm, *Music in Late Medieval Bruges* (2/1990), 27, 257. As with an earlier case (see the note at the end of Appendix 4, below), I question whether the appellation '*magister*' always necessarily indicates an adult at this period.

[86] Frank A. D'Accone, 'The Singers of San Giovanni in Florence during the 15th Century', *Journal of the American Musicological Society* 14/3 (1961), 332 and 355–6.

[87] Stefano Davari, *La musica a Mantova* (Mantua, 1884), 64. The intriguing correspondence between Isabella and Johannes Martini in October 1491 may highlight a new terminological ambiguity: that the top part of a 'low' choir is referred to as a *superius/sovrano* but is sung by a singer otherwise categorized as a *contratenor altus/contralto*. Alternatively, this could be a very early instance of falsetto singing being considered as a possible makeshift for that of a boy; ibid., 63.

('Boys' Changing Voices'), inc. Illus. 3.4, where the four singers appear to be three men and a youth.

VOCES MUTATAE

THE appearance in Trent Codex 87 of the words *'mutate voces'* – literally, 'changed voices' (i.e. men's 'broken' voices) – has long been known to scholars, and its significance in the present discussion cannot be overestimated. David Fallows writes:

> it is easy enough to demonstrate that the highest voice of early 15th-century three-voice sacred polyphony was normally sung by men in a 'falsetto' register. The key documents here are two pieces in the Trent codices that specifically alternate sections for *mutate voces* and for *pueri* in the same register ...[88]

In fact, while both works mention *pueri* (boys), only one of them also mentions *'mutate voces'*: the *Gaude virgo mater Christi* by a Liégeois composer, 'H. Battre' (see Illus. 3.3). Located in a portion of the codex copied in or near Namur around 1435, the antiphon

> opens with a three-part section in which the upper part is marked *'mutate voces'* – changed or broken voices. The next section is written on the facing page: here the clefs have changed and all three voices are marked *'pueri'*. How the broken voices and the boys are distributed in the remainder of the piece is not always entirely clear.[89]

The general layout of the piece, showing how the singers fall into two distinct groups, is represented in Table 3.3a.

With the piece sounding at a pitch level feasible for the *pueri*, it is argued, 'the *mutate voces* would involve at least some degree of falsetto or head-voice – as indeed the very existence of the marking might imply'.[90] Although Fallows does not go so far as to equate the expression directly with 'falsetto voices', others have chosen to do so in later contexts – and with calamitous results: the belief that 'Vicentino uses *a voce mutata* and *voce mutabile* to denote high parts sung in falsetto' has rendered critical passages of his *L'antica musica ridotta alla moderna prattica* (1555) incomprehensible and nonsensical in translation, all apparently without drawing scholarly comment.[91]

---

[88] Fallows, 'Contradistinctions', 381. In 'Specific Information' (at pp. 124–5) Fallows discusses three further works that seem similarly to juxtapose two kinds of choir: Dufay's Sanctus 'Papale' and a Gloria–Credo pair by Binchois.

[89] Fallows, 'Specific Information', 122–3.

[90] Fallows, 'Specific Information', 123.

[91] See n. 103, below.

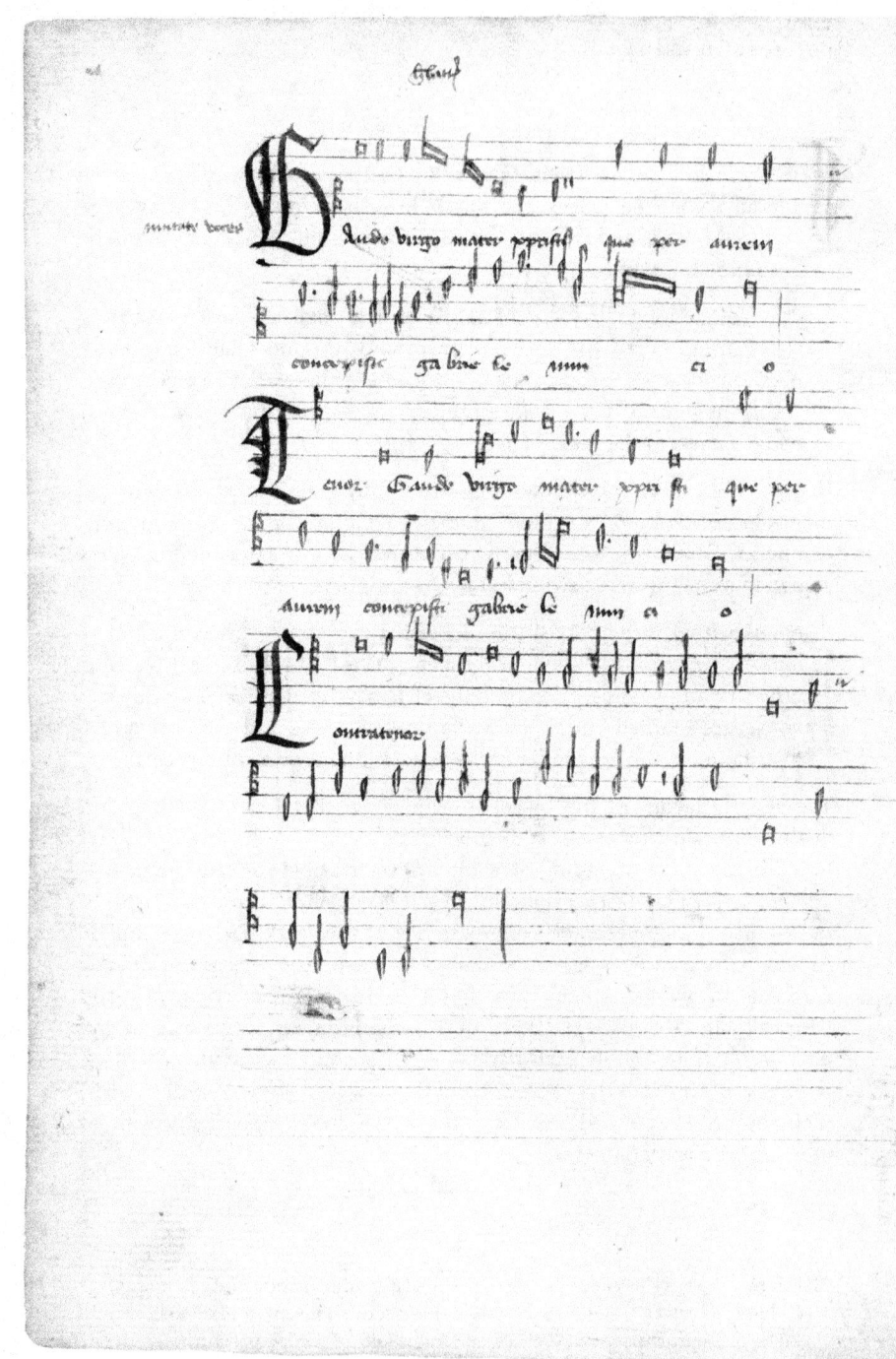

Illus. 3.3 H. Battre, *Gaude virgo mater Christi*, I-TRmp 87, fols. 262v–263

Table 3.3 H. Battre, *Gaude virgo mater Christi* (*I-TRmp* 87, fols. 262v–264v)

(a)

Bar	Text	Men	Clef	Boys	Range
1–13	*Gaude virgo*	mutate voces [S]	C2	–	c'–c''
		Contratenor	C4	–	d–e'
		Tenor	C4	–	d–d'
14–29	*Gaude quia deo*	–	C1	Pueri	d'–d''
		–	C2	Pueri	a–$b(\flat)'$
		–	C2	Pueri	c'–c''
30–72	*Gaude quia tui nati*		C1	Pueri 37–46 only	d'–d''
		[S]	C2 C3		f–g'
		Contratenor	C4		c–e'
		Tenor	C4		c–f'
73–80	*ubi fructus*	–	C2	[Pueri]	d'–a'
		Contratenor	C4		g–d'
		Tenor	C4		d–d'
81–108	*Per te*	[?S]	C1	Pueri [?]	c'–d''
		Contratenor	C3		d–g'
		Tenor	C4		c–d'

(b)

$$
\begin{array}{lll}
\text{pueri} & a\text{–}d'' & \uparrow 4 = d'\text{–}g'' \\
\left[\begin{array}{l}\text{[superius]} \\ 15/16 \ \ \text{contratenor} \\ \text{tenor}\end{array}\right. & \begin{array}{l}f\text{–}c''\,[?d''] \\ c\text{–}g' \\ c\text{–}f'\end{array} & \left.\begin{array}{l}\downarrow 5 = B\flat\text{–}f'\,[?g'] \\ \downarrow 5 = F\text{–}c' \\ \downarrow 5 = F\text{–}b(\flat)\end{array}\right] 23
\end{array}
$$

The expression – or rather its application in Battre's composition – puzzled me, I confess, for many years.[92] That *mutatus* ('changed') implies adult males is not in question. In 1411 the boy and men singers at Notre-Dame in Paris are classed respectively as *pueri* and 'voces quae mutatae dicuntur' ('voices which are called "changed"');[93] in 1421 an endowment at St Donatian in Bruges uses the corresponding French verb *muer* in calling for four choirboys whose voices are 'not yet changing';[94] and by the 16th

---

[92] Even Praetorius struggled to make sense of the related 'choro mutato': 'I have found this [expression] in Hieronimus Iacobus but cannot yet really be certain how he means it to be understood'; Praetorius, *Syntagma musicum* iii (Wolfenbüttel, 1618), 127 (*recte* 107). His source was Girolamo Giacobbi, *Prima parte dei salmi concertati* (Venice, 1609), preface, where the composer is evidently referring to a 'low' choir.

[93] F.-L. Chartier, *L'Ancien Chapitre de Nôtre-Dame de Paris* (Paris, 1897), 67–8 n. 1. If 'voces mutatae' were to be interpreted here as 'falsettists', then the cathedral's adult choir would have to be understood to have comprised falsettists *exclusively*.

[94] '... ayant une voix claire qui ne mue encore' (French *muer* = Latin *mutare*); Wright, 'Performance Practices', 301 n. 11.

century the *duodeni mutati* of the cathedral in Battre's native Liège are known to have been former choirboys aged between 20 and 30 whose role was no longer musical.[95] But for the word to indicate here a *doubly* changed voice – a changed voice changed from a natural into a falsetto voice – would be somewhat odd. The solution to this minor part of the puzzle (if I am right) lies in the observation that the words *mutate voces*, found only at the start of the piece, are almost certainly not intended to apply exclusively to the upper voice part (which would not normally carry any designation) but to *all three* in the first group (the column headed 'men' in Table 3.3a), in order to distinguish them from the *pueri* (the 'boys').[96] Support for this interpretation comes both from later definitions of the term (see below) and from a similar use of the word 'chorus' in the other Trent Codex work explicitly involving an independent body of *pueri*, the Gloria by Bourgois (*I-TRmp* 87), where the marking appears not only against the *superius* part but also against the *tenor*; see Appendix 6. Of course, it does not follow from this that falsetto voices are necessarily excluded from the generality of 'changed voices'. Thus the central question remains: how can boys' voices and men's natural voices reasonably occupy the same singing range in polyphony of this kind? The short answer is, of course, that they cannot. The conundrum may nevertheless be approached in two ways: first by examining other uses of the expression *mutate voces* (*voci mutate* etc.), and then by considering a notational issue faced by pioneers of the full choir ('full' as described above).

Some 70 years after Battre's early experiment in alternating (and combining) boys and changed voices within a single work the term *voci mutate* in its various forms begins to appear regularly in designations of certain compositions of narrow overall compass.[97] In Petrucci's first collection of *Frottole* (1504) an item spanning just 12 notes is headed 'A voce mutate',[98] and other works from the same decade with ranges of 15[+] notes are similarly marked.[99] Clarification of the meaning of the term and of music so labelled is duly provided by Pietro Aaron in 1516:

---

[95] Bénédicte Even-Lassman, *Les Musiciens liégeois au service des Habsbourg* (2006), 35, 41.

[96] The use of a plural ('voces') may point in the same direction: polyphony of this sort is far more likely to have been sung with just one singer per part, at least by adults. See, for example, Bowers II, *passim*.

[97] See Carey, 'Composition for Equal Voices', 300–42.

[98] Michele Pesenti, *Sì, me piace el dolce foco*, in Petrucci, *Frottole*, bk 1 (Venice, 1504), fols. 39v–40. The clefs used are C3 C3 C3 C4.

[99] Innocentius Dammonis, *Sol, mi sol, disse Holoferno* ('a voce mudade'), in Petrucci's *Laude*, bk 1 (Venice, 1508); and Noel Bauldeweyn (*fl.* 1509–13), *Missa sine nomine* ('a voce mutata'). Amongst unlabelled works of narrow compass from this period are Josquin's *Alma redemptoris* (14 notes) and *Domine ne in furore* (15 notes); Fallows, 'The Performing Ensembles in Josquin's Sacred Musc', 46.

Voices of that kind are called 'changed' because they cannot reach as high as the other [kind], those of boys. In this kind of composition the *cantus* itself, because it is usually made for lower parts, could not be sung by a boy's or a feigned [= falsetto] voice; rather, it is sung by a man's voice, in other words by those who normally sing alto or bass [parts].

Voces eiusmodi ob id quidem mutatae appellantu[r], quod secundum aliarum puerilium vocum ascensum attolli nequeunt: Cantus enim ipse in eiusmodi cantilenis: quia gravioribus solito in partibus constituitur: cum puerili voce, vel ficta cani non possit: virili canitur eorum scilicet: qui vel Altos, vel Bassos canere consueverunt.[100]

(The almost incidental reference to a 'feigned' voice is, I believe, the earliest-known reliable evidence of falsetto singing.) Put differently, Aaron states that the top part of compositions for *voci mutate* is not in the usual soprano range but lower and beneath the reach of both boys' and falsetto voices; instead, all parts – *cantus* included – are conceived for men's natural voices and consequently lie within a limited overall range of 15 to 17 notes.[101] Three key points emerge:

- feigned voices are associated with *superius* parts
- voices associated with alto parts are not feigned voices
- *voci mutate* are men's (natural) voices singing in lower ranges than boys' voices or feigned voices.

In 1555 Nicola Vicentino confirms Aaron's understanding of *voci mutate*[102] and goes on to describe a method of writing which allows for

---

[100] Pietro Aaron, *Libri tres de institutione harmonica* (Bologna, 1516), fol. 52 (ch. 46 'De modo et compositione vocum quae mutate dicuntur'). For apparently different but not entirely clear usages of the expression 'a voce mutata' see Jonathan Glixon, 'A Musicians' Union in 16th-Century Venice', *Journal of the American Musicological Society* 36/3 (1983), 400–2; and James H. Moore, *Vespers at St Mark's* i (1981), 80. In 1587 (and again in 1631 and beyond) the boys of the French chapel royal were evidently being supported by 2 or 3 cornetts and/or *dessus mués*, presumably adult falsettists. Peter Bennett, 'Collaborations between the Musique de la Chambre and the Musique de la Chapelle at the Court of Louis XIII', *Early Music* 38/3 (2010), 372.

[101] Aaron might be read as suggesting that this low *cantus* part could be sung by either an alto or a bass, but he seems merely to be defining 'manly' voices in general, ignoring the tenor simply because his range rarely differs from that of the alto.

[102] 'When you compose a composition *a voce mutata*, that is, without a soprano [part], take care that the extremes do not go beyond 15 notes, and at most to 16 with the semitone' (*quando si comporrà una compositione à voce Mutata, cioè, senza soprano; s'avvertirà che gli estremi non passino quindeci voci, & al più in sedeci con il semitono*). Nicola Vicentino, *L'antica musica ridotta*

performance both 'à voce piena, & à voce mutata' (both 'by "full" voices and by "changed" voices'), i.e. scored either for all voice ranges or just for lower voices (men only). A soprano part

> is put down an octave and converted into a tenor, while the alto part becomes in effect the soprano of the changed-voice version ...
>
> *si farà un soprano, & poi il medesimo si abbasserà per Ottava quello si convertirà in Tenore, & il Contr'alto sarà come soprano à voce mutata ...*[103]

By the simple expedient of having a tenor sing a soprano part an octave lower than written, a scoring *à voce piena* becomes one *à voce mutata*, a 22-note compass is reduced to one of 15 notes, and a four-part composition for SATB voices is transformed into one for ATTB, with the 'A' part now functioning as a *superius*. (The process can also work in reverse.) No written transposition is involved, nor does a reallocated part require mental transposition in any familiar sense: it is simply to be sung at the octave corresponding to the singer's natural range (an option nowadays indicated, for example, by 𝄞 or 𝄞). In this respect it is no different from what happens today in congregational hymn singing, or when any mixed group sings 'in unison', and it occurred naturally whenever boys sang plainchant together with men,[104] since 'a childe voys is 8 notis above a manes voyce, they [= though] it seme that they sing both in one voice'.[105] A more conscious use of the same principle also featured in certain types of improvised polyphony:

---

    alla moderna prattica (Rome, 1555), fol. 84v (bk 4, ch. 26). See also Gioseffo Zarlino, *Le istitutioni harmoniche* (Venice, 1558), 263 (pt 3, ch. 65).

[103] Vicentino, 'Regola di comporre ogni compositione che si potrà cantare à voce piena, & à voce mutata', *L'antica musica*, fol. 92v (bk 4, ch. 38). Through misunderstandings of each of these terms Vicentino has been represented as contrasting two manners of singing rather than of composition, 'in full voice' (a misleadingly literal translation) and 'in falsetto' (in effect, an opposite of the intended meaning). As a consequence Vicentino's clear description of how one scoring can be converted to another (by dropping a soprano part an octave so that it becomes a tenor part, or *vice versa*) is entirely destroyed. Maria Rika Maniates, *Nicola Vicentino: Ancient Music Adapted to Modern Practice* (1996), 229 n. 2; see also 265–8, 294–7.

[104] At Notre Dame in Paris the boy choristers 'were expected to join in the performance of all choral chants such as the Psalms, the hymns, the antiphons, the refrains of responsories, and the five parts of the Ordinary of the Mass'; Craig Wright, *Music and Ceremony at Notre Dame of Paris, 500–1550* (1989), 180–1.

[105] Anon., 'A short treatise of the rule of discant' (MS, 15th c.); Manfred Bukofzer, *Geschichte des englischen Diskants und des Fauxbourdons nach den theoretischen Quellen* (Strasbourg, 1936), 144–5.

> the discantor of the trebill shall begynn his discant with the plainsong in syght ... and the 8 abowe in voce ...
>
> (Anon., early 15th c.)[106]

> [the added 'unison' part] is an 8ve above, for it only looks like a unison, but in sound is an 8ve ...
>
> (Burzio, 1487)[107]

In short, octave 'displacement' – or whatever we may wish to call it – could occur in plainchant, in improvised polyphony and (under specific circumstances) in composed polyphony, too.

Viewed against this background, the critical and long-standing puzzle of Battre's *Gaude virgo mater Christi* arguably dissolves. The men's changed voices (*mutate voces*) sing within their usual collective range, and the boys (*pueri*) sing within theirs. Although the whole piece is notated within a conventional narrow compass, each group performs its music in its own natural range, and thus at different octaves. In other words, the written 15$^+$–note compass is employed in Battre's piece to represent a wider sounding compass of 22$^+$ notes – and in the most economical fashion possible (merely through the added designations 'mutate voces' and 'pueri'), neatly obviating any necessity to employ new or unfamiliar clefs or notes.[108]

Needless to say, this straightforward interpretation is incompatible with any preconception that Battre's intended sounding pitch must have been broadly similar to today's.[109] A rough indication of possible equivalent ranges at today's pitch is therefore given in Table 3.3b, and the openings of the first two sections, as we might wish to notate them today, are shown in Ex. 3.2. (The reader will, I trust, be clear that these transpositions do not in any way suggest that 'transposition' would have been required of Battre's singers.) For a parallel account of the other Trent Codex work in which 'pueri' are mentioned, see Appendix 6 ('The Gloria by Bourgois').

---

[106] Anon., 'A short treatise', 145.

[107] '... *quantum ad visum unisonus sed in sono diapason*'; Nicolò Burzio, *Musices opusculum* (Bologna, 1487), bk 2, ch. 6.

[108] The opposite process occurs – for no evident good reason – in an anonymous 16th-century English organ Magnificat (copied ?c. 1548). Its written compass is an unusually wide 31 notes, since three sections are written 'high' and three 'low'. However, two of the high sections bear the instruction 'play both parts viii nots lower' (as most probably should the third), which brings them to the level of the remainder and reduces the overall compass by an octave. *Early Tudor Organ Music I: Music for the Office*, Early English Church Music 6, ed. J. Caldwell (1966), 23–8.

[109] A by-product of this investigation is the recognition that a 'low' pitch a 4th or so below today's fits well not only with Schlick's comments on organ pitch but also with the origins both of the divergent organ/choir pitches in England and of the diverse clef-configurations employed in polyphonic music (the so-called *chiavette*).

Ex. 3.2 H. Battre, *Gaude virgo mater Christi*, opening sections (renotated ↓5 and ↑4 respectively)

[Musical score with three vocal parts: (top staff) Gau-de vir-go ma-ter Chri-sti | Pueri: Gau-de qui-a de-o ple-na; Contratenor: Gau-de vir-go ma-ter Chri-sti | Pueri: Gau-de qui-a de-o ple-na; Tenor: Gau-de vir-go ma-ter Chri-sti | Pueri: Gau-de qui-a de-o ple-na pe-pe-ri-sti]

ENGLAND: ORGAN PITCH

THE present investigation has thus far found nothing of substance to suggest that falsetto singing was practised anywhere in continental Europe before the 16th century. It lies well beyond the scope of this essay to chart subsequent developments in its various regions – the slow emergence of the voice, first as a *soprano*[110] (often standing in for the boy's voice) and only later as an alto, and its eventual eclipse by the castratos. Instead, some of the necessary building blocks of two such histories are set out in Appendix 7 ('Boys and Falsettists in 16th- and Early 17th-Century Italy and Germany').

As for 'the golden age of English music' and its reputed standard-bearer the falsettist countertenor,[111] almost a century and a half stands between Aaron's mention of a *vox 'ficta'* (1516) and the first clear indication of falsetto singing on English soil:[112]

---

[110] The high a'' expected of today's soprano sounds a 3rd or so above the top notes of most 16th-century Continental soprano parts (allowing not only for different pitch standards but also for high-cleffed notation; for which see, for example, Parrott, 'A Brief Anatomy of Choirs', 12–14). For Vicentino (1555) the soprano's usual top written note was e'', for Praetorius (1618) e''/f''.

[111] '... a long-lost voice-type intimately associated with the golden age of English music of the 16th and 17th centuries, ... resurrected unwittingly by the self-taught Deller in our own time'; Michael and Mollie Hardwick, *Alfred Deller: A Singularity of Voice* (1968), ix.

[112] I am aware of just three earlier references to possible falsetto singing, none of them in an ecclesiastical context. (1) Thomas Campion, 1613 (*The Entertainment at Caversham*): 'Here standing on a smooth greene, and environed with the Horse-men, they present a Song of five Parts, and withall a lively Silvan-dance of six persons: the *Robin-Hood*-men faine two Trebles, one of the Keepers with the *Cynick* sing two Countertenors, the other Keeper the Base; but the Traveller being not able to sing, gapes in silence, and expresseth his humour in Antike gestures'; *The Works of Thomas Campion*, ed. W. R. Davis (1967), 238. Were the Robin Hood men

for above a Year after the Opening of His Majesties Chappel [in 1660], the Orderers of the Musick there, were necessitated to supply the superiour Parts of their Musick with *Cornets*, and *Mens feigned Voices*, there being not one Lad, for all that time, capable of Singing his Part readily.

(Matthew Locke, 1673)[113]

'singing softly' or just 'pretending' to sing while others supplied their parts? Were they boy singers, or were their 'treble' parts simply the 'top' parts of a men-only line-up? Is this an early instance of falsetto being used for comic effect? Only one thing seems reasonably certain: the 'faining' singers were not singing the countertenor parts. (2) Mathurin Marie, 1634: a Frenchman who was amongst Queen Henrietta Maria's servants newly arrived from Navarre in 1625, Marie took the solo treble part of 'Justice' in James Shirley's masque *The Triumph of Peace*; see *A Biographical Dictionary of English Court Musicians, 1485–1714*, compiled A. Ashbee et al. (1998). Marie was presumably either a castrato or a *dessus mué* (see n. 100). (3) Ralph Kettell, President of Trinity College, Oxford, ?c. 1641–3: 'He sang a thin shrill high Treble, but there was one J. Hoskyns who had a higher, and was wont to playe the wag with the Doctor, to make him straine his voyce up to his'; John Aubrey, *Brief Lives* ii, ed. A. Clark (Oxford, 1898), 24. John Hoskins was a contemporary of Aubrey at the college. While there is no mention of 'feigning', he and Kettell may well have been singing in falsetto (which, of course, does not make them 'countertenors') – though possibly just for fun. And again, 'treble' may simply be Aubrey's casual way of indicating the (non-falsetto) top parts of music for men only; see Morley, p. 86 below.

[113] Matthew Locke, *The Present Practice of Musick Vindicated* (London, 1673), 19. For a similar practice at the French chapel royal see n. 100. The expedient of 'feigned voices' is very likely to have been the idea of Henry Cooke, Master of the Children of the Chapel from 1660, and 'esteem'd the best singer after the *Italian* manner of any in *England*' (*The Diary of John Evelyn* iii, ed. E. S. de Beer (1955/R2000), for 28 November 1654). The 'feigned voice' crops up around the same time in John Playford's *An Introduction to the Skill of Musick* (London, 1664), which includes '*A Brief Discourse of, and Directions for Singing after the* Italian *manner ... Written some time since by an* English *Gentleman who lived many years in* Italy, *and Taught the same here in* England' (p. 57). This is essentially a translation of Giulio Caccini's preface to his *Le nuove musiche* (Florence, 1602), and the expression 'feigned voice' is employed wherever Caccini writes '*voce finta*' or '*voci finte*', for example: '... Increasing of the Voyce in the *Treble* Part [?register], especially in feigned Voyces, doth oftentimes become harsh, and unsufferable to the Hearing, as upon divers occasions I have heard' (p. 64). The singer of solo songs should 'choose for himself such a Tune [?pitch] wherein he can sing to his full and natural Voice, to avoid feigned Tunes of Notes. ... from a feigned Voice can come no noble manner of singing, which proceeds from a natural voice, serving aptly for all the Notes which a man mannage according to his ability' (pp. 74–5). (Might the anonymous translator, who Playford tells us was no longer alive, have been Walter Porter, who died in 1659, supposedly studied with Monteverdi in Venice and was a leading figure in Charles I's Chapel Royal where, according to Anthony Wood, Cooke was 'bred up originally'?)

(Here, too, the voice is assigned to *top* parts, substituting for boys.)[114] Furthermore, the English traveller Thomas Coryat, despite his years at Winchester and Oxford during the 1590s, gives the distinct impression of having been wholly unfamiliar with falsetto singing before reaching Venice in 1608:

> I alwaies thought that he was an Eunuch, which if he had beene, it had taken away some part of my admiration, because they do most commonly sing passing wel; but he was not, therefore it was much the more admirable. Againe it was the more worthy of admiration, because he was a middle-aged man, as about forty yeares old. For nature doth more commonly bestowe such a singularitie of voice upon boyes and striplings, then upon men of such yeares.[115]

No comparably informative allusion to falsetto singing is known from earlier English sources.[116] As for the countertenor, we learn from Charles Butler (1636) simply that the part

> answereth the Tenor; thowgh commonly in higher keyz: and therefore is fittest for a man of a sweete shril voice. ... in Harmoni it hath the greatest grace: specially when it is sung with a right voice: which is too rare.[117]

---

[114] For developments later in the 17th century see Andrew Parrott, 'Performing Purcell', in *The Purcell Companion*, ed. M. Burden (1995), 415–24 (reprinted in this volume, Ch. 9).

[115] Thomas Coryat, *Coryat's Crudities* (London, 1611), 252–3. The singer in question can be identified as a priest known as 'il falsetto di Piove'; Denis Arnold, 'Music at the Scuola di San Rocco', *Music & Letters* 40/3 (1959), 238. Misleadingly, Arnold goes on to describe a second singer, the alto Bartolomeo Barbarino, as 'The *other* countertenor' [my italics].

[116] Some readers may be recalling an image from 'The Miller's Tale' of Absalon making music: 'He played a two-stringed fiddle, did it proud,/ And sang a high falsetto rather loud'. These, of course, are not Chaucer's words but those of the well-known translation by Neville Coghill; Geoffrey Chaucer, *The Canterbury Tales*, trans. N. Coghill (1951), 106. The original reads: 'And pleyen songes on a smal rubible;/ Therto he song som tyme a loud quynyble'; *The Works of Geoffrey Chaucer*, ed. F. N. Robinson (2/1974), 49 (lines 3331–2). Noting Chaucer's fondness for musical allusions, Charles Burney reports (with some justification) that the Pardoner, 'just come from Rome, without a beard, sings in Falset'; *A General History of Music* ii (London, 1782); ed. F. Mercer (London, 1935) i, 661. Chaucer's own words are these: 'A voys he hadde as smale as hath a goot. ... I trowe he were a geldyng or a mare.' *The Works*, ed. Robinson, 23 ('General Prologue', lines 688, 691).

[117] Butler, *The Principles of Musik*, 41–2. Butler entered Magdalen Hall, Oxford, in 1579 and moved from the city only in 1593.

('Shrill', today an opposite of 'sweet', seems mostly to have had the force of 'sonorously high',[118] and the rarity of 'right' voices is generally true of all but middle-range voices.) The author of British Library MS Royal 18. B xix (?1620s) evidently found nothing distinctive about countertenors other than that they were 'lesse lowe and more higher then Tenors',[119] though lines from an earlier Scottish song are rather more evocative: 'The *Counter* is the prince of all/ Whilk does require a mighty voce.'[120]

The subject clearly needs to be approached in other ways, and for this two factors prove critical: the 'mean' voice and, even more important, organ pitch.

OVER the past half century much of the thinking – and much of what is consequently expected of the music itself by editors, performers and listeners – has been coloured by the supposition of an English organ pitch a minor 3rd above modern pitch.[121] (In England, as opposed to most other European countries, not one church instrument has survived reasonably intact from before the Civil War.) My own understanding has always been both that this was a highly questionable calculation, overshooting the mark significantly (by up to a tone), and also that the mere equating of a written f with the pitch of a 2½-foot pipe (as in the key source)[122] was in any case never intended as a formula for defining a

---

[118] Cf. 'My brest is shryll. *Vox mea est sonora*' – John Stanbridge, *Vulgaria* (1519), 19; 'All voyces, great and small, base & shrill' – Roger Ascham, *Toxophilus* (London, 1545), ed. E. Arber (London, 1869), 43; in Rome a church is reported as using clerical assitants 'of shril and sounding voyces ... the one for Latin, the other for Italian, to pronounce and to tel the people in both languages one after an other, what everie relike is' – Gregory Martin, *Roma Sancta* (MS, 1581), ed. G. B. Parks (1969), 52; 'At last they heard a horne, that shrilled cleare/ Throughout the wood' – Edmund Spenser, *The Faerie Queene* (London, 1590), bk 2, canto iii, lines 20–1; '*Sonoreux*: ... Sonorous, lowd, shrill, roring, ringing' – Randle Cotgrave, *A Dictionarie of the French and English Tongues* (London, 1611).

[119] London, British Library, MS Royal 18. B xix, fol. 8v.

[120] Anon., 'Nou let us sing' (?late16th), verse 4, in *Music of Scotland, 1500–1700*, ed. K. Elliott, Musica Britannica 15 (3/1975), 170 (no. 48). This accords with George Wither's 'Seas, and Flouds, from Shore to Shore,/ Shall the COUNTER-TENOUR roare', in *A Sonnet, Wherein All Creatures are Provoked to Ioyne Together, in Prayse of their Almightie Creator*, in *Preparation to the Psalter* (London, 1619), sig. Avii.

[121] 'We have hard evidence that English church organ pitch was a minor 3rd higher above modern pitch'; Wulstan, 'The Problem of Pitch', 98.

[122] The claim stems from a single sentence (in Latin) found in a copy of the *pars organica* of Thomas Tomkins, *Musica Deo Sacra* (London, 1668). This was first reported in the preface to *A Collection of the Sacred Compositions of Orlando Gibbons*, ed. the Rev. Sir Frederick A. Gore Ouseley (London, 1873), where it is reckoned that a written f would have sounded as 'a somewhat sharp G' (presumably in relation to a' = 455; cf. n. 124).

pitch in precise terms, but rather as a convenient and conventional way of pointing to a known approximate pitch standard (in this case, 'choir' pitch).[123] The first point was clarified as long ago as 1880, when Alexander J. Ellis adjudged Gore Ouseley's earlier estimate to be 'slightly incorrect' and instead proposed $a' = 474$, somewhere between a semitone and a tone above today's pitch.[124] (Regrettably, Ellis's well-informed estimate lay buried in the 42 densely packed columns of tables appended to his 1880 paper, where it evidently failed to attract sufficient attention to supplant Ouseley's reading.) More recently, scrupulous calculations from three marked pipes originally belonging to Robert Dallam's organ of c. 1630 for Magdalen College, Oxford, have emphatically confirmed Ellis's estimate, with results in the region of $a' = 475-7$.[125] Directly comparable evidence from the early 16th century is lacking, but it is more than likely that organ pitch was generally the same or very similar, since both a 1519 contract and a contemporary organ case show that their pipes, like Dallam's, were somewhat longer than their nominal '5-foot' lengths.[126]

The relevance of all such information has recently been sharply challenged: 'In no sense ... was singing pitch determined by organ pitch.'[127]

---

[123] More specifically, it alerts the organist to the fact that the music before him is written at *choir* pitch and therefore must be transposed if played on an instrument built to the older *organ* pitch. (The relationship between 'quire pitch' and 'ye keys & musiks' of organs need not occupy us further here.) A full and clear explanation of this and of related matters is provided by Andrew Johnstone, '"As it was in the beginning": Organ and Choir Pitch in Early Anglican Church Music', *Early Music* 31/4 (2003), 506–25, with the quoted words from Nathaniel Tomkins's letter (1665) at p. 515. See also J. Bunker Clark, *Transposition in 17th-Century English Organ Accompaniments and the Transposing Organ* (1974).

[124] Alexander J. Ellis, 'On the History of Musical Pitch', *Journal of the Society of Arts*, 5 March 1880; Ellis and Mendel, *Studies in the History of Musical Pitch* (1968), 48. Ellis describes his estimate as 'only a semitone sharper than our present concert pitch' (which may be taken to have been $a' = 455$); ibid., 23.

[125] The pipes in question are now at St Nicholas, Stanford on Avon, Northamptonshire; A. Johnstone, '"As it was in the beginning"', 508–9 and 521. The pitches they yield also have the merit of being only a little above the most recent estimates of the pitch Praetorius decribes as 'now in use in Italy and England as well as with princely *Capellen* in German lands' (which was probably nearer $a' = 460$); Praetorius, *Syntagma musicum* ii, 15; and Bruce Haynes, *A History of Performing Pitch* (2002), 79–82.

[126] Dallam's '5-foot' pipe measures 5' 1½", the early 16th-century organ case at St Mary's, Old Radnor, Powys, seems designed to allow 5' 2" for its largest pipe, and Anthony Duddyngton's contract with All Hallows by the Tower of London (1519) specifies a longest pipe of 'x foot or more'. Johnstone, '"As it was in the beginning"', 509.

[127] And in similar vein: 'there is no reason whatever to imagine that the singing voices were trussed into any sort of mandatory congruity with the pitch of the organ'; Bowers, 'Chains', 15. The strength of this [recent] disavowal arises

Well, yes and no. Uniformity of pitch between organs – to the degree of precision now measurable – was clearly never absolute. In Oxford in 1662 the organist of Christ Church suggested that a proposed new instrument for New College should be 'half a note lower' than that of his own college (which presumably was inconveniently high), 'but Mr. Dalham supposed that a quarter of a note would be sufficient'.[128] Nor was any one instrument as stable as we might imagine. When in the mid-18th century Robert Smith measured the pitch of the organ at Trinity College, Cambridge, on cold, temperate and hot days of the year, his results ranged over roughly a semitone.[129] Yet it was precisely on account of these and other variables, and in the interests of singers, that transposition – written and unwritten – played an important role in the organist's art. Thomas Morley's 'Master', inspecting a short four-part compositional exercise by 'Polymathes', criticizes the unnecessary complexity of its written pitch level (which involves a two-flat signature and additional A flats):

> The musick is in deed true, but you have set it in such a key as no man would have done, except it had beene to have plaide it on the Organes with a quier of singing men, for in deede such shiftes the Organistes are many times compelled to make for ease of the singers ...[130]

By explicitly acknowledging singers' precedence in matters not only of notation but also of performance pitch,[131] Morley (a former organist

from an evident conflict between Bowers's recognition that the 'high' organ pitch is no longer credible and his adherence to the 'high' vocal ranges to which it gave birth. Ibid., 12 (fig. 2(d)).

[128] Stephen Bicknell, *The History of the English Organ* (1996), 111. Christ Church still has in its possession a fine pair of treble cornetts bought by the College in 1605, presumably for use at a service 'mixt with instrumental and vocal musick' on the occasion of a visit from James I. Their pitch was measured for me in 1978 (by Bruce Dickey, Teresa Caudle and Jeremy West) and found to be very slightly below/above $a' = 440$ with/without the silver mounts. This could imply that they were pitched a tone lower than an organ somewhat sharper than was evidently common (in order to be compatible with it). See also Julian Drake, 'The Christ Church Cornetts, and the Ivory Cornett in the Royal College of Music, London', *Galpin Society Journal* 34 (1981), 44; and Jamie Savan and Ricardo Simian, 'CAD Modelling and 3D Printing for Musical Instrument Research: The Renaissance Cornett as a Case Study', *Early Music* 42/4 (2014), 539.

[129] The organ's d sounded variously at 254, 262 and 268 Hz. Robert Smith, *Harmonics or, The Philosophy of Musical Sounds* (Cambridge, 1749), 202–6 and 223–4.

[130] Thomas Morley, *A Plaine and Easie Introduction to Practicall Musicke* (London, 1597), 156.

[131] '... the verie sight of those flat cliffes (which stande at the beginning of the verse or line like a paire of staires, with great offence to the eie, but more to the amasing of the yong singer) make them mistearme their notes and so go

of St Paul's Cathedral) highlights the close relationship that necessarily existed between the two parties. In continental Europe organs were commonly built or adapted explicitly to facilitate this necessary collaboration:

- Valencia (Cathedral), 1460/68: one department of the instrument is tuned to *'cant d'orgue'* ('polyphony').
- 's-Hertogenbosch (Cathedral), c. 1500: '*Item* the great organ must have a new keyboard beginning at *effaut* ... for one must often use that *effaut* and it fits the choir in polyphony [*discant*].'
- Padua (S Maria di Monteortone), 1507: 'The pitch should be that of the human voice or of the choir' (Item *sea coristo a voce de homo over da coro*).
- Schlick, 1511 (*Spiegel der Orgelmacher*): an organ 'should be suitably tuned to the choir for the singing; for where this is not taken into account the people often have to sing too high or too low'. The scaled-down pipe-length for a *'ein geschickt gut chor moß'* ('a fittingly good choir pitch') is then given by means of a printed line.
- Innsbruck (St Jacob Pfarrkirche), 1513: a new department is to be added 'in order that when His Imperial Majesty's choir sings in the said church, they shall have in the two organs two different pitches [*chormass*] side by side'.
- Modena (S Pietro), 1519: the exact pitch is to be 'according to needs of the choir' (*secundo il bisogno del Coro*).
- Bergamo (S Maria Maggiore), 1546: the organ of 1498 is lowered 'because when following the present pitch of this organ the result is great strain for the singers or great discord' (*quia sequendo tonum presentem ipsius organi fit magna vis cantoribus in canendo aut fit magna dissonantia*).[132]

English organs and organists had no less a need to accommodate vocal pitch levels. Norwich Cathedral's statutes of 1608 specify that the organist

out of tune'. The corrected exercise is then presented one tone higher (with a single-flat signature); Morley, *A Plaine and Easie Introduction*, 156. Cf. Butler, *The Principles of Musik*, 86: 'wheither the Key bee high or low; it resteth in the Discretion of the *Chanter*, to set the Tunes, according to the *Ambitus* or Compas of his Voices.'

[132] Spanish and Italian items – Mendel, 'Pitch in Western Music', 37, 39 and 42; 's-Hertogenbosch item – Nicolas Meeùs, 'Some Hypotheses on the History of Organ-pitch before Schlick', *The Organ Yearbook* 6 (1975), 46 and 51 n. 23; Arnolt Schlick, *Spiegel der Orgelmacher und Organisten* (Speyer, 1511), 2 [sig. Bii] (ch. 2); Innsbruck item – A. Mendel, 'Devices for Transposition in the Organ before 1600', *Acta musicologica* 21 (1949), 32 [from Hans Joachim Moser, *Paul Hofhaimer* (Berlin, 1929), 177].

'shall give with the organ the proper sound to the choir',[133] while in 1570 his opposite number at Lincoln Cathedral – one William Byrd – was instructed to play before the various Office canticles, though 'merely for the guidance of the choir'.[134] Earlier still, at a time when the organ's principal role was to alternate with singers in the performance of plainchant, intriguing indications – 'in A re' and '(Ut in) C fa ut' – appear against four polyphonic Magnificats (by Horwood, Cornysh, Turges and Ludford),[135] suggesting that these unaccompanied vocal works may have been pitched with reference to the organ (or some other source of fixed pitch).

Choir pitch and organ pitch in England lay a 4th/5th apart from each other, and organists were familiar with transposing between the two,[136] but they also knew that in certain circumstances further (or secondary) transposition might be needed for smaller adjustments.[137] Choir pitch thus represented a norm, but one which when necessary (and within certain practical limits) organists could adjust for the benefit of singers.

ENGLAND: THE 'MEAN' VOICE

How then to judge what would and would not benefit singers? There is currently a measure of agreement that the bewildering variety of written ranges and clef configurations found in English church music of the 16th and early 17th centuries masks a notably consistent use of no more than five categories of voice.[138] Defining these categories, however, continues to divide opinion and is an issue at the heart of this essay – whence the second critical question mentioned earlier: who sang 'mean' parts? Was the *medius* of the Eton Choirbook and its successors designed for boys or for men (falsettists) – or for either or both?

---

[133] Statutes, ch. 5. Noel Boston, *The Musical History of Norwich Cathedral* (1963), 45.

[134] '... *quod exinde organista dicte ecclesiae cathedralis sub forma sequenti tantum modo ad regimen chori in dicta ecclesia organa modulabitur viz ante inchoacionem cantici vocati Te Deum* ...'; John Harley, *William Byrd: Gentleman of the Chapel Royal* (1997), 39; cf. Bowers VI, 67 [= 'Lincoln Cathedral: Music and Worship to 1640', in *A History of Lincoln Minster*, ed. D. Owen (1994)].

[135] Horwood's Magnificat is found in the Eton Choirbook, the others in the Caius Choirbook.

[136] In transpositions of a 4th or 5th, up or down, only one degree of the scale changes. For a detailed explanation of the processes involved, see Johnstone, '"As it was in the beginning"', 511–18.

[137] As in Morley's examples, any 'secondary' transposition of this sort was almost inevitably restricted to the interval of a tone, by the nature of meantone tuning and not least because early English organs are not known to have possessed split keys (even for G#/A♭).

[138] See Parrott, 'A Brief Anatomy of Choirs', 12–14.

Today's Anglican choirboys are almost invariably required to sing as trebles, yet it is undeniable that plenty of boys more naturally sing in a lower range. (Are all female singers sopranos?) Continental composers soon settled for a lower top part than their English counterparts, rarely using a full three-octave choral texture,[139] and have left a few examples of divided parts for boys where one is set lower still:

- Ockeghem, *Missa Fors seulement* (*a*5), Credo: 'secundus puer' 4/5 notes lower
- Regis, *Celsitonantis* (*a*5): 'secundus puer' 3 notes lower
- Obrecht, *Salve regina misericordiae* (*a*6): 'puer' (beneath a 'secundus puer') 3 notes lower.

By contrast, boys' voices in England were regularly classified as high and low, treble and mean:

- Wells Cathedral, 1460 (Bishop Thomas de Bekynton's *Regulae et ordinationes*): 'The Master or Undermaster ... should teach the boys clearly and distinctly in plain and prick song, taking care to give them high or low parts according to the range of their voice.'[140]
- Northumberland Household Book, *c.* 1505: 'Childeryn of the chapell v viz ij Tribills and iij Meanys'; ?*c.* 1518: 6 boys – 3 trebles, 3 'second trebles.'[141]
- Llanthony Secunda Priory, 1533: John Hogges as Master of the Lady Chapel choir was to provide 'foure childerne ... too meanys and too trebles' for the daily Lady Mass and evening votive antiphon.[142] (The Priory, on the outskirts of Gloucester, was the country's sixth-largest Augustinian house.)
- Peterhouse partbooks (Cambridge), ?1530s: Taverner, *Meane Mass* 'for iiij men and a childe' (19 notes). Three of the 71 pieces (mostly of 21–3 notes) have ranges of just 15 or 16 notes and are specially marked 'men' in each index – implying that elsewhere

---

[139] According to Vicentino, 'the extreme limits of soprano and bass parts should be 19 notes, or 20 with the semitone', even though their combined clefs make 21 notes readily available (*l'estremo del soprano con il Basso, dè essere xix. voci, & xx. con il semitono*). For compositions in eight or more parts this can be extended to 22 notes. *L'antica musica*, bk 4, ch. 17.

[140] Cosyn MS (Wells), fol. 176v; *Dean Cosyn and Wells Cathedral Miscellanea*, ed. Dom A. Watkin, Somerset Record Society 36 ([Frome], 1941 [i.e. 1943]), 105.

[141] See Bowers III, 57–64; also 68–76 (Appendix: 'An Evaluation of the Evidence of the 'Northumberland Household Book' Relating to the Constitution, *c.* 1505–*c.* 1525, of the Household Chapel of Henry [Percy], Fifth Earl of Northumberland').

[142] Bowers II, 35.

'parts higher than *tenor* and *contratenor* ... were performed by boys'.[143]

- *Audivi vocem/Media nocte* and *Hodie nobis celorum rex/Gloria in excelsis*: settings by Cowper, Sheppard, Tallis and Taverner (all *a4*, mostly a pair of high voices a 4th/5th above a pair of low voices; 14–16 notes) match the liturgical stipulation that these texts are to be sung by boys only.[144]
- Gyffard partbooks, 1553–8 (*or* 1570s): Taverner, *In pace* 'for iij men and a childe' (19 notes) – the 'child' part being a mean.[145]
- Salisbury Cathedral, 1580: John Farrant ('the elder') was to 'furnishe the quier of the said Cath[edral] churche with eight choristers havinge good and commendable voyces for trebles and meanes'.[146]
- Thomas Morley, 1597: 'compositions for men onely to sing ... never passe this compasse' (15 notes; G–g') and do not include a mean part.[147]
- London, British Library, MS Royal 18. B xix, c. 1620–30: 'of Childrens voices there are two kyndes, viz: Meane voyces (which are higher then mens voyces) and Treble voices.'[148]
- Charles Butler, 1636: the mean part lies 'betweene the Countertenor (the highest part of a man) and the Treble'.[149]

Weighed against this ample documentation of the boy mean, the total absence of comparable evidence for an adult mean is quite striking. Neatly complementing the view (as represented by Wulstan) that the falsettist has a role elsewhere (on *contratenor* parts), acknowledgment of the boy *medius* manifestly collides with the alternative prevailing view (that of Bowers). On the basis of putative earlier practice, this view strenuously asserts that from before *c*. 1547 'there is no reason whatever to imagine that the singing of ... *medius* parts in 5-part three-octave scoring was committed to anyone other than ... adult falsettists'.[150] The claim is

---

[143] Bowers III, 65. Cf. n. 132.

[144] See Bowers II, 38–9.

[145] Bowers defends his position by arguing that 'the atypical allocation of this part to a boy's voice instead of to an adult alto ... had specifically to be directed by a written note' (and similarly in the case of Taverner's *Meane Mass* 'for iiij men and childe'; see above); Bowers II, 51–2.

[146] Bowers II, 39 n. 99.

[147] Morley, *A Plaine and Easie Introduction*, 166.

[148] London, British Library, MS Royal 18. B xix, fol. 8v.

[149] Butler, *The Principles of Musik*, 42.

[150] Bowers, 'Chains', 11 (and 16 n. 25); see also *point 8.* in 'Lines of Reasoning', above. Bowers insists that the boy mean 'was used as a substitute for the adult alto, whose line and part it took over in choirs in which the men were

then said to be 'corroborated' by the terms of Bishop Robert Sherburn's endowment at Chichester Cathedral (1526), which provides for

> four lay clerks with well-formed voices and well-versed in music, of whom one at least should always be of a natural and [clearly] audible bass voice, while the voices of the other three should be sweet and melodious, such that by the combined singing of the voices they may be able naturally and freely to extend to 15 or 16 notes ...
>
> *quatuor clerici laici concinnas voces habentes et musice docti. quorum unus ad minus semper sit basse naturalis. et audibilis vocis. aliorum vero trium voces sint suaves et canore. ita quod a communi vocum succentu possint naturaliter et libere ascendere ad quindecim vel sexdecim notas ...*[151]

The significance of the 15/16 notes will be familiar from earlier in this study. Here the issue is whether the required compass is intended to be that of all four singers or of only 'the other three'. Since the passage as a whole concerns *four* new singers (as stated clearly in its heading), a natural expectation is created that the mention of 'combined singing' does the same. For Roger Bowers, however, 'the plainest sense of the Latin original' is that the stipulated range of 15/16 notes excludes the bass singer and applies 'expressly' to the other three men, whom he presumes to be required for three higher voice parts (*tenor, contratenor* and *medius*); *ergo*, an adult (falsettist) mean is intended.[152] As far as I am aware, however, it

> sufficiently few, and the boys sufficiently many, to make this particular device at least expedient, and in some cases essential'; Bowers III, 67. This hypothesis, which may or may not match the relevant statistics, relies on further uncertain matters – of availability as opposed to participation, and of numerical as opposed to acoustical 'balance'. Elsewhere, in order to accommodate the documented boy mean, Bowers makes the unfounded assertions that 'from the early 16th century onwards the boys' voices of all the greater churches were trained to render both treble and alto parts, and that the ability to do so was ubiquitous'; Bowers II, 39. While acknowledging that 'the professional historian would never base a contention on the lack of evidence that, viewed objectively, it would be unreasonable to expect to be able to find anyway', Bowers claims that 'Happily, the *circumstantial* evidence ... in favour of the ecclesiastical use of the adult male alto as early as the 1560s [*sic*] is abundant and compelling'; Review of recordings, *Early Music* 18/2 (1989), 276.

[151] Harrison, *Medieval Britain*, 181 n. 5 (with 'concinuas' and 'musica' changed in line with Oxford, New College, archive 9432, fol. 21v). The passage is headed '*Fundatio quatuor clericorum laicorum*'.

[152] Having initially acknowledged that 'the Latin is not totally unambiguous', Bowers now argues strenuously, if unconvincingly, that 'the chosen phraseology ruled out all chance of ambiguity'. Bowers III, 51 n. 29; and Bowers, 'Chains', 11; see also Bowers II, 34–5. Be that as it may, if the legalistic Latin is considered to be that of a non-musician (specifically a

would be unique for a specification of this sort to apply to an incomplete vocal scoring.[153] More significantly, and regardless of any other ambiguity, Sherburn clearly stipulates *at least* one proper bass (presumably to ensure a firm foundation for a 'full' choir), with the possible consequence that only two singers might then be available to cover the three parts predicated by Bowers. A straightforward and more plausible reading (that of, amongst others, the scholar whom Bowers justly considers to have been 'the greatest expert in this field', Frank Ll. Harrison)[154] is that the four singers were to include at least one strong bass and to have a collective range of two octaves or so – the standard combined range of *bassus*, *tenor* and *contratenor* parts and of all music explicitly designated for men only. (For higher voices Chichester Cathedral could call on eight boy choristers.)[155]

As this prolonged and difficult cross-examination nears its conclusion, it will be abundantly clear that the continuing non-appearance of the star witness – the quintessentially English falsettist 'countertenor' – has major implications for our understanding of large tracts of early vocal music (and not just from from Britain). While the picture that emerges for pre-Commonwealth music may not accord with current Anglican practice or with its familiar non-ecclesiastical offshoots, it is, I believe, one that matches the music with telling simplicity. The 'ordinari compas of humane voices (i.e. from the lowest Note of a Mans Base, unto the highest of a Boyz Treble)' is, was and will continue to be roughly three octaves ('althowgh there ar found soom Bases that reach below, and soom Trebles that arise aboov this ordinari compas').[156] Before the falsettist entered the equation, men's voices were considered to occupy just the two lower octaves or so, and boys the upper two. In the early 16th century the potential combined compass was exploited to the full by English composers (though rarely by those on the Continent), initially employing just four basic ranges but

lawyer), it is not unreasonable to wonder how precise its author's grasp of such musical intricacies may have been. Tightly worded legal documents down the centuries have not infrequently been found to be open to interpretation. For the role of punctuation in interpreting the Chichester ordinance see Simon Ravens, '/ – . : ; , or ?', *Early Music Review* 164 (February 2015), 6–8.

[153] Vicentino, in setting out the limits of the various parts, explicitly measures each range from the lowest note of the bass; *L'antica musica*, bk 4, ch. 17 ('*De i termini & Modi, che si debbono tenere nel comporre le parti*'). See n. 139 above.

[154] Harrison is perhaps best remembered as editor of the Eton Choirbook and author of *Medieval Britain* (in which see p. 181); Bowers, 'Chains', 11 n. 5.

[155] Bowers II, 34.

[156] Butler, *The Principles of Musik*, 9. For a discussion of how the specific ranges of 'humane voices' today may differ from those of our ancestors, see Simon Ravens, *The Supernatural Voice: A History of High Male Singing* (2014), 38–44.

Table 3.4 16th- and early 17th-century English vocal scoring

		c. 1500	c. 1540	c. 1547 and beyond	
15 BOYS	Triplex	d'–g"	d'–g"		
				c'–d"*	Mean
	Medius	g–c"	g–c"		
15/16 MEN	Contratenor	c–f'	e–g'	e–g'	Countertenor
	Tenor	c–f'	c–f'	c–d'	Tenor
	Bassus	F–b	F–b	F–a	Bass

Totals (brackets): 23 = 15 + 15/16; right-side brackets: 9 + 16 = 20.

* Shading indicates the two significant changes of range.

soon preferring the idea that 'Nature ... [has] disposed all voices both of men and children into fyve kindes'.[157] The various usual written ranges are shown in Table 3.4.[158] Two principal modifications occurred in the course of the century. First the *contratenor* moved up a little from its equal pairing with the *tenor*, then the two distinct boys' parts merged to form a single part of intermediate range. (This second development could well have been prompted both by the example of Continental vocal writing and by a decline in the musical training of boys.)[159] The bass part remained one 'to be sung with a deepe, ful, and pleasing Voice', while the tenor – 'neither ascending to any high or strained note, nor descending very low' – settled as one which 'may bee sung by an indifferent voice'.[160] (Reviewing Salisbury Cathedral's choir in 1634 Archbishop Laud insisted 'that there be not more of tenors therein, which is an ordinary voice, then there be of baces and counter-tenours, which doe best furnish the quire'.)[161] The

---

[157] London, British Library, MS Royal 18. B xix.

[158] The ranges shown in Table 3.4 are all adopted from Bowers, 'Chains', 12.

[159] '... even so do I wysshe from the bottome of my heart, that the laudable custome of Englande to teache chyldren their plainesong and priksong, were not so decayed throughout all the realme as it is'; Roger Ascham, *Toxophilus* (London, 1545), ed. E. Arber (London, 1869), 41. While Wulstan argues that 'the change from Latin to English at the Reformation would have resulted in considerable dulling of the vowel spectrum' (*Tudor Music*, 229), Bowers goes further, claiming that 'by the introduction of the English vernacular Book of Common Prayer in 1549' the overall compass of choral music shrank at both ends, partly in order 'to obviate difficulties in articulating at the extremes of range the vowels of vernacular English' ('Chains', 12). It is difficult to see how these claims can hold up, given that singers had already been using English vowels in Latin; see Harold Copeman, *Singing in Latin* (2/1992), 134.

[160] Butler, *The Principles of Musik*, 41.

[161] *Fourth report of the Royal Commission on Historical Manuscripts* (London, 1874), 128 (Visitation Articles). For Laud's similar advice to Wells Cathedral in 1636 see Peter Le Huray, *Music and the Reformation in England, 1549–1660* (1967), 120–1. (The tenor's 'ordinariness' has on occasion been misunderstood as implying that voices equivalent to the modern tenor were

treble, revived occasionally during the early decades of the 17th century, called for 'a high cleere sweete voice',[162] but the *'very* high treble' seems to be a 20th-century invention,[163] evidently born of the high-pitch hypothesis and of a modern appetite for 'extra and desirable brilliance'.[164]

THE reading proposed here has the merit of producing no apparent need for the piecemeal scoring, anomalous pitching, part-swapping and part-sharing involved in some of today's performances.[165] Nor does it require any of the special pleading encountered elsewhere for

- the absence of basses from earlier polyphony
- adult *medius* singers in pre-Reformation music
- a major upheaval of scoring and pitch following the Reformation

common in the early 17th century.) 'Some are ashamed to sing tenor as being too common a voice', declared Heinrich Glarean (*Tenorem quosdam pudet canere, utpote vocem nimis vulgatam*); *Dodecachordon* (Basel, 1547), 178 (bk 2, ch. 38). Lodovico Zacconi considered the tenor range (rarely exceeding written *c–f'*) to be 'natural' – as opposed to high or low – 'because almost all men are naturally suited to this voice part' (*perche quasi tutti gli huomini naturalmente convengano in quella voce*); *Prattica di musica* (Venice, 1596), fol. 51v.

[162] Butler, *The Principles of Musik*, 41. From between 1547 and 1643 there are just two dozen or so liturgical works with treble parts.

[163] As far as I can ascertain, 'very high' is never used of trebles in early writings but may be found in David Wulstan, 'Vocal Colour in English 16th-Century Polyphony', *Journal of the Plainsong and Medieval Society* 2 (1979), 17; in Bowers, 'The Performing Pitch', 25 and 28; and in Bowers II, 39. Similarly, the claim that 'many foreigners remarked on the high trebles ... in 16th-century English choirs' appears to be entirely without foundation; Peter Phillips, 'Performance Practice in 16th-Century English Choral Music', *Early Music* 6/2 (1978), 198.

[164] Peter Phillips argues that 'at written pitch' (i.e. at a' = 440) the top part 'will never go above G' (i.e. g''), whereas 'almost everybody correctly called "soprano" can sing a 4th higher than this'. (In other words, he believes the part needs to be pitched significantly higher.) See Peter Phillips, 'Treble or Soprano? Performing Tallis', *Early Music* 33/3 (2005), 500. Praetorius, on the other hand, was of the opinion 'that the human voice, when it enters the middle and slightly low [register], is much more pleasant and lovely to listen to than high up when it has to shout and scream beyond its capacity' (... *daß auch die Menschen Stimme/ wenn sie im Mittel und etwas tieff herein gehet/ viel anmütiger und lieblicher anzuhören/ als wenn sie in der höhe/ uber vermügen oben hinaus ruffen/ und schreien muß*); *Syntagma musicum* ii, 15.

[165] Peter Phillips writes: 'In my experience any mixture of contraltos, falsettists and high tenors make perfect *"contratenors"* at high pitch'; 'Treble or Soprano?', 498.

- 'high pitch', a minor 3rd above today's
- 'very' high trebles
- dual-register or 'gear-changing' altos
- undocumented falsetto singing[166]

Furthermore, a falsettist-free pre-Restoration choir agrees very satisfactorily with the general sounding pitch suggested by those surviving organ pipes (see 'England: Organ Pitch', above). Indeed, much the same pitch can also be inferred simply by matching duly aligned ranges to the vocal categories as understood here. Which, as it happens, is exactly how I first arrived at an approximate 'working' pitch of an equal semitone above a' = 440 (within a quarter-tone of the organ pipes), one I have adopted for performance fairly consistently since the early 1970s.[167]

CONCLUSION

No music written before *c.* 1500 can be shown either to imply or to demand falsetto singing, nor is there any convincing contemporary record of its cultivation. Subsequent first sightings, moreover, are associated not with alto parts but with the upper parts usually sung by boys (*cantus/discantus/supremus*). It follows that many familiar assertions can no longer be regarded as safe:

> Whereas the alto falsettist had been traditionally accepted both in France (from at least the time of Perotin) and Italy (the Trecento), his sound was not remarkable enough to elicit comment.[168]

> Falsetto singing has been the most common source of alto voices in all-male choirs throughout the history of Western music.[169]

---

[166] For an excellently thorough and up-to-date account of these various matters see Scott Metcalfe, 'Performance Practice in Peterhouse's Chapel: Scoring, Voice Types, Number of Singers, and Pitch', in *Music, Politics, and Religion in Early 17th-Century Cambridge: The Peterhouse Partbooks in Context*, ed. Scott Mandelbrote (forthcoming 2015).

[167] In preparing this essay I came across a published letter I had written in 1979, sharing a previous correspondent's 'dissatisfaction' with the prevalent 'minor 3rd up' practice, pointing out the 'equally unsatisfactory' nature of the supporting evidence, mentioning Gore Ouseley as its apparent originator, apologizing for failing to publish the 'counter-arguments' and recommending 'a sampling of the wonderfully natural, if less sensational, sound of Tallis sung just a semitone up' at an imminent Taverner Choir performance; *Early Music News*, September 1979, 11.

[168] Rebecca Stewart, 'Voice Types in Josquin's Music', *Tijdschrift van de Vereniging voor Nederlandse Muziek Geschiedenis* 35/1–2 (1985), 125.

[169] Owen Jander, 'Contratenor altus', in *The New Grove* 2 vi, 374.

Contemporary [early 16th-century English] documentary sources identified as available the four timbres of boy treble, falsetto alto, tenor, and bass ...[170]

See also Appendix 8 ('English (and Scottish) Music: Dubious Inferences and Assertions').

Falsetto singing and the singing of an alto part (*contratenor*) have quite separate stories, although in some traditions they eventually converge. In England, long seen as the home of the falsettist countertenor, a transition towards this new voice-type began only in the late 17th century. Almost all of Purcell's writing for solo countertenor nevertheless seems still to have been intended for an equivalent of today's (high) tenor,[171] as does Handel's until at least 1719.[172] (It should not be forgotten, of course, that 'countertenor' could on occasion apply equally well to a castrato or to the likes of 'Signora Merighi, a Woman of a very fine Presence, an excellent Actress, and a very good Singer – A Counter Tenor'.)[173] In Germany in the early 1600s the falsettist may have been known primarily as a recent Italian phenomenon: the soprano *Falsetista* appears in Praetorius's table of voice-ranges, bracketed with *Eunuchus* and *Discantista*, but is neither mentioned in the preceding discussion (which includes details of Lasso's celebrated choir at Munich)[174] nor considered in the requirement that a singer should

> choose a voice part – *cantus, altus* or *tenor* etc. – which he can sustain with a full and clear sound, without falsetto (i.e. a half and forced voice).[175]

---

[170] Bowers, 'Chains', 12. This is in effect a description of today's Anglican choir and could therefore be viewed as reflection either of its venerable ancestry or of preconceptions that have inadvertently shaped much of the thinking about its pioneering ancestor.

[171] Parrott, 'Performing Purcell', 417–24.

[172] See, for example, Handel's 'Chandos' anthems. The belief that the 'countertenor' was already necessarily a falsettist has given rise to an imagined conundrum: 'The fact that [Richard] Elford [d. 1714] had a range as low as A at the bottom of the Bass Stave is a musicological red herring for either Elford was a tenor ... in which case he should not have called himself a counter tenor, or, more likely, this note was falsetto'; G. M. Ardran and D. Wulstan, 'The Alto or Countertenor voice', *Music & Letters* 48/1 (1967), 22.

[173] *Daily Journal*, 2 July 1729; Otto Erich Deutsch, *Handel: A Documentary Biography* (1955), 243.

[174] Praetorius, *Syntagma musicum* ii, 20 and 17–18, respectively. See also Appendix 7.

[175] '... *daß ein Sänger ... eine Stimm als* Cantum, Altum *oder* Tenor &c. *erwehlen/ welche er mit vollem und hellem laut/ ohne Falsetten/ (das ist halbe und erzwungene Stimme) halten könne*'; Praetorius, *Syntagma musicum* iii, 231.

(Praetorius's alto is thus confirmed as a non-falsettist.) Earlier still, in mid-16th-century France, tenor and countertenor were explicitly considered 'alike in all respects', despite slightly differing ranges and tessituras:

> whoever knows how to sing the one ... will also do the other ...; for whoever has a strong voice that works well low down should sing tenor rather than countertenor, [and] contrariwise whoever has a delicate and lofty voice should sing countertenor, as all good masters will show you.[176]

This almost equal pairing represents what appears to have been a norm for most vocal music of the same period, and in all parts of Europe. By the mid-18th century, however, the picture had changed significantly under the powerful influence of the Italians, who had earlier embraced the use of falsetto, initially as a solo 'soprano'-range voice and then as a legitimate technique for extending all natural voices upward:

> The Italians and several other nations unite this falsetto with the chest voice, and make use of it to great advantage when singing: with the French, however, this is not customary ...
>
> (Quantz, 1752)[177]

At a time when the English falsettist countertenor had finally arrived (though not on the operatic stage),[178] the much-misunderstood French *haute-contre* remained the staunch upholder of an older and strictly falsetto-free tradition of alto singing and was simply what we would call a (high) tenor.[179]

---

[176] 'La taille, & la haute contre sont semblables en toutes choses'; 'qui saura chanter ... l'une, aussi fera il lautre. ... celuy qui a forte voix fornissant bien en bas doit plustost chanter la taille que l'haute contre, au contraire celuy qui a la voix delicate & hautaine doit chanter l'haute contre. comme tous bons maistres vous le monstreront bien'; Philibert Jambe de Fer, *Épitome musical* (Lyons, 1556), 51–2.

[177] 'Die Italiäner, und einige andere Nationen vereinigen dieses Falset mit der Bruststimme, und bedienen sich dessen, bey dem Singen, mit großem Vortheile; Bey den Franzosen aber ist es nicht üblich'; Johann Joachim Quantz, *Versuch einer Anweisung die Flöte traversière zu spielen* (Berlin, 1752), 47.

[178] Not once, over the course of his long and well-documented career, did Handel employ a falsettist countertenor for an operatic role.

[179] See A. Parrott, 'Falsetto and the French: "Une toute autre marche"', *Basler Jahrbuch für historische Musikpraxis* 26 (2002), 129–48 (reprinted in this volume, Ch. 4). The particular confusion surrounding French and English voices is reflected in the statement that Purcell's 'One charming night' in *The Fairy Queen* (1692) is 'set for a male alto voice, modeled perhaps on the French *haute-contre* but sung in the "head voice" or "falsetto" range throughout'; Richard Taruskin, *The Oxford History of Western Music* ii (2005), 130.

WHY might any of this matter? There are, of course, many who believe that none of it does: 'All we can do with voices is guess ... I don't think trying to replicate ['original choral sound'] would be at all a good idea.'[180] Yet in the case of early 16th-century English polyphony, for example, today's choral performances commonly shun (reasonably low) basses and (reasonably high) tenors, promote a vocal production (falsetto) that was not then cultivated and assign the falsettist either to a part meant for boys or alternatively to a lower part using a medium-to-low register but intended for the medium-to-high register of a natural voice. All of which may in turn encourage a higher sounding pitch than intended and thence a *very* high top part, where words are predictably harder to enunciate. Put more simply, when an unneeded falsetto voice is shoe-horned into a vocal texture there is an inevitable knock-on effect for all other voice parts, perpetuating in the case of Tallis's music, for instance, the unfortunate impression that 'there is no easy answer to the problem posed by his ranges'.[181] Difficult though this is to put into words, such inadvertent interference with the carefully calibrated sonorities and textures evolved by composers who were themselves singers and whose knowledge and understanding of the choral medium has rarely been matched is hardly likely to lead to an improvement on their original intentions.

With solo writing the corresponding impact may be more obvious. Heroic theatrical or celebratory solo writing designed to exploit the top register of a man's natural voice will clearly have a very different effect, however well sung, when placed in the medium-to-low range of a falsetto voice. And whole repertories that depend on speech-like naturalness and directness of verbal communication – English lute songs, consort songs and verse anthems, for example – risk being jeopardized by an 'unnatural' voice singing well above the pitch of its owner's speaking voice.

Falsetto singing has its place in musical history. A muddled understanding of what that place was, however, has encouraged its colonization of whole repertories in which it originally played no part. More seriously, the very process of accommodating the modern 'countertenor' to those repertories may have further distorted our perceptions of the music itself.

---

[180] Peter Phillips, review ('Hip Replacements'), *The Musical Times* 155/3 (2014), 98. 'I had done my research into the period ... learnt what there was to be learnt about voice-types ... and concluded that I should (and could) go my own way'; ibid., 99. With admirable candour Phillips has declared that as conductor of 16th-century polyphony he aims simply to create a choral 'sound' he likes, rather than to engage in any attempt at recovering the practices of its composers: 'the quest for this sonority should start with the contratenor part. ... the countertenors stitch the ensemble together'; Phillips, 'Treble or Soprano?', 499.

[181] Phillips, 'Treble or Soprano?', 496.

APPENDICES

Translations from Latin by Hugh Griffith

APPENDIX 1

Four Early Sources

A Cistercian Order, 1134

It is right that men should sing in a manly voice, and should not in womanish fashion with tinkling voices [notes] ('false', as they are commonly called) imitate the wantonness of minstrels. We therefore decree that moderation must be preserved in the chant, that it may keep a serious flavour and devotion may be maintained.

Viros decet virili voce cantare, et non more femineo tinnulis, vel ut vulgo dicitur falsis vocibus veluti histrionicam imitari lasciviam. Et ideo constituimus mediocritatem servari in cantu, ut et in gravitatem redoleat, et devotio conservetur.[182]

B Gilbertine Order, c. 1148

We utterly forbid, to all our members of both sexes, the use in divine office of organum and descant, *fausetum* and *pipeth*.

Organum tamen et decentum, fausetum et pipeth, omnino in divino officio omnibus nostris utriusque sexus prohibemus.[183]

C Ekkehard V (of St Gall), between 1210 and 1220 (*Instituta Patrum de modo psallendi sive cantandi*)

Minstrelish voices [notes], those that chatter, that belong on hillsides or mountains, that thunder or whisper [hiss], or neigh like a she-ass, that low or bleat like cows and sheep; likewise womanish ones and all 'falseness' of voices [notes], ostentation and novelty: it is our intention to abominate and forbid these in our choirs. For voices [notes] of this kind savour of vanity and folly rather than religion ...

Histrioneas voces, garrulas, alpinas, sive montanas, tonitruantes, vel sibilantes, hinnientes velut vocalis asina, mugientes, seu

---

[182] *Statuta capitulorum generalium ordinis Cisterciensis ab anno 1116 ad annum 1786* i, ed. J.-M. Canivez (Louvain, 1933–41), 30. It has been argued that this and other early 12th-century foundation statutes 'remained in circulation, and to a large extent in force, throughout the 15th century and beyond'; Bowers, 'False Voices', 74. The statutes of 1258 deal in very similar terms with the same issue of maintaining moderation in the performance of chant but without any mention of 'false voices'; *Statuta capitulorum* ii, 435–6.

[183] W. Dugdale, *Monasticon Anglicanum* iv, new edn by J. Caley *et al.* (London, 1817–30), pt 2, 42 (between 945 and 946).

balantes quasi pecora; sive foemineas, omnemque vocum falsitatem, iactantiam seu novitatem detestemur, & prohibeamus in Choris nostris; quia plus redolent vanitatem & stultitiam quam religionem ...[184]

D Roger Bacon, 1267

... in our time there has gradually spread through the Church a bad practice in the chant, which has declined from the gravity and uprightness of old and lost its gentle and natural goodness through sinking into shameless effeminacy. This is evident in the passion for new harmonies, the dangerous devising of new proses, and an unseemly delight in multiple melodies. The same thing is shown above all by $\frac{\text{notes}}{\text{voices}}$ *in falseto* debasing the manly and holy harmony, immoderate as boys and licentious as women, throughout almost the entire Church.

*... jam per ecclesiam paulatim crevit abusus cantus, qui a gravitate et virtute antiqua cecidit, et in mollitiem inverecundam lapsus, mansuetam et naturalem probitatem amisit; quod novarum harmoniarum curiositas, et prosarum lubrica adinventio, multipliciumque cantilenarum inepta voluptas manifestat. Et super omnia voces *in falseto harmoniam virilem et sacram falsificantes, pueriliter effusæ, muliebriter dissolutæ fere per totam ecclesiam comprobant illud idem.*[185]

* One source gives *insulsae* ('absurd') in place of *in falseto*: 'above all by absurd $\frac{\text{notes}}{\text{voices}}$ debasing the manly and holy harmony'.

APPENDIX 2

Music and Effeminacy

St Ambrose, late 4th c.

The voice itself should be not weak, not feeble, nor sounding at all womanish ... but maintaining a certain form and pattern and a manly vigour.

Vox ipsa non remissa, non fracta, nihil femineum sonans, qualem multi gravitatis specie simulare consuerunt, sed formam quamdam et regulam ac sucum virilem reservans.[186]

The passage comes from a section on general deportment and echoes Plato.

---

[184] M. Gerbert, *Scriptores Ecclesiastici* i, 8.

[185] Roger Bacon, *Opus tertium*; *Fr. Rogeri Bacon opera quaedam hactenus inedita*, ed. J. S. Brewer (London, 1859) i, 297.

[186] St Ambrose, *De Officiis*, bk 1, ch. 19 §84; ed. I. J. Davidson (2002), 166.

Boethius, 6th c.

> ... Plato considers that music of the finest nature, chastely formed, is a powerful protection for the republic, provided it be moderate, simple and masculine, not effeminate, wild or full of variety.

> ... *magnam esse custodiam rei publicae Plato arbitratur musicam optime moratam pudenterque coniunctam, ita ut sit modesta ac simplex et mascula nec effeminata nec fera nec varia.*[187]

Ailred of Rievaulx, c. 1145

> Why that contracting and breaking up of the note? ... Sometimes, it is shameful to say, [the voice] is forced into a horse's whinny, sometimes, with manly strength laid aside, it is sharpened into the thinness of a woman's voice ...

> *Ad quid illa vocis contractio et infractio? ... Aliquando, quod pudet dicere, in equinos hinnitus cogitur, aliquando virili vigore deposito in femineae vocis gracilitates acuitur ...*[188]

This splendid diatribe was repeated almost verbatim by Hübner in Silesia (c. 1400) and by William Prynne, *Histriomastix* (London, 1633).

Bernard of Clairvaux, c. 1150

> I urge you, dear friends, always to participate in the divine praises with a pure and active spirit: active, so as to assist the Lord both reverently and promptly, not lazy, not sleepy, not sluggish, not sparing your voices, not cutting words off in the middle, not leaving them out completely, not stuttering some womanish thing through the nose with feeble and slack voices, but with manly sound and attitude, as is right, producing voices filled with the Holy Spirit; and pure, that when you chant you think of nothing but that which you chant.

> *Unde vos moneo, dilectissimi, pure semper ac strenue divinis interesse laudibus: strenue quidem, ut sicut reverenter, ita et alacriter Domino assistatis, non pigri, non somnolenti, non oscitantes, non parcentes vocibus, non praecidentes verba dimidia, non integra transilientes, non fractis et remissis vocibus muliebre quiddam balba de nare sonantes, sed virili, ut dignum est, et sonitu, et affectu voces Sancti*

---

[187] Boethius, *De institutione musica*, bk 1, ch. 1; ed. G. Friedlein (Leipzig, 1867), 181.

[188] *Speculum charitatis*, bk 2, ch. 23, §23; Ailred of Rievaulx, *Opera omnia*, ed. Dom A. Hoste and C. H. Talbot (1971), 97–8.

Spiritus depromentes; pure vero, ut nil aliud, dum psallitis, quam quod psallitis cogitetis.[189]

John of Salisbury, 1159

> It defiles the very practice of religion that in the sight of God and in the very heart of the sanctuary, by the wantonness of their lascivious voices, by their showing off, by their womanish manner of making little notes and their chopping up of phrases, they try to enervate dazed little minds. If you heard the effete strains of those intoning and responding, uniting and descanting, interposing and interrupting, you would think it the music of Sirens, not of men ...

> *Ipsum quoque cultum religionis incestat quod ante conspectum Domini in ipsis penetralibus sanctuarii lascivientis vocis luxu, quadam ostentatione sui, muliebribus modis notularum articulorumque caesuris, stupentes animulas emollire nituntur. Cum praecinentium et succinentium, concinentium et decinentium, intercinentium et occinentium praemolles modulationes audieris, Sirenarum concentus credas esse non hominum ...*[190]

(In the same context it is made clear a little later that the 'dazed little minds' are those of the listeners.)

Robert of Courson, c. 1210

> ... the services of masters of *organum* who set scurrilous and effeminate things before young and ignorant persons, in order to feminize their minds, are not licit ...

> *... illicite sunt opere magistrorum organicorum qui scurrilia et effeminata proponunt iuvenibus et rudibus ad effeminandos animos ipsorum ...*[191]

Jacques de Liège, c. 1330

> Who can deny that the moderns have taken music, which was originally wise, noble, simple, masculine and virtuous, and made it too sensual?

> *Nonne Moderni musicam, quae in suo exordio fuit prudens, honesta, simplex et mascula et bene morata, lascivam nimium reddiderunt?*[192]

---

[189] Bernard of Clairvaux, 'Sermon on the Song of Songs', no. 47 §8, in *Sancti Bernardi opera*, ed. J. Leclercq *et al.*, ii (Rome, 1958), 66.

[190] John of Salisbury, *Policraticus* (MS, 1159); ed. K. S. B. Keats-Rohan, i (1993), 48–9 (bk 1, ch. 6). John of Salisbury was Secretary to the Archbishop of Canterbury and later Bishop of Chartres.

[191] Robert of Courson, *Summa* (MS, c. 1210); Christopher Page, *The Owl and the Nightingale: Musical Life and Ideas in France, 1100–1300* (1989), 145.

[192] *Jacobi Leodiensis Speculum musicae* vii, ed. R. Bragard (1973), 94.

APPENDIX 3

The Burgundian Court Ordinances of 1469

Item: for *chant du livre* there shall be at least Six high voices, Three tenors, Three low contratenors and two *moiens* not including the four chaplains for High Mass or the *sommeliers* who whenever they are not occupied at the altar or in some other reasonable way shall be required to serve with the above-mentioned.

Item pour le chant du livre y aura du moyns Six haultes voix, Troys teneurs, Troys basses contres et deux moiens sans en ce comprendre les quatre chapelains des haultes messes ne les sommeliers lesquelz toutefoys silz ne sont occupes a lautel ou autrement Raisonnablement seront tenus de servir avec les dessus ditz.[193]

As David Fallows has observed, 'a document that assumes four-voice polyphony in 1469 is forward-looking'.[194] These Burgundian ordinances appear not only to be such a document but also to provide 'evidence that the minimum preferred distribution of singers in four-voice polyphony was three on the Bassus, three on the Tenor, two on the Contra and six men on top', a total of 14.[195] (This is not the place to discuss the number and distribution of these voices, but it should not be overlooked that, rather like Bach's 1730 *Entwurff*, these ordinances deal essentially with staffing and organization rather than with the specifics of any individual musical performance, much as we may wish it were otherwise.) Fallows proceeds to demonstrate convincingly that in 1469 all the possible court singers (chaplains and *clercs*) were adult men.[196] However, if one is to accept his conclusion that 'the six men on top were certainly falsettists', it is obviously necessary to know the exact nature of the repertory concerned.

The terms used for polyphonic singing in the 1469 ordinances are variously *deschant*, *chant du livre* and *chanterie du livre* ('singing from

---

[193] Oxford, Bodelian Library, MS Hatton 13, fol. 13r–v; cf. Fallows, 'Specific Information', 149.

[194] Fallows, 'The Performing Ensembles', 43. Elsewhere Fallows has noted that in the case of Cambrai Cathedral 'there must be some doubt whether they really sang four-part polyphony' as early as 1457; 'Specific Information', 121.

[195] Fallows, 'The Performing Ensembles', 42.

[196] Fallows, 'Specific Information', 112–4. The Duke was fully aware that elsewhere there were choirboys eminently capable of singing new polyphony: 'Charles, count of Charolais, son of Philip, duke of Burgundy, etc., composed a motet and all the music, which was sung before him after Mass in the the venerable church of Cambrai by the master and the choirboys in the year 1460, October 23, which is the day of St Severin'; marginal note on a manuscript at the Bibliothèque municipale, Cambrai; Craig Wright, 'Dufay at Cambrai: Discoveries and Revisions', *Journal of the American Musicological Society* 28/2 (1975), 209.

the book').[197] None is easy to define with complete certainty, but – more importantly – none necessarily implies polyphony of the kind we may be hoping to identify. In his *Musices opusculum* of 1487 Nicolò Burzio devotes a chapter to 'The counterpoint of singers and its use among the ultramontane, especially the French', in which he outlines how note-against-note counterpoint is improvised above a chant: 'These principles ... are used daily in the chapels of princes.'[198] According to Tinctoris in 1477, 'counterpoint ... which is extemporized is called absolute counterpoint, and this is the sort of thing that is commonly called *cantus super librum*'. He continues:

> when two, three, four or more people sing together over the book, they are not subject to one another. In fact, it is enough for each of them to accord with the tenor in regard to the rule and ordering of consonances. However, I consider it no cause for reproach but rather great praise if those singing together take care as a group to avoid duplicating the choice and ordering of consonances. For by doing so they will make the harmony much fuller and sweeter.
>
> *Sed duobus aut tribus, quatuor aut pluribus super librum concinentibus alter alteri non subicitur. Enimvero cuilibet eorum circa ea, quae ad legem ordinationemque concordantiarum pertinent, tenori consonare sufficit. Non tamen vituperabile immo plurimum laudabile censeo si concinentes similitudinem assumptionis ordinationisque concordantiarum inter se prudenter evitaverint. Sic enim concentum eorum multo repletiorem suavioremque efficient.*[199]

Indeed, 'Singing *super librum*, as Tinctoris knew it, was the pinnacle of achievement in the art of improvisation'[200] and as such is likely to have been highly prized at the Burgundian court. Perhaps 'chant(erie) du livre' naturally embraces both types of sung polyphony, composed and improvised. I would hazard a guess, though, that newly composed polyphony, whether in three or four parts, would generally have been sung by a select one-to-a-part group chosen in advance from the 'pool' of singers. They would expect to have rehearsed, would be able to deal individually with any open questions of underlay, *musica ficta* and ornamentation, and would also have no difficulty reading from relatively small musical

---

[197] Fallows, 'Specific Information', 147–9. As far as I am aware, *chant* au *livre*, *chant* du *livre*, *chant* sur le *livre* and *cantus super librum* are synonymous expressions.

[198] Nicolò Burzio, *Musices opusculum* (Bologna, 1487), bk 2, ch. 6.

[199] Johannes Tinctoris, *Liber de arte contrapuncti* (MS, 1477), bk 2, ch. 20.

[200] Bonnie J. Blackburn, 'On Compositional Process in the 15th Century', *Journal of the American Musicological Society* 40/2 (1987), 258–9. See also Ross W. Duffin, '*Contrapunctus simplex et diminutus*: Polyphonic Improvisation for Voices in the 15th Century', *Basler Jahrbuch für historische Musikpraxis* 31 (2007), 69–90.

sources. Larger and flexible numbers of singers would more often be suited to improvised chant-based singing.²⁰¹ Here, large chant books would commonly be used, no rehearsal would have been expected and, assuming a firm chant line (perhaps sung by several voices), 'balance' would scarcely be an issue. Admittedly, this more inclusive method of music-making could prove problematic at times, as at Rouen Cathedral in 1483:

> *Item, magister* Carolus Paon, when he stands in the choir with the other musicians, often tries to sing in the manner of [improvised] counterpoint, and otherwise, and because he is greatly discordant with the others and hinders and disrupts the singers, to the disgrace and dishonour of the church, the said lords ... have forbidden him on pain of judgement to sing any more in the group with the others, and he has promised to abide by this.²⁰²

Do the ordinances really imply four-part singing (whether composed or improvised)? Taking the view that *moiens* ('means') are 'presumably contratenors' Fallows concludes that

> four-part polyphony is intended because the names *teneur, basse contre* and *moien* can surely refer only to the voice-names in four-part polyphony.²⁰³

He may well be right, but I am not alone in finding the designation *moiens* 'a little unusual',²⁰⁴ and there are further reasons to question its interpretation. Nowhere in the document does the term reappear,²⁰⁵ nor is any musical definition known to dictionaries of early French. According to Godefroy's *Dictionnaire*, however, *moien* (variously spelt) could denote an 'ecclésiastique de second ordre', as in the allegorical poem *Le Besant de Dieu* (1226–7) by Guillaume le Clerc de Normandie:

> Archdeacons and deans,/ And officials and the *moiens*/ Who are masters in the chapters.
>
> *Arcediacres e diens,/ E officiaus e les maiens/ Qui as chapitres sont les sires.*²⁰⁶

---

²⁰¹ Singing *sur le livre* by as many as '30 or so' is reported as common in some mid-18th-century French churches. For this and a very short sketch of improvised 'choral' singing, see Parrott, 'A Brief Anatomy of Choirs', 7–9.

²⁰² Rouen Cathedral, chapter acts (19 May); from the Latin in Rob C. Wegman, 'The Testament of Jean de Saint Gille (†1501)', *Revue de Musicologie* 95/1 (2009), 31.

²⁰³ Fallows, 'Specific Information', 110–11.

²⁰⁴ Strohm, 278 n. 21. Defining a singer – as opposed to a voice part – as a *medius* or *moien* would certainly be exceptional at this early date.

²⁰⁵ Earlier there is reference to '*tel nombre de haultes voix, teneurs et contres que cy apres est ordonnes*', where *contres* is suitably ambiguous; Fallows, 'Specific Information', 148.

²⁰⁶ Guillaume le Clerc de Normandie, *Le Besant de Dieu*, ed. Ernst Martin (Halle, 1869), 20 (lines 673–5); Frédéric Godefroy, *Dictionnaire de l'ancienne*

Assuming the continuance of this usage into the 15th century, might the two *moiens* in the ordinances perhaps be those in charge of the singing – in effect, 'masters of the choir'? If so, the justification for focussing on four-part music would disappear.

In seeking to identify composed works with possible connections to the court of Charles the Bold, Fallows points to a set of six four-part masses in *I-Nn* MS VI E 40, a manuscript dating from perhaps almost a decade after the ordinances.[207] Each mass has an overall range of 18 or 19 notes, putting it beyond the plausible reach of natural voices alone.[208] All are based on the cantus firmus *L'homme armé* and have consequently been associated with the Order of the Golden Fleece.[209] While this may well tie them intimately to the Duke, it also makes them less likely to conform to the norms laid down in the court ordinances, since they 'may well have been intended for the singers at the Marian chapel of the Golden Fleece in Dijon, rather than for Charles's regular chaplains'.[210]

Be this as it may, a distinctly more reliable indication of relevant repertory has been identified since Fallows first explored the ordinances in the early 1980s. The 'original nucleus' of the choirbook *B-Br* MS 5557 (fols. 2–48), which contains five masses by English composers, may be 'reasonably assumed' to have been commissioned for the Burgundian court chapel, 'most probably' in preparation for the marriage of Charles the Bold and Margaret of York, which took place in Damme and Bruges in 1468.[211] Furthermore, 'numerous traces ... indicate that the manuscript must have been used very intensively' and that it was 'intended for use, not for display', on account of 'the relatively up-to-date quality of the compositions contained in it'.[212] All but one of these English masses

---

langue française (Paris, 1888).

[207] The date of the manuscript is given as 'perhaps *c*. 1477–8' in the MS Database of the *Digital Image Archive of Medieval Music* [accessed February 2015].

[208] Fallows, 'Specific Information', 111–12, 115–17.

[209] The masses have been described as 'votive masses that for all their beauty are, by comparison with festal settings, modest and rather private works'; Alejandro E. Planchart, 'The Origins and Early History of *L'homme armé*', *Journal of Musicology* 20/3 (2003), 354.

[210] Howard Mayer Brown, 'Music and Ritual at Charles the Bold's Court: The Function of Liturgical Music by Busnoys and his Contemporaries', in *Antoine Busnoys: Method, Meaning, and Context in Late Medieval Music*, ed. P. Higgins (1999), 59.

[211] Rob C. Wegman, *Choirbook of the Burgundian Court Chapel: Brussel, Koninklijke Bibliotheek MS. 5557* (1989), i (introduction).

[212] Rob C. Wegman, 'Concerning the Origins and Chronology of Brussels, Koninklijke Bibliotheek, Manuscript 5557', *Tijdschrift van de Vereniging voor Nederlandse muziekgeschiedenis* 36 (1986), 15.

turn out to be in three parts rather than four and to have overall ranges realizable by men's natural voices:[213]

Walter Frye:			
Nobilis et pulcra	C2 C4 C5 [– T C]	A–b♭'	16 notes
Summa Trinitati	C1 C3 C4 [– T C]	c–d"	16 notes
Flos regalis (a4)	C1 C3 C3* C4 [– C T B]	c–e"	17 notes
Richard Cox:			
Sine nomine	C1 C3 C3 [– C T]	f–e"	14 notes
John Plummer:			
Sine nomine	C3 C5 F4 [– C T]	G–a'	16 notes

* Underlining indicates that the parts are paired.

Furthermore, although Frye's four-part mass exceeds the compass of the others by a tone, it nevertheless remains within the reach of natural voices alone.[214] Thus, in contrast to the *L'homme armé* masses on which Fallows based his interpretation of the ordinances, none of those in this Brussels manuscript can be shown to demand the falsetto voice.[215]

In sum, even if the Brussels manuscript's claim to represent the Burgundian court chapel's repertory *c.* 1469 is dismissed, various critical areas of uncertainty remain: was the polyphonic music they sang in three or four parts, composed or improvised, of 15^+- or 18^+-note compass? Fallows's conclusion that the six '*haultes voix*' of the chapel were 'certainly falsettists' must now be considered doubtful. In this respect the Burgundian ordinances signally fail to add to Tinctoris's definition of the voice part taken by those 'high voices':

> The *supremum* is that voice part of a composed song which goes higher than the others.
>
> *Supremum est illa pars cantus compositi: quae altitudine caeteras excedit.*
>
> (*Terminorum*, 1495)[216]

---

[213] See *Fifteenth-Century Liturgical Music: III – The Brussels Masses*, ed. G. Curtis, Early English Church Music 34 (1985).

[214] It does so by virtue of keeping within the limits implied by its clefs, which are the same as in his *Summa Trintitati* mass, though with the middle one duplicated.

[215] A subsequent layer of the choirbook (its fifth gathering) 'probably existed prior to the original nucleus' and contains Dufay's mass *Ecce ancilla Domini* (a4), a work known to have been copied at Cambrai in 1463–4; Wegman, 'Concerning the Origins', 16. Its compass is wider – 18^+ notes – as is the span of its clefs (C2 to F4), implying that the top part is intended for a voice-type higher than a man's natural voice. There is, however, no reason to assume that the work had entered the repertory of the Burgundian court chapel by the time the ordinances were drawn up in 1469.

[216] Tinctoris, *Terminorum*, ch. 17.

APPENDIX 4

The 'High' Choir

- Siena Cathedral, 1451: 'three boys and their tenor and contratenor' are approved for employment.[217]
- Ghent, 1458: at his entry into the city on 23 April Duke Philip the Good of Burgundy was greeted by *'deux hommes et quatre enffans, qui chanterent une nouvelle et joyeuse chanson'* from within a castle astride an elephant.[218]
- Prince Don Juan (of Aragon), 1490s: the crown prince reportedly enjoyed singing tenor together with his *maestro de capilla* (Juan de Anchieta) and four or five *'muchachos, moços de capilla'*.[219]
- Robinet Testard, c. 1500: a miniature (detail) shows three tonsured boys and two men apparently singing polyphony from a choirbook (see Illus. 3.2).
- ?Venice, ?early 1500s: a woodcut shows a youth and two men evidently singing *laude* before an image of the Virgin.[220]
- Speyer, 1511: the frontispiece to Arnolt Schlick's *Spiegel der Orgelmacher und Organisten* shows three boys and two men singing from a single sheet of music (see Illus. 2.1).[221]
- London, 1520s: Nicholas Ludford's cycle of three-part Lady Masses, with overall compasses of 18 or 19 notes was evidently designed to be sung at St Stephen's, Westminster, by the boy choristers (of whom there were seven) together with their Instructor (Ludford himself).[222]

Not included above is the three-part *'capella'* proposed for the Florence Baptistry in 1469 by Jacques de Marville (whom we have encountered above). It was to comprise a tenor, himself as contratenor and three *canti*

---

[217] Frank A. D'Accone, *The Civic Muse: Music and Musicians in Siena during the Middle Ages and the Renaissance* (1997), 189, 213. A group of five Polish singers – ?two men and three boys – had arrived in Siena the previous year; ibid., 187, 213.

[218] Jean Chartier, *Chronique de Charles VII*, ed. V. de Viriville (Paris, 1858) iii, 86–7.

[219] According to Gonzalo Fernández de Oviedo; Fallows, 'Specific Information', 137.

[220] Reproduced on the title-page of *Die mehrstimmige italienische Laude um 1500*, ed. K. Jeppesen and V. Brøndal (Leipzig, 1935) but without identification. See under 'Lauda' in *Musik in Geschichte und Gegenwart* viii (1960), 313.

[221] Reproduced in Parrott, 'A Brief Anatomy of Choirs', 11.

[222] See Bowers II, 38. Christopher Tye's *Gloria laus et honor* (a Palm Sunday processional hymn) has a similar scoring; ibid., 39 n. 99.

(sopranos), with the possible addition of a bass 'when we wish to sing *a quattro voce*'.[223] However, it is not entirely clear whether the three *canti* were boys or adults: the first of them is named as 'maestro Jacobo franzose', while both they and the tenor are described as 'gioveni compagni'. If all were men, there is no reason to infer that the *canti* must have been falsettists; like *superius*, the term simply applies to the top part of the music performed (about which nothing is known), and at this period four-part singing (perhaps improvised) is still perfectly likely to have been commonly contained within a two-octave compass and to have included a *contratenor bassus* part.

In addition to the example of Dufay's four-part *Ave regina celorum* (see main text) the emergence of the 'full' choir with an 18–23-note range may be reflected in the following early references:

- Urbino, 1482–1508: the singers of Duke Guidobaldo's court *cappella* comprised 5 pages (*paggi di canto*) and 3 adults.[224]
- Tyrol, 1492: Venetian ambassadors are entertained by 'the singing of 5 boys and 3 masters'.[225]
- Bruges, 1499/1500 (St Donatian): 'it is understood that the same choirmaster [Obrecht] is obliged to bring with him, in every Salve, in addition to the children, four of the best companion singers of the church ... But now most of the time there are rarely more than two or three singers, which frequently causes great confusion [*groote confusie*], so that it would be better ... not to sing the Salve than to sing it.'[226]

---

[223] '... *una capella de bono tenore principaliter con tre boni canti da bone costume et con loro contratenore*' · '*uno tenore, con una voce grossa, alta e bassa, e duolce e sufficiente ...; e tre canti altissimi colle voce bone, piene e suave e yo per contre[-tenor], e in fra questo mezzo quando noy vorrimo cantare a quattro voce, Bartholomeo farà lo contre-basso*'; Bianca Becherini, 'Relazioni di musici fiamminghi con la corte dei Medici', *La Rinascita* 17 (1941), 99–100. Cf. Fallows, 'Specific Information', 121–2.

[224] *Ordini et Offitij alla corte del Serenissimo Signor Duca d'Urbino*, ed. G. Ermini (Urbino, 1932), Appendix, vii.

[225] Moser, *Paul Hofhaimer*, 14.

[226] Rob C. Wegman, *Born for the Muses: The Life and Masses of Jacob Obrecht* (1994), 305 (Flemish, 373 (doc. 49)).

APPENDIX 5

Boys' Changing Voices

- Avignon, 1372: at a 'Presentation' the role of *Ecclesia*, which included the singing of a substantial solo, was taken by 'a very good-looking youth, about 20 years old and beardless' (*pulcerrimus iuvenis circa xx. annos sine barba*).[227]
- Rome, 1425: Barthélemy Poignare is admitted as one of the *iuvenes cantores* at the papal chapel (under Nicholas Grenon) at the age of 16 or 17.[228]
- Windsor, 1461–99: account rolls show that at St George's Chapel the choirboys' voices generally broke at 14 or 15.[229]
- Edward IV, c. 1471–2 (*Liber niger domus regis*, §59 'Children of Chapell viii'): 'Also when they be growen to the age of xviij yeres, and than theyre voyces be chaunged, ne can nat be preferred in this chapell nor within this court, the numbyr beyng full, then, if they wull assent, the king assigneth every suche child to a college of Oxenford or Cambridge, of the kinges fundacion, there to be in finding and study sufficiauntly tyll the king otherwise list avaunce hym.'[230]
- Galeazzo Maria Sforza's secretary, early 1470s: Cicco Simonetta instructs Filippo Macerata to send from Venice 'a boy aged between 12 and 15 and not more ... who knows how to sing well, has a good voice and also a grounding in and understanding of music'.[231]
- Benvenuto Cellini, c. 1523: in his autobiography (c. 1560) Cellini tells of a prank he played at a meeting of an artists' club, by taking with him 'a 16-year-old lad' (*un giovinetto de età di sedici anni*) disguised as a woman – 'After we had dined came some admirable vocal music together with instruments; and because they were singing and playing with books before them, my beauty begged to sing her part' – which s/he duly did, presumably in

---

[227] Richard Rastall, *The Heaven Singing: Music in Early English Religious Drama* (1996), 312–13.

[228] Alejandro E. Planchart, 'Music for the Papal Chapel in the Early 15th Century', *Papal Music and Musicians in Medieval and Renaissance Rome*, ed. R. Sherr (1998), 97.

[229] Bowers III, 48 n. 23.

[230] A. R. Myers, *The Household of Edward IV* (1959), 137. Cf. Bowers III, 48 n. 23, where Wulstan's inferences from this source are challenged.

[231] '... *qualche garzone de xij fino in xv anni et non più ... quale sapesse ben cantare, havesse bona voxe et anchora fondamento et raxone del canto*'; Emilio Motta, *Musici alla Corte degli Sforza* (Milan, 1887), 554–5.

character and with an unbroken voice (and 'almost better than the others').[232]

- Rotherham, 1545–6: College of Jesus – '6 pore chyldren, chorysters, to be chosen in to the sayd College by the sayd provoste, of the pore sorte, which be apte to lernyng ... The same chyldren to be brought up in knowledge of grammar, song, and wrytynge, untyll the age of 18 yeres.'[233]
- Stoke next Clare, 1547–8: at the College of St John the Baptist four boys are named and listed in a Chantry Certificate as 'Choristres, of the age of 15 yeres'.[234]
- Durham, c. 1555: while poor scholars [*discipuli*] previously could not be admitted at 15 or over, the cathedral's Marian statutes state that 'Nevertheless we permit Choristers of the said Church to be admitted as scholars even if they have passed their 15th year, and we will that if they be suitable and shall have served the Choir well by being very proficient in music, these shall be preferred to others'.[235]
- Durham, 1541–1637: Brian Crosby has reportedly been 'able to establish the dates of birth of 79 out of 186 choristers' at the cathedral, and that on leaving '19 were under 15, 60 were 15 or over, and of these 60, 27 were over 18' and the two oldest over 21.[236]
- Cosimo de' Medici, 1565: The Duke asks his ambassador in Rome to find 'either a boy [*putto*] or a castrato [*eunuco*]' who can represent 'a youth [*giovane*] of 15 or 16 years' in a Florentine *intermedio* (see also Appendix 7).[237]
- Thomas Whythorne, c. 1576: 'after [*th*]e age of chyldhod (which kontyneweth from *the* infancy untill fyfteen) beginneth *the* age named *Adolescency*. which kontineweth untill twenty and fyv.'[238]

---

[232] 'Dipoi che avemmo cenato, venne un poco di mirabil musica di voce insieme con istrumenti; et perché cantavano et sonavano con i libri inanzi, la mia bella figura chiese da cantare la sua parte'; Benvenuto Cellini, *La Vita*, ed. L. Bellotto (1996), 106, 110 (bk 1, ch. 30).

[233] Arthur F. Leach, *English Schools at the Reformation* (London, 1898), pt 2, 292–3.

[234] Leach, *English Schools*, pt 2, 219.

[235] *The Statutes of the Cathedral Church of Durham*, ed. A. H. Thompson, Surtees Society 143 (Durham, 1929), 144–5 (ch. 28).

[236] Metcalfe, 'Performance Practice in Peterhouse'.

[237] Tim Carter, 'Giulio Caccini (1551–1618): New Facts, New Music', *Studi musicali* 16 (1987), 14.

[238] *The Autobiography of Thomas Whythorne*, ed. J. M. Osborn (1961), 19.

- Johann Hermann Schein, 1599: Schein was admitted at 13 to Dresden's *Hofkapelle* as a *Discantist*, and according to Mattheson 'occupied the position for four years' (i.e. until he was 16 or 17).[239]
- Adriano Banchieri, 1614: 'nowadays ... lads of about 13 are losing their unbroken voices.'[240]
- Durham, 1634: Thomas Wilson was paid as a chorister at the cathedral up to the end of September, when he was approximately 16½.[241]
- Bénigne de Bacilly, 1668: 'when one has taken great pains to train a boy's voice, it disappears as the voice breaks, which usually happens between the ages of 15 or 20.'[242]
- John Blow, 1664: he was dismissed from the Chapel Royal at Christmas, aged 15 but closer to 16. (He was baptized on 23 February 1649.)[243]
- Pelham Humfrey, 1664: he was discharged from the Chapel Royal at Christmas, aged either 16 or 17. (He was born sometime between 15 July 1647 and 13 July 1648.)[244]
- Henry Purcell, 1673: in early December, when he was just over 14, court records refer to Purcell as a 'late child of his Majesty's Chappell Royall, whose voice is changed, and gon from the Chappell'.[245]
- *Der simplicianische Welt-Kucker*, 1677: the central character of Johann Beer's novel – Jan Rebhu – is a pubescent 15-year-old, with smooth skin and unbroken voice.[246]
- J. S. Bach, 1700: Bach was already 15 when he took up a place as a soprano in Lüneburg.[247]

---

[239] Johann Mattheson, *Grundlage einer Ehren-Pforte* (Hamburg, 1740), 315.

[240] '... al giorno odierno ... i giovineti di tredici in circa anni, mutano la voce'; Adriano Banchieri, *Cartella musicale* (Venice, 1614), 18.

[241] Brian Crosby, *The Choral Foundation of Durham Cathedral, c. 1350–c. 1650* (D.Phil. dissertation: University of Durham, 1993) ii, 133.

[242] Bénigne de Bacilly, *Remarques curieuses sur l'art de bien chanter* (Paris, 1668), 80–1.

[243] *A Biographical Dictionary* i, comp. Ashbee *et al.*, 161.

[244] Peter Dennison, *Pelham Humfrey* (1986), 5.

[245] Henry C. de Lafontaine, *The King's Musick* (London, 1909), 263; see also *Records of English Court Music*, ed. A. Ashbee, i (1986), 131; and v (1991), 162.

[246] Stephen Rose, *The Musician in Literature in the Age of Bach* (2011), 50.

[247] *Bach-Dokumente* ii (1969), 8. It is not known when Bach's voice broke, other than that it was 'some time later' ('einige Zeit später'); *Bach-Dokumente* iii (1972), 82.

- Martin Heinrich Fuhrmann, 1706: 'the usual age at which an alto becomes a tenor is over 18.'[248]
- Johann Kuhnau, 1709: reminding Leipzig's Town Council of the difficulty of maintaining the musical standards of the Thomasschule boys, Kuhnau points out that 'their voices always change, and after losing their good *Discant* they remain completely mute for several years'.[249]
- Leipzig (i), 1729: all eight or so sopranos who auditioned successfully for J. S. Bach at St Thomas's were aged 13 or 14.[250] (ii), 1731: Christian Friedrich Schemelli, described by Bach as a soprano, enters the school, already aged 17 (or perhaps 18).[251] (iii), 1763: Johann Friedrich Doles junior, then nearly 17 years old, sings solo soprano in a cantata celebrating the end of the Seven Years War.[252]
- Chapel Royal, London, 1699–1758: the dates at which boys were formally discharged from the Chapel show that 39 of them (out of 53) were probably in the 16–19 age range.[253]
- Joseph Haydn, ?1749 (autobiographical sketch, 1776): 'Until my 18th year I sang soprano with great success, not only at St Stephan's [Vienna] but also at court.'[254] (Haydn was born on 31 March 1732, and his '18th year' therefore ran from April 1749 to March 1750.)
- J. F. Agricola, 1757: 'the high voice turns into a lower one around one's 14th year approximately.'[255]
- Salzburg, 1767: in Mozart's youthful *intermedium Apollo et Hyacinthus* K38 performed at the Benedictine University, four of the solo roles were sung by boys from the Gymnasium – the

---

[248] Martin Heinrich Fuhrmann, *Musikalischer-Trichter* (Frankfurt an der Spree, 1706), 36.

[249] '... weil sie [die Schul Jugend] auch immer die Stimme mutiret, und manche jahre nach dem verlohrnen guten Discant ganz stum bleibet...'; Johann Kuhnau, Erinnerung §12, in *St Thomas zu Leipzig, Schule und Chor: Stätte des Wirkens von Johann Sebastian Bach*, ed. B. Knick (1963), 126.

[250] See Bach's audition reports, in Andrew Parrott, *The Essential Bach Choir* (2000), 159–62 (app. 2). Two altos were 14 and a third 16.

[251] *Bach-Dokumente* i (1963), 145, where Schemelli's age is taken as 'an explicit reference to his [Bach's] use of falsetto singers'.

[252] Helmut Banning, *Johann Friedrich Doles: Leben und Werke* (Leipzig, 1939), 65.

[253] Donald Burrows, *Handel and the English Chapel Royal* (2005), 573–5.

[254] '... ich sang allda sowohl bey St: Stephan als bey Hof mit grossen Beyfall bis in das 18te Jahr meines alters den Sopran'; *Joseph Haydn: Gesammelte Briefe und Aufzeichnungen ... H. C. Robbins Landon*, ed. D. Bartha (1965), 77.

[255] Johann Friedrich Agricola, *Anleitung zur Singkunst* (Berlin, 1757), 28.

princess Melia by a 15-year-old soprano, and Zephyrus by a 17-year-old alto.[256]

- Wolfgang Mozart, 1770: in a letter to his wife (25 August) Leopold Mozart reports from Bologna that Wolfgang – then 14½ – 'now has no singing voice whatsoever. It is completely gone. He has neither a deep one nor a high one, and not even five notes'.[257]

- R. J. S. Stevens, 1773: a week after turning 16 the St Paul's Cathedral choirboy writes to his father 'I am this Day to leave the Surplice'.[258]

- J. F. Oest, 1787: 'In particular one should keep an eye on boys who sing *Diskant* in towns where there are so-called choirs. If before their 17th year their *Diskant* voice drops noticeably and they are otherwise observing the dietary rules of a soprano, then one knows what to make of it' – i.e. this is a consequence of indulgence in 'the secret vice'![259]

APPENDIX 6

The Gloria by Bourgois

In contrast to Battre's *Gaude virgo mater Christi*, where the designation 'mutate voces' is found solely at the opening, the troped Gloria by Bourgois in *I-TRmp* 87 carries the marking 'chorus' in four places. (The unattributed version of the same music in *I-TRmp* 88 lacks all such markings.) The first occurrence is not until 'bar 19', where the word appears just against the tenor of the voices labelled *A* in Table 3.5a – a feature duly noted by Fallows as 'unexplained'.[260] I suggest that the combined three voice parts of *A* represent a conventional 'chorus' (one of changed voices), which in this Gloria is juxtaposed with one headed by boys (labelled *B*), and that the particular purpose of the first 'chorus' marking may have been to ensure

---

[256] Stanley Sadie, *Mozart: The Early Years, 1756–1781* (2006), 121.

[257] '*Stimme zum singen hat er itzt gar keine: diese ist völlig weg; er hat weder dieffe noch höhe, und nicht 5 reine Töne*'; *Mozart Briefe und Dokumente – Online-Edition* [accessed 4 February 2015].

[258] *Recollections of R. J. S. Stevens: An Organist in Georgian London*, ed. M. Argent (1992), 14.

[259] Johann Friedrich Oest, 'Versuch einer Beantwortung der pädagogischen Frage: wie man Kinder und junge Leute vor dem Leib und Seele verwüstenden Laster der Unzucht ... verwahren ... könnte?', in *Allgemeine Revision des gesamten Schul- und Erziehungswesens* vi, ed. J. H. Campe (Hamburg, 1787), 165. For this together with useful data from the 19th century see Herbert Moller, 'Voice Change in Human Biological Development', *Journal of Interdisciplinary History* 16/2 (1985), 241.

[260] Fallows, 'Specific Information', 123 n. 36.

Table 3.5 Bourgois, *Gloria* (*I-TRmp* 87, fols. 39v–43r)

(a)

Bar	Text	A	Clef	B	Range*
1–91	*Et in terra pax*	[S]	C2	–	g–d̲"
		Contra	C4	–	A̲–f̲'
		chorus Tenor	C4	–	c–d'
92–109	*Spiritus*	–	C2	Pueri	g–c"
		–	C2	Contra	g–g'
		–	C2	Tenor	f–b♭'
110–24	*Domine Deus*	*chorus* [S]	C2	–	c'–b♭'
		Contra	C4	–	B♭–e[♭]
		Tenor	C4	–	d–d'
125–36	*Primogenitus*	–	C2	Pueri	c'–d"
		–	C3	Tenor	g–g'
		–	C3	Contra	f–g'
137–51	†*Qui tollis ... miserere*	–	C2	Pueri	c'–c"
		–	C3	[Tenor]	g–g'
		Contra	C4		c–d'
		Tenor	C4		d–e̲'
152–67	*Qui tollis ... suscipe*	[S]	C2	–	c'–c"
		Contra	C4	–	B̲–e'
		Tenor	C4	–	g–f̲'
168–76	*Ad Mariae gloriam*	Contra	C4	–	c–a
		Tenor	C4	–	e–c'
177–96	*Qui sedes*	[S]	C2	–	c'–c"
		Contra	C4	–	c–g'
		Tenor	C4	–	c–d'
197–207	*Mariam sanctificans*	–	C2	Pueri	c'–c"
		–	C3	Contra	g–g'
		–	C3	Tenor	g–g'
208–14	*Tu solus dominus*	*chorus* [S]	C2	–	d'–c"
		Contra	C4	–	c–d'
		Tenor	C4	–	g–e̲'
215–28	*Mariam gubernans*	–	C2	Pueri	c♯–c"
		–	C3	Contra	g–a'
		–	C3	Tenor	g–a̲'
229–38	*Tu solus altissimus*	*chorus* [S]	C2	–	a–a'
		Contra	C4	–	c–e̲'
		Tenor	C4	–	d–c'
239–48	*Mariam coronans*	–	C2	Pueri	b–c"
			C4	Contra	f̲–g'
		–	C4	Tenor	g–e'
		Contra	C4		B♭–d'
249–65	*Cum sancto spiritu*	[S]	C2	–	b–c"
		Contra	C4	–	B̲–d'
		Tenor	C4	–	B♭–e̲'

* Underlining indicates the highest and lowest notes of each voice-part.
† The version of this Gloria in *I-TRmp* 88 sets out *Qui tollis ... miserere* for just three voices (fols. 325v–326r).

Table 3.5 *continued*

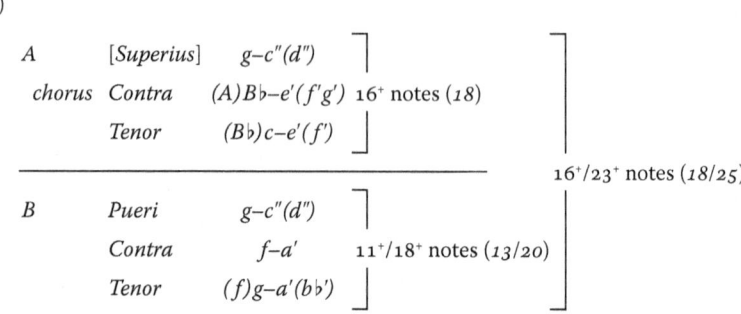

that the singer(s) of its tenor part would proceed with the new section ('Laudamus te') rather than rest in the mistaken belief that the alternating group was to take over at this point. (The term *'chorus'* is most likely to indicate a three-person entity rather than one comprising multiple singers per part; see n. 96.) The three subsequent appearances of the marking, all against the *superius* of group *A*, each directly follow a section sung by the other group. Loose and inconsistent though they may be, these markings seem intended simply to help clarify for the singers what is an exceptional and potentially confusing distribution of six voice parts rather than the usual three.

The manner in which the music is apportioned to the two separate vocal groups is set out in Table 3.5a. Composite individual and collective ranges are given in Table 3.5b, where alternative readings (e.g. 11⁺/18⁺) represent performance with the *pueri* part sung 'as written'/at the higher 8ve (see main text).

APPENDIX 7

Boys and Falsettists in 16th- and Early 17th-Century Italy and Germany

Italy

- Florence, 1501: the re-established polyphonic choir at the cathedral is to contain seven sopranos including 'Ser Raphaelle di Piero Cortesi' – thus apparently six boys and one adult.[261] (Cf. Florence, 1510, below.)

---

[261] '... *dua tenori, dua contrialti, dua contribassi, uno maestro di chierici di canto figurato, sette sovrani tra quali sia uno ser Raphaello di Piero Cortesi, cappellano di decta chiesa*'; Frank A. D'Accone, 'The Musical Chapels at the Florentine Cathedral and Baptistry during the First Half of the 16th Century', *Journal of the American Musicological Society* 24/1 (1971), 37.

Illus. 3.4 Title-page from Andrea Antico, *Canzoni nove* (Rome, 1510). Universitätsbibliothek Basel, Sign. kk II 32

- Ferrara, [1504]: two related documents from a court emissary concern the recruitment of singers in Picardy – [doc. A] 'there are two excellent sopranos, both of them boys; one is called Johannes' (*el ge dui/ belissimi sovrani tuti doi puti; uno se chiama Johannes*); [doc. B] 'there are two good sopranos in the cathedral church; the one is called Jannes and is a priest' (*sono/ dui sovrani boni, ne la ecclesia cathedrale; l'uno se chiama/ Jannes et e prete*).[262]

- Rome, 1510: Andrea Antico's early anthology of four-part frottolas includes a woodcut illustration of a group of four male singers, seemingly three men and a youth (see Illus. 3.4).[263]

---

[262] Lewis Lockwood, '"Messer Grossino" and Josquin Desprez', in *Studies in Renaissance and Baroque Music in Honor of Arthur Mendel*, ed. R. Marshall (1974), 16–17. I have not been able to check the originals, but their significance would be very different if document A's '*puti*' were to prove to be a mistranscription of '*preti*'.

[263] Andrea Antico, *Canzoni nove con alcune scelte de varii libri di canto* (Rome, 1510), title-page.

- Florence, 1510: singers at the Baptistry were to include 'ser Raffaele di Piero as soprano together with at least six choristers [*cherici*] or others of those who might sing if chosen by the said *ser* Giovanni Serragli, master of your choristers' school'.[264]
- Pietro Aaron, 1516: his implication is that it is generally possible for *cantus* parts to be sung 'by a boy's or a feigned [= falsetto] voice' (*cum puerili voce, vel ficta*). See main text (under 'Voces mutatae').
- Milan, 1534: amongst the four listed altos at the cathedral is 'D. Battista de Bussero, contraalto seu falseto'.[265] Differentiated thus from his alto colleagues, he is almost certainly to be understood as a (natural) alto capable of being deployed as a falsettist (soprano).
- Giovanni Camillo Maffei (physician and musician), 1562: 'Since if someone wanted to feign [a high voice] in his own way, having by nature a bass voice and feigning it for lack of a soprano, he could achieve his purpose by making the movement of air faster. And this manner of feigning the voice was granted to the man alone, especially when in argument he wishes to persuade and move and express his will.' (*Che se volesse alcuno à suo modo fingerlo, si come havendo di natura il basso, e per mancamento di soprano fingesse la voce, chiamata falsetto, potria con fare il movimento dell'aere piu veloce, à posta sua farlo. E questo modo di fingere la voce fù solo à l'huomo conceduto, massimamente quando egli ragionando desidera persuadere, e movere, & isprimere il voler suo.*)[266]
- Cosimo de' Medici, 1565 (to his ambassador in Rome): 'you should have a few words there with those musicians of the Pope, or with [Giovanni] Animuccia, *maestro di cappella* of St Peter's, and see whether they might accommodate us either with a boy [*putto*] or with a castrato [*eunuco*] from those of the *cappella* who might be judged suitable to do this [i.e. to sing soprano in *intermedi* for a forthcoming Medici wedding] ... He will have to represent a youth [*giovane*] of 15 or 16 years, we would like him to have a beautiful voice and gracefulness in singing with embellishments in the Neapolitan fashion, and the voice should be natural, not falsetto [*naturale non falsetto*].' (In the end it was the 14-year-old

---

[264] D'Accone, 'The Musical Chapels', 40 (doc. 5).

[265] Christine Getz, 'The Milanese Cathedral Choir under Hermann Matthias Werrecore, Maestro di Cappella 1522–1550', *Musica Disciplina* 46 (1992), 177–82.

[266] *Delle lettere del Sor Gio. Camillo Maffei*, ed. V. de' Paoli (Naples, 1562), 26.

Giulio Caccini who was sent to Florence, and the role he sang was that of Psyche.)[267]

- Camillo Capilupi and Scipione Gonzaga, 1586 (three references to Giovanni Luca Conforti as a singer): (i) 'in private the best falsettist there is in Rome, and a contralto in chapel.'[268] (ii) 'In full voice he sings contralto, and that is how he sings in the Papal Chapel; in private and in oratories he sings soprano and goes quite high.'[269] (iii) 'His usual part is the soprano, yet when he was in the Papal Chapel I believe he always sang contralto, perhaps in order not to join his falsetto to the natural voices of the castratos.'[270]

- Rome, 1589: Pope Sixtus V's bull reorganizing the Cappella Giulia at St Peter's stipulates 4 basses, 4 tenors, 4 altos 'and in addition for the voice called soprano 4 eunuchs if skilled ones can be found; if not, 6 boys'.[271]

- Alfonso Fontanelli, 1594 (describing the musical abilities of Ettore Gesualdo): 'He has quite a good tenor voice. He also sings soprano, but in this part his voice is not very true, even though it is graceful.'[272]

- Rome, late 16th and early 17th century: there were 'many sopranos, such as Giovanni Luca [Conforti, *fl.* 1580–1608], Ottavio Durante [*fl.* 1608–18], Simoncino, Ludovico [?Gualtero],

---

[267] Carter, 'Giulio Caccini', 14, 18–19.

[268] '... in camera il falsetto il miglior che sia in Roma, et contralto in capella'; Iain Fenlon, *Music and Patronage in 16th-century Mantua* i (1980), 191 (letter of 22 March).

[269] '... egli a voci piene canta contralto, e cosi cantò in cappella di N. S.re in camera e in oratori canta soprano, et và alto asai'; Richard Sherr, 'Gugliemo Gonzaga and the Castrati', *Renaissance Quarterly* 33 (1980), 54 (letter of 5 April). (For 'a voci piene' Iain Fenlon gives 'à voce piena'; Fenlon, *Music and Patronage*, 190.)

[270] '... la sua parte ordinariamente è di soprano tuttavia nel tempo che egli stette in cappella di N. S.re cantò sempre, si come intendo, il contralto, forse per non accoppiar il suo falsetto alle voci naturali de' castrati'; Sherr, 'Gugliemo Gonzaga', 43 (letter of 29 March).

[271] Bull '*Cum pro nostro pastorali munere*' (27 September), in *Collectionis Bullarium, brevium, aliorumque diplomatum sacro sanctae Basilicae Vaticanae* iii (Rome, 1752), 172.

[272] 'Ha voce di tenore assai buona. Canta anco il soprano ma la voce in questa parte non è tanto sincera, benchè egli sia graziosa'; Anthony Newcomb, 'Carlo Gesualdo and a Musical Correspondence of 1594', *The Musical Quarterly* 54/4 (1968), 434 (letter of 9 October).

who sang *in voce da falsetto*, and many eunuchs of the [Papal] Capella' (Giustiniani, c. 1628).²⁷³

- Pietro Della Valle, 1640: three notable Roman 'falsetti' from the early years of the century are mentioned – 'Lodovico [?Gualtero]', 'Giovanni Luca' [Conforti], 'a great singer of *gorge* and *passaggi*, who went as high as the stars [*che andava alto alle stelle*]', and 'Orazietto' [?Orazio Griffi], 'a very good singer in falsetto or in tenor'. • 'Your Lordship wishes to compare the falsettists of those times with natural sopranos, the castratos that we now possess in such abundance. ... The most that could be done then was to have a competent boy [*un buon fanciullo*]; but as soon as they began to develop some understanding they lost their voice; and during the period that they still had it they naturally, because of their age, had no discrimination, so they always sang with no taste or feeling for beauty, as though everything had been learned by rote, and hearing them sometimes strained my nerves quite unbearably.' (Della Valle proceeds to discuss the castratos and, in particular, 'those women singers that today we have with singular excellence'.)²⁷⁴

- Luigi Zenobi, c. 1600 (on the qualities of the perfect musician): the soprano voice – 'To please the listener it must above all be a natural one, or that of a boy [*naturale, o puerile*] ...'²⁷⁵

- Giulio Caccini, 1602: 'this increasing of the voice in the soprano part, especially in feigned voices, very often becomes shrill [*acuto*] and unbearable to the ear, as I have heard on many occasions.' • The singer 'will be well advised to choose for himself a pitch at which he can sing in a full and natural voice so as to avoid feigned notes; since in feigning them, or if he forces the notes, he will find himself relying on the breath to prevent them sounding very obvious (because for the most part they tend to offend the ear) ... For feigned notes cannot engender nobility of

---

²⁷³ Vincenzo Giustiniani, *Discorso sopra la musica* (MS, 1628, §5); Angelo Solerti, *Le origini del melodramma* (Turin 1903), 110. Musicians who welcomed pilgrims from Perugia at Rome's Archiconfraternità all'Ave Maria in 1600 (Jubilee Year) included *'falsetti rarissimi'*, not least *'il S. Lodovico gratiosissimo che con gorga e passaggi mostrava quanto valesse in questa professione'*; [Marc'Antonio Masci], *Descrittione del Peregrinaggio ... l'anno 1600*, in Christopher F. Black, *Early Modern Confraternities in Europe and the Americas* (c. 2006), 119.

²⁷⁴ Pietro Della Valle, *Della musica dell'età nostra* (MS, 1640); Solerti, *Le origini del melodramma*, 161–2, 163.

²⁷⁵ Bonnie J. Blackburn and Edward Lowinsky, 'Luigi Zenobi and his Letter on the Perfect Musician', *Studi musicali* 22 (1993), 82–4.

singing, which grows out of a natural voice that is comfortable through its whole range.'[276]

- Lodovico Viadana, 1602: 'In these concertos falsettists [*i Falsetti*] will make a better effect than natural sopranos [*i Soprani naturali*], because for the most part boys [*i Putti*] sing carelessly and with little grace; also because distance is reckoned to lend more charm; there is no doubt, however, that a good natural soprano does not come cheap; but there are few to be found.'[277]

- Agostino Agazzari, 1607: in accompanying singers, continuo players should constantly avoid playing in high registers when the voices, 'especially *i soprani, ò falsetti*', are occupying them.[278]

- Scipione Cerreto, 1608: 'nowadays falsetto singers have a higher standing than [boy] sopranos do, not only because they are of a more mature age but also because such voices when they sing give greater satisfaction and bring greater sweetness to the ears of their listeners.' (*al tempo d'hoggi gli Cantori di Falsetto stanno con maggior prerogatiua, che non stanno gli Soprani, non solo perche sono di età più matura, ma ancora perche tali voci mentre cantano danno maggior sodisfatione, e rendono maggior dolcezza all'orecchie de gli ascoltanti.*)[279]

- Adriano Banchieri, 1608: a drinking song has five voices/characters – 'Canto, Falsetto, Alto, Tenor e Basso'. Canto and Falsetto are two more or less equal soprano parts, both in C1; Falsetto's range is $e'-d''$.[280]

- Thomas Coryat, 1608 (at the Scuola di S Rocco, Venice): see main text (under 'England: Organ Pitch').

- Pietro Cerone, 1613 (advice for young singers 'not to sing in a forced way on high notes'): 'with a low/bass voice [*voz baxa*], those high [notes] should not be forced if they don't come easily: for it is better to feign or mute them [*fingirlas ò callarlas*] than to sing them harshly.'

- Bellerofonte Castaldi, 1623 (a collection of songs): 'And because they treat either of Love or of the disdain that the Lover has for the object of love, they are represented in the tenor clef, the intervals of which are proper and natural to masculine speech, as it seems to the present author a laughable matter that a man

---

[276] Giulio Caccini, *Le nuove musiche* (Florence, 1602), '*A i lettori*', sig.Bv · sig.C2r.

[277] Lodovico Viadana, *Cento concerti ecclesiastici* (Venice, 1602), organ part-book, 3 ('*A' benigni lettori*', Avertimento 11).

[278] Agostino Agazzari, *Del sonare sopra'l Basso* (Siena, 1607), 6.

[279] Scipione Cerreto, *Dell'arbore musicale* (Naples, 1608), 29.

[280] Adriano Banchieri, *Festino nella sera del giovedì grasso avanti cena* (Venice, 1608), no. 18 ('*Vinata di brindesi e ragioni*').

with a feminine voice should begin to reason with his beloved and demand compassion from her in falsetto.'[281]

- Lodovico Casali, 1629: The perfect *maestro di cappella* 'should, and this matters more than any other concern, be careful to work the [boy] sopranos very hard in their training, knowing how worthy is music with natural sopranos and not false ones'.[282]

- Verona, 1630: 'Prete Girolamo Falsetto/ P Simo Contralto/ Paris Tenore/ Prete Gier.º Ratario Basso.'[283]

Germany

- Andreas Ornithoparcus, 1517 (trans. Dowland, 1609): '*Discantus* is the uppermost part of each Song. Or it is an Harmony to be song with a Childs Voyce.'[284]

- Dresden (St Ann in Annaberg), c. 1510–30: in a source of the missa 'Une mousse de Biscaye' (attrib. Josquin) Christe I and the opening of the Gloria are designated '*Quattuor puerorum*' ('4 of the boys'), while Christe III is designated '*Quattuor [s]ocio[r]um*' ('4 of the fellows').[285]

- Heinrich Glarean, 1547: 'Boys are the most able to sing the highest voice part, or would be if only they were not so often ignorant of singing.' (*Supremam vocem pueri maximè canere possunt, si non ijdem frequenter ignari cantus essent.*)[286]

- Gallus Dressler, 1563: 'What is the *discantus*? ❋It is the highest voice part of any vocal work, for a boy's voice to perform.' (*Quid est discantus? ❋Est cuiuslibet cantilenæ vox suprema, puerili voce modulanda.*)[287]

---

[281] '... *cosa da ridere che un huomo con voce Feminina si metta a dir le sue ragioni, e dimandar pietà in Falsetto ala sua innamorata*'; Bellerofonte Castaldi, *Primo mazzetto di fiori* (Venice, 1623), [63] ('*A chi legge*').

[282] *Generale invito alle grandezze, e maraviglia della musica* ... (Modena, 1629), 52, 54; Anne Schnoebelen, 'Cazzati vs. Bologna: 1657–1671', *The Musical Quarterly* 57/1 (1971), 27–8 (translation only).

[283] Inga Mai Groote, *Musik in italienischen Akademie*n, Studien zur institutionellen Musikpflege 1543–1666 = *Analecta musicologica* 39 (2007), 58.

[284] '*Discantus est cuiuslibet cantilene pars suprema. Vel est harmonia puellari voce modulanda*'; Andreas Ornithoparcus, *Musicae activae micrologus* (Leipzig, 1517), sig. Liiiv; trans. J. Dowland, (London, 1609), 83 (bk 4, ch. 5).

[285] Dresden, Sächsische Landesbibliothek, MS mus. 1/D/506 (*olim* Annaberg, Bibliothek der St. Annenkirche, MS. 1126); T. L. Noblitt, *Musica Disciplina* 28 (1974), 86.

[286] Glarean, *Dodecachordon*, 178 (bk 2, ch. 38).

[287] Gallus Dressler, *Praecepta musicae poeticae* (MS, 1563), ed. R. Forgács (2007), 120.

- Munich, 1569: Troiano names several of the bass, tenor and alto singers then in the court *Capelle*, merely describing its 12 sopranos as 'discepoli/discipulos' (pupils) of Lassus.[288] Similarly, for a performance of Brumel's missa *Et ecce terrae motus* (a12) under Lassus's direction around the same time, the manuscript Munich, Bayerische Staatsbibliothek, Mus. Ms. 1 bears the names of all the bass, tenor and alto singers involved, while the sopranos – presumably boys only – remain unnamed.[289] (Just a few years later, in 1573–4, castratos as well as boys are reported.)[290]
- Joachim Burmeister, 1606: 'The *discantus* ... is suited to a boy's age and to the female voice ...' (*Discantus ... ætati puerili femineæque voci convenit ...*).[291]
- Michael Praetorius, 1618: a 'Universal Table' sets out the ranges of the four principal vocal categories: bass, tenor, alto and – under a single heading – 'Eunuchus, Falsetista, Discantista' ('castrato, falsettist, [boy/female] soprano').[292] As with the ranges of the various instruments, the usual limits are shown in void notes, while black notes indicate unusual and exceptional 'falsetto notes above *and below*' which 'not everyone can always attain or reach' [my italics]. (In this context 'falsetto' clearly does not imply the technique by which such notes are produced). The usual soprano range is given as $c'-e''/f''$ (at *Cammerthon*), and the extensions as b below and g''/a'' above.[293]

---

[288] Massimo Troiano, *Dialoghi di Massimo Troiano* (Venice, 2/1569), fol. 42v (bk 1).

[289] *Antoine Brumel: Collected Works* iii, ed. B. Hudson (1970), ix–x.

[290] Wolfgang Boetticher, *Orlando di Lasso und seine Zeit: 1532–1594* i (1958), 441. Cf. Praetorius, *Syntagma musicum* ii, 17.

[291] Joachim Burmeister, *Musica poetica* (Rostock, 1606), 11 (ch. 2, 'De Vocibus').

[292] Praetorius, *Syntagma musicum* ii, 20 ('Tabella Universalis IV: Vox viva seu humana').

[293] '*Falset* Stimmen/ oben und unten'; 'dieselbige ... ein jeder allezeit nicht *assequiren* oder erreichen kan'; Praetorius, *Syntagma musicum* ii, 19.

APPENDIX 8

English (and Scottish) Music: Dubious Inferences and Assertions

- 'The ranges of the parts [in 15th-century English liturgical music] are not generally those of the modern voices, and a countertenor should be used if possible.'[294]
- 'This appears to be a Mass for male voices (two high countertenors, one low countertenor)' – an early 16th-century setting.[295]
- 'By "counter bass" he could mean counter tenor ... [possibly] to suggest the traditional bass–alto relationship'[296] – an interpretation of Nicolo Sagudino's report of a High Mass 'sung by the King's choristers' at the English court in 1515. (Their voices were 'more divine than human; and as to the counter bass voices, they probably have not their equals in the world.')[297] Sagudino, secretary to the Venetian ambassador, uses the conventional Italian '*contrabasso*' (from *contratenor bassus*), simply meaning 'bass'.
- '... many foreigners remarked on the extraordinary phenomenon of the high *trebles* (a technical term for this high part) in 16th-century English choirs.'[298] (I am not aware of any such remarks.)
- 'A letter about Taverner's appointment as master of the choristers at Cardinal College ... specifies that he must have "both his breste [?tenor or bass voice and falsetto voice] att will, the handling of an instrument, pleasure, cunning and exercise in teaching".'[299] As glossed thus, the word 'breste' (breast = singing voice) is treated as though it were plural rather than singular. However, it seems more likely that the preceding 'both' (which need not imply just two things) here introduces the three required areas of expertise: singing, playing and teaching.

---

[294] *Fifteenth-Century Liturgical Music: I – The Antiphons and Music for Holy Week & Easter*, ed. A. Hughes, Early English Church Music 8 (1968), xv.

[295] *Music of Scotland, 1500–1700*, ed. K. Elliott, Musica Britannica 15 (1957), 1. The anonymous three-part mass has a 16-note compass and is notated in high clefs: G2 G2 C2/C1.

[296] Peter Giles, *The Countertenor* (1982), 35.

[297] *Calendar of State Papers ... Venice* ii: *1509–1519*, ed. R. Brown (London, 1867), #624.

[298] Phillips, 'Performance Practice', 198.

[299] John Stevens, *Music and Poetry in the Early Tudor Court* (2/1979), 309. Later (at p. 312) he writes: 'almost certainly a choir-singer had to be versatile enough to sing either in a true or a falsetto voice'.

- 'In effect [Tudor] countertenors were hired both for their falsetto voices and for their chest voices.'[300]
- 'For some time it has been the editor's belief, based on his own experience, that the singing men of the Chapel Royal [during Tallis's lifetime] took either the bass, tenor, or countertenor part as was convenient on any given occasion.'[301]
- The first appearance of the 'very high boy's treble, singing in the range $f'-b''$ flat or even c''' ... can apparently be dated with some confidence to the 1570s'.[302]
- 'Sir Francis Drake, no less, is thought to have been a countertenor singer in addition to his professional sea-faring career.'[303]
- 'Shakespeare surely had a countertenor in mind when he wrote: "O stay and hear your true love's coming that can sing *both high and low*" [my italics][304] – commentary on Feste's song 'O mistress mine', in Shakespeare's *Twelfth Night*.
- English sources show that 'there were as many countertenors in choirs as tenors and basses put together. This fact makes it unlikely that they were eunuchs or eunuchoid high tenors. The obvious conclusion is that they were, like their Italian counterparts, falsettists'.[305]

---

[300] Phillips, 'Performance Practice', 198.
[301] Thomas Tallis, *Early English Sacred Music: I – Anthems*, ed. Leonard Ellinwood, Early English Church Music 12 (1971), xv.
[302] Bowers, 'The Performing Pitch', 25.
[303] Giles, *The Countertenor*, 35.
[304] Giles, *The Countertenor*, 35.
[305] Ardran and Wulstan, 'The Alto or Countertenor Voice', 17.

4
Falsetto and the French: 'Une toute autre marche'

FEW areas of musical study have engendered as much confusion as the (sometimes) interrelated topics of the 'falsetto' voice and the singing of 'alto' parts in earlier centuries. Some of this confusion is entirely understandable: at almost every turn we may encounter unknowable pitch standards, terminological riddles, or a sheer dearth of evidence. Much of it, however, is of our own making: in particular, the endemic failure to distinguish different repertories, different traditions, or different periods, coupled not infrequently with an apparent belief in a single 'true countertenor' of the past.

My broad aim is thus to encourage some fundamental rethinking about the place of falsetto singing – if any – in a number of specific vocal traditions. But on the present occasion I shall limit myself to a single period and country (18th-century France), one which, despite an abundance of relatively clear documentation, has nevertheless remained prone to misunderstanding. My approach has been to keep speculative interpretation to a minimum and, wherever possible, to allow the sources to speak for themselves. (All are given both in their original language and in translation.) More specifically, this study aims to take a fresh look at the nature of the *haute-contre* in this period.

With his admirably succinct article 'The Enigma of the Haute-Contre' (1974), Neal Zaslaw sought to clear up 'the vexed question of whether the *haute-contre* – the designation of the voice to which the leading male roles in French opera from Lully to Rameau were usually assigned – was a natural or a falsetto voice'.[1] He concludes: 'a balanced appraisal of all the historical evidence seems to suggest that the *haute-contre* in 18th-century French music was sung falsetto only by rare exception' – in other words, that the voice was essentially the same as our high tenor. Mary Cyr (1977) concurred and presented further valuable information, adding: 'it remains to be determined what unusual circumstances might have prompted the use of falsetto, when, and by whom.'[2]

First appeared in *Basler Jahrbuch für historische Musikpraxis* 26 (2002), 129–48.

[1] Neal Zaslaw, 'The Enigma of the Haute-Contre', *The Musical Times* 115 (1974), 939–41.
[2] Mary Cyr, 'On Performing 18th-Century Haute-contre Roles', *The Musical Times* 118 (1977), 291–5.

René Jacobs (1983) sees things differently:[3] the *haute-contre* was indeed a high tenor, but one that was significantly different from those we know today.[4] All Baroque singers, he believes, cultivated 'the ability to unite chest voice and falsetto' – the French *haute-contre* (or 'countertenor') included: 'If modern falsettists would abandon their preconceptions and would use their chest voice to their individual limits, and if some high tenors would develop their falsetto range, then the rebirth of the true Baroque countertenor might occur.'[5]

Pursuing these various issues turns out to have interesting implications not only for singers of *haute-contre* parts, but for all voice-types. And it is not only our understanding of French but also of Italian singing that is affected.

CATEGORIES OF VOICE

CONTEMPORARY comparisons of French and Italian music in the 18th century – most of them from a French perspective – have left us with some very clear descriptions of the perceived distinctions between their vocal practices. A fundamental point to emerge from these sources is that the two countries favoured quite different vocal ranges and scorings: according to de Brosses (1739/40) the three top parts in Italian music (soprano, contralto, tenor) lay 'a 3rd or a 4th higher than ours' (*dessus, haute-contre* and *taille*).[6] As a consequence, alto parts – 'contralto' to the Italians, 'haute-contre' to the French – were conceived for and executed by wholly different categories of singer:

> [Italian contraltos] are not of the same kind as ours: no type of French voice could render their song well. They are female *bas-dessus* voices, lower than any of ours ...

> [*Les hautes-contre italiens*] *ne sont pas du même genre que les nôtres; aucune espèce de voix françoise ne pourroit bien rendre leur chant. Ce sont des voix de femmes en bas-dessus plus bas qu'aucun des nôtres* ...

> (Charles de Brosses, 1739/40)[7]

---

[3] René Jacobs, 'The Controversy Concerning the Timbre of the Countertenor', in *Alte Musik: Praxis und Reflexion*, ed. P. Reidemeister and V. Gutmann (1983), 288–306.

[4] Jacobs, 'The Controversy', 298.

[5] Jacobs, 'The Controversy', 289, 306.

[6] '*Ces trois premiers genres de voix ont une tierce ou une quarte d'élévation plus que chez nous*'; Charles de Brosses, *Lettres familières écrites d'Italie en 1739 et 1740* ii (ed. R. Colomb; Paris, 4/1885), 317.

[7] de Brosses, 317–8.

> In Italian music this part, which they call contralto and which corresponds to the *haute-contre*, is nearly always sung by *bas-dessus*, be they women or castratos.[8]
>
> *Dans la Musique Italienne, cette Partie, qu'ils appellent* Contr'alto, & *qui répond à la* Haute-contre, *est presque toujours chantée par des* Bas-dessus, *soit femmes, soit Castrati.*
>
> (Jean-Jacques Rousseau, 1768)[9]
>
> The [Italians'] contraltos are *second dessus* voices of women [and of castratos].
>
> *Les* contralti *[des Italiens] sont des voix de femmes [et de castrats] en second dessus.*
>
> (Jérôme de Lalande, 2/1787)[10]

This distinction still held good at the end of the century, as we see from Framery's 'Contralto' entry in the *Encyclopédie méthodique: Musique* (1791):

> an Italian word which corresponds to our word *haute-contre*; but the two voices are nevertheless not the same, and their ranges are rather different. The Italian contralto is performed by castratos whose voices have become lower with age, or by women who have particularly cultivated the low range and who are, properly, what we call *bas-dessus*. ... One can therefore conclude that in their choirs the Italians are wholly unacquainted with the *haute-contre* and that they have substituted for it the *second dessus*, while continuing to call it 'contralto'.
>
> *mot italien qui répond à notre mot haute-contre; mais les deux voix ne sont pourtant pas les mêmes, & leur diapason est assez différent. Le* contralto *italien est exécuté par des castrati à qui l'âge a rendu la voix plus grave, ou par des femmes qui ont particuliérement* [sic] *cultivé les cordes basses, & qui sont proprement, ce que nous appellons des bas-dessus. ... On peut donc conclure que les Italiens ne connoissent point dans leurs chœurs la haute-contre, & qu'ils lui ont substitué le second-dessus, en continuant de le nommer* contralto.[11]

---

[8] The 'Haute-contre' article in *The New Grove Dictionary of Music and Musicians*, ed. S. Sadie (2/2001) mistakenly represents Rousseau as saying that 'the haute-contre is a male voice *equivalent in range* to the contralto or second soprano parts sung by women or castratos' [my italics]. As de Brosses and others make clear, it is merely the *name* of the part which 'corresponds', not its range.

[9] Jean-Jacques Rousseau, *Dictionnaire de musique* (Paris, 1768), 248. The *Dictionnaire* is based on articles originally written for Diderot's and d'Alembert's *Encyclopédie* (Paris, 1751–65).

[10] Jérôme de Lalande, *Voyage en Italie* v (Yverdon, 2/1787) 447.

[11] *Encyclopédie méthodique: Musique* i, ed. N. E. Framery and P. L. Ginguené (Paris, 1791), 315–16 ('Contralto').

In other words, *haute-contre* and contralto corresponded only in *name* (both deriving ultimately from the Latin 'contra[tenor] altus'). In *range* (and general voice-type) the Italian contralto's closest equivalent was the *second* (or *bas-*) *dessus*, while the *haute-contre* was best equated with the Italian tenor. French practice and terminology, Framery argues, were connected in a way the Italian was not:

> From the compass of the C3 [or 'alto'] clef, which serves both types of voice, it is evident that it is the French who use the true *haute-contre* and that Italian contraltos are just *seconds dessus*, as this clef goes down to *e* or *d* and up to *a'* or *b'*. ... This is in effect the [pitch] area which a man's voice can comfortably cover when it is a high and clear one; but the Italians call this voice *tenore*, without distinguishing it from the other type [*tenore secundo*] whose sound is deeper and fuller.
>
> *A considérer le diapason de la clef d'ut sur la troisième ligne, qui sert aux deux espèces de voix, il est évident que ce sont les François qui emploient la véritable haute-contre, & que les* contralti *italiens ne sont que des seconds-dessus, car cette clef descend jusqu'au* mi *ou au* re, *& monte jusqu'au* la *& au* si. ... *Tel est en effet l'espace que peut parcourir à son aise la voix d'homme quand elle est aiguë & claire; mais cette voix, les Italiens l'appellent* tenore, *sans la distinguer de cette autre dont le son est plus grave & plus nourri.*[12]

The Italian *tenore*, declares Lalande (2/1787), 'c'est la haute-contre françoise'.[13] To illustrate the point as clearly as possible, he invokes two of the century's most celebrated *hautes-contre*, Pierre de Jélyotte and his younger contemporary Joseph Legros, whose combined careers spanned several decades (from 1738 to 1783) and witnessed the creation of an impressive number of leading operatic roles in Paris, from Rameau to Gluck. In Italian terms,

> Jélyotte and Legros would have been called 'tenors' and not 'contraltos', even though one may be accustomed to translate this word as *haute-contre*.
>
> *Geliot & Legros auroient été appellés* tenori, *& non pas* contralti, *quoiqu'on ait coutume de traduire ce mot par haute-contre.*[14]

This is plain enough and readily suggests that we too would recognize those eminent *hautes-contre* as tenors. But are we also to assume that Italian and French singers used these 'tenor' voices in more or less the same fashion as each other?

---

[12] *Encyclopédie méthodique: Musique*, ed. Framery and Ginguené, 315.
[13] Lalande, *Voyage*, 446. He introduces his subsequent comments (see below) in more or less identical fashion: '*J'ai dit que le tenore des Italiens étoit la haute-contre des François*' (p. 447).
[14] Lalande, *Voyage*, 447.

RANGES

LALANDE continues his comparison of *haute-contre* and *tenore* with some very specific information on ranges. But when we look at it, we shall need to remind ourselves that such ranges – whether expressed in note names or in musical notation – are of only limited use unless we understand the pitch standards that inform them.

Fortunately, it is possible to be reasonably certain both of the pitch standard adopted by Lully in performances of his own *tragédies en musique* during the 1670s and 80s and of subsequent practice at the Paris Opéra, where his works long remained core repertory. Lully's standard, it seems, lay roughly a tone beneath today's a' = 440 and was still in use at the Opéra as late as 1770.[15] By 1766, though, Dom Bédos de Celles could write that '*ton de l'Opéra* ... is not a fixed pitch; it is raised and lowered by a quarter of a tone, or even more, depending on the compass of the voices.'[16] The ranges of Italian singers given by Lalande are less straightforward, as his information was presumably collected in Italy in the 1760s;[17] but it seems reasonable to suppose that such a sophisticated writer (musical amateur though he was) would base his remarks on a single pitch standard, one that his French readers would most readily understand.

As a solo voice the French *haute-contre* first rose to prominence with the dozen or more heroic parts written for it by Lully.[18] Roles such as those of Perseus, Phaeton, Atys, Roland and Amadis typically range from g up to a' (plus the occasional b') and have a consistently fairly low tessitura.[19] (The voice of Antoine Boutelou, 'the celebrated *haute-contre* of Louis XIV's chapel', was said to have been full but 'not high', extending to $b\flat'$ 'only in passing'.)[20] By the 1730s Rameau had adopted a higher tessitura and very slightly wider compass when writing for Denis-François Tribou (Hippolytus, Castor); the Act IV air in *Hippolyte et Aricie*, for example, extends from f up to $b\flat'$.[21] A generation or so further on, both Corrette (1758) and Rousseau (1768) set the *haute-contre*'s upper limit still higher, at c'' (with g and f respectively as the lowest

---

[15] Bruce Haynes, *A History of Performing Pitch*, 100–2, 116, 275–7, 308–10.

[16] '... le ton de l'Opéra ... n'est pas un ton fixe; on le hausse ou le baisse d'un quart de ton, ou même plus, selon la portée des voix': Dom François Bédos de Celles, *L'Art du facteur d'orgues* ii (Paris, 1770), 432.

[17] Haynes, *Pitch*, 269–73.

[18] *New Grove 2*, 'Haute-contre', 154.

[19] Cyr, 'Haute-contre Roles', 292.

[20] '... célebre haute-contre de la chapelle de Louis XIV ... Sa voix n'était pas haute, & il n'allait au si♭ qu'en passant; mais le son en était si plein'; Jean-Benjamin de La Borde, *Essai sur la musique ancienne et moderne* iii (Paris 1780), 498.

[21] Cyr, 'Haute-contre Roles', 293.

notes).²² As we have already seen, Framery (1791) links the range of the voice to the natural span of the C3 clef (e up to a') with an extra tone at each end (low d and high b').²³

And now Lalande (2/1787): 'our *haute-contre* ... ascends in full voice to bb'.' Exceptionally, Legros went to c'' and Jélyotte a further tone to d'', though 'in all countries these vocal qualities are very rare'. Others were successful as *hautes-contre* despite distinctly restricted upper limits: 'Lainez goes up to a forced a', Rousseau [a young singer in Paris from 1780] to a somewhat forced ab', Dufrenoy up to a forced g'.'²⁴ But because many important roles had been created for the exceptionally high voices of Jélyotte and Legros in particular, 'all who succeeded Legros are obliged to shout in order to reach the pitch of the *haute-contre*, except for Rousseau, but he has a smaller tone.'²⁵ Gluck's *Orphée* (1774) proved particularly problematic in this respect. In revising *Orfeo ed Euridice* for Paris, the composer had contrived to give Legros some top c''s (in the Act III duet) and even a fleeting d'' (at 'L'excès de mes malheurs' in Act II). Others later attempted the part as written, but pitch at the Opéra had risen²⁶ and by the time Louis Nourrit took on the role in 1809 many downward transpositions were deemed necessary.²⁷

REGISTERS

NEAL Zaslaw (1974) argues that the 18th-century *haute-contre* used falsetto 'only by rare exception'.²⁸ For his part, René Jacobs (1983) claims that the *haute-contre*, like all 'Baroque male alto' voices, 'has always

---

²² Michel Corrette, *Le Parfait maître à chanter* (Paris, 1758), 20; Rousseau, *Dictionnaire*, planche F, fig. 6. In the latter, the manner of notating the ranges is explained thus: '*Les Notes blanches montrent les Sons pleins où chaque Partie peut arriver tant en haut qu'en bas, & les Croches qui suivent montrent les Sons où la Voix commenceroit à se forcer, & qu'elle ne doit former qu'en passant*' ('The white notes indicate the full sounds which each part can reach both at top and bottom, and the quavers that follow indicate the sounds where the voice begins to force and which it should not employ except in passing'); p. 368, 'Partie'.

²³ *Encyclopédie méthodique: Musique*, ed. Framery and Ginguené, 315.

²⁴ '... notre haute-contre ... monte en pleine voix jusqu'au si♭ ... A Paris, Geliot avoit la même étendue qu'Amorevoli [jusqu'à re], & Legros avoit celle des deux premiers [Babbi & Caribaldi, jusqu'à ut]; ces qualités de voix, dans tous les pays, sont très-rares: Lainez va jusqu'au la forcé, Rousseau jusqu'au la♭ un peu forcé, Dufrenoy jusqu'au sol forcé'; Lalande, *Voyage*, 447; see also n. 93.

²⁵ '... tous ce qui ont succédé à Legros, sont obligés de crier pour arriver au ton de la haute-contre, excepté Rousseau; mais il a le timbre plus petit'; Lalande, *Voyage*, 447.

²⁶ Haynes, *Pitch*, 308–10, 329–32.

²⁷ Patricia Howard, *C. W. von Gluck, Orfeo* (1983), 75.

²⁸ Zaslaw, 'The Enigma', 941.

been a *voce mezzana*' (a rather murky term borrowed from Zacconi, 1596)[29] and that all such voices 'united their chest voice with their falsetto in the way described by García'.[30] (Manuel García published his theory of registers in the 1840s; it is, Jacobs tells us, 'still very much in the tradition of 18th-century castrato teachers, e.g. Tosi, Porpora and Mancini'.)[31] But just how relevant are these Italianate theories to an earlier *French* vocal tradition, one rooted in Lully's time and long regarded as quite distinct from Italian practice?[32]

In a chapter on declamation, Jean-Léonar le Gallois de Grimarest (*Traité du récitatif*, 1707) sets out an interesting principle:

> An actor must carefully avoid having two different tones of voice, viz. pronouncing in a natural tone at certain points and falling into falsetto when he is obliged to raise [his voice]. This unpleasantness is very shocking to the listener.
>
> *Un Acteur doit éviter avec soin d'avoir deux tons de voix différens: c'est à dire, de prononcer dans un ton naturel en de certains endroits, & de tomber dans le fausset, quand il est obligé de s'élever. Ce desagrément est tres-choquant pour l'Auditeur.*[33]

This has been translated as 'A *singer* must take care to avoid using two different voices: that is, ... falsetto when he is obliged to *sing* higher' [my italics].[34] However, while the term 'acteur' undoubtedly embraces 'l'Acteur qui chante', and while this actor-singer was explicitly required to observe the rules of good declamation,[35] Grimarest's comments – despite the reference to falsetto – are probably best understood in relation to the speaking actor. (Only the subsequent and final chapter of the *Traité* is specifically concerned with recitative 'dans le Chant'.)[36] It could in any case be argued that the very mention of the 'defect' of register switching implies that it happened rather frequently, or perhaps that Grimarest's view was purely 'theoretical' or idiosyncratic. Nevertheless, it may

---

[29] Jacobs, 'The Controversy', 289.

[30] Jacobs, 'The Controversy', 306.

[31] Jacobs, 'The Controversy', 290. García was born in 1805 and first studied singing in Naples with his eminent (Spanish) father.

[32] Zaslaw warns against undue reliance on 'the testimony of a generation of musicians [Castil-Blaze, Choron, Fétis] who may have lived too late to know the true haute-contre tradition except by hearsay'; 'The Enigma', 941.

[33] Jean-Léonar le Gallois de Grimarest, *Traité du récitatif* (Paris, 1707), 133 (ch. 7, 'De la Déclamation').

[34] James R. Anthony, letter to *The Musical Times* 116 (1975), 237.

[35] '... l'Acteur qui chante doit absolument suivre toutes les regles de la Déclamation'; Grimarest, *Traité*, 222.

[36] Cf. David Tunley, 'Grimarest's *Traité du récitatif*: Glimpses of Performance Practice in Lully's Operas', *Early Music* 15/3 (1987), 361–4.

well be that French vocal music observed a comparable underlying principle.

Powerful evidence of French preference for a single register comes from no lesser authority than Johann Joachim Quantz (1752), a well-placed and astute observer of practical musical matters French and Italian:

> The voice is of two types, chest voice and falsetto or fistula. ... The Italians and several other nations unite this falsetto with the chest voice, and make use of it to great advantage when singing; with the French, however, it is not customary ...

> *Die Stimme besteht aus zweyerley Arten, aus der Bruststimme, und aus dem Falset, oder Fistel. ... Die Italiäner, und einige andere Nationen vereinigen dieses Falset mit der Bruststimme, und bedienen sich dessen, bey dem Singen, mit großem Vortheile; Bey den Franzosen aber ist es nicht üblich ...*[37]

With this we come, I believe, to the heart of the matter. From the documentary evidence presented in this brief study it emerges – quite plainly, it seems to me – that the use or non-use of falsetto (in the sense of head voice, as most of us would call it) was seen as a central factor in the polarization of Italian and French vocal traditions. Its cultivation, throughout the 18th century (and beyond), was seen as a defining characteristic of Italian singing, one which distinguished it sharply from French practice.[38] Even Rousseau, a vociferous critic of French music, was not comfortable with its use. Referring in his *Dictionnaire de musique* (1768) to a table of ranges for each principal voice part (*dessus, haute-contre, taille* and *basse*), he writes:

> Italian voices nearly always exceed this range at the top, especially the *dessus*; but then the voice becomes a sort of falsetto, and however artfully this defect may be disguised, it certainly is one.

> *Les Voix Italiennes excèdent presque toujours cette étendue dans le haut, sur-tout les Dessus; mais la Voix devient alors une espèce de* Faucet, *& avec quelqu'art que ce défaut se déguise, c'en est certainement un.*[39]

This 'sort of *falsetto*' not only made for a very different colour in the upper reaches of a voice (a colour the Italians liked and the French generally did not), but also extended the potential range upwards by a significant

---

[37] Johann Joachim Quantz, *Versuch einer Anweisung die Flöte traversiere zu spielen* (Berlin, 1752), 47.

[38] I am unaware of this distinction being emphasized in the secondary literature, though I cannot claim to have searched extensively. It is, however, absent from general surveys such as those in the *New Grove* handbook on *Performance Practice: Music after 1600*, ed. H. M. Brown and S. Sadie (1989).

[39] Rousseau, *Dictionnaire*, 368 ('Partie').

amount. As Quantz puts it, judicious use of falsetto enabled one, 'without doing oneself violence, to produce several more notes at the top than is possible with chest voice'.[40] (Over-indulgence in this register, perhaps when embellishing, is presumably what Jommelli meant (1769) by 'the usual defect of modern tenors of wanting to contralto-ize [*contraltiggiare*] too much'.)[41] In comparing the French *haute-contre* voice with its closest Italian equivalent Lalande is admirably clear on this crucial distinction in technique:

> The [Italian] *tenore* goes from C to g' in full voice and up to d'' in falsetto or *fausset*; after g' our *haute-contre* ordinarily ascends in full voice to $b\flat'$, whereas after g' the *tenore* enters into falsetto – but that is not without exception: Babbi ascended to c'' in full voice, like Caribaldi, until the age of 48. Amorevoli, who was a little older, went up to d''.[42]
>
> *Le tenore va de* ut *à* sol *en pleine voix, & jusqu'à* re *en* falzetto *ou* fausset: *notre haute-contre, ordinairement après le* sol, *monte en pleine voix jusqu'au* si♭; *au lieu que le* tenore, *après le* sol, *entre dans le fausset; mais cela n'est pas sans exception: Babbi montoit jusqu'à* ut *en pleine voix, de même que Caribaldi, jusqu'à l'âge de quarante-huit ans. Amorevoli, qui étoit un peu plus ancien, alloit jusqu'à* re.[43]

In a response (1754) to Rousseau's *Lettre sur la musique françoise* an anonymous writer reported an 'experiment' aimed at identifying the cause of French 'antipathy' towards Italian singing and made with the help of 'people I knew could not bear' it.[44] This antipathy he duly ascribed, in part, to 'the custom of using falsetto and of making an artificial voice [which] must make a much more disagreeable impression on the ear than would

---

[40] '... ohne sich Gewalt anzuthun, in der Höhe einige Töne mehr, als mit der Bruststimme möglich ist, herausbringen'; Quantz, *Versuch*, 47.

[41] Cyr, 'Haute-contre Roles', 294.

[42] Mancini mentions (but does not discuss) 'some rare examples of somebody receiving from Nature the most singular gift of being able to execute everything with just chest voice' (*qualche raro esempio, che qualcheduno riceve dalle natura il singolarissimo dono di poter eseguir tutto colla sola voce di petto*); Giovanni Battista Mancini, *Pensieri, e riflessioni pratiche sopra il canto figurato* (Vienna, 1774), 43.

[43] Lalande, *Voyage*, 447. Jacobs appears to regard this comparison as demonstrating that *both* types of voice combined chest and falsetto, with the Italian tenor doing so 'in perhaps a less perfect manner'; 'The Controversy', 298.

[44] '... des personnes que je sçavois ne pouvoir souffrir le Chant Italien'; [Élie-Catherine Fréron and Jean-Jacques Baudinet], *Suite des lettres sur la musique françoise* (1754), 33 (Lettre IV).

have been made by a natural sound.'⁴⁵ This association of falsetto with Italian singing (and, perhaps, a consequent Gallic distrust of it) is still found alive and well towards the end of the century in Meude-Monpas's definition (1787) of '*Fausset*':

> Voice-type which is not natural: for, instead of singing from the throat, one gives the impression, so to speak, of singing from the top of one's head. This method of singing falsetto comes to us once again from Italy.
>
> *Genre de voix qui n'est pas naturel: car, au lieu de chanter du gosier, on a, pour ainsi dire, l'air de chanter du toupet. Cette méthode de chanter le fausset nous vient encore d'Italie.*⁴⁶

And indeed this is an aspect of technique which is consistently addressed in Italian sources from at least Tosi (1723) to Mancini (1774)⁴⁷ and well beyond. (The origins of this Italian tradition are, of course, another story altogether, and we may briefly note Giulio Caccini's well-known advice at the start of the previous century that the solo singer should choose 'a pitch at which he can sing in a full and natural voice in order to avoid feigned notes'.)⁴⁸ In stark contrast, Jean-Antoine Bérard, author of *L'Art du chant* (1755)⁴⁹ and a former solo *haute-contre* at the Paris Opéra, makes no mention whatsoever of the falsetto register.

Unlike our French writers, Quantz (1752) had no qualms about endorsing the Italian approach, when setting out 'what is required of a good singer':⁵⁰

> It is further required that a singer know how to unite the falsetto with the chest voice so as for it to be imperceptible where the latter leaves off and the former commences ...

---

⁴⁵ '... *j'ai trouvé que la coutume de se servir du fausset & de se faire une voix factice devoit faire sur l'oreille une impression d'autant plus désagréable, qu'elle venoit d'être affectée par un son naturel*'; [Fréron and Baudinet], *Suite des lettres*, 34.

⁴⁶ J. J. O. de Meude-Monpas, *Dictionnaire de musique* (Paris, 1787), 60 ('Fausset').

⁴⁷ Mancini, *Pensieri*, 43–6 (articolo IV, 'Della voce di petto, e di testa, o sia falsetto').

⁴⁸ '... *un tuono, nel quale possa cantare in voce piena, e naturale per isfuggire le voci finte*'; Giulio Caccini, *Le nuove musiche* (Florence, 1602), 'A i lettori', sig.C2r. By taking '*le voci finte*' to mean 'falsettists' (rather than the more probable 'falsetto notes' – Playford's 'feigned Tunes of Notes'), and by overlooking the force of the verb '*isfuggire*', Jacobs is able to argue thus: 'Caccini doesn't attack the *voce di testa o falsetto*, the register that in a good voice is always connected with the *voce piena o naturale*; he attacks the *voce finte* [sic], or falsettists'; 'The Controversy', 303.

⁴⁹ Jean-Antoine Bérard, *L'Art du chant* (Paris, 1755).

⁵⁰ 'Von einem guten Sänger wird erfodert ...'; Quantz, *Versuch*, 281.

> *Es wird weiter erfodert, daß ein Sänger das Falset mit der Bruststimme so zu vereinigen wisse, damit man nicht merken könne, wo die letzte aufhöret, und das erstere anfängt ...*[51]

By the 1750s this Italianate manner of vocal production was evidently already in vogue at Germany's cosmopolitan courts, though not in 'most towns':

> From choir- or school-singers one can still even now gather an impression, in most towns, of the nature of the Germans' singing style in times past. ... Uniting chest voice with falsetto is as unknown to them as [it is] to the French.
>
> *Wie die Singart der Deutschen in den alten Zeiten beschaffen gewesen sey, kann man, noch bis auf diese Stunde, in den meisten Städten, an den Chor- oder Schul-Sängern abnehmen. ... Die Vereinigung der Bruststimme mit dem Falset ist ihnen eben so unbekannt, als den Franzosen.*[52]

PERCEPTIONS

IF asked to differentiate between quintessential Italian and French voices of the 18th century, many of us today would perhaps be tempted to characterize the former as the more robust, not least on high notes, the latter as generally lighter and somewhat thin, especially at the top. Contemporary descriptions, however, frequently run counter to these preconceptions:

> French singing demands full lung power, the full range of the voice; louder, our singing masters tell us, swell the sounds, open the mouth, use the whole of your voice. Softer, say the Italian masters, don't force, sing freely, make your notes soft, flexible and flowing, save the outbursts for those rare and fleeting moments when you must astonish and overwhelm.
>
> *Le chant François exige tout l'effort des poumons, toute l'étendue de la voix; plus fort, nous disent nos Maîtres, enflez les sons, ouvrez la bouche, donnez toute votre voix. Plus doux, disent les Maîtres Italiens, ne forcez point, chantez sans gêne, rendez vos sons doux, flexibles & coulans, reservez les éclats pour ces momens rares & passagers où il faut surprendre & déchirer.*
>
> (Rousseau, 1753)[53]

We then entered into a great debate; I told him that they [two young

---

[51] Quantz, *Versuch*, 281–2.
[52] Quantz, *Versuch*, 326.
[53] Rousseau, *Lettre sur la musique francoise* ([Paris], 1753), 30.

ladies who had been brought from Italy] had made their voices much bigger down low and a great deal softer up high; he [the Marquis of Varennes] asked me in reply whether I wished the Italians might do as the French, who howl like a wolf when dealing with a high note; I replied to him that what I favoured was not that the voice be forced but that its beauty be made apparent through a natural brilliance, and that there was more pleasure in hearing a large voice than a small one; I also added that mention was [regularly] made of *Mlle Lemaure, M. Muraire, M. Jélyotte, MM. Benoit* and *Maligne* etc., who have made themselves charming through the beauty and large volume of their voices, and that no one ever mentioned a small one ...

The Italians ... can be enticed only by a small voice, which never fills the ear like a large one; they don't even care to have one, but [are happy] to transgress nature; for I have just seen a soprano arietta in a modern Italian opera covering two and a half octaves, which is almost impossible to execute.

Nous entrâmes d'abord dans une grande dispute; je lui dis qu'elles [deux Demoiselles qu'on avoit fait venir d'Italie] avoient fort grossi leur voix dans le bas, & qu'elles l'avoient fort adoucie dans le haut, il [Mr. le Marquis de Varene] me repondit si je voulois que les Italiens fissent comme les François, qui crient au loup, lorsqu'il s'agit de donner un ton en haut; je lui repliquai que je n'aprouvois pas qu'on forçât la voix, mais qu'on en fît paroître la beauté par un éclat naturel, & qu'il y avoit plus de plaisir à entendre une grande voix qu'une petite: Je lui ajoutai encore que l'on faisoit mention de Mademoiselle Le More, *de* Mr. Muraire, *de* Mr. Gelliotto, *de* Mrs. Benoit *&* Maligne, *& autres qui se sont rendus charmans par la beauté & le grand volume de leur voix, & qu'on n'avoit jamais fait mention d'une petite ...*

Les Italiens ... ne peuvent avoir l'apas que d'une petite voix, qui ne remplit jamais l'oreille comme une grande, ils ne se piquent pas même d'en avoir, mais de forcer la nature; car je viens de voir dans un Opera Italien moderne, une ariéte de dessus qui va deux octaves & demi, ce qui est presque impossible à exécuter.

(A. P., 1754)[54]

[54] Mr. l'A*** P******, *Dissertation sur la musique françoise et italienne* (Amsterdam, 1754), 35–7; reproduced in *La Querelle des Bouffons*, ed. D. Launay (1973) iii, 1704 (no. 55). (Launay proposes the Abbé Pellegrin as author, but he had died in 1745; might it perhaps be another literary and musical Abbé, Prévost?) According to Dufort de Cheverny, Jélyotte was a particularly powerful singer: 'Sa voix dans Pygmalion *couvrait tellement le chœur qu'on n'a jamais entendu rien de pareil; et dans* Zoroastre, *tout Paris courait entendre, au milieu du tonnerre: "Ciel! Thémire expire dans*

Although the Italians may be more accustomed than the French to singing with a small amount of voice and at high pitches, the latter, according to my observations, manage to produce cadenzas with just as much elegance and perfection as the former.

Quoique les Italiens soient plus accoutumés à chanter avec un petit volume de Voix & à sons aigus que les François, ceux-ci à l'aide de mes Observations, réussiront à former le Point d'Orgue avec autant de graces & de perfection que ceux-là.

(Bérard, 1755)[55]

The general disposition of French composers is always to force the voices in order to make them shout rather than sing ...

L'esprit général des Compositeurs François est toujours de forcer les Voix pour les faire crier plutôt que chanter ...

(Rousseau, 1768)[56]

The repugnance which Italians have for strong, firm voices, such as our *basses-taille* and even our *hautes-contre*, makes them regard the use of castratos as necessary for their pleasures; it would, however, be better for humankind if one were accustomed, as we are, to finding pleasure in voices that are natural, male, brilliant and that have all their strength ...

La répugnance qu'ont les Italiens pour les voix fortes & dures, telles que nos basses-tailles & même nos hautes-contres, leur fait regarder comme nécessaire à leurs plaisirs l'usage des Castrati*: il vaux mieux cependant pour la nature humaine que l'on soit accoutumé, comme nous, à trouver du plaisir dans les voix naturelles, mâles, éclatantes, & qui ont toute leur force ...*

(Lalande, 2/1787)[57]

Although seemingly widespread, the idea that the French had stronger voices was for Rousseau (1753) a misperception which – not entirely convincingly – he endeavours to correct:

it is erroneous to believe that Italian singers generally have less voice than the French. On the contrary, they need to have the strongest and most melodious tone quality in order to make themselves heard

mes bras!"'; *Mémoires de Dufort de Cheverny: La Cour de Louis XV*, ed. J.-P. Guicciardi (1990), 2012. ('In *Pygmalion* his voice covered the choir to such an extent that one has never heard the like; and in *Zoroastre* the whole of Paris ran to hear in the midst of the thunder: "Ciel! Thémire expire dans mes bras!"') De Cheverny's recollection is not wholly accurate, as the line he quotes does not appear in *Zoroastre*.

[55] Bérard, *L'Art du chant*, 35.
[56] Rousseau, *Dictionnaire*, 545 ('Voix').
[57] Lalande, *Voyage*, 441–2.

in the immense theatres of Italy, without ceasing to nurture the sounds, as Italian music requires.

c'est un erreur de croire qu'en général les Chanteurs Italiens ayent moins de voix que les François. Il faut au contraire qu'ils ayent le timbre plus fort & plus harmonieux pour pouvoir se faire entendre sur les théatres immenses de l'Italie, sans cesser de ménager les sons, comme le veut la Musique Italienne.[58]

A further aspect of the evident difficulty the French had with Italian singing was that, however smooth the transition between high and low registers, the two could seem disconcertingly disparate:

> the older of these two young ladies [who had been brought from Italy] sang a recitative in which her voice turned out to be more of a bass than a *dessus*; in it I recognized perfectly the singing of our rustics [in Provence]; she then sang an arietta, in which she made her voice a great deal softer for the highest notes and rendered the low ones disagreeable by making them bigger and by digging them out like *basses-taille* ... Next ... the younger sister sang a recitative in which she made her voice much bigger in the low parts and a great deal softer in the high parts of the arietta, just as her elder had done. ... The Italians set no limits either for their *symphonies* or for their vocal music; they make them go so high that they have to make their voices a great deal softer in order to reach the high pitches of their ariettas ...

> *l'aînée de ces deux Demoiselles [qu'on avoit fait venir d'Italie] chanta un recitatif, où sa voix paroissoit plûtôt une voix de basse que de dessus; je reconnus là parfaitement le chant de nos rustiques [de Provence]; elle chanta ensuite une ariéte, où elle adoucit beaucoup sa voix dans ses tons les plus hauts, & rendoit désagréables ceux d'en bas, en les grossissant & creusant comme des basses-tailles ... Ensuite ... la cadete chanta un recitatif où elle grossit fort sa voix dans le bas, & l'adoucit beaucoup dans le haut de l'ariéte, ainsi qu'avoit fait son aînée. ... Les Italiens ne mettent point de bornes à leurs symphonies, ni à leurs chants, ils les font aller si haut qu'il faut qu'ils adoucissent beaucoup leur voix pour atteindre à la hauteur de leurs ariétes ...*

(A. P., 1754)[59]

But it was not only in Italian music that ranges were being expanded. In a small book on the 'corruption' of musical taste, Bollioud de Mermet (1746) deplores – amongst other things – the vogue among contemporary French composers for extending vocal as well as instrumental ranges upwards:

---

[58] Rousseau, *Lettre*, 30.

[59] A. P., *Dissertation*, 34–6; ed. Launay, 1702–4.

> Since extremely high voices are rare, and rarely beautiful in the upper reaches, if musicians tune instruments to a higher pitch than the natural one and in composing take parts above the stave [i.e. above the natural range of a given clef], they expose the most defective extreme end of ordinary voices. The throat being more contracted in high notes, the fibres of the glottis more tense, the breath more violently emitted – this produces forced sounds, sometimes less in tune and always contrary to what is natural. In this manner one no longer sings, one shouts: these are no longer the full and mellow sounds of a voice which is free within its range – this is yelling [and] wailing.
>
> *Comme les Voix extrémement hautes sont rares, & rarement belles dans les derniers sons aigus, les Musiciens qui portent dans l'accord des Instrumens le ton plus haut que le naturel, & qui élévent, en composant, les parties au-dessus de leur portée, font paroître à découvert l'extrémité la plus défectueuse des Voix ordinaires. Le gosier étant plus serré dans les tons hauts, les fibres de la glotte plus tendues, l'air frapé plus violemment, produit des sons forcés, quelquefois moins justes, & toujours contre le naturel. On ne chante plus par ce moyen, on crie: ce ne sont plus des sons pleins & moileux d'une Voix libre dans son étenduë; ce sont des clameurs, des gémissemens.*[60]

Although at the end of the century the *haute-contre* could still be defined as 'a voice which is bright and which goes up high with ease',[61] persistent criticisms begin to be voiced in the middle of the century – by the French themselves – of problems associated with the upper part of the voice, and especially that of the *haute-contre*. We have already encountered Lalande's observation that Legros's successors were 'obliged to shout to reach the pitch of the *haute-contre*'; others are equally outspoken:

> Indeed, the *haute-contre* in a man's voice is not natural; one has to force in order to carry it to this register: whatever one may do, it always has a sharp-edged quality and rarely good intonation.
>
> *En effet, la* Haute-contre *en Voix d'homme n'est point naturelle; il faut la forcer pour la porter à ce Diapason: quoi qu'on fasse, elle a toujours de l'aigreur, & rarement de la justesse.*
>
> (Rousseau, 1768)[62]

---

[60] Louis Bolliloud de Mermet, *De la corruption du goust dans la musique françoise* (Lyon, 1746), 25–6.

[61] '"Contralto": *une voix claire & s'élevant facilement dans le haut*'; *Encyclopédie méthodique: Musique*, ed. Framery and Ginguené, 315.

[62] Rousseau, *Dictionnaire*, 248 ('Haute-contre, Altus ou Contra').

> The *haute-contre* is an artificial voice, it is not in nature: ... the *haute-contre* always has a sharp-edged quality and rarely good intonation.
>
> *La haute-contre est une voix factice, elle n'est pas dans la nature: ... la haute-contre a toujours de l'aigreur, et rarement de la justesse.*
>
> (Meude-Monpas, 1787[63] – in a clear echo of Rousseau)

> Several [*hautes-contre*], in order to reach the top notes, are obliged to force their natural means by contracting the throat; but they thereby lose in charm what they gain in range, for these strangulated sounds lack gentleness and purity.
>
> *Plusieurs [hautes-contre], pour parvenir aux sons les plus aigus, sont obligés de forcer leurs moyens naturels en se resserrant le gozier; mais ils perdent ainsi en agrément ce qu'ils gagnent en étendue, car ces sons étranglés manquent de douceur & de pureté.*
>
> (Framery, 1791)[64]

(These words of Framery's readily bring to mind Rossini's famous reaction to Duprez's chest-voice c''s in *Guillaume Tell* in 1837, which he is said to have likened to 'the squawk of a capon whose throat is being cut'.)

As time went on singers evidently experienced increasing difficulty with the higher *haute-contre* parts. It is therefore striking that not one of the above sources mentions recourse to falsetto. Or, at least, not explicitly so; in concluding that the *haute-contre* may occasionally have employed falsetto – if 'only by rare exception' – Zaslaw had in mind Rousseau's use of the words 'not natural' and '*forcer*' in describing these difficult top notes (1768, see above), terms he found 'strikingly similar to those which J. G. Walther had used in defining the falsetto voice'.[65] While the observation is perfectly accurate, the usages are, I believe, reasonably distinct. After all, Rousseau himself also refers to *composers* 'forcing' voices and to an Italian emphasis on 'unforced' singing (see above); and elsewhere we may read of an *orchestra* 'forcing the sounds' (i.e. 'making a crescendo'). The French, I suggest, considered it 'unnatural' for a voice to go above 'natural' limits by whatever means, whether by 'forcing' (straining, pushing, shouting) – as

---

[63] Meude-Monpas, *Dictionnaire*, 76.

[64] *Encyclopédie méthodique: Musique*, ed. Framery and Ginguené, 315 ('Contralto').

[65] Zaslaw, 'The Enigma', 939. Johann Gottfried Walther, *Musicalisches Lexicon* (Leipzig, 1732), '*Falset*-Stimme, *Falsetto*', 239: '*Bey erwachsenen Sängern, wenn sie an statt ihrer ordentlichen* Bass- *oder* Tenor-Stimme, *durch Zusammenzwingen und Dringen des Halses, den Alt oder Discant singen. Man nennet es auch deswegen eine unnatürliche Stimme*' ('Of adult male singers, when instead of their normal bass or tenor voices they sing alto or soprano by constraining and forcing the throat. It is also called an unnatural voice for that reason').

some of their own singers clearly did on occasion – or in the mellifluous fashion favoured by the Italians.

In fact, it was the very avoidance of falsetto in French singing that gave rise to these problems:

> With the French ... it is not customary: because of which their singing in the high register often turns into disagreeable shouting ...
>
> *Bey den Franzosen ... ist es nicht üblich: weswegen sich dieser ihr Singen, in den hohen Tönen, öfters in ein unangenehmes Schreyen verwandelt ...*
>
> (Quantz, 1752)[66]

Not until near the end of the century do we find unmistakable signs that the French tradition had begun to bow to the inevitable. In a brief note at the end of Framery's article on 'Fausset' (1791), his colleague Jean-Louis Castilhon adds:

> Note that by dint of practice one can succeed in singing four or even five falsetto notes without the listener's perceiving any change of voice, an advantage which is not to be scorned.
>
> *Remarquez qu'à force d'exercise on peut parvenir à chanter quatre, & même cinq tons du fausset, sans que l'auditeur s'aperçoive du changement de voix, avantage qui n'est pas à mépriser.*[67]

Yet, from the perspective of an Italian singing teacher based in Paris, there was still some way to go. Florido Tomeoni (1799) writes:

> The *haute-contre* voice does not extend at all into the low register; but in compensation it reaches up to the fourth *B* on the keyboard [i.e. *b'*]: its partisans claim that the top register is always produced in the chest; but in reality it is produced in the throat and is always more or less nasal. In Italy voices of this sort are excluded from the theatres and banished from concerts: they are admitted only into the cathedrals, to which they have been relegated by good taste and the natural principles of music. But in France, where another path altogether is followed, they are on the contrary cherished voices. They are admitted on to the stage, they are sought out in concerts; indeed, they occupy the first rank there, which more justly would be accorded the tenor voice.
>
> *La voix de haute-contre n'a point d'étendue dans les sons bas; mais en revanche elle monte jusqu'au quatrième si du clavier: ses partisans prétendent que les sons les plus élevés se forment toujours de la*

---

[66] Quantz, *Versuch*, 47.
[67] *Encyclopédie méthodique: Musique*, ed. Framery and Ginguené, 550 ('Fausset').

poitrine; mais ils se forment réellement dans le gosier, et sont toujours plus ou moins nasillards. En Italie ces sortes de voix sont exclues des théâtres et bannies des concerts: elles ne sont admises que dans les cathédrales, où les ont reléguées le bon goût et les principes naturels de la musique. Mais en France, où l'on suit encore une toute autre marche, ce sont au contraire les voix chéries. On les admet sur les Théatres, on les recherche dans les concerts; elles y occupent enfin le premier rang, que l'on accorderait avec plus de justice à la voix de ténor.[68]

In Tomeoni's eyes the (Italianate) tenor was altogether superior:

> The tenor voice is the widest in range, and one wouldn't know how to fix limits for it: it is as pleasant in the low register as in the high one, where it employs falsetto ... In France it is scarcely made use of in choirs; it seems to be admitted into them only out of pity: for the sake of good taste one hopes that its fate may change soon and that it may not be proscribed and misunderstood any longer.
>
> *La voix de ténor est la plus étendue, et on ne saurait pas en fixer les bornes: elle est aussi agréable dans les sons bas que dans les sons les plus hauts, où elle emploie le* fausset *... En France à peine s'en sert-on dans les chœurs; elle n'y semble admise que par commisération: il est à désirer pour le bon goût que son sort change bientôt, et qu'elle ne soit pas plus long-tems proscrite et méconnue.*[69]

If I am correct, the 18th century's first mention of falsetto in reference to any of the principal solo voice-types in France – haute-contre included – occurs (with Castilhon) around the time of the Revolution, some four decades on from Rameau's operatic heyday and more than a century after the death of Lully.

A very different view has been put forward by René Jacobs (1983): 'The haute-contre didn't use falsetto occasionally at the top of his range, but at the top of his range *whenever* he wanted to use this colour in service of the particular expressive need of the music at the moment' [my italics].[70] This may or may not hold true in the case of the early 19th-century haute-contre,[71] but if Jacobs's statement is intended to apply to the voice in Rameau's day, yet alone Lully's, it must surely be regarded as entirely fanciful.

---

[68] Florido Tomeoni, *Théorie de la musique vocale* (Paris, 1799), 56–7.

[69] Tomeoni, *Théorie*, 57.

[70] Jacobs, 'The Controversy', 296.

[71] 'The haute-contre gradually fell out of use and practice, and the term came to connote an unusual extension of the tenor range'; Cyr, 'Haute-contre Roles', 293. Cf. Zaslaw, 'The Enigma', 940–1.

FALSETTISTS

ONE further issue remains: would 18th-century France have recognized today's countertenor – whether one of the current 'army of falsettists'[72] or one who draws liberally on chest voice as well as falsetto (as Jacobs advocates)? If so, what name did the voice carry, what music did it sing and how was it regarded?

Most of what has been said above is concerned with solo singing. Choral practice is less well documented, but the broad definition of any voice-type may generally be assumed to apply in both contexts. With choral singing, however, the 'defect' of switching registers is more easily disguised, particularly in the case of an inner part and especially within a large chorus. It is also true that, following the dictates of good part-writing and chordal spacing, a choral alto line may frequently inhabit a higher tessitura than the corresponding solo writing. In such circumstances it is therefore entirely possible that a choral *haute-contre* singer might commonly have felt at liberty to shift into falsetto (head voice or otherwise) for high-lying passages. Although this is, of course, entirely conjectural, it is interesting to learn (from Lalande, 2/1787) that comparable expedients were not unknown:

> we have many [castratos] in Paris among the female singers of the choirs; they are often put in unison with the *hautes-contre*, but they are never made to sing solo.
>
> *nous ... avons beaucoup [de castrats] à Paris parmi les chanteuses des choeurs; on les met souvent à l'unisson des hautes-contre, mais on ne les fait jamais chanter seules.*[73]

These choral castratos, then, who were classed with the '*chanteuses*' as *dessus* and *bas-dessus*, may 'often' have been reassigned to *haute-contre* parts, especially perhaps when these parts lay uncomfortably high for the *hautes-contre* themselves.

One further category of choral singer has not yet been mentioned:

> In the reigns of Louis XIV and XV, some persons who sang falsetto were sometimes added to them [the Italian castratos], but very few. Moreover, it is very bad practice, and the Italians are better value because the falsettists' voices are neither as pleasant nor as durable as theirs.
>
> *Soux le regne de louis 14, et celuy de louis 15, on leur [= aux italiens] a adjoints quelques fois des personnes qui chantoyent le fausset mais tres peu. D'ailleurs, cela est un tres mauvais usage et les italiens*

---

[72] Jacobs, 'The Controversy', 305.
[73] Lalande, *Voyage*, 447.

vallent mieux parce que les voix des faussets ne sont ny si agreables ny si durables que les leurs.

Thus Marc-François Bêche (*c.* 1770), sketching the musical history of the French royal chapel, where he had long sung as an *haute-contre*.[74] (We may note in passing that he makes no mention of these court falsettists' ever having been 'put in unison' with himself and his fellow *hautes-contre*, in the way Lalande describes.) Over the near-century 'from 1674 up to the present', these occasional falsettists at the chapel had numbered 'at most seven or eight' (Bêche tells us),[75] though at the time of the 1702 *Etat de France* the *dessus* section included three of them, alongside six castratos ('*italiens*').[76] (A similar mix appears also to have been adopted on occasion for mid-century stage productions at court.)[77]

The chorus of the *Concert spirituel* in Paris perhaps represented something of a special case in the 1750s and 60s. In sharp contrast to the Opéra, where choral (and solo) *dessus* parts were entrusted 'almost entirely to women',[78] it was apparently falsettists who predominated: *premier* and *second dessus* in 1751, for example, comprised respectively four men and two women, and four men and three women. Subsequently, though, the ratios became reversed, and by 1778 the number of adult male *dessus* (now listed explicitly as '*fauçets*') had dwindled to three (as against eight women).[79] Whether these falsettists are likely ever to have been 'put in unison with the *hautes-contre*', as their castrato colleagues sometimes were (see above), is once again a moot point, but in the *Encyclopédie méthodique* (1791) Framery makes this intriguing remark:

> Men who sing falsetto partake of both types of voice [i.e. 'the French *haute-contre* and the Italians' *contralto*'] and can serve as liaison between [them].
>
> *Les hommes qui chantent le fausset, participent aux deux espèces de voix, & peuvent servir de liaison entre la haute-contre françoise & le contralto des Italiens.*[80]

---

[74] Lionel Sawkins, 'The Brothers Bêche: An Anecdotal History of Court Music', *Recherches sur la Musique française classique* 24 (1986), 219 [original, 106].

[75] '... *depuis 1674 jusqu'à ce moment ... tout au plus le nombre de sept ou huit fauçets*'; Sawkins, 'The Brothers Bêche', 32.

[76] Lionel Sawkins, 'For and Against the Order of Nature: Who Sang the Soprano?', *Early Music* 15/3 (1987), 318.

[77] Sawkins, 'For and Against', 318.

[78] Sawkins, 'For and Against, 322. Before the early 1720s there was also 'a small number of male sopranos, presumably falsettists', according to Lois Rosow, 'Performing a Choral Dialogue by Lully', *Early Music* 15/3 (1987), 327.

[79] Zaslaw, 'The Enigma', 940; and Sawkins, 'For and Against', 324 n. 50.

[80] *Encyclopédie méthodique: Musique*, ed. Framery and Ginguené, 316 ('Contralto').

Just how this 'liaison' was supposed to function is unfortunately not made clear, though elsewhere the same author tells us a little more:

> The adult male falsetto voice does not resemble a woman's voice precisely. It is rounder [and] fuller and is closer to that of the castratos who sing *second dessus*. It also has an extremely limited range, being unable to go up very high and merging with the tenor voice at the low end. Falsettists ordinarily sing the contralto part.
>
> *La voix de fausset des hommes ne ressemble pas précisément à la voix d'une femme. Elle est plus ronde, plus nourrie, & s'approche davantage de celle des Castrats, qui chantent le second dessus. Elle a aussi fort peu d'étendue, ne pouvant s'élever très-haut, & se réunissant dans le grave à la voix de Ténor. Les faussets chantent ordinairement la partie de contralto.*[81]

If the 'voix de fausset des hommes' is thus taken to be one that does not confine itself to the use of falsetto – thereby satisfying Jacobs's criteria for a 'voce mezzana' (see above) – we must also acknowledge that what is being described has nothing whatsoever to do with the *haute-contre*: not only does Framery liken this 'fausset' voice to the sound of 'castratos who sing *second dessus*', he also assigns the voice to the 'contralto part' (as opposed to *haute-contre*) – which, as we have seen at the outset, equates in range with *second dessus*. Moreover, the 18th-century French falsettist seems to have had little or no place as a solo singer.

In practice, neither falsettist nor castrato seems to have appealed much to French taste. With evident relief the *Mercure de France* (April 1765) describes the voice of an eminent *taille* (Richer) as 'without the sharp-edged quality of falsetto, without the sterility of voices conserved against the order of nature'.[82] Even a century earlier, opinions on falsetto singing had been divided, as Bénigne de Bacilly (1668) makes clear:

> Those who have a natural voice despise falsetto voices for being out of tune and strident; and the latter hold that the essence of a song is much more apparent with a brilliant voice, such as those of falsetto singers, than with a natural *taille* voice, which ordinarily does not have so much brilliance, even though it may have better intonation.
>
> *Ceux qui ont la Voix naturelle, méprisent les Voix de Fausset, comme fausses & glapissantes; & ceux cy tiennent que le fin du Chant paroist bien plus dans une Voix éclatante, telle que l'ont ceux qui chantent*

---

[81] *Encyclopédie méthodique: Musique*, ed. Framery and Ginguené, 550 ('Fausset').

[82] '... *sans l'aigreur du fausset, sans l'aridité des voix conservées contre l'ordre de la nature*'; *Mercure de France* ii (April 1765), 70.

en Fausset, que dans une Voix de Taille naturelle, qui pour l'ordinaire n'a pas tant d'éclat, bien qu'elle ait plus de justesse.[83]

Rousseau was certainly no admirer of the falsetto voice. Although he considered 'Fausset' a topic meriting inclusion in his *Dictionnaire de musique* (1768),[84] he pointedly fails to ascribe to the voice any role in the music-making of his own time:

> In vocal music the *dessus* is performed by women's and children's voices and also by castratos ...
>
> Dans la Musique vocale, le Dessus s'exécute par des voix de femmes, d'enfans, & encore par des Castrati ...[85]

The *Concert spirituel*'s falsettist sopranos had not escaped his attention, however. Expressing an unabashed preference for the female voice, Rousseau (under 'Voix') compares the different species of high voice, last amongst them the falsetto:

> ... and as for falsetto, it is the most disagreeable of all the colours of the human voice: to concur with this it suffices to hear the choruses of the *Concert spirituel* in Paris and to compare the *dessus* with those of the Opéra.
>
> ... & pour le Faucet, c'est le plus désagréable de tous les Tymbres de la Voix humaine: il suffit, pour en convenir, d'écouter à Paris les Chœurs du Concert Spirituel, & d'en comparer les Dessus avec ceux de l'Opéra.[86]

---

[83] Bénigne de Bacilly, *L'Art de bien chanter* (Paris, 1668), 35–6.

[84] Rousseau, *Dictionnaire*, 219 ('Fausset'): 'C'est cette espèce de voix par laquelle un homme, sortant à l'aigu du Diapason de sa voix naturelle, imite celle de la femme'. ('It is that species of voice by means of which a man, going out of his natural voice at the top of his compass, imitates a woman's'.)

[85] Rousseau, *Dictionnaire*, 143 ('Dessus'); cf. 368 ('Partie').

[86] Rousseau, *Dictionnaire*, 543 ('Voix').

FALSETTISTS sang *dessus*, and *hautes-contre* were not falsettists – this much is not really in dispute. But because the word we most often use for the falsettist is 'countertenor', and because this word doubles as the correct historical equivalent of '*haute-contre*', these two quite distinct voice-types have tended to become linked (and frequently confused) with each other.

René Jacobs treats the two as a single family of alto voices, albeit a heterogeneous one in which there are 'high' and 'low' types. This he is able to do by arguing that all – in England, France, Germany and Italy alike and from at least the 16th century – cultivated two overlapping registers, chest and falsetto, and employed them extensively.[87] This in turn sustains the notion of a 'real/true countertenor'[88] (neither today's high tenor nor a mere falsettist) and brings within reach a multiplicity of repertories – not least that of yet another voice-type, the operatic castrato.

This line of thinking leads Jacobs to some generalized conclusions which flatly contradict some of the historical evidence reviewed above:

Jacobs: A good alto voice is never a one-register voice.[89]

Quantz: Uniting chest voice with falsetto is … unknown … to the French.

Jacobs: What we have lost is the ideal of the alto as a *hermaphrodite* voice.[90]

Lalande: [The French delight] in voices that are natural, male, brilliant and that have all their strength …

Ironically, a rare point of convergence occurs when Jacobs objects that *haute-contre* parts are 'too high for modern tenors':

Jacobs: Today … *haute-contre* parts are sung by tenors who often force their voices in the high notes …[91]

Framery: Several [*hautes-contre*], in order to reach the top notes, are obliged to force their natural means …

An aura of mystery has long surrounded the *haute-contre*, and the documented shortcomings of some singers – beginning only in the middle of the 18th century, in the fading years of the Baroque – have also tended to obscure our view of French vocal ideals. But what is abundantly clear is that, while the exploitation and unification of falsetto and head registers

---

[87] Jacobs, 'The Controversy', 289.
[88] 'The loss of real countertenors … of true *voce mezzane* [sic], as Zacconi calls them, is a disaster'; Jacobs, 'The Controversy', 305.
[89] Jacobs, 'The Controversy', 306.
[90] Jacobs, 'The Controversy', 306.
[91] Jacobs, 'The Controversy', 288.

is correctly regarded as 'a basic principle of *bel canto* for every voice-type'[92] in 18th-century Italy, the French manifestly followed 'another path altogether'.[93]

---

[92] Jacobs, 'The Controversy', 289.

[93] As this article goes to press, my attention has been drawn to a passage in the anonymous *Lettre sur le méchanisme de l'opéra italien* (Naples/Paris, 1756), where the author – probably the francophile Count Giacomo Durazzo – confirms some of the points raised above: '*dans ces six ou sept voix, on n'y souffre au plus qu'une Taille; & si belle qu'elle soit, c'est toujours la voix qui y brille le moins, rapport à la nature de la Musique Italienne, si l'on en excepte cependant quelques-unes de ces voix rares comme Babbi, Amorevoli, Raaff, &c. qu'une extrême agilité a rendus célèbres, & qui font communément plus d'usage du Fausset, que de la voix naturelle. On n'y entend point de Haute-contres; le climat apparemment n'en produit point. Les Italiens ont bien la Haute-contre; mais c'est ce que nous appellons* Bas-dessus'; pp. 30–1. (The Italians 'can bear no more than just one of these six or seven voices [in operas] to be a *taille*; and, however beautiful it may be, this is always the voice that shines the least (in keeping with the nature of Italian music) – with the exception, however, of some of those rare voices such as Babbi, Amorevoli, Raaff [who had studied with Bernacchi in Bologna] etc., [voices] which extreme agilty has made famous and which commonly make more use of falsetto than of the natural voice. *Hautes-contre* are not heard there at all; apparently the climate produces none. The Italians do have the *haute-contre*, but it is what we call *bas-dessus*.')

5
Transposition in Monteverdi's Vespers of 1610

OURS is an essentially conservative musical climate, and attempts to reproduce historical styles of performance still tend to be viewed with suspicion. It is therefore not surprising that to transpose parts of a recognized masterpiece should be regarded by some almost as an act of heresy. I first directed a performance of Monteverdi's 1610 Vespers in 1977, and on that occasion,[1] as on subsequent ones, the psalm *Lauda Jerusalem* and the Magnificat *a7* were given a 4th below their written pitch. (The discussion that follows is quite independent of absolute pitch standards appropriate to Monteverdi's music: the issue is that of the relative pitch levels of the various Vespers movements.) Reactions to the idea of the transpositions have been predictably mixed: one of our best-known Monteverdi conductors has described them as an 'aberration',[2] while others find the results revelatory. But if the very familiarity of the work makes objective assessment difficult, it has also the advantage of focusing attention on a vital but neglected area of historical performance practice, one of direct relevance to a host of less well-known pieces. With the release of my recording of the 1610 Vespers,[3] the time is obviously ripe for a detailed defence of the practice.

Monteverdi has had the misfortune to be labelled a Baroque composer and a Venetian composer, despite the facts that he published six collections before the 17th century even began and that he worked in Mantua until he was 45. Consequently his music has often been viewed in a false light. Instrumental writing of the kind illustrated in Ex. 5.1 would perhaps have seemed unexceptional in its technical demands to a musician of the early 18th century; in 1610 it would undoubtedly have seemed

First appeared in *Early Music* 12/4 (1984), 490–516.

[1] A BBC Promenade Concert, July 1977. The performers were the Taverner Choir and Players with various soloists. I am indebted to Hugh Keyte for instigating the performance and for his encouragement and advice at all stages. I am also grateful to many other colleagues, especially Clifford Bartlett, Bruce Dickey and Graham Dixon, for their assistance.

[2] John Eliot Gardiner, programme notes for performances in 1984 of the 1610 Vespers. In an interview for BBC Radio 3 (July 1984), Gardiner put forward his objections to the transpositions. First, 'such an academic formula seems to me foreign to his [Monteverdi's] nature'. Second, 'it would involve using a lower cornetto'. Third, 'I just think it sounds dull and wrong'.

[3] EMI Reflexe (1984), later Virgin Veritas.

Ex. 5.1 Monteverdi, *Vespers* (1610), Magnificat *a7*, 'Deposuit'; (a) Cornett I, and (b) Violin I

Ex. 5.2 High and normal clef-configurations

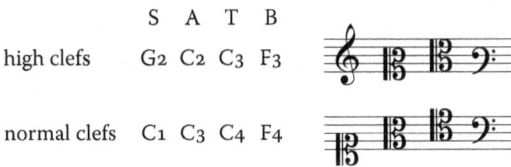

revolutionary in its high tessitura. And there lies the crux of the matter. Do the high vocal and instrumental ranges of the Magnificat *a7* serve a new dramatic function through an (as it were) Beethovenian stretching of existing conventions? Or is this all an illusion, caused by a trick of notation that would have ruffled none of Monteverdi's contemporaries?

Lauda Jerusalem and the Magnificat *a7* lie consistently at a higher written pitch level than the other Vespers movements, a fact which is reflected in (or caused by) the choice of a different set of clefs. These high clefs and what I shall call normal clefs are shown in Ex. 5.2. (The anachronistic terms *chiavette* and *chiavi naturali* need not be used.)[4] There are variants of both sets of clefs, but the configuration in use may generally be identified quite easily from the clef of the lowest part: normal clefs have the bass clef (F4), while high clefs have a baritone, tenor or even alto clef (F3 [=C5], C4 or C3). The presence or absence of a key signature with a particular clef or set of clefs can affect the implications for transposition and will be indicated in subsequent examples by (♭) or (–) after each clef.

In his 1610 publication Monteverdi uses high clefs not only for these two movements but also for the alternative Magnificat *a6*, and for the whole of the six-part Mass *In illo tempore* which takes pride of place in the collection.[5] Again we must ask whether the clefs simply reflect the composer's decision to write in a higher tessitura than elsewhere (perhaps

---

[4] The terms seem to derive from Giuseppe Paolucci, *Arte pratica di contrappunto* (Venice, 1765–72); see Siegfried Hermelink, 'Chiavette', in *The New Grove Dictionary of Music and Musicians*, ed. S. Sadie (1980).

[5] Claudio Monteverdi, *Sanctissimae virgini missa senis vocibus ad ecclesiarum choros ac vespere pluribus decantandae, cum nonnullis sacris concentibus,*

in response to the texts) or whether the use of such clefs is the result of certain theoretical conventions which, though of little consequence to the singer, acted as a clearly understood signal to the instrumentalist to transpose. Although an understanding of these general questions is fundamental to the performance of Renaissance polyphony, there has been very little serious research of practical value since the late 1940s, when Arthur Mendel published his findings.[6] Performers for the most part have been seemingly oblivious to the problems, and editors have perpetuated this state of affairs by failing to offer transposed editions of high-clef works, perhaps because of a horror of offending established scholarly principles.

In this article I shall try to show that 'obligatory transposition' is implicit in the notation of much vocal music of the late 16th and early 17th centuries and that some of Monteverdi's music (notably *Lauda Jerusalem* and the Magnificat *a7*) requires it. I shall suggest that downward transposition of a 4th brings those Vespers movements into line with what is known both of contemporary vocal types and of instrumental technique, and I shall therefore need to demonstrate that instrumentalists were equipped to transpose. Finally, I shall speculate briefly on Monteverdi's reasons for choosing to notate certain pieces at what is, to us, the 'wrong' pitch. But before looking in any detail at Monteverdi's works, the considerable evidence for conventions of transposition during the composer's lifetime (1567–1643) must be examined. I shall concentrate on Italian and German sources; the latter (in particular the writings of Michael Praetorius) are often concerned with Italian practices and are therefore an invaluable supplement. These sources fall broadly into three categories: theoretical writings, keyboard instruments and musical sources.

THEORETICAL WRITINGS

In his *Dimostrationi harmoniche* (1571) the Venetian composer and theorist Zarlino considers the possible written transposition of each of his 12 modes either up or down an octave, or ↑4th or ↓5th; that is, to just one alternative level, if we exclude octave transpositions. Almost in parenthesis he comments:

> We organists know how useful these transpositions are, and how they can be made ...

---

ad sacella sive principum cubicula accommodate (Venice, 1610) (title from *Bassus generalis*; the other seven partbooks omit 'ad ecclesiarum choros').

[6] Alexander J. Ellis and Arthur Mendel, *Studies in the History of Musical Pitch* (1968); Mendel's contribution consists largely of reprints of his invaluable 'Pitch in the 16th and Early 17th Centuries', *The Musical Quarterly* 34/1–4 (1948), 28–45, 199–221, 336–57, 575–93. His later 'Pitch in Western Music since 1500: A Re-examination', *Acta musicologica* 50/1–2 (1978), 1–93, covers much of the same ground but often in less detail; all references to Mendel are therefore to his earlier work and give the pagination of the 1968 reprint.

Noi altri Organisti lo sapiamo, quanto sia di utile queste trasportationi: & come si possino fare ...[7]

For a player fluent in all the clefs, transposition ↓5th is a simple matter of substituting one clef for another and of adjusting the signature;[8] an organist playing from a high-clef bass line written in C4 would, for example, imagine an F4 clef (plus ♭) in its place (Ex. 5.3):

Ex. 5.3

$$= c' \text{ or } f$$

The organist's concept of transposition as the alteration of written pitches by a particular interval was not shared by the singer of the 16th and 17th centuries, for whom written notes represented not fixed pitches but a series of intervallic relationships. The position of the clef and the presence or absence of a flat dictated where the semitones occurred among the tones and hence the appropriate solmization. Cerone (1613) gives a table of those clefs that are equivalent in terms of solmization (Ex. 5.4) and comments:

> We may conclude, then, that some clefs [including their signatures] look exactly alike in everything that concerns reading and the placing of the mutations; they differ solely in the letters and positions [i.e. pitch-names]; this difference (as I said) is of no concern to the singer, who is concerned only to sound his notes correctly, observing the intervals of tones and semitones.
>
> *Concluyremos pues que algunas Claves, puntualmente se parecen, en todo lo que toca al leer, y al hazer de las Mutanças; mas diffieren solamente en las letras y posiciones; la qual differença (como dixe) no es de consideracion à cerca del Cantante; el qual no considera otra cosa mas, que entonar sus vozes rectamente, con la observacion de los intervalos de Tono y Semitono.*[9]

Ex. 5.4 Clef equivalences, from Cerone, *El melopeo y maestro* (Naples, 1613), 494

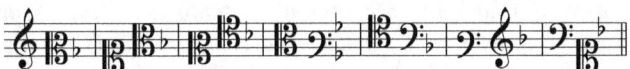

Thus, if an organist chooses to accompany voices at a pitch other than the written one, he is involved in a transposition, but the singers are not. (For convenience, the term 'transposition' is used in this article for vocal and

---

[7] Gioseffo Zarlino, *Dimostrationi harmoniche* (Venice, 1571), 309 and 311.

[8] Michael Praetorius describes this procedure for enabling a tenor trombonist to read correctly when playing bass trombone; *Syntagma musicum* ii (Wolfenbüttel, 1618), 31.

[9] Pietro Cerone, *El melopeo y maestro* (Naples, 1613), 494.

instrumental music alike, but this distinction in procedure should always be understood.) This should not beguile us into thinking of the singer as someone unconcerned with pitch level: as we shall see, several theorists are quite explicit in saying that the organist's transpositions are made precisely to suit the voices.

The surprisingly wide range of intervals of transposition cultivated by organists in particular may misleadingly give the impression of complete flexibility. It is important, rather, to think of these transpositions as being in two separate categories which sometimes overlap: first, the larger intervals of transposition (of a 4th or 5th) necessary to reconcile most high-clef music with normal vocal ranges; second, those fine adjustments (generally of a tone) that take into account the tessitura of a particular work or the pitch of a particular organ. Our main interest here is with the first category. (Transposition of a minor 3rd may have been considered a combination of the two categories – a primary transposition of a 4th, modified by a tone – while in some contexts transposition of a 4th consists of a primary transposition of a 5th, adjusted by a tone.)

This division seems to be acknowledged by Diruta (1609), who devotes a chapter of his keyboard treatise, *Il transilvano*, to 'the true formation, recognition and transposition of all the Tones, whether of polyphony or of chant: a matter concerning every organist when he is giving the pitch to the choir' (*la vera formatione, cognitione, e transportatione di tutti i Tuoni, si del Canto figurato, come anco del Canto fermo: Cosa appartenente ad ogni Organista per lasciare in Tuono al Choro*).[10] After illustrating the Tones and their transpositions a 4th higher or 5th lower, he writes:

> it is necessary to understand another sort of transposition in order to be able to respond to the choir at a convenient pitch level, whether in polyphony or in chant. And because the majority of organs are high and not at choir pitch, the organist needs to become accustomed to playing outside [the usual keys], a tone and a 3rd lower.
>
> *vi è necessario intendere un'altra sorte di trasportationi per poter rispondere al Choro in voce commoda, tanto nel Canto figurato, quanto nel Canto fermo. E perche la maggior parte de gl'Organi sono alti, fuora del Tuono Choristo, bisogna che l'Organista si accommodi à sonare fuor di strada, un Tuono, & una Terza bassa.*[11]

Diruta then gives short, two-voice musical examples in the 12 modes, each with one, two or three transpositions '*per commodità del Choro*': except in the case of Tone 2, all the transpositions are downwards, and, predictably, transposition ↓2nd or a (minor) 3rd is common. In Tones 5, 7, 9 and 12,

---

[10] Girolamo Diruta, *Seconda parte del transilvano* (Venice, 1609), bk 3, 1.

[11] Diruta, *Seconda parte del transilvano*, bk 3, 4.

where G2 clefs are used for the upper parts, the intervals of transposition are wider (↓4th, 5th and, once, a minor 7th).[12]

Such transpositions were by no means new.[13] Galilei (1581) mentions in passing that 'skilled organists' (*i periti Organisti*) are accustomed to transpose 'for the convenience of the chorus, by a tone, a 3rd or some other interval' (*per comodità del coro per un Tuono, ò per una Terza, ò per altro intervallo*).[14] But the full range of transpositions was not possible on instruments tuned in meantone temperaments. G. P. Cima (1606) recognized and attempted to solve the problem by giving directions for the wholesale retuning of accidentals for each semitonal transposition. (Although he is addressing organists, his rules are for the tuning of '*un Clavicordo*'.)

> Recognizing as I do how important it is for organists to know how to play at any pitch level and interval on our instrument for the convenience of singers in their *concerti*, it seemed to me laudable to make known a means by which one may easily put this into practice ... That this practice is necessary is shown clearly in book 4, chapter 17 of the famous Zarlino's *Istitutioni harmoniche*.
>
> *Conoscendo io di quanta importanza sia à gli Organisti, per commodità de Cantori ne i concerti loro, il saper sonare in qual si voglia luogo, & intervallo del nostro Instrumento; m'è parso lodevol cosa dare in luce il modo; con che si possa agevolmente far questa prattica ... Et che questa pratica sia necessaria, lo mostra chiaro il famoso Zerlino nel quarto libro delle sue Institutioni armoniche al capitolo 17.*[15]

Even if Cima's recommended procedure is impracticable for organs – and no other musician or theorist of the Baroque is known to have described it – he does unequivocally expect organists to be able to play in the remoter keys.

---

[12] Diruta treats the eight Magnificat Tones similarly; *Seconda parte del transilvano*, bk 4, 7–16.

[13] Juan Bermudo, *El libro llamado declaración de instrumentos musicales* (Osuna, 1555), fols. 73v–74r (bk 4, ch. 26), gives instructions for playing the modes ↑2nd, ↑4th and ↑5th, and ↓2nd and a minor 3rd. Later, Thomas Morley writes that certain transpositions were often required for ease of the singers (*A Plaine and Easie Introduction to Practicall Musicke* (London, 1597), 156). Jean Denis, *Traité de l'accord de l'espinette* (Paris, 2/1650), 19, tells how his teacher, the organist of the Ste-Chappelle in Paris, Florent le Bienvenu (1568–1623), would play the Magnificat chant in one key '*pour la commodite des Chantres*', but his solo verses in another, avoiding 'bad' keys.

[14] Vincenzo Galilei, *Dialogo della musica antica et della moderna* (Florence, 1581), 87.

[15] Gian Paulo Cima, *Partito de ricercari & canzoni alla francese* (Milan, 1606), 73.

Each untransposed Tone and its prescribed transposition admitted of a few specific accidentals only. In the *Intonationi d'organo* (1593) by Andrea and Giovanni Gabrieli,[16] there are therefore just six different accidentals altogether: B natural, the flats on B and E and the sharps on F, C and G. Certain transpositions, though, inevitably introduced further, unfamiliar 'accidentals' such as A flat and D sharp. The occasional written appearance of these new keys in vocal polyphony had already drawn adverse comment from Zarlino (1558)[17] and Galilei (1581),[18] though Rodio (1609)[19] explains how singers can simplify the solmization process by substituting high for normal clefs and vice versa. Cerone (1613) summarizes the position as follows:

> These [extraordinary accidentals], though, are used more by organists to suit the choir better than by composers in composing their works, because of the difficulty singers have when they see so many flats and so many naturals or sharps and have to sing on unfamiliar staff-degrees; ... all the [species] that are notated with a single B flat, or with its octave, are the accidental ones most used by composers. I say most used by composers, because all [the above transpositions] are practised and used equally easily by excellent organists: that is, now one and now another according to the high or low pitch of the organ, always using the one that best suits the choir.
>
> *Los quales [accidentals extraordinarios], aunque son mas usados de los Organistas para accomodarse mejor con el Choro, que de los Compositores para componer sus obras, por la dificultad que tienen los Cantores de ver tantos Be moles, y tantos Be quadrados ò Sostenidos, y de cantar fuera de las cuerdas ordinarias; ... todas las [Sequencias] que apuntadas estan con esta b señal en una sola posicion de befabemi, ò con su Octava, son las accidentales mas usadas de los Compositores. Digo mas usadas de los Compositores, porquanto de los eccelentes Organistas todas indifferentemente son praticadas y usadas: es asaver, quando uno y quando otro, y esto segun el Tono alto ò baxo del Organo, usando siempre de aquel que sale mas comodo para el Choro.*[20]

---

[16] Andrea and Giovanni Gabrieli, *Intonationi d'organo* i (Venice, 1593).

[17] Zarlino, *Le istitutioni harmoniche* (Venice, 1558), 319–20.

[18] Galilei, *Dialogo*, 87.

[19] Rocco Rodio, *Regole di musica* (Naples, 1609), 86–8 (this edition also bears the date 1611 on its final page). The section in question, headed '*Come per musica finta si ponno fare gl'istessi tuoni in altri luoghi*', is an addition to the original publication of 1600. See Mendel, *Musical Pitch*, 153–4, who takes Rodio as providing evidence against the principle of the downward transposition of high-clef music; in fact, the subject is not mentioned.

[20] Cerone, *El melopeo*, 922 and 925.

Clearly there was resistance to the use of complicated keys in vocal notation. In Agazzari's essay on continuo playing (1607) we may also detect a reaction against the remoter unwritten transpositions sometimes practised:

> Finally, one must know how to transpose pieces from one degree to another so that all the consonances are correct, and proper to the given Tone. Otherwise one must not transpose, because, as I have sometimes observed, it makes a very disagreeable sound[, for example,] to transpose a first or second Tone, naturally pleasing because of its many B flats, to some degree whose Tone requires B natural; it will be difficult [even] for the careful player to avoid stumbling against some conflicting note. And thus the ensemble is spoiled and the listeners are offended with such crudity, while the natural character of the given Tone never appears. Most natural and convenient of all is transposition by a 4th or 5th, and sometimes a note higher or lower; in short, one must see which is most appropriate and suitable to the given Tone, not as some do who pretend to play every Tone at every level, for if I could argue at length, I would show them their impropriety and error.

> *Finalmente conviene saper anco trasportare le Cantilene da un tasto ad un 'altro, quando però vi sono tutte le consonanze naturali, e proprie di quel tono; perche altrimenti non si debbon trasportare, perche fa brutissimo sentire, come io alle volte ho osservato, che trasportando un primo, over secondo tono, che sono di natura soave, per le molte corde di B. molle, in qualche tasto, ch'l suo tuono sia di B. quadro, difficilmente potrà, chi suona, esser tanto cauto, che non inciampi in qualche contraria voce; e così vien à guastarsi il conserto, et offender l'udito de gl'ascoltanti con tal crudezza; anzi mai mostra la naturalezza di quel tuono. Trasportar alla quarta, ò quinta, è più naturale, e commodo di tutti: e tal volta una voce più giù, ò più sù; ed in somma convien veder quel più proprio e conferente à quel tuono: e non come fanno alcuni, che pretendono suonar ogni tuono in ogni corda; perche s'io potessi disputar alla lunga, gli mostrarei l'impropietà* [sic], *ed error loro.*[21]

We should note here the emphasis given to the 'basic' intervals of transposition: a 4th, 5th and tone.

If none of these Italian theorists unequivocally associates downward transposition with high-clef music, there may be good reason. First, as I have shown, the concept of transposition did not exist for the singer, and thus the theoretical writing on singing does not touch on the subject. Second, organists themselves may perhaps have scarcely regarded such manœuvres as transposition – they, too, thought largely in terms of

---

[21] Agostino Agazzari, *Del sonare sopra'l basso* (Siena, 1607).

solmization syllables – and in any case were so thoroughly schooled in the art of transposition for the purpose of accommodating vocal ranges that the need would have been obvious. The Italian theorists never concern themselves with explaining exactly when transpositions are necessary; they merely assert that they are necessary and advise how to make them.

It is Praetorius (1618) who, in characteristically thorough and practical fashion, clarifies the matter:

> Every vocal piece in high clefs, i.e. where the bass is written in C4 or C3, or F3, must be transposed when it is put into tablature or score for players of the organ, lute and all other foundation instruments, as follows: if it has a flat, down a 4th *in durum*, but if it has no flat, down a 5th *in mollem, naturaliter*. Yet if some modes, e.g. Mixolydian, Aeolian and Hypoionian, are transposed by a 5th, a duller and worse harmony is produced because of the lower sounds; hence it is much better, and the piece becomes much fresher and more spirited to listen to, if these modes are transposed by a 4th, *ex duro in durum*.

> *Ob zwar ein jeder Gesang/ welcher hoch* Claviret*, das ist/ da im Baß das* C *uff der ander oder dritten Lini von oben an zu zehlen/ oder das* 𝄢 *uff der dritten Lini also* [notation] *befunden wird; Wenn er* b mol*, per quartam inferiorem in durum; Wenn er aber* ♮ dur*, per quintam inferiorem in mollem, naturaliter in die* Tabulatur *oder* Partitur *von* Organisten/ Lauttenisten und allen andern/ *die sich der* Fundament Instrumenten *gebrauchen/ gebracht unnd* transponiret *werden muß: So befindet sich doch/ daß in etlichen* Modis, Als in Mixolydio, Aeolio und Hypojonico, *wenn sie* per quintam transponiret, *eine* languidior & pigrior harmonia propter graviores sonos generiret *werde: Darumb es dann ungleich besser/ und wird auch der Gesang viel frischer und anmuthiger zuhören/ wenn diese* Modi per quartam ex duro in durum transponiret *werden.*[22]

Later, in a section on organ continuo, these principles are taken almost for granted:

> But this especially must be observed and taken note of here: that in those songs which, [being] in Mixolydian, Aeolian and Hypoionian modes, are to be transposed a 4th lower (because down a 5th, as shown above, may be too sleepy, and down a 4th sounds rather fresher and more pleasant, especially on harpsichords) a sharp is marked at the beginning beside the clef ...

> *Dieses aber muß sonderlich allhier* observiret *und in acht genommen werden/ daß in denen Gesängen/ welche* Mixolydij, AEolij *und* Hypojonici Modi, in quartam inferiorem *(weil es in der* Quint, *wie*

---

[22] Praetorius, *Syntagma musicum* iii (Wolfenbüttel, 1618), 80–1.

oben angezeigt/ allzuschläfferig seyn möchte/ und in der Quart *sich etwas frischer und anmutiger/ sonderlich uffn* Instrumenten *hören lest)* transponiret *werden/ forn an bey dem* Clave Signata 𝄢 *die Diesis ♯ bezeichnet ...*[23]

(We should note in passing the special importance of transposition ↓4th.) If Praetorius seems rather dogmatic, we must at least acknowledge that none of the Italian theorists contradicts him in any way.[24] A decade or so later another German theorist, Wolfgang Schonsleder (1631), gives a complete set of high clefs (G2 C2 C3 F3) and declares that he is 'amazed to see the majority of musicians customarily writing many of their songs in them, although they know that if anyone wishes to sing them they will have to be transposed downwards'.[25]

With the development of instrumental music, free of vocal models, the concept of fixed pitches began to predominate; hence in due course the problem of understanding the different notated pitch levels of earlier periods. But a tradition of performing this earlier repertory would appear to have continued through the 17th century, and, with it, the necessary skills of transposition. Penna's *Li primi albori musicali* (1672)[26] emphasizes the importance of downward transposition of a 4th and 5th in association with high-clef bass parts but also gives various transpositions for normal-clef bass parts. Similarly, Bismantova's *Compendio musicale* (1677–9) gives instructions as part of the *'Regole; p[er] suonare il Basso Continuo'*[27] for transposing ↓4th and ↓5th (although without reference to high clefs), and then proceeds to describe other transpositions too. Later, Samber (1707)[28] specifically associates the high-clef notation of 'old Introits, Graduals and Counterpoint-Masses' with downward transposition (when the lowest clef is F3, by a 4th; when C4, by a 5th). And much later still, Paolucci (1772)[29] gives examples from Palestrina, Benevoli and Colonna of high-clef music and calls for transposition ↓4th or ↓5th.

---

[23] Praetorius, *Syntagma musicum* iii, 136.

[24] Only Morley in England seems to advise against such transpositions; he thus at least implies the existence of such a practice.

[25] Volupius Decorus [= Wolfgang Schonsleder], *Architectonice musices universalis* (Ingolstadt, 1631), 66 ff.; cited in Mendel, *Musical Pitch*, 230, in an addition to his original article.

[26] Lorenzo Penna, *Li primi albori musicali* (Bologna, 5/1696), 188–96.

[27] Bartolomeo Bismantova, *Compendio musicale* (MS treatise, Ferrara, 1677–9), [84–6] ('Del suonare Spostato').

[28] Johann Baptist Samber, *Continuatio ad manuductionem organicam* (Salzburg, 1707), 143; cited in Mendel, *Musical Pitch*, 140.

[29] Paolucci, *Arte pratica* i, 184–5, 231; iii, 173–4, 215; cited in Mendel, *Musical Pitch*, 130.

KEYBOARD INSTRUMENTS

From the theoretical material we move to the second category of evidence, which though small is significant: the nature of certain 16th- and early 17th-century keyboard instruments. (For this section a brief departure from the self-imposed restrictions to Italian and German practices seems justified.)

The notion that downward transposition, in particular that of a 4th, is regularly required in the performance of late Renaissance and early Baroque music receives strong support from the disposition of the contemporary Flemish two-manual harpsichord. With a slightly patronizing air, Quirinus van Blankenburg (1739) looks back to the early 17th century:

> At that time, they were so inexperienced in transposition that in order to be able to transpose a piece a 4th downwards they made a special second keyboard in the harpsichord for the purpose. This seems incredible, but the proof, which is very remarkable, will show that the famous Ruckers family from the beginning of the last century for more than 30 years made nothing else.
>
> *In die tyd was men in de Transpositie zo onërvaren dat men om eenig spel een quart lager te konnen transponeren expres een byzonder tweede clavier in de clavicimbel maakte, Het schynt ongelooflyk, maar 't bewys't welk zeer aanmerkensweerdig is, zal 't zelve bewaar heiden, dat de vermaarde Ruckerssen van 't begin der voorlede eew af tot meer als 30 jaren daar na niet anders hebben gemaakt.*[30]

On a normal double-manual Ruckers harpsichord the shorter upper keyboard stood at 'standard' pitch and the lower one a 4th lower, with the upper c' key aligned with the lower f' and sounding the same strings. (Some earlier organs may well have had a similar disposition.)[31] Only one such harpsichord survives in its original state, the 1638 Joannes Ruckers in the Russell Collection, Edinburgh University[32] (see Illus. 5.1), but more than a dozen others by members of the Ruckers family from before 1642, plus a 1646 Joannes Couchet, show signs of having originally been transposing instruments. Furthermore, although double-manual instruments without this feature can be shown to have been in existence by 1620, the earliest surviving example, by Hans Moermans the Younger,

---

[30] Quirinus van Blankenburg, *Elementa musica* (The Hague, 1739), 142; cited in Mendel, *Musical Pitch*, 179.

[31] See Mendel, *Musical Pitch*, 170–86.

[32] *The Russell Collection and other Early Keyboard Instruments in Saint Cecilia's Hall, Edinburgh* (1968), 12–15.

Illus. 5.1 Two-manual harpsichord by Joannes Ruckers, 1638
(Russell Collection, University of Edinburgh)

dates only from 1642.[33] So though Blankenburg may not necessarily be right in regarding the principal function of these instruments to be transposition,[34] their nature clearly facilitates it. Other fragments of organological information also hint at the coexistence of two pitch standards a 4th or so apart from each other. Although much of the history of the Italian harpsichord is still rather obscure, it has been plausibly suggested that surviving instruments were built at pitches a 4th or 5th apart;[35] unfortunately the issue is complicated by the fact that strings of brass and steel imply different optimum pitch levels.[36] Clearly there was

---

[33] John Henry van der Meer, 'More about Flemish Two-Manual Harpsichords', *Keyboard Instruments: Studies in Keyboard Organology, 1500–1800*, ed. E. M. Ripin (1971), 50–2.

[34] See Richard T. Shann, 'Flemish Transposing Harpsichords: An Explanation', *Galpin Society Journal* 37 (1984), 62–71.

[35] John D. Shortridge, *Italian Harpsichord Building in the 16th and 17th Centuries* (1960), J. Barnes, 'Pitch Variations in Italian Keyboard Instruments', *Galpin Society Journal* 18 (1965), 110–16, and J. Barnes, 'The Specious Uniformity of Italian Harpsichords', in *Keyboard Instruments*, ed. Ripin, 1–10.

[36] William R. Thomas and John J. K. Rhodes, 'The String Scales of Italian Instruments', *Galpin Society Journal* 20 (1967), 48–62; and John Henry van der Meer, 'Harpsichord Making and Metallurgy: A Rejoinder', *Galpin Society Journal* 21 (1968), 175–8.

great diversity of pitch standard; but, equally clearly, there was broad understanding of how these pitches were related. Banchieri (1608), for example, in tuning an organ or 'quilled keyboard instrument' (*strumento da penna*), recommends starting with an F, 'which you set at the natural pitch of the instrument, [whether] at choir pitch or a tone lower or a 4th higher or lower' (*quella si pone in tuono della natura dell'instromento in voce corista overo un tuon più basso overo 4. superiore, o inferiore*).[37] Similarly, Praetorius describes the *spinetta* as being an octave or 5th above 'normal' pitch[38] and labels his woodcut of a harpsichord 'Harpsichord, a 4th lower than choir pitch' (*Clavicymbel, so eine Quart tieffer als Chor-Ton*).[39]

There were also some single-manual keyboard instruments that could be set at different pitch levels. A Venetian harpsichord now in Cambridge, probably 16th-century, may perhaps have had a third set of strings of a different scale from the others and possibly tuned a tone higher,[40] while a 17th-century regal in the Heyer Collection had a keyboard that could be shifted by a tone.[41] The principle of the sliding keyboard was evidently known in Germany as early as 1537,[42] and Carl Luython's *clavicymbalum universale*, which Praetorius describes,[43] had a keyboard (with 19 keys to the octave) that could be set in any of seven positions, covering a major 3rd. A little later G. B. Doni (1635)[44] mentions a harpsichord by a Florentine maker, Iacopo Ramerino, 'in which, ingeniously, just by moving the register the same strings will give you the pitch of Rome, that of Florence and that of Lombardy' (*nel quale ingegnosamente con muover solo la chiave del Registro, l'istesse corde serviranno al tuono di Roma, a quel di Firenze, & a quel di Lombardia*).

---

[37] Adriano Banchieri, *Conclusioni nel suono dell'organo* (Bologna, 1608), 94–5. Cf. the interrelationship of the different-sized instruments built by the Ruckers family; see G. G. O'Brien, 'Ioannes and Andreas Ruckers', *Early Music* 7 (1979), 453–66.

[38] Praetorius, *Syntagma musicum* ii, 62.

[39] Praetorius, *Theatrum instrumentorum* (Wolfenbüttel, 1620), pl. 6.

[40] Trevor Beckerleg, 'The Fitzwilliam Museum Harpsichord', *Italian Music at the Fitzwilliam* (Cambridge, 1976), 24–5. Beckerleg's assessment has subsequently been queried.

[41] See Georg Kinsky, *Musikhistorisches Museum von Wilhelm Heyer in Cöln: Katalog* i (Cologne, 1910), no. 310.

[42] The harpsichord by Hans Müller (Leipzig, 1537), now in the Museo degli Strumenti Musicali in Rome, has a keyboard that could be shifted by a tone. See Luisa Cervelli and John Henry van der Meer, *Conservato a Roma il più antico clavicembalo* (1967).

[43] Praetorius, *Syntagma musicum* ii, 63–6. Giovanni Valentini is known to have performed on this instrument in 1617.

[44] Giovanni Battista Doni, *Compendio del trattato de' generi e de' modi della musica* (Rome, 1635), 70.

DISCREPANCIES IN MUSICAL SOURCES

Having discussed theorists and instruments, we now turn to the third category of evidence: the musical sources. Numerous instances could be cited of works (masses and other cyclic compositions) with some movements in high and some in low clefs, producing implausibly wide vocal ranges (e.g. Palestrina's four-part *Missa de beata Virgine* (1567),[45] Le Jeune's three-section 'Aeolian' piece from his *Dodécacorde* (1598),[46] and Landi's *Il Sant'Alessio* (1634)).[47] These certainly suggest the need for transposition but do not provide conclusive proof of it, so I shall confine this discussion to examples that offer more explicit evidence.

Occasional discrepancies between keyboard intabulations and their vocal counterparts suggest a pattern of transposition consistent with Praetorius's rules. For example, a version in organ tablature of the Kyrie and Gloria from Jacob Handl's *Missa 'Adesto dolori meo'* lies a 4th lower than the original, which uses the clefs G2 G2 C2 C3 F3 (♭).[48] Printed anthologies of intabulations confirm that such transpositions are not made simply to accommodate the pitch of a particular instrument. The first section of Bernhart Schmid's 1577 collection[49] contains 20 works: 19 motets and a chanson. Of the eight originally notated in high clefs, four remain untransposed, two are put ↓5th and two ↓4th. (The two ↓5th have no signature in the original; of the two ↓4th, one has a flat, the other does not.) There are no obvious reasons for this inconsistency of approach to high-clef music. Jacob Paix's volume of six years later[50] is rather more revealing. Of 24 motets, seven in normal clefs are untransposed, while

---

[45] Giovanni Pierluigi da Palestrina, *Missarum liber secundus* [Rome, 1567], in *Le opere complete* iv, ed. R. Casimiri et al. (Rome 1939), 1–25.

[46] Claude Le Jeune, *Dodécacorde* (La Rochelle, 1598).

[47] Stefano Landi, *Il Sant' Alessio* (Rome, 1634).

[48] Wrocław, *olim* Stadtbibliothek, MS mus. CI. 1238 (presumably destroyed in World War II); and Jacobus Gallus [Handl], *Missarum V. vocum liber III* (Prague, 1580), no. 9; *Denkmäler der Tonkunst in Österreich*, 119, 30 ff. and 103 ff.

[49] Bernhart Schmid, *Zwey Bücher. Einer neuen kunstlichen Tabulatur auff Orgel und Instrument* (Strasbourg, 1577). Contents listed, with details of transposition, in Wilhelm Merian, *Der Tanz in den deutschen Tabulaturbüchern* (Leipzig, 1927). All the works are by Lassus, except for Crecquillon's chanson *Si me tenes* (RISM, 1545[14]), fol. 14, and the motet *Hierusalem luge* (RISM 1532[9]), fol. 49, by Richafort or Lupus.

[50] Jacob Paix, *Ein schön nutz unnd gebreüchlich Orgel Tabulaturbuch* (Lauingen, 1583). The index, listing transposition degrees, is reprinted in Merian, *Der Tanz*, 116. The 24 motets are mostly by Lassus and Palestrina, with one each by Josquin, Senfl and Clemens non Papa. In addition, there are three whose original I have been unable to trace: two by Paix himself (*Jubilate Domino* and *Domine quid multiplicati sunt*) and an *Ave Maria* by one 'Riccius' (perhaps Teodore Riccio). Although the transposition degree of these three

16 in high clefs are transposed ↓4th or ↓5th. (Of these, all 12 with a flat signature are ↓4th, whereas the four without are transposed ↓5th.) Only one piece with high clefs is left untransposed. It could be argued that all these intabulations are independent of their models and that any adjustments of pitch are merely examples of editorial taste. Against this must be set the very considerable number of differences of pitch level that occur not between different sources but within a single piece.

Publications for lute and voice(s) are invaluable in this respect; a vocal part may be notated in one key, while the tablature of its accompaniment implies another. (Adriaenssen's *Pratum musicum* (1584) gives intabulations of high-clef works generally ↓4th but sometimes ↓5th.)[51] The Roman publisher Simone Verovio issued several collections which offer examples of both lute and keyboard versions alongside their vocal originals. The first of these, *Diletto spirituale* (1586) contains 21 three- and four-voice

---

is known, the original clefs are not, so they are omitted from the statistics. (One is untransposed, one ↓4th and one ↓5th.)

[51] Emanuel Adriaenssen, *Pratum musicum* (Antwerp, 1584); partly edited in *Monumenta musicae belgicae* (1966). Contents listed in Howard Mayer Brown, *Instrumental Music Printed before 1600: A Bibliography* (1965), 334–7 (1584⁶). The 27 items discussed below are nos. 6–32 in Brown. Adriaenssen prints a lute intabulation and the top and bottom parts of 27 madrigals and chansons. Those which I have checked (nos. 6–8, 10–11, 14, 16, 21–2, 24–5, 27–31) retain their original clefs, so it seems likely that the others do. There are 15 with clefs C1 and F4 (i.e. normal clefs); of these, 14 have the lute part at the same pitch (assuming a lute in G tuning), and one has the lute a tone higher. (It could be argued that this is to avoid the difficulty of playing a piece in F on an instrument with a bottom string G; but elsewhere Adriaenssen uses a seventh course.) There are 10 with high clefs (eight have G2 and F3 and two have G2 and C4): all are transposed downwards. Two (both with flat signatures) are transposed down a tone; both are in G minor, so there would have been difficulties in keeping the bass notes on the instrument, had they been put ↓4th into D minor. Two (both without flat signatures) are transposed ↓5th. Six are transposed ↓4th (three with a flat and three without). In addition, there is one with C1 and C4 clefs, which goes ↓4th, and one (Lassus's popular *Susann' un jour*), using G2 and C4 clefs, which goes down a tone.

The rest of the publication clearly shows that high-clef pieces are lowered, though it offers no examples of transposition ↓5th. A group of three-voice works mostly in C1, C2 or C3, and C4 clefs is transposed down a tone, though two examples with a G2 clef go ↓4th; the two famous pieces by Hubert Waelrant for 4 voices and 4 lutes, in normal clefs, are untransposed if we assume lutes in G, F, D and C, or up a tone if the lutes are in A, G, F and D. The two settings for two lutes a tone apart (nos. 33 and 34) require instruments in A and G to give the expected transposition of ↓4th for the first and to preserve the original pitch for the second. Whatever the absolute pitch relationship between lute tuning and the pitch implied by the vocal notation, the intention to bring high-clef works to the level of normal-clef ones is clear.

devotional pieces, each printed in parts on a left-hand page, and opposite them, versions for keyboard and for lute in G (Illus. 5.2).[52] There is a clear pattern of transposition, identifiable in this case from the clef of the top part and the signature: when the clef is C1, there is no transposition, when it is G2 (–), transposition is ↓5th, and when G2 (♭), ↓4th. (The single exception may be an error: Nanino's *Jesus in pace imperat*, which has a G2 clef, has a transposed lute intabulation but an untransposed keyboard version.) The secular music of Verovio's similar *Lodi della musica* (1595) follows exactly the same system; of the 18 items, 9 are transposed.[53] The six madrigals '*per cantar nel Chittarrone*' in Salamone Rossi's first published collection[54] also follow this pattern. The tablature for chitarrone (in A) matches the pitch of the four madrigals that use C1 and F4 clefs, whereas the two that use G2 and F3 clefs (♭) appear a 4th lower in the tablature.

Although most organists would have been fluent in at least a few transpositions, written-out transpositions in staff notation are not uncommon. Among the solo items of the *Cento concerti ecclesiastici* (1602) of Lodovico Viadana are six which, exceptionally, have the voice part in a high clef (G2 for soprano, C2 for alto and C3 for tenor, all (♭)) written a 4th higher than the organ part.[55] There are comparable examples elsewhere in the collection, among the works for several voices. Similarly, two isolated items in G. F. Anerio's *Antiphonae, seu sacrae cantiones* (1613) have organ continuo parts a 4th below the voice parts,[56] and in the set of Magnificats published by Johann Stadlmayr the following year, there is one in high clefs with its two organ parts notated a 4th lower.[57]

---

[52] Simone Verovio, *Diletto spirituale* (Rome, 1586, 2/1592). There was also an edition of 1586 without the keyboard and lute versions. Nanino's *Jesu spes penitentibus* and four other items from the collection are transcribed in Helmut Haack, *Anfänge des Generalbass-satzes* (1974), Notenteil, 82–6.

[53] Simone Verovio, *Lodi della musica* (Rome, 1595); contents listed in Brown, *Instrumental Music*, 406 (1595¹⁰). Verovio's *Ghirlanda di fioretti musicali* (Rome, 1589) contains similar examples.

[54] Salamone Rossi, *Il primo libro de madrigali* (Venice, 1600).

[55] Lodovico Viadana, *Cento concerti ecclesiastici* (Venice, 1602; ii, 1607; iii, 1609); later German reprints combine all three volumes. Two earlier instances may be added: (i) MS sources of Philippe Rogier's mass 'Domine Dominus noster' (*a*12), composed in the early 1590s, give both the organ part of choir I and the 'guion' part a 4th lower than the high-cleffed voice parts, and (ii) an item in Gabriele Fattorini's *I Sacri Concerti* (Venice, 1600) does the same; Noel O'Regan, 'What Can the Organ *Partitura* to Tomás Luis de Victoria's *Missae, Magnificat, motecta, psalmi et alia quam plurima* of 1600 Tell us About Performance Practice?', *Performance Practice Review* 14/1 (2009), 11–12.

[56] G. F. Anerio, *Antiphonae, seu sacrae cantiones* (Rome, 1613), no. 42, *Tanto tempore*, for 2 altos (C2 (♭)) and no. 157, *Qui sequitur me*, for 2 tenors (C3 (♭)).

[57] Johann Stadlmayr, *Super magnae matris divino carmine Magnificat* (Innsbruck, 1614), no. 3; Magnificat '*Laudans exultans*' *a*8 (based on

Illus. 5.2 Simone Verovio, *Diletto spirituale* (Rome, 1586), for voices (left), keyboard (top right) and lute (bottom right); London, British Library, MS K.8.d.8, fol. 19

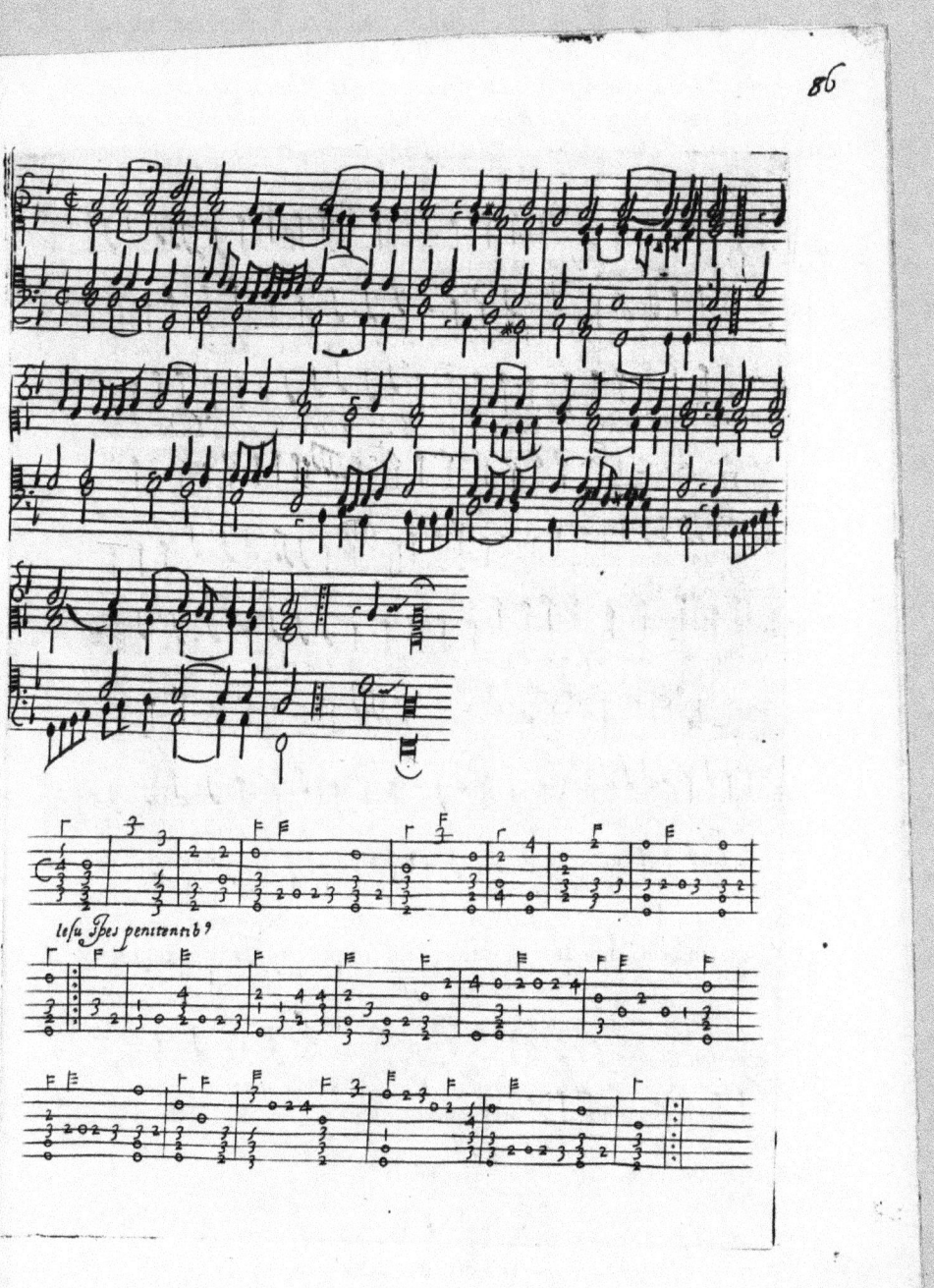

We now come to the music of Heinrich Schütz, who studied in Venice with Giovanni Gabrieli and later perhaps also with Monteverdi himself, and whose substantial output is particularly valuable in establishing principles of transposition. His setting of Psalm 111, *Ich danke dem Herrn*,[58] is in fact a reworking of Giovanni Gabrieli's double-choir madrigal '*per cantar et sonar*', *Lieto godea a8*;[59] in the original, each choir has the high-clef configuration G2 C2 C3 F3 (–), while in Schütz's version the clefs are C1 C3 C4 C5 (♭) and the music is a 5th lower. More revealing still is the notation of Schütz's *Musicalische Exequien* (1636), where the voices are in high clefs (in A minor), but the continuo part is printed a 4th lower (in E minor). Schütz himself explains:

> For the benefit of the singers and in order to have the chords I prefer in this work played on the organ, I have transposed the basso continuo down a 4th, although I am well aware that it would go more naturally on the organ a 5th lower, thereby perhaps making things easier for the inexperienced organist.

> *Den* Bassum Continuum *habe ich den Sängern zum Vorteil/ und zu berürung deren auff der Orgel zu diesen Wercke mir gefälligen* chorden *eine* Quarta *niedriger transponiret, ohngeachtet mir nicht ohnwissend/ daß* ad Quintam inferius, *es auff der Orgel natürlicher kommen/ damit auch vielleicht den ohngeübten Organisten eines theils besser gedienet gewesen were.*[60]

At first glance, it may seem that Schütz is simply explaining the transposition as a step taken 'for the benefit of the singers'. But the point at issue is that he is taking for granted downward transposition by a 5th for a work in high clefs (without signature); he thinks, however, that in this case the pitch then becomes too low for his singers and so he transposes ↓4th instead, thus making things more difficult for 'the inexperienced organist', who now has to read a part with the still unusual signature of one sharp.[61] We find the same transposition ↓4th (from A minor to E minor) in

---

a motet by Giovanni Croce); in *J. Stadlmayr: Selected Magnificats*, ed. H. Junkermann, *Recent Researches in the Music of the Baroque Era* 35 (1980), 74–105. The clefs of the voice parts are G2 C2 C3 F3 (♭) for each of the two choirs.

[58] Schütz, *Psalmen Davids* (Dresden, 1619), no. 13.

[59] Andrea and Giovanni Gabrieli, *Concerti ... continenti musica di chiesa, madrigali, & altro* (Venice, 1587).

[60] Schütz, *Musicalische Exequien* (Dresden, 1636), Ordinantz, §4.

[61] It is not clear whether the inexperienced organist finds the notation difficult with a sharp signature, or whether Schütz is thinking of his difficulties with the 'bad' notes of a mean-tuned instrument. Diruta touches on the subject briefly (*Seconda parte del transilvano*, bk 4, 16) and Praetorius more fully (*Syntagma musicum* iii, 81).

the seventh of the *Zwölf geistliche Gesänge* (1657),[62] where the vocal parts are notated in high clefs (without signature) and the organ part has one sharp. It is perhaps a little surprising that in the second half of the 17th century Schütz should still expect singers to be aware of the transposing convention and to prefer to avoid a sharp signature.[63] But there is one important additional feature: the work is explicitly headed '*ad Quartem inferiorem*' (a 4th lower).

INSTRUCTIONS IN MUSICAL SOURCES

WE have seen examples of discrepancies between two independent sources (suggesting a convention of transposing) and of discrepancies within a single source (revealing the clear necessity of transposing). In a last glance at the evidence of contemporary musical sources, we turn to those which contain explicit instructions or advice on the subject. The earliest example would appear to be from the first publication of sacred music to include a basso continuo, Viadana's collection of 1602, already cited.[64] There the third and fourth items, *Fratres, ego enim accepi* and its second part *Accipite et manducate*, are intended for '*Canto solo over cornetto*', while the organ part (written a 4th lower) bears the rubric 'When playing this concerto with cornett, the organist will play a 4th higher, thus' (*Sonando questo Concerto co'l Cornetto l'Organista*

---

[62] Schütz, *Zwölf geistliche Gesänge* (Dresden, 1657); no. 7, *Meine Seele erhebt den Herren*, is for four voices in the clefs G2 C2 C3 C4 (–), with the basso in continuo in F4 (♭).

[63] This is the only work in the set notated with a G2 clef in the top part; it is this clef that is the clearest indicator, not that of the lowest voice, which is F4 in seven of the other motets, F3 in three and C4 in one. Another work of Schütz's to use this transpositional convention is *Also hat Gott die Welt geliebt* (no. 12 of *Geistliche Chor-Music* (Dresden, 1648)), which has voices in G2 C2 C3 C3 F3 clefs (–), while the basso continuo has an F4 clef (♯) and is transposed ↓4th. Five different intervals of transposition are evidently called for in Constantijn Huygens's anthology of solo songs, *Pathodia sacra et profana* (Paris, 1647). Before each item the singer's initial note is given in lute tablature, despite the fact that the accompaniment is simply a bass line in staff notation. Assuming a G tuning, 21 of the 39 songs are untransposed and a further 11 are down a tone. Most of the basses use F4; the remainder are as follows:

F3 (–) ↓2nd
F3 (♭) ↓4th
F3 (–) ↓5th
C4 (–) ↓(×3)
C4 (–) ↓major 6th

[64] See n. 55. More recently it has been pointed out that earlier uses of the rubric '*Ad quartam inferiorem*' occur with two masses by Victoria (1600); O'Regan, 'The Organ *Partitura* to Victoria's *Missae*', 7, 10–11.

sonarà la quarta alta così); there follow the first few notes a 4th higher. In other words, the piece may be performed either vocally (at the lower pitch) or instrumentally (at the higher pitch).

Caspar Vincentius evidently preferred to leave certain options of transposition open to the organist. In a preface to the *bassus generalis* part prepared by him for part 2 of Abraham Schadaeus's anthology *Promptuarium musicum* (1611) he writes:

> I have not used any transposition of the pieces, but in the notation I have left them all in their clefs, as they stand in the originals. So, anyone may transpose as he pleases by either a 4th or a 5th, especially those *cantiones* given with the C4 clef (–). Furthermore, because the *calculi* or keys of organs and harpsichords in these areas are so designed that we do not have the major 3rd *in # duro* [i.e. above B♮], the organist will easily imagine the clef C4 (–) to be F4 (♭) and will have the lower 5th.

> *nullâ usus sum harmoniarum transpositione: sed in descriptione singulas in suis, ut in exemplari extant, reliqui Clavibus. Quilibet igitur pro suo lubitu, praesertim hac Clavi* 🎼 *signatas cantiones, vel per Quartam vel per Quintam transponat. Praeterea quia in his regionibus organorum atque instrumentorum Calculi sive Claves ita conficiuntur, ne in ♯ duro tertiam majorem habeamus Organista facilè sibi imaginabitur* 🎼 *clavem, esse* 🎼 *& habebit Quintam inferiorem.*[65]

Casually read, this may appear to suggest that transposition is at the player's discretion; but it is only the choice of interval (a 4th or 5th) that is in fact free. Vincentius sees no point in notating a transposition of a 5th when this can easily be achieved by a simple clef-substitution and prefers to avoid those transpositions of a 4th which introduce the tuning problems of sharp keys.[66]

---

[65] Abraham Schadaeus, *Promptuarium musicum* (Strasbourg, 1611); cited in Mendel, *Musical Pitch*, 149.

[66] Attempts to solve this problem by making instruments with separate keys for D♯ and E♭ (and also G♯ and A♭) evidently date from the 15th century in Italy but seem to have been rarer in Germany (see Praetorius: *Syntagma musicum* iii, 81). The 1480 contract for an organ at Lucca cathedral specifies this solution (see M. Lindley, '15th-Century Evidence for Meantone Temperament', *Proceedings of the Royal Musical Association* 102 (1975–6), 37), and more than a century later Diruta (*Seconda parte del transilvano*, bk 4, 16) records that 'In some organs there are split keys' (*In alcuni Organi vi sono li tasti scavezzi*). See also Wolfgang Caspar Printz, *Phrynis oder Satyrischer Componist* (Quedlinburg, 1676), ch. 11, §12 ff.; cited in Mendel, *Musical Pitch*, 230. Italian harpsichords with keyboards of this type were quite common. As early as 1548 Zarlino had commissioned one with 19 notes to the octave (*Le istitutioni*, 140).

In contrast, G. F. Anerio seems to leave no choices to the player, and we have already noted two examples in his *Antiphonae, seu sacrae cantiones* where a transposition is written out. The collection is an exceptionally large one and therefore of exceptional value in assessing any systematic approach.[67] Of the 244 works, 37 use high clefs; these are all marked '*Alla quarta*' or '*Alla 4*' in the *bassus ad organum* partbook, and no other interval of transposition occurs. A further 14 items have the rubric 'play it as it stands' (*sonate come stà*); these are works, without vocal bass and with the continuo part in a C4 clef, which might otherwise appear to be high-clef pieces needing transposition. The importance of three features of Anerio's collection cannot be over emphasized. First, the complete consistency of clef and transposition: all high-clef pieces are to be transposed, and none of those in normal clefs. Second, the exclusive importance of transposition ↓4th, whichever clef is used for the continuo part (C3, C4 or F3); Verovio's and others' distinction between pieces without signature (↓5th) and those with one flat (↓4th) is not observed here. Third, the implication contained in the phrase '*sonate come stà*' that a bass part in a C4 clef would automatically suggest transposition to a keyboard player.

A slightly more complicated but consistent picture emerges from a study of *Polyhymnia caduceatrix et panegyrica* (1619), Michael Praetorius's large collection of polychoral music[68] issued in the same year as the last volume of his *Syntagma musicum*. There are eight works notated in high clefs, all without signature, and against all but one of these in the *bassus generalis* is the instruction 'a 4th or 5th lower' (*quartam vel quintam inferiorem*). In notes preceding nos. 15 and 16, *Aus tiefer Not* and *Nun freut euch*,[69] the composer reiterates the point made in his treatise[70] that here transposition ↓4th or ↓5th must be made, the former being better for the voices. The exception – no. 6, *Allein Gott in der Höh sei Ehr*, the Lutheran versification of the Gloria – is simply marked '*per quartam inferiorem*', and in a separate note preceding no. 5, *Teutsche Missa: O Vater allmächtiger Gott*, we may discover why transposition ↓5th is here ruled out:

> In churches where the Gloria is sung in front of the altar, one must omit the *Preis sei Gott* and immediately begin the *Allein Gott in der Höh sei Ehr a6 & 12*; but it must be performed a 4th lower, so that

---

[67] See James Armstrong, 'The *Antiphonae, seu Sacrae Cantiones* (1613) of Giovanni Francesco Anerio: A Liturgical Study', *Analecta musicologica* 14 (1974), 89–150.

[68] Michael Praetorius, *Polyhymnia caduceatrix et panegyrica* (Wolfenbüttel, 1619); the original clefs are listed at pp. xxxi–xxxiii.

[69] Quoted in full below.

[70] See above.

it agrees in pitch [or key] with the preceding *Kyrie, O Vater, Christe*, etc.

In denen Kirchen/ do das Gloria *vor dem Altar gesungen wird/ muß man das (Preiß sey Gott) aussen lassen/ und so bald das Allein Gott in der höh sey Ehr/ à 6. & 12. anfangen/ Aber es muß umb eine* Quart tieffer *musicirt werden/ darmit es in dem rechten Thon mit dem vorhergehenden* Kyrie, O Vater/ Christe/ *etc. uberein komme.*

In other words, if the Kyrie (which is in normal clefs) and Gloria (in high clefs) were to match in key, avoiding a downward shift of a tone, the interval of transposition would necessarily be a 4th, not a 5th.

Comparable instructions, though without elaboration, are found in Schütz's *Kleine geistliche Concerte* I (1636). Here, the only three pieces written in high clefs, all without signature, are to be transposed ↓4th or ↓5th, according to instructions given in the continuo part (e.g. '*Organum ad quartam inferius*').[71] For whatever reasons, there may have been an increasing desire or need for composers and publishers of the 17th century to be more explicit about the intended pitch levels of their music. The substantially revised 1661 reprint of Schütz's *Psalmen Davids*, op. 5 (the Becker Psalter),[72] originally published at Freiburg in 1628, strongly hints at such a change of approach, and several errors suggest a last-minute change of policy concerning the method of presenting the various transpositions.[73] With 30 psalms in high clefs and over 100 transposition instructions, these 158 pieces probably represent the richest surviving source of information on this subject.[74]

In the publication as a whole, which contains several new items, transposition ↓4th is indicated 35 times, with transposition ↓(as a second option) 17 times; each is almost always associated with high-clef notation. Appropriately, transposition ↓3rd (which occurs 17 times, eight of them with high clefs) is mostly a second option and is often marked 'for the experienced' (*pro exercitatis*).[75] Adjustments of a tone are also frequent; upwards 12 times and downwards 29 times. (It could be argued that the quite high incidence of transposition down a tone is related to the rather

---

[71] Schütz, *Kleine geistliche Concerte* i (Leipzig, 1636), nos. 7, 8 and 18.

[72] Schütz, *Psalmen Davids* (Dresden, 3/1661) – simple, four-voice settings of Cornelius Becker's versification of the psalms, not the polychoral settings of the 1619 *Psalmen Davids*.

[73] Mendel's analysis of the revisions (*Musical Pitch*, 144–7) is unfortunately based on the misleading edition by Philipp Spitta (H. Schütz, *Sämtliche Werke* xvi). See Siegfried Hermelink, 'Bemerkungen zur Schütz-Edition', in *Musikalische Edition im Wandel des historischen Bewusstseins*, ed. T. G. Georgiades (1971), 207–9 and 214–5.

[74] See Ulrich Prinz, 'Anmerkungen zur Neuausgabe des "Beckerschen Psalters" von Heinrich Schütz', *Musikforschung* 25 (1972), 175–81.

[75] See Praetorius's comments in *Syntagma musicum* ii, 16–17

high pitch of German organs; Praetorius also suggests this transposition for music of a wide range where the cantus is high.)[76] The purpose of these various transpositions is explained by Schütz in a note at the end of the *bassus continuus* part:

> For this little work, such transpositions (especially in those with high clefs) are often not only very necessary but also comfortable for the singers' voices and fall all the more pleasantly on the ear.
>
> *Solche* Transpositionen *bey Gebrauch dieses Werckleins (bevorab in denen hoch-gezeichneten Systematis) offtermals nicht alleine hochnötig/ sondern auch der* Cantorum *Stimmen bequem/ und dem Gehör desto angenehm fallen.*

All this may appear to indicate a new level of sophistication; but 80 years earlier Galilei (and before him Bermudo) had expected 'skilled organists' to be familiar with these various intervals of transposition. What is new is that the composer's own precise wishes are made explicit. (This in itself may perhaps suggest a greater degree of pitch standardization than in the earlier period.) Superficially, it may be taken to undermine the simple principle that high-clef music be transposed to the 'normal' level. In fact, by allowing subtle adjustments to individual pieces (while retaining a relatively simple notation), it reinforces the idea of small, well-defined ranges for each category of voice and thereby the absolute necessity of reconciling high- and normal-clef music. The two categories of transposition described above have merely merged. In other words, where some composers would confine themselves to indicating 'obligatory' transposition of a 4th or 5th, leaving organists to make smaller adjustments of pitch to allow for vocal range and so on, here Schütz for normal-clef pieces suggests the smaller adjustments, while for high-clef pieces he gives only the 'resultant' transposition, for example, a 4th down (obligatory) and a tone up (adjustment), producing a downward transposition of a minor 3rd.

Before finally focusing our attention on the music of Monteverdi, it will be as well to look back briefly at the evidence so far presented. From Zarlino (1571) to Cerone (1613) the theorists merely tell us that organists should be capable of transpositions (often quite complex ones), while Praetorius (1618) explains exactly where transposition ↓4th or ↓5th is necessary. The fact that almost all two-manual Flemish harpsichords before the mid-17th century incorporated two different pitches a 4th apart emphasizes the importance of transposition by a 4th. Keyboard and lute intabulations from before 1600 show transposition of high-clef pieces ↓4th and ↓5th (and sometimes a tone), while organ continuo parts from

---

[76] Praetorius, *Syntagma musicum* iii, 82. See also Praetorius's arguments in favour of a choir pitch a tone lower than the prevailing *Cammerthon* (*Syntagma musicum* ii, 15–16).

Viadana (1602) to Schütz (1657) reveal written-out transposition ↓4th and instructions or recommendations for transposition ↓4th (notably in Anerio (1613)) and, to a lesser extent, ↓5th. One of Schütz's last publications (1661) shows a greater variety of intervals of transposition, but is wholly consistent with the idea of bringing high-clef writing down to the more normal written levels, a principle (or at least a practice) that was still familiar in the 18th century to Samber (1707) and even Paolucci (1765–72).

MONTEVERDI'S 1610 MASS AND VESPERS: VOICES

MONTEVERDI'S 1610 publication contains four pieces notated in high clefs (Table 5.1):

Table 5.1

	S	A	T	B
Mass	G2 G2	C2	C3 C3	F3 (–)
Lauda Jerusalem	G2 G2	C2 C2	C3	F3 F3 (–)
Magnificat *a7*	G2 G2	C2	C3 C3	F3 F3 (♭)
Magnificat *a6*	G2 G2	C2	C3 C3 (&F3)[77]	F3 (♭)

There are no instructions for transposition and the *bassus generalis* is consistently at the written pitch level of the other parts. Following Praetorius's clear-cut rules, the continuo player should play the Mass and *Lauda Jerusalem* either ↓5th or ↓4th, and the two Magnificats ↓4th. (In practice, smaller intervals of transposition, of a tone and a minor 3rd, are perhaps feasible for the Magnificat *a6* but would place the virtuoso obbligato instrumental writing of the related Magnificat *a7* in wholly unacceptable keys; for *Lauda Jerusalem*, and perhaps even for the Mass, transposition down a minor 3rd cannot be completely ruled out.) But does Monteverdi's music in general show any evidence of conforming to the conventions we have found documented and practised by Praetorius and others?

In the large posthumous collection of Monteverdi's church music (1650) is a setting of *Laudate pueri* 'a 5 voci da Capella'[78] notated in the clefs and signature of the two 1610 Magnificats (G2 C2 C3 C3 F3 (♭)) and in the same key (G minor). Here the *basso continuo* part contains the unambiguous instruction '*Alla quarta Bassa*'. Whether or not this was originally the composer's own marking, the suggested transposition was clearly considered reasonable by his editor (or at least by the user of the copy which the publisher had acquired). A comparison of the written vocal ranges of this psalm and of those of the Magnificat *a6* reveals a predictable similarity and an identical overall compass (Ex. 5.5). Thus if the

---

[77] The tenor part uses F3 just in 'Sicut locutus est'.
[78] *Messa a Quattro voci et salmi* (Venice, 1650).

Ex. 5.5 Vocal ranges in Monteverdi:
(a) *Laudate pueri* (1650), and (b) Magnificat *a6* (1610)

In this and subsequent examples, the notes in parentheses occur once only.

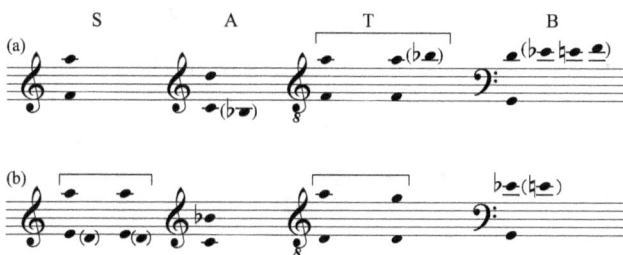

1650 *Laudate pueri* is to be transposed ↓4th, should not the Magnificat *a6* follow its example?[79]

The 1610 Mass, as we have observed, is notated in such a way as to suggest downward transposition by either a 4th or a 5th. The ranges of the work would clearly seem to rule out the lower option because of the lower extremities of each voice (Ex. 5.6). They do, however, match those of the 1650 *Laudate pueri* sufficiently for a performance at the same pitch as that, i.e. ↓4th, to be plausible. This possibility receives very strong support from two musical sources. In his *Esemplare ossia saggio fondamentale pratico di contrappunto sopra un canto fermo* of 1775 the eminent musical historian G. B. Martini quotes the Agnus Dei *a6* of Monteverdi's 1610 Mass ↓4th,[80] and in Brescia there exists an organ score by Lorenzo Tonelli from the late 17th or early 18th century of the complete Mass, also ↓4th.[81]

Ex. 5.6 Vocal ranges in Monteverdi, Mass *In illo tempore* (1610)

The ranges in square brackets are those of the extra parts which appear in the 'Crucifixus' (alto) and final 'Agnus Dei' (bass).

[79] Viewing the Magnificat *a6* in isolation from the other Vesper music, however, a 'skilled organist' might perhaps be tempted to consider the alternative interval of a minor 3rd, as the alto part does not lie at all high, and the three lowest voices descend rather low.

[80] Giovanni Battista Martini, *Esemplare* ii (Bologna, 1775), 242–50.

[81] See Jeffrey G. Kurtzman, *Essays on the Monteverdi Mass and Vespers of 1610* (1978), 9 and 38. These late transpositions are unlikely to have been affected directly by changes in pitch standard in the century and a half after 1610, when pitch seems rather to have moved downwards (by perhaps as much as a tone); it might be argued, though, that such a change would have ruled out transposition ↓5th.

Ex. 5.7 Vocal ranges in Monteverdi, *Vespers* (1610):
(a) *Lauda Jerusalem*, and (b) other movements

Excluded are the motets (except the portion *a*6 of *Audi coelum*) and, of course, the two high-clef Magnificats. Conflations have been made, since Monteverdi sometimes has more than one alto and bass part and also more than two tenor parts, but such doubles tend to move in the same range.

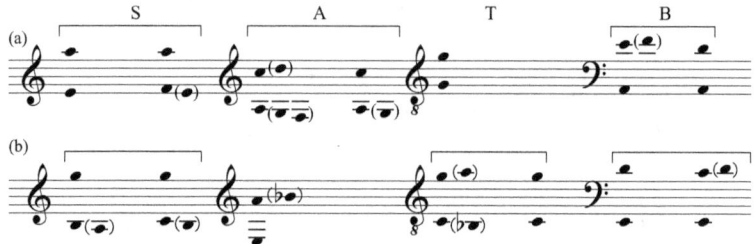

For *Lauda Jerusalem* we have no such corroborative evidence. Ex. 5.7 compares its vocal ranges with those of other movements of the 1610 Vespers. To leave *Lauda Jerusalem* at its written pitch is to expand ranges which are already wide for the period by a small but critical amount; all except the tenor and second bass would extend above their ranges elsewhere in the Vespers. But if the psalm is transposed ↓4th, all its ranges (apart from two unique low notes in the alto part) are contained within the extremities of those found elsewhere. Ex. 5.8, which compares these transposed ranges with those of the Mass and of the 1650 *Laudate pueri*, shows a similarly telling consistency. Although here the evidence is suggestive rather than conclusive, surely *Lauda Jerusalem* is intended to be performed at the lower pitch.[82]

Despite the logic of these arguments, the reader may well find that the evidence presented withers into insignificance when weighed against the aural memory of the Vespers with all sections at their relative notated pitches. It may be tempting to protest that Monteverdi surely intended a new, high tessitura for his final psalm, and that to seek mere consistency in range may be to miss his point. No doubt these low ranges also prompt other questions. What happens to all the brilliance and brightness of *Lauda Jerusalem* at the low pitch? Was Monteverdi's pitch standard perhaps much higher than our present $a' = 440$? The twin subjects of voice-types and pitch standards in early 17th-century Italian music each require at least as much attention as do the conventions of transposition, and this is clearly impractical in the present article; moreover, they should

---

[82] The possible temptation to lower *Lauda Jerusalem* by a minor 3rd rather than a 4th can easily be resisted because of the prominent major triads on F♯ that this would create for the continuo, quite apart from the probability of an uncomfortable transition from a closing F♯ major chord to the ensuing antiphon or antiphon substitute. (In the publication the psalm is followed by the *Sonata sopra Sancta Maria*, which opens in G major.)

Ex. 5.8 Vocal ranges, transposed down a 4th: (a) *Lauda Jerusalem* (1610), (b) Mass *In illo tempore* (1610), and (c) *Laudate pueri* (1650)

not be allowed to confuse the issue of transposition, which is essentially quite distinct. Consideration of the topic may become easier, however, if the different voices are not thought of in terms of the modern SATB choir. In particular, Monteverdi's altos at Mantua are more likely to have been of the usual Renaissance type (i.e. what we call high tenors) than the falsettists or castratos who superseded them, while the contemporary tenor corresponded in range if not in timbre to our baritone. Greater emphasis on naturalness of diction and less on sheer power of singing, combined with a general fondness for low sonorities, encouraged vocal ranges lower than those familiar to us from the music of later eras.

Nowhere is familiarity such a barrier to comprehension as in the case of the celebrated Magnificat *a7* with which most modern concert performances of the 1610 Vespers close. Its untransposed and transposed voice ranges are given in Ex. 5.9. The lower set scarcely seems designed to create the brilliant climax that we may have come to expect of the work, but it does accord closely with the ranges of the two high-clef works by Monteverdi for which we have evidence of transposition: the 1650 *Laudate pueri* and the 1610 Mass. If the presence of a low *A* for tenor causes some surprise, one need look no further for precedent than to the solo tenor

Ex. 5.9 Vocal ranges in Monteverdi, Magnificat *a7* (1610): (a) as notated, and (b) transposed down a 4th

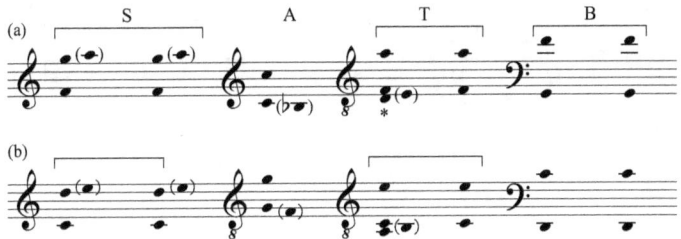

* The (low) written *d* occurs only once but is sustained.

Ex. 5.10 Monteverdi: (a) Magnificat *a7* (1610), 'Et misericordia', at 'timentibus eum', transposed down a 4th, and (b) Gloria *a7* (1640), at 'pax hominibus voluntatis', as notated

Ex. 5.11 Complete vocal ranges in the *Vespers* and Mass *In illo tempore* (1610), as notated

* Here and in Ex. 5.12 void notes indicate extremities found only in the untransposed 1610 Mass.

writing in *Audi coelum* from the same publication;[83] but such a note is rare in Monteverdi's liturgical output.[84] (In his 1614 collection Caccini goes much further: he includes 'two special arias for tenor which explore the bass register' (*due Arie Particolari per Tenore, che ricerchi le corde del Basso*), combining tenor and (low) bass ranges.)[85] The abandon with which Monteverdi appears to call for (low) Ds in the vocal bass may cause rather more surprise. But in addition to those arising from transposing the 1650 *Laudate pueri* and 1610 Mass, there are instances in five polyphonic works from the 1640–1 collection[86] and three from the 1650 collection.[87] More sensational still, with their low Cs and 16-note range up to d', are the solo motet *Ab aeterno*[88] and the role of Neptune in *Il ritorno d'Ulisse*.[89] Pluto's comparable two-octave compass (D–d') in *Il ballo delle ingrate*,[90] a Mantuan work dating from 1608, exactly matches the 1610 Vespers' transposed bass range. Clearly such solo writing is of a different kind from that of 'Et misericordia' and 'Sicut erat', where transposition results in low Ds, but even such low, sober counterpoint is not without its equivalents, as comparison with the Gloria *a7* (1640–1)[91] shows (Ex. 5.10).

How does transposition of the Magnificat *a7* affect the ranges of the publication as a whole? Ex. 5.11 gives the written ranges of all the polyphonic music in the Vespers. With *Lauda Jerusalem*, the two Magnificats and the Mass transposed ↓4th, the results are those given in

---

[83] On the words 'aurora' and 'coelos', bars 14 and 22.

[84] The note occurs once in *Selva morale e spirituale* (Venice, 1640–1), in *Laudate pueri* ii (*Tutte le opere* xv, 472, bar 127) and once in *Messa a Quattro voci et salmi* (1650), in *Dixit* [i] (*Tutte le opere* xvi, 73, bar 116); both occurrences are brief. When transposed, the 1610 Mass has two Gs (Gloria, bar 42, and Credo, bar 34) and one A (Agnus Dei *a7*, bar 49); these are also brief.

[85] Giulio Caccini, *Nuove musiche e nuova maniera di scriverle* (Florence, 1614), 33–8.

[86] Gloria *a7*, *Dixit* II, *Beatus* II, *Laudate pueri* II and *Magnificat* I.

[87] Both settings of *Dixit*, and *Beatus vir*.

[88] *Selva morale* (1640–1). Cf. the bass parts in Schütz, *Kleine geistliche Concerte* (Leipzig, 1636).

[89] See especially the opening bars of Act I, scene 5.

[90] Monteverdi, *Madrigali guerrieri et amorosi* (Venice, 1638).

[91] *Selva morale* (1640–1); *Tutte le opere* xv, 117–77.

Ex. 5.12 Complete vocal ranges as in Ex. 5.11, but with the Mass, *Lauda Jerusalem* and the Magnificats *a6* and *a7* transposed down a 4th

Ex. 5.13 Vocal ranges given in Praetorius, *Syntagma musicum* ii, 20

* See n.92

Ex. 5.12. The comparison perhaps proves little; in the transposed table the bass range is slightly narrower, the tenor range wider, while alto and soprano are much the same. In fact, we may well be inclined to favour the untransposed ranges on account of their greater familiarity from more recent music. It will therefore be of value to compare these tables with a contemporary one, that given by Praetorius in *Syntagma musicum* ii (Ex. 5.13). (It may be tempting to postulate a higher pitch standard for Praetorius than for Monteverdi, yet Praetorius specifically equates his with that of Italy.)[93] In both transposed and untransposed forms, two of Monteverdi's voice ranges exceed those of Praetorius: his soprano goes lower and his tenor higher. Without transposition, the upper end of both alto and bass is significantly higher; with transposition, soprano and alto go lower and the tenor both higher and lower.

---

[92] For the bass voice Praetorius also gives an F' which evidently some singers tried to reach, though without real success. He goes on to name three basses reputed to have been able to sing $E\flat'$ (*Syntagma musicum* ii, 17).

[93] *Syntagma musicum* ii, 15. The question of absolute pitch-standards in the early 17th century is, of course, an extremely complex one. William R. Thomas and John J. K. Rhodes ('Schlick, Praetorius and the History of Organ-pitch', *Organ Yearbook* 2 (1971), 58–76) have used the evidence of Praetorius's woodcut of pipe dimensions (*Syntagma musicum* ii, 232) to propose roughly $a' = 428$ as his reference pitch. Recently, Herbert W. Myers ('Praetorius's Pitch', *Early Music* 12/3 (1984), 369–71) has pointed out that the large majority of Praetorius's scale illustrations of wind instruments correspond closely to surviving examples of about $a' = 460$; this may be the standard of most Nuremberg trombones, which Praetorius considered the most reliable guides to his own pitch (*Syntagma musicum* ii, 232). This is quite likely to have been roughly the same as Venetian pitch, but we cannot assume that it was therefore in use in Mantua too; Giovanni Battista Doni (*Annotazioni sopra il compendio* (Rome, 1640), 181–2; Mendel, *Musical Pitch*, 236) differentiates – by suspiciously neat semitones – between the prevailing pitch standards of Naples, Rome, Florence, Lombardy and Venice, from low to high respectively (see also above and n. 44).

Ex. 5.14 (a) Magnificat *a7* (1610), 'Quia fecit', transposed down a 4th, and (b) Gloria *a7* (1640), 'Qui sedes', as notated

This is also inconclusive perhaps, but consistency of range is a matter not only of extremities but also of tessitura. Although more difficult to demonstrate on the page, the gains in consistency of the tessitura resulting from the transpositions are considerable. At the lower pitch the bass duet writing in the Magnificat *a7*, for example, reveals its close ties with that of the later Gloria *a7* (Ex. 5.14). The character of the solo tenor writing is still more revealing: although the introduction to the doxology of the Magnificat *a7* loses a certain amount of its presumed 'brilliance' by downward transposition, it now has much more in common with *Audi coelum*, *Duo seraphim* and, significantly, with the two principal tenor roles in the same composer's *L'Orfeo*. (See Ex. 5.15a–d.) *L'Orfeo* was published in 1609, just one year before the Vespers. The opera had been performed first in February 1607 and it is very likely that music for the 1610 publication was assembled, if not all composed, over the following three years.[94] These two works represent the twin peaks of Monteverdi's Mantuan output, and from the moment of the opening respond's reworking of the toccata from *L'Orfeo*, the Vespers invites comparison with its secular predecessor. One may reasonably conjecture that Monteverdi had some of the same singers specifically in mind. Was, for example, the original Orfeo, the great Florentine singer Francesco Rasi,[95] also the inspiration for

---

[94] See Iain Fenlon, 'The Monteverdi Vespers: Suggested Answers to Some Fundamental Questions', *Early Music* 5/3 (1977), 380–7. Fenlon conjectures that a first performance took place in Mantua at S Andrea on 25 May 1608, but Kurtzman's objection (*Essays*, 42) that such an occasion would not account for the dedication of the Vespers to the Virgin is a strong one. Cf. Roger Bowers, 'Monteverdi at Mantua, 1590–1612', in *The Cambridge Companion to Monteverdi*, ed. J. Whenham and R. Wistreich (2007), 53–75.

[95] For Rasi as Orfeo, see Tim Carter and David Butchart, correspondence, *The Musical Times*, 118 (1977), 393. Marco da Gagliano mentions in the preface to

Ex. 5.15 (a) Magnificat *a7* (1610), 'Gloria', tenor I; (b) *Audi coelum* (1610), tenor I; (c) *Duo seraphim* (1610), tenor I; (d) *L'Orfeo*, Act V; (e) *L'Orfeo*, Act III; (f) *Audi coelum* (1610), tenor I

Ex. 5.16 Tenor ranges in (a) *Nigra sum, Duo seraphim* and *Audi coelum* (1610), and (b) *L'Orfeo*

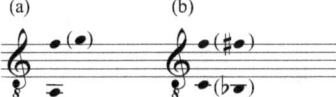

Audi coelum? (See Ex. 5.15e–f.) The conflated ranges of *Nigra sum, Duo seraphim* and *Audi coelum* offer a further point of comparison with the role of Orfeo (Ex. 5.16).

Such comparisons may well tip the scales back in favour of the transposed version, especially as Praetorius explains that in Italy a low pitch standard, well below his own, was also often used:

> Some Italians, not unreasonably, take no pleasure in high singing, believing that it is unseemly, also that the text cannot be properly grasped, that high up one squawks, shrieks and sings just like [?]sparrows.

> *Sintemahl etliche* Itali *an dem hohen singen/ wie nicht unbillich/ kein gefallen/ vermeynen es habe keine art/ könne auch der* Text *nicht recht wol vemommen werden/ man krehete/ schreye und singe in der höhe gleich wie die Grasemägde.*[96]

INSTRUMENTS AND TRANSPOSITION

BEFORE looking for similarities or inconsistencies in the instrumental writing of *L'Orfeo* and the 1610 Vespers, we obviously need to ask whether instrumentalists other than continuo players would ever have been expected to transpose. After all, keyboard or lute tablature incorporates an appropriate transposition, a two-manual Flemish harpsichord gives the player a choice of pitch level, and an organist, reading from staff notation, is specially trained in transposition to suit voices, while a singer is simply unencumbered by the concept of a fixed pitch. But why should a violinist ever be required to play a 4th lower than the given notes normally suggested?

The only other high-clef work with obbligato instrumental parts in Monteverdi's output is the madrigal *A quest'olmo* ('*a sei voci,*

La Dafne (Florence, 1608) that Rasi participated in the original performance in mid-February 1608; for the date, see Stuart Reiner, 'La vag'Angioletta', *Analecta musicologica* 14 (1974), 53–6. Gagliano's solo writing is much more restrained than that of Monteverdi, so a more restricted range is to be expected.

[96] Praetorius, *Syntagma musicum* ii, 16. The translation of 'Grasemägde' is uncertain; cf. Mendel (*Musical Pitch*, 112, n. 45).

concertato'),⁹⁷ which has parts for 2 violins and 2 '*flauti o fifara*' [*sic*]; the ranges, however, are restricted and work either at pitch or lower and so are of no assistance to us. One answer may be that the players were not in fact required to transpose at sight. Praetorius expects many organists to prepare for a performance by writing out a tablature for themselves from the parts (see above); might violinists also perhaps expect to copy out parts, at whatever pitch was appropriate, from the printed source? The 1610 Vespers partbooks may be regarded as a compact repository of the musical text, from which parts were to be prepared if and as necessary. Although these eight partbooks are so arranged that a performance from them (with one voice or instrument to a part) can just be managed, further copying is essential if any degree of spatial separation is required. (If, for example, in *Ave maris stella* the two four-part choirs are to be separated, the instrumental group(s) for the ritornello (*a5*) will be divided between them.) It would thus have been perfectly natural for instrumentalists (or a copyist on their behalf) to write out new parts where necessary.

An alternative option open to Monteverdi would have been to present vocal parts at one pitch and instrumental parts at another. Already amply illustrated in connection with basso continuo parts, this is the approach adopted in Schütz's *Nun lob mein Seel den Herren*:⁹⁸ the two vocal choirs are notated in high clefs (in C), while the two instrumental choirs are set a 4th lower (in G) – the clearest possible demonstration of (vocal) transposition theory in practice. A similar procedure is followed in the Mass from the Venetian composer Giovanni Antonio Rigatti's *Messe e salmi* (1640):⁹⁹ while the two violin parts are notated in G2 clefs at a normal level (in D), all the voice parts and the remaining instrumental parts (continuo and three 'viola'/trombone parts) stand a 4th higher (in G) in high clefs (G2 C2 C3 F3), all without signature.

These examples may on balance seem to argue against the idea of instrumentalists transposing. So perhaps does Viadana's *Fratres, ego enim accepi/Accipite et manducate* (see above):¹⁰⁰ it is for '*canto solo over cornetto*', and the higher pitch, giving a range of d' to a'', clearly suits the instrument better. Yet as early as the mid-16th century we find Ganassi¹⁰¹ instructing viol players in the art of transposition – for that is one of the functions of his fingering charts – albeit mostly by a tone up or down, though in one instance ↑4th. Virgiliano

---

⁹⁷ Monteverdi, *Concerto: Settimo libro de madrigal* (Venice, 1619). The violin parts go up to c''' (which, at pitch, would have been manageable in first position, with extension) and down to e'.

⁹⁸ Schütz, *Psalmen Davids* (Dresden, 1619), no. 20.

⁹⁹ G. A. Rigatti, *Messe e salmi* (Venice, 1640); information from Jerome Roche.

¹⁰⁰ See text above. The original notation is with G2 clef (♭); the organ part is a 4th lower but is also cued at the same pitch as the upper part if it is to be played with a cornett.

¹⁰¹ Sylvestro di Ganassi dal Fontego, *Regola Rubertina* (Venice, 1542).

Table 5.2 Virgiliano's directions for transposition in *Il dolcimelo* (c. 1600)

	Normal clefs		High clefs	
	up	down	up	down
viol	2nd	2nd, min. 3rd	–	4th, 5th, maj. 6th, min. 7th
cornett & trombone	2nd	2nd, min. 3rd	–	4th, 5th, maj. 6th, min. 7th
cornett	2nd, 5th	2nd, min. 3rd	2nd	4th, 5th, maj. 6th, min. 7th
flute	4th	4th, 5th	–	4th, 5th
recorder	2nd	2nd, min. 3rd, 4th	–	4th, 5th, maj. 6th, min. 7th

(c. 1600)[102] gives comparable directions for players of the viol, cornett, recorder and trombone, but with a much wider range of transposition (see Table 5.2). (It is worth noting that the 'easy' transposition ↓3rd, once mistakenly associated with high-clef notation,[103] occurs only in connection with normal clefs.) Virgiliano also gives 13 solo ricercares for a choice of instrument (recorder, flute, cornett, violin and 'similar' instruments). One, lacking any indication of instrumentation, uses G2 and C3 clefs alternately and has a range of *g* to *c"*,[104] while all the others are notated in C1, twice in alternation with C4, both (♭) and (–). Those that specify flute, violin and cornett have the range *d* to *g"*, which suits only the flute (more particularly, the instrument which Praetorius calls a tenor/alto flute in D, sounding an octave higher)[105] and is clearly impossible for violin or cornett without transposition upwards. (Transposition ↑4th aligns these ranges reasonably well with those of the other ricercares.)

At first sight, the phrase '*Va sonata alla quarta alta*' against three items in Salamone Rossi's first collection of *Sinfonie et gagliarde* (1607)[106] may also appear to demand upward transposition. However, the pieces (two of which are for 2 '*viole*' or 2 cornetts and basso continuo) are already in high clefs and the rubric is evidently a warning *against* (otherwise customary) downward transposition of a 4th: 'To be played at the pitch level which is a 4th up'. Thus, a further high-clef piece, with an even higher range for the top part and *no rubric*, may be taken to imply the usual downward transposition.

---

[102] Aurelio Virgiliano, *Il dolcimelo* (MS, c. 1600: Bologna, Civico Museo Bibliografico Musicale), [98–9, 102–3, 105, 109, 111]. See also below.

[103] See Mendel, *Musical Pitch*, 129–32.

[104] Virgiliano, *Il dolcimelo*, [70]. This is an incomplete diminution on Palestrina's *Vestivi i colli*; the key and high clef derive from the original madrigal.

[105] Praetorius, *Syntagma musicum* ii, 22.

[106] Salamone Rossi, *Il primo libro delle sinfonie et gagliarde* (Venice, 1607). Rossi, it should be remembered, was one of Monteverdi's colleagues at Mantua, though it is unlikely that, as a Jew, he would have been involved in any church music-making.

The ability of instrumentalists to transpose is even more certainly presupposed in Besard's *Novus partus* (1617).[107] The first section consists of 12 items involving three lutes (two of which can be shown to be in G, the other a 4th lower). Eleven of these, including dances and *simphoniae*, also have two or three parts in staff notation (in five instances for voices or instruments *ad libitum*). The apparent pitch of these parts coincides fully with that of the lutes in only two instances; all three pieces in high clefs (G2 and C4) lie a 5th above the lutes, while five in normal clefs lie a tone above. The remaining item, *Lachrimae J. Dooland*, has one part (in G2) a tone above the lutes and another (in F4) at the lutes' pitch. Thus Besard presumably expects transposition down a 5th and a tone to cause no difficulty.

The players most likely to have been fluent in the art of transposition, especially ↓4th and ↓5th, are those cornettists, trombonists and others who played regularly with choirs. As *maestro di cappella* at St Mark's, Venice, Zarlino (1558) must have expected this fluency from his colleagues:

> such transpositions [↑5th or ↓4th] are useful and highly necessary both to every skilled organist involved with choral music and similarly to other instrumentalists playing other sorts of instruments, in order to match their sound to voices, which sometimes cannot go as high or as low as the proper positions of the modes require when played on the said instruments.
>
> *tali Trasportationi sono utili, & sommamente necessarie anco ad ogni perito Organista, che serve alle Musiche choriste; & ad altri Sonatori similmente, che sonano altre sorti di istrumenti, per accommodare il suono di quelli alle Voci, le quali alle volte non possono ascendere, o discendere tanto, quanto ricercano i luoghi propij delli Modi, accommodati sopra i detti istrumenti.*[108]

These ideas are elaborated by Zacconi (1592):

> And everyone [should] note that, just as voices can sing a song a tone higher or lower according to what proves comfortable for them and what seems pleasing to them, instruments too can similarly play a piece now in one Tone and now in another, remembering that universally they are all high in relation to voices. And thus, when you want to accompany voices with instruments, in order to accommodate them you mostly play [at the distance of] a tone, 3rd or 4th etc. And therefore, in this case, those who wish to join in (if they have no further particular knowledge of it) should at least know that you can generally play the musical Tones given in their

---

[107] Jean-Baptiste Besard, *Novus partus, sive Concertationes musicae* (Augsburg, 1617). See Julia Sutton, 'The Music of J. B. Besard's *Novus partus*, 1617', *Journal of the American Musicological Society* 19 (1966), 182–204.

[108] Zarlino, *Le istitutioni*, 319.

natural positions one tone lower and the transposed ones a 4th or
5th [lower], as anyone who has to consider these matters for himself
would imagine.

> *Et averta ogni uno che si come le voci humane, possano cantar una
> cantilena un Tuono piu alto, & un Tuono piu basso che li torna
> commodo & che li pare è piace, che cosi ancora gl'Istrumenti possano
> sonar una cosa hora in un Tuono & hora nell'altro, per rispeto che
> tutti universalmente sono alti rispetto alle voci. Et cosi quando che
> con gl'Istrumenti si vogliano accompagnar le voci il piu delle volte per
> accommodarle, le si sonano alle seconda, alla terza, alla quarta & c.
> E però in questo caso quelli che li vogliano adoprare: se non ne hanno
> altra particular cognitione: almeno sappiano generalmente che i
> Tuoni harmoniali posti & collocati dentro alle lor corde naturali: si
> possano sonar un Tuono piu basso: & che li trasportati si possano
> fare alla quarta & alla quinta come si presuppone ch'egli da se stesso
> habbia da considerar queste cose.*[109]

While in theory instrumentalists working with voices would be familiar
with several intervals of transposition, in practice experience obviously
varied from player to player:

> For if any cantor follows the organist in the wrong key and initiates
> the singing before the wind players join in and begin, or before they
> blow their cornett or trombone and give the cantor the correct
> choral key, they cannot proceed, especially on cornetts or violins
> already tuned to the choir and to the correct key, because they are
> not very familiar with transposition by a tone or a 3rd; since for
> some it is painful and difficult enough to transpose a part by a 4th
> or a 5th, and they therefore cause quite a confusion, or at least do a
> miserable job.

> *Denn wenn irgend ein* Cantor *so denen Organisten im unrechten*
> Clave *folget/ und dem singen den Anfang machet/ ehe die
> StadtPfeiffer darzu kommen und mit anfangen/ oder ehe sie zuvor
> in den* Cornett *oder Posaun stossen und den rechten Chormessigen*
> Clavem *dem* Cantori *geben/ können sie sonderlich auff den* Cornetten
> *oder Geigen/ so vor sich zum* Chor *und rechten* Clave *gestimmet/
> nicht fort kommen/ weil ihnen die* transpositio *per Secundam
> und* Tertiam *nicht wol bekant/ Sintemahl es etlichen sawer und
> schwehr gnug wird/ einen* Cantum *per Quartam oder* Quintam *zu
> transponiren, und machen also wol gar eine* Confusion, *oder doch
> sonsten erbärmliche Arbeit.*[110]

Evidently then, experienced players could be expected to transpose by
a 4th or 5th when necessary, even if other intervals were generally to be

---

[109] Lodovico Zacconi, *Prattica di musica* i (Venice, 1592), fol. 218v.
[110] Praetorius, *Syntagma musicum* ii, sig. 9r.

avoided. In *Polyhymnia caduceatrix et panegyrica* (1619), Praetorius again presupposes some facility with transposition on the part of his instrumentalists:

> Now, as these and all other *cantiones* in the Hypoionian mode must necessarily be transposed down a 4th or 5th – at the 4th the piece always becomes fresher and more spirited, but it is rather more difficult for the organists and instrumentalists than at the 5th – I intended to have the instrumental choirs and the continuo part printed a 5th lower. But as I have discovered that instrumentalists who are not so very experienced can manage almost less [well] than when it stays in its proper key and also for some such a Tone appears much more comfortable to deal with from the 5th than from the 4th – also the pitch of the organs will often not permit anything else – I have therefore left it in its proper key, so that each can proceed and act as he pleases and according to circumstance.

> *Dieweil auch diese und alle andere* Cantiones in Modo Hypojonico in Quartam *oder* Quintam inferiorem *nothwendig* transponiret *werden müssen: und* in Quarta *der Gesang allezeit frischer und anmutiger/ den Organisten und* Instrumentisten *aber etwas schwerer als* in Quinta *ankömpt: so bin ich willens gewesen/ die* Choros Instrumentales *und* Bassum Generalem, in Quintam inferiorem *gesetzet drucken zu lassen. Dieweil ich aber befunden/ daß nicht so gar sehr geubte* Instrumentisten *sich fast weniger darein richten können/ als wann es in seinem rechten* Clave *bleibt: und auch manchen solcher* Tonus *viel bequemer auß der* Quinta *als auß der* Quart *zu* tractiren *vorkömbt, auch offt die höhe der Orgeln es nicht anders leiden wil: so habe ichs in seinem rechten* Tono *bleiben lassen/ darmit ein jeder nach seinem eignen gefallen und guten gelegenheit darmit* procediren *und gebaren könne.*[111]

Although some of Praetorius's statement may seem rather obscure, the opening is crystal clear and confirms the points made in *Syntagma musicum* (see above). Three of the high-clef pieces in question call for instrumental doubling of the vocal parts, while the remaining four have independent instrumental parts; all are in C major. It is difficult to imagine any notational problems resulting from a written-out transposition ↓5th to F major, whereas G major, with its sharp signature, may well have been considered less comfortable.[112] It seems at least possible that a misprint causes the apparent obscurity: if, after the words 'Bassum Generalem', 'in Quartam' were to replace 'in Quintam', Praetorius would appear to say that his intended transposition ↓4th created more (notational and technical) problems for the inexperienced player than an

---

[111] Praetorius, *Polyhymnia*, no. 15, introductory note §6.
[112] Cf. Schütz's observations above.

Table 5.3 Distribution of parts in Cesis, *Hodie gloriosus Pater* (*a*8)

Choir I	Choir II
C1 [voice]	C2 *per il cornetto alla quarta bassa, ma però sempre si sona sù l'ottava alta*
C2 [voice]	C4 *altus per il Trombone all quarta bassa*
C3 *tenor all'ottava alta*	C4 *per il trombone alla quarta bassa*
F3 *alla quarta bassa per il violone*	F4 *Contra basso alla quarta per l'Arciviolone*

unwritten transposition ↓5th and was in any case not low enough for some organs.[113]

One important final example will serve to show incontrovertibly that in Italy, too, a composer of Monteverdi's time would expect instrumentalists to be able to transpose, at least ↓4th, just as Virgiliano's treatise implies (see above). *Hodie gloriosus Pater* (*a*8) from a volume of motets by Sulpitia Cesis (1619)[114] is for two choirs: Table 5.3 shows the distribution of the parts. Despite the 'normal' upper and lowest clefs (C1/C2 and F4), the piece is to be performed ↓4th; hence the unusually precise instructions. Choir I is for three voices (all female?) and '*violone*', while choir II is purely instrumental. The cornett effectively transposes ↑5th (as does the vocal 'tenor'), one of the intervals of transposition given by Virgiliano for the cornett (see above), while the two trombones and the two stringed instruments play ↓4th.

MONTEVERDI'S MAGNIFICAT *A*7: INSTRUMENTS

JUST as we have conjectured that *L'Orfeo* and the 1610 Vespers were written with some of the same singers in mind, so we may imagine that perhaps some of the same virtuoso violinists and cornettists took part in each work. Ex. 5.17 gives the ranges of five of the instruments in the Magnificat *a*7: (a) at notated pitch, and (b) transposed ↓4th; these may be compared with their equivalents in (c) the *Sonata sopra Sancta Maria* and in (d) 'Possente spirto' from *L'Orfeo*, Act III. The consistency in range demonstrated by this transposition is quite striking; the consistency of tessitura is no less impressive (see Ex. 5.18).

---

[113] There is reason to believe that early 17th-century organ pitch in Germany tended to approximate the highest levels known in Italy; thus, transposition ↓5th might have been more useful and therefore more common there. See n. 93.

[114] Sulpitia Cesis, *Motetti spirituali* (Modena, 1619). Cesis was a nun at the convent of S Agostino in Modena.

Ex. 5.17 Instrumental ranges in (a) Magnificat *a7* (1610), as notated, (b) Magnificat *a7* (1610), transposed down a 4th, (c) *Sonata sopra Sancta Maria* and (d) *L'Orfeo*, 'Possente spirto'

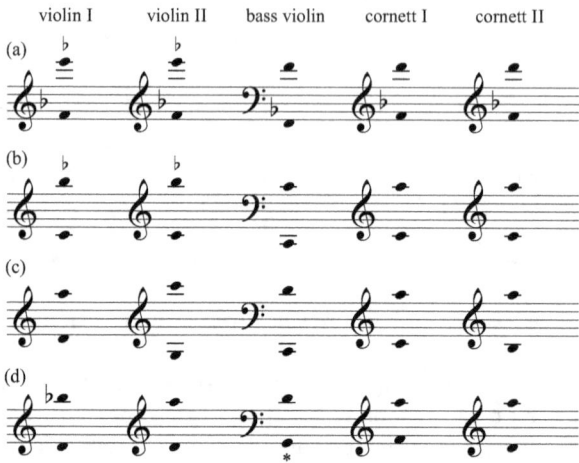

* Elsewhere in *L'Orfeo* (in the ritornello which opens Acts V) the bass violin is taken down to *D*.

Ex. 5.18 (a) and (c) Magnificat *a7* (1610), 'Deposuit', transposed down a 4th; (b) and (d) *L'Orfeo*, Act III

Let us look in a little more detail at some of the technical aspects of these instruments. First, the cornett. Zacconi (1592),[115] Praetorius (1618)[116] and Rognoni (1620)[117] all write of a basic two-octave range of a–a'' which can be extended upwards according to individual ability by four and even six notes. (Mersenne (1636–7) gives the instrument's range as c'–d''',[118] while Bismantova (1677–9)[119] describes the high a''–d''' as 'note sforzzate'; for Speer (1697)[120] the upper limit is c'''.) Yet the surviving music of Giovanni Gabrieli,[121] who had at his disposal possibly the best wind players in Italy, never exceeds b''; and, typically, that note occurs just once in the virtuoso cornett writing of Praetorius's elaborate setting of *Wachet auf*.[122] In the solo cornett literature of the early 17th century, where one may expect to find innovations and displays of virtuosity, c''' appears infrequently and d''' not at all; Marini (1617) writes only up to b'',[123] while Picchi (1625),[124] Marini (1629)[125] and Fontana (1641)[126] seem to be the earliest to write c''' (Marini also has a $c\sharp'''$). As Ex. 5.17 shows, the unprecedentedly virtuoso writing of the *Sonata sopra Sancta Maria* and also of *L'Orfeo* takes the instrument only to a''. (An isolated b''' occurs in *Deus in adiutorium* (*Domine ad adiuvandum*), which in any case is in origin a trumpet part a tone lower.) Untransposed, the two cornett parts in the Magnificat *a7* are clearly anomalous.

In a transposed Magnificat *a7*, however, the low range of cornett III may cause some disbelief (see Ex. 5.19). Yet the cornett III part of Giovanni Gabrieli's equally 'brilliant' motet *In ecclesiis a15*[127] has a similar tessitura and range (see Ex. 5.20). It may well be that in both cases a tenor cornett is intended; just as the term 'viola' or 'viola da brazzo' in the 1610 publication serves without further qualification for two (or probably

---

[115] Zacconi, *Prattica di musica* i, fol. 218v.

[116] Praetorius, *Syntagma musicum* ii, 36.

[117] Francesco Rognoni Taeggio, *Selva de varii pasaggi* (Milan, 1620), pt 2, [2].

[118] Marin Mersenne, *Harmonie universelle* iii (Paris, 1636–7), 273. Later (p. 275), Mersenne mentions that Quiclet and others can reach two notes higher.

[119] Bismantova, *Compendio*, [108–9].

[120] Daniel Speer, *Grundrichtiger ... Unterricht der musicalischen Kunst, oder Vierfaches musicalisches Kleeblatt* (Ulm, 1697), 232.

[121] See the parts with designations in Giovanni Gabrieli, *Sacrae symphoniae* (Venice, 1597) and *Canzoni et sonate* (Venice, 1615).

[122] Praetorius, *Polyhymnia*, no. 21.

[123] Biagio Marini, *Affetti musicali* (Venice, 1617).

[124] Giovanni Picchi, *Canzoni da sonar* (Venice, 1625)

[125] Marini, *Sonate, symphonie ... e retornelli* (Venice, 1629).

[126] Giovanni Battista Fontana, *Sonate* (Venice, 1641). This is a posthumous publication; the composer died c. 1630.

[127] Giovanni Gabrieli, *Symphoniae sacrae* ii (Venice, 1615), no. 26.

Ex. 5.19 Range of cornett III in the Magnificat *a7* (1610): (a) as notated, and (b) transposed down a 4th

Ex. 5.20 Range of cornett III in G. Gabrieli, *In ecclesiis*

three)[128] different sizes of instrument, so 'cornett' may refer generically to the family of instruments rather than to a specific size. The tenor cornett was certainly more common than modern performances of late 16th- and early 17th-century music might suggest,[129] but low playing on the treble cornett is also a possibility, especially as the doubling of vocal parts in C1 and C2 clefs had long been one of the instrument's main functions. Virgiliano seems to give a fingering for low *g*,[130] Praetorius recognizes both

---

[128] (Excluding its exceptional use for violin II at the start of the Magnificat *a7*.) I leave aside here the question of a 'tenor' or 'small bass' violin (tuned an octave or a 9th below the treble violin), which I believe was common at this period in Italy and which must be the intended alternative to trombone II in the *Sonata sopra Sancta Maria*.

[129] An inventory of the Stuttgart *Hofkapelle* in 1589 lists '4 big straight cornetts, 3 notes lower [than the previously mentioned 6 mute cornetts at choir pitch], to be used in the Kapelle for the alto part' (*4 grosse gerade Zinken, 3 Tonos niederer, seindt in der Kappel zu dem Alt zu gebrauchen*); see Gustav Bossert, *Württembergische Vierteljahrsheft für Landesgeschichte*, n.s. 21 (1912). Viadana, in a note in the *Basso generale per l'organo* book of his *Salmi a Quattro chori* (Venice, 1612), recommends '*Cornetti storti*' ('crooked' cornetts) for C2 and C3 parts in two of the four choirs. Praetorius, however, had reservations about the instrument (*Syntagma musicum* ii, 36): 'The *corno* or *cornetto torto*, also called *cornon*, is a large cornett, shaped rather like an S, and is a 5th lower than the ordinary cornett; and although some maintain that it has no more than 11 natural notes, and no falsetto above, this in fact not the case, for just like the ordinary cornett it has 15 notes. But because the resonance is quite unlovely and horn-like, I consider it better to use a trombone in its place.' (Corno vel Cornetto torto, sonsten Cornon *genand/ ist ein grosser Zinck/ bald wie ein S formiret/ unnd ist ein* Quint *Tieffer, alß ein rechter gemeiner Zinck; unnd wie vol etzliche meynen/ dieser gebe nicht mehr aß 11. Natürlicher Thon oder Stimmen/ und kein* falsett *drüber; So befindet sichs doch anders/ denn er gleicher gestald/ als die gemeine Zincken 15. Thon von sich gibet. Aber weil der Resonanz gar unlieblich und hornhafftig/ so halt ich mehr darvon, das man eine Posaun an dessen stad gebrauche.*) The range Praetorius gives for the instrument is *c/d–d"* (*Syntagma musicum* ii, 22), while Zacconi gives the narrower range up to *g'* (*Prattica* i, fol. 218v).

[130] Virgiliano, *Il dolcimelo*, [102–3].

g and f as possibilities,[131] and Marini writes g once and a several times in the fourth part of his *Canzone prima per quatro Violini ò Cornetti* (1629).[132] These two notes occur only in Monteverdi's final 'Amen' (the g twice and the f once), where the instrument is doubling a vocal line, and in any case the player could without difficulty play in the higher octave, as Cesis specifies (see above) and as Praetorius may imply;[133] such octave doubling is, after all, not uncommon in polychoral music of the time.[134]

The pairs of wind instruments that make brief appearances in 'Quia respexit' may seem to contribute little to the argument, as flutes (if indeed the terms 'fifara' and 'pifara' here indicate flutes), trombones and recorders of appropriate sizes can be chosen to serve the music well at either pitch (Ex. 5.21). But the ordinary flute of the early 17th century was the tenor/alto in D with a normal range of two octaves ($d'-d'''$).[135] It was treated as an octave transposing instrument, and thus the untransposed writing of the Magnificat *a7* would either exceed the normal upper limit by a few notes or, exceptionally, have to be played at the lower octave. Transposed, the parts lie comfortably in the upper half of the flute. On the other hand, it is true that, after transposition, the lower trombone part in this section has a range which might make us expect the designation '*trombone doppio*' (as in the *Sonata sopra Sancta Maria*), rather than merely '*trombone*'[136] (see Ex. 5.22), but as with the violin and cornett families, a complete and consistent nomenclature is not to be expected; after all, the lowest of the three trombone parts in the opening respond ('Domine ad adiuvandum') is also marked simply '*trombone*'.[137]

Next, the strings. In first position, the violin's highest note is b'', but an extension makes c''' possible without shifting.[138] The violin writing

---

[131] Praetorius, *Syntagma musicum* ii, 36.

[132] Marini, *Sonate*.

[133] Praetorius allows certain alto or tenor parts to be sung an octave up by a boy (*Syntagma musicum* iii, 158), and Viadana suggests performing a C3 part 'con Violini all'ottava' (*Salmi a Quattro chori*).

[134] In Schütz's reworking of Giovanni Gabrieli's *Lieto godea*, *Ich danke dem Herrn* (see n. 58), the instruments simply double the voices, mostly up an octave, and in Giovanni Gabrieli's *Jubilate Deo a10* (*Symphoniae sacrae* ii (1615)) a cornett doubles a lower part two octaves higher.

[135] See, for example, Praetorius, *Syntagma musicum* ii, 22.

[136] The range in the other movement of the Magnificat *a7* in which the instrument appears, 'Sicut locutus est', is similar, but with some written top d's.

[137] Praetorius's '*trombone doppia*' is a lower instrument than Monteverdi's music requires, but he also describes the more common '*Quart*-Posaun', a 4th or 5th below the ordinary (tenor) trombone, with a normal range of over two octaves down from c' (*Syntagma musicum* ii, 31–2); this seems best suited to Monteverdi's music.

[138] This semitone extension is shown by the figure '5' in the tablatures found in Gasparo Zannetti, *Il scolaro* (Milan, 1645).

Ex. 5.21 Instrumental ranges in the Magnificat *a7* (1610): (a) as notated, and (b) transposed down a 4th

Ex. 5.22 Range of trombone in (a) the Magnificat *a7* (1610) as notated, (b) the Magnificat *a7* (1610) transposed down a 4th, and (c) *Sonata sopra Sancta Maria*

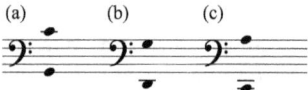

in *L'Orfeo* has b'' as its top note, while c''' comes just once in the *Sonata sopra Sancta Maria*[139] and is used sparingly by Monteverdi elsewhere in his output.[140] The note d''' is even rarer[141] and no higher written note occurs anywhere in his surviving work outside the Magnificat *a7*. By contrast, in the untransposed Magnificat *a7* c''' appears regularly, violin I has d''' in four of its five obbligato sections (see Ex. 5.1b), violin II has the note in two sections, and both have one eb'''. I have already noted an instrumental work of 1607 by the Mantuan composer Rossi requiring downward transposition; its violin part goes to written d''', a note which appears nowhere else in the publication. Even a decade later in his op. 1 (1617), Biagio Marini,[142] then a violinist under Monteverdi at St Mark's, Venice, does not write beyond first position; b'' is his normal top note and c''' occurs in just one item. But by the time of the same composer's op. 8 (1629), c''' has become the most frequent upper extreme, while two pieces go to d''' and one as far as e'''.[143] Comparable ranges are called for by another composer with Mantuan connections, Giovanni Battista

---

[139] Bar 49, violin II.

[140] For example, in only three passages in *Selva morale*.

[141] It occurs in one passage in *Selva morale*, in one bar in the posthumous *Messa et salmi*, and just once in *Madrigali guerrieri et amorosi* (Venice, 1638). The instrumental parts Malipiero prints in Act II, scene 3 of *L'incoronazione di Poppea* (*Tutte le opere* xiii, 130–4) come from the Naples manuscript – the 'autograph' has a bass line and blank staves above – so the d''' cannot be cited as Monteverdi's.

[142] Marini, *Affetti*.

[143] Marini, *Sonate*.

Buonamente (1626),[144] and by Tarquinio Merula (c. 1631–3),[145] and it may be significant that all three composers had by then spent several years working north of the Alps. Despite some apparent anomalies in Giovanni Gabrieli's posthumous *Canzoni e sonate* (1615),[146] it would seem from a provisional survey of early 17th-century Italian string music that composers probably did not begin to write for the violin beyond first position until sometime in the 1620s. Even then it was very much the norm not to demand shifting; Castello's music (1621 and 1629), for example, never exceeds c'''[147] and even Merula (1637) stays within this limit.[148] Against this background, it seems strange that Monteverdi (and his Mantuan players) might have been responsible for initiating these revolutionary experiments in violin technique, only to abandon them almost wholly to younger colleagues.

Only one other stringed instrument is called for in the Magnificat *a7*: a bass '*Viuola da Brazzo*'. Here there are perhaps fewer easy points of comparison because of the general confusion surrounding the terminology and nature of bass stringed instruments at this time. But downward transposition has two clear effects on the part. First, it brings all the music into first position, in line with all Monteverdi's other writing for the instrument (notably in the *Sonata sopra Sancta Maria*); second, it gives the instrument a single, idiomatic C (almost certainly its lowest open

---

[144] Giovanni Battista Buonamente, *Il quarto libro de varie sonate, sinfonie, gagliarde, corrente, e Brandi* (Venice, 1626).

[145] Tarquinio Merula, *Il secondo libro delle canzoni da suonare* (c. 1631–3; Venice, 2/1639).

[146] There are 16 parts labelled 'violino', of which four go beyond c'''; three of these are in the G1 clef and have d''' as their top note, while the remaining one, evidently in the otherwise usual G2 clef, also has an e'''. Granted the loose terminology of the period and the youthfulness of the violin family in the early 1600s, one must at least consider the possibility that these parts were intended for Praetorius's 'Klein Discant Geig', tuned a 4th above the common violin (*Syntagma musicum* i, 6; and *Theatrum instrumentorum*, pl. 21). However, Zacconi, in a slightly confusing passage (*Prattica* i, fol. 218), says that 'through skill and judgement' (*per artificio & giuditio*) the violin's range of a 17th can be extended by 'some' extra notes; it does not follow, though, that these notes would appear in compositions or even occur in performance (cf. Praetorius's exceptional low notes for the bass voice, above). Similarly, Mersenne (*Harmonie*, 179) observes that 'excellent violinists ... can ascend each string up to the octave'.

[147] Dario Castello, *Sonate concertate in stil moderno* i (Venice, 1621); and ii (Venice, 1629).

[148] [Merula], *Canzoni overo sonate concertate per chiesa e camera* iii (Venice, 1637).

Ex. 5.23 Magnificat *a7* (1610), 'Fecit potentiam', transposed down a 4th: (a) viuola da brazzo, and (b) bassus generalis

string and in any case a note that occurs in the *Sonata*) at a place where the organ has *c* (see Ex. 5.23).[149]

To transpose Monteverdi's Magnificat *a7* ↓4th is thus to remove several apparent anomalies (and probable anachronisms) from the instrumental writing without creating any new ones (unless the lowness of cornett III be such). This in itself is surely suggestive, as the similar transposition of any comparably complex instrumental music (for example, the *Sonata sopra Sancta Maria*) would almost inevitably produce insoluble problems.

HIGH-CLEF NOTATION

IT would be unreasonable to conclude without touching briefly on the question of why Monteverdi used high clefs in the first place. With Schonsleder (1631),[150] we may well still find ourselves 'amazed to see the majority of musicians customarily writing many of their songs in them, although they know that if anyone wishes to sing them they will have to be transposed downwards'. The subject is a vast and intricate one, and as yet there has been no definitive study. Matters of compositional technique, notational practice, modal theory and pitch-standard are all involved, and the four high-clef pieces in Monteverdi's 1610 Mass and Vespers perhaps reflect some of this diversity.

The 1610 Mass is a rigorous reworking of 10 *fughe* from Gombert's motet *In illo tempore*. Parody works of this type almost always retain the notated pitch level, and therefore clefs, of their models; Monteverdi's is no exception and we therefore need look no further for an explanation of his choice of high clefs in that work.

In the conservative *Lauda Jerusalem* the chant is presented in the tenor, first untransposed and later a 4th higher; these are its two traditional written levels (the only ones that remain strictly within the gamut) and it may well be that Monteverdi chose the written pitch of his setting accordingly. In both the Mass and psalm, to have written at the intended sounding pitch (a 4th lower) would not only have altered the given

---

[149] Elsewhere Monteverdi writes down to C in the *bassus generalis*, too; the note was generally available on Italian organs of the time.

[150] See above and n. 25.

material but, more important, would also have introduced an undesirable signature of one sharp.

The apparent incongruity of dazzling, up-to-date instrumental writing cast in imminently obsolete high-clef notation may seem a central problem with the Magnificat *a7*. Yet, particularly if we are correct in thinking that Monteverdi intentionally reproduced Gombert's written pitch in his Mass, an explanation may be that here, too, he wished to preserve the written pitch of his model. Analysis of the two Magnificats 'strongly suggests that the smaller six-voice setting served as the basis for the larger one with instruments',[151] and thus it would have been natural for Monteverdi to compose his more elaborate work at the pitch of the earlier one.

One puzzle remains. Why is the Magnificat *a6* in high clefs? Here the chant (Psalm Tone 1) is mostly used transposed ↑4th, often in alternation with an untransposed version. However, the traditional alternative level of the chant is not up but down a 4th. Has Monteverdi chosen to transpose the chant up only for performers to perform it down? There are no obvious notational difficulties with the lower (performing) pitch as there are in the Mass and *Lauda Jerusalem*; the flat signature would simply disappear and the remotest accidental would sharpen G rather than C. Either the choice of high clefs was almost arbitrary – it was a perfectly common form of notation presenting no problems to singers or organist – or it was dictated by reasons of modal theory still obscure to us. (Interestingly enough, it seems that 'as the 16th century wore on interest in and evidence for modality of any kind in the polyphonic repertory increased rather than lessened'.)[152]

Considerations of this nature may seem to conflict with the modernity and freedom of Monteverdi's *concertato* music, but more probably they were ingrained in the thinking of a composer in his early 40s whose first publication[153] had pronounced him a pupil of Marc'Antonio Ingegneri. In any case he was undoubtedly sensitive to the criticisms by Giovanni Maria Artusi of his contrapuntal procedures,[154] and an express purpose of the 1610 publication was, according to its preface, that 'the mouths of those speaking unjustly against Claudio may be closed' (*claudantur ora in Claudium loquentium iniqua*).

It is perhaps ironic that one of the more conservative features of such an innovatory publication should have caused Monteverdi to be so badly misrepresented later on.

---

[151] Kurtzman, *Essays*, 71.

[152] See Harold S. Powers, 'Tonal Types and Modal Categories in Renaissance Polyphony', *Journal of the American Musicological Society* 34 (1981), 467.

[153] Monteverdi, *Sacrae cantiunculae* (Venice, 1582).

[154] See, for example, Claude V. Palisca, 'The Artusi–Monteverdi Controversy', in *The Monteverdi Companion*, ed. D. Arnold and N. Fortune (1968), 133–66.

6

Monteverdi's Vespers of 1610 Revisited

IN this short anniversary paper I wish to offer some observations on three aspects of the Vespers music contained in Monteverdi's great 1610 publication.[1] All have received much less scholarly attention than they merit for the simple reason, certainly in two cases, that they are seen as belonging primarily to the world of the performer rather than to that of the scholar/editor. And because both scholars in general and editors in particular usually feel at liberty to side-step such questions, performers (who may or may not possess musicological skills) are themselves tempted to follow suit, tacitly encouraged in believing the matters to be of only peripheral importance, or at least unsusceptible to historical clarification. The three subjects under discussion here are (1) implied transpositions, (2) historical pitch standards and (3) contemporary liturgical practice (specifically, the function of the *Sonata sopra Sancta Maria*).

TRANSPOSITION PRACTICE

IT is now over a decade since I published a lengthy and detailed argument for the downward transposition (by a 4th) of certain movements in Monteverdi's 1610 collection – the Mass, *Lauda Jerusalem* and both Magnificats[2] – and the best part of two decades since I first put forward the same ideas in performance.[3]

Yet, despite my use of a sledge-hammer to crack a nut (as one friend put it), and despite subsequent endorsement from many scholars (Fallows, Kurtzman, Roche) and specialist performers (Dickey, Holloway, Wistreich), the issue is still considered controversial and opinion is divided. Several noted directors (Gardiner, Harnoncourt, Savall) have chosen to persist in presenting the *Lauda Jerusalem* and the Magnificat *a7* untransposed – a

---

First appeared in *Performing Practice in Monteverdi's Music: Proceedings of the International Congress, Goldsmith's College, University of London, December 1993*, ed. R. Monterosso (1995), 163–74; reprinted in *The Musical Times* 136/10 (1995), 531–5.

---

[1] Claudio Monteverdi, *Sanctissimae virgini missa ... ac Vespere* (Venice, 1610).

[2] Andrew Parrott, 'Transposition in Monteverdi's Vespers of 1610: An 'Aberration' Defended', *Early Music* 12/4 (1984), 490–516; reprinted in this volume, Ch. 5).

[3] BBC Promenade Concert, July 1977, St Augustine's, Kilburn (London), with the Taverner Choir and Players and various soloists. A recording for EMI was issued in 1984 and later transferred to Virgin Veritas.

course of action happily condoned by all but a few critics – even though there has apparently been no written critique of the arguments by any of the rumoured dissenting scholars.[4]

A partial exception, misleadingly described as having 'significant ramifications for … spurious notions of transposition',[5] is a still unpublished paper given in 1992[6] by the American scholar Stephen Bonta. This valuable study of 'Clef, Mode, and Instruments in Italy, 1540–1650' mainly explores the theoretical background to Monteverdi's use of high clefs for mode-1 pieces such as the two Magnificats, and thus addresses what is perhaps a central question for us today: why might a composer choose to notate music at one particular pitch level even if instrumentalists are required to realize it at another? Bonta's work also serves to emphasize the exceptional nature of the Magnificat *a7*, with its conjunction of *concertato* instruments and high-clef notation. (High clefs were in due course abandoned altogether, but not before Schütz and Rigatti, and perhaps others, had dealt with the same problem in a different way, by using a 'bitonal' notation with instrumental parts in one key – 'at pitch' – and high-clef vocal parts in another).[7]

But part of Bonta's purpose is also 'to point out some of the difficulties' in the idea of downward transposition of Monteverdi's Magnificat *a7*. In my 1984 article I had drawn attention to one of Viadana's *Cento concerti ecclesiastici* for '*canto solo over cornetto*' where vocal and instrumental alternatives are unambiguously intended to sound a 4th apart (the cornett at pitch, the voice a 4th lower, the organ accommodating either).[8] In arguing, quite correctly, that higher-sounding keys may commonly have been preferred for instruments, Bonta cites further vocal works explicitly suitable also for instrumental performance at levels well above their sung pitch: Croce's 'Percussit Saul' ('*Alla quinta bassa, e in tuono per sonare*')[9] and three mode-1 pieces by Banchieri ('*In tuono per cantare, & una quarta superiore per gli stromenti*', etc.).[10] What he crucially neglects to point

---

[4] Indeed, it would be quite wrong to assume that all those who resist the idea of the transpositions are even familiar with the underlying reasoning, as discussion at the Congress clearly revealed; see Andrew Parrott, 'Signifying Nothing', *The Musical Times* 136/6 (1995), 267. Roger Bowers first addressed the subject in print in 2003; cf. Andrew Parrott, 'Monteverdi: Onwards and Downwards', *Early Music* 32/2 (2004), 303–17; reprinted in this volume, Ch. 7).

[5] Tim Carter, 'Fifth Biennial Conference on Baroque Music', *Early Music* 20/4 (1992), 697.

[6] Fifth Biennial Conference on Baroque Music, Durham, July 1992.

[7] See Parrott, 'Transposition', 505.

[8] Parrott, 'Transposition', 505.

[9] Giovanni Croce, *Motetti, a8* (Venice, 1594).

[10] Adriano Banchieri, *Ecclesiastiche sinfonie, a4* (Venice, 1607). Four further items, to be sung low ('*trasportato alla quinta per le voci*', etc.), are implicitly

Ex. 6.1 Ranges of treble instruments in (a) Banchieri, *Ecclesiastiche sinfonie* (1607), as explicitly intended, (b) Monteverdi, Magnificat *a7* (1610) transposed down a 4th, and (c) Monteverdi, Magnificat *a7* (1610) as notated

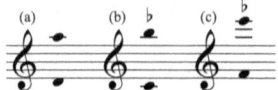

out, however, is that none of the resultant 'high' instrumental ranges is in any way comparable to the exceptionally high notated ranges found in Monteverdi's Magnificat *a7*; Croce's top part rises only to f'' and none of Banchieri's exceeds a''. In other words, the instruments' sounding ranges are completely conventional for the period and lie effectively *a 4th lower* than Monteverdi's notated ones (see Ex. 6.1). Moreover, even the five normal-clef, mode-2 pieces in Banchieri's collection – which rise only to eb'' – were evidently not considered appropriate for upward transposition (*'In tuono per voci & stromenti'*).

It should be clearly understood that each of Bonta's examples concerns performance by instruments *alone*, rather than by mixed vocal and instrumental forces. Having set up a false dichotomy between needs of voices and instruments in the case of the Magnificat *a7*, Bonta goes on, naturally enough, to ask: which should have priority? But rather than answer by drawing attention to the considerable body of evidence for instrumental transposition to accommodate voices,[11] he leaves the question hanging. Bonta's line of thinking would seem to be leading him to a rather implausible suggestion that the two versions of the Magnificat, *a7* and *a6*, be sung a 4th apart. Also, far from undermining the proposition that instruments must adopt the lower, 'vocal' pitch, Banchieri's collection self-evidently helps to emphasize just how common the idea of transposition was for most instrumentalists (and not just for continuo players), thereby answering another of the principal objections.

Bonta's paper concludes by resurrecting a couple of questions to be 'addressed in detail on a later occasion'. These concern the upper limits of Monteverdi's writing for violin and for soprano. With distinctly dubious logic Bonta appears to suggest that 'the highest note for violin in the Magnificat is not all that unusual' *because* the (single) c''' in the *Sonata sopra Sancta Maria* (violin II) is 'only a major second lower'. This completely ignores the moot point of whether in 1610 Monteverdi expected violinists to play outside first position, and is also both misleading and inaccurate: d''' is extremely rare even in Monteverdi's later violin writing (it appears in one passage in *Selva morale e spirituale* (1640), in one bar in *Messa et salmi* (1650) and just once in *Madrigali guerrieri et amorosi* (1638), for example), and the Magnificat's top note (for both

to be played higher, at written pitch.

[11] Parrott, 'Transposition', 492–4, 497, 500, 506–7.

violins) is in any case not d''' but $e\flat'''$, which is unique in the composer's output. To my earlier brief observations about Monteverdi's violin writing[12] I might add that for Zacconi (1592)[13] a violin's range extended only to b''. Clearly, violin playing developed rapidly in the early years of the 17th century, but in this context the exceptionally high writing looks suspiciously like just one more anomaly.

While accepting my points about (in)consistency of vocal ranges within the 1610 publication Bonta objects that 'Parrott's context is essentially limited to this one print'. (In practice, although my 1984 article was necessarily quite specific, I have always paid rather close attention to matters of vocal range, not least in 16th- and 17th-century Italian music, and it was precisely this broader interest that first made me aware of the various problems in the 1610 print.) Although a'', found in the high-clef soprano parts, may arguably be 'not that unusual in Monteverdi's secular music', its absence from *L'Orfeo* (published in 1609) is conspicuous, and, more to the point, in the remainder of Monteverdi's substantial sacred output – setting aside a handful of high-clef pieces without *concertato* instruments – the note appears just twice (for a fleeting quaver in one phrase and its repetition).[14] Certainly, high tessituras are very rare. Bonta finds further support for his views in the soprano lines of Giovanni Gabrieli's *Sacrae symphoniae* (1597 and 1615), but he falls, I believe, into the trap of assuming them to be intended for voices merely because they are texted; none is ever labelled *voce* and, as various circumstances make clear, they are almost certainly instrumental lines, to be taken, as a matter of course, by treble cornett. (Gabrieli's 16-part madrigal 'Udite chiari e generosi figli'[15] makes the point quite neatly: all parts are marked 'Voce' except for the top one – in a G2 clef, rising frequently to a'' – which is labelled 'Cornetto muto' but is also texted.) Bonta's final argument is quite simply that boy sopranos, 'the most likely performers', are demonstrably capable of singing a''s. Again, the premise is questionable; such virtuoso music is much more likely to have been entrusted to castratos or falsettists, and in any case Praetorius's table of voice ranges gives for 'Eunuchus/Falsetista/Discantista' alike an upper limit of e'' or f'', with g'' and a'' only as exceptional possible extensions.[16] And just how valuable were such high notes considered to be?

> For some Italians, not unreasonably, take no pleasure in high singing, believing that it is unseemly, also that the text cannot be properly

---

[12] Parrott, 'Transposition', 509–10.
[13] Lodovico Zacconi, *Prattica di musica* i (Venice, 1592), fol. 218v.
[14] Claudio Monteverdi, *Selva morale e spirituale* (Venice, 1640–1), 'Ut queant laxis', bars 20 and 56.
[15] Found in a Kassel source but not suggesting 'German' scoring.
[16] Michael Praetorius, *Syntagma musicum* ii (Wolfenbüttel, 1618), 20. The ranges are shown in Chapter 5 of this volume, Ex. 5.13.

grasped, that high up one squawks, shrieks and sings just like *Grasemägde* [?sparrows].[17]

These remarks of Praetorius's, which should be read against the background of his table of ranges and which are a seemingly accurate reflection of Italian practice of Monteverdi's time and circle, lead us closer, perhaps, to the heart of the matter. 'Why', asks Jordi Savall, 'should the Magnificat drop down a 4th at the very moment that requires the greatest splendour and magnificence of sound...?'[18] In the first place, this movement (like *Lauda Jerusalem*) does not, of course, 'drop down a 4th' but, if transposed, merely does not rise above the general tessitura of the others. Second, I very seriously question the assumption that it is meant to be 'splendid' and 'magnificent' in the ways that untransposed performances compel it to be. Only verses 1 and 12 use tutti forces; the remainder, apart from a magical dialogue (*a6*) between upper and lower voices ('Et misericordia'), are vocal solos, duets and trios embellished by kaleidoscopic instrumental writing almost in the manner of 'Possente spirto' (*L'Orfeo*). Devotional intimacy, sensuous ornateness and subtlety of expression, far more than grandeur, are Monteverdi's chosen means of making the Canticle 'magnificent'. Third, the equation of splendour and magnificence with a higher than usual pitch is in any case suspect and, in my view, quite foreign to the aesthetic of Monteverdi's music. It is worth noting that his only other surviving *concertato* Magnificat, a setting *a8*, lies comfortably within the tessitura of the other Vespers music in *Selva morale* (1640–1), as does Cavalli's setting (*a6*) supplied to complete the posthumous *Messa et salmi* (1650) (see Ex. 6.2). Indeed, if space permitted, I believe it would be possible to demonstrate convincingly that many of the high textures which may thrill audiences today would have been regarded in the 17th century as coarse and unacceptably vulgar.

PITCH STANDARDS

Many who acknowledged the force of my earlier arguments for transposition in Monteverdi's 1610 publication have nevertheless sought some sort of middle ground because of discomfort with the unfamiliar lowness of the two Vespers movements, especially of 'Et misericordia' in the Magnificat *a7*. Amongst those who require this Magnificat to be climactic, thrilling and *therefore* high are not a few who are reasonably happy with the lower *Lauda Jerusalem*. Others hanker

---

[17] '*Sintemahl etliche* Italia *an dem hohen singen/ wie nicht unbillich/ kein gefallen/ vermeynen es habe keine art/ könne auch der* Text *nicht recht wol vernommen werden/ man krehete/ schreye und singe in der höhe gleich wie die Grasemägde*'. Praetorius, *Syntagma musicum* ii, 16.

[18] Jordi Savall, notes for the recording on Astrée (later transferred to Alia Vox Heritage).

Ex. 6.2 Vocal ranges from Monteverdi, *Selva morale e spirituale* (1641) of (a) Vespers music other than Magnificats,* and (b) Magnificat *a8*; and from *Messa et salmi* (1650) of (c) Vespers music by Monteverdi,† and (d) Cavalli, Magnificat *a6*

* excluding *Ut queant laxis* (see above and n. 14)
† excluding *Laudate pueri*, which is in high clefs with the rubric '*Alla quarta Bassa*'

after some lesser interval of transposition than a 4th. (In practice, the only vaguely plausible alternative key to the written G minor and sounding D minor of the Magnificat *a7* is E minor, a poor key for an organ in quarter-comma meantone, an unusual and ungrateful one for most winds and strings at this period, and therefore a highly implausible one for a movement that revels in instrumental display.) Extraordinary as it may seem, there are also those who are evidently content to believe that these transpositions are an entirely optional matter – as if Bach, Beethoven, and Brahms were to have left to the discretion of performers the choice of performing movements from the Mass in B minor, the *Missa Solemnis* and the *Deutsches Requiem* a 4th higher/lower than notated. The 'solution' to this 'problem' of lowness is widely believed to be a high pitch standard of a semitone or more above $a' = 440$: '[Despite] what seems unassailable evidence in favour of transposition [in Parrott's article], one can see [Savall's] point … The only real solution is … to adopt for the work as a whole the higher pitch level that Monteverdi would surely have expected and then transpose the Psalm and Magnificat in relation to that.'[19] (Those who espouse this idea of a higher pitch and at the same time reject the idea of downward transposition will, I trust, consider the consequences very carefully before attempting *Lauda Jerusalem* in particular.)

In the very first paragraph of my 1984 article I pointed out that the ensuing discussion was 'quite independent of absolute pitch standards

---

[19] Graham Sadler, review, *Early Music* 18/2 (1990), 341.

appropriate to Monteverdi's music', and in due course I gave a lengthy talk on '17th-Century Pitch Standards in Italy: Speculation, Fact and Hearsay' at a Royal Musical Association conference in Cambridge (April 1990). (Alas, my intention to present a written-up version of the detailed findings I presented on that occasion remains unfulfilled.) The evidence, though abundant, is complex and fragmentary and in need of very careful interpretation. The possibility of an intended high pitch standard certainly cannot be lightly dismissed but, in short, it is my view that the well-documented pitch standard of roughly $a' = 466$ (an equal semitone above $a' = 440$) was only one of several in use in Monteverdi's Italy and one that had no direct relevance either to his Mantuan or, more surprisingly perhaps, even to his Venetian output.[20]

These conclusions are in sharp contrast to some of the ideas prevalent in musical circles. According to David Fallows, for example, 'it seems likely that Monteverdi's pitch-standard [for the 1610 Vespers] ... was between a tone and a minor 3rd higher than ours. That would bring all the voices into a more comfortable, brighter, range.'[21] This is seriously wide of the mark. At the very least, pronouncements of this sort stem from dangerously selective readings of the available evidence. But even if we were to suppose that such high instrumental pitch standards were relevant to Monteverdi's music-making, it would be irresponsible to ignore the strong evidence that they would have occasioned almost automatic downward transposition 'for the ease of the singers' (Zarlino, Zacconi, Bontempi, *et al.*). (Such transposition would be essentially independent of any caused by clef.) It must also be said that the preconceptions of voice-types and singing that underlie such thinking are distinctly dubious. (The nature of the soprano voice is touched on above, but the detailed analysis the subject deserves unfortunately cannot be presented here.)

LITURGY AND THE *SONATA SOPRA SANCTA MARIA*

WHILE an article setting out in full the intricate web of arguments on pitch standard will again have to wait for another occasion, I can in the meantime at least offer one small, new observation relating to a third aspect of the 1610 Vespers – the general question of the order of the items in the publication and the specific function of the *Sonata sopra Sancta Maria*.

---

[20] It is gratifying to find Bruce Haynes (private communication) reaching similar conclusions.

[21] *Choral Music on Record*, ed. Alan Blyth (1991). In the preface (p. vi) to his edition of the *1610 Vespers* (1994), Jerome Roche also asserts that 'it is quite likely that the pitch standard current in northern Italy at the time was a tone higher, if not more, than $a' = 440$'; as with Fallows, no source for this idea is given.

Whatever the precise origins of Monteverdi's 1610 Vespers music, its publication was explicitly intended for feasts of the Blessed Virgin, and 'it is now generally accepted that the Vespers may legitimately comprise all items in Amadino's 1610 print except the Mass *In illo tempore*'.[22] It scarcely needs to be said that the only context in which anything approaching a complete performance can have taken place is that of the liturgy; to view the works as somehow standing above or beyond the liturgical realities of the day is surely fanciful and is to fail to appreciate the skill with which Monteverdi embellishes his liturgical framework. But there are problems: *Duo Seraphim*'s Trinitarian text is quite implausible as an antiphon substitute in this Marian context (whatever its original associations with S Barbara),[23] and the remaining four antiphon substitutes are distributed in an apparently arbitrary fashion, leaving a particularly conspicuous gap after the Magnificat.

While the scholar is free to contemplate these intriguing matters at leisure, the performer is compelled to make decisions: whether simply to ignore the problems (the popular choice) or to wrestle with various alternative possibilities. In my performances and recording I have aimed to explore as fully as possible the implications of a liturgical context. With one conspicuous exception, this approach has drawn little comment: 'I find my critical sensibilities offended by Andrew Parrott's changing the order of movements, and interpolating other pieces', writes Philip Brett.[24] Without any elaboration, he goes on to assert that these things have been

---

[22] Sadler, review, 341. Earlier doubts about the inclusion of the *concerti* and *Sonata* were countered by Stephen Bonta, 'Liturgical Problems in Monteverdi's Marian Vespers', *Journal of the American Musicological Society* 20 (1967), 87–106. In 1960 Denis Stevens had written: 'Let us state then, quite categorically, that the following texts are not antiphons, nor have they any connection with Vespers of the Blessed Virgin: *Nigra sum*; *Pulchra es*; *Duo Seraphim*; *Audi coelum*; *Sonata sopra Sancta Maria*'; preface to his edition of the *1610 Vespers* (1961). In 1994 the same writer talks of his 'deliberately setting aside evidence' of the use of antiphon substitutes, and furthermore appears to attribute the exclusion of the five items from his 1961 version to Westminster Abbey's 'limited toilet facilities'; Denis Stevens, 'Monteverdiana 1993', *Early Music* 21/4 (1993), 570–1. More recently Joshua Rifkin has also argued that the *concerti* had no intended connection with the Vespers compositions: '17th-century users – if not their modern successors – would have understood that Monteverdi never meant this [printed order of items] as a sequence for performance; as a new examination of the source confirmed, the concertos owe their position to nothing more than exigencies of formatting'; private communication (2015).

[23] See Graham Dixon, 'Monteverdi's Vespers of 1610: "della Beata Vergine"?', *Early Music* 15/3 (1987), 386–9; and Tim Carter, 'Monteverdian Encounters', *Early Music* 22/1 (1994), 184.

[24] Philip Brett, 'Text, Context, and the Early Music Editor', in *Authenticity and Early Music*, ed. N. Kenyon (1988), 113.

done 'on the basis of a normalizing[25] theory of contemporary liturgical practice that does not take into account the evident special nature of that work and its publication'. Moreover, Brett considers the approach to be an act of 'aggression' towards Monteverdi and as such 'an unattractive feature of our discipline' that 'reflects insecurity and fear more than strength'[26] on the part of the performer.[27]

Needless to say, the view that the special nature of the 1610 Vespers is somehow compromised by an attempt to use the music in ways a contemporary *maestro di cappella* might have done is one I do not share. Quite the reverse: one is led to appreciate all the more keenly how superbly well Monteverdi's music serves the liturgy. While criticism from a recognized scholar may generally be assumed to carry some scholarly weight, Brett's, for all its academic veneer, is little more than a simple (if strong) emotional response,[28] and as such it inevitably fails to make any discernible contribution to the understanding of the matter in hand. Worse, its sheer negativity also gratuitously threatens to discourage and impede the process of further experiment and discovery.

The inclusion of additional pieces – in this instance to replace chant – is of course an entirely optional matter, and one on which I am certain Monteverdi would have been much less squeamish than Brett. I shall therefore limit my comments here to one aspect of the reordering of

---

[25] Elsewhere – in connection with clefs – Brett admits to 'a strong aversion to the word ['normal'] on account of its modern heterosexist quality'; see n. 12 to his 'Pitch and Transposition in the Paston Manuscripts', in *Sundry Sorts of Music Books; Essays on the British Library Collections presented to O. W. Neighbour on his 70th birthday*, ed. C. Banks, A. Searle and M. Turner (1993), 116.

[26] Brett, 'Text, Context', 113–14. Interestingly enough, the essay is itself an unashamed exploration of its author's own considerable 'fear and insecurity' as an editor.

[27] Brett had already toyed with this notion in an earlier article ('Facing the Music', *Early Music* 10/3 (1982), 347–50). Here too I was the object of a sustained if veiled attack. Finding a performance of mine – of Striggio's *Ecce beatam lucem* – not conventionally 'choral', Brett pronounced that the work was 'not well enough known yet for anyone to risk distorting it with a partially informed instrumentation and thereby sabotaging the composer's intentions' (p. 349). (For an account of the reasoning behind the instrumentation, see Andrew Parrott, 'A Tale of Five Cities Revisited', *Early Music* 9/3 (1981), 342–3.) I can only hope that such blatant casuistry does not seduce the casual reader. Given Brett's low opinion of the piece in question, I assume that he has made no attempt to get to know it better through performance. For my own part, I find the most 'unattractive feature of our discipline' to be an intellectual cowardice born of an unwillingness or inability to listen and think afresh.

[28] This presumably springs from what Brett calls 'a strong intuitive feeling for the music itself' ('Text, Context', 114). Needless to say, there can be no monopoly on such feelings.

movements. For my recording of the work I followed a suggestion of Hugh Keyte's in placing the *Sonata* to function as an antiphon substitute after the Magnificat, 'where it fits admirably, seeming to pick up and amplify techniques in the Canticle itself'.[29] Working quite independently and from a broader study of the litany, David Blazey subsequently came to exactly the same conclusion about the relationship of Magnificat and *Sonata*:

> I submit ... that, far from expecting the local *maestro* to provide a makeshift substitute for the missing Magnificat antiphon [as suggested by Bonta (1967)], Monteverdi intended the *Sonata sopra Sancta Maria*, a succint evocation of one favourite Marian text through the associated medium of another, to provide the most fitting response to his equally grand Magnificat, and that no qualms of conscience need accompany translating it in performance to its most appropriate musical and liturgical position.[30]

This convergence of research and hypothesis, each based on a good general understanding of contemporary practice, not only encourages us to look afresh at Monteverdi's masterpiece but also serves to alert us to possible additional clues elsewhere.

A further, and quite telling, reason for associating Magnificat and *Sonata* has duly presented itself in a contemporary source that has recently come my way. Viadana's Vespers collection *Salmi a quattro cori* (1612) concludes with a Magnificat *Sexti toni*, in which the composer assigns the 'Sicut locutus est' verse to a solo bass beneath a 'hidden soprano' (*Soprano da nascosto*). While the bass carries the Magnificat text, the soprano part consists of three statements of 'Sancta Maria ora pro nobis' to the same melodic formula used by Monteverdi (see Ex. 6.3). Whether this is regarded as an anticipation of the litany or as a telescoping of the two items – in other words, whether or not the litany is subsequently heard – there could scarcely be a closer association of Magnificat and litany text.

An increased awareness and a better understanding of such liturgical conventions and of all aspects of performance practice surely play a vital part in revealing more fully the undoubtedly 'special nature' of Monteverdi's publication. Any complacency on the part of either performers or scholars would certainly be a poor tribute to *il divino Claudio*.

---

[29] Hugh Keyte's notes to the recording; see n. 3 above.
[30] David Blazey, 'A Liturgical Role for Monteverdi's *Sonata sopra Sancta Maria*', *Early Music* 17/2 (1989), 175–82. See also Jerome Roche's observation, in the preface (p. vi) to his edition of the *1610 Vespers*, that the Marian antiphon *Sancta Maria succurre miseris* 'prescribes the particular ending of tone 1 that Monteverdi uses for his cantus firmus'.

Ex. 6.3 Viadana, *Salmi a quattro chori* (1612), Magnificat *Sexti toni*, 'Sicut locutus est'

7

Monteverdi: Onwards and Downwards

FRESH from directing a performance of Monteverdi's 1610 Vespers in New York, I was a little surprised to read in Roger Bowers's article in last November's *Early Music* that downward transposition by a 4th of its high-clef movements was supposedly no more than 'theoretically' possible.[1] While Bowers argues that 'the properties of the music itself deny its applicability',[2] my own recent experience (with both *Lauda Jerusalem* and the Magnificat *a7* down a 4th) had been of an ease and naturalness that seemed to render further theoretical justification wholly unnecessary.[3] Bowers wholeheartedly accepts the need for downward transposition; it is the appropriate *interval* of transposition that he calls into question.[4] Where I have long advocated downward transposition of a 4th (↓4th), Bowers now proposes a whole tone (↓2nd).

This turn of events – somewhat unexpected after two decades – has had the entirely healthy effect of sending me back to my original *Early Music* article,[5] as well as to a pile of notes on subsequent findings. Rather than delay in order to accumulate yet more material (while readers mislay their copies of Bowers's article, forget the details of its contents or simply lose interest), I have chosen to respond swiftly and as succinctly as the subject permits, focusing on the Magnificat *a7*. The present contribution therefore reiterates very little of my previous article and should be regarded as supplementary to it. New material is marked with an asterisk (*).

First appeared in *Early Music* 32/2 (2004), 303–17.

---

[1] Roger Bowers, 'An "Aberration" Reviewed: The Reconciliation of Inconsistent Clef-Systems in Monteverdi's Mass and Vespers of 1610', *Early Music* 31/4 (2003), 527–38, at 532.

[2] Bowers, 'An "Aberration" Reviewed', 533. The argument is surely circular: 'such transposition cannot be applied in instances, such as *1610*, in which the properties of the music itself deny its applicability.'

[3] The New York Collegium, St Ignatius Loyola, New York, 8 October 2003. The *New York Times*'s review (15 October) makes no mention of the transpositions: 'The listener had the sense of being surrounded, physically immersed in the music, and it was thrilling.'

[4] Bowers, 'An "Aberration" Reviewed', 527, 537.

[5] Andrew Parrott, 'Transposition in Monteverdi's Vespers of 1610', *Early Music*, 12/4 (1984), 490–516; reprinted in this volume, Ch. 5.

Revisiting the subject in this way and with the benefit of others' more recent research into related matters of mode[6] has left me with a much clearer understanding of certain critical points. As a consequence I am now distinctly more confident than before that the only plausible transposition for these high-clef movements really is ↓4th. Attractive though Bowers's suggestion may appear, I can discern no basis for it in the practice of Monteverdi's time. Even though I argue for its rejection, my hope is that the reasons for doing so will help clarify an issue which has ramifications far beyond this one publication and its composer.

BOWERS'S APPROACH

ACKNOWLEDGING that music variously written in high clefs and 'normal' clefs (= Bowers's 'low' clefs)[7] represents 'not two distinct pitch levels, but a single pitch level diversely notated' (see Table 7.1), Bowers observes that in Monteverdi's publication (hereinafter *1610*) transposition ↓4th 'fails to accomplish a perfect or all-but-perfect reconciliation' of the two pitch levels.[8] His analysis of the vocal ranges aims to show that there is a differential of only a 2nd between the two configurations.[9] Since transposition by this interval is said to 'receive some support from contemporary local theory',[10] and since the resultant instrumental writing presents 'no problem that was actually insurmountable',[11] the intended 'solution' must be to transpose *1610*'s high-clef movements ↓2nd.

Bowers does not seek to introduce new historical information (theoretical or musical), nor does he choose to re-examine any source

---

[6] See in particular Patrizio Barbieri, '*Chiavette* and Modal Transposition in Italian Practice (*c*. 1500–1837)', *Recercare* 3 (1991), 5–69. See also Stephen Bonta, 'Clef, Mode, and Instruments in Italy, 1540–1650', unpublished paper delivered at the Fifth Biennial Conference on Baroque Music, Durham (1992); Jeffrey G. Kurtzman, 'Tones, Modes, Clefs and Pitch in Roman Cyclic Magnificats of the 16th Century', *Early Music* 22/4 (1994), 641–64; Rudolf Rasch, 'Modes, Clefs, and Transpositions in the Early 17th Century', *Théorie et analyse musicales, 1450–1650*, ed. A.-E. Ceulemans and B. Blackburn (2001), 403–32.

[7] 'It would be anachronistic to identify either of these clef-configurations as "normal"'; Bowers, 'An "Aberration" Reviewed', 528. In fact, by the early 1600s the lower clef-configuration had established itself as easily the more common one, as *1610*'s Vespers music testifies. Describing the lower clef-system as 'low' can moreover both suggest *undue* lowness (as opposed to a 'normal' pitch level) and create confusion with yet another clef-configuration (C2 C4 F3 F5), which is lower still.

[8] Bowers, 'An "Aberration" Reviewed', 528.

[9] Bowers, 'An "Aberration" Reviewed', 532, 535.

[10] Bowers, 'An "Aberration" Reviewed', 533.

[11] Bowers, 'An "Aberration" Reviewed', 537.

Table 7.1 Voice parts in high and normal clefs

	S	A	T	B
High clefs	G2	C2	C3	F3/C4
Normal clefs	C1	C3	C4	F4

other than *1610*. Instead he sets out to isolate *1610* from the available contemporary material, discounting an 'array' of comparative vocal ranges as 'exceptional' and dismissing a 'cornucopia' of evidence on transposition as inapplicable to 'North Italian practice on the Mantua–Venice axis' (*exeunt* all Romans, plus Praetorius, Schütz *et al.*).[12] Even the testimony of Monteverdi's own high-clef *Laudate pueri a5* (1650) – unequivocally marked to be performed ↓4th – is disregarded.[13] As a consequence, Bowers's case rests not on historical foundations of the usual sort, but on his own 'additional body of data', a new analysis of *1610*'s vocal (and instrumental) ranges. Indeed, it is no exaggeration to say that the case he presents depends utterly on the presumed absence of historical evidence 'relevant' to *1610*.

Any conclusion based on such an approach naturally needs to be treated with extreme caution. We may begin therefore by asking whether there is precedent, first, for the specific transposition proposed (↓2nd) and, second, for the resultant 'key'. (Bowers provides instances of neither.)

CLEFS AND TRANSPOSITION ↓2ND

FLUENCY in transposing was cultivated by most professional instrumentalists.[14] Such is the sheer abundance of evidence for the practice that we may wish to imagine there to have been little restriction on *what* could be transposed and *by how much*. Thus, in support of his proposal, Bowers merely cites my earlier 'copious' examples, and reports that 'Italian theorists of the late 16th and early 17th centuries ... specifically mention downward transposition by one tone.'[15]

But matters are not quite so simple. High clefs and low clefs were in fact each associated with their own set of transpositions, as Virgiliano (c. 1590) shows perhaps most clearly;[16] see Illus. 7.1 and Table 7.2, which indicates how cornettists and trombonists may transpose.

---

[12] Bowers, 'An "Aberration" Reviewed', 532–3.

[13] Parrott, 'Transposition', 501–2. Bowers also ignores examples of transposition ↓4th found in Venetian publications of works of Rossi (1600), Viadana (1602) and Rigatti (1640); see Parrott, 'Transposition', 496, 498, 505.

[14] Parrott, 'Transposition', 505–8.

[15] Bowers, 'An "Aberration" Reviewed', 535, 533.

[16] Aurelio Virgiliano, *Il dolcimelo* (MS treatise, c. 1590; R/1979), [102–3, 105]; see also Parrott, 'Transposition', 506 (Table 2).

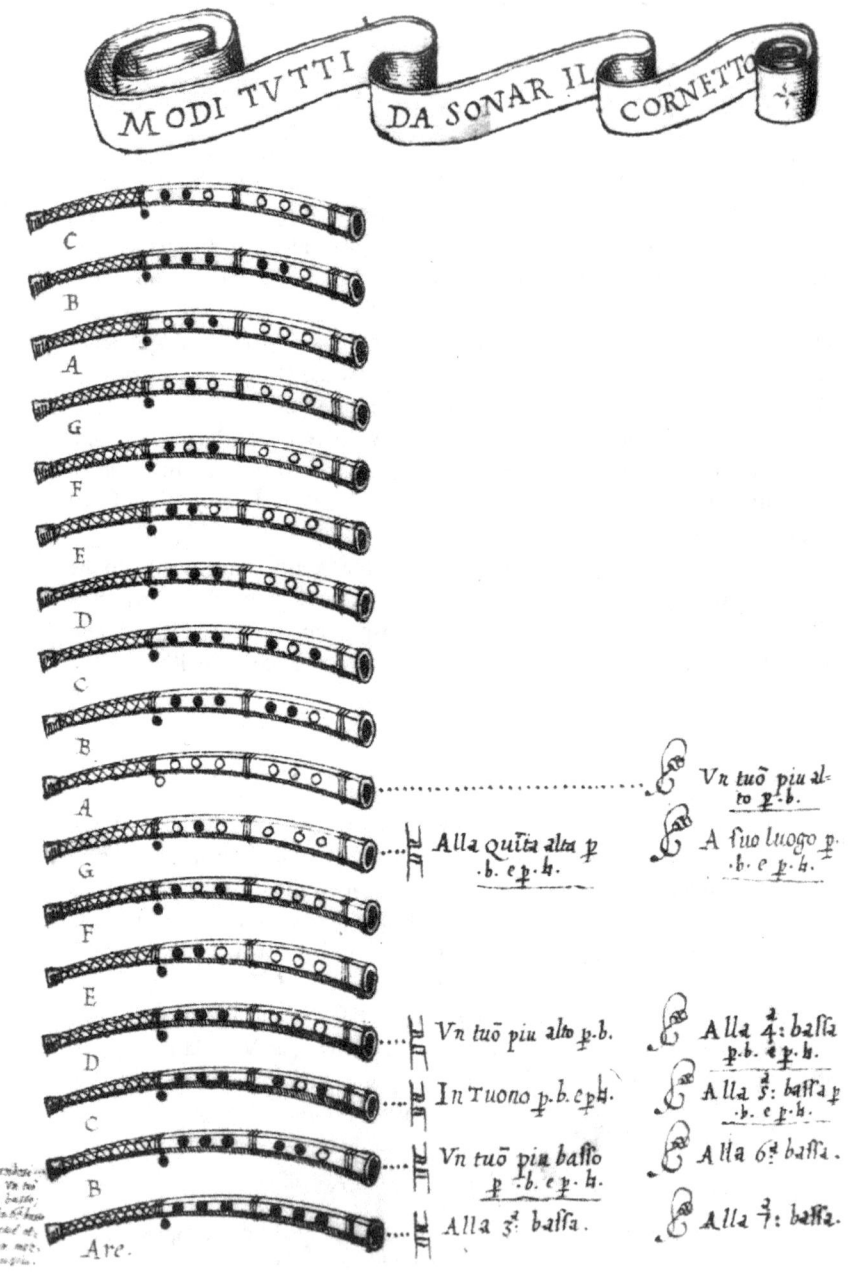

Illus. 7.1 'Modi tutti da sonar il cornetto', from Aurelio Virgiliano, *Il dolcimelo* (MS, c. 1590), [105]

Table 7.2 Transpositions for wind players, after Vigiliano

	Normal clefs	High clefs
up (↑)	2nd*	—
down (↓)	2nd, 3rd	4th, 5th, 6th, 7th

* also ↑5th for cornett but not for trombone

Here, as with Virgiliano's other instruments, transposition ↓2nd does not occur with high clefs, and is instead linked exclusively to normal-clef writing, just as it is in Diruta's explicit instructions for organists (1609).[17] Equally, both writers specifically associate music written in high clefs (usually with one flat) with the wider transposition ↓4th. Zacconi (1592) expresses it thus:

> you can generally play the musical Tones given in their natural positions [i.e. in normal clefs] a 2nd lower and [those in high clefs] a 4th or 5th [lower] ...[18]

This is not abstract theory but practical information for instrumentalists. It therefore comes as no surprise to find these principles confirmed in the musical sources themselves. One of the very earliest publications to include an organ bass – and therefore one of the very earliest sources in which one might hope to find evidence of such transposition – is *Croce (1594), a collection of motets *a8 'comodi per le voci, e per cantar con ogni stromento'* by the then *vicemaestro di cappella* of St Mark's, Venice.[19] All but two of its 17 items are supplied with instructions for transposition, mostly as a pair of options such as *Alla quarta, e quinta bassa* (↓4th & ↓5th); see Table 7.3.

---

[17] Girolamo Diruta, *Seconda parte del transilvano* (Venice, 1622), bk 3, 4–11; cf. Parrott, 'Transposition', 492.

[18] Lodovico Zacconi, *Prattica di musica* (Venice, 1592), fol. 218v; see Parrott, 'Transposition', 506–7. The transposed Dorian of Monteverdi's two Magnificat settings is not listed by *Praetorius among those modes that sometimes go ↓2nd; Michael Praetorius, *Syntagma musicum* iii (Wolfenbüttel, 1619), 82.

[19] Giovanni Croce, *Motetti a8* (Venice, 1594/?1607). Bowers gives a publication date of 1594, but Martin Morell has argued that the organ book is evidently a later addition; correspondence in *Music & Letters* 72 (1991), 516–7. See Bonta, 'Clef, Mode, and Instruments', table 13; and Andrew Parrott, 'High Clefs and Down-to-Earth Transposition', *Early Music* 40/1 (2012), 85 n. 4.

Table 7.3 Transpositions in Giovanni Croce, *Motetti* (1594)

	Normal clefs	High clefs
up (↑)	–	–
down (↓)	–/2nd (×6), 3rd (×2), –/3rd/4th (×1), 3rd/4th (×1)	4th/5th (×4), 5th (×1)

The two main points to observe here are that transposition ↓2nd again occurs *only with normal clefs*, and that high-clef writing in each case goes ↓4th *at least*.[20] The additional flexibility of Croce's collection does not in any way conflict with these broader principles. As Agazzari (1607) puts it:

> one must see which [transposition] is most appropriate and suitable *to the given Tone*, not as some do who pretend to play every Tone at every level, for if I could argue at length, I would show them their impropriety and error [my italics].[21]

In short, while the general practice of transposing is handsomely documented, the specific transposition which Bowers proposes – of high-clef music ↓2nd – is conspicuously absent not only from Zacconi, Croce, Virgiliano and Diruta, but also from all other relevant contemporary sources I have so far encountered.[22]

IF the Magnificat *a7* is to be transposed ↓2nd from its written level, it moves – in instrumental terms – from G minor into an outlandish F minor (with a signature of three flats but plenty of additional D♭s). This is barely mentioned by Bowers.[23] If there is any string or wind music from this period – let alone any comparably sophisticated and virtuoso writing – specifically intended for this remote and problematic key, I have yet to see it. (It does not appear even amongst Diruta's 23 written-out examples of organ transposition.)[24] On the other hand, in D minor (i.e. ↓4th)

---

[20] We may also note that *downward* transposition – never upward – is an option for all 10 normal-clef pieces, and that in only one of 12 cases do Croce's alternative pitch levels lie more than a tone apart.

[21] Agostino Agazzari, *Del sonare sopra'l basso* (Siena, 1607); see Parrott, 'Transposition', 493.

[22] Diruta, moreover, regards ↓2nd not as a 'primary' or mandatory transposition but as an expedient to compensate for the *unduly high* pitch of some organs; Parrott, 'Transposition', 492. Bowers's proposition goes in the opposite direction: while accepting that downward transposition is required by the notation, he seeks to avoid unduly low ranges by adjusting the resultant pitch *upward* (reducing the conventional interval of a 4th to a 2nd).

[23] See Bowers, 'An "Aberration" Reviewed', 535 and n. 19.

[24] See n. 18 above, but see also Giovan Paolo Cima, *Partito de ricercari & canzoni alla francese* (Milan, 1606), ex. 4.

Ex. 7.1 Passages from *L'Orfeo* (a, c, e) and the 1640 Gloria *a7* (g), compared with 1610, Magnificat *a7* (↓4th) (b, d, f, h)

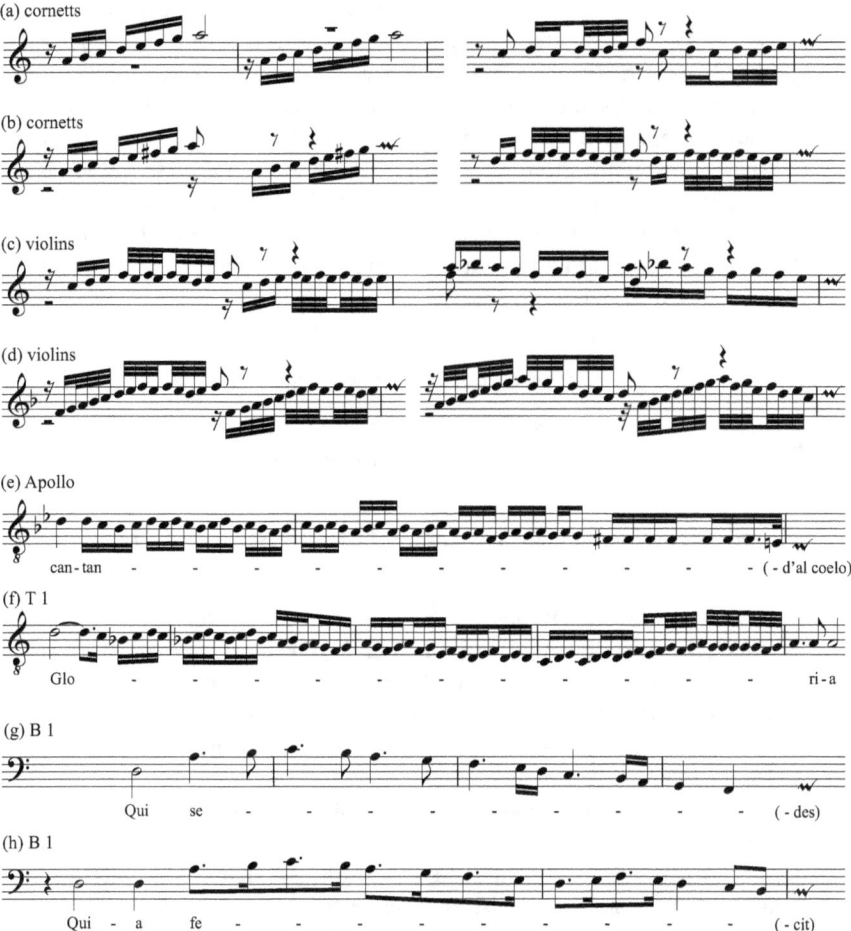

Monteverdi's writing for violins and cornetts not only lies completely naturally and idiomatically under the fingers, but also emerges as a strikingly exact counterpart in range, tessitura and character to passages in his *L'Orfeo* (performed 1607, published 1609); see Ex. 7.1, which also shows some parallels of vocal writing.[25] Bowers offers no comment on this phenomenon.

Experienced organists and others probably did find themselves in F minor from time to time. But if so, they are more likely to have arrived there by a different route from the one Bowers proposes, perhaps by taking a *normal-clef* G minor piece ↓2nd.[26] And, just as we are more accustomed

---

[25] Also given in Parrott, 'Transposition', 508 (as ex. 18).
[26] See Virgiliano, *Il dolcimelo*; and Diruta, *Il transilvano*.

to transposing hymns or simple anthems than intricate cantatas, it is conservative vocal polyphony rather than elaborate concerted music that is most likely to have attracted such transposition. For any composer of Monteverdi's day to write a virtuoso vocal and instrumental showpiece specifically *intended* to be played in F minor (whatever its notated level) would presuppose some very special circumstance. To write such a work without any apparent concession to the particular nature of this highly unusual key would also be quite remarkable.[27] And, not least, to do so without including any instruction to alert performers to the need for a wholly exceptional form of transposition – *un tuono più basso* from high-clef notation – would be to court disaster, causing performers instead to adopt a conventional one.

TRANSPOSITION ↓4TH

ACCORDING to Bowers there is only one unequivocal source for the degree of transposition appropriate to high clefs: namely, Praetorius (1619). A key passage begins thus:

> Every vocal piece in high clefs ... must be transposed ... as follows: if it has a flat, down a 4th ...[28]

This major source is then rejected as 'peripheral' to Monteverdi's practice on the grounds that 'Praetorius was no Italian': only the music and writings of Northern Italy should be taken into consideration – and these are said to be silent on the matter. 'If ever it turns out that some writing of Michael Praetorius happens to match and coincide with this prime evidence, then well and good.'[29]

By these means Bowers argues himself into a position where the only evidence that counts is his own analysis of *1610*'s vocal ranges. The vast body of information enshrined in the works of Heinrich Schütz, for example, is therefore disregarded in its entirety[30] – despite the composer's five or so years of study in Italy (mostly in Venice), first with Giovanni Gabrieli (whose high-clef *Lieto godea* he reworked ↓5th)[31] and later perhaps with Monteverdi himself.[32] Ruled out similarly for geographical

---

[27] Bowers argues that 'these unconventional demands were ... intentional and genuine'; 'An "Aberration" Reviewed', 537. The composer's contemporaries, on the other hand, would (I suspect) have regarded any such writing as something of an aberration; see also below.

[28] Praetorius, *Syntagma musicum* iii, 80–1; Parrott, 'Transposition', 493–4.

[29] Bowers, 'An "Aberration" Reviewed', 532–3.

[30] Parrott, 'Transposition', 496–7, 500.

[31] Parrott, 'Transposition', 497.

[32] Schütz also knew Praetorius personally, while Praetorius himself was evidently familiar at least with *1610*'s *Ave maris stella*; Praetorius, *Syntagma musicum* iii, 128–9 [*recte* 108–9].

reasons is the testimony of Roman publications such as G. F. Anerio's (1613), with its 37 high-clef pieces, each and every one bearing an instruction for transposition either ↓4th or ↓5th.³³ But is modal theory, which lies at the heart of transposition practice,³⁴ really so particular about geography?³⁵ Roman practice demonstrably accords with that of Germany, for example.³⁶ Bowers (beyond his analysis of 1610's vocal ranges) offers no evidence to suggest that Northern Italy followed a separate path.

Fortunately the matter need not remain purely conjectural, as 'prime' evidence from Northern Italy turns out not to be lacking. Asked by his *discepolo* about high clefs, the *maestro* in *Banchieri (Bologna, 1601), for example, answers in terms that correspond exactly to those of Praetorius (1619):

> when the G2 clef has a flat, then ... the notes are to be taken a 4th lower.³⁷

(From Naples *Picerli (1631) says the very same thing: 'when the composition uses ... the G2 clef, it is to be transposed, mentally or in writing, down a 4th or 5th ... with B♭ it is to be transposed down a 4th.')³⁸ And for two examples of comparable evidence from the musical sources we may turn first to the instructions given in *Croce (1594), where – as we have seen above – all five high-clef pieces are marked to go ↓4th *at least*. (Even if Croce's practice here is seen as somewhat more flexible than Banchieri's and Praetorius's theory, there is no disguising the fact that it also flatly contradicts Bowers's proposal.) A more orthodox example is found in *Palestrina (1608), a Venetian reissue of his fourth book of motets *a5* (1584): complete with organ continuo, all 23 original high-clef items have here been transposed and renotated in normal clefs, ↓4th in the case of each of the 15 motets with a signature of one flat.³⁹

---

³³ Two further items in Giovanni Francesco Anerio's collection – *Antiphonae, seu sacrae cantiones* (Rome, 1613) – have organ parts written ↓4th from the high-clef vocal parts; Parrott, 'Transposition', 496, 498.

³⁴ Barbieri, 'Chiavette', 17–35.

³⁵ See Rasch, 'Modes', whose examples are of music from the Netherlands.

³⁶ Parrott, 'Transposition', 496–500.

³⁷ '*Quando poi la Chiave di G sol re ut sarà per b molle, all'hora ... pigliorassi le voci una quarta bassa*'; Adriano Banchieri, *Cartella overo Regole* (Bologna, 1601), 23.

³⁸ '... *quando la compositione si canta ... per la chiave di G sol re ut, la compositione si trasporta mentalmente, ò in scritta, una quarta, ò una quinta sotto ... si trasporta una quarta sotto, quando si canta col b molle*'; Silverio Picerli, *Specchio secondo di musica* (Naples, 1631), 192 (quoted from Barbieri, 'Chiavette', 44).

³⁹ Giovanni Pierluigi da Palestrina, *Mottetti a5*, bk 4 (Venice, 1608). The remaining eight motets (without flat) have been transposed ↓5th; Barbieri, 'Chiavette', 51.

THE 'RECONCILIATION OF INCONSISTENT CLEF-SYSTEMS'

In Bowers's view, when Monteverdi's high-clef movements are set ↓4th, the 'tessituras of all the voices emerge as gratingly low compared with those of the generality of the rest of the movements'.[40] With this we come to the heart of the matter. It is this perception – shared perhaps by many – that generates the search for 'an alternative solution'. But what degree of uniformity is it reasonable to expect between one piece and the next?

Monteverdi's publication is a dazzling catalogue of styles and techniques, and the individual characteristics of its component parts naturally give rise to – and result from – differing tessituras. Thus, when the normal-clef movements are compared with each other, we find that some lie significantly higher than others (compare *Laetatus sum* and *Ave maris stella*),[41] while the tessituras of individual voice parts can vary by a good minor 3rd; see Ex. 7.2. To think purely in terms of *composite* tessituras – the aggregates of several movements – is therefore potentially misleading. And while *1610*'s high-clef writing (when ↓4th) may well end up lower than the 'generality' of its normal-clef pieces, the Magnificat *a7* nevertheless does align revealingly well with two other individual items, namely *Audi coelum* and *Ave maris stella*; see Ex. 7.3. If, even after transposition ↓4th, the Magnificat *a7* proves so remarkably similar in tessitura to these two movements, are they, too, to be considered implausibly low? (And, if so, are we to start transposing all such movements at will in order to bring them in line with a supposed norm?) Or is it merely the Magnificat's wider – and lower – bass range that puts it beyond the pale?

Before looking at vocal scoring in general, and at these bass parts in particular, we may query the underlying assumption of Bowers's article, that 'the perfect or all-but-perfect reconciliation of pitch levels ... is the objective sought by the application of some degree of transposition'.[42] Are we really justified in demanding that high and normal clefs always yield virtually identical sounding ranges?

Clefs and clef-combinations served, in part, as compositional tools to regulate vocal (and instrumental) ranges. Having chosen one or other set of clefs, a composer was assured that workable ranges for each voice (and appropriate relative ranges for the voices as a whole) could be achieved through the simple expedient of not writing above or below a stave; any need for ledger lines acted as a warning that normal modest limits were being exceeded. Individual and overall ranges from Monteverdi's time

---

[40] Bowers, 'An "Aberration" Reviewed', 531.

[41] *Laetatus sum* has an overall range of bass *F* to soprano *g″*, while that of *Ave maris stella* is *E–d″*.

[42] Bowers, 'An "Aberration" Reviewed', 528.

Ex. 7.2 Divergent ranges within *1610*

Ex. 7.3 Voice ranges in *1610* compared:
(a) *Audi coelum*, (b) *Ave maris stella*, (c) Magnificat *a7* (↓4th)

are therefore much more intimately related to clefs than in most later repertoires. As Ex. 7.4 shows, if two hypothetical compositions are compared – one in high clefs, the other in normal clefs, each employing the full extent of its staves – we find that to transpose the former ↓4th *necessarily* produces a lower tessitura (by one degree) than that of the latter, for the simple reason that the two systems themselves do not lie a 4th apart but only a 3rd.[43] It follows that conventional transposition

[43] Just as the lines of a stave represent steps of a 3rd, so too are the various clefs separated from each other by 3rds. From this it follows that any written-out transposition ↓4th (from high to normal clefs) will necessarily shift the notes one degree lower on the stave. (Transposition by a 3rd or a 5th can be achieved simply by substituting a different clef and signature, while keeping the notes in exactly the same position on the stave; with transposition of a 2nd or a 4th, however, the notes inevitably shift their position on the stave, irrespective of any change of clef.) By the same token, any note or phrase in

Ex. 7.4 High and normal clef-configurations compared

(a) high clefs

(c)

(b) normal clefs

In (a) o = written pitch; in (c) these pitches are shown transposed ↓4th following the normal clef-range of each voice.

↓4th is no guarantee of an exact alignment of ranges and that the sort of 'mismatch' (of roughly a tone) that may seem puzzling in *1610* is almost intrinsic to the process.[44] In short, high clefs tend quite naturally – if somewhat paradoxically – to yield *lower* tessituras than normal clefs.

CORE VOCAL RANGES

'THE starting-point for a fresh evaluation of the evidence', writes Bowers, is the 'identification of the core ranges' (as opposed to total ranges) of *1610*'s vocal writing; this 'can usefully be undertaken in respect only of the movements composed for chorus or ensemble of non-specialist voices'.[45]

In the context of the Vespers music this use of the word 'chorus' is not intended (I trust) to carry any necessary implication of more than one singer per part. While the idiom of *1610*'s Mass does suggest such an ensemble, the remainder of the music gives not the slightest indication that Monteverdi had anything other than solo voices in mind.[46] What is more striking, though, is the notion that 'non-specialist voices' ('standard voices') might have had a role in courtly concerted music-making of this

a particular position on the stave will also end up sounding one degree lower after such transposition.

[44] A good test of this would be the 244 compositions in Anerio (1613), where all 37 high-clef items are marked to be transposed ↓4th; see Parrott, 'Transposition', 498.

[45] Bowers, 'An "Aberration" Reviewed', 528–9.

[46] For a brief outline of the Italian origins of German one-to-a-part practice in concerted music see Andrew Parrott, *The Essential Bach Choir* (2000), 29–32. At the New York performance mentioned above (see n. 3) Monteverdi's music was sung entirely by solo voices and with no unspecified instrumental doubling.

sort. Certainly some sections demand less virtuosity than others (just as some lie higher than others), but there are no serious grounds for imagining that Monteverdi is writing for two distinct groups of singers, 'virtuoso voices' and a 'non-virtuoso ensemble'.

Unfortunately, this spurious distinction seriously undermines the value of Bowers's analysis: in order to achieve 'the most secure conclusions', all virtuoso writing is excluded from consideration. The reader, however, is left in considerable doubt as to what remains in and what is out; mention is made only of 'the solo motets (including the first section of *Audi coelum*) and certain Magnificat sections'.[47] Are the duetting tenors in *Laudate pueri* ('Excelsus super omnes gentes dominus') and all the cascading voices of *Laetatus sum* ('Illuc enim') therefore presumed to be 'non-specialist'? And if the tenor's solo opening of *Audi coelum* has been discounted, why does its single fleeting top f' remain to define the upper limit of tenor 'core range' for that movement?

Core range, rather than 'the rare liberties represented by the extremes of range', is justifiably considered to be the critical indicator of a composer's understanding of voice-types,[48] but Bowers's analysis contains noticeable inconsistencies. With *Dixit Dominus* a unique and quite short $f\sharp'$ (in S1 only) is allowed to represent the upper end of the soprano core range; similarly, a single (semiquaver) bass high c' is retained for *Laetatus sum*.[49] As it happens, the effect of both oversights, and of that in *Audi coelum*, is to create the misleading impression of a somewhat higher tessitura than is actually the case. (All three are normal-clef movements.)

With the Magnificat *a7* the picture is more seriously distorted. If its 'non-virtuoso ensemble movements' have been omitted from consideration, we need to know which they are; are we left with seven of the 12 sections, or just three?[50] Clearly, the duetting basses of 'Quia fecit' have been ruled out; the conspicuous absence of their repeated high written f's ($\downarrow$4th = c') at 'fecit mihi magna' causes an entire minor 3rd to be chopped off the top of the movement's bass core range. Here, then (in this high-clef movement), the impression is given of a *lower* tessitura than is actually the case.

VOCAL SCORING AND RANGES

TRANSPOSITION was not a free-for-all, nor was vocal scoring. Uncertainty about pitch standards and (as we have seen) a lack of familiarity with the practical implications of the different clef-systems have conspired to cloud the issue for us. But another factor complicates matters

---

[47] Bowers, 'An "Aberration" Reviewed', 529.
[48] Bowers, 'An "Aberration" Reviewed', 529.
[49] Bowers, 'An "Aberration" Reviewed', 529, ex. 1.
[50] Bowers, 'An "Aberration" Reviewed', 529.

further: the simple assumption that Monteverdi's vocal categories equate directly with our own.

Instead of needing to scrutinize each vocal line in the time-consuming way that both Bowers and I have done, musicians of Monteverdi's time understood that clefs were a succinct indicator both of core ranges and of vocal scoring. In each system a particular clef identifies a specific voice-type – soprano, alto, tenor, bass (as in Table 7.1) – and also broadly prescribes its potential range, which is roughly that of the stave itself (as in Ex. 7.4). (As the distances between clefs also show the relationships of the various parts, we may note that alto and tenor lie closer to each other than other voices.)

*Banchieri (1614) is rather more specific about vocal ranges: for each voice he gives both a (core) range of a 10th – for the *Cantore perfetto* – (see Ex. 7.5, range (a)), and one of a 12th – for the *Cantore perfettissimo* – extending a degree further in each direction (range (b)).[51] Naturally enough, it is in solo writing that we can most often expect to encounter these wider ranges. Particularly convenient for comparison with Banchieri are the *Cento concerti ecclesiastici* by *Viadana (1602), a collection which opens with short solo items for each voice-type in turn (10 apiece, plus *falsobordoni*).[52] While Viadana's soprano and alto conform fairly closely to Banchieri's wider limits, his tenor reaches down as far as 'bass' F in two separate items (albeit briefly) and his bass extends both higher and lower (touching low D on two separate occasions);[53] see Ex. 7.5, range (c). Not surprisingly these composite ranges from Viadana turn out to be wider for each voice than for any individual Vespers item in *1610*, including the Magnificat *a7*. Indeed, both tenor and bass require what Bowers describes as 'gigantic overall ranges of two complete octaves', something

---

[51] Adriano Banchieri, *Cartella musicale* (Bologna, 1614), '146' [recte 138]; reproduced in Barbieri, 'Chiavette', 36. I have corrected what I take to be errors in Banchieri's bass column, where the use of black and void noteheads seems to have become muddled.

[52] Lodovico Viadana, *Cento concerti ecclesiastici* (Venice, 1602). In five cases there is 'bitonal' notation, where a high-clef vocal line is unambiguously intended to sound at the lower written pitch of the organ part – specifically, ↓4th.

[53] This data meets Bowers's objection ('An "Aberration" Reviewed', 532) that my earlier 'array of instances' of very low vocal pitches cannot be found 'within any single and cohering body of music issued at a single date as a single publication'. Should further evidence be needed, it may also be found in Giovanni Gabrieli's posthumous *Sacrae symphoniae* ii (Venice, 1615). In *Jubilate Deo*, for example, both optional vocal bass parts (*si placet*) contain several low Ds and one of them eight Cs. With more obvious textual justification the soprano part (C1) of *Misericordia tua* descends at the word 'inferiori' to semibreves on low *a* and *g*(♯), while in *Quem vidistis* the soprano (G2) touches low *g* at 'in terris' and two of the tenors descend to low G at 'humiliter'.

Ex. 7.5 Voice ranges compared: (a) Banchieri, *Cantore perfetto*, (b) Banchieri, *Cantore perfettissimo*, (c) Viadana, *Cento concerti ecclesiastici*, (d) Monteverdi, *1610*, Magnificat *a7* (↓4th), (e) Monteverdi, *1610*, Magnificat *a7* (↓2nd), (f) Palestrina, *Vergine saggia* (○ = written note, ● = sounding note, after Doni (1640))

he regards as intrinsically 'neither very practical nor very probable' for *1610* as a whole.[54] Although Monteverdi calls more frequently for bass low *D* (with the movement set ↓4th), all his ranges lie comfortably within those of Viadana; see range (d). By contrast, the effect of Bowers's proposed narrower transposition ↓2nd – range (e) – is to nudge each of Viadana's (already wide) ranges discernibly upwards, consistently creating new upper limits and scarcely approaching the lower ones.

From today's perspective normal-clef music from the late 16th and early 17th centuries may generally appear to lie rather low for voices, and anything lower is certainly liable to be regarded with scepticism.[55] Clearly, differences in pitch standard need to be taken into account (see below), but the matter is further complicated by a natural tendency to assume that the terms 'soprano, alto, tenor, bass' carried more or less the same connotations then as they do for us today. In particular, while the alto in church music of Monteverdi's time is commonly taken to have been either a falsettist or a castrato (as in some later traditions), the weight of evidence points instead to a voice that we would call a (high) tenor.[56] (Bowers, who probably has the falsetto voice in mind, notes that 'for some reason as yet undetermined' Monteverdi's normal-clef alto parts are relatively narrow, with a usual upper limit of *a'*,[57] while their close proximity to

---

[54] Bowers, 'An "Aberration" Reviewed', 531–2.

[55] The apparent sacrifice of a 'high' piece through downward transposition is particularly likely to meet with stout resistance.

[56] There is insufficient space to elaborate here, but I think it better to alert the reader to the issue (and to some of my conclusions) than to ignore it.

[57] Bowers, 'An "Aberration" Reviewed', 530. The alto part of *Laetatus sum* has a single brief *bb'*.

Table 7.4 Varying understandings of SATB

	Mixed voices c. 2000	Anglican choir c. 2000	Italian vocal ensemble c. 1600
S	woman (high)	boy (high)	man (falsetto)/castrato
A	woman (low)	man (falsetto)	man (high)
T	man (high)	man (high)	man (medium/high)
B	man (low)	man (low)	man (low)

tenor parts removes the need for much use of the lower range, it is easy enough to see why the non-falsetto alto's upper range would be restricted in this way.) Falsettists and castratos were both still associated with soprano (rather than alto) parts, while boys who could hold their own in elaborate concerted music were probably a rarity.[58] The remaining male voices were divided not into two categories (tenor and bass) but into three (high, medium/high and low), with the range of the middle voice perhaps best described as that of a baritonal tenor.[59] This understanding of early 17th-century practice in Italy is compared in Table 7.4 with the more familiar distribution of voices in two types of present-day choir – the mixed-voice choir and the Anglican cathedral or collegiate choir.

The implications of this are considerable. As an illustration we may take Palestrina's setting of Petrarch's *Vergine saggia*; see Ex. 7.5, range (f). Apart from a rather high-lying bass part the madrigal's written ranges conform tolerably well to modern expectations of SATB scoring, such that today's editors would probably be loath to transpose it more than, say, ↓2nd. (And at such a level it would neatly match Bowers's proposed transposition of the 1610 Magnificat *a7*; see range (e).) However, *Giovanni Battista Doni (1640) is adamant not only that Palestrina's madrigal should be transposed – 'because it is notated high, as they say, and would prove too uncomfortable if it were sung as it stands' – but also that the 'most usual type of transposition' (in this instance) is of altogether another order: namely, ↓5th.[60] Our present SATB paradigms, it seems, are very unreliable guides to early 17th-century vocal scoring.

---

[58] For some observations on soprano parts see Andrew Parrott, 'Monteverdi's Vespers of 1610 Revisited', *Performing Practice in Monteverdi's Music*, ed. R. Monterosso (1995), 165–7 (= *The Musical Times* 136/10 (1995), 532); reprinted in this volume, Ch. 6.

[59] On the survival of a comparable distribution of voices into the late 17th and 18th centuries, see Andrew Parrott, 'Performing Purcell', *The Purcell Companion*, ed. M. Burden (1995), 417–24; and Andrew Parrott, 'Falsetto and the French: "Une toute autre marche"', *Basler Jahrbuch für historische Musikpraxis* 26 (2002), 129–48 (both reprinted in this volume, Chs. 9 and 4, respectively).

[60] '... perche è segnato all'alta, come dicono, & riuscirebbe troppo scommodo, se si cantasse, come stà', 'alla quinta bassa, ch'è la maniera più consueta di

Ex. 7.6 Monteverdi, Gloria *a7*, 'pax hominibus'

BASSES AND PITCH STANDARDS

A SPECIFIC effect – or aim – of Bowers's proposal (Ex. 7.5, range (e)) is to eliminate the bass low *D*s that result from transposition ↓4th (range (d)). These notes, which many still find perplexing, are all doubled by organ and are almost wholly confined to the Bassus part (B1) of 'Et misericordia', a slow-moving dialogue between three upper and three lower voices.[61] (It may be helpful to remind readers that the music under consideration here is concerted music and thus primarily, if not exclusively, the preserve of select solo voices; see n. 46.) In my earlier article I pointed to no fewer than 10 other sacred works by Monteverdi himself that unambiguously call for this note.[62] Ex. 7.6 reproduces a telling extract from his 1640 Gloria *a7* ('pax hominibus'), where the seven voices, each in its

---

trasportatione'; Giovanni Battista Doni, *Annotazioni sopra il compendio* (Rome, 1640), 250, quoted in Barbieri, '*Chiavette*', 45. I am grateful to Hugh Griffith for his help with this passage in particular.

[61] There is a single *D* for B2 (*Sextus*) in 'Et misericordia' and a further one each for B1 and B2 at the start of 'Sicut erat'. In the *1610* Mass, the same transposition produces just four *D*s.

[62] Parrott, 'Transposition', 502. See also Parrott, 'Vespers Revisited', 168.

lowest register, combine to produce a dark, sober texture unmistakably similar to that of 'Et misericordia' (↓4th), complete with low Ds[63] – and thus, despite the composer's full authority, 'gratingly low' in Bowers's terms.

In questioning the significance of these and other instances of low vocal ranges, Bowers suggests that 'each represents not conventional but *exceptional* practice' and should thus be excluded from the Vespers.[64] (Interestingly, the very opposite argument is employed in defence of some wholly unprecedented instrumental writing: the instrumental demands of the Magnificat *a7* are, he claims, 'not routine but genuinely exceptional', and must therefore be allowed to stand as testament to Monteverdi's genius.)[65] Let me nevertheless briefly offer two further instances of low bass writing in Venetian publications. In *Ercole Porta's *Missa secundi toni* (1620) the Kyrie, Gloria and Credo each require the bass voice, in their very opening bars, to descend to low *D* ('elei-*son*', 'Et in terra *pax*', 'et ter-*rae*'),[66] while in *Giovanni Valentini's *Missae quatuor* (1621) two specified transpositions for optional organ (↓4th and ↓5th) take the bass part respectively to low *D* (*Missa Susanna*) and, further still, to *C* (*Missa Stabat mater*).[67]

Little is known, sadly, of Mantua's bass singers in the early 1600s, but some decades later *Doni (1640) commented that Monteverdi had had 'certain very low basses' at his disposal there.[68] Moreover, in 1614, shortly after the composer's departure for Venice, *Ferdinando Gonzaga's agent in Rome reported having found there *un Basso per camera*, a new bass singer for the court's chamber singing, and commented that 'he goes down to low *D*' (*va basso sino al ottava di D sol re*).[69]

Exactly how low might Monteverdi have expected this *D* to sound? The question has been deferred until this point because Bowers's subject – and mine – is the *relation* in pitch between high- and low-clef movements in *1610*, a matter which is indeed 'preliminary to, and entirely independent of, identification' of an appropriate pitch standard.[70] Suffice it to say that all salient information on Italian pitch standards for the period

---

[63] The two passages are compared in Parrott, 'Transposition', 503 (ex. 10).

[64] Bowers, 'An "Aberration" Reviewed', 532.

[65] Bowers, 'An "Aberration" Reviewed', 536.

[66] *Seventeenth-Century Italian Sacred Music* ii, ed. A. Schnoebelen (1995).

[67] Hellmut Federhofer, 'Zur Chiavetten-Frage', *Anzeiger der österreichischen Akademie der Wissenschaften: Philosophisch-historische Klasse* 10 (1952), 148–50.

[68] '... *certi Bassi molto profondi*'; Doni, *Annotazioni sopra il compendio*, 155.

[69] Paolo Faccone (1614), writing from Rome to Ferdinando Gonzaga in Mantua; S. Parisi, 'Acquiring Musicians and Instruments in the Early Baroque: Observations from Mantua', *Journal of Musicology* 14 (1996), 137. Parisi gives '*Dessore*' for what I take to be '*Dsolre/D sol re*'.

[70] Bowers, 'An "Aberration" Reviewed', 527.

has helpfully been brought together by Bruce Haynes[71] and that the two strongest candidates in the case of *1610* appear to be, in approximate terms, $a' = 440$ and one semitone above $a' = 440$. (For what it is worth, the 1565 Graziadio Antegnati organ in Mantua's court chapel of Santa Barbara has been restored in recent years to its original condition, reportedly at the higher pitch.)[72] Having performed the Vespers music at both pitch levels, but always with the same principles of vocal scoring (see above), I merely offer two observations: that, while on balance the higher pitch is probably somewhat easier for most voices, the overall width of ranges has never proved problematic, and that the *relative* pitch levels of high- and normal-clef movements (with the former ↓4th) have always felt utterly convincing.

INSTRUMENTS

IF I have scarcely touched on the obbligato instrumental writing in the Magnificat *a7*, this is primarily because I have dealt with the matter at length elsewhere.[73] But it is also the least persuasive part of Bowers's argument: his suggestion that the very real problems caused by transposition ↓2nd can be solved by 'the simple engagement of instruments of a size identified as capable of realizing the sounding of these particular parts transposed down by one tone' side-steps too many issues and is in any case far from 'simple'.[74] And, while the very basis of his analysis of ranges is that *1610* is written for 'a single unchanging vocal ensemble' (of 'non-specialist' singers?),[75] the reader is required to imagine that by contrast the corresponding instrumental ensemble has one set of instruments for *Domine ad adiuvandum, Dixit Dominus, Ave maris stella* and the *Sonata sopra Sancta Maria* but a second set especially for the Magnificat *a7*. (This would certainly put a damper on another – and, in my view, more plausible – hypothesis, that the *Sonata*, despite its printed position in *1610*, was intended to function as an antiphon substitute at the Magnificat's conclusion;[76] with half a dozen or so virtuoso players needing to switch instrument, it would be hard to avoid either an unseemly delay or an unholy scramble.)

Almost as if seeking refuge from these imponderables, Bowers proceeds to justify the presence in *1610* of the second Magnificat (*a6*) – a related work without obbligato instruments – on the grounds that 'for many

---

[71] Bruce Haynes, *A History of Performing Pitch* (2002), 58–75.
[72] Haynes, *Performing Pitch*, 73; see also Parrott, 'Vespers Revisited', 169–70.
[73] Parrott, 'Transposition', 508–10 and Parrott, 'Vespers Revisited', 164–6.
[74] Bowers, 'An "Aberration" Reviewed', 535. For a discussion of related matters see Nicholas Mitchell, 'Choral and Instrumental Pitch in Church Music, 1570–1620', *Galpin Society Journal* 48 (1995), 13–32.
[75] Bowers, 'An "Aberration" Reviewed', 528.
[76] Parrott, 'Vespers Revisited', 170–4.

ensembles, and perhaps for most,' the more elaborate setting was 'simply out of reach' on account of Monteverdi's 'unconventional' instrumental demands.[77] A more satisfactory explanation of 'the ostensible enigma' of the two Magnificats[78] is, in my view, that the composer's intention was the wholly practical one of providing a complete Vespers that could be performed either with or without instrumental ensemble: instead of the grand toccata-like setting, the usual simple chant could be reinstated for the opening Response, the ritornellos in *Dixit Dominus* and *Ave maris stella* could be omitted (as sanctioned by the composer himself in the case of the former),[79] and the liturgically inessential *Sonata* could safely be dropped altogether.

Neither the flaunting of extreme (if 'playable') top notes nor the mere avoidance of 'insurmountable' problems is a hallmark of Monteverdi's other known instrumental writing, not least the virtuoso *Sonata sopra Sancta Maria*.[80] Yet to perform the Magnificat *a7* ↓4th would, Bowers suggests, reduce 'the capacities required of the players of violin and cornett to those of entirely conventional performers'.[81] Given its striking similarities (at this lower pitch) with passages for the same instruments in *L'Orfeo* (see Ex. 7.1), the claim would also require us to imagine that Monteverdi had been content to supply his Orpheus with undemanding writing for 'entirely conventional' instrumentalists at the very moment (in Act III) when music's powers are being tested to the full. The wholesale transfer of idiomatic figuration to a higher and distinctly less grateful key scarcely seems how a composer of Monteverdi's subtlety would choose to demonstrate 'the brilliance of his artistic imagination'.[82]

Despite its modest role, the third cornett part in the Magnificat *a7*, which lies exactly a 5th beneath the others, has attracted attention on account of what Bowers calls its 'anomalous low pitches' (↓4th).[83] While the part *can* be played on a treble instrument,[84] a low range of this sort may well be unexpected. However, a glance at the double-choir 'echo' canzona *a10* in *Giovanni Gabrieli (1597) demonstrates that our

---

[77] Bowers, 'An "Aberration" Reviewed', 537.

[78] Bowers, 'An "Aberration" Reviewed', 536.

[79] In *1610*'s Bassus generalis this movement is headed: 'The ritornellos can be played or omitted as desired' (*Li Ritornelli si ponno sonare & anco tralasciar secondo il volere*).

[80] Bowers, 'An "Aberration" Reviewed', 536–7.

[81] Bowers, 'An "Aberration" Reviewed', 537.

[82] Bowers, 'An "Aberration" Reviewed', 537.

[83] Bowers, 'An "Aberration" Reviewed', 534; see also Parrott, 'Transposition', 509.

[84] The sackbut player Mack Ramsey (Boston, USA) plays this part on treble cornett.

expectations may need some revision.⁸⁵ Here, no fewer than eight cornetts are seen at work – four in each choir, with four different clefs (G2, G1, C2, C3) and four distinct ranges, the top one playing a full octave higher than the lowest (but – we may note – only up to a'').⁸⁶ All are simply labelled 'cornetto', as are Monteverdi's, although it seems very unlikely that all are intended for *treble* cornetts. An *inventory from Stuttgart (1589) lists a cornett 'two tones lower than the treble cornett',⁸⁷ and among the musical details of a *Florentine wedding celebration (1608) is reference to a '*Cornetto Torto p[er] un Contralto*', apparently a tenor instrument playing an alto part.⁸⁸ But perhaps even more important than the size of the instrument is the player's embouchure and ability to play in the particular register (see n. 84). Certain players undoubtedly specialized in inner/lower parts, and Bologna's municipal wind ensemble (the Concerto Palatino), for example, included a position for *contralto di cornetto*.⁸⁹ An intriguing detail of *1610*'s *Sextus* part-book may support the idea that Monteverdi was thinking along similar lines. At 'Quia respexit' the cornett III part shares a stave with trombone I, making it entirely feasible in this verse for one and the same player first to play cornett (of one size or another), then tenor sackbut, and finally cornett again, using the intervening woodwind duets to switch instruments.

From around the time of *1610*'s composition and compilation there is overwhelming evidence not only that vocal music notated in high clefs was generally understood by Italian musicians to demand downward transposition, but also that the expected interval of transposition was most frequently a 4th and sometimes a 5th.⁹⁰ Thus, when high-clef madrigals by Monteverdi turn up in a collection of spiritual contrafacta by *Aquilino Coppini (1607), it is no surprise to find that – without comment – the *Partito* (score) sets two of them ↓4th (and not less) from the pitch of the

---

⁸⁵ Giovanni Gabrieli, *Sacrae symphoniae* (Venice, 1597), Canzon in echo duodecimi toni.

⁸⁶ Similarly, the cornett and violin parts in two '*Simphonie*' from *G. F. Anerio's, *Teatro armonico* (Rome, 1619) go up to a'' but not beyond; Barbieri, 'Chiavette', 60.

⁸⁷ 'Cornetto', in *The New Grove Dictionary of Music and Musicians*, ed. S. Sadie (2/2001).

⁸⁸ Tim Carter, 'A Florentine Wedding of 1608', *Acta musicologica* 55 (1983), 107; '*Un cornetto muto p[er] contralto*' is also mentioned.

⁸⁹ Osvaldo Gambassi, *Il concerto palatino* (1989), 196, 212.

⁹⁰ To the already abundant evidence cited in Parrott, 'Transposition', and above, the following sources may be added: *Usper's *Vulnerasti cor meum* (1614), *Rigatti's *Laudate pueri* (1640), and the collections of *Orfeo Vecchi (1600), *Assandra (1609), *Osculati (1615) and *Cesis (1619).

vocal part-books.[91] Only later in the century did a narrower downward transposition (↓3rd) begin to be associated with high-clef pieces.[92] By contrast, transposition ↓2nd was seen not as a primary transposition required by the notation and essential for correct vocal (and instrumental) scoring, but as a secondary one which, at the discretion of the performer, could in some circumstances effect a helpful small adjustment (where, for example, an organ's pitch was unusually high). For all its originality, Monteverdi's Magnificat *a7* possesses no exceptional features that would have obliged, encouraged or even allowed contemporary performers to override these fundamental principles.

What of *1610*'s three other high-clef movements? Despite its lack of obbligato instruments, the less well-known Magnificat *a6* is in notational terms identical with its sibling *a7*; consequently, the same conventional transposition is almost certainly to be understood. In both the Mass and *Lauda Jerusalem*, however, the absence of a flat signature would, according to theory, indicate a wider transposition (↓5th),[93] though in practice this particular rule was increasingly ignored in favour of transposition ↓4th (as is seen, for example, in much of the *Vesperi* by the Milanese composer *Serafino Cantone, 1602).[94] In Monteverdi's case, and especially for the Mass, the voice ranges suggest that performers of the composer's time are most likely to have taken the higher option – as does the later Brescian organ score of the Mass.[95]

Innumerable untransposed performances over the past 70 years have doubtless helped establish the view that 'extrovert brilliance' epitomizes the 'particular characteristics' of the Magnificat *a7*.[96] The perceived threat to these supposedly intrinsic characteristics is perhaps the biggest obstacle to any objective re-evaluation of the question of its transposition.[97] We therefore do well to remind ourselves that specific expectations of this sort derive in most cases not from acquaintance with the notated music or with the performance conventions on which the composer's notation depended, but from the infinitely more potent experience of hearing it (perhaps repeatedly) as performed by musicians of our own time. But this

---

[91] Aquilino Coppini, *Musica tolta dai madrigali di Claudio Monteverdi e d'altri autori* (Milan, 1607); the two retexted madrigals in question, from bk 5 (1605), are *Qui pependit/Ecco Silvio* and *Pulchrae sunt/Ferir quel petto*. Their ranges after transposition ↓4th are once again consistently lower than those proposed by Bowers for the Magnificat *a7*.

[92] See Barbieri, 'Chiavette', 53; and Rasch, 'Modes', 405.

[93] See Parrott, 'Transposition', 491–4; and Barbieri, 'Chiavette', 42–4.

[94] See Barbieri, 'Chiavette', 52. We may also note that *Descendit Angelus* from Croce, *Motetti a8*, a high-clef piece without flat signature, is marked 'Alla quarta, e quinta bassa'; Bonta, Clef, Mode, and Instruments', table 13.

[95] See Parrott, 'Transposition', 501.

[96] Bowers, 'An "Aberration" Reviewed', 535.

[97] See Parrott, 'Vespers Revisited', 167–8.

questionable familiarity is by no means the only barrier to understanding Monteverdi's Magnificat *a7* more fully: while the niceties of 16th- and 17th-century transposition practice are simply too remote from current modes of thinking to attract widespread attention,[98] critical differences between earlier and current conventions of vocal scoring have scarcely begun to be acknowledged. Small wonder then if the idea of transposing the movement downward (especially by as much as a 4th) appears, to some, 'still controversial'.[99]

The present discussion will, I hope, contribute to a somewhat clearer understanding of high-clef notation. If so, its usefulness need not be thought to be confined to a single composition (the Magnificat *a7*), to a single collection (*1610*) or to a single composer's output (Monteverdi's): vast quantities of high-clef Renaissance and early Baroque vocal music – a good two-thirds of Palestrina's output, for example[100] – await re-exploration in fuller awareness of the notation's practical significance.

---

[98] Rasch ('Modes', 403), noting 'quite divergent' scholarly opinions, begins his essay thus: 'All three key words mentioned in the title of the present contribution – modes, clefs, and transpositions – are controversial'.

[99] Bowers, 'An "Aberration" Reviewed', 527.

[100] Siegfried Hermelink, *Dispositiones modorum: Die Tonarten in der Musik Palestrinas und seiner Zeitgenossen* (1960), 21.

8

High Clefs and Down-to-Earth Transposition: A Brief Defence of Monteverdi

'SOME favour a perfect 4th; I a major 2nd.' Thus Roger Bowers, embarking on a recent second attempt to promote a rather idiosyncratic hypothesis of downward transposition for Monteverdi's high-clef writing, notably in the 1610 Magnificat *a7* (see Bowers, '"The high and lowe keyes come both to one pitch": Reconciling Inconsistent Clef-Systems in Monteverdi's Vocal Music for Mantua', *Early Music* 39/4 (2011), 531–46). Undeterred by the fact that in similar contexts the composer's contemporaries appear invariably to have avoided the smaller interval of transposition (↓2nd), Bowers elaborates a theory manifestly born of a strong personal aversion to the conventional larger interval (↓4th) when applied to these particular works: 'the entire tessitura is dragged bodily downwards ... and the overall sound is effectively decapitated', all of which 'traduces the music without appearing to make any compensatory rational sense'.

Readers who may not wish to revisit the byways of opposing thinking on this issue[1] will perhaps do well to rest content with the testimony of a man who knew more about early 17th-century Italian music and its workings than most of us today: Monteverdi's contemporary, the eminent and versatile German composer, theorist, organist and *Capellmeister*, Michael Praetorius (1571–1621):

> Every vocal piece in high clefs, i.e. where the bass is written in C4 or C3, or F3, must be transposed when it is put into tablature or score for players of the organ, lute and all other foundation instruments, as follows: if it has a flat, down a 4th ... but if it has no flat, down a 5th.[2]

This is neither second-hand dogma nor casual oversimplification.

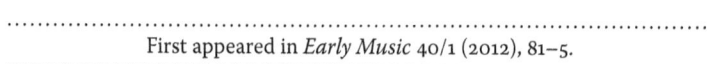

First appeared in *Early Music* 40/1 (2012), 81–5.

---

[1] Andrew Parrott, 'Transposition in Monteverdi's Vespers of 1610: An "Aberration" Defended', *Early Music* 12/4 (1984), 490–516 (reprinted in this volume, Ch. 5); Roger Bowers, 'An "Aberration" Reviewed: The Reconciliation of Inconsistent Clef-Systems in Monteverdi's Mass and Vespers of 1610', *Early Music* 31/4 (2003), 527–38; Andrew Parrott, 'Monteverdi: Onwards and Downwards', *Early Music* 32/2 (2004), 303–17 (reprinted in this volume, Ch. 7).

[2] Parrott, 'Transposition', 493–4.

Table 8.1 Evidence for transposition ↓4th (and ↓5th) from high-clef notation

Theoretical sources	Compositions (sacred music)	
Zacconi (Venice, 1592)	Rogier (1590s)[a]	1 item
Virgiliano (MS, c. 1600)[b]	Victoria (Madrid, 1600)	2
Banchieri (Bologna, 1601)[c]	Fattorini (Venice, 1600)	1
Banchieri (Bologna, 1613)	Viadana (Venice, 1602)	6
Angleria (Milan, 1622)	Puliti (Milan, 1602)	1
Picerli (Naples, 1631)	Banchieri (Bologna, 1607)	4
G. B. Doni (Rome, 1640)	[Coppini] (Milan, 1607)	2 (Monteverdi madrigals)[d]
	Croce (Venice, ?1607)	5[e]
	Palestrina (Venice, 1608)	23
	G. F. Anerio (Rome, 1613)	37
	Leoni (Venice, 1613)	1
	Stadlmayr (Innsbruck, 1614)	1 (Croce, Magnificat)
	Usper (Venice, 1614)	1
	Osculati (Venice, 1615)	5
	Schütz (Dresden, 1619)	1 (G. Gabrieli, Lieto godea)
	Valentini (Venice, 1621)	2
	Rigatti (Venice, 1640)	3
	Monteverdi (Venice, 1650)	1 (Laudate pueri)

[a] Italics indicate items by non-Italian composers.
[b] See n. 5.
[c] See Bowers, 'The high and lowe keyes', 539.
[d] Spiritual contrafacta; see Parrott, 'Monteverdi: Onwards and Downwards', 314, 317.
[e] See n. 4.

Unanimous confirmation of these clear principles comes from copious Italian sources, emphatically answering Bowers's question: 'what did north Italian musicians of c. 1600–10 expect to be told by the clefs of the music they were performing?' As a sample, Table 8.1 lists almost 100 documented cases of the explicit link between high-clef notation and transposition ↓4th (and ↓5th). By contrast, not a single contemporary example of downward transposition by as little as a tone (↓2nd) has thus far been identified in association with high clefs.[3] Arguing nevertheless for a 'fluidity' of transposition practice that would allow this smaller interval, Bowers cites the organ book of a motet collection by Giovanni Croce, where a variety of options is given.[4] What he inexplicably fails to point out, however, is that *all* of its high-clef items are marked to go ↓4th and/or ↓5th – and

[3] In the case of standard clefs transposition ↓2nd was perfectly common. With high clefs, however, it would at this period have constituted an anomaly requiring clear signalling.

[4] Giovanni Croce, *Motetti a8* (Venice, ?1607); Bowers gives a publication date of 1594, but Martin Morell has argued that the organ book is evidently a later addition; correspondence in *Music & Letters* 72 (1991), 516–17.

none ↓2nd. The option of *un tuono basso* (↓2nd) is reserved exclusively for *standard*-clef pieces.[5]

It is thus no mere coincidence that, when transposed ↓4th, Monteverdi's high-clef Magnificat *a7* reveals unmistakable and telling parallels of range and tessitura, both vocal and instrumental, with prominent solo passages in the same composer's *L'Orfeo*, published just one year earlier.[6] Yet, when comparing this transposition of the Magnificat with standard-clef items elsewhere within the 1610 Mass and Vespers collection, Bowers sees not only 'a major degree of inconsistency' but the 'wilful eschewment and suppression of a rationally consistent level of sounding pitch'.

Two broad questions immediately arise: what constitutes undue 'inconsistency' (and how is this measured), and did Monteverdi really leave it to performers to 'probe, resolve and extinguish' any such perceived inconsistency in pursuit of 'an exact alignment' of ranges? For a 'direct answer' to this second question (and also for his title), Bowers turns to an Englishman, Thomas Morley:[7] 'the high and lowe keyes [clefs] come both to one pitch.' What Morley actually writes is that 'the high and lowe keyes come both to one pitch, *or rather compasse*' [my italics], which arguably sheds a slightly different light on the sentence. Addressing students of composition (rather than performers),[8] might he merely be pointing out that the two clef-systems are 'of equal compass', each defining a 21-note span (irrespective of sounding pitch)?[9] Be that as it may, no writer –

---

[5] See Parrott, 'Monteverdi: Onwards and Downwards', 315 n. 20. The illustration by Aurelio Virgiliano (*c.* 1600) of five clefs with associated transposition options may appear to include an exception to the rule ('Segni per conoscer tutti i Modi da sonar qualsi voglia Instrumento'; Virgiliano, *Il Dolcimelo*, facs. (1979), [97]). However, his subsequent tables for viols, trombones (with cornett), cornett (separately), flutes and recorders all clearly and consistently contradict this ([98–111]).

[6] See Parrott, 'Transposition', 504–5, 508. Bowers offers no comment on these parallels.

[7] This marks something of a *volte-face* from Bowers, who previously has allowed as primary evidence only 'the music and theoretical and other writing of contemporary Northern Italy', discounting the testimony of Praetorius as 'emanating from a distinct and distant musical culture working to different rules'; see his 'An "Aberration" Reviewed', 533.

[8] Part 3 of Morley's book 'entreateth of composition'; Thomas Morley, *A Plaine and Easie Introduction to Practicall Musicke* (London, 1597), 166. For his interpretation of 'compasse' as 'sounding compass' Bowers ('An "Aberration" Reviewed', n. 34) draws on subsequent comments of Morley's. Only a little earlier, however, the illustration of 'the high key' is introduced with the words 'here is the compasse of your musicke' (p. 165). In short, this portion of Morley's treatise regrettably proves not quite 'plain enough' for present purposes and in any case, *pace* Bowers, probably has no direct connection with early 17th-century Italian (and German) transposition practice.

[9] Ironically, Morley's high and low clef-systems in fact differ slightly, spanning 21 and 20 notes respectively. For more on clefs and vocal scoring, see

including Morley – appears to demand of performers that they seek absolute equivalence of high- and standard-clef ranges.

Armed with questionable measurements of 'core' vocal ranges (see Appendix, below) Bowers sets out to demonstrate that transposition ↓4th produces implausibly low vocal ranges a minor 3rd below those of standard clefs, and – further – that this discrepancy is 'an anomaly to be investigated and dissolved'. Yet, as Monteverdi's publication amply illustrates, it is entirely natural for diverse modes, styles, scorings and sung texts to generate diverse ranges.[10] Amongst its ensemble movements in standard clefs we find both differing overall ranges[11] and numerous related 'inconsistencies' – lowest bass notes a clear minor 3rd apart, for example, and the highest soprano note of one item fully a 4th above that of another.[12] With so little consistency among standard-clef pieces, what exactly is the transposed Magnificat *a7* supposed to be consistent with?

While the issue of 'high instrumental registers' raises its head yet again (see Appendix), the ever-present organ remains crucially neglected. When transposed ↓2nd the 1610 Magnificat *a7* finds itself in a key akin to our F minor, with a 3-flat signature and recurrent additional D♭s. To any musician of Monteverdi's day a major stumbling block will have been instantly apparent: the overwhelming majority of organs simply did not possess the note D♭ in any octave, let alone throughout the compass. Although split keys for the more remote notes of mean-tone temperament were certainly available on many important Italian organs, it seems to have been general for there to be just D♯/E♭ and G♯/A♭ and only in the lower half of a keyboard (see Illus. 8.1 for a late 16th-century Italian organ with this disposition).[13] A third split key adding D♭ to the usual C♯ was evidently an

---

Andrew Parrott, 'A Brief Anatomy of Choirs', in *The Cambridge Companion to Choral Music*, ed. A. de Quadros (2012), 12–16 (reprinted in this volume, Ch. 2).

[10] For the influence of clef-systems themselves on ranges, see Parrott, 'Monteverdi: Onwards and Downwards', 308–9.

[11] The ranges of individual items in the 1610 collection are variously between 20 and 23 notes, while collectively they cover 24.

[12] Soprano *g"* in *Laetatus sum* and *d"* in *Ave maris stella*; bass *E* in *Audi coelum* and *G* in *Laudate pueri*.

[13] Shortly after the passage quoted in the second paragraph (above), Praetorius stresses the need in concerted music for an organ to possess split keys for D♯/E♭ and 'where possible' also for G♯/A♭; no mention is made of any further keys; Michael Praetorius, *Syntagma musicum* iii (Wolfenbüttel, 1619), 81. For photographs showing split *D♯/E♭* and *G♯/A♭* keys on restored organs by Graziadio Antegnati (1565) at S Barbara, Mantua, and by Giovanni Guglielmi (1612) at S Maria in Vallicella, Rome, see <www.antegnatisantabarbara.it> and <www.ruffatti.com/restauro_organi_storici.htm> [accessed 26 January 2015]. For an illustration of the keyboard of a harpsichord by G. B. Boni (Rome, 1619), see *The New Grove Dictionary of Music and Musicians*, ed. S. Sadie (2/2001), 'Enharmonic keyboard'.

Illus. 8.1 *(top)* The Gospel organ (1596) by Baldassarre Malamini in the Basilica di San Petronio, Bologna; *(bottom)* the lower half of the keyboard, showing its three split keys: *D♯/E♭, G♯/A♭* and *d♯/e♭*

extreme rarity. To play the organ part with the many essential D♭s either omitted or replaced by C♯s would make a mockery of the music. Even on an instrument with all the necessary flats, this strange and remote key would have constituted an unusual and unwelcome obstacle course for the most experienced organist. Diruta (1609), in his 26 examples of assorted transpositions, knew better than to demand a single D♭.[14]

---

[14] Girolamo Diruta, *Il transilvano* (Venice, 1609), bk 4, 7–15.

It may be helpful at this point to move on from the tangled web of argument to the firm evidence provided by Monteverdi's own music. While the vocal compass of the transposed Magnificat *a7* (↓4th) – extending from (low) bass *D* up to (modest) soprano *e"* – may well seem unusually low to us today, it is by no means unique in Monteverdi's output; no fewer than six other church pieces are absolutely identical in this respect (five of them in standard clefs, one in high clefs explicitly marked *Alla quarta bassa*).[15] Even the contentiously low six-part texture at 'Et misericordia' has its standard-clef twin elsewhere in his music.[16] Other bass parts, too, similarly employ low *D*s quite freely, as well as commonly extending upwards the best part of two octaves; indeed the later *Selva morale* Magnificat I has a bass part exactly matching the 14-note sounding range of the 1610 setting (↓4th).[17] (There is thus no justification for regarding the writing in 'Quia fecit' as taking the basses 'notably higher' than normal, or in supposing it to have been composed for particular singers 'who happened to possess a presentable baritonal quality'.) Equally, we may easily imagine 'the conventional higher reaches of the soprano register' to include *a"* and certainly *g"*. Yet in the ensemble movements of Monteverdi's 1610 collection (excepting those in high clefs) even this *g"* occurs nowhere other than in the suitably joyous setting of *Laetatus sum*.[18] Moreover, in only one of the composer's 30 or so other comparable church works does this note ever make more than a single appearance;[19] in fact, almost half of all such soprano parts never rise above *e"*.

That 'a prominently lowered pitch' (as Bowers sees it) is neither a trick of Monteverdi's notation, nor a 'mirage created by over-enthusiastic downward compensation', is surely confirmed in the work of a younger composer close to Monteverdi. In 1626 Giovanni Rovetta, a bass singer at St Mark's, Venice, and Monteverdi's eventual successor as *maestro di cappella*, published as part of his opus 1 a *Confitebor tibi Domine a5* notated in high clefs and employing a written 22-note compass of

---

[15] *Beatus vir* II and *Laudate pueri* II from *Selva morale e spirituale* (Venice, 1640–1), *Dixit Dominus* I, *Dixit Dominus* II, *Beatus vir* and *Laudate pueri* (↓4th) from *Messa et salmi* (Venice, 1650). The Magnificat *a8* (*Selva morale*) stretches an extra semitone to a single *f"*.

[16] The *Gloria a7* (at the words 'pax hominibus voluntatis'); see Parrott, 'Transposition', 502–3 (inc. ex. 10).

[17] Comparably wide-ranging bass parts prove not at all hard to find in the music of Monteverdi's contemporaries, though Banchieri's set of ranges fails to reflect this (see Bowers, 'An "Aberration" Reviewed', 535). To citings of low *D*s given in Parrott, 'Transposition', 502, and Parrott, 'Monteverdi: Onwards and Downwards', 311–12, we may add others found in Giovanni Paolo Cima (1610) and Rovetta (1626).

[18] The *g"* in *Laetatus sum* appears there only infrequently: four times in S1, just twice in S2.

[19] *Confitebor* III *alla francese* (*Selva morale*) – in effect a solo item with 4-part instrumental or vocal accompaniment.

G–g''.[20] What marks the piece out for special attention here is not its range – which almost exactly matches that of the 1610 Magnificat *a7* (though each of Monteverdi's sopranos is also given an isolated a') – but the accompanying rubric: *Alla Terza, & quarta Bassa*. This is one of the very earliest known high-clef pieces specifically to admit downward transposition by less than a 4th,[21] and it gives rise to three particular observations: 1) both transpositions result in keys favourable for the organ (no obbligato instruments are involved);[22] 2) the lower specified pitch (↓4th) is at exactly the level vehemently rejected by Bowers; and 3) even the higher option (↓[minor] 3rd) fails to bring the voice ranges into line with those proposed by Bowers for the Magnificat *a7*.

The key to understanding all this is a recognition that the vocal ensemble implied by a work such as the 1610 Magnificat *a7* has very little in common with the solo-and-choral set-up we may have come to expect. Seven expert singers are called for, and no more. And of their four basic categories – soprano, alto, tenor, bass – none may safely be assumed to correlate directly with those we currently cultivate.[23] In particular, the lower bass register was exploited more freely than is now common, and soprano parts conventionally occupied a more middling range, with only rare excursions to the higher registers routinely demanded of today's female sopranos and boy trebles. Inconsistencies of vocal range following transposition ↓4th are more apparent than real, and few will have been either undue or unintended. Moreover, Monteverdi's instrumental parts in the Magnificat *a7* all emerge idiomatically pitched, grateful to play, and utterly consistent with those elsewhere both in the 1610 Vespers music and in *L'Orfeo*. Whatever the intended interval of transposition, we may be sure that the composer would not have allowed it to compromise either his vocal or his instrumental writing. In addition, if for any reason Monteverdi had intended such an extraordinary composition as the Magnificat *a7* to receive some *exceptional* degree of transposition, we may be quite sure that he would never have risked publishing it without a firm indication of those intentions.

---

[20] Giovanni Rovetta, *Salmi concertati* (Venice, 1626).

[21] See Patrizio Barbieri, '*Chiavette* and Modal Transposition in Italian Practice (*c.* 1500–1837)', *Recercare* 3 (1991), 53; and Rudolf Rasch, 'Modes, Clefs, and Transpositions in the Early 17th Century', *Théorie et analyse musicales, 1450–1650*, ed. A.-E. Ceulemans and B. Blackburn (2001), 405.

[22] The piece has a signature of one flat and F as its final.

[23] See Parrott, 'Monteverdi: Onwards and Downwards', 309–12; and Parrott, 'A Brief Anatomy of Choirs', 14–16.

APPENDIX

Core Vocal Ranges

The 'core' ranges produced by Bowers (see his Exx. 1 and 4) are the tools employed by him to measure 'inconsistency' of vocal range. But how, one must ask, does the highest note of the entire standard-clef writing in the 1610 publication (soprano g'') meaningfully represent its highest *core* note, given that it is unique to just one of the ensemble movements?[24] And why then exclude the bass low E found in three such items?[25] Lapses of this sort again distort their author's findings,[26] encouraging him to conclude that transposition ↓4th from high clefs produces an 'irrational' discrepancy (of a minor 3rd) with standard-clef writing. Yet, if in standard-clef pieces the same difference exists between, for example, the soprano parts of *Laudate pueri* and *Laetatus sum* (top notes e'' and g'' respectively) and between the bass parts of *Laudate pueri* and *Ave maris stella* (bottom notes G and E), why should similar differences between standard-clef and transposed high-clef pieces be viewed as undue inconsistencies?

Instruments and Transposition

For instruments the practical consequences of transposition ↓2nd in the 1610 Magnificat *a7*, as proposed by Bowers, appear to be as follows.[27] Violinists and cornettists have two options (both lacking notational warrant): (1) to employ an unprecedented transposition instead of a routine one, and to play in a bizarre and extremely ungrateful key – for no apparent reason – and in an unusually high register; (2) to turn to differently pitched instruments (a step lower than those used elsewhere in the publication, and, in the case of mute cornetts, less suited to high registers), not to transpose at all (despite the expected requirement

---

[24] See n. 18 above.

[25] *Dixit Dominus*, *Audi coelum* and *Ave maris stella*. Similarly the low G shown in Ex. 1b does not accurately represent the 'core' range of high-clef movements, as the bass of *Lauda Jerusalem* descends only to A.

[26] See Parrott, 'Monteverdi: Onwards and Downwards', 309.

[27] *Pace* Bowers, I have never claimed that the written high notes for violin and cornett in the Magnificat *a7* were 'unplayable', rather that Italian composers 'probably did not begin to *write* for the violin beyond first position until sometime in the 1620s', and that 'In the solo cornett *literature* of the early 17th century ... c''' appears infrequently and d''' not at all' [my italics]. There is little to add to what I have written in Parrott, 'Transposition', 508–10, and Parrott, 'Monteverdi: Onwards and Downwards', 313–14, other than that Giovanni Gabrieli's very occasional high violin writing may deserve further consideration in the light of what Praetorius calls a '*Discant*-Geig ein *Quart* höher'. My understanding of Salamone Rossi's notation remains unchanged (see Parrott, 'Transposition', 506).

with high-clef vocal music), and to play in an even higher and more exceptional register. The organist's sole option meanwhile is to cope (in unspecified ways) with the handicap of an intractable and most probably unplayable key.

If we are to believe that Monteverdi presented his various virtuoso colleagues with novel challenges of this sort in the crowning movement of his 1610 Vespers music, we must also ask why he evidently chose never to repeat the experiment.

9

Performing Purcell

Musick (... after all the learned Encomions that words can contrive) commends it Self best by the performance of a skilful hand, and an angelical voice.

(Henry Purcell)

THE anniversary in 1959 of Purcell's birth was also that of Handel's death, and for any assessment of the current state of our knowledge of Purcellian performance practice Handelian scholarship provides a useful yardstick. As a result particularly of further Handelian celebrations in 1985, a great deal of detailed research was undertaken that can now assist the performer and thereby illuminate in performance the music of England's great adopted son, while even with plans for 1995 firmly in place, it is clear that the pace of equivalent research into our Orpheus Britannicus has been decidedly slower. It may be argued, though, that substantial advances in understanding, while perhaps not yet reflected in musicological literature, are evident in live performances and recordings, especially in those involving period instruments. Yet it is not long since, in a prestigious London concert of Purcell's church music, given by an all-male choir and a period-instrument band, that oboes were unapologetically added to Purcell's strings and several pieces tacitly transposed. More disturbingly, these and other questionable decisions seem to have passed entirely without comment. The example – by no means isolated – serves to illustrate two general points. First, that in the absence of any sophisticated appreciation of Purcellian conventions, performers will tend to fall back on more familiar Handelian practices. Second, that details of performance practice can rarely be viewed in isolation: dubious instrumentation, for instance, may lead to the adoption of an inappropriate pitch standard, and in turn to wholesale transpositions, both of which will influence intonation, colour and balance.

In short, much work lies ahead if full justice is to be done in performance to Purcell's rich legacy, and in this chapter I can only hope to take the process a few steps further. A straightforward summary of published research would achieve little; instead I have chosen to concentrate on issues that seem to me to be of critical importance and to demand particular attention, ignoring other broad areas of performance

---

First appeared in *The Purcell Companion*, ed. M. Burden (1995), 387–444.

practice (notably rhythm[1] and tempo[2]) and many very specific ones, too. I have also aimed to draw together as much of the available evidence as possible and to allow it to speak for itself.

It should be said at the outset that the sources for such a study as this are for the most part frustratingly disparate and inadequate. Purcell's own work on the 12th edition (1694) of Playford's *An Introduction to the Skill of Musick* is disappointingly unenlightening in matters of performance practice,[3] and, after Christopher Simpson's *The Division-Viol*, first published in the year of Purcell's birth, and Thomas Mace's conservative *Musick's Monument* (1676),[4] no major practical treatises were published in England in the course of Purcell's lifetime. On the other hand, Roger North's voluminous manuscript writings begun around the time of Purcell's death are perhaps ample compensation and are extensively quoted here. North was just a few years older than Purcell, was acquainted with him, lived in London from 1669 until the early 1690s, was 'a medler with most sorts of instruments'[5] (harpsichord, organ, violin, bass viol), sang a little, and, above all, possessed a keen ear and a lively pen. Also invaluable are the organographical data collected some time in the 1690s by the Cambridge scholar James Talbot, a 'friend & admirer' of Purcell's.[6] But in general we must rely on the musical sources themselves (and in particular on performance materials), on court archives, on a range of isolated documents, on diaries (especially John Evelyn's), and on a handful of surviving instruments.

---

[1] For Roger North's observations on the use of dotted rhythms ('tho Not Expres't') to give 'a life and spirit' to passages written 'plaine', see *The Works of Henry Purcell* v, The Purcell Society (2/1976), xiii.

[2] See Purcell's address 'To the Reader' in the *Sonnata's of III Parts* (1683), his discussion 'of the Moods, or Proportions of the Time or Measure of Notes' in ch. 9 of *An Introduction to the Skill of Musick* (London, 12/1694), and the 'Instructions for Learners' in *The Harpsichord Master* (1697). See also Klaus Miehling, 'Das Tempo bei Henry Purcell', *Basler Jahrbuch für historische Musikpraxis* 15 (1991), 117–47; and A. Margaret Laurie, 'Continuity and Tempo in Purcell's Vocal Works', in *Purcell Studies*, ed. C. A. Price (1995), 192–206.

[3] See W. Barclay Squire, 'Purcell as Theorist', *Sammelbände der Internationalen Musik-Gesellschaft* 6 (1904/5), 521–67.

[4] Evidently 'wholly *Compos'd*' in 1672; see Thomas Mace, *Musick's Monument* (London, 1676), 45.

[5] *Roger North on Music*, ed. J. Wilson (1959), xxii; hereinafter cited as *North I*.

[6] Robert Unwin, '"An English Writer on Music": James Talbot 1664–1708', *Galpin Society Journal* 40 (1987), 59.

KEYBOARDS:
INSTRUMENTS, FINGERING, ORNAMENTS

As a composer Purcell himself knew that 'after all the learned Encomions that words can contrive [Musick] commends it Self best by the performances of a skilful hand, and an angelical voice',[7] and throughout his short life he was intimately involved in practical music-making at the highest professional level. Versatility was commonplace and many of his contemporaries doubled as singer/instrumentalist, wind/string player, performer/composer, or player/maker. As an executant Purcell was presumably best known in his own day as an organist, both at Westminster Abbey (from 1679) and with the Chapel Royal (from 1682). But the instruments he would have played are remarkably poorly documented: we know little more than that Robert Dallam's 'faire Double Organ for the use of his Ma^{ts} Chappel in Whitehall'[8] was ready for use in 1664 and survived until the palace fire of 1698,[9] and that the Abbey's organ was overhauled and enlarged by Bernard Smith in 1694–5.[10] (Purcell himself provided an additional instrument for the coronations of 1685 and 1689.)[11] Moreover, although there are a few stop-lists, not a single contemporary church organ survives intact.[12]

From 1681 Bernard Smith ('Father' Smith) held the post of organ-maker to the court,[13] and as part of the protracted and very partisan contest between him and Renatus Harris in the 1680s to build an organ for the Temple Church, London,[14] Draghi evidently played for Harris (a fellow Catholic), while both Purcell and Blow publicly showed off (the

---

[7] *Sonnata's of III Parts* (1683), preface.

[8] Andrew Ashbee, *Records of English Court Music* i (1986), 69–70. At an early stage Dallam made 'an Addition to the said Organ and a new Stopp with Conveyances and another sett of keyes'.

[9] Peter Williams, *A New History of the Organ* (1980), 135. In 1687 Purcell claimed that 'The organ is at present so out of repair that to cleanse, tune and put in good order will cost £40'; J. A. Westrup, *Purcell* (1937; 4/1980), 57.

[10] Westrup, *Purcell*, 79–80; and James Boeringer, *Organa Britannica* iii (1989), 256–9.

[11] Ashbee, *Records* v, 273, 276. In 1685 'A little Organ for the Kings Choir' was placed in a gallery overlooking the Abbey's high altar on the south side (see the 'Ground-Plot' given in Francis Sandford, *The History of the Coronation of James II and Queen Mary* (London, 1687)).

[12] See Stephen Bicknell, 'English Organ-Building, 1642–1685', *Journal of the British Institute of Organ Studies* 5 (1981), 19–21, etc.

[13] Ashbee, *Records* i, 195. He had been described as 'the King's organ maker' at least a decade earlier and had built a one-manual instrument for the King's private chapel at Windsor in 1673.

[14] See *North I*, 354.

Table 9.1 Specification of Bernard Smith's organ for the Temple Church, London

Great Organ		Choir Organ	
Prestand of mettle	12'	Gedackt wainescott	12'
Holflute of wood and mettle	12'	Holflute of mettle	6'
Principall of mettle	6'	A Sadt of mettle	6'
Quinta of mettle	4'	Spitts flute of mettle	3'
Super octavo	3'	A Violl and Violin of mettle	12'
Cornett of mettle	2'	Voice humane of mettle	12'
Sesquialtera of mettle	3'		
Gedackt of wainescott	6'		
Mixture of mettle	3'		
Trumpett of mettle	12'		

Ecchos	
Gedackt of wood	6'
Sup. Octavo of mettle	3'
Gedackt of wood	–
Flute of mettle	–
Cornett of mettle	–
Sesquialtera	–
Trumpett	–

Source: Edmund Macrory, *Notes on the Temple Organ* (London, 3/1911), 33–4.

Protestant) Smith's 23-stop instrument,[15] with its '3 full setts of keyes and quarter notes' (see Table 9.1).[16] The half-dozen extant organ pieces by Purcell scarcely hint at such an elaborate instrument; only the Voluntary for Double Organ (z719) demands more than one manual, and the Cornet solos of the Voluntary on the Old Hundredth (z721) – by Blow? – were probably intended for a single manual with divided stops. Sweet and brilliant wooden pipes were evidently a hallmark of Father Smith's work and the Temple organ's 'sweetnes and fulnes of Sound' drew comment;[17] apart from a few domestic instruments, the most reliable witness now is perhaps the restored 1698 organ in the University Church, Cambridge.[18]

Towards the end of 1685 Purcell added to his two positions as organist that of 'harpsicall' player in James II's private music.[19] While his first

---

[15] According to Thomas Tudway, quoted in Sir John Hawkins, *A General History of the Science and Practice of Music* ii (London, 1875), 691.

[16] William Leslie Sumner, *The Organ* (4/1973), 158–9.

[17] Edmund Macrory, *Notes on the Temple Organ* (London, 3/1911), 24.

[18] Nicholas Thistlethwaite, 'ORGANO PNEUMATICO: The Construction and Design of Bernard Smith's Organ for the University Church, Cambridge, 1698', *Journal of the British Institute of Organ Studies* 2 (1978), 31–62.

[19] Ashbee, *Records* ii, 3–4.

published keyboard music was 'for the Virginals, Harpsichord, and Spinet' (*The Second Part of Musick's Handmaid*, 1689), that of the posthumous *A Choice Collection of Lessons* (1696) specifies just harpsichord and spinet, reflecting a shift in fashion away from the rectangular virginal and towards the tonally very different wing-shaped spinet.[20] At Purcell's death 'the organ, the double spinet, [and] the single spinet'[21] in his possession passed to his son, but again, little is known about the particular instruments he would have played. While Purcell was assistant keeper of the King's instruments, the purchase (for £30) was recorded of 'a greate Harpsichord with 3 ranks of strings for his Ma^{ts} musick in ye hall and in ye privy lodgings'.[22] The maker of what was almost certainly still a single-manual instrument is not named, but around the same time Charles Haward, 'ye virginall maker', had been brought in by Hingeston to repair 'ye Harpsicords & pedalls'.[23] As it happens, an instrument by Hawood, altered in the 18th century but dated 1683 and now at Hovingham Hall, is the only fully attested English harpsichord to have survived from the second half of the 17th century. Its original specification was an Italianate 8'8' with, perhaps surprisingly, a lute stop. The case for associating Hawood more closely with the court and thus with Purcell is strengthened by two further details: Queen Anne is known to have owned a virginal by him,[24] and recurrent references in court documents to 'pedalls' lead indirectly to the elder Hawood, John, himself a distinguished maker.[25]

---

[20] This shift had begun *c*. 1670. Stephen Keene's two known virginals are dated 1668 and 1675, while from 1685 onwards only spinets by him survive.

[21] Franklin B. Zimmerman, *Henry Purcell, 1659–1695: His Life and Times* (1983), 314.

[22] Ashbee, *Records* i, 157.

[23] Ashbee, *Records* i, 156–7. Pepys in 1668 'called upon one Haywood that makes virginalls, and did there like of a little Espinettes and will have him finish them for me; for I had mind to a small Harpsicon, but this takes up less room'; *The Diary of Samuel Pepys* ix: *1668–1669*, ed. R. Latham and W. Matthews (1976), 148–9 (4 April 1668). See also 10, 13 and 15 July 1668; pp. 259, 261 and 262.)

[24] Edward F. Rimbault, *The Pianoforte: Its Origin, Progress and Construction* (London, 1860), 68.

[25] Ashbee, *Records* v, 125; i, 209. Said by Mace, *Musick's Monument*, 235–6, to have been 'of a *Late Invention*, contriv'd (as I have been inform'd) by one Mr. *John Hayward* of *London*', the instrument was 'in *Shape and Bulk* just like a Harpsicon', but with 'several *Various Stops* at Pleasure; and all *Quick and Nimble*, by the *Ready Turn* of the Foot ... *Wonderfully Rare, and Excellent*: So that doubtless It *Excels* all *Harpsicons*, or *Organs* in the World, for *Admirable Sweetness and Humour, either for a Private, or a Consort use*.' A quarter of a century later another commentator observed that 'The *Harpsicon* is of late mightily Improved, by the Invention of the Pedal, which brings it so near to the Organ, that it only seems to come short of it in Lungs'; Michael Tilmouth, 'Some Improvements in Music Noted by William Turner in 1697', *Galpin Society Journal* 10 (1957), 58. A 'Fantasia for

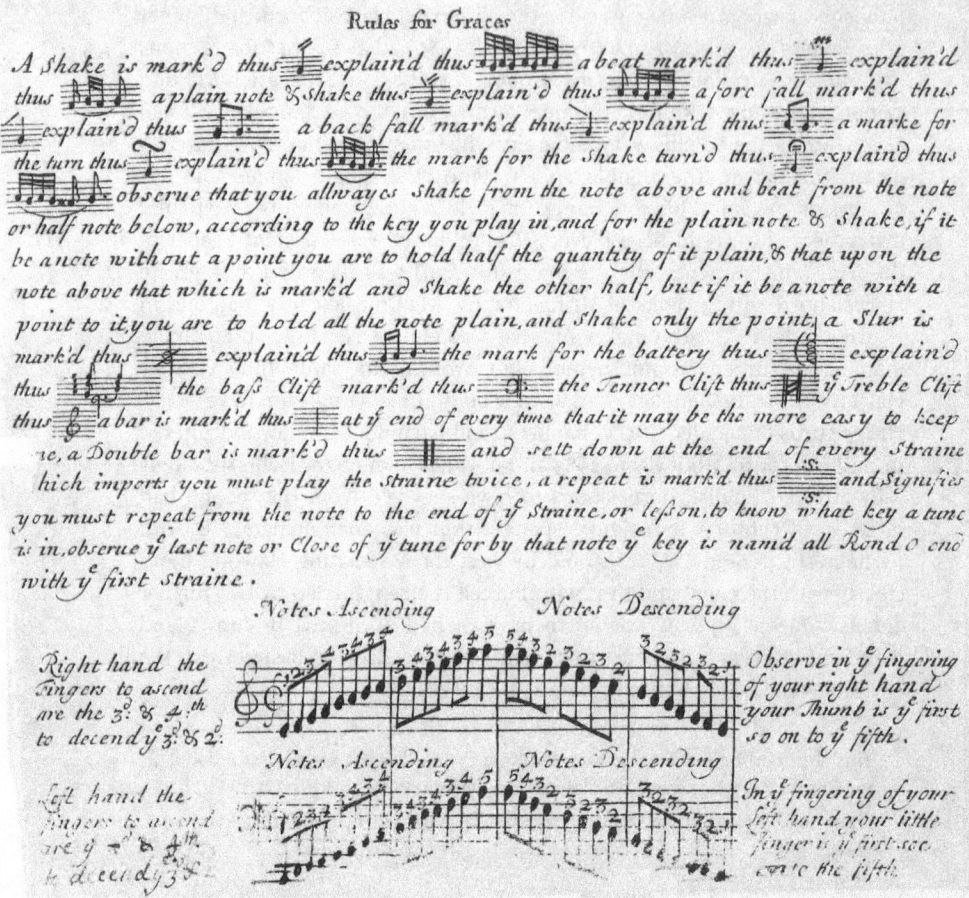

Illus. 9.1 [?Henry Purcell], 'Rules for Graces', in *The Harpsichord Master* (London, 1697)

Two years after Purcell's death a modest volume of 'y^e newest Aires & Song Tunes' was published by Walsh under the title *The Harpsichord Master*.[26] Its interest for us here lies in the prefatory material, some 'plain & easy Instructions for Learners on ye Spinnet or Harpsicord', and especially in the portion on ornament signs and fingering (Illus. 9.1). (These instructions were reprinted in the 1699 edition of *A Choice Collection of Lessons*, but without attribution.) Moreover, the first item purports to be a 'Prelude for ye fingering by Mr H: Purcell' (Ex. 9.1). The style of fingering matches at least three Italian sources of the 17th century[27]

one Violin, Base Viol, a Pedall Harpsicord, or Organ' by Hingeston survives (Oxford, Bodleian Library, MS Mus. Sch. e 382).

[26] *The Harpsichord Master* (London, 1697).

[27] Banchieri (1611), Penna (1672) and Bismantova (1677); see Maria Boxall, '"The Harpsichord Master 1697" and its Relationship to Contemporary

Ex. 9.1 Henry Purcell, 'Prelude for yᵉ fingering', from *The Harpsichord Master* (London, 1697)

* The fingering for the LH in the original used the system in which the thumb is 5, the little finger is 1, and so on.

and suggests a possible link with Italian players such as Draghi and Bartolomeo Albrici, who were both domiciled in England from *c.* 1666.

The ornament signs that abound in both the organ and harpsichord sources are inherited directly from Locke (*Melothesia*, 1673) and others. All are included in the 'Rules for Graces', and only three require any comment. The explanation of the *battery* sign (= modern ⦃) is surely just a garbled attempt to notate a simple arpeggiated chord, whereas both the *beat* and the *plain note & shake* really do deserve to be taken at face

Instruction and Playing', *The English Harpsichord Magazine* 2 (1981), 178–83. See also *North I*, 57, for examples of Prendcourt's fingering.

value: the latter does not require a tie between the first two notes[28] and, tempting though it may be to regard the *beat* simply as a mordent (🎵), the presence of an initial lower auxiliary is implied by Carr (1686) and specified by Blakeston (1694), Prendcourt (*c.* 1700) and North (*c.* 1710).[29] (Perhaps surprisingly, there is no contemporary evidence for the simple mordent in English keyboard music.) The compound ornament 🎵, found quite frequently in Purcell's solo keyboard music, would thus sound 🎵, with a reiterated lower auxiliary.

Many other keyboard ornaments were, of course, 'seldome or never exprest in wrighting, for they are in the hand and the player takes them of course'.[30] North's writings on 'The Art of Gracing', while not confined to keyboard matters, are a salutary reminder of this hidden world.[31] 'A Table of Graces proper to the Viol or Violin', more or less identical to Simpson's, is found in *An Introduction to the Skill of Musick*,[32] and a pithy and informative set of 'Rules for gracing on the flute' survives from the 1690s.[33]

---

[28] Howard Ferguson renames this a '*backfall and shake*' and, by analogy with the French *tremblement appuyé*, adds a tie; *Keyboard Interpretation* (1975), 150.

[29] H. Diack Johnstone, 'The English Beat', in *Aspects of Keyboard Music*, ed. R. Judd (1992), 34–44. Ferguson, writing before the rediscovery of *The Harpsichord Master* (1697), argued that the printer may accidentally have jumped from this sign to the next explanation but one, thereby omitting such an interpretation of the *beat*, together with a following term and its sign – in other words, that the explanation shown was intended for a missing 🎵 (*forefall and beat*); Ferguson, *Keyboard Interpretation*, 148–52.

[30] *North I*, 155.

[31] *North I*, 149–73.

[32] See also Peter Holman, *Four and Twenty Fiddlers: The Violin at the English Court, 1540–1690* (1993), 377, for an illustration of ornaments from John Lenton's violin tutor, *The Gentleman's Diversion* (London, 1694).

[33] London, British Library, Add. MS 35043, fol. 125, 'Never shake first nor last [note]. Never shake nor beat 2 notes in the same place. all Ascending Prick't notes are Beaten. all Descending are shaked; all sharpes are shaked ascending or falling. Never shake a quaver nor Semiquaver. – Take breath after all Long notes; Prepare all Longe shakes; Raise all Long Beats afterwards Sweeten –; if you meet wth 3 Crotchetts Descending Beat ye first shake ye second & play the third plaine. – The Note before a Close is to be shaked; Double Relish all Long Shakes if ye Note after ascend but not if it descend – where there is a Prickt Crotchett quaver & Crotchett stay Long upon ye Prickt Crotchet. If y be 3 Crocthets [*sic*] ascending Divide ye first into 2; Double rellish the 2, & play the 3^d plaine. – If 2 thirds Descending shake the one & Leave ye other; if but one Either shake or Slur. Shake no Ascending flatts. all Descending flatts are to be shaked – Naturall sharpes when they are made flatt must be raised when they are beaten – all shakes are taken from ye Note above, after a Shake keep ye finger, downe, All Beats are taken from ye Note below, after a beat keep the finger up. F.Fa.Ut & G.Sol, Re, Ut in alt are allwaies Beaten wth the

TEMPERAMENTS

A PASSING observation by North on ornaments raises the issue of keyboard tuning systems: 'Another use of the semitonian temperings is to abate the rancor of the scismes'[34] – in other words, an ornament involving a neighbouring semitone can help to disguise out-of-tune intervals. What temperament(s) then did Purcell favour for his instruments?

The source closest to Purcell himself is Dr William Holder's *A Treatise of the Natural Grounds, and Principles of Harmony* (1694), written 'for the Sake and Service of all Lovers of Musick, and particularly the Gentlemen of Their Majesties Chapell Royal'. Holder, Purcell's senior by 50 years and himself a competent composer, had been Sub-Dean of the Chapel (from 1674 until *c.* 1688) and his explanation of how 'to put an Organ or Harpsichord into more general usefull Tune'[35] is explicitly not innovative: his aim was rather to describe actual practice in physical terms. What emerges is a meantone with the 5ths (up to) a ¼ comma narrow and with the 'Anomalies ... thrown upon such Chords as are least used for the Key: as ♯G, ♭E, &c' (i.e. with the 'wolf' between G♯ and E♭). Interestingly, Holder goes on to comment that, except at cadences, even these bad notes 'the Ear will bear with, as it doth with other Discords in binding [= chromatic] passages'. North, who later (1726) described an irregular meantone, argued that the 'bad' keys 'by meer out-of-tuned-ness have certein caracters, very serviceable to the various purposes of Musick', and warned against the use of more 'equal' temperaments.[36]

It has been shown that, with some retuning, all of Purcell's solo harpsichord music is playable in meantone temperament;[37] apart from C♯, E♭, F♯, G♯ and B♭, the only chromatic notes to occur are A♭ (but never in conjunction with G♯) and D♯ (never with E♭). In most circumstances such retuning is obviously out of the question for an organ (or, at least, for all

---

forefinger; There are but 3 notes Naturally sharp. Viz. A La.Mi Re. B.fa Bi Mi & E.La. A Prick behind a Note makes it half as Long againe.' See Thurston Dart, 'Recorder "Gracings" in 1700', *Galpin Society Journal* 12 (1959); see also Holman, *Four and Twenty Fiddlers*, 375–6, for ornament signs used in the 'Tune for the flutes' from John Blow's *Venus and Adonis*, Act I.

[34] *North I*, 155.

[35] William Holder, *A Treatise of the Natural Grounds, and Principles of Harmony* (London, 1694), 180–2.

[36] *North I*, 208–12. See also the 'Rules for Tuning a Harpsicord or Spinnett' in Godfrey Keller's *A Compleat Method for attaining to play Thorough Bass upon either Organ, Harpsicord or Theorbo-Lute* (London, 1705); and Peter Williams, 'Equal Temperament and the English Organ, 1675–1825', *Acta Musicologica* 40 (1968), 53–65.

[37] John Meffen, 'A Question of Temperament: Purcell and Croft', *The Musical Times* 119 (1978), 504–6. For a different view, see J. Murray Barbour, 'Bach and the Art of Temperament', *The Musical Quarterly* 33 (1947), 77–8.

but a modest domestic instrument), yet of Purcell's six surviving organ pieces three require D♯ (z719, which also uses E♭, z720 and z721), and one of these (z721) the even more problematic A♯ and E♯. The 'quarter notes' on Smith's Temple organ, mentioned above, were split keys (and additional pipes) for G♯/A♭ and D♯/E♭, and were considered a novelty.[38] But although John Player and others are also said to have built harpsichords and spinets with quarter-notes,[39] split keys were only one (partial) solution: an experienced keyboard player would probably instinctively release 'bad' notes early wherever possible or, in realizing a basso continuo, perhaps avoid them altogether. Or when G♯, was too low to function as a reasonable A♭, for example, the player could 'favor', or ornament, it 'by a mixture with the note above (that is with ♮A), be it a back-fall or slight trill'; this would 'make the pipe or string sound as being a little sharper'.[40]

An understanding of the niceties of tuning was, of course, not confined to keyboard players. Indeed, Purcell's contemporary Pier Francesco Tosi would later argue that keyboard instruments tended to undermine a singer's proper understanding of the different sizes of semitone:

> Every one knows not that there is a Semitone Major and Minor, because the Difference cannot be known by an Organ or Harpsichord, if the Keys of the Instrument are not split ... this Knowledge ... [in] Songs accompanied with Bow Instruments ... becomes so necessary, that if a *Soprano* was to sing *D* sharp, like *E* flat, a nice Ear will find he is out of Tune, because this last rises.[41]

Tosi goes on to advise his readers to 'consult the best Performers on the Violin' on the matter. Woodwind fingering charts, such as that for 'the Hoboy' in *The Second Book of Theatre Music* (1699), similarly distinguish between D♯ and E♭ and between G♯ and A♭, with the flats sounding higher than the sharps.[42] And although equal temperament was a natural system for fretted instruments, which 'all our Violls, Lutes, Gitares, and the like

---

[38] 'The Organ at the Temple hath quarter notes, which no organ in England hath, and can play any tune; as, for instance, yᵉ tune of yᵉ 119 Psalm [in F minor], and severall other services set by excellent musicians, which no [other] organ will do'; Macrory, *Temple Organ*, 35; see also *North I*, 212.

[39] Ambrose Warren, *The Tonometer* (London, 1725), 7.

[40] *North I*, 155.

[41] Pier Francesco Tosi, *Opinioni de' cantori antichi e moderni, o sieno Osservazioni sopra il canto figurato* (Bologna, 1723); English translation, *Observations on the Florid Song*, trans. J. E. Galliard (London, 2/1743), 19–21; see also 36–7.

[42] See Bruce Haynes, 'Beyond Temperament: Non-keyboard Intonation in the 17th and 18th Centuries', *Early Music* 19/3 (1991), 359–61. See also the tablature by 'Mr La Riche' reproduced in Anthony Baines, 'James Talbot's Manuscript', *Galpin Society Journal* 1 (1948), 14.

instruments do follow',[43] there was considerable interest in setting such instruments unequally.[44]

These matters of tuning have interesting implications for continuo practice, especially in Purcell's extended works. The title page of *Orpheus Britannicus* (1698) informs us that the songs 'are placed in their several Keys according to the Order of the *Gamut*' — surely a convenience for performers rather than a theoretical scheme. But it is highly unlikely that a harpsichordist would have been expected to retune in the course of *Hail! bright Cecilia!* (1692), which uses nine keys, or between the two scenes of *Dido*'s Act II, which require E♭, A♭, D♭ and C♯, G♯, D♯ respectively. In the absence of split keys, might two instruments with complementary tunings have been used, by one or two players? (There are records from the early 1670s of London theatres hiring two harpsichords, and in the early 18th century two instruments were normally used for English dialogues.)[45] Was the harpsichord indeed the predominant continuo instrument of the time? And is it even correct always to assume the presence of a chordal instrument?

CONTINUO PRACTICES

THERE are no definitive answers to most of these questions, but the performer will perhaps be better equipped to find reasonable conjectural solutions with a fuller understanding of English continuo practice in general. In particular, it is well worth asking whether the presence of a keyboard instrument is justified in the first place. Table 9.2 lists the various continuo options given on the title pages of extant song publications issued during Purcell's lifetime.[46] Theorbo(-lute) is named in all but one.[47] Bass viol is absent only once, but is absent, too, from the

---

[43] London, British Library, Add. MS 4388, 42–3. See Mark Lindley, *Lutes, Viols & Temperaments* (1984), 45; see also 33–6.

[44] See Thomas Salmon, *A Proposal to perform Musick in Perfect & Mathematical Proportions* (London, 1688). The following year Richard Meares (the elder) advertised that he would fret instruments according to Salmon's system, 'approved by the Mathematical Professors of both Universities'; Michael Tilmouth, 'A Calendar of References to Music in Newspapers Published in London and the Provinces, 1660–1719', *Royal Musical Association Research Chronicle* 1 (1961), 8. See also Lindley, *Temperaments*, 68–9.

[45] Ashbee, *Records* i, 156; and Judith Milhous and Curtis A. Price, 'Harpsichords in the London Theatres, 1697–1715', *Early Music* 18/1 (1990), 38–46.

[46] The information is drawn principally from Cyrus Lawrence Day and Eleanore Boswell Murrie, *English Song Books, 1651–1702, and their Publishers* (London, 1936).

[47] The implications of the various terms are still not fully understood, partly because no English lutes survive from this period, but the English theorbo differed from the Italian *tiorba/chitarrone* in having shorter diapasons and a

Table 9.2 Continuo options from song publications issued during Purcell's lifetime (*NB* Only first editions and the first volumes of series are included.)

1673	[John Playford], *Choice Songs and Ayres*	T-L or B-V
1678	John Banister and Thomas Low, *New Ayres, Dialogues, and Trialogues*	T-L or B-V
1685	[Henry Playford and Richard Carr], *The Theater of Music*	T or B-V
1685	John Blow et al., *A Third Collection of New Songs*	T and B-V
1687	[John Carr and Samuel Scott], *Comes amoris*	H, T or B-V
1687	[John Carr and Samuel Scott], *Vinculum societatis*	H, T or B-V
1687	[John Crouch], *A Collection of the Choyest* [sic] *and Newest Songs*	H, T or B-V
1688	[Henry Playford], *The Banquet of Musick*	T-L, B-V, H or O
1688	[Henry Playford], *Harmonia sacra*	T-L, B-V, H or O
1690	John Wolfgang Franck, *Remedium melancholiae*	H T or B-V
c. 1692	Robert King, *Songs for One Two and Three Voices*	O or H
1693	[John Hudgebut], *Thesaurus musicus*	H, T or B-V
1695	[Henry Playford], *Deliciae musicae*	T-L, B-V, H or O
1695	[Henry Playford], *The New Treasury of Musick**	T(-)L or B-V, H or Spinnet

* A compilation from *The Theater of Musick* I, II and IV, and *Choice Ayres* IV and V.

B-V = Bass-Viol   H = Harpsichord   O = Organ   T(-L) = Theorbo(-Lute)

substantial posthumous *Orpheus Britannicus*, with its bass 'Figur'd for the Organ, Harpsichord, or Theorbo-Lute'. Only from 1687 does harpsichord occur consistently (and Book IV of *The Theater of Music* from that year expands to include harpsichord),[48] while organ appears fairly regularly from the following year.[49] Despite a rather narrower range of comfortable keys than on keyboard instruments, the theorbo was undoubtedly the

more lute-like body and perhaps tone. For Mace, '*The Theorboe*, is no other, than *That* which we call'd *the Old English Lute* ... [but] *is Principally us'd in Playing to the Voice, or in Consort; It being a Lute of the Largest Seize; and we make It much more Large in Sound*, by contriving unto *It a Long Head, to Augment and Increase that Sound, and Fulness of the Basses, or Diapasons,* which are a great Ornament to the Voice, or Consort'; Mace, *Musick's Monument*, 207.

[48] Earlier, William King's *Songs and Ayres* (1668) had added 'Harpsecon' to the otherwise standard alternatives of theorbo/bass viol.

[49] Chamber organs were to be found not only at Court and in grand houses, but also in humbler settings – occasionally even in taverns; John Harley, *Music in Purcell's London: the Social Background* (1968), 138. Purcell owned one (see above), and John North as a Cambridge student in the 1660s had 'got a small organ into his chamber at Jesus Colledge'; *North I*, 252.

most flexible and subtle instrument of vocal accompaniment through most of this period, and it is presumably the theorbo that is generally to be understood in connection with those singers known to have accompanied themselves on the 'lute' – John Abell, Arabella Hunt,[50] and Mrs Knepp[51] among them.[52] For Mace the norm was a double-strung instrument in G (or, if necessary, A), whereas for Talbot it could be either single- or double-strung, in either tuning.[53] The archlute, which seems to have come to England from Italy very late in the century and which in a short space of time largely displaced the theorbo,[54] does not appear in these title pages at all, nor in court documents, nor among the instruments to be taught at the proposed 'Royal Academies' in 1695,[55] but it was known to Talbot, who measured an instrument belonging to 'Mr [John] Shores'.[56] The suspicion that the instrument established itself just too late to have influenced Purcell's music-making is reinforced by its absence from (and the theorbo's

---

[50] The mezzotint made by John Smith in 1706, a year after Arabella Hunt's death, from a portrait by Godfrey Kneller depicts her playing 'an 11-course French lute', which is essentially a solo instrument.

[51] Curtis A. Price, *Music in the Restoration Theatre* (1979), 78.

[52] See also *North I*, 16 n. 15. According to Pepys, Reggio 'sings Italian songs to the Theorbo most neatly'; *Pepys* v, 217 (22 July 1664).

[53] For a discussion of the use of fingernails or flesh for plucking, see Peter Walls, 'The Baroque Era: Strings', in *Performance Practice: Music after 1600*, ed. H. M. Brown and S. Sadie, New Grove Handbooks (1989), 74.

[54] See Robert Spencer, 'Chitarrone, Theorbo and Archlute', *Early Music* 4/4 (1976), 417. An isolated early appearance of the term archlute is found in the 'Advertisements to the Reader' of Matthew Locke's *Melothesia* (London, 1673), which mention 'Rules for Playing on a *Continued Bass* ... equally fit the *Theorbo, Arch-Lute, Harp*, or any other Instrument capable of performing Duplicity of Parts'.

[55] 'Mr Purcell' was one of four listed teachers of organ and harpsichord, while 'Lute, Guittar and Theorbo' were to be taught by 'Mr De la Tour, Mr Dupre, Mr Crevecoeur'; see Michael Tilmouth, 'The Royal Academies of 1695', *Music & Letters* 38 (1957), 327.

[56] Michael Prynne, 'James Talbot's Manuscript IV: Plucked Strings – The Lute Family', *Galpin Society Journal* 14 (1961), 60. Not long after Purcell's death one commentator observed that 'The *Theorbo*, which is no other than an Arch-Lute, keeping to the old Tuning, is still generally made use of in Consorts'; see Tilmouth, 'Some Improvements', 58. In the late 1720s North wrote of 'Dr. Walgrave [c. 1636–1701], a prodigy of an archlutinist'; *Roger North's 'Cursory Notes of Musicke' (c. 1698–c. 1703): A Physical, Psychological and Critical Theory*, ed. M. Chan and J. C. Kassler (1986), 269, hereinafter cited as *North II*. However, John Evelyn in 1685 wrote of Walgrave's accompanying Mr Pordage 'with his *Theorba Lute*'; *The Diary of John Evelyn* iv, ed. E. S. de Beer (1959), 403 (27 January). Elsewhere North described 'Dr. Waldegrave' as one of 'a set of men who advanced much the Italian way, and slighted the French'; *North II*, 285 (see also *North I*, 308). According to Pepys, he was 'an Englishman bred at Rome'; *Pepys* v, 119 (12 April 1664).

presence in) the intended 'Accompaniment' to Talbot's 'An Ode for the Consort at York Buildings upon the death of Mr. H. P.'.[57]

These song-book title pages also make no mention of the fashionable guitar,[58] which, especially among actor-singers, remained a popular instrument of self-accompaniment, being relatively easy both to play (especially the 'brushing way', i.e. strummed) and to carry.[59] As Purcell's apparently limited use of the instrument suggests, it was regarded very much as a dance instrument and traditionally had erotic associations. In *Hail! bright Cecilia!* a guitar's participation is implied by the text of the duet (with recorders), 'In vain the am'rous flute and soft guitar,/ Jointly labour to inspire wanton heat and loose desire'; but only in *Dido and Aeneas* is the instrument expressly called for by Purcell, where the 1689 libretto specifies 'A Dance Gittars Chacony' (at the end of Act I) and 'Gitter Ground a Dance' (in the middle of Act II).[60] (There is surely no 'missing' music at these points, as has commonly been supposed; rather, the dances would have been improvised above Purcell's given ground basses, those of the Triumphing Dance and 'Oft she visits this lone mountain'.)[61]

The harpsichord, too, was used by singers to accompany themselves. Evelyn heard the castrato Siface at Pepys's home in 1687 and observed: 'He touch'd the Harpsichord to his Voice rarely well.'[62] Similarly, Evelyn's daughter Mary often 'play'd a through-base on the Harpsichord' to her own 'incomparable sweete Voice'.[63] These reports share an interesting feature with others of the period – of John Abell 'being accompanied with

---

[57] New Haven, CT, Yale University, Music Library (K. Foxwell/26835d); see Robert Unwin, 'James Talbot', 67–9.

[58] 'The guitarre was never so much in use & credit as it is at this day'; Nicola Matteis, *The False Consonances of Musick* (1682), 2. In 1680 Reggio 'sung admirably to a *Guitarr*' at Evelyn's home; *Diary of John Evelyn* iv, 220 (23 September 1680). In 1686 Abell received £10 'for a Gittarr by him bought for his Ma^ts service in his Bed-Chamber'; Ashbee, *Records* ii, 17, 38. According to Hawkins (*A General History*, 693), the Duke of York would accompany the singing of Charles II and Gostling on the guitar. In 1690 Benjamin Garrot offered instruction in 'playing upon the Gittar, either by Letters or Notes'; *The London Gazette*, 10 November; see Tilmouth, 'A Calendar', 10.

[59] See Price, *Restoration Theatre*, 78. The guitar was played either the 'brushing way' or the 'pinching way'; see Tilmouth, 'Some Improvements', 58.

[60] One guitar or several? In Staggins's and Crowne's *Calisto* (1674) four guitars were involved, probably playing onstage for dances; Ashbee, *Records* i, 146. See also Holman, *Four and Twenty Fiddlers*, 368–9.

[61] This solution is adopted in both recordings of *Dido and Aeneas* by Andrew Parrott with the Taverner Choir and Players (Chandos, 1981, and Sony/Avie, 1999/2014).

[62] *Diary of John Evelyn* iv, 547 (19 April 1687).

[63] *Diary of John Evelyn* iv, 421 (14 March 1685). Also, Catherine Shore, said by Burney to have been 'a scholar of Purcell in singing and playing of the harpsichord', appeared in her husband Colley Cibber's *Woman's Wit: or, The*

Signor *Francesco* on the *Harpsichord*' in 1682 and Mr Pordage singing with 'Signor Jo: Baptist [Draghi], playing to it on the Harpsichord' in 1685[64] – and with Hawkins's anecdotal description of Purcell accompanying Gostling and Mrs Hunt on the harpsichord at court in 1691 or 1692;[65] in none of these accounts is any mention made of a supporting bowed string instrument. This accords with the clear implications of the information in Table 9.2, that in the song repertoire a bass viol was intended invariably not as a supplementary instrument to a chordal one but as a self-sufficient alternative. The possible objection that this is too literal an interpretation of a casual turn of phrase must vanish when we find certain songs described as 'Composed to be sung either to the Theorbo-Lute, or Bass-Viol'.[66] A viol can, of course, play occasional chords, and Roger North used to accompany his elder brother Francis's singing in this fashion:

> And it being necessary to the sound of a voice, whatever it is, to have an instrument to accompany, and I being well habituated to the viol and the fingering, I used to touch the principall notes as well as I could, and by degrees to putt in cords, and at last to full harmony, as the instrument would afford.[67]

This form of accompaniment probably became less fashionable with time but apparently persisted even after Purcell's death (see, for example, Matteis's *A Collection of New Songs*, 1696).

Does this preference for a single continuo instrument apply also to purely instrumental chamber music? In his preface to the *Sonnata's of III Parts* for 'TWO VIOLLINS And BASSE:/*To the* Organ or Harpsecord' (1683), Purcell attributes a delayed publication date to the fact 'that he has now thought fit to cause the whole Thorough Bass to be Engraven, which was a thing quite besides his first Resolutions'.[68] In other words, a generously figured 'Basso Continuo' part is given in addition to the original unfigured 'Basso' partbook. That two bass instruments are required is clear from the title of the posthumous *Ten Sonatas of Four Parts* (1697), with its 'Through Bass for the *Harpsichord*, or *Organ*', which is presented in the same way. Moreover, a uniquely documented performance of (presumably)

Lady in Fashion (1697), first playing and then singing, presumably to her own accompaniment; Price, *Restoration Theatre*, 80.

[64] *Diary of John Evelyn* iv, 270 (27 January 1682), and 404 (28 January 1685).

[65] Hawkins, *A Genral History*, 564.

[66] John Banister and Thomas Low, *New Ayres, Dialogues, and Trialogues* i (1678). Almost twenty years earlier John Gamble's *Ayres and Dialogues* (1659) were similarly intended 'To be Sung either to the THEORBO-LUTE or BASSE-VIOL'.

[67] *North I*, 26.

[68] The *London Gazette*, 28 May 1682, had announced that copies of Purcell's 'Sonata's of three Parts for two Violins and Base to the Harpsicord or Organ' were 'compleately finished'; Tilmouth, 'A Calendar', 5.

the earlier works (*c.* 1683) points, albeit somewhat ambiguously, to four players: Francis North, who was also a keen viol player, 'caused the devine Purcell to bring his Itallian manner'd compositions [to his home]; and with him [Purcell] on his harpsicord, my self [Roger North] and another violin, wee performed them more than once'.[69] The possibility nevertheless remains that instrumental chamber works with a single bass part may require just a single bass instrument, and not necessarily a chordal one.[70]

In an orchestral context the harmonic need for a chordal instrument is often slight. Is the High Baroque norm of an ever-present chordal continuo necessarily appropriate in Purcell's case? An engraving of the 1685 coronation feast in Westminster Hall affords a rare glimpse of the royal violin band ('ye Musick') in action – 20 players and apparently no continuo instruments.[71] At the start of Locke and Shadwell's version of *The Tempest* (1674) we read of 'the Band of 24 Violins, with the Harpsicals and Theorbo's which accompany the Voices'.[72] The wording seems exactly to describe the Lullian operatic model, in which continuo instruments were usually reserved for vocal sections (including choruses); *airs de ballet* and many other independent *symphonies* (including overtures) contain no figuring.[73] But the picture is less clear with Restoration theatre music where conventions were more fluid and evidence is limited. In a few individual cases the presence in the sources of autograph or early contemporary figuring can settle the matter: the 1691 printed score of *Dioclesian*, for example, contains two revealing bars of figuring in the overture. But this need not imply the same practice for a slightly earlier work such as *Dido* (before 1689?)[74] or for non-theatrical works. Furthermore, it seems that even 'in early 18th-century London theatres the harpsichord was used exclusively to accompany the voices'.[75] (But by the second decade of the 18th century North was writing of the harpsichord that 'in a great consort, tho' struck full at every note, it is lean and

---

[69] *North I*, 47.

[70] *The Loyal Post*, 28 October 1682, announced Gerhard Diessener's recently published 'consort of Musick for three parts (*viz*). Two Violins, and a Base Viol'; Tilmouth, 'A Calendar', 5.

[71] Sandford, *Coronation*, pl. 4, 'A Prospect of the Inside of Westminster Hall'; reproduced in Holman, *Four and Twenty Fiddlers*, as fig. 13.3.

[72] Price, *Restoration Theatre*, 79.

[73] Graham Sadler, 'The Role of the Keyboard Continuo in French Opera, 1673–1776', *Early Music* 8/2 (1980), 148–57; see also Holman, *Four and Twenty Fiddlers*, 384–5.

[74] On the dating of the first performance of *Dido and Aeneas* see various contributions to *Early Music*: 20 (1992), 372, 392, 703; 21 (1993), 510; 22 (1994), 115, 365, 469; 23 (1995), 188.

[75] Milhous and Price, 'Harpsichords', 43. See also Peter Holman, 'Reluctant Continuo', *Early Music* 9/1 (1981), 75–8.

soundless. If one can but say there is such an instrument heard amongst them, it is all.')[76]

The figuring of bass parts from Purcell's time is in general very sparse and frequently non-existent.[77] Consequently, writers on continuo practice concentrate on harmonic matters: Locke's *Melothesia, or, Certain General Rules for Playing upon a Continued-Bass* (1673) and Blow's manuscript 'Rules for playing of a Through Bass upon Organ & Harpsicon' do just that.[78] But

> whether figured or not, it is certein, a thro-base part may best be played from the score: and if there were nothing else to recomend it but the capacity of a nicer waiting on the parts then displayed, by seeing their movement, it's enough.[79]

Organ parts copied by Blow for three of Purcell's anthems arranged without strings, and those of a dozen collected by Gostling,[80] adopt a quite plain style and the fairly familiar two- or three- (and occasionally four-) part texture of other late 17th-century organ books, with occasional harmonic enrichment. But what of stylistic matters in theorbo and harpsichord realizations? While admitting 'That *the Greatest Excellency* in *This Kind of Performance*, lies beyond whatever *Directions* can be given by *Rule*', Mace provides 21 useful examples of how to 'Amplifie your Play' on the theorbo, by '*Breaking* your *Parts*, or *Stops*, in way of *Dividing-Play* upon Cadences, or Closes'.[81] Handwritten realizations of five songs

---

[76] *North I*, 248.

[77] Curtis A. Price, *Henry Purcell and th141 London Stage* (1984), 243.

[78] See Franck Arnold, *The Art of Accompaniment from a Thorough-Bass* (London, 1931), 154–72. (Blow's instructions are from London, British Library, Add. MS 34072, fols. 1–5.) See also Godfrey Keller, *A Compleat Method for attaining to play a Thorough Bass upon either Organ, Harpsicord or Theorbo-Lute* (London, 1705), described by Arnold (pp. 247–50); and Prendcourt's 'The treatis of the continued or through basse' (London, British Library, Add. MS 32549, fols. 17–30v).

[79] *North I*, 249.

[80] See *Works II* xiii (1988), 69–87, 133–41.

[81] Mace, *Musick's Monument*, pt 2, ch. 43, esp. 217, 221–4. An early example of a written-out accompaniment for theorbo is found in Lady Ann Blount's Song Book, for the anonymous 'Sing aloud harmonious spheres'. Locke points out that 'When a *Bass* hathe many swift Notes running one after another ... for the *Theorbo* &c. it is sufficient to Play single Notes' (Arnold, *The Art of Accompaniment*, 157). Matteis's 'Instructions for playing a true Base upon the Guitarre' and other instruments include a brief discussion of the rate of chord-playing (*The False Consonances of Musick* (1682), 19–20; cf. Mace, *Musick's Monument*, 229); this matches Blow's advice to keyboard players that 'If your Bass move by Quavers or Semiquavers, you need not play wth your right hand more than on^{ce} to four quavers, or once to two quavers, being the same as if your Bass had been Minums or Crochets' (Arnold, *The*

including Purcell's 'How pleasant is This flowry Plain and Grove!' are found in a copy of *The Banquet of Musick* (1688–92), but they are undated and may well have been intended for archlute; their style is quite active and melodic.[82] Specifically for harpsichord is the simple realization in a contemporary source of a three-bar modulatory continuo phrase in the ode 'From Hardy Climes' (1683; Ex. 9.2). But rather more revealing are two short solo harpsichord pieces (ZT681 and 682), both grounds, derived from vocal models (Ex. 9.3). Both alternate a simple melodic line (at the higher octave) with a written-out continuo part essentially in two parts (occasionally three) in the middle register, and use 'broken' rhythms and more or less exact repetitions. This style would seem to have much more in common with North's view (*c.* 1710–20) that the harpsichord excelled in 'humouring a solo or single voice, where there is much of interlude, which lets that instrument in to shew itself':

> For the sprinkling or *arpeggio*, the proper genius of it, must have pauses, for liberty of that kind, which hath an egregious effect, as either in leading the air, to possess a voice with its key, [or] to enter *petit* fuges or intersperse *ritornello's*.[83]

North goes on to emphasize the need to be 'a master of composition in generall':

> For there is occasion of so much management in the manner of play, sometimes striking onely the accords, sometimes *arpeggiando*, sometimes touching the air, and perpetually observing the emphatick places, to fill, forbear, or adorne with a just favour, that a [mere] thro-base master, and not an ayerist, is but an abcdarian ...

He also maintains that:

> it is not allow'd a thro-base part to break and adorne while he accompanys, but to touch the accords onely as may be figured, or [as] the composition requires. Yet there is a difference in the management when the upper parts move slow, and when they devide, or when they are full, or pause. In that latter case, somewhat more airey may be putt in, and often there is occasion to fill more or less.[84]

Art of Accompaniment, 166). See also Nigel North, *Continuo Playing on the Lute, Archlute and Theorbo* (1987), 196.

[82] Oxford, Bodleian Library, MS Mus. 8 c.2. See Peter Holman, 'Continuo Realizations in a Playford Songbook', *Early Music* 6/2 (1978), 268–9. For the opening of the Purcell song, see Ian Spink, *English Song: Dowland to Purcell* (1974), 216.

[83] *North I*, 247–8.

[84] *North I*, 249.

Ex. 9.2 Henry Purcell, 'From Hardy Climes' (z325/4a), bars 1–3

Ex. 9.3 (a) Henry Purcell, *Ground* (zT681), bars 1–6;
(b) Henry Purcell, *A New Ground* (zT682), bars 1–5

As a continuo instrument the 'Noble Base Viol' seems, for the most part, to have held its own against 'the harsh volon' (bass violin).[85] We have already seen that a viol very probably played in a contemporary performance of the earlier trio sonatas, and a subsequent advertisement

---

[85] *North I*, 227. Of viol-only accompaniments there appear to be no written-out examples from so late in the century.

for the set confirms this scoring;[86] the undesignated bass of the later collection, similarly, is labelled 'Viol di gambo' in an early 18th-century source.[87] But Purcell's later years may well have been a period in which the virtual monopoly of the bass viol as a bowed string continuo instrument began to be challenged by the bass violin. The latter, generally bowed underhand, was for a long time associated exclusively with professional musicians, often 'some hireling drudge' (like the 'Fat-Red-Fac'd-Fidler that plays upon the Base' in Otway's *Friendship in Fashion*, 1678), and was considered 'a cours instrument', which, 'as then used [in the 1670s], was a very hard and harsh sounded base, and nothing so soft and sweet as now [*c*. 1726]'.[88]

By 1692 Purcell could confidently specify a bass violin to support two violins in the duet 'Hark! each tree' (*Hail! bright Cecilia!*), and at a private gathering in Oxford the following year; in the company of 'Mr Shore [and] Monseur la Rich', Francis Withey observed that 'Monse Diseb plais on ye Base Violin Ex[cellently]'.[89] Two tell-tale *BB*♭s occur in the bass (bars 10 and 46) to the bass solo (again with 2 violins) 'The father brave' ('A Song for the Duke of Gloucester's Birthday', 1695), as does a *BB* in the D major '3 parts upon a Ground' (z731). (Talbot gives the lowest note of the bass violin as *BB*♭, without mentioning *C* as an alternative; the lower note appears in Purcell's orchestral music – for example, in the overture to *The Indian Queen* and in the symphony to 'A Song for the Duke of Gloucester's Birthday' – but only seldom.)[90] In the anthems with strings it would seem that, as a rule, the (unspecified) bowed string bass played only with the upper strings, in purely instrumental sections and tuttis, and that the continuo for solo sections was provided by organ, often with theorbo(s). In addition, viols may have doubled the choral bass.[91]

Before turning from matters of continuo practice, it may be worth asking whether an 8′ 'great' bass viol, like Orlando Gibbons's 'great Dooble

---

[86] '*Sonnata's* of three Parts, for two *Violins* and *Bass-Viol*, with a Through-Bass for the *Organ* or *Harpsichord*', in [J. Playford], *Choice Ayres, and Songs and Dialogues* v (1684), 63.

[87] Low *C* occurs in no. 4 (2, bar 38) of the 1683 set, but nowhere in the 1697 set. It was not uncommon for the bass viol to tune its lowest string down a tone; see Christopher Simpson, *The Division-Viol* (London, 1667), 8; and Robert Donington, 'James Talbot's Manuscript II: Bowed Strings', *Galpin Society Journal* 3 (1950), 33.

[88] Price, *Restoration Theatre*, 266; and *North I*, 304. See also *Roger North's The Musicall Grammarian 1728*, ed. M. Chan and J. C. Kassler (1990), 265, hereinafter cited as *North III*.

[89] Robert Thompson, '"Francis Withie of Oxon" and his Commonplace Book, Christ Church, Oxford, MS 337', *Chelys* 20 (1991), 11. 'Diseb' was probably Desabay(e); see Ashbee, *Records* ii, 16, 19, 91, 102.

[90] See also Holman, *Four and Twenty Fiddlers*, 406–7.

[91] Holman, *Four and Twenty Fiddlers*, 318–19.

Basse', survived in use from the earlier part of the century.[92] Certainly, the 'Double Base' writing in Blow's 'Lord, who shall dwell in thy tabernacle?' (from the early 1680s?) need not imply a 16' instrument.[93] The six-string 'Violone or Double Bass' viol mentioned by Talbot (and labelled by him as 'German') has its lowest string tuned to low GG,[94] and, like the theorbo, would be capable of occasionally dropping an octave to enrich a bass line. The advantage of such a viol as continuo instrument would be not so much its range as the quality of sound in the bass register:

> Lent the noble *viola* or double base viol: the strings have length in proportion to their magnitude and tension, which makes the tone sweet and loud. The base-violin is too short and strong, therefore harsh, whatever of organ or harpeggia there is. Let the double base viol governe the *basso continuo*, and if one be not enough let there be more.[95]

Was this 'double bass' viol the 8' instrument which survived, at least in Germany and Austria, into the 18th century,[96] and might such an instrument therefore have had a place in Purcell's music?[97] Specifically, might this have been the type of viol employed by the Chapel Royal to support the choral voices? 'I cannot but commend the double base, or standing viol, for plaine bases,' wrote North (c. 1695), 'especially for accompanying voices, because of its softness joyned with such a force as helps the voice very much'.[98]

---

[92] In his family portrait (c. 1650) Sir Peter Lely, a close friend and benefactor of Roger North's, depicts himself playing a large viol of a size intermediate between that of the normal bass and a 16' violone. See Holman, *Four and Twenty Fiddlers*, pl. 5a. For a more recent survey of 'Large Bass Instruments' at this period see Peter Holman, *Life After Death: The Viola da Gamba in Britain from Purcell to Dolmetsch* (2010), 43–5.

[93] Similarly, the 'Great Basse' in George Jeffreys's 'Felice Pastorella'; see also Holman, *Four and Twenty Fiddlers*, 216–17. In the case of some sonatas by Keller the term 'double basses' appears merely to indicate the inclusion of a pair of (identical) bass parts, specifically for 'Organo e Violoncello'; Godfrij Keller, *Six Sonatas/ The First Three/ For a Trumpett, Houbois or violins/ with Doubble Basses. The Other Three/ For two flutes, and two Haubois/ or two violins with Doubble Basses* (Amsterdam, 1699 or 1700).

[94] Donington, 'Bowed Strings', 33.

[95] *North I*, 274 (written sometime in the first six years after Purcell's death).

[96] Walls, 'Strings', 46.

[97] Two German viol players who worked in England were Theodore Steffkin (until 1673) and (from c. 1685) Gottfried Finger. The viol teachers at the proposed Royal Academies in 1695 were to have been Finger and 'Mr Stephkins', presumably either Frederick or Christian, the sons of Theodore; Tilmouth, 'The Royal Academies', 327.

[98] *North I*, 16.

ORCHESTRAS AND STRING PLAYING

ONLY two aspects of Purcell's string orchestra need special attention here: its bass line and its strength. As we have seen, a bass violin tuned a tone below the cello is implied even in music from the composer's last year. But what of a 16′ bass? Convincing evidence for the use of any form of 16′ orchestral bass seems to be wholly absent from the music of Purcell and his immediate contemporaries. Anthony à Wood, noting the rise of the violin band in the 1650s, wrote: 'only violins used, as treble, tenor, and bass-violin',[99] and court archives for the remainder of the century record the purchase of 'Base violins' (and strings for them), but of nothing obviously larger.'[100] Even in post-Purcellian Italian operas 'the instrumental part' was, at least in retrospect, considered 'under based', because bassoons failed to 'urge the other instruments, as the [new 16′?] double violls doe'.[101] On the other hand, a 'double bass' by Edward Lewis, dated 1695, has survived, and Talbot measured a five- or six-string fretted 'double bass viol' with a body-length of over 5 feet, belonging to Gottfried Finger. As far as I can ascertain, the first known specialist double-bass player in England was probably Giuseppe Fedeli, known as Joseph Saggione, a composer and member of Christopher Rich's Drury Lane company orchestra in the early 1700s.[102] Significantly, it was Saggione, together with Montéclair, who was later credited with having introduced the instrument to the Paris Opéra c. 1701.[103]

It would seem then that, in this one respect at least, orchestras in England mirrored the French model throughout Purcell's lifetime.[104] At

---

[99] Oxford, Bodleian Library, MS Wood D. 19 (4), fol. 32v.

[100] See also Tilmouth, 'Some Improvements', 58; and Talbot's 'tuning of the violins' (Donington, 'Bowed Strings', 29), where the double bass is conspicuous by its absence.

[101] *North I*, 274.

[102] See also Ashbee, *Records* ii, 102, where 'Sig^r Sajony' is listed with the 'Instrumentall Musick' of the Queen's Theatre, Haymarket, in 1710.

[103] Michel Corrette, *Méthode pour apprendre à jouer de la contre-basse* (Paris, 1773), 1. See also Mary Cyr, 'Basses and *basse continue* in the Orchestra of the Paris Opéra, 1700–1764', *Early Music* 10/2 (1982), 155–70.

[104] Whatever the French influences on the early Restoration Court string band, it was 'Cremona' instruments that were occasionally imported (Ashbee, *Records* i, 15, 37, 60; and *Records* v, 110, 112, 133), although from Purcell's time at Court we know of only 'a Cremona Base Violin' bought for £20 in 1680 (Ashbee *Records* i, 92). In 1692 'a number of Curious Violins, Cremonia and others' were advertised for sale (*The London Gazette*, 15 December; see Tilmouth, 'A Calendar', 13). Later, North commented: 'some say England hath dispeopled Italy of viollins' (*North III*, 272). Talbot's measurements of a violin lent by 'Banister' apparently resemble those of the 'grand pattern' Amati (Donington, 'Bowed Strings', 27, 29, 30; David D. Boyden, *The History of Violin Playing from its Origins to 1761* (1965), 202), but surviving

Whitehall the full body of the Twenty-Four Violins may occasionally have taken part in the various birthday and welcome odes, but from 1668 the players were organized into two groups to 'wait & attend upon his Ma^ty ... 12 one moneth & 12 ye other'.[105] Also, when the court was at Windsor only 12 players were usually available.[106] For the 1685 coronation there were some 35 instrumentalists (in addition to the trumpeters),[107] and the violinist and Master of the Musick Nicholas Staggins received payment for 'faire writing of a composition for his Majesty's coronation day from the originall in score the 6 parts, for drawing ye said composition into forty severall parts for trumpetts, hautboyes, violins, tennors, bases'.[108] (Staggins's bills for music-copying in 1675–6, incidentally, confirm that his players did not normally share copies but that 'every man [had] a part to himselfe'.)[109] In theatres such a large group would have been almost unheard of.[110] At Wren's Dorset Garden theatre, which probably accommodated 700 or 800 spectators, the 'musick room' above the proscenium arch perhaps measured roughly 25' by 8'.[111] Nor would other buildings associated with the performances of Purcell's odes and secular public pieces generally have demanded large forces. Although the brief reduction to 2 violins and violas per part in the opening chorus of the richly scored *Hail! bright Cecilia!*[112] suggests at least 14 string players for the first performance in Stationers' Hall, a repeat given in York Buildings

English instruments show more Northern European influences. Notable contemporary makers were William Baker of Oxford (*c.* 1645–85), Edward Pamphilon (*fl. c.* 1670–95), Thomas Urquhart (*c.* 1650–80) and the young Barak Norman (*c.* 1670–1740). Both gut and silk strings overwound with 'Small Wire' were known in England from at least 1664 but were not necessarily in common use; their increased density enabled thinner and therefore tonally 'better and lowder' strings to be used in the bass of an instrument (Michael G. Lowe, 'The Historical Development of the Lute in the 17th Century', *Galpin Society Journal* 29 (1976), 24).

[105] Ashbee, *Records* i, 83. See also Holman, *Four and Twenty Fiddlers*, appendix D; and Mace, *Musick's Monument*, 233.

[106] See Ashbee, *Records* i, 184, 187, etc.

[107] Holman, *Four and Twenty Fiddlers*, 401.

[108] Ashbee, *Records* ii, 12. Note again the absence of a double bass.

[109] Ashbee, *Records* i, 155–6. But cf. Peter Holman, 'Original Sets of Parts for Restoration Concerted Music at Oxford', in *Performing the Music of Henry Purcell*, ed. M. Burden (1996), 9–19.

[110] Price, *Restoration Theatre*, 8, 82, 267; and *North I*, 274.

[111] Mark A. Radice, 'Theater Architecture at the Time of Purcell and its Influence on his "Dramatick Operas"', *The Musical Quarterly* 74 (1990), 111, 126, 129.

[112] *Works II* viii (1978), 13–14. A comparable reduction from 'full' to 'single' strings is indicated in an early score of *King Arthur* (see *Works II* xxvi (1971), 18–20), and in Grabu's 'From harmony, from heavenly harmony' (1687); see Holman, *Four and Twenty Fiddlers*, 427–8.

in 1693 cannot have involved more than 20 or so performers *in toto*: there 'the Great Room' seems to have been just 32′ 4″ long, 31′ 6″ broad, 21′ high, with 'a Semicircle of Seats, and stands for Musick' in a raised alcove 15′ 9″ deep and 17′ in diameter.[113]

While coronation verse anthems such as 'My Heart is Inditing' (for James II) and 'Praise the Lord, O Jerusalem' (for William and Mary) would have been played by the full Twenty-Four Violins, it may well have been simple lack of space in the chapel at Whitehall Palace that led to the 'orchestrally' accompanied anthems by Purcell and others being played there by a mere handful of players, situated probably in the music room that opened on to the chapel at first-floor level. (The choir was in stalls below, but verse sections may usually have been sung from the gallery.)[114] The chapel itself, 'panelled round almost up to the roof', cannot have measured much more than 75′ by 30′ or so.[115] Four to six 'violins' plus two viols – 'a select number of his [Majesty's] private music'[116] – served there on a rota system, and the almost inescapable conclusion is that they played with just one player per part.[117]

From 1674 and for the remainder of Purcell's lifetime, the court band was in the charge of Staggins, who had travelled in 'France ... Italy, & other Forrin Parts, to capacitate & make my self fit for ye Service of His Late Ma^{ty} Kg Charles ye Second'.[118] And among the court violinists from 1681 was John Lenton, whose modest *The Gentleman's Diversion, or the Violin*

---

[113] *North I*, 306. Mace gives a plan for an 18-foot square 'Musick-Roome, w^{ich} would have none in It besides the Performers', surrounded by 12 galleries which, 'though but little, will (I believe) hold 200 *Persons* very well, without *Crowding*'; *Musick's Monument*, 239, 241. Advertisements for weekly music-making in the Great Room, Lambeth Wells, in 1697 mention 'Vocal and Instrumental Musick, consisting of about Thirty Instruments and Voices, after the method of the Musick meeting in York Buildings'; Tilmouth, 'A Calendar', 19; such a total need not imply the simultaneous involvement of all performers.

[114] Holman, *Four and Twenty Fiddlers*, 398–9, 404–5. For the 1685 coronation in Westminster Abbey the spatial separation between the three special galleries accommodating the musicians was considerable. The 'Kings Choir' and the 'Master and Kings Choir of Instrumental Musick' were diagonally across from each other near the high altar, while the Abbey's own choir was just west of the transepts, next to 'The Great Organ' on the north side of the choir. The 'whole *Consort* of *Voices* and *Instruments*' performed Blow's 'God Spake Sometimes in Visions' and Purcell's 'My Heart is Inditing'; see Sandford, *Coronation*, 99, 101, etc.

[115] Holman, *Four and Twenty Fiddlers*, 389, 391.

[116] Thomas Tudway, preface to 'Services and Anthems' ii (1716), London, British Library, MS Harleian 7338, fols. 2v–3; also printed in Ian Spink, *Restoration Cathedral Music, 1600–1714* (1995), 437.

[117] See also Holman, *Four and Twenty Fiddlers*, 397–400; and Ashbee, *Records* i, 108–9, 113.

[118] Ashbee, *Records* v, 91.

explained (1693) apparently has the distinction of being the first extant violin tutor in any language.[119] Rejecting both the older example of Matteis, who 'rested his instrument against his short ribbs',[120] and the newer chin-on technique, Lenton considered that 'the best way of commanding the instrument will be to place it something higher than your Breast'.[121]

Christopher Simpson's instructions (1659) for holding and using a viol bow (including gracing 'by the bow') were echoed by both Playford and Mace[122] and seem to have been regarded as models through the remainder of the century. Comparably detailed information for violin bowing is harder to find. Lenton scarcely gives any, on the grounds that 'The humours of Masters being very Various ... what is approved by one would be condemned by another',[123] but the instructions he does give match the Rule of the Down Bow, and include the characteristically French [⊓ V ⊓ | ⊓] for triple time.[124] North considered the 'bipedalian' bow used by Matteis 'very long' and 'as for a base violl',[125] but Talbot gives 2 feet as the 'usual length of the Consort Bow' (in line with Lenton's view that 'your Bow be as long as your Instrument') and an extra 2 or 3 inches as the 'length of the Bow for Solo's or Sonata's'.[126] Lenton recommends that the elbow is held no higher 'than necessity requires' and describes a bow grip with the thumb on the hair at the frog,[127] despite North's assertion that Matteis had 'taught the English to hold the bow by the wood onely and not to touch the hair, which was no small reformation'.[128] Certainly, Matteis's playing seems to have epitomized the refinement that well-modulated bowing could achieve; in 1674 Evelyn

> heard that stupendious Violin Signor Nicholao ... whom certainly never mortal man Exceeded on that Instrument: he had a stroak so

---

[119] Two earlier English tutors, from the 1680s, are apparently not extant; see Malcolm Boyd and John Rayson, 'The Gentleman's Diversion: John Lenton and the First Violin Tutor', *Early Music* 10/3 (1982), 329–32.

[120] *North I*, 309 and n. 63.

[121] Lenton, 'The Gentleman's Diversion', 11; see Boyd and Rayson (cf. n. 115). According to John Playford, the violin was 'rested on the left breast, a little below the shoulder'; *An Introduction to the Skill of Musick* (London, 7/1674), 114.

[122] Playford, *An Introduction*, 101–4; and Mace, *Musick's Monument*, 248.

[123] Walls, 'Strings', 45.

[124] Walls, 'Strings', 51.

[125] *North I*, 168, 309.

[126] Donington, 'Bowed Strings', 29.

[127] Walls, 'Strings', 49. The title page of John Playford's *The Division-Violin* (London, 2/1685) clearly illustrates bow shapes.

[128] *North I*, 309.

sweete, & made it speake like the Voice of a man; & when he pleased, like a Consort of severall Instruments ...[129]

VIBRATO

THE expressive skills and vocal qualities exhibited by Matteis bring us to the matter of vibrato. It was doubtless with the same violinist in mind that North wrote:

> The Italians have brought the bow to an high perfection, so that nothing of their playing is so difficult as the *arcata* or long bow, with which they will begin a long note, clear, without rubb, and draw it forth swelling lowder and lowder, and at the ackme take a slow waiver; not [a] trill to break the sound or mix 2 notes, but as if the bird sat at the end of a spring [and] as she sang the spring waived her up and downe, or as if the wind that brought the sound shaked, or a small bell were struck and the sound continuing waived to and againe – so would I express what is justly not to be shewn but to the ear by an exquisite hand.[130]

This form of vibrato was evidently quite new to English players at the time, and even *c.* 1715–20 North was writing of 'the late invention they call a wrist-shake'.[131] Its function was, he wrote, 'that the sound may waive, but not stopp or vary its tone' (i.e. pitch). The point is amplified elsewhere:

> It is rarely observed, but lett it pass for a truth upon my word, that the greatest elegance of the finest voices is the prolation of a clear plain sound. And I may add, that in voice or instrument (where the hand draws the sound) it is the most difficult part to performe ...
>
> Therefore as to the *pratique*, I would have a voice or hand taught, first to prolate a long, true steddy and strong sound ... to superinduce [on a plain note] a gentle slow wavering, not into a trill, upon the swelling the note; such as trumpetts use, as if the instrument were a litle shaken with the wind of its owne sound, but not so as to vary the tone [i.e. pitch], which must be religiously held to its place, like a pillar on its base, without the least loss of the accord. This waving of a note is not to be described, but by example. But as wee often use odd similes to express our meaning and help the imagination, take these images of sound by lines, which represent the humour of sound judiciously mannaged:

---

[129] *Diary of John Evelyn* iv, 48 (19 November 1674).

[130] *North I*, 164.

[131] *North I*, 167. Later still, around 1726, he complained of its overuse (*North I*, 164–5).

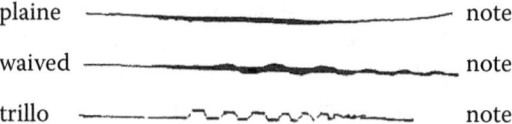

The latter is the trill, which, as you see, breaking the tone [i.e. pitch] and mixing with another, is dangerous for a scollar to medle with, till he hath the mastery of the sound, else it will make him apt to loose the principall tone: and that spoiles all.[132]

Vibrato was clearly regarded as an ornament (or grace), and one especially associated in instrumental use with the violin:

There is another sort of trill, which varyeth not the tone, but sounds as if the air shakt, as when an upright tree plays a litle in the air. Few instruments [have it] except the violin, upon which it is used to perfection. The trumpet hath it also, and the viol in some degree; the rowl of the finger without stop, gives it upon the violin, but upon the viol gentle touches very neer the stop, but that is not so perfect as the other. It is rather a soft and lowd then a trill, but extraordinary gratefull, and setts off a plaine tone to a wonder as may be heard but not described.[133]

---

[132] *North I*, 17–18 and pl. 2; see also *North I*, 128.

[133] *North II*, 223. The viol's equivalent to which North refers was a two-finger vibrato, described by Simpson: '*Close-shake* [Tremor pressus] is that when we shake the Finger as close and near the sounding Note as possible may be, touching the String with the Shaking finger so softly and nicely that it make no variation of Tone [i.e. pitch]. This may be used where no other Grace is concerned ...'. This 'explanation' is effectively identical with one given earlier by Playford; Simpson classifies it as one of the 'more smooth and Feminine' graces, 'which are more natural to the *Treble*, or upper parts' (Simpson, *The Division-Viol*, 11–12). (However popular the ornament may have been among viol players – and it is mentioned in connection with the bass viol as late as c. 1726 by North, who calls it a 'close beat' – the sign itself is not known to occur in contemporary musical sources.) The now normal one-finger vibrato, found alongside the close shake in French sources (de Machy, 1685; Marais, 1686; and Rousseau, 1687) is not mentioned by the English viol players, but the apparent familiarity of the English lutenists with it may suggest that it was not unknown in English viol technique of the period. Mace (*Musick's Monument*, 109) informs us that in lute playing: 'The *Sting*, is another very Neat, and Pritty Grace; (But not *Modish* in *These Days*) ... first strike your *Note*, and so soon as It is struck, hold your *Finger (but not too Hard) stopt upon the Place* (letting your *Thumb loose*) and *wave your Hand, (Exactly) downwards, and upwards, several Times, from the Nut, to the Bridge*; by which *Motion*, your *Finger will draw, or stretch the String a little upwards, and downwards*, so, as to make the Sound seem to *Swell*.'

264 Composers' Intentions?

The analogous form of vibrato for woodwind instruments is the finger-vibrato, found in Hudgebut's *Vade mecum* (1679), Salter's *Genteel Companion* (1683) and *The Compleat Flute-Master* (1695), where it is called 'an open shake or sweetning', achieved by 'shaking your finger over the half hole immidiately below yᵉ note to be sweetned ending with it off'.[134]

A different form of vibrato, explicitly called for in Purcell's music as a special effect, is the easily misinterpreted tremolo (♩♩♩♩), which occurs in writing both for bowed strings and for voices (Ex. 9.4), and which 'resembles the shaking stop of an organ'.[135] For string players, the 'Italians *tremolo*', probably learnt from Matteis, was not a *tremolando* (♩) but a bow vibrato made by playing an even rhythm 'with the same bow, but distinguishing the notes' (♩♩♩♩).[136] For voices it was presumably an equivalent gentle rearticulation (from the diaphragm or throat) or rhythmic pulsation, on a single pitch and syllable. A further occurrence of '*Tremulo*' (but without its symbol) seems to have attracted little attention: the canzona for flat trumpets that concludes the Funeral Music for Queen Mary (1695) appears as in Ex. 9.5 in Oxford, Oriel College, MS U a 37. Here a breath vibrato in all parts is surely implied for groups of repeated notes (starting ♩ ♩ ♩ ♩), the first notes tongued, the remainder articulated from the diaphragm or throat.

---

[134] See Greta Moens-Haenen, *Das Vibrato in der Musik des Barock* (1988), 88–93; and Bruce Dickey, 'Untersuchungen zur historischen Auffassung des Vibratos auf Blasinstrumenten', *Basler Jahrbuch für historische Musikpraxis* 2 (1978), 88–91.

[135] *North I*, 186. See also Simpson, *The Division-Viol*, 10.

[136] *North I*, 22–3, 227, 355. See also Stewart Carter, 'The String Tremolo in the 17th Century', *Early Music* 19/1 (1991), 53–5; and Lionel Sawkins, '*Trembleurs* and Cold People: How Should they Shiver?', in *Performing the Music of Henry Purcell*, ed. M. Burden (1995).

Ex. 9.4 Henry Purcell, *King Arthur, or the British Worthy* (z628): (a) Prelude while the Cold Genius rises (z628/20a), bars 1–3; (b) 'What power art thou' (z628/20b), bars 1–5; (c) 'See, we assemble thy revels to hold' (z628/24b), bars 1–3

Ex. 9.5 Henry Purcell, Canzona from the Funeral Music for Queen Mary (z860/2), bars 1–8

Tremulo

WIND INSTRUMENTS

Early in 1690 Purcell found himself in a position to write for an orchestra that had expanded from a string group, with occasional 'flutes' (recorders)[137] and on just one brief occasion a single oboe,[138] to one which could normally include both oboes and trumpet(s). Clearly trumpet playing had reached a new level of sophistication:

> While the company is at table the hautboys and trumpets play successively. Mr Showers [Shore] hath taught the latter of late years to sound with all the softness imaginable.[139]

[137] The 'bass flute' that makes an appearance in 'Hark! each tree' from the 1692 ode 'Hail! bright Cecilia!' must be Talbot's 'pedal or double bass' recorder (in C), as the part descends beneath (written) *F*, as does the 'bass flute' part in Blow's 'Lord, who shall dwell in thy tabernacle?'. Some figuring in the part shows that this very delicate instrument (and effect) would have been supported by a continuo instrument.

[138] In 'Swifter, Isis' (1681).

[139] *The Gentleman's Journal*, January 1692. In 1699 Godfrey Keller wrote that the 'Trumpet [is] an Instrument formerly practis'd in yᵉ rough Consorts of yᵉ Field but now instructed in gentler Notes, it has learnt to accompany yᵉ softest

Ex. 9.6 Henry Purcell, 'Hail! bright Cecilia!' (z328/11b), bars 71–3

[Adagio]

loud
loud
loud

This 'softness' was no doubt a principal reason for the trumpets' gaining admission to an orchestral context, and the development of the 'flat' trumpet, which Purcell called on twice in his last year or so, was itself a reflection of a new sophistication. This instrument, by means of a double-slide which draws back towards the player's head (rather than away from it, as on the trombone), could play certain 'exotick notes'[140] and thus in minor ('flat') keys, 'it being a thing formerly thought impossible upon an instrument designed for a sharp [major] key'.[141] It has even been argued that these 'flat trumpets were used routinely in the English orchestra of the Purcell period', in normal ('sharp') trumpet music,[142] thereby facilitating quick changes – from C to D tuning (or *vice versa*) as in all four semi-operas – or obviating any such necessity – as in *The Libertine* where only some of the writing is obviously for flat trumpets. More importantly, the occasional prominent non-harmonic note such as that marked with an asterisk in Ex. 9.6 would cease to be problematic.[143]

Flutes and can join with the most charming Voices'; dedication to an 'English Princess' of three trumpet sonatas; see Edward Tarr, *The Trumpet* (1988), 135.

[140] *North II*, 119.

[141] *The Gentleman's Journal*, January 1692. The instrument was a particular speciality of John Shore's and of perhaps a small handful of his close colleagues'. In the March and Canzona the three upper parts use only slide positions 1–3, while the bass, which lies fairly high, goes as far as position 5 and may have been played (on a flat trumpet) by a sackbut player. The simple homophonic anthem 'Thou knowest Lord', which according to Tudway in 1717 was 'accompanied wth flat Mournfull Trumpets', would, if played, take the bass to position 6 and the tenor to 4 (Thomas Tudway, 'Services and Anthems' iv (1717), London, British Library, Harleian MS 7340, fol. 264v); what was meant, almost certainly, was not that trumpets *doubled* the voices but simply that the anthem was sung *in conjunction with* the brass pieces.

[142] Andrew Pinnock, 'A Wider Role for the Flat Trumpet', *Galpin Society Journal* 42 (1989), 107.

[143] See Peter Downey, 'What Samuel Pepys Heard on 3 February, 1661: English Trumpet Style under the Later Stuart Monarchs', *Early Music* 18/3 (1990), 417–28; Andrew Pinnock and Bruce Wood, 'A Counterblast on English Trumpets', *Early Music* 19/3 (1991), 437–43; Peter Holman, 'English

Purcell's earliest notated kettle-drum parts are those of *The Fairy Queen* (1692), and, while it is possible that the earlier use of trumpets implies the presence of drums too, Purcell's writing is rarely so formulaic or so simple harmonically that a part could have been easily improvised. (The notion that kettle-drums would have played in the March and Canzona for flat trumpets at Queen Mary's funeral cannot be sustained, but it seems that the March was performed in procession to the sound of side drums.)[144]

The possibility of unnotated parts, or rather of unspecified instruments, arises in several further cases. Trumpet writing from the last year and a half or so of the composer's life almost always lacks a second trumpet part, which could perhaps be merely a notational quirk of the surviving sources.[145] Within works which use oboes there are also occasional ambiguities over their possible involvement in string-only movements; but certainly the addition of oboes to the string writing of, for example, *Dido and Aeneas* is gratuitous and anachronistic. Similarly, the appearance of a bassoon (with an independent part) in *Dioclesian* (1690) – together with a 'tenor hautboy' – may mark Purcell's first use of the instrument[146] and its first occurrence in an English score[147] but should not be taken to imply its presence alongside oboes on every occasion, least of all perhaps in non-orchestral movements.

These woodwind instruments would have been of the new 'Baroque' type developed in France in the 1650s and 1660s and evidently first heard in England in 1673.[148] The players, too, were mostly from France: the group of five 'Hooboys that were in Holland' with William III in 1691 consisted of George Sutton (the first known English player) and four Frenchmen, among them François Le Riche and Paisible's 'good friend, Peter Bressan, the instrument maker' (1663–1731).[149] It was Le Riche who supplied Talbot

Trumpets – A Response', *Early Music* 19/3 (1991), 443. See also Crispian Steele-Perkins, 'Practical Observations on Natural, Slide and Flat Trumpets', *Galpin Society Journal* 42 (1989), 122–6; David Rycroft, 'Flat Trumpet Facts and Figures,' *Galpin Society Journal* 42 (1989), 134–42; and Frank Tomes, 'Flat Trumpet Experiments', *Galpin Society Journal* 43 (1990), 164–5.

[144] See Bruce Wood, 'The First Performance of Purcell's Funeral Music for Queen Mary', in *Performing the Music of Henry Purcell*, ed. M. Burden (1995).

[145] Peter Downey, private communication. See also Rebecca Herissone, 'Robert Pindar, Thomas Busby, and the Mysterious Scoring of Henry Purcell's "Come ye sons of art"', *Music & Letters* 88/1 (2007), 1–48.

[146] David Lasocki, 'The French Hautboy in England, 1673–1730', *Early Music* 16/3 (1988), 341.

[147] Price, *Henry Purcell*, 263.

[148] David Lasocki, 'Professional Recorder Playing in England, 1500–1740 II: 1640–1740', *Early Music* 10/2 (1982), 183; and Lasocki, 'The French Hautboy', 339. See also Bruce Haynes, *The Eloquent Hautboy: A History of the Hautboy, 1640–1760* (2001), 145–52.

[149] Ashbee, *Records* ii, 35–6, 38–41; *The New Grove Dictionary of Music and Musicians* iii, ed. S. Sadie (1980), 263.

with a tablature of oboe fingerings and also, quite probably, the 'French hautbois' which Talbot measured; the oboe itself was by Bressan, as were other woodwind instruments Talbot inspected. At least 36 recorders and three flutes by this maker are known to survive, and a recent tentative suggestion that the 'Galpin' oboe (now in the Bate Collection, Oxford)[150] could be an early instrument of his[151] leads directly to discussion of a central issue in Purcellian performance practice: that of pitch.

PITCH STANDARDS

PRACTICALLY all Purcell's large-scale compositions from 1690 onward make use of the oboe. (The instrument was presumably still unavailable in Dublin where 'Great Parent, Hail!' was first performed in 1694; for the *Te Deum* and *Jubilate*, first heard at St Bride's in London's Fleet Street later the same year, it may have been ruled out by an incompatible organ pitch or by the players' Catholicism.) As there is no reason to believe that the oboe was treated as a transposing instrument, it follows that the pitch standard for these works would have been dictated by the new 'French' woodwind instruments. Whatever its precise origin, the 'Galpin' oboe seems to be a unique survival from the 17th century and is generally agreed to date from the 1680s or 1690s and to play at approximately $a' = 392$, a well-documented contemporary 'French' pitch.[152] It is certainly the longest instrument known, together with one of a similar date by Naust which plays at the same pitch (an equal tone beneath $a' = 440$). Furthermore, although Talbot's Bressan was shorter, the difference is mainly in the bell and the sounding length does not suggest that the pitch was different; in any event, 'it is likely that it played at something considerably lower than the usual 'Baroque' standard of the present'[153] ($a' = 415$).

Low pitches ($a' = 390-8$) were by no means exclusive to France and are found both where the influence of the new French woodwind instruments was felt (as in some German circles) and also quite independently, for example in Rome. Nor were they confined to the 17th century: Brook Taylor's calculations (1713) reliably show that his harpsichord sounded just above $a' = 390$ or even lower,[154] and later still Robert Smith (1749) reported that the 1708 organ of Trinity College, Cambridge (by Bernard Smith and

---

[150] See Anthony Baines, *The Bate Collection of Historical Musical Instruments: Catalogue of the Collection* (1976), 18 (no. 200).

[151] Bruce Haynes, 'Bressan, Talbot and the "Galpin" Oboe', *Galpin Society Journal* 43 (1990), 112.

[152] Players who have found this the instrument's most likely intended pitch include Paul Goodwin, Bruce Haynes, Michel Piguet and Anthony Robson. See also Bruce Haynes, *A History of Performing Pitch* (2002), 97, 115–7.

[153] Haynes, 'Bressan, Talbot', 117.

[154] Cary Karp, 'Pitch', in *Performance Practice: Music after 1600*, ed. H. M. Brown and S. Sadie, New Grove Handbooks (1989), 160.

Christopher Shrider), stood at approximately $a' = 393$, having at some stage been lowered (by a tone?) 'to the Roman pitch, as I judge by its agreement with that of the pitch-pipes made above 30 years ago'.[155] And at a time when pitches in the region of $a' = 420-426$ may have become reasonably standard, William Tansur (1746) observed that 'our new *Consort-Pitch* is more fitter for *Vocal Performance* than the *old Consort Pitch*, which is half a Tone lower'.[156] This 18th-century evidence points to an earlier 'consort pitch' below $a' = 400$. In practice, the low French-influenced standard seems to have risen slowly in the early years of the new century,[157] and a fascinating letter (dated January 1712) from a French oboist working in London reveals that a pitch almost a quarter of a tone higher than at the opera in Paris was by then in use: this suggests a level of $a' = 400-406$,[158] which matches several instruments both by Bressan and by Thomas Stanesby senior (c. 1668–1734). It must be emphasized, though, that the evidence for this slightly higher 'low' pitch seems to come entirely from after Purcell's death.[159] For a precise definition of orchestral pitch in the 1690s, then, there seems to be no more tangible evidence than that of the 'Galpin' oboe, corroborated by Talbot's measurements of a Bressan oboe. (And, as we shall see, written vocal ranges support the idea that the advent of such instruments caused a substantial shift in orchestral pitch.) For clues about church pitch(es), we must turn first to organs.

From extant pipework and recorded measurements of pipes it can be shown that (in terms of 'quire pitch') four important organs built in the 1660s, at Exeter, Gloucester, and Worcester Cathedrals and at New College, Oxford, played at levels from roughly $a' = 440$ to a semitone higher.[160] This 'high' pitch, most probably echoing a pre-Commonwealth standard, came to be regarded as too high for convenience, and both Smith and Harris are known to have lowered the pitch of older instruments: in the 1670s Smith was responsible 'for taking half a note lower the Organ in ye Chappell' at

---

[155] Cary Karp, 'Pitch', 160.

[156] William Tansur, *A New Musical Grammar* (London, 1746), 57.

[157] French pitch itself also rose in due course, according to Quantz (1752) and Agricola (1757); see Arthur Mendel, 'On the Pitches in Use in Bach's Time, Part II', *The Musical Quarterly* 41 (1955), 469–70.

[158] Tula Giannini, 'A Letter from Louis Rousselet, 18th-Century French Oboist at the Royal Opera in England', *Newsletter of the American Musical Instrument Society* 16/2 (June 1987), 10–11.

[159] A possible exception is the 15-stop, 2-manual house organ at Adlington Hall, Cheshire, believed to have been built around 1693, which now plays at about $a' = 407$; see John Mander, 'Some Notes on the Organ in Adlington Hall', *Journal of the British Institute of Organ Studies* 10 (1986), 68.

[160] Dominic Gwynn, 'Organ Pitch in 17th-Century England', *Journal of the British Institute of Organ Studies* 9 (1985), 65–78.

Whitehall,[161] and in 1684 he undertook 'to take down sink and Reduce the said halfe note throughout the whole Organ' at Canterbury too;[162] for his part, Harris agreed with Magdalen College, Oxford, in 1690 to 'alter the pitch of the said organs half a note lower than they now are', and again, significantly, with New College in 1713 'to make ye Organ one note lower'.[163] In general, Harris seems to have favoured a standard lower than Smith's, one which may, incidentally, be seen as an important antecedent of the more familiar mid-18th-century 'consort' pitch (see above). But the majority of Purcell's church music was tailor-made either for Whitehall Chapel or for Westminster Abbey, and he would almost certainly have regarded the pitch of Smith's organs as normal and appropriate. This has often been described as 'high',[164] yet in 1847 Sutton observed that 'Schmidts's Organs were generally below concert pitch, and great numbers have been altered by cutting the pipes'.[165] The better documented instruments by Smith suggest a norm of approximately $a' = 442$ (see Table 9.3).[166]

If organs and woodwind instruments can provide some firm evidence of pitch standards, it is clearly for vocal music that an understanding of pitch is most critical. And vocal ranges themselves can in turn add to

---

[161] Andrew Freeman, *Father Smith otherwise Bernard Schmidt, being an account of a Seventeenth Century Organ Maker* (London, 1926), 13.

[162] Sidney W. Harvey, 'Two Unpublished Records of Father Smith', *The Organ* 1 (1921), 98.

[163] Gwynn, 'Organ Pitch', 76 nn. 20 and 21.

[164] Edward J. Hopkins and Edward F. Rimbault, *The Organ: Its History and Construction* (London, 3/1877), 107.

[165] Sir John Sutton, *A Short Account of Organs built in England* (London, 1847), 37. Sutton's 'concert pitch' could have been anything from $a' = 433$ to $a' = 453$; see Alexander J. Ellis, 'The History of Musical Pitch', *Journal of the Society of Arts*, 5 March 1880, 305.

[166] Discrepancies of pitch between organs are undoubtedly the reason for similar discrepancies of notation among contemporary sources. Most anthems with organ accompaniment would have worked reasonably well at either Harris's or Smith's pitch, but a handful would not. In these instances, an organist playing on an instrument tuned in ¼-comma meantone, or in most other unequal temperaments, can almost never risk transposition by a semitone, whereas a shift of a tone is quite often practicable. Thus Jeremiah Clarke's 'He shall send down from on high', for example, was probably written originally in A minor (three sources) for Smith's (high) pitch but then put into B minor (five sources) for lower-pitched organs, the intermediate B♭ minor being both practically and notationally out of the question. Similarly, the Richard Ayleward Organ Book, associated with Norwich Cathedral (and therefore with Harris's 1689 instrument), includes upward transpositions as alternatives for five of its 19 anthems. Winchester, Chapter Library, MS A.3.10, an organ score, has Purcell's 'Blessed is the Man' ('Composed for the Charter House') in D minor, a tone higher than in 11 other sources, and 'Thy way, O God, is Holy' in C minor, a tone lower (surprisingly) than in seven other sources.

Table 9.3 Approximate pitches of organs by Bernard Smith and Renatus Harris

Maker	Date	Location	Pitch
Bernard Smith	1683–7	London, Temple Church	$a' = 442$
	1690	Hampton Court	$a' = 442$
	[1690	London, St Mary at Hill	'Common Church']
	1708	Cambridge, Trinity College	$a' = 442$
Renatus Harris	1670	Newcastle, St Nicholas	$a' = 429$
	(?)1689	Norwich Cathedral	$a' = 427$
	1696	London, St Andrew's, Undershaft	$a' = 428$

Source: This table is based primarily on the data given in Alexander J. Ellis, 'On the History of Musical Pitch', *Journal of the Society of Arts*, 5 March 1880, 293–336, but represents only the most reliable of the relevant measurements and calculations found there.

Note: Talbot's (slightly ambiguous) organ-pipe measurements, which come perhaps from the St Paul's Cathedral instrument by Smith (1694–9), may suggest a pitch of $a' = 428$–437, intermediate between the pitches of Smith's and Harris's instruments as tabulated here; see Peter Williams, 'The First English Organ Treatise', *The Organ* 44 (1964), 20–2, 27–9, 32.

Table 9.4 Vocal ranges of datable choral writing by Purcell

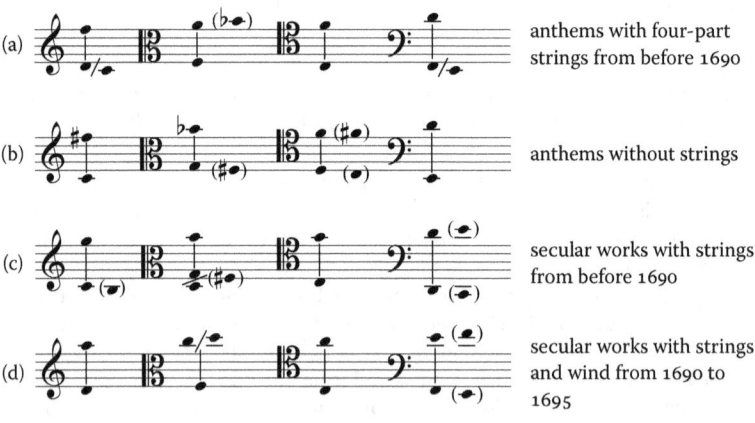

this understanding. Table 9.4 shows the choral ranges of datable works by Purcell. The similarity of (a) and (b) suggests that the string group at the Chapel Royal tuned to the organ. Though the wider ranges of the secular works make exact comparisons with the anthems difficult, (c), despite its low bass notes, seems overall to imply a very similar (or perhaps a slightly lower) pitch standard. The clearest point to emerge is that the presence of woodwind instruments from 1690 onwards must have required strings to play at a substantially lower pitch – in the region of a tone lower – than formerly. Confirmation of this shift of pitch standard is to be found in Purcell's writing for William Turner, practically the only solo singer named in works from both before and after the introduction of oboes; the later writing lies exactly a tone higher.[167] The shift also offers an explanation for Gostling's apparent loss of low notes around this time.[168]

In broad terms, we may be reasonably confident that there are at least two pitch standards implicit in Purcell's music: an organ pitch very close to modern pitch and, from 1690 onward, an orchestral pitch the best part of a tone beneath it. (The higher and lower organ pitches also in use may not have influenced his compositional practice.) Before 1690 orchestras may normally have played either at (Smith's) 'organ' pitch, as did the strings at the Chapel Royal, or possibly somewhat lower, perhaps at the pitch used by Harris.

VOICE-TYPES

WITH this framework in mind we are in a better position to understand the types of voice for which Purcell wrote. Solos for soprano rarely rise higher than their choral counterparts, and then only by a step, and never in a way that would be likely to jeopardize either tonal or verbal delivery. Bass solos, whether or not intended for 'That stupendious Base' John Gostling,[169] tend to have much wider ranges and often require an agility not always associated with basses (Ex. 9.7). Solo writing for tenor is comparatively rare, and it is the much-misunderstood Purcellian countertenor that merits most attention here.

The 1680s and 1690s seem to mark an historical mid-way point in the evolution of the countertenor, with the emergence of the later, and indeed current, falsettist countertenor overlapping with the glorious last years of an earlier tradition in which – contrary to popular belief – the voice was,

---

[167] Three works from the period 1685–7 have the range g–bb', and three from 1690–93 a–c''.

[168] See Bruce Wood, 'Purcell's Odes: A Reappraisal', in *The Purcell Companion*, ed. M. Burden (1995), 236.

[169] *Diary of John Evelyn* iv, 404 (28 January 1685). See also Westrup, *Purcell*, 5 (quoted in n. 218 below), and 196; and Hawkins, *A General History*, 693.

Ex. 9.7 (a) Henry Purcell, 'I will give Thanks unto Thee, O Lord' (z20/10), bars 244–6; (b) Henry Purcell, 'Hail! bright Cecilia!' (z328/2a), bars 1–6

in modern terms, essentially a (high) tenor.[170] In his solo writing Purcell appears to differentiate between the two types, while his choral parts tend to amalgamate them. The generally quite high tessitura of these choral lines often suggests falsetto singing, but the frequent low phrases within them surely demand some use of chest voice (Ex. 9.8).

While a choral texture helps to disguise any necessary mixing of techniques, a solo context is much less accommodating. Consequently most of Purcell's solo writing divides fairly clearly into high or low parts. Most are low and, after allowances for any differences of pitch standard, have every appearance of being suited to what we call (high) tenors – and of being implausibly low for even the most accomplished of today's (falsettist) countertenors. Ex. 9.9 gives just a few of the many conspicuously low-lying phrases.

By writing in a higher clef than usual (C2 rather than C3) and by using an exceptional designation ('High Contra tenor for Mr Howel'), Purcell himself seems to be differentiating the upper part of the duet 'Hark! hark! each Tree' (*Hail! bright Cecilia!*) from these normal 'low' countertenor solos (Ex. 9.10).[171] In the duet 'Sound the trumpet' ('Come Ye Sons of Art', 1694), where the text justifies both countertenors singing at the very tops of their voices, Purcell arguably parades the two types side by side: the written ranges lie a third apart ($c\#'$–e'' and a–b' plus a single brief $c\#''$). Evelyn apparently chose to describe the higher type not as a countertenor at all but as a 'treble':

[170] The first unequivocal reference to falsetto singing in England appears to be in Matthew Locke's comment that 'for above a Year after the Opening of His Majesties Chappel, the Orderers of the Musick there, were necessitated to supply the superiour Parts of their Musick with Cornets and Mens feigned Voices'; *Present Practice of Musick Vindicated* (London, 1673), 19.

[171] There are similar solos specifically for Howell in 'Love's Goddess' (1693) and 'A Song for the Duke of Gloucester's Birthday' (1695).

Ex. 9.8 (a) Henry Purcell, *Funeral Sentences*, second working (z17b), bars 49–51; (b) Henry Purcell, 'Bow Down Thine Ear, O Lord' (z11/6), bars 98–101; (c) Henry Purcell, *Dido and Aeneas* (z626/7b), bars 65–72; (d) Henry Purcell, *Dido and Aeneas* (z626/27), bars 11–12; (e) Henry Purcell, 'Hail! bright Cecilia!' (z328/5), bars 30–1

(a)

(b)
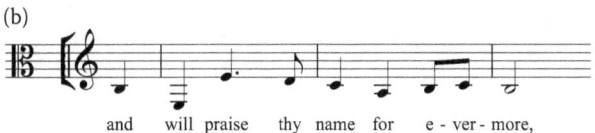

(c)
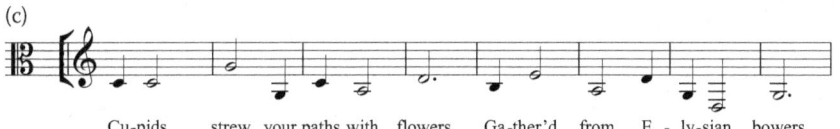

(d)

(e)
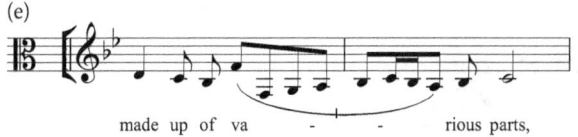

After supper, came in the famous Trebble *Mr. Abel* newly return'd from *Italy*, & indeede I never heard a more excellent voice, one would have sworne it had ben a Womans it was so high, & so well & skillfully manag'd ...[172]

(Purcell's writing in the 1687 welcome song for James II, 'Sound the Trumpet', takes Abell up to written b' and down only to a, while the song 'Aloud proclaim', 'set and sung by Mr. Abell' himself and published in 1702, rises to a d'', a sounding difference of perhaps only a semitone.)

But are there reasons of a less subjective nature for viewing so much of Purcell's countertenor writing as not having been intended for falsettists? (This of course invites the question of exactly what reasons there may be, apart from the word's subsequent connotations, for taking the still conventional opposite view.) Although Burney's later testimony may not

---

[172] *Diary of John Evelyn* iv, 270 (27 January 1682).

276   *Composers' Intentions?*

Ex. 9.9 (a) Henry Purcell, 'O Lord', first working of the second verse (z13a), bars 13–17; (b) Henry Purcell, *King Arthur* (z628/30bc), bars 60–9; (c) Henry Purcell, 'Hail! bright Cecilia!' (z328/4), bars 27–9; (d) Henry Purcell, 'Who Can from Joy Refrain?' A Birthday Song for the Duke of Gloucester (z342/7), bars 9–13

Ex. 9.10 Henry Purcell, 'Hail! bright Cecilia!' (z328/3b), bars 136–43

be wholly reliable, he felt confident to write that William Turner 'was sworn in gentleman of the Royal Chapel 1669, as a countertenor singer, his voice settling to that pitch; a circumstance which so seldom happens, naturally, that if it be cultivated the possessor is sure of employment';[173] from a later 18th-century perspective a non-falsettist countertenor was indeed a rarity. Certainly the oft-repeated notion that Purcell himself was a (falsettist) countertenor who also sang bass does not stand up to scrutiny. According to an account in *The Gentleman's Journal*, the second stanza of *Hail! bright Cecilia!* ("Tis Nature's voice') 'was sung with incredible Graces by Mr. *Purcell* himself';[174] did he actually sing, or merely compose, the ornamentation? Despite the presence of Mr Pate's name against the line in the autograph score,[175] Purcell probably really did sing this exceptionally florid (low) countertenor solo at its first performance (to his own accompaniment?) in 1692.[176] But his place among the basses in the 1685 coronation procession was surely a matter of pure convenience, 'simply to make up a complete file';[177] indeed, the last file of 'basses' consisted of four senior musicians, Blagrave, Staggins, Blow and Child.[178] On the other hand, the case of Mr Pordage, whom Evelyn recorded as singing 'with an excellent voice both Treble and Base' in 1685,[179] may well be an exception – that is, unless Evelyn simply meant that Pordage had an unusually wide vocal range. Interestingly, it is not the term 'countertenor' but 'treble' that is again being used to describe what may have been falsetto singing, and indeed Locke had earlier associated the use of 'Mens feigned Voices' with

---

[173] Charles Burney, *A General History of Music* [London, 1776–89] ii, ed. F. Mercer (London, 1935), 36.

[174] *The Gentleman's Journal*, November 1692, 19.

[175] Oxford, Bodleian Library, MS Mus. c. 26; this was probably used for at least one repeat performance.

[176] Two early printed sources (London, c. 1693) present Purcell's song as 'sung by himself at St. Cecilia's Feast'.

[177] Jeremy Noble, 'Purcell and the Chapel Royal', in *Henry Purcell, 1659–1695: Essays on his Music*, ed. Imogen Holst (1959), 62.

[178] Sandford, 'Coronation', 71.

[179] *Diary of John Evelyn* iv, 403 (27 January 1685).

'superiour Parts' ordinarily sung by boys.[180] In either case, the notion of countertenor/bass interchangeability being a common occurrence cannot be sustained.

If the (low) 'countertenor' corresponded to today's (high) tenor, what was the nature of the 'tenor' voice? The modest upper limits of Purcell's tenor parts, and perhaps also the relative scarcity of solo writing for that voice, imply in turn that it was thought of as a more baritonal 'second' tenor rather than as an equivalent of the modern tenor. But although Pietro Reggio had 'a perfect good tenor & base &c',[181] and John Bowman, Purcell's favourite high bass, may have also sung a tenor part in *King Arthur*,[182] tenor and countertenor voices, interestingly enough, seem generally to have enjoyed a much closer relationship than bass and tenor.[183] In an affidavit of 1664 Thomas Richardson refers to 'the next place of a lay tenor or counter tenor that shall be voyd', and the following year Andrew Carter was sworn in as a Gentleman of the Chapel Royal 'to come into pay w*h*en the next tenor or counter tenor's place shalbe voyde'.[184] These may have been purely administrative manœuvres, but they are wholly exceptional in mentioning two voice-types. (In practice, both Carter and Richardson, who is elsewhere listed as a countertenor, evidently succeeded countertenors.)[185] Thomas Heywood, who had entered the Chapel Royal in 1678, 'in place of Cha: Husbands', a countertenor,[186] was listed among the countertenors in the 1685 coronation procession,[187] although at the same time he held a place as tenor in the Private Musick (alongside Abell, Turner, Gostling and Bowman).[188]

The case for believing countertenor and tenor voices to have been almost indistinguishable on occasion is further strengthened by the evidence of several musical sources. In an early manuscript source of Purcell's 1687 welcome song for King James the name [Anthony] Robert appears against a tenor solo,[189] while in three other works from the 1690s the same singer is allocated (low) countertenor parts. (Ironically, the tenor solo may well in practice have been the highest of these parts.) The

---

[180] Locke, *Present Practice*, 19.
[181] *Diary of John Evelyn* iv, 220 (23 September 1680).
[182] Price, *Henry Purcell*, 299.
[183] See Noble, 'Chapel Royal', 62–4. Also, the *tenor cantoris* I of 'Blow up the Trumpet in Sion' is notated in the C3 clef with the instruction, 'The contratenor & tenor for this anthem are here to sing together' (*Works I* xxviii (1959), 193).
[184] Edward F. Rimbault, *The Old Cheque-Book, or Book of Remembrance of the Chapel Royal from 1561 to 1744* (London, 1872), 14, 112.
[185] Ashbee, *Records* i, 136.
[186] Ashbee, *Records* v, 73; and Rimbault, *Old Cheque-Book*, 13, 16, 112.
[187] Sandford, 'Coronation', 70.
[188] Ashbee, *Records* ii, 3, 122.
[189] *Works II* xviii (2004), 153, 219.

actor-singer John Pate is known to have sung both a tenor role (Kalib) in *The Indian Emperor* in 1692 and two countertenor roles (Mopsa and Summer) in the 1693 revival of *The Fairy Queen*. Furthermore, in Purcell's autograph score of *Hail! bright Cecilia!* Pate's name is found against not only "Tis Nature's voice' (a countertenor solo) but also the tenor part of a brief duet within the opening chorus.[190] (It may be worth pointing out that Pate's singing of the roles of Kalib 'in the shape of a Woman' and of the rustic Mopsa 'in Woman's habit' – and subsequently of 'a Lusty Strapping Middle ag'd Widdow all in Mourning' – no more demands the use of falsetto than does the role of the Sorceress in *Dido and Aeneas* when taken by a man.)[191] 'Celebrate this Festival' (1693) similarly contains both a countertenor and a tenor solo evidently sung by the French-born Alexander Damascene; in four other works by Purcell Damascene sang countertenor solos. Of all Purcell's countertenor soloists the most frequently named is John Freeman; an isolated tenor part sung by him in 1694 (as St George) in the duet 'Genius of England' from *Don Quixote* part II lies no lower than many of his other solos and is identical in range with three sung by him the following year in *The Indian Queen*.[192] (He was also named as a tenor in Draghi's 1687 St Cecilia's Day Ode.) This tenor/countertenor connection continued throughout Purcell's lifetime: John Church, who as a 19- or 20-year-old took a tenor role (Second Aerial Spirit) in *The Indian Queen* (1695), sang as a countertenor later the same year in a *Te Deum* by Blow, and again in Clarke's 'A Song on New Year's Day 1706'.[193]

VOCAL PRACTICES

IN at least one respect the comparison of the (low) countertenor with today's tenor is perhaps misleading: the physical stamina and sheer power that enable some of today's singers to project successfully over a symphony orchestra and to fill large opera houses are never demanded by Purcell's music. Indeed, a big voice was sometimes considered a liability: after listening to a French boy with 'a delicate voice', Evelyn

> also heard Mrs Packer (daughter to my old friend) sing before his Majestie & the Duke privately, That stupendious Base Gosling, accompanying her, but hers was so lowd, as tooke away much of the sweetnesse; certainly never woman had a stronger, or better [voice]

---

[190] *Works II* viii (1978), 17 bars 43–7.
[191] Olive Baldwin and Thelma Wilson, 'Alfred Deller, John Freeman and Mr. Pate', *Music & Letters* 50 (1969), 107; Curtis A. Price and Irena Cholij, 'Dido's Bass Sorceress', *The Musical Times* 127 (1986), 615–18.
[192] *Works II* xvi (2007), 178; and *Works II* xix (1994), 12, 34, 67.
[193] London, British Library, Add. MSS 31457 and 31813.

could she possibly have govern'd it: She would do rarely in a large Church among the Nunns.[194]

Many singers specialized in this 'private' singing:[195] Arabella Hunt, who possessed a voice 'like the pipe of a bullfinch',[196] moved exclusively in court circles and among her wealthy friends, never appearing on the public stage.[197] For women, this was largely a matter of social decorum, but even in private there were strict codes of behaviour that affected performance. Evelyn admired his daughter Mary's poise:

> the sweetnesse of her voice, and manegement of it, adding such an agreablenesse to her Countenance, without any constraint and concerne, that when she sung, it was as charming to the Eye, as to the Eare ...[198]

In the louder singing that theatres required, such facial control was more difficult to maintain, and when in *King Arthur* that 'capital, and admired Performer' Mrs Butler 'in the person of Cupid' chose to ignore stage convention and 'turne her face to the scean, and her back to the theater', North ascribed the admirable results ('even beyond any thing I ever heard upon the English stage') 'to nothing so much as the liberty she had of concealing her face, which she could not endure should be so contorted as is necessary to sound well, before her gallants, or at least her envious sex'.[199]

An inhibited delivery may well have been a common failing among female singers; in North's view 'The English have generally voices good enough, tho' not up to the pitch of warmer countreys', 'But come into the theater or musick-meeting, and you shall have a woman sing like a mouse in a cheese, scarce to be heard, and for the most part her teeth shutt.'[200] He was also critical of singing masters who 'begin to teach with tunes, whereas they should begin with pronunciation'.[201]

In the theatres, actor-singers performed alongside more specialist singers. The leading actress of her day, also admired for her singing, was Mrs Bracegirdle, and it was a mad-song by Eccles 'so incomparably well sung, and acted' by her that was the inspiration for Purcell's song upon

---

[194] *Diary of John Evelyn* iv, 404 (28 January 1685).

[195] *The London Gazette* for 11 June 1694 announced a 'consort' in which 'a Gentlewoman Sings that hath one of the best Voices in England, not before heard in publick'; Tilmouth, 'A Calendar', 15.

[196] Hawkins, *A General History*, 761.

[197] Olive Baldwin and Thelma Wilson, 'Purcell's Sopranos', *The Musical Times*, 123 (1982), 602.

[198] *Diary of John Evelyn* iv, 421–2 (14 March 1685).

[199] *North I*, 217–18.

[200] *North I*, 215; see also 216; and Playford, *An Introduction*, 20.

[201] *North I*, 216.

'Mrs Bracegirdle Singing (I burn &c) in ye play of Don Quixote'.²⁰² Indeed, Dryden's verdict on the music in *The Richmond Heiress* (1693) was that Mrs Bracegirdle and Thomas Doggett 'sung better than Redding and Mrs Ayloff, whose trade it was'.²⁰³ Mrs Butler, Purcell's leading soprano for three years from 1689, similarly 'prov'd not only a good Actress, but was allow'd, in those Days, to sing and dance to great Perfection'.²⁰⁴ More remarkable still was the actress-singer for whom Purcell wrote so many fine soprano songs during the last eight months of his life: Miss Cross claimed to be only 12 years old in 1695 and was in any case no more than 14.²⁰⁵ (The other singers in the company were the countertenor Freeman and the bass Leveridge, both in their 20s, and the boy Jemmy Bowen.)

In contrast to Bracegirdle, Butler and Cross, Mrs Ayliff was primarily a singer, though she did occasionally take acting roles.²⁰⁶ Possibly the finest of Purcell's sopranos (*pace* Dryden), she is also the only female singer named in the odes: she sang 'Thou tun'st this world' in *Hail! bright Cecilia!* and both a solo and a duet (with 'the Boy') in 'Celebrate this Festival'. Of the song 'Ah me! to many deaths decreed', 'set by *Mr. Purcell* the *Italian* way' in Crowne's *Regulus* (1692), *The Gentleman's Journal* wrote: 'had you heard it sung by Mrs *Ayliff* you would have own'd that there is no pleasure like that which good Notes, when so divinely sung, can create.'²⁰⁷

While there have always been those who 'despair of ever having as good Voices among us, as they have in *Italy*',²⁰⁸ 'the *Italian* way' of singing was certainly cultivated by many. Reggio, who settled in London in 1664, taught singing there for over 20 years (young Mary Evelyn was one of his pupils), and published a treatise on *The Art of Singing* (Oxford, 1677).²⁰⁹ The castrato Siface (Giovanni Francesco Grossi), who 'came over from Rome, esteemed one of the best voices in *Italy*',²¹⁰ made quite an impression on London society, although he seems to have spent just five months in England (in 1687). His 'holding out & delicatenesse in extending & loosing a note with that incomparable softnesse, & sweetenesse' Evelyn

---

²⁰² Price, *Henry Purcell*, 215.

²⁰³ Letter to William Walsh (9 May 1693), in *The Letters of John Dryden*, ed. C. E. Ward (1942), 52–3.

²⁰⁴ Colley Cibber, *An Apology for the Life of Mr. Colley Cibber* (London, 1740), 97.

²⁰⁵ Baldwin and Wilson, 'Purcell's Sopranos', 607. *The London Gazette*, 26 November 1694, announced 'the Addition of two new Voices' to the Charles Street consort, 'one a young Gentlewomans of 12 years of Age'; Tilmouth, 'A Calendar', 15.

²⁰⁶ Baldwin and Wilson, 'Purcell's Sopranos', 603.

²⁰⁷ *The Gentleman's Journal*, August 1692

²⁰⁸ Preface to *The Fairy Queen*.

²⁰⁹ *Diary of John Evelyn* iv, 421, 427–8 (14 March 1685). There were believed to be no extant copies of Reggio's *The Art of Singing* until one was put up for auction at Sotheby's in 1997.

²¹⁰ *Diary of John Evelyn* iv, 537 (30 January 1687).

found admirable,[211] while Tosi commented that, although he had 'the most singular Beauty' of voice, his 'Manner of Singing was remarkably plain [i.e. unembellished], consisting particularly in the *Messa di Voce*, the putting forth his Voice, and the Expression'.[212] Tosi was himself a castrato, who arrived in London in 1692 and soon began giving weekly concerts and teaching singing;[213] his use of *rubato* ('The Breaking and yet Keeping Time') particularly impressed North,[214] and his 'Observations on the Florid Song', dedicated to the Earl of Peterborough, is perhaps the single most valuable treatise on mid-Baroque Italian vocal style. But then, as now, the best way of assimilating an Italian style of singing was to visit Italy. John Abell was 'newly return'd from Italy' when Evelyn heard him in 1682[215] (and after the revolution he spent more than a decade abroad). Three years later Evelyn was 'invited to heare that celebrated voice of Mr. *Pordage*, newly come from *Rome*',[216] and later still, in 1698, he

> dined at Mr Pepyss, where I heard that rare Voice of Mr. *Pate*, who was lately come from *Italy*, reputed the most excellent singer, ever England had: he sang severall compositions of the last Mr. Pursal, esteemed the best composer of any Englishman hitherto.[217]

Where modern practice for large-scale vocal works is to use the minimum practicable number of soloists, Purcell clearly revelled in opportunities to display as many different voices as possible – in *Hail! bright Cecilia!* at least a dozen, half of them countertenors, and in 'Celebrate this Festival' a similar number. (Most, if not all, probably sang in the choruses, too.) Almost invariably, these will have been close colleagues whose voices he knew intimately.[218] Certainly Purcell understood better than anyone that 'the compass of a good tone, and extent in the scale, are very different',[219] and the two versions of 'You twice ten hundred deities' (*The Indian Queen*) show the lengths to which he could go to accommodate different singers.[220] It is hardly surprising therefore that, apart from an occasional 'loud' or 'soft', the vocal music

---

[211] *Diary of John Evelyn* iv, 547 (19 April 1687).
[212] Tosi, *Observations*, 102.
[213] Tilmouth, 'A Calendar', 13.
[214] *North I*, 151.
[215] *Diary of John Evelyn* iv, 270 (27 January 1682).
[216] *Diary of John Evelyn* iv, 403 (27 January 1685).
[217] *Diary of John Evelyn* v (1959), 289 (30 May 1698).
[218] A letter from Thomas Purcell to Gostling in 1679 reports that 'my sonne is composing wherein you will be chiefly concern'd'; Westrup, *Purcell*, 5.
[219] *North I*, 262.
[220] Price, *Henry Purcell*, 130.

Ex. 9.11 Henry Purcell, 'If music be the food of love' (z379c), bars 14–18

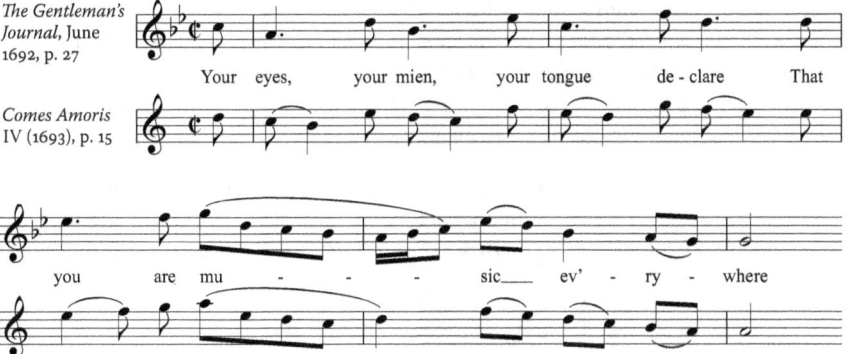

generally lacks expressive directions.²²¹ Several ornaments familiar from keyboard practice – the shake (⁄⁄), beat (∼), forefall (⁄) and backfall (⁄) – were part of a singer's vocabulary too, and their signs appear from time to time in the sources, but, although Purcell's vocal lines incorporate much ornamentation, further embellishment would often have been added as a matter of course. (The composer's own G minor version of 'If music be the food of love' (setting I) reveals a particular fondness for backfalls, but interestingly this may predate the plainer, A minor, version; see Ex. 9.11.)²²² It is difficult to gauge the exact relevance to Purcell's music of Caccini's instructions given in translation in all editions of Playford's *Brief Introduction to the Skill of Musick* from 1664 to 1694 and summarized in the *Synopsis of Vocal Musick* (1680):

> An Exclamation is a slacking of the voice to reinforce it afterwards ... A Trillo is a shaking of the Uvula on the Throat in one Sound or Note, as the Gruppo is in two Sounds or Notes, the one being by one degree higher than the other, and are commonly used in cadences and closes. These Ornaments are not to be used in Airy Songs ... but in Passionate Musick, wherein ... the ordinary measure of Time is here less regarded, for many times is the value of the Notes made less by half, and sometimes more, according to the conceit of the words, with a graceful neglect.²²³

(Caccini's *trillo* was eventually replaced in Playford's 1697 edition: 'Of the TRILL or SHAKE, Directions for learning it is only this, To move your

---

[221] Exceptions include 'sighing and languishing by degrees' in ''Tis Nature's voice' from 'Hail! bright Cecilia!'.
[222] *Works II* xxv (1985), 157–61, 300.
[223] *Synopsis of Vocal Musick ... By A. B. Philo-Mus* (London, 1680), 44.

Voice easily upon one Syllable the distance of a Note ... *slow*, then *faster* by degrees.')²²⁴

A common failing among those 'who court a voice' was that 'in learning they have cheif regard to ornaments, such as are called graces, and pretty devisions, which makes them neglect the art of sounding full and true, and that onely renders a voice musicall'.²²⁵ The young Jemmy Bowen was presumably well past this stage when he sang as a boy for Purcell:

> He, when practising a Song set by Mr. *Purcell*, some of the Music told him to grace and run a Division in such a Place. *O let him alone*, said Mr. *Purcell; he will grace it more naturally than you, or I, can teach him.*²²⁶

(By 1698 Bowen was singing as a countertenor and one can only guess at his age. Purcell's own voice seems to have broken relatively early, when he was just 14; Blow was evidently 15 and Humfrey 17, while in France around the same time Bacilly observed that the change 'usually comes about between the ages of 15 and 20 in males'.)²²⁷

Most of Purcell's male soloists also sang as members of the Chapel Royal. At full strength this choir, which sang not only for services but in the various court odes, consisted of 10 or 12 boys and between 20 and 30 men.²²⁸ But these numbers are perhaps deceptive and ignore in particular a rota system for the Gentlemen in operation on 'working days'.²²⁹ A more typical strength for a Sunday or major feast day would perhaps have been 8 or 10 boys and 15 to 20 men, facing each other in Decani and

---

²²⁴ John (and Henry) Playford, *A Brief Introduction to the Skill of Musick* (London, 13/1697), 31.

²²⁵ *North III*, 99.

²²⁶ Anthony Aston, quoted in *A Brief Supplement to Colley Cibber, An Apology*, ed. R. W. Lowe (London, 1889; 2/1966), 312.

²²⁷ Bénigne de Bacilly, *Remarques curieuses sur l'art de bien chanter* (Paris, 1668), 36.

²²⁸ The full group of 32 Gentlemen of the Chapel Royal listed by Francis Sandford (*Coronation*, 70–1) includes five who in 1685 were almost certainly non-singing members: Blagrave, Staggins, Blow, Child and Purcell himself ('Organist of Westminster').

²²⁹ Christopher Dearnley, *English Church Music, 1650–1750* (1970), 32. A Memorandum of April 1693 established a system of fines for 'whatever Gentleman of the Chappell in waiting should absent himself from the practice of the Anthem on Saturdays or other holiday eves, when the King or Queen were to bee present on the morrow, or upon any other occasions before the Wednesdays and Fridays in Lent, being thereto ordered by the Subdean to appear'; Rimbault, *Old Cheque Book*, 86. Court odes, incidentally, appear to have had three 'practices' prior to performance; see Westrup, *Purcell*, 57.

Cantoris stalls.[230] Westminster Abbey supported 8 'Quiristers' and 12 or 16 'Quiremen',[231] and a reduced section in the opening chorus of *Hail! bright Cecilia!* for 'trebles' and two of each other part may imply a similar body of 20 or more singers. But undoubtedly in humbler institutions and on lesser occasions choirs would often have been smaller still: in the early 1670s Mace was lamenting the fact that 'in most [*Cathedral*] *Quires* there is but allotted *One Man to a Part*'.[232] Furthermore, some works often assumed to be choral – notably Purcell's two Latin psalm settings, *Beati omnes* and *Jehovah, quam multi sunt hostes mei* – were surely intended as vocal chamber music, for private or devotional rather than church performance, and thus to have had just one voice to a part.[233]

THOUGH I have chosen to end this survey of issues of Purcellian performance practice with a discussion of vocal matters, it is with these that most performers of Purcell's music must normally start. Yet for the most part scholars and performers have scarcely begun to address the subject, partly perhaps because of a natural scepticism that anything of substance awaits discovery. Of course, none of the practical issues touched on in this chapter will on its own lead us to the heart of Purcell's music, but cumulatively the fragments of information that have come down to us can enable performances to develop from a starting-point nearer to that of the close circle of professional musicians for whom Purcell wrote. And – at least in my own view – a deeper understanding of the supreme craftsmanship which informs his work will almost inevitably assist today's performers in releasing the essence of Purcell's glorious music to the full.

---

[230] Ashbee, *Records* i, 136 and *passim*. The fifth edition of Edward Phillips's *The New World of Words* (London, 1696), to which Purcell contributed, defines an anthem as 'a divine Song consisting of Verses sung alternatively by the two opposite Quires, and Chorus's'.

[231] Sandford (*Coronation*, 70) lists 16 men for James II's coronation (1685), but there were 12 for that of William and Mary (1689); see Franklin B. Zimmerman, 'Purcell and the Dean of Westminster – Some New Evidence', *Music & Letters* 43 (1962), 13.

[232] Mace, *Musick's Monument*, 23.

[233] The autograph manuscript of these two works (London, British Library, Add. MS 30930) contains no verse/chorus indications.

SUBSEQUENT RELATED LITERATURE

A. Margaret Laurie, 'Continuity and Tempo in Purcell's Vocal Music', in *Purcell Studies*, ed. C. A. Price (1995), 192–206.

Dominic Gwynn, 'Purcell's Organ at Westminster Abbey', *Early Music* 23/4 (1995), 550.

Lynda Sayce, 'Continuo Lutes in 17th- and 18th-Century England', *Early Music* 23/4 (1995), 666–84.

Performing the Music of Henry Purcell, ed. M. Burden (1996), comprising P. Holman, 'Original Sets of Parts for Restoration Concerted Music at Oxford' • D. Gwynn, 'The English Organ in Purcell's Lifetime' • J. Dilworth, 'Violin Making in England in the Age of Purcell' • P. Downey, 'Performing Mr Purcell's "Exotick" Trumpet Notes' • B. Wood, 'The First Performance of Purcell's Funeral Music for Queen Mary' • H. Diack Johnstone, 'Ornamentation in the Keyboard Music of Henry Purcell and his Contemporaries' • O. Baldwin and T. Wilson, 'Purcell's Stage Singers' • T. Morris, 'Voice Ranges, Voice Types and Pitch in Purcell's Concerted Works' • M. Burden, 'Purcell Debauch'd; The Dramatick Operas in Performance' • A. Walking, 'Performance and Political Allegory: What to Interpret and When on the Restoration Stage' • R. Semmens, 'Dancing and Dance Music in Purcell's Operas' • R. E. Ronen, 'Of Costume and Etiquette: Staging in the Time of Purcell' • R. Savage, 'Calling up Genius: Purcell, Roger North and Charlotte Butler' • J. and F. Muller, 'Purcell's Dioclesian on the Dorset Garden Stage' • L. Sawkins, 'Trembleurs and Cold People: How Should they Shiver?'

Peter Trevelyan, 'How Did 17th-Century English Violins Really Sound?', in *From Renaissance to Baroque: Change in Instruments and Instrumental Music in the 17th Century*, ed. J. Wainwright and P. Holman (2005), 167–72.

Dominic Gwynn, 'From Stops Organical to Stops of Variety: The English Organ from 1630 to 1730', in *From Renaissance to Baroque*, 211–25.

Rebecca Herissone, 'Robert Pindar, Thomas Busby, and the Mysterious Scoring of Henry Purcell's "Come ye sons of art"', *Music & Letters* 88/1 (2007), 1–48.

Peter Holman, 'The Sale Catalogue of Gottfried Finger's Music Library: New Light on London Concert Life in the 1690s', *Royal Musical Association Research Chronicle* 43 (2010), 23–38.

Olive Baldwin and Thelma Wilson, 'Henry Purcell's Countertenors and Tenors', in *Der Countertenor: Die männliche Falsettstimme vom Mittelalter zur Gegenwart*, ed. C. Herr, A. Jacobshagen and K. Wessel (2012), 79–98

Stephen Rose, 'Performance Practices', in *The Ashgate Research Companion to Henry Purcell*, ed. R. Herissone (2012), 115–64.

10

How Many Singers?

MASSED voices will always be a potent musical medium. But performances [of J. S. Bach's 'choral' works] by 16 or so singers have now become commonplace (and some of us use fewer), reminding us that Bach's music can speak equally powerfully in many ways. So, with choir size, is personal taste all there is to it?

At the heart of Bach's incomparable output of church music stands the choir. And, just as we rightly expect Abbado, Rattle *et al.* to know a thing or two about Mahler's orchestra, so ought we to be able to assume that our Bach experts know their Bach choir. Yet, for all the recent advances in Baroque instrumental practice, this central vocal medium has rarely received serious attention. Conventional thinking rests content with the idea that a small choir of 12 or 16 fits the historical facts adequately. Unfortunately, it doesn't.

A century before Bach, composers such as Praetorius and Schütz knew two quite distinct types of vocal choir. The *capella* sang mostly chorales and straightforward types of motet and, like our 'chamber' choirs, might vary in size but would generally have several voices per part. The other type might not look like a choir at all to us, yet this *Favoritchor* – a select group of solo voices – was the 'favoured' medium of the new Italianate concerted music, and the music it sang was technically much more demanding. When in large-scale concerted works these two types of choir appeared side by side, it was always the 'solo' choir (a one-to-a-part 'consort', as we might call it) that was the main protagonist; the larger choir generally functioned as a wholly subsidiary *ripieno* group, 'filling out' the texture from time to time.

Bach, together with most of his contemporaries, was a direct heir to these 17th-century traditions. Of course much had changed, but the underlying principles remained constant; elaborate concerted music was essentially for soloists, simpler and more conservative idioms were choral (in the modern sense). At Leipzig, where Bach spent the last 27 years of his life, the larger groups sang the old motets on an almost daily basis but played little or no part in concerted music-making. (Clearly, by Mendelssohn's day, another 100 years on, things had changed substantially.)

Indeed, the very complexity of Bach's choral writing argues that it remained the province of the select few; after all, the choruses are often just as difficult to sing as the arias. This group of 'concertists' – perhaps typically three of the best from amongst the Thomasschule's 55 or so pupils

First appeared in *BBC Music Magazine* 9/1 (2000), 38–9.

(aged approximately 13 to 21) plus a bass from the university – stood at the front of the ensemble and sang choruses and solo movements alike (as their surviving copies show). Occasionally a second vocal quartet, standing elsewhere and singing from a separate set of copies, might be added as a ripieno group in some (though rarely all) of the choral writing. Other pupils, as Bach himself clearly tells us, took no part in this repertoire *as singers* but were deployed instead as instrumentalists alongside the municipal musicians.

Thus, the medium Bach habitually worked with at Leipzig comprised four select singers (concertists), sometimes joined by another four (as ripienists), and 20 or more instrumentalists. An ensemble of this sort, as abundant documentary sources and pictures show, was wholly typical of its time. To think of this vocal quartet as a 'minimal' – let alone 'minimalist' – choir, pared down for economy, misses the point completely. A string quartet is not a minimal string orchestra but a different medium altogether. A group of concertists was simply the natural and expected vehicle of 18th-century Lutheran concerted music. 'Current orthodoxy', by contrast, promotes something of a hybrid: a quite plausibly Bachian orchestra grafted on to an unmistakably Handelian oratorio choir that has more to do with Anglican than with Lutheran practice.

How did things get so muddled? First, we have all been mesmerized by the idea that a choir must by definition consist of more than one singer per part, and that difficult vocal writing demands the mutual support of many, rather than the expertise of one. (The Mendelssohnian Bach revival casts a long shadow.) Second, in our natural preoccupation with Bach's own music, we have interpreted his demand for choirs of 12 or 16 singers (three of each voice-type) as a simple prescription for the performance of his own music, rather than as an attempt to secure larger 'pools' of pupils and thereby to ease the year-round problems of illness and absences and to ensure the regular singing of eight-part motets. (The more players Manchester United has on its books, the easier it is for the club to field a strong team throughout the season.)

But does this really work in practice? In over-resonant acoustics Bach's music is never heard to advantage, whatever the forces; it is simply too 'intricate' (Bach's own word). But in suitable buildings, with good singers, refined trumpet-playing and sensitive placement of performers, there are handsome dividends: Bach's glorious music acquires an ever-sharper focus. Fullness of sound is still there when needed, achieved not by multiple voices but by Bach's skilful scoring. (In any case, three voices on a part turn out – surprisingly perhaps – to be scarcely any louder than one; their main effect is a change of colour.)

More important still is a dimension we otherwise lose completely, of interplay between solo voices and full ensemble. A fugue, for example, will start with concertists alone (plus continuo) and then slowly and magnificently expand to involve everyone. The result is greater clarity, not only of sound (and text) but also of structure.

Does all this sound familiar? As long ago as 1981 Joshua Rifkin put these ideas forward to his uncomprehending musicological colleagues – and was duly pilloried for his heretical 'hypothesis'. One contemporary of Darwin's reacted to his theory of evolution by saying: 'Let us hope it is not true, but if it is, let us hope it will not be generally known.' Whether or not future generations find today's vehement resistance to the choir-as-consort idea amusing or puzzling, it is high time to explore the rich possibilities inherent in a more sophisticated understanding of Bach's chosen medium. Bach is still performed on the modern piano – and why not? – but no one pretends that he wrote for it. Our best musical offering to Bach (250 years after his death) might be to explore his music without its usual Handelian overlay. *Vive la différence.*

11

Vocal Ripienists and
J. S. Bach's Mass in B minor

> ... it is the present aim once again to demonstrate emphatically that today's universal custom of performing Bach's cantata choruses with choral scoring throughout ... sacrifices a multitude of fine and considered details to a craving for monumentality at any price.

NOT my words but those of the eminent Bach scholar Arnold Schering, written some 90 years ago.[1] While 'monumentality' may be less prevalent today, the 'continuously choral scoring' to which Schering objected is still routinely promoted as Bach's own preferred practice. In this, the Mass in B minor differs not at all from the composer's other church works. Yet, in common with an overwhelming majority of those works, early sources for the Mass contain no suggestion whatsoever of any requirement for ripieno singers. (A brief reminder: the ripienist's role was to *reinforce* – not to *replace* – the concertist in choral movements.) Both in the composer's autograph score of the complete Mass and in the set of parts of the *Missa* prepared for Dresden, vocal tutti indications are entirely absent; moreover, neither this set nor that associated with C. P. E. Bach's 1786 Hamburg performance of the *Credo* – both apparently complete (with 21 and 20 parts respectively) – includes any copies for ripienists.[2] This conspicuous absence of direct evidence for vocal ripienists necessarily forms the starting-point for the present investigation.

DESPITE its unique (if problematic) status within Bach's output, the Mass in B minor has proved fertile ground for previous exploration of the composer's choral writing and its implied mode(s) of performance. Indeed, Joshua Rifkin's searching reassessment of the nature of Bach's choir was for some time widely perceived to relate almost exclusively to

---

First appeared in *Eighteenth-Century Music* 7/1 (2010), 9–34.

---

[1] '... es ist Zweck dieser Zeilen, mit Nachdruck einmal wieder darauf hinzuweisen, daß die heute allgemein übliche Art, Bachs Kantatenchöre durchweg in chorischer ... Besetzung aufzuführen, dem Stile der Zeit nicht immer entspricht und der Sucht, um jeden Preis Monumentalität herauszuschlagen, eine Menge feiner und wohlbedachter Einzelzüge opfert'; Arnold Schering, 'Die Besetzung Bachscher Chöre', *Bach-Jahrbuch* 17 (1920), 77–8.

[2] Berlin, Staatsbibliothek, Mus. MS Bach P 180; Sächsische Landesbibliothek – Staats- und Universitätsbibliothek, Mus. 2405–D–21; Berlin, Staatsbibliothek, Mus. MS Bach St 118.

the Mass through his recording of the work, even though his original 1981 paper had barely made any mention of it.³ In the same year, however, the Austrian-born American conductor Erich Leinsdorf specifically challenged (albeit in a much broader context) 'the customary division of Bach's B minor Mass into sections for full chorus and for soloists':

> For well over 200 years it has been taken for granted that the solo voices sing only the arias and duets. Yet there is no indication whatever in the original score to justify the arbitrary divisions that have become almost universally accepted. ... To anyone reading the score without preconceptions it appears quite clear that Bach assigned a considerably larger portion of the Mass to soloists.⁴

(Leinsdorf proceeds to identify various 'solo' passages in *Kyrie* I, *Et in terra pax*, *Cum sancto spiritu* and *Et resurrexit*.) Behind Leinsdorf's thinking undoubtedly lies that of others, perhaps Wilhelm Ehmann's in particular, whose extensive work on the distribution of concertists and ripienists in the Mass first aroused my own curiosity in the matter.⁵ Although Ehmann's contribution starts from the usual 'choral' standpoint and is marred by his emphasis on a proposed tripartite division of Bach's vocal forces – soloists, small choir (*Chorsoli*) and large choir (*Ripieni*)⁶ – it nevertheless stands as a serious attempt to take the subject further. Much earlier still Schering, having noted evidence for ripieno participation in BWV21, 24 and 110, reached this conclusion:

> Much more numerous [than this handful of unambiguous cases], however, are those instances where direct indications ... are lacking but the 'concertato' mode of performance must nevertheless be employed.⁷

---

³ Joshua Rifkin, 'Bach's Chorus', in Andrew Parrott, *The Essential Bach Choir* (2000) [hereinafter *EBC*], 189–208 (app. 6). Reference to the Mass in B minor occurs only at p. 190, with table I.

⁴ Erich Leinsdorf, *The Composer's Advocate: A Radical Orthodoxy for Musicians* (1981), 98.

⁵ Wilhelm Ehmann, '"Concertisten" und "Ripienisten" in der h-moll-Messe Joh. Seb. Bachs', *Musik und Kirche* 30/2–6 (1960).

⁶ This proposal picks up on a practical suggestion from Schering, 'Die Besetzung Bachscher Chöre', 88. Acknowledging that there was no evidence from Bach's time for this tripartite division, Ehmann subsequently defended it against crticism from Alfred Dürr as a means of bridging the gap between solo and choral sections in an age when the ratio of soloist to choir singer had turned from Bach's supposed 1:3 to 1:15 or even 1:30; Wilhelm Ehmann, 'Noch einmal zum Problem: "Concertisten–Ripienisten"', *Musik und Kirche* 31/6 (1961), 269.

⁷ '*Sehr viel größer aber ist die Zahl der Fälle, wo solche direkten Hinweise fehlen und dennoch die „konzertierende" Vortragsweise zur Anwendung kommen muß*'; Schering, 'Die Besetzung Bachscher Chöre', 79.

The Mass in B minor, he points out, has 'some classic passages' where choral writing seems clearly intended for concertists alone, above all the continuo-accompanied opening of the *Cum sancto spiritu* fugue:

> if it is executed by the solo quintet in the manner of many similar passages in the cantatas, there is then an elemental build-up from the chorus entry at 'Amen' through to the repetition of the fugue by the full choir.[8]

(Schering's alertness here and elsewhere to the musical impact of these principles is well worth noting.)

Underlying this early recognition that choruses were not necessarily intended to be sung exclusively 'chorally' is the seemingly reasonable assumption of an ever-present larger body of singers (a 'choir') for whom choral writing is primarily designed. Rifkin's achievement, the product of a rigorous investigation of all the relevant performance material, has been to show just how fragile that assumption is and to recognize the central place that concertists occupied in the singing of choruses. With an ever-present team of solo voices (concertists), one for each vocal line, and perhaps the occasional option of additional singers (ripienists), the procedure is, from our perspective, simply the reverse of what had been assumed: rather than (re)allocating certain portions of choral movements to 'soloists', we need to ask exactly *where* – and (not least) *whether* – it might or might not be appropriate to add vocal ripienists to the team of concertists.

Lacking only chorales and *turba* movements, the Mass in B minor is a veritable compendium of Bach's choral writing and contains a higher proportion of choruses than the only two other works of comparable scale, the *St John* and *St Matthew Passions*. Of its 16 choruses – 18 if one includes the repeated *Osanna* and the return at *Dona nobis pacem* of the *Gratias* music – no more than two seem to have been newly composed (*Confiteor* and perhaps *Et incarnatus*), while of the earlier models all but one (for *Crucifixus*) may date from Bach's Leipzig years; see Table 11.1. Of particular value to this study are those nine choruses known in versions performed under Bach's supervision; see Table 11.2. In the circumstances it is scarcely surprising that none of the choral writing in the Mass, even if written with Dresden or some other musical centre in mind, appears to imply either vocal forces or conventions of vocal scoring that differ in any significant way from Bach's usual Leipzig practice.

The principal aim of the present discussion is to explore the diverse implications of all this choral writing, with a specific view to establishing what role – if any – a vocal ripieno group might have played in Bach's

---

[8] '*Zunächst den continuobegleiteten Anfang der* 'Cum sancto spiritu'-*Fuge; wird er nach Art vieler ähnlicher Stellen in den Kantaten vom Soloquintett ausgeführt, so ergibt sich über den Choreinsatz des* 'Amen' *hinweg bis zur Wiederholung der Fuge durch den Gesamtchor eine elementäre Steigerung*'; Schering, 'Die Besetzung Bachscher Chöre', 87.

expectations. Background information on the broader subject of Bach's choir, summarized and reviewed in the light of recent commentary and research, may be found in the Appendix.

Table 11.1 Choruses in the Mass in B minor

Movement	Model; related version
I Missa (1733)	
1 *Kyrie*	? [?1725/1726]
3 *Kyrie*	? [?1723/1724]
4 *Gloria*	? [*a*4; ?1723<]; BWV191/1 (?1745)*
5 *Et in terra pax*	? [*a*4]
7 *Gratias agimus*	?; BWV29/2 (1731)
9 *Qui tollis*	BWV46/1 (1723)
12 *Cum Sancto Spiritu*	? [*a*4; ?1723<]; BWV191/3 (?1745)
II Symbolum Nicenum (1748/1749)	
13 *Credo*	Credo/G Mixolydian
14 *Patrem*	?; BWV171/1 (?1729)]
16 *Et incarnatus est*	perhaps new
17 *Crucifixus*	BWV12/2 (1714)
18 *Et resurrexit*	? [*a*4; ?1723<]
20 *Confiteor*	new
21 *Et expecto* (c. 1742)	? [*a*4] BWV120a/1 (?1729); BWV120/2
III Sanctus (1748/1749)	
22 *Sanctus*	Bach-Compendium E 12 (1724)
IV Osanna, Benedictus, Agnus Dei et Dona nobis pacem (1748/1749)	
23, 25 *Osanna*	BWV Anh. 11/1 (1732); BWV215/1 (1734)
27 *Dona nobis pacem*	7 Gratias agimus (above)

* On this table the sign < means 'or later'.

Table 11.2 Related choruses performed under Bach's supervision

BWV232/movement	BWV	First perf.	Occasion	Extant parts
17 *Crucifixus*	12/2	1714	Jubilate	SATB and bc only
9 *Qui tollis*	46/1	1723	Trinity X	complete (no ripieno parts); cf. Schering, 'Die Besetzung Bachscher Chöre', 83
22 *Sanctus*	–	1724	Christmas	complete (no ripieno parts)
14 *Patrem*	171/1	1729	New Year	–
21 *Et expecto*	120/2	?1729	Ratswahl	–
7, 27 *Gratias, Dona nobis*	29/2	1731	Ratswahl	complete (includes ripieno parts)
23, 25 *Osanna*	215/1	1734	Königswahl Anniversary	complete (includes 2 × SATB)
4 *Gloria*	191/1	?1745	?Christmas	–
12 *Cum Sancto Spiritu*	191/3	?1745	?Christmas	[*Note* ⁓⁓ in autograph score]*

* By analogy with BWV71, the wavy line (⁓⁓) that appears from time to time at the foot of the page may indicate passages where ripienists might sing and/or where the organ's registration might be fuller (*EBC*, 37). See also Joshua Rifkin, *Bach's Choral Ideal* (2002), 59 n. 111; and n. 26, below.

A SHORT preliminary test case serves to demonstrate the pitfalls of presuming a 'choir' (in the current sense) to be the intended vehicle of Bach's choral writing. In common with manuscript parts for well over 100 other cantatas, the rare printed set for the Mühlhausen cantata *Gott ist mein König*, BWV71, includes none for ripienists.[9] Nevertheless, one might reasonably expect the performance of a large-scale early 18th-century work employing trumpets and drums and designed for an occasion of civic ceremony to be capable of incorporating a vocal ripieno body if suitable singers were available. BWV71 proves to have been no exception, as we learn both from Bach's autograph performing parts and from his outstandingly informative autograph score. Yet, as the composer himself specifies, the participation of the ripieno group is entirely *optional*: 'se piace'. More important still, the ripienists are actually *excluded* from much of the choral writing. Far from giving them prime responsibility for all choruses, Bach limits their involvement to well under half the work's choral singing, calling on them only for sporadic appearances in two of the four choruses and for none whatsoever in a third.[10]

[9] See *EBC*, 141–2.
[10] See *EBC*, 36–7, 68, 141–2.

This test case brings into focus two questions of overriding importance concerning ripieno participation in Bach's choral output as a whole, and hence in the Mass in B minor. Each proves significantly more fruitful than merely asking how many performers may have been *available* at Leipzig, Dresden or elsewhere:

1. How much in Bach's output actually demands vocal ripienists (as opposed to simply providing or allowing for them as an option)?
2. When ripienists are explicitly provided for, how does Bach choose to deploy them?

While I assert above that 'early sources for the Mass contain no suggestion whatsoever of any requirement for ripieno singers', Christoph Wolff's edition of the work appears to tell us otherwise. At two points in the Dresden performing parts of the *Missa* the autograph inscription 'Solo' is found, against the alto's *Qui sedes* and against the bass's *Quoniam*. This, it is claimed, implies the presence elsewhere of a 'vocal tutti ensemble', which indeed it does. But to imagine that such an ensemble necessarily comprises more than one singer for each vocal line (Wolff promptly invokes the 'three to four singers per part' of Bach's 1730 *Entwurff*)[11] is mere wishful thinking:[12] 'all' five concertists singing together also constitute a 'tutti', and the concertist's brief always includes the singing of tutti sections, whether or not ripienists are also present.

It might be argued that, when a work lacked ripieno parts or failed to specify them in some way, it would have been entirely natural for a Cantor or *Capellmeister*, at least on occasion, to have considered adding some. Just as certain acoustical spaces call for more violins than others, or for a stronger instrumental bass line, there are conditions in which it may at times be helpful to reinforce the vocal lines. More richly scored compositions or grander circumstances might also suggest the use of increased numbers of both instruments and voices: of the 15 Bach works indicating ripieno participation no fewer than 11 feature trumpet(s), the majority of them written for events outside the routine of Sunday worship.[13] Performance choices of this sort – unlike W. F. Bach's addition of trumpets and drums to BWV80 – leave the compositional fabric of a work intact and thus do not in themselves constitute arrangements or (arguably) even different versions of a work, merely different realizations.

---

[11] Kurtzer, '*iedoch höchstnöthiger Entwurff einer wohlbestallten Kirchen Music*'; in *Bach-Dokumente* i, ed. W. Neumann and H.-J. Schulze (1963), 60. See *EBC*, 163 and 167.

[12] J. S. Bach, *Messe in h-Moll*, BWV232, ed. Christoph Wolff (1994), 408. See also Rifkin's review of facsimile editions of the Mass in B minor, where Wolff is also quoted as saying that the markings 'are in themselves ... a strong argument against Joshua Rifkin's view'; *Notes* 44/4 (1988), 797–8.

[13] *EBC*, 61–2.

And is this not exactly what today's performances generally do? By replacing (or at least expanding) the concertists' choir with a larger body of singers, are we not simply adapting Bach's rather modest forces in the very same spirit, perhaps to suit today's concert halls, while according these great works – through sheer admiration – a greater audible 'status' than their original circumstances may have merited? Perhaps so, but there is, of course, a big catch to all this. Without due understanding of the conventions that governed ripieno writing, there will always be a distinct risk (to repeat Schering's words) of sacrificing 'a multitude of fine and considered details' to a desire for our own slimmed-down version of 'monumentality'. Rather than allowing the composer's work to flourish in something like the manner he might have hoped for (if those are our aspirations), undue intervention – however well-intentioned – may inadvertently result in distortion.

With this in mind, we may set about the task of understanding Bach's own occasional use of ripienists,[14] in order to see what, if anything, might prove applicable – speculatively – to the Mass in B minor. In similar vein, George Stauffer asks: 'If we ... assume that Bach had at his disposal a modest-sized choir divided into concertists ... and ripienists ..., to what extent might he have used the former to create solo effects in the chorus movements of the B-minor Mass?'[15] Setting aside any image this may evoke of a hypothetical single body of singers containing both concertists and ripienists, the question is more correctly put the other way around: to what extent might Bach have used ripienists to create fuller tutti sections in choruses?

A simple but fundamental principle underlies ripieno usage, and its importance can scarcely be overemphasized. A ripieno choir – a distinct body of singers whose function is to 'fill out' or 'strengthen' the vocal texture – 'sings with' or 'joins in' with concertists 'only occasionally' or 'now and then'. These expressions, reminiscent of Johann Gottfried Walther's in his *Musicalisches Lexicon* of 1732,[16] are all drawn from Johann Heinrich Zedler's *Universal-Lexicon* (1731–54), where, for example, *canto ripieno* is defined as 'a *Discant* for filling out [the texture], which joins in just occasionally'.[17] As surviving parts show, supplementary voices of this sort were not necessarily expected either to sing throughout choruses, or

---

[14] See *EBC*, 59–92.

[15] George Stauffer, *Bach: The Mass in B minor* (1997), 214.

[16] See *EBC*, 35–6.

[17] '... *ein zur Ausfüllung dienender Discant, der nur bißweilen mit einfällt*'; 'Canto ripieno', in Johann Heinrich Zedler, *Universal-Lexicon* (Leipzig, 1731–54). The corresponding definitions of alto, tenor and bass 'Ripieno' also variously employ *zur Verstärckung, mitsingen/mitgehen* and *dann und wann* in equivalent contexts.

even to take part in all of them.[18] (At least one writer today nevertheless regularly misuses the term *ripieno* simply to mean 'the choir that sings choruses'.)[19] Bach's own fairly consistent practice[20] may be summarized as follows:

(1) ripienists are likely to double concertists throughout in
   (a) chorales
   (b) turba choruses
   (c) *stile antico* and *alla breve* writing;
(2) ripienists may be added at select points in
   (a) concerto-like ritornello forms
   (b) fugues;
(3) ripienists are likely to be excluded from
   (a) 'solo' passages
   (b) lightly accompanied passages
   (c) certain types of initial statement
   (d) *affettuoso* movements.

Before examining how some of these practices might influence our understanding of the various choruses in the B minor Mass, three interrelated questions must briefly be addressed. To what extent did such conventions vary from one town to another? Did court chapels operate quite differently from town churches? Is the process of extrapolation from a mere handful of works a reliable guide to what might have happened in others?

Despite differing local conditions, most conventions of musical notation, composition, theory and practice were understood across (and beyond) German-speaking lands, as the circulation of music, books on music and musicians themselves attest. To answer the first question as it relates to ripieno practice, we may glance back at the subject of the test case above: *Gott ist mein König*, BWV71, written at Mühlhausen in 1708. Here, despite inevitable stylistic differences, there is little in the way the ripieno writing is handled that is not matched by Bach's later usage at Leipzig:[21]

---

[18] The evidence of these parts confirms that Walther's and Zedler's 'occasionally' does not mean merely 'whenever a chorus occurs amidst arias and so forth'.

[19] Thus in one instance 'ripieno singing' stands for the singing of choruses, while elsewhere we are told that 'the four soloists double up as ripienists in the choruses and chorales'; *BBC Music Magazine*, July 2007, 71.

[20] See *EBC*, 59–92.

[21] In his review of the German edition of *EBC* (*Bachs Chor: Zum neuen Verständnis* (2003)) Hans–Joachim Schulze claims that 'large parts of

/1 As in the larger-scale rondeau structure of BWV23/3, the intermittent inclusion of ripienists serves to underscore the 'motto' theme of the movement's A B A' C A form.

/3 Comparison is not possible in this instance, as entire choruses where instruments other than continuo are not employed are very rare (one thinks of *Sicut locutus est* in the Magnificat, BWV243), and the group of works with known ripieno involvement contains no such movement. Here, ripienists – like most of the instrumental ensemble – remain silent for the whole movement.

/6 Although marked 'Affettuoso e larghetto', the movement has clear stylistic parallels with chorale settings such as BWV76/7 where the vocal writing, usually doubled by instruments, is similarly homophonic. Ripienists double the concertists throughout.

/7 The fugue (bars 40–88) follows the familiar pattern whereby ripienists enter at the second exposition,[22] while in the flanking sections they are reserved for those few moments where most or all of the instruments are also engaged.

A second test case, while again touching on the matter of location, addresses the objection that musical practices at court chapels may have differed crucially from those of town churches.[23] Over the course of a decade *Ich hatte viel Bekümmernis*, BWV21, travelled with Bach from Weimar via Cöthen (and Hamburg) to Leipzig, where the composer added ripieno parts.[24] In other words, at the court of Weimar (1714) and for the probable performance at one of Hamburg's churches (1720)[25] the cantata seems to have been performed in the same way: without ripienists. While some courts evidently used ripieno singers on a fairly regular basis, others did not, and from one town church to the next there was probably a similar diversity. Resources are not the issue here: ripieno voices were almost always considered optional, and musicians of the day knew how to deploy

---

Parrott's book have no bearing on the matter in hand, as they transfer the performance data of, say, Mühlhausen or Weimar indiscriminately [*ungeprüft*] to Leipzig'; *Bach-Jahrbuch* 89 (2003), 270. Schering is rather more relaxed when explaining the concerted style: 'This practice was naturally introduced in Leipzig, too'; 'Die Besetzung Bachscher Chöre', 77.

[22] See *EBC*, 64–5 *et seq*.

[23] '*Methodisch problematisch erscheint zudem die Annahme einer an höfischen Kapellen wie städtischen Kantoraten identischen Verfahrensweise bei der Darbietung von figuraler Kirchenmusik*'; Andreas Glöckner, 'Alumnen und Externe in den Kantoreien der Thomasschule zur Zeit Bachs', *Bach-Jahrbuch* 92 (2006), 9.

[24] Joshua Rifkin, 'From Weimar to Leipzig: Concertists and ripienists in Bach's *Ich hatte viel Bekümmernis*', *Early Music* 24/4 (1996), 591.

[25] Christoph Wolff, *Johann Sebastian Bach: The Learned Musician* (2000), 211–15.

them if they were available and if they would benefit a particular work or performance. In the case of BWV21 Bach chose to use his added ripienists at Leipzig (1723) in all four choruses, but to different extents:

/2 Ripienists sing throughout.

/6 Concertists alone introduce both the first section and the fugue.

/9 A chorale tune in the first section of the movement is given to both concertist and ripienist tenors; the remaining ripienists join only later when instruments enter.

/11 The opening is sung by all, after which a fugue is led off by concertists.

More critical, perhaps, is the third question: can we safely second-guess the manner in which Bach might have chosen to add ripienists to his Mass in B minor? (There is, of course, no solid justification for assuming that he even considered the matter.) The discovery in 2000 of a set of ripieno parts to *Du wahrer Gott und Davids Sohn*, BWV23, presented an almost unique opportunity to test earlier predictions, if only on a modest scale.[26] It comes as no surprise to find that ripienists 'fill out' the cantata's concluding chorale (/4) and that the duet passages of the chorus (/3) – which account for a good third of the movement – are left to concertists. But what is not anticipated in any modern edition of the work – and remains unmentioned in Wolff's report of the discovery – is that the opening choral statement (bars 9–17) is also left to the four concertists. Having observed this feature of Bach's ripieno usage elsewhere – in BWV21/6 (1723) and BWV195/5 (c. 1742) – I had earlier hazarded a guess that here, too, 'any ripieno parts would have begun [only] with the instrumentally doubled repetition of this phrase at bar 24'.[27] While this chance confirmation is perhaps of little consequence in itself (there is

---

[26] Christoph Wolff, 'Originale Ripienstimmen zu BWV23', in Wolff *et al.*, 'Zurück in Berlin: Das Notenarchiv der Sing-Akademie. Bericht über eine erste Bestandaufnahme', *Bach-Jahrbuch* 88 (2002), 167–9, 179. Earlier the existence of such parts had been doubted: 'If vocal *ripieno* parts for BWV23 have been lost, Bach may have had 16 or more singers. Considering the seemingly complete set of performance parts, however, such a loss is not very likely'; C. Wolff, *Bach: Essays on his Life and Music* (1991), 135. Rifkin, however, thought it likely that ripieno parts would have been used for the 1723 performance (see Joshua Rifkin, *Bach's Choral Ideal* (2002), 31, first presented as a paper at the 1990 Royal Musical Association conference), and has since identified the rediscovered parts as dating from that year (Wolff had concluded that they dated from the repeat performance in 1724) and thus within the short period after which such ripieno parts 'disappear all but totally'; Joshua Rifkin, 'Bach's Chorus: Some New Parts, Some New Questions', *Early Music* 31/4 (2003), 573–4.

[27] Andrew Parrott, 'Bach's Chorus: Beyond Reasonable Doubt', *Early Music* 26/4 (1998), 653 n. 22; see also *EBC*, 75. Schering, I have subsequently noticed, makes exactly the same observation; 'Die Besetzung Bachscher Chöre', 83.

no comparable passage in the Mass), it does reinforce the belief that ripieno practice in general, and Bach's in particular, merit closer attention than they have generally received. It suggests that careful extrapolation from Bach's own ripieno writing can go some way towards providing a reasonably secure framework for a better understanding of his choir. More specifically, it also suggests that in other respects, too, today's ripienists-with-(almost)-everything mentality may not accurately reflect Bach's own subtle understanding of vocal scoring.

It is well known that the choruses of the Mass in B minor are written variously in four, five, six and eight parts. This does not mean, however, that there are just four vocal scorings (with or without possible ripieno reinforcement). There are in fact six, as Bach's four-part writing appears in three forms: first with S1 and S2 sharing a single line, then with S1 *tacet*, and finally with the two four-part choirs singing together; see Table 11.3. (The first and last of these variants also occur elsewhere in Bach's output, both with and without the aid of ripienists.)[28] These distinctions are easily overlooked, especially in today's conventionally choral performances. To hear (and see?) now four, now five, six or eight individual singers is inevitably quite different from experiencing all choruses tackled by a uniform choral body (generally with no more than a left-right division for the double-choir *Osanna*), and is a distinctly richer experience, I would venture to suggest. The effect, if less monumental, is unquestionably more dynamic.

Commenting on the total absence of tutti indications in the Dresden vocal parts for the *Missa*, Rifkin writes:

> A scribe trying to extract *ripieno* parts from all this would have found it difficult indeed, especially in the absence of a score: at the very least, the task entailed a laborious collation of the parts already present. Hence, short of conjuring up a set of autograph *ripieno* parts left at Dresden but subsequently lost, we have no way of supposing that Bach envisaged more singers for the *Missa* than the existing materials allow for.[29]

---

[28] In BWV31/9 the two soprano parts are amalgamated, as they are for all chorales, in the motet *Jesu, meine Freude*, BWV227. Bach's normal ripieno practice is, of course, to double all four parts, but the same effect is produced when, for example, in the *St Matthew Passion* the two independent choirs are brought together in four-part writing; see Daniel R. Melamed, *Hearing Bach's Passions* (2005), 49–65.

[29] Rifkin, review in *Notes* (1988), 797. He continues: 'It stands to reason, I need hardly add, that any obstacles to the copying of vocal *ripieno* parts would equally diminish the possibility – a strictly hypothetical one in any event ... – of having extra singers read from the same parts as the soloists.'

Table 11.3 Vocal scorings in the Mass in B minor

Voice parts	Movement	
a4 S1/2 A T B	3, 7; 14	S1, S2 in unison
a4 – S2 A T B	9; 17	S1 tacet
a4 S1/2 A1/2 T1/2 B1/2	27	two choirs in unison
a5 S1 S2 A T B	1, 4–5, 12*; 13, 16, 18, 20, 21	
a6 S1 S2 A1 A2 T B	22	
a8 S1 A1 T1 B1 S2 A2 T2 B2	23, 25	two choirs in dialogue

* At bars 21–24 of movement 12, where S1 and S2 are in unison, the writing is briefly a4.

(As he also observes, 'we know today that a performance of the *Missa* using exactly the forces that a strict reading of the Dresden parts would yield poses no practical difficulties'.)[30] The circumstances of the later and larger Mass in B minor, for which there is no equivalent set of parts, are of course less cut and dried. Nevertheless, my aim is not to promote the use of ripienists in the work, let alone to prescribe their hypothetical use; rather it is to help clarify the principles of Bach's own practice. After all, a good understanding of these principles can be the only basis for any serious speculation on the possible inclusion of vocal ripieno forces in performances of the Mass in B minor. Various general issues will be discussed as they arise in a survey of individual movements. To that end it will be helpful to consider the choruses under four broad stylistic headings: *stile antico*, *concertato*, *concertato* with fugue, and (for want of a better term) *affettuoso* style; see Table 11.4.

[30] Rifkin, review in *Notes* (1988), 797.

Table 11.4 Choral writing in the Mass in B minor

Movement	No. of parts	Orchestral support (besides basso continuo)	Comments
stile antico (all in ₵)			
/3 Kyrie	a4 (S1 + 2)	throughout (strict)	alla breve
/7 Gratias	a4 (S1 + 2)	throughout (strict)	alla breve
/13 Credo	–	none	violins only
/20 Confiteor	–	none	orchestra tacet; *Note* Adagio ending (affettuoso style)
/27 Dona nobis	(as /7)	(as /7)	S1/2 A1/2 T1/2 B1/2
stile concertato (i)			
/4 Gloria	–	occasional, free	–
/18 Et resurrexit	–	occasional, free	*Note* 'Et iterum' (B)
/21 Et expecto	–	occasional, free	–
/23 Osanna, /25 (repeat)	a8 (SATB × 2)	occasional, free	–
stile concertato (ii) with fugue			
/1 Kyrie	–	none 30–44; otherwise free but continuous	–
/5 Et in terra	–	none 20–34; otherwise free but almost continuous	–
/12 Cum Sancto Spiritu	–	none 37–64; otherwise free and intermittent	*Note* transition from /11
/22 Sanctus	a6 (inc 2 × A)	none 48–71; continuous 115–68; otherwise intermittent	–
/14 Patrem	a4 (S1 + 2)	almost throughout	–
affettuoso style			
/9 Qui tollis	a4 (S1 tacet)	occasional, free	flutes, strings; *note* transition from /8
/16 Et incarnatus	–	none	violins (unison except bars 45–8)
/17 Crucifixus	a4 (S1 tacet)	none	flutes, strings

STILE ANTICO

COMPOSITION in *alla breve* style or *stile antico* is well represented in the Mass in B minor. Although idioms of this sort stand in clear contrast to the younger *concertato* styles, they always coexisted with them. Thus we may look back, for example, to Giovanni Rovetta's collection of *Salmi Concertati a Cinque et Sei Voci* (Venice, 1626) which also includes two non-*concertato* psalms, marked *'Per Cantar alla Breve con le parte Radoppiate Se piace'*.[31] Here, as elsewhere, doubling of parts is specifically associated with *alla breve* settings, even though it remains strictly optional; for Rovetta's concerted psalms, on the other hand, it appears not even to have been an option. This conventional distinction in manner of performance was still drawn in Bach's Germany (see Appendix) and the underlying reasons are succinctly articulated by Walther when he chooses 'da Capella' writing, with its avoidance of small note values, to exemplify a compositional style that is appropriate 'if many voices and instruments are to do one and the same thing accurately together'.[32]

/3 Kyrie The explicit presence of 'Stromenti in unisuono' makes it a natural candidate for the optional addition of ripieno voices. With S1 and S2 assigned to a single vocal line (as in /7 and /14), the soprano line is indeed already reinforced.

/7 Gratias agimus Again, S1 and S2 share a single vocal line. The continuous *colla parte* instrumental doubling of the vocal lines would also seem to allow further doubling by ripieno voices, as suggested by the ripieno parts to *Wir danken dir, Gott*, BWV29/2 (1731). The music's return in another guise, however, raises some questions (see /27 below).

/13 Credo in unum Deum According to *The New Bach Reader* Carl Friedrich Cramer (1786) expressed the opinion that in performing 'the five-part Credo of the immortal Sebastian Bach ... the vocal parts must be presented in sufficient numbers [*hinlänglich besetzt*], if it is to show its full effect'.[33] Not for the first time we encounter a translation that reflects a critical preconception rather than the original text. Cramer's report of C. P. E. Bach's Hamburg performance continues: 'Our good singers proved again, especially in the Credo, their known skill in performing securely the most difficult passages.'[34] As Rifkin has shown, the 'staunch' (*brav*) singers in the *Credo* are most likely to have comprised five of Emanuel's usual team of eight (just five copies were prepared), while Cramer's admiration of their 'skill' in undeniably 'difficult' music most naturally relates to

---

[31] Basso continuo book, 61 (*Tavola Delli Salmi*).
[32] *EBC*, 64.
[33] *The New Bach Reader*, ed. H. T. David and A. Mendel, rev. C. Wolff (1998), 371.
[34] *The New Bach Reader*, 371.

Credo in unum Deum	1	**T**				
	3	T + **B**				
	6	T B + **A**				
	9	A T B + **S1**				
	12	S1 A T B + **S2**				
	14	S1 S2 A T B + **v1**				
	17	S1 S2 A T B	v1 + **v2**			
Patrem omnipotentem	1	<u>S1/2 A T B</u>	v1 v2 + **va ob1 ob2**			
	29	<u>S1/2 A T B</u>	v1 v2	va ob1 ob2 + **tr1**		
	65	<u>S1/2 A T B</u>	v1 v2	va ob1 ob2	tr1 + **tr2**	
	67	<u>S1/2 A T B</u>	v1 v2	va ob1 ob2	tr1 tr2 + **tr3/timps**	

Fig. 11.1 Vocal and instrumental scoring in the *Credo in unum Deum* and *Patrem omnipotentem*. The underlining indicates where the vocal parts might reasonably attract ripieno vocal doubling, at least from the successive fugal entries at bars 1, 7, 11 and 17.

his immediately preceding remark that the vocal parts be 'assigned adequately' (*hinlänglich besetzt*), that is, given to suitably capable singers. Certainly, there is no mention of 'numbers', and it rather looks as though commentators and translators may have confused quality with quantity.[35]

Yet at Hamburg, as many will be aware, C. P. E. Bach did choose to reinforce the vocal lines with instruments, both here and in the *Confiteor*. George Stauffer has proposed that these two movements belong to a tradition in which instrumental doubling was routinely added.[36] There are good reasons nevertheless for not viewing this first movement of the *Credo* in the same light as, for example, the *Gratias/Dona nobis pacem* – not least the absence of any notational warrant for *colla parte* instrumental doubling. In addition, by holding a full, independent instrumental accompaniment in reserve, Bach is surely creating a forward momentum from this movement to the *Patrem omnipotentem* which is only dulled by employing fuller forces from the start. (This cannot be disregarded merely on the basis of a perceived similarity to 'a 19-century-oriented crescendo'.)[37] Begun – even before the continuo enters – with a single voice as by a celebrant, the *Credo*'s intended progress to an eventual tutti could scarcely be more palpable; see Fig. 11.1.

There are also grounds of a less subjective nature for believing that ripieno voices would have been considered inappropriate in the *Credo in unum Deum* – and these have implications that reach far beyond this particular movement. The first dozen or so bars, as we can see, lack any instrumental accompaniment beyond that of the basso continuo, and

---

[35] Joshua Rifkin, '"... wobey aber die Singstimmen hinlänglich besetzt seyn müssen...": Zum Credo der h-Moll-Messe in der Aufführung Carl Philipp Emanuel Bachs', *Basler Jahrbuch für historische Musikpraxis* 9 (1985), 157–72.

[36] Stauffer, *Bach: The Mass in B minor*, 224–31.

[37] Stauffer, *Bach: The Mass in B minor*, 229.

even the contrapuntal lines subsequently given to the violins cannot be considered as accompanimental to or supportive of the voices in any usual way. In effect, the movement consists of seven equal 'voices' (the two highest being necessarily instrumental) over an independent bass. The question raised is this: does choral writing in which the instrumental ensemble is silent (or, as in this exceptional case, only partially involved and in an atypical fashion at that) ever attract ripieno voices in Bach's output? Just as instrumental doubling of one sort or another is a valuable guide to the plausibility of possible vocal reinforcement, is the absence of such instrumental support an indicator that concertists were expected to be left untrammelled by additional voices? The 15 works with known ripieno involvement give a fairly clear answer: extended passages – let alone entire movements – where ripienists sing but the instrumental ensemble is silent are conspicuously absent. And what seems to be easily Bach's longest stretch of writing for more than one voice on a part with just continuo comes from elsewhere: the exceptionally turbulent opening 16 bars of 'Sind Blitze, sind Donner in Wolken verschwunden' in the *St Matthew Passion*, BWV244/27b. These meagre statistics are set out in Table 11.5 and may be compared both with BWV71/3, a complete 38-bar movement explicitly intended for just four singers, and with other similarly telling examples given in Table 11.6.

/20 Confiteor See below.

/27 Dona nobis pacem At its second appearance the vocal scoring has subtly shifted to take account of the three voice parts first added at the *Sanctus* (A2, T2 and B2). Thus, it is now not only the top vocal line which is doubled (with S1 and S2 in unison, as before), but each of the four: A1 with A2, T1 with T2, and B1 with B2. The 'discrepancy' between the two vocal scorings of the same music may be viewed as a mere notational nicety resulting from Bach's shift from the predominantly five-part vocal texture of the *Kyrie, Gloria* and *Credo* to the six and then eight parts of the *Sanctus* and *Osanna*. As such it may appear to be of little practical consequence, in that the addition of ripienists for the *Gratias* would have been regarded as a perfectly conventional option which (assuming a conventionally small number of ripienists) would make only a modest difference to the texture. Alternatively, the distinction might be seen as entirely purposeful on Bach's part, implying just the expected five singers for the *Gratias* and then eight for the *Dona nobis pacem*, as a means of creating a cumulative effect for the conclusion of the Mass.

Table 11.5 *Choral passages for more than one voice per part with continuo only*

BWV	Title	Movement	Length of passage(s) bars*	Length of movement (bars)
71	Gott ist mein König	1	<1	38
		6	–	37
		7	1<	103
22	Jesus nahm zu sich die Zwölfe	1	–	92
23	Du wahrer Gott und Davids Sohn	3	–	153
		4	–	58
75	Die Elenden sollen essen	1	–	105[a]
76	Die Himmel erzählen die Ehre Gottes	1	<3	137
21	Ich hatte viel Bekümmernis	2	–	58
		6	1<	75
		9	–	216
		11	1<	68
24	Ein ungefärbt Gemüte	3	5	104
63	Christen, ätzet diesen Tag	1	<9	84[b]
		7	<14	67 (+ *da capo*)
245	St John Passion	1	–	95 (+ *da capo*)
		24	18[c]	[191]
		39	~25[d]	124 (+ *da capo*)
244	St Matthew Passion	1	–	90
		27b	16	73[e]
		29	–	99
110	Unser Mund sei voll Lachens	1	–	189
201	Der Streit zwischen Phoebus und Pan	1	11<	150 (+ *da capo*)
		15	–	65 (+ *da capo*)
29	Wir danken dir, Gott	2	0	91
215	Preise dein Glücke	1	<2	237 (+ *da capo*)
195	Dem Gerechten muß das Licht	1	6	120
		5	–	134 (+ *da capo*)
191	Gloria in excelsis	3	–	134
234	Mass in A major	6	<1	54

* On this table the sign < means 'slightly fewer/less than' when placed before the numeral, and 'slightly more than' when placed after.

[a] From the 'tutti' at bar 83
[b] Counted as 6/8 bars
[c] The fleeting SAT interjections – 'Wohin?' – in the bass aria 'Eilt, ihr angefochtnen Seelen'
[d] Never more than 4 bars in succession
[e] 'Sind Blitze, sind Donner in Wolken verschwunden'

Table 11.6 Choral passages for concertists and continuo alone in works employing a ripieno

BWV	Title	Movement	Bars
71	Gott ist mein König	3	entire movement (38 bars)
		7	5–22, 23–30, 88–94 (in dialogue with instruments); 40–56/64 (fugal exposition)
22	Jesus nahm zu sich die Zwölfe	1	42–56< (fugal exposition)
23	Du wahrer Gott und Davids Sohn	3	9–17 (initial statement), 72–6, 85–96, 105–16 (duets)
75	Die Elenden sollen essen	1	11–17 (initial duet); 68–77< (fugal exposition)
76	Die Himmel erzählen die Ehre Gottes	1	13–16 (initial solo), 67–93< (fugal exposition)
21	Ich hatte viel Bekümmernis	6	1–4 (initial statement); 43–50/53 (fugal exposition)
		9	1–116 (first half of a bipartite movement)
		11	12–25 (fugal exposition)
24	Ein ungefärbt Gemüte	3	36–54/58 (fugal exposition)
195	Dem Gerechten muß das Licht	1	21, 23–4, 26–30 (fugal exposition)
		5	21–8 (initial statement), 58–67, 99–110
234	Mass in A major	6	4–5 (initial solo)

On this table the sign < means 'and over the next few bars'.

STILE CONCERTATO (I)

/4 Gloria Bach's use of the same material in BWV191/1 dates from just three years or so before work on the complete Mass in B minor began. No parts survive for the cantata, but an autograph score does: unlike the last movement (= /12 *Cum Sancto Spiritu*; see below), the first contains no hints of ripieno involvement. (Any conjectural ripieno parts reflecting Bach's own practice elsewhere would most probably have to exclude at least the brief introductory duets at 25–8 and 41–4 and the four successive entries at 69–76.)

/18 Et resurrexit One feature of this movement demands particular attention. At the words 'Et iterum venturus est' the bass part is given an extended 12-bar 'solo' – except that nowhere is the passage actually marked *solo*, nor are there any complementary tutti indications. Multi-voiced renditions are still heard in some of today's period-instrument performances, yet most scholars and performers (if not all bass choristers) probably acknowledge that the passage is really intended for a single singer.[38] Similar 'soloistic' bass writing in BWV195/5 (from *Dem Gerechten muß das Licht*) may be seen to support this: at bars 72–8 the corresponding ripieno bass part (*c.* 1742) is given rests. Unless Bach's notation in the Mass is to be regarded as deficient, the straightforward inference is that the whole movement (and indeed the entire work) is intended – at least primarily and essentially – for single voices. (Bars 9–14 and 93–7 have no obvious parallels in Bach's ripieno parts, and as a general rule any movement which does not clearly suggest where ripienists might and might not sing is likely to be one in which their participation was not anticipated.)

/21 Et expecto Related sources shed no light on possible ripieno usage in this movement; passages that are accompanied by no more than continuo – and occasional flutes (bars 17–24, 41–9, 61–9) – lack any real precedent for ripieno doubling (see above).

/23 (and /25) Osanna in excelsis Surviving parts for Bach's earlier use of this music in *Preise dein Glücke, gesegnetes Sachsen*, BWV215/1 – apparently a complete set – include just a single copy for each of the eight vocal parts (2 × SATB). Moreover, the strong possibility that the second choir in the *St Matthew Passion* originated as a one-to-a-part ripieno choir[39] suggests that of all choruses in the Mass this is perhaps the least likely to have attracted ripieno doubling.[40]

---

[38] A comparable but even longer passage for bass occurs in BWV110/1 (*Unser Mund sei voll Lachens*) at bars 128–47, but there is no bass copy in the ripieno set to confirm it as a solo.

[39] See Melamed, *Hearing Bach's Passions*, 49–65.

[40] At the same time, suspicion may be aroused that the additional voices required to supplement the five (and six) concertists would have been

STILE CONCERTATO (II) WITH FUGUE

IN fugues, Schering tells us, 'Bach often reserves the instruments for the entry of the choral voices'.[41] Several decades earlier Wilhelm Rust, however, had more correctly put it the other way round: Bach's ripieno parts show that his common practice in fugues was to hold back these extra voices until the instruments enter at the second exposition, thus leaving the first exposition to concertists and continuo alone.[42]

/1 Kyrie Questions of vocal scoring present themselves even in the very first two bars of the Mass. If we first compare S2 in bar 1 with the doubling wind parts, and then S1 in bar 2 with the corresponding wind parts, we must surely ask why the rising figures on 'e-[le-i-son]' are left to the respective voices, undoubled. An undoubled vocal ensemble of concertists renders these pregnant phrases – effectively and affectingly – as solos. With additional singers, the choice is either to create ripieno parts which match the doubling instruments (leaving the three-note figures to the concertists) or, questionably, to treat the phrases as brief if conspicuous choral 'solos'.

Similar apparent ambiguity confronts us in the spacious fugue that follows. By any reckoning the first four fugal entries, which are free of instrumental doubling, must be considered as intended for concertists alone. But the fifth entry (for bass voice at bar 45) confuses the picture, in that it is supported not only by continuo but also by viola and appears to do double duty as the first of another set of similar leads. If we are to introduce a ripieno bass, the temptation would be to do so here. However, this would not only deprive the concertist of his anticipated 'solo' entry, it would also set up the expectation of ripieno entries in all voices, when in practice no appropriate entry points exist for tenor and alto at this stage in the movement. At the next set of entries (from bar 81) no such problems arise, despite the unusual absence of instrumental doubling for the tenor line. Only for the second half of the fugue would the hypothetical involvement of ripienists make sense.

/5 Et in terra pax In the fugal writing the situation here is relatively clear-cut: the first exposition (bars 20–37) leaves the subject free of instrumental doubling and keeps the accompaniment light, whereas the second exposition (bars 43–60) is consistently doubled by instruments and would therefore admit similar vocal doubling. As for the ritornello

---

expected to take some earlier role as ripienists. The arithmetic does not work, however, unless we speculate further and summon up two more sopranos for a five-part ripieno earlier in the Mass.

[41] Schering, 'Die Besetzung Bachscher Chöre', 79.

[42] *Johann Sebastian Bachs Werke* v, ed. Wilhelm Rust, Bach-Gesellschaft zu Leipzig (1855), xviii.

elements of the movement, there are no such clear guidelines – reminding us that none of these 'problems' need exist if we accept that Bach's writing does not actually *require* a ripieno.

/12 Cum Sancto Spiritu In the autograph score of the related BWV191/3 a wavy line (∼∼∼) appears from time to time at the foot of the page. A similar line in BWV71 appears in conjunction with the word 'Capella', seeming to indicating passages where the vocal ripieno joins the concertists.[43] In the case of the *Cum Sancto Spiritu* it would not be the usual straightforward matter to create satisfactory ripieno parts, whether *a*5, following the existing scoring, or *a*4, following both the conjectured original scoring and the conventional composition of ripieno groups. On the other hand, it is tempting to imagine Bach himself doing so with relish, as the placement of the line in BWV191/3 clearly has some musically strategic purpose. (The absence of the line at the equivalent of bars 81–105 nevertheless points more towards its being a possible guide for a bassoon part.)[44] On the principle outlined above, the fugal section at bars 37–64 (now without BWV191/3's light instrumental accompaniment) would in any event preclude ripienists.

/14 Patrem omnipotentem As in /7, S1 and S2 sing in unison, meaning that the soprano line is already doubled. Here, though, the instrumental doubling of vocal lines is both fluid and intermittent. Unusually, all fugal entries (with the common exception of some in the bass part) are supported by instruments, which would make ripieno reinforcement more plausible than in many other places, especially following the concertists-only *Credo in unum Deum* (see /13 above). Differentiated ripieno parts do not readily suggest themselves, and no original performing material survives for the related BWV171/1 to inform our speculation.

/22 Sanctus In its earlier independent form (scored for SSSATB rather than SSAATB) the *Sanctus* survives in a full set of parts with just one for each of the six voices.[45] The writing at the opening is in any case far too subtle to lend itself to any straightforward ripieno doubling, and at the 'Pleni sunt coeli' a 24-bar stretch with ripienists but no instruments other than continuo would be unprecedented (see /13 and Table 11.5 above).

---

[43] *EBC*, 62, table 3B note *d*.

[44] The wavy line has alternatively been interpreted as a possible guide for a bassoon part (though in the case of BWV71 a bassoon is already present), while a third possibility is that it indicates passages in which a fuller organ registration is to be used. In practice, these three interpretations need not be seen as mutually exclusive: the line corresponds to those passages where a fuller sonority may be desirable. See Rifkin, *Bach's Choral Ideal*, 59 n. 111.

[45] 'An attempt to fit these forces into the 12-voice choir so long regarded as the norm for Leipzig comes up either with a grotesque imbalance between upper and lower voices – or with an ensemble including one singer for each line'; Joshua Rifkin, 'Bach's Chorus: A Preliminary Report', *The Musical Times* 123/11 (1982), 754.

AFFETTUOSO STYLE

/9 Qui tollis Bach's model for this movement, BWV46/1 (*Schauet doch und sehet*), dates from Bach's first summer at Leipzig and from a month or so after he evidently ceased providing ripieno copies on a regular basis; the surviving set of parts – quite possibly a complete one – includes none for ripienists. For the four-part writing of /3, /7 and /14 Bach brings his two soprano parts together on a single line; here he does not. The most uncomplicated explanation for this is that the intimate character of the vocal writing (marked *p* in BWV46/1) would simply be diminished by anything more than the occasional doubled phrase in one or other string part. The particular expressiveness demanded by both text and music lies naturally in the province of solo voices.

/16 Et incarnatus est Individually and collectively, the spare accompaniment (just unison violins and pulsating bass line), the intensely expressive vocal lines and the tortuous harmony all suggest that ripienists would not merely be redundant but would prove an encumbrance to the concertists. When at the end, with the reduction from five- to four-part writing for the ensuing *Crucifixus*, one singer drops out from a five-person ensemble, the effect is distinctly more potent than any corresponding reduction in conventional choral numbers.

/17 Crucifixus Here, too, and for similar reasons, there are no real grounds for considering ripieno participation. At Weimar, where Bach first used this music more than 40 years earlier in BWV12/2 (*Weinen, Klagen, Sorgen, Zagen*), a ripieno group does not appear to have been much used.[46] The extant performing material to the cantata comprises only a basso continuo part and a set of four for concertists.

/20 Confiteor It may be unexpected to see this extraordinary movement, the only incontestably new composition in the whole Mass, grouped here with the *Qui tollis*, *Et incarnatus* and *Crucifixus* settings. In five rather than four parts, it is rigorously contrapuntal in nature and with no instrumental accompaniment other than continuo. Where Stauffer again argues for the addition of *colla parte* instruments (as well as the ripieno voices he presumes),[47] I would strongly suggest the opposite approach: that nothing more is implied than a five-part ensemble of concertists with continuo, and that this is exactly what J. S. Bach intended – even if one of his sons took a different line some 40 or more years later (see /13 above). Several reasons may be given. We have seen the evident care Bach took in assigning the soprano line in four-part writing (not just to 'soprano' but to S1 and S2 together, or to S2 alone); to have made no mention of *colla*

---

[46] For the cantata movement's middle section, not used in the Mass in B minor, the *Neue Bach Ausgabe* supplies editorial instrumental doubling of all vocal lines.

[47] Stauffer, *Bach: The Mass in B minor*, 224–31.

parte instruments, let alone of how they should be distributed, would by contrast have been a major oversight. While instrumental doubling might in principle suit the fugal writing and its plainchant cantus firmus, its continued use in the ensuing highly charged Adagio ('Et expecto resurrectionem mortuorum') would surely be counterproductive. One of the miracles of the *Confiteor* is the manner in which this new section emerges from the fading counterpoint. The removal of instrumental doubling at any point during this transition would be an unwelcome distraction, and the only plausible place for this to happen would be bar 123, two bars after the *Adagio* has already begun.

BWV71/3, 'one of the few purely vocal Bach cantata choruses',[48] provides a perfectly sound model for entrusting an entire movement of this sort – where the instrumental ensemble rests – to concertists alone (see /13 and Table 11.5 above). Put another way: there is no known instance of ripienists taking part in this admittedly rare type of chorus. Earlier I cited the parallel scoring of BWV243/11, the *Sicut locutus est* of the D major Magnificat. The movement also offers a parallel context: just as *Sicut locutus est* (another fugal movement notated in ¢) prepares the way for the tutti *Gloria*, so too does the *Confiteor* lead us dramatically into the tutti *Et expecto*. Maximum contrast of scale between adjacent movements is surely intended. Just as *Credo in unum Deum* and *Patrem omnipotentem* form a *stile antico–stile moderno* pair, so do *Confiteor* and *Et expecto*. From this Stauffer procedes to argue that in order for the two styles to appear on 'an even footing' and equally 'important', they should sound comparably 'weighty', producing 'a symmetrical *plenum* sound closer to Baroque convention'.[49] This, it seems to me, again confuses quality with quantity and hints at a familiar underestimation of the sheer excellence in ensemble singing that will have been expected, for example, from Dresden's top five Italian singers.

One final reason for ruling out ripienists from the *Confiteor* relates to a notable feature of the Adagio – the enharmonic C/B♯ in the first soprano part (bars 138–9). In 1786, the year of his Hamburg performance of the *Credo*, C. P. E. Bach wrote:

> Singers are just as able to sing in tune as instrumentalists are to play in tune, but in enharmonic contexts it is well-nigh impossible, especially with several together, for everyone to hit the same precise interval that is required. One performer or many makes a big difference in this respect.
>
> *Sänger können so wohl als Instrumentisten rein singen und spielen, aber bey enharmonischen Fällen ist es beynahe unmöglich, daß,*

---

[48] Alfred Dürr, *The Cantatas of J. S. Bach*, rev. and trans. R. D. P. Jones (2005), 724.

[49] Stauffer, *Bach: The Mass in B minor*, 227, 229.

zumahle wenn mehrere zusammen sind, alle auf einen und den gehörigen kleinen Punkt des Intervall rücken. Ein Ausführer, oder viele machen einen großen Unterschied hierin.[50]

How this observation might relate to his experience of performing the *Confiteor* is anyone's guess. *Pace* Fux (1725), who regarded *colla parte* doubling as appropriate to chromatic and modulatory writing,[51] my own strong suspicion is that Bach *père*, rather than adding another 'full' chorus to the work, was drawing on the unmatchable potential of a good team of concertists for suppleness and expressivity – and fine tuning. To ignore this by adding either instruments or (second-rank?) voices risks flattening out, rather than enhancing, the magnificent array of vocal scorings and textures that comprise Bach's Mass in B minor.

WHILE the 1733 *Missa* is preserved in a carefully prepared set of performing parts, the autograph score of the complete Mass necessarily leaves many more performance issues open. If the work's sheer length and grandeur tempt us to explore what an unspecified vocal ripieno group might bring to a performance, we must surely start with a thorough understanding of how Bach himself might have approached the matter – but also with a clear awareness that he might well have regarded the exercise as merely incidental, even pointless or perhaps utterly undesirable. This awareness might in turn edge us just a little closer towards understanding Bach's B minor Mass.

APPENDIX

In reviewing some of the broader underlying issues, and for ease of reference, I indicate those chapters in *The Essential Bach Choir* (*EBC*) where topics are addressed at greater length, and draw attention (by underlining key words) to various sources of information introduced here for the first time.

Repertoires (*EBC*, 17–27) Chant, chorales, motets and concerted church music formed a hierarchy of distinct repertoires, of ascending technical difficulty. At Leipzig Bach allegedly considered it 'beneath his dignity' to be required to direct mere chorales, while motets – drawn from an anthology already over 100 years old – were routinely left to the prefect. Cantatas could be 'as hard again' as motets, and Bach himself tells us that his own music, written only for the first of the four choirs under his control,

---

[50] C. P. E. Bach, *Zwey Litanien aus dem Schleswig-Holsteinischen Gesangbuch, 1785* (Copenhagen, 1786), preface. See also *Briefe von Carl Philipp Emanuel Bach an Johann Gottlob Immanuel Breitkopf und Johann Nicolaus Forkel*, ed. E. Suchalla (1985), 515.

[51] See Stauffer, *Bach: The Mass in B minor*, 225.

was 'incomparably harder and more intricate' than the concerted music entrusted to the second choir.[52]

Instances of large numbers of singers performing older polyphony or even chant have mistakenly been taken as confirmation that Bach would have wished to use comparably large vocal ensembles in his own music. But distinct repertoires made distinct musical demands and commonly presupposed distinct vocal forces. The traditional motet repertoire, as Johann Mattheson tells us, possessed 'a wholly other character' than concerted music,[53] and its relative simplicity invited relatively large vocal forces.[54]

---

[52] Although the repertoire of this second choir does not directly concern us, we may briefly note that Bach considered himself obliged to choose it 'according to the capabilities of those who are to execute it' (*EBC*, 19). The idea nevertheless circulates that for his all-important first choir Bach, by contrast, 'seems deliberately to engineer a bad-sounding performance by putting the apparent demands of the music beyond the reach of his performers and their equipment' (Richard Taruskin, *The Oxford History* ii (2005), 370) – a perverse strategy which would immediately have drawn attention to itself. It certainly runs counter to Daniel Speer's advice to avoid 'overly artificial and difficult pieces when one does not have the people for them ... one should always take full account of the people at one's disposal and avail oneself of such pieces as one may be able to bring off and deliver without upset, so that no offence is given to the congregation in their prayers and devotions' (... *allzukünstliche und schwere Stuck/ wann sie nicht Leute darzu haben ... sondern es soll ein jeder nach seinen unter sich habenden Leuten sich richten/ und solche Stuck ergreiffen/ die er ohne Anstoß fortbringen und hinauß führen könne/ damit der Gemein in ihrer Bet- und Audienz-Andacht kein Aergernus gegeben werde*); Daniel Speer, *Musicalisches Kleeblatt* (Ulm, 1697), 18.

[53] '*Eine gantz andre Beschaffenheit*'; Johann Mattheson, *Der vollkommene Capellmeister* (Hamburg, 1739), 222.

[54] Thomas Selle in 1642 declared that 'For motets there must be as many [singers] again' as for concerted music (*EBC*, 29), and a *Chorordnung* from the town church of Darmstadt from 1721 stipulates 'that the *chorus musicus* be staffed only with capable persons who apply themselves to music, of whom for every voice part, excluding the four concertists, three or four would be used when and where desired, so that they can sing and execute a complete motet or artful aria in various parts *figuraliter*' (... *daß man den chorum Musicum mit lauter tüchtigen und zur Music sich applicirenden Subjectis bestelle, deren bey jeder Haupt-Stimme ohne die 4 Concertisten 3 oder 4 zu gebrauchen wären, damit sie, wann und wo es begehret wird eine vollständige Mottette oder geschickliche Arie mit zusammen gesetzten Stimmen figuraliter absingen und bestellen können*); Elisabeth Noack, *Musikgeschichte Darmstadts vom Mittelalter bis zur Goethezeit* (1967), 202. Casually read, this may appear to match modern expectations of a (small) 'choir' and (independent) 'soloists', as in most Bach cantata performances of today. In fact, a rather large choir (of 12 or more) is being associated here – quite explicitly – not with concerted music but with the distinctly more workaday motet and (chorale-like) choral aria repertory.

Concertists and Ripienists (*EBC*, 29–41) Even when a vocal 'Capella' or ripieno group was also present, it was the concertists who constituted 'the principal choir'[55] and who as such retained prime responsibility for choruses, not just intervening in them from time to time (as both Schering and Ehmann seem to imply) but singing from start to finish.[56] From Martin Heinrich Fuhrmann, for example, we learn that

- concertists sing throughout all choruses;
- ripienists do not (often) do so;
- ripieno parts are (usually) optional.[57]

(The second point is examined in the main text, above. As to the third point, we have noted Bach's explicit treatment of BWV71's ripieno parts as optional, following a tradition that reaches back to Michael Praetorius; in at least two other cases, moreover, the ripieno set is believed to have been added some years after the work's first performance.)[58] As with Fuhrmann, so with Bach. For concertists to sing throughout all choruses was incontestably standard practice in Bach's own works, as it was for all vocal concerted music of his time, whether or not ripienists were also participating.[59] (Universally acknowledged in Bach scholarship, this critical feature of the concertist's role is nevertheless almost the exact reverse of most current practice:[60] 'soloists' have been rendered redundant – and

---

[55] 'Das Haupt-Chor'; Johann Mattheson, *Das neu-eröffnete Orchestre* (Hamburg, 1713), 158.

[56] At one point Schering writes of 'the introduction of a quartet of soloists' into a particular chorus (*Die Einführung eines Solistenquartetts*); 'Die Besetzung der Bachscher Chöre', 88.

[57] Martin Heinrich Fuhrmann, *Musikalischer Trichter oder Anleitung zur Singekunst* (Frankfurt an der Spree, 1706), 80.

[58] See *EBC*, 61.

[59] In parallel with the instrumental *concerto grosso*, where the *concertino* forms the backbone of an entire work and does not rest during tutti sections, 'Canto Concertante' is defined in 1724 as 'the Treble of the little Chorus, or the Part, that sings throughout'; [Johann Christoph Pepusch], *A Short Explication of Such Foreign Words, as are Made Use of in Musick Books* (London, 1724), 18. 'Concertante' by itself is explained as 'those Parts of a Piece of Musick which play throughout the whole, to distinguish them from those which play only in some Parts' (p. 23).

[60] The issue of stamina, however, has been cited as a 'loose end' in the argument for single voices (Yo Tomita, review of *EBC*, *The Musical Times* 141 (Summer 2000), 66), though I am not certain how well it would stand up to historical scrutiny. What we must surely presume, though, is that a singer lacking the necessary stamina to be a concertist is unlikely to have been selected for that role (see *EBC*, 84 n. 22). On the related matter of balance see *EBC*, ch. 10, and for some comments on Bach's younger singers at Leipzig see *EBC*, pp. 12–13 and appendix 2. (My own experience from directing performances of the most extended works – the Mass in B minor and the

mute — in choruses by the encroachment of ever-present 'choirs', giving us the musical oxymoron of 'tutti' sections no longer performed by 'all'.)

Furthermore, there are no grounds for imagining that Bach's ripieno group would necessarily have been any larger than the one-to-a-part concertists' choir that it supported. The Württemberg court's eight singers were sufficient for a '*quatuor* with its ripieno' in 1714 (see below, under 'Rosters and Additional Performers'),[61] and in three instances Bach himself uses the term 'Ripieni' all but explicitly to denote individual singers in a vocal quartet.[62] Not only did a ripieno group commonly mirror the formation of the concertists' choir (thus SATB in Bach's case), it also sang as a discrete unit 'separately positioned in a place apart from the concertists', as Fuhrmann puts it.[63] This principle runs right through concerted music-making from its inception; Ignatio Donati, for example, informs us in 1623 that the optional ripieno parts he provides can form a second choir '*sù la cantoria*',[64] while Mattheson in 1713 simply allocates

---

two Passions — is that perceived problems of stamina for single-voice choirs prove almost wholly illusory.)

[61] Even the otherwise exceptional vocal scoring of *Der Streit zwischen Phoebus und Pan*, BWV201 (1729), seems to imply an eight-singer line-up of this sort: for the work's two choruses, the solo voices of the six named characters (SATTBB) are joined by just two ripieno parts (SA), suggesting a total of two singers of each voice-type (*EBC*, 61, 63). Equally unusual (by Bach's standards) is Zelenka's oratorio *Gesù al Calvario*, written in Dresden in 1735. Of the apparently complete set of surviving vocal parts, five are for soloists (SSAAA), while a further six serve for the 'Ripieni per i Cori' (SATTBB), suggesting a probable ensemble of 3S 4A 2T 2B for the four-part choruses. See Janice B. Stockigt, *Jan Dismas Zelenka (1679–1745): A Bohemian Musician at the Court of Dresden* (2000), 239; and Joshua Rifkin, 'Zelenkas Chor: Der Blick von 1725', in *Provokation und Tradition: Erfahrungen mit der Alten Musik (Festschrift Klaus Neumann)*, ed. H.-M. Linde and R. Rapp (2000), 246–50.

[62] On Bach's use of the expression 'à 4 voci' Ton Koopman writes: 'Did this really mean only a solo quartet ...?' If so, he continues, how are the surviving 'six vocal parts' for BWV21 to be explained?; 'Bach's Choir, an Ongoing Story', *Early Music* 26/1 (1998), 114. Yo Tomita claims I have not answered Koopman's question (review of *EBC* in *The Musical Times* [see n. 60], 66). Born of an elementary misunderstanding, the question addresses a claim that has never been made and therefore surely merits little serious attention; my earlier treatment of it is nevertheless duly noted (*EBC*, 40 n. 37). (In 1998 I pointed out that 'it has nowhere been suggested that [the expression] *necessarily* does mean "only a solo quartet"'; Parrott, 'Bach's Chorus: Beyond Reasonable Doubt', 638.) It may be added that BWV21 has not six but *eight* surviving vocal copies (*EBC*, 178, where there is also a reference to Rifkin's eminently clear explanation of the cantata's complex origins).

[63] '... *an einem* a parten *Ort von den* Concertisten *abgesondert gestellt*'; Fuhrmann, *Musikalischer Trichter*, 80.

[64] Ignatio Donati, *Salmi Boscarecci concertati a Sei Voci, con aggiuntà, se piace, di altre sei voci* (Venice, 1623), A2, 3.

his 'Capella' singers and his concertists to separate 'choirs'.⁶⁵ Similarly, any additional ripienists, rather than simply swelling the ranks of the existing body (as in today's choral practice), might equally well form a further discrete one in yet another location.⁶⁶ This additive process of expanding vocal forces is presumably what is represented in the oft-reproduced frontispiece to *Unfehlbare Engel-Freude* (1710), where, as Schering points out, three vocal quartets are plainly visible.⁶⁷

Copies and copy-sharing (*EBC*, 43–57) Placing concertists and ripienists in discrete choirs inevitably dictates that each group be provided with its own set of parts. Surviving performance materials of Bach's choral works, however, include very few ripieno parts (see further below), leading Schering to surmise that '*if need be*, the tutti singers could also sing from the concertists' parts, in the event that time did not permit the copying out of the other [parts]'.⁶⁸ To remedy the lack of written indications in these circumstances, 'A sign from the conductor sufficed to bring the ripienists back in at the desired place'.⁶⁹ Yet when this idea is traced back to Praetorius and ultimately to Viadana in 1612, we find that it merely relates to the routine cueing of ripienists who are standing in separate choirs and are therefore necessarily equipped with their own copies.⁷⁰ (As Rifkin puts it: 'The situation resembles that of the present-day timpanist who has to count huge stretches of rest and surely appreciates a confirmatory nod from the conductor.')⁷¹ If we are to imagine that Schering's conjectural stopgap was ever adopted outside truly exceptional circumstances, we must surely ask: would it really have taken Bach so long to add a dozen or so valuable solo/tutti indications to a set of concertists' parts? One minute? Five minutes?⁷²

---

⁶⁵ Mattheson, *Das neu-eröffnete Orchestre*, 158.

⁶⁶ See, for example, Mattheson, *Das neu-eröffnete Orchestre*, 158–9.

⁶⁷ *EBC*, 51–6.

⁶⁸ My italics. '*Es konnten aber die Tuttisänger zur Not auch aus den Konzertatstimmen singen, falls etwa die Zeit das Ausschreiben der andern nicht gestattete*'; Schering, 'Die Bestezung der Bachscher Chöre', 80.

⁶⁹ '*Ein Zeichen des Dirigenten genügt, um die Ripienisten an der gewünschten Stelle wieder einfallen zu lassen*'; Arnold Schering, *Johann Sebastian Bachs Leipziger Kirchenmusik* (Leipzig, 1936), 31 n. 3. Compare Schering, 'Die Bestezung der Bachscher Chöre', 80.

⁷⁰ '*E quando si faranno i Ripieni, [il Maestro di Capella] volterà la faccia a tutti i Chori, levando ambe le mani, segno che tutti insieme cantino*'; Ludovico da Viadana, *Salmi a quattro chori* (Venice, 1612), preface ('Modo di concertare i detti salmi a quattro chori'). Compare Michael Praetorius, *Syntagma musicum* iii (Wolfenbüttel, 1619), 126 [*recte* 106].

⁷¹ Rifkin, 'From Weimar to Leipzig', 601 n. 49.

⁷² There is only a single instance (BWV24) where *solo–tutti* markings are found in a set of concertists' parts for which no companion ripieno set has survived.

The still widely accepted hypothesis of a 'group of three' singers reading from a single (concertist's) part[73] has long ceased to be regarded as the emergency measure originally proposed by Schering. It now forms a cornerstone of the 12-strong Bach choir and has even been quietly extended to accommodate '16 or more singers' on those occasions when Bach *did* have time to prepare a set of ripieno parts.[74] Yet Schering's memorable image not only stands in contrast to the 'groups of four' in quartet formation that he himself identifies in the engraving from *Unfehlbare Engel-Freude* but appears to remain uncorroborated by any other relevant source. Attempts to introduce iconographic evidence of copy-sharing are once again undermined by the failure to differentiate between the conventions of distinct repertoires; why else would an essay on Bach's forces for concerted music lead with an engraving of a Cantor and half a dozen or more men and boys singing around a lectern from a large book of monophonic chant?[75]

The copies used by Bach's concertists bear no signs of having been shared, and actually give strong indications that they were not.[76] Similarly,

> In other words, the rare occurrence of such markings in concertists' parts correlates pretty exactly with the apparently equally rare occasions on which ripieno parts were provided, suggesting (as Rifkin has persuasively argued) that the markings served not for singers but for copyists preparing ripieno parts.

[73] '... wenn hier [in bwv24] wie anderswo diese Stimmen den Ripiensängern mit galten, so konnten es solcher höchstens zwei sein: der eine blicke rechts, der andere links vom Konzertisten mit ins Notenblatt' ('... if here [in BWV24] and elsewhere these copies also served for the ripieno singers, there could be at most two of them, the one sharing the music from the concertist's right, the other from the left.'); Schering, 'Die Besetzung der Bachscher Chöre', 81. '... die Aufstellung [muß] so gewesen sein, daß der mittelste Sänger jeder Dreiergruppe – der "Solist" oder "Konzertist" – das Notenblatt hielt, in das bei Chorsätzen je ein Nachbar zur Rechten und zur Linken als "Ripienist" mit hineinschaute' ('... the arrangement [must] have been such that the middle singer of each group of three – the "soloist" – held the copy which in choral movements was also read by a ripienist on each side, one on the left and one on the right'); Schering, *Johann Sebastian Bachs Leipziger Kirchenmusik*, 30.

[74] 'If [once existent] vocal *ripieno* parts to BWV23 have been lost, Bach may have had 16 or more singers'; Wolff, *Bach: Essays*, 135.

[75] *Die Welt der Bach Kantaten* iii, ed. C. Wolff and Ton Koopman (1999), 232; engraving by Christoph Weigel (1698), heading Ton Koopman, 'Bachs Chor und Orchester', 233–49. See also the illustrations chosen at pp. 243–4.

[76] See Rifkin, 'Bach's Chorus' (*EBC*, app. 6) and elsewhere. Uwe Wolf, however, has argued that 'the evidence of the sources is not capable of demonstrating single-voice choral scoring'; 'Von der Hofkapelle zur Kantorei: Beobachtungen an den Aufführungsmaterialien zu Bachs ersten Leipziger Kantatenaufführungen', *Bach-Jahrbuch* 88 (2002), 191. In response, Rifkin shows that a dubious comparison of like with unlike lies at the heart of Wolf's 'sweeping assertion': *solo-tutti* indications in Bach's parts for

a careful study of the 800 or so Telemann cantatas at Frankfurt am Main concludes 'that only one singer sang from each part, and that concertists and ripienists did not share parts'.[77] If this is so, then why are there so few ripieno copies amongst Bach's own performance material?[78] Of almost 150 extant sets, just 10 include parts for ripienists.[79] To believe it 'likely that many ripieno parts were indeed produced ... and subsequently lost or disposed of' is merely to reiterate the unsubstantiated belief that Bach's own performances involved a ripieno choir on a regular basis.[80] Schering's explanation is that 'less importance may have been attached to their preservation' than to those for concertists, because, by contrast,

> concertists cannot be expected to have had the same force as in those of Gottfried August Homilius designed for ripienists. By contrast, ripieno parts by both composers clearly support the view 'that ripieno singers sang from ripieno parts that told them exactly what to do'; Rifkin, 'Bach's Chorus: Some New Parts, Some New Questions', 573–80.

[77] Jeanne Swack, '"Telemanns Chor": Aufführungspraxis und Stimmensätze in Telemanns Frankfurter Kantaten', *Telemann-Konferenzbericht* 13 (2007), 295–314. See also *EBC*, 218, and Swack, *Composition and Performance in the Music of Georg Philipp Telemann* (forthcoming). If the presumption of copysharing amongst singers supports a belief in larger vocal forces, larger forces may themselves seem almost to presuppose the practice of copy-sharing. However, any such easy assumption should perhaps be measured against what is known of German practice from both before and after Bach's lifetime. In mid-17th-century Halle, for example, polychoral music often called for '30, 40 and more persons', yet according to the organist Johannes Zahn in 1641, 'each person must have his own [material] specially written out' (*Weil die itzige art der Music auf viel Chor gesetzet undt oftmahls auf 30, 40 und mehr Personen gerichtet, und einem Jeden das seine absonderlich vorgeschrieben werden muß*; quoted in Walter Serauky, *Musikgeschichte der Stadt Halle* ii/1 (1939), 116–17; and given again in Barbara Wiermann, *Die Entwicklung vokalinstrumentalen Komponierens im protestantischen Deutschland bis zur Mitte des 17. Jahrhunderts* (2005), 61.) More surprisingly perhaps, we find that only a few years after his epoch-making 1829 performance of the *St Matthew Passion* by a reported 150 or so singers (*EBC*, 3), Mendelssohn still had in his possession no fewer than 140 vocal parts for the work (a list of *Noten Sachen* drawn up in 1835 by his sister Fanny Hensel; Peter Ward Jones, *Catalogue of the Mendelssohn Papers in the Bodleian Library, Oxford* iii (1989), 302).

[78] Any regular use of more than one ripieno group would, of course, make the scarcity of such parts even more puzzling. Bach's few ripieno parts survive in single sets, a partial exception being BWV76, which has two soprano ripieno copies, one of them – like the alto ripieno part – incomplete (*EBC*, 181).

[79] A further five works by Bach suggest ripieno participation in different ways (*EBC*, 59–62). For what it is worth, a similar survival rate of ripieno copies is found in the smaller body of works by Carl Gotthelf Gerlach, organist at Leipzig's Neue Kirche from 1729: of 26 extant sets just two include parts for ripienists; Andreas Glöckner, *Die Musikpfege an der Leipziger Neukirche zur Zeit Johann Sebastian Bachs*, Beiträge zur Bach-Forschung 8 (1990), 153–4.

[80] Tomita, review of *EBC*, 66.

they would not have contained all sung portions of a work.[81] Yet if these hypothetical ripieno parts really had been considered musically desirable for performance (let alone essential), it seems strange that so many would apparently have gone missing, at least at an early stage.[82]

The *Entwurff* (*EBC*, 93–102) If the careful examination of Bach's performance material has opened up the nature of his vocal forces for reconsideration, it is the composer's 1730 'Entwurff einer wohlbestallten Kirchen *Music*' that remains the bedrock of traditional thinking on the subject. The document's concerns, however, are fundamentally logistical rather than artistic: how to maintain the forces necessary to provide music year round in four different churches, given an official total strength of just eight town musicians and 32 (of 55) *alumni* (only 17 of them 'usable' in either of Bach's top two choirs). How the music is to be performed is never directly addressed, only how to keep the show on the road:

> Each 'musical' choir must have at least 3 sopranos, 3 altos, 3 tenors, and as many basses, so that even if one person falls ill ... at least a two-choir motet can be sung.[83]

Describing the *Entwurff* as the 'most telling' documentation of 'the puny resources Bach had to work with, and those that he would have thought adequate if not ideal', Richard Taruskin proceeds to quote a parenthetical passage which has long appeared to offer a uniquely authoritative and

---

[81] '*Da diese Tutti- oder Ripienstimmen den Gesangsteil nicht* in toto *enthielten, also gleichsam unvollständig waren, mag man auf ihre Erhaltung weniger Gewicht gelegt haben als auf die andern mit der vollständigen Musik*'; Schering, 'Die Besetzung Bachscher Chöre', 80.

[82] Mattheson writes of 'keeping together the parts that have been copied out (which is an important part of the prefect's official duty)' (... [*die*] *Zusammenhaltung der ausgeschriebenen Stimmen (welches ein wichtiges Stück ist, so zum Am[t] des Vorgesetzten gehöret)*); *Der vollkommene Capellmeister*, 481.

[83] *EBC*, 167 ('*Zu iedweden* musica*lischen* Chor *gehören wenigstens 3* Sopran*isten, 3* Altist*en, 3* Tenor*isten, und eben so viel* Baß*isten, damit, so etwa einer unpaß wird ... wenigstens eine 2* Chörigte Motette *gesungen werden kan.*'; *Bach-Dokumente* i, 60, and *EBC*, 163–4). Ironically, it turns out that virtually the only thing we can learn of performance practice from the *Entwurff* is that double-choir motets (of the pre-Bachian type suitable for *larger* choirs) may in fact be performed with single voices on at least most parts. Interestingly enough, Schering was prepared to go even further. Elsewhere in the *Entwurff* Bach explains that 'Concertists are ordinarily four [in number], and even five, six, seven and as many as eight – if one wishes, that is, to perform [concerted] music *per choros*' (*EBC*, 167). Arnold Schering comments: 'That means: in double-choir pieces each part is taken by a solo voice' (*Das bedeutet: bei doppelchörigen Stücken wird jede Stimme solistisch besetzt*); *Johann Sebastian Bachs Leipziger Kirchenmusik*, 30–1. Cf. Rifkin, *Bach's Choral Ideal*, 27–9.

clear-cut statement on performance: with four singers for each voice, Bach appears to say, one 'could *perform every chorus* with 16 persons'.⁸⁴ This critical mistranslation, long identified as such, comes straight out of the old *Bach Reader* of 1945. From *The New Bach Reader* of 1998, on the other hand, we learn that Bach is in fact merely addressing the organizational matter of how many singers should belong to each of the Thomasschule's three 'musical' choirs: with four singers of each voice-type one 'could *provide every choir* with 16 persons'.⁸⁵ This may be disappointing, as it hardly answers our questions, but it should not really be surprising, since the section in which the passage appears has no demonstrable connection with the performance of concerted music in the first place.

---

⁸⁴ *The Bach Reader*, ed. H. T. David and A. Mendel (1945), 121 [my italics]. Taruskin, *The Oxford History* ii, 362.

⁸⁵ *The New Bach Reader*, 146. In linguistic terms the revised understanding of the sentence in question – a direct product of Rifkin's close reading of the whole document – turns on two words: *Chor* and *bestellen* (Rifkin, *Bach's Choral Ideal*, 16–29, especially pp. 21–3). The passage from Bach's *Entwurff* reads: '*Wiewohln es noch beßer, wenn der* Coetus *so beschaffen wäre, daß mann zu ieder Stimme* 4 subjecta *nehmen, und also ieden* Chor *mit 16. Persohnen bestellen könte*' (*EBC*, 164). *Chorus* (or *Chor*), as Mattheson observes, means several things 'promiscuously', notably either the body of performers, or 'that part of the work where all participate' ('*Es kan noch angemercket werden/ daß das Wort* Chorus *promiscuè, bißweilen ... die Musicirenden/ oder denjenigen Theil des Stückes/ wo alles gehet/ bedeute*'); *Das neu-eröffnete Orchestre*, 159. In Bach's immediate context the word is used unambiguously in the former sense, and his continued use of the same meaning is confirmed by its time-honoured association with the verb *bestellen* (most commonly 'to appoint' or 'to set in order'). Thomas Selle in 1642 and Johann Gottfried Walther in 1732 employ the two words in the same way; see Rifkin, *Bach's Choral Ideal*, 21–2. Beer (?1690s), in similar vein, writes: 'In Halle war die Capell sehr stark bestellt'; *Johann Beer: Sein Leben, von ihm selbst erzählt*, ed. A. Schmiedecke (1965), 22. In discussing his Hamburg 'Chor' (used here in the broader sense of a complete vocal-instrumental body), Telemann in the late 1720s adopts the same usage as Bach: the vacant place of a deceased wind player should be filled by a violinist, otherwise '*der Chor für unsere neuere Music* [*wäre*] *viel zu schwach bestellet*'; *Georg Philipp Telemann: Briefwechsel*, ed. H. Grosse and H. R. Jung (1972), 32. Mattheson's admiring reference to Handel's 'Chor, von mehr, als hundert ausgesuchten Personen' on the occasion of the 1727 coronation in London is mistakenly used by Günther Wagner to imply 'more than a hundred' *singers*, when in fact it refers to the entire ensemble; 'Die Chorbesetzung bei J. S. Bach und ihre Vorgeschichte: Anmerkungen zur "hinlänglichen" Besetzung im 17. und 18. Jahrhundert', *Archiv für Musikwissenschaft* 43/4 (1986), 286. Compare Donald Burrows, *Handel and the English Chapel Royal* (2005), 258–9, 274–9.

Rosters and Additional Performers (*EBC*, 103–15) The *Entwurff* has usually been taken at face value as indicating poor performance conditions,[86] and – as often as not – it is the 'small numbers' of musicians at Bach's disposal that are taken to exemplify these poor conditions. Thus:

> By Bach's own avowal ... he considered 34 persons (plus himself and another keyboard player, who went without saying) to be the bare minimum required for a performance of a maximal piece like Cantata No. 80 ['in his son's "big band" arrangement'] – and that number would have been thought puny indeed at any aristocratic, let alone royal, court.[87]

This recent reading by Taruskin will stand for many. Its purpose is to show that Bach 'never had at his disposal the musical forces that could do anything approaching justice to this mighty fortress of a chorus'[88] – the opening movement of *Ein feste Burg ist unser Gott*, BWV80, in the version with trumpets and drums. (Perhaps we are meant to understand that Bach's forces were so inadequate that he even had to make do without these posthumously added instruments.)[89]

Several things are wrong here. In addition to inflating the instrumental tally (albeit mildly)[90] and assuming in familiar fashion that a full quota of 12 singers would necessarily all be 'required' to perform a chorus of this sort, Taruskin has mistakenly treated the list of instruments in the *Entwurff* as a simple minimum.[91] Bach's overall figures – purely

---

[86] 'However, all these petitions [from Kuhnau, Gerlach, Bach] are better seen as skillful devices of politically resourceful musicians to extract funds from reluctant councilors'; Tanya Kevorkian, 'Changing Times, Changing Music: "New Church" Music and Musicians in Leipzig, 1699–1750', in *The Musician as Entrepreneur, 1700–1914*, ed. W. Weber (2004), 77.

[87] Taruskin, *The Oxford History* ii, 362.

[88] Taruskin, *The Oxford History* ii, 362.

[89] See Dürr, *The Cantatas*, 709.

[90] It is curious how often the composer of the Mass in B minor is thought to have been inept in matters of simple arithmetic. The *Entwurff*'s total of 'at least 18 persons for the instrumental group' makes perfect sense when it is recognized that the optional third players on violins I and II and the two allocated to a seldom needed viola II part are in effect the same players, as Bach's subsequent tables of players and vacancies confirm (*EBC*, 168); see Ulrich Siegele, 'Bachs Endzweck einer regulierten und "Entwurff einer wohlbestallten Kirchenmusik"', in *Festschrift Georg von Dadelsen zum 60. Geburtstag*, ed. T. Kohlhase and V. Scherliess (1978). Similarly, his third oboe and second bassoon parts are extremely likely to have been covered by a single player. On the commonplace practice of such doubling see *EBC*, 14–15; and also Dieter Kirsch, *Lexikon Würzburger Hofmusiker vom 16. bis zum 19. Jahrhundert* (2002), 13 (and compare pp. 14–15).

[91] Bach qualifies his *summa* of '18 persons for the instrumental group' with the words 'at least' (*EBC*, 167), evidently in order to take account of the

	oboes	bassoons	horns	trumpets
Dresden (1745)	5	5	2	12 (including 'field' as well as 'musical' players)
Fireworks (1749)	24	12 + contra	9	9

Fig. 11.2 A comparison of instrumental resources

aspirational as they may have been – are certainly no 'bare minimum'; rather, they represent his considered view of 'a properly constituted church musical establishment', one which naturally enough could encompass even a 'maximal' scoring with 3 oboes, trumpets and drums.[92] Achieving these numbers, at least with adequate quality, manifestly posed a major challenge to Bach – though hardly with the alarming results Taruskin alleges: 'as Bach complains, most of the time some parts had to be omitted from the texture altogether due to absences.'[93] If anything had to go, it would naturally be the optional vocal ripieno group, leaving the compositional texture intact.

So, just how 'puny' would a musical establishment of 12 singers and 20 or so instrumentalists have seemed to a contemporary court? Curiously, the comparison Taruskin offers (see Fig. 11.2) is with Handel's *Fireworks* music, an occasional piece written for outdoor performance in London by a quite exceptional 55-piece wind band made up of both court and freelance players.[94] Even northern Europe's most glittering court in Dresden would have been hard put to muster anything remotely comparable.[95]

Whether or not the numbers outlined by Bach 'would be considered stingy for a professional performance today',[96] they correspond reasonably

occasional third oboe and second bassoon, which, though listed, are not included in his total. Moreover, he proceeds directly to mention the further possible addition of a pair of recorders or flutes (which Taruskin supplements with his own 'etc.'), thus making not '20 at least' but '20 instrumentalists *in all*' [my italics]. In other words, Bach's earlier qualification most obviously allows just for those wind instruments that are not part of the core ensemble of 18; it does not imply any interest in a larger string section, nor is this hinted at elsewhere in the document.

[92] See *EBC*, 117.
[93] Taruskin, *The Oxford History* ii, 363 n. 17, where he cites Joshua Rifkin, 'Bach's Chorus: A Preliminary Report', adding: 'the controversy over this article has lasted more than twenty years and generated a sizeable literature of books, articles and manifestoes [sic]'.
[94] See Donald Burrows, *Handel* (1994), 297–8.
[95] See Stockigt, *Jan Dismas Zelenka*, 238. (Trumpets are listed separately on p. 75.)
[96] Taruskin, *The Oxford History* ii, 363.

closely to those of musical establishments at several major German courts in Bach's own time. The Württemberg court in 1714, for example, maintained a 35-strong *Kapelle*, and a document from Würzburg (1740) outlines a 'most compendious court *Kapelle* or church musical establishment' of 36 persons, comprising

- 12 singers
- 12 strings
- 6 woodwinds
- 4 brass
- organ, theorbo.[97]

On a more modest scale, Mattheson nevertheless reflects the steady expansion of instrumental resources both at courts and in towns during the first half of the century. Rejecting Beer's earlier model of a seven-person nucleus for a *Kapelle*, he proposes instead a body of at least 23[98] – which 'in republics can be more easily increased than at courts, if one wishes to do anything about it'.[99]

However common they may have been in Bach's lifetime, ensembles of these dimensions have come to be viewed with a pitying eye: 'circumstances in many other cities were hardly better [than at Leipzig] and in many cases worse: had Bach gone to the Jacobikirche, Hamburg, in 1720, he may have had no more than half a dozen adult singers and 15 or so instrumentalists, plus trumpeters on occasion.'[100] The example usefully highlights another aspect of these comparisons: that in these various musical establishments singers were routinely outnumbered by instrumentalists – and usually by a significant margin. Given that the full rosters may be considered unduly 'small' today (especially for the performance of 'great' music), it is no surprise to find their vocal contingents so often dismissed as positively 'inadequate'. Yet a figure of eight singers 'seems to have represented something of a traditional norm'.[101] At one end of the spectrum Mattheson's four were still evidently considered sufficient for concerted music,[102] and at the other the suggested 16 for Leipzig would have eclipsed even Würzburg. Whereas by statute

---

[97] 'Zur Einrichtung einer Compendiosesten Hoff-Capell oder Kirchen Musique werden erfordert...'; Kirsch, *Lexikon Würzburger Hofmusiker*, 13 (compare pp. 14–15). See also Lorenz Christoph Mizler's lists in the *Neu eröffnete musikalische Bibliothek* (Leipzig) iii/1 (1746) and iv/1 (1752).

[98] Mattheson, *Der musicalische Patriot* (Hamburg, 1728), 64. See *EBC*, 118; and Rifkin, *Bach's Choral Ideal*, 34.

[99] 'In Republicken läßt sie sich eher vergrössern, als an Höfen, wenn man was darauf wenden will'; Mattheson, *Der musicalische Patriot*, 64.

[100] Peter Williams, *J. S. Bach: A Life in Music* (2007), 273.

[101] Rifkin, 'Bach's Chorus: A Preliminary Report', 750; compare *EBC*, 97–8.

[102] See *EBC*, 118.

each of Bach's choirs comprised just eight singers,[103] his stables of 'at least' 12 were explicitly designed, as we have seen, to provide insurance against absences ('so that even if one person falls ill …'). With only eight the Württemberg *Kapelle* remained vulnerable:

> We have so few vocalists that we can just fill a *quatuor* with its ripieno in the *Hofkapelle*, and should any of them fall sick, even this is not then possible, so that one can do something, say, with only two or three, which is certainly not becoming for such a noble Princely *Kapelle* …
>
> Vocalisten *haben wir so wenig, das wür just, ein* quatuor *mit seiner* Ripien *in der Hof*cappella *khönnen besetzen, solte aber ein oder der ander Krankh werden, so khan dises auch nicht geschehen, das mann als nur mit 2: oder 3: etwas machen khan, welches ja für eine so vornembe Hochfürstl:* Cappella *nicht anständig ist* …[104]

It is clear that none of these figures measures up to today's expectations of a 'proper' choir, causing many commentators to invoke various categories of additional singer – sometimes whole ranks of choirboys (at Weimar,[105] Dresden[106] and Hamburg, for example), and at Leipzig individual *externi* (day-boys) and university students.[107] As a counterbalance, we may note the widespread use of 'choirboys' as instrumentalists rather than as singers – at the Württemberg court, where in 1717 its two *Kapellknaben* both played viola in concerted music,[108] at Dresden, where the young Franz Benda did the same in the early 1720s,[109] and – not least – in Bach's Leipzig.[110] Indeed, it seems that at Hamburg later in the century the majority of boys played no role whatsoever in concerted music-making, as we learn from the responses to a series of questions put to C. P. E. Bach's daughter at his death in 1788 concerning the nature of his church duties:

---

[103] See *EBC*, 96.

[104] Johann Christoph Pez in 1714; Samantha Owens, 'Professional Women Musicians in Early 18th-Century Württemberg', *Music & Letters* 82/1 (2001), 33 (see also p. 32). By 1717 there were 10 singers (p. 36).

[105] See Joshua Rifkin, 'Bassoons, Violins and Voices: A Response to Ton Koopman', *Early Music* 25/2 (1997), 306–7.

[106] See Rifkin, 'Zelenkas Chor', 242.

[107] *EBC*, 104–11. Despite the reasonably clear stipulation at Leipzig in 1723 that 'none apart from *Inquilini* [boarders] … be admitted to the first *Cantorey*' (*EBC*, 105), there remains an apparent desire amongst scholars to enlist *externi* posthumously to its ranks; see Peter Williams, *J. S. Bach: A Life in Music*, 272.

[108] Owens, 'Professional Women Musicians', 36–7.

[109] Franz Benda, [Autobiography] (Potsdam, 1763), cited in Stockigt, *Jan Dismas Zelenka*, 69. For precedents at Dresden in 1652 see Mary E. Frandsen, *Crossing Confessional Boundaries* (2006), 444.

[110] See *EBC*, 13–15 and 98.

Q. Did he include the [14] choirboys in choruses etc., and how much did he pay them? A. No; one boy, named as choirboy in the accounts, is supported by what he receives from the board and the churches. He has to take care of the small jobs such as carrying the music to the church and back home, bringing the warming-pan to the choir loft and so on. The remaining choirboys are no concern of the director's.

Ob er die [vierzehn] Chor Knaben mit zu Chören usw. gebraucht habe, und wie viel er solche bezahlt? · Nein, von dem was er von der Kammer und den Kirchen erhält, wird ein Knabe[,] der eigentlich in den Rechnungen Chorknabe genennet wird, gehalten. Dieser muß die kleinen Geschäfte besorgen, z. B. die Noten in die Kirche und zu Hause tragen, den Feuerschapen ins Musik Chor bringen u. dgl. Die übrigen Chorknaben gehen den Director nichts an.[111]

Rosters (and payment lists) rarely tell the whole story. Certain categories of additional performer may well remain undocumented,[112] but, equally, even a complete documented body of performers had to accommodate both absences (particularly, in the case of singers, through illness) and the diverse musical requirements of different repertoires (from chant to elaborate concerted music). Whilst Bach's *Entwurff* catalogues various 'troublesome aspects of the organizational structure' of one such body (of a size perfectly in keeping with Leipzig's status), it 'simply does not allow for a reconstruction of the composition of the actual vocal-instrumental ensemble' used in Bach's own performances – not because 'essential groups of musicians' (real or imagined) are omitted,[113] but because this administrative memorandum did not need to explain what even unmusical town councillors would already have observed from week to week: that, in contrast to chorales and motets, the defining characteristic of concerted church music of the time was that it offered a platform not only to an instrumental ensemble but also to 'the selected best singers' – a choir of (four or so) concertists.[114]

---

[111] Reginald Sanders, 'Carl Philipp Emanuel Bach's Ensemble for Liturgical Performances at the Hamburg Principal Churches', *Hamburger Jahrbuch für Musikwissenschaft* 18 (2001), 394–5. In an appended 'Verzeichnis der Chorknaben', setting out in colourful detail the boys' characters, behaviour, absences and payments, there is no information of any musical nature, while the usual two *Discantisten* who sang concerted music are accounted for separately.

[112] See *EBC*, 103–15.

[113] Christoph Wolff, 'Bach's Chorus: Stomach Aches May Disappear', *Early Music* 26/3 (1998), 540 [letter].

[114] See *EBC*, 34.

Instrument/Singer Ratios (*EBC*, 117–29) If the *Entwurff* gives us a reasonable idea of Bach's aspirations for an instrumental ensemble at Leipzig but is reticent on what role(s) his vocal resources might play in concerted music, we may enquire whether the instrumental proportions themselves suggest anything about singer numbers. Conventional wisdom is that larger instrumental forces dictate larger vocal forces.[115] Generally neglected in this context are those sources – both documentary and iconographic – that detail actual performing ensembles, as opposed to musical 'establishments'. Seven clear-cut examples from Germany (from the 1720s to about 1750) show instrumentalists and singers in ratios of 2.5:1 up to 6:1,[116] including the ensemble sent from Dresden to perform in the chapel at the Hubertusburg palace under Zelenka's direction in 1739, which consisted of 14 instrumentalists and 5 singers (a ratio of almost 3:1).[117] Comparisons using estimates for five selected Leipzig works by Bach point clearly in the same direction: numbers of instruments drawn from the *Entwurff*, when set alongside numbers of singers assuming 4 concertists with or without 4 ripienists, produce ratios of the same order: from almost 2:1 up to 6:1.[118] Revealingly, similar calculations based on 12-strong and 16-strong choirs diverge quite sharply from the evidence of these sources. However numerous the instruments, a small group of concertists singing one to a part (with or without the occasional addition of a similar group of ripienists) seems to have been what concerted vocal music in Bach's time was all about.

---

[115] See most recently, for example, Uwe Wolf, 'Von der Hofkapelle zur Kantorei', 181–91. See also Rifkin's response in 'Bach's Chorus: Some New Parts, Some New Questions', 576–7.

[116] *EBC*, 128 (table 9); I have removed the two ambiguous Jena examples from consideration here.

[117] Janice B. Stockigt, 'Bach's *Missa* BWV 232^1 in the Context of Catholic Mass Settings in Dresden, 1729–1733', in *Exploring Bach's B-minor Mass*, ed. Y. Tomita, R. A. Leaver and J. Smaczny (2013), 52–3.

[118] *EBC*, 128 (table 10); I have taken account of an estimate for BWV22 based on eight singers, rather than just four.

12
Bach's Chorus: The Leipzig Line

When the facts change, I change my mind. What do you do, sir?

(John Maynard Keynes)[1]

READERS who might have preferred the so-called debate on Bach's choir to have concluded long ago – myself included – may nevertheless be curious to understand why it has dragged on for almost 30 years. The foregoing article by Andreas Glöckner may help to supply an explanation.* It illustrates how a handful of highly influential German scholars have responded to the challenge of reassessing old certainties, while its studied scepticism invites doubt: is it shaped more by scholarly thinking, or by a simple desire to bury the subject as far beyond the reach of scrutiny as possible?

This response will not restate the detailed case for single-voice choirs, which can readily be found elsewhere, but will merely explore the opposing line of thinking, represented here by Glöckner. A preliminary reminder of the divergent conclusions may not come amiss. At Leipzig the bulk of the élite Choir I's duties consisted of chant, chorales and a fairly undemanding repertoire of traditional motets, all handled not by Bach himself but by the choir's Prefect.[2] In addition, Choir I also sang Bach's own music, 'incomparably harder and more intricate' even than other concerted music allocated to Choir II.[3] This belonged to a higher order of music-making, featuring a substantial and independent instrumental ensemble and also providing a vehicle for *select* singers – a concerto for vocal concertists.[4] One argument is that these singers were responsible not

---

* This essay was written in response to Andreas Glöckner, 'On the Performing Forces of Johann Sebastian Bach's Leipzig Church Music', *Early Music* 38/2 (2010), 215–22, and first appeared adjacently in *Early Music* 38/2 (2010), 223–35.

---

[1] In reply to criticism during the Great Depression for having changed his position on monetary policy; Alfred L. Malabre, *Lost Prophets: An Insider's View of the Modern Economists* (c. 1994), 220.

[2] See Andrew Parrott, *The Essential Bach Choir* [hereinafter *EBC*] (2000), 9–12 and ch. 3 ('Repertoires').

[3] Bach's own description; *EBC*, 19.

[4] In this sense Bach's vocal *Concert Musique* may be seen as an heir to Michael Praetorius's *Concert*: 'from a whole company of musicians one selects a certain number – and especially the best and most distinguished members – and has them alternating vocally and with all manner of instruments' (*Wenn*

only for solos and duets but also – as Joshua Rifkin has reminded us[5] – for all choruses (as in much Italian oratorio and opera of the period),[6] whether with or without an occasional vocal ripieno group to 'fill out' certain types of choral writing. Traditional thinking, by contrast, holds it as self-evident that Bach would always have wanted his own choral music to be sung by all available singers, and at Leipzig preferably by 16 or so.

As we shall see, much of the effort invested in defending the conventional choir can only throw light on the following question:

> What vocal forces did Bach consider necessary in order to meet the various musical requirements of the Leipzig churches for which the Thomasschule's four choirs were responsible?[7]

That, however, is not the same as the question we are supposed to be trying to answer, which is this:

> What vocal forces did Bach choose to use in his concerted music at the two Leipzig churches served by Choir I?

The two questions are entirely distinct, yet it is repeatedly assumed that an answer to the first somehow disposes of the second as well. This necessary distinction is further obscured if we fail to differentiate between repertoires, in particular between the musical requirements of (old) polyphonic motets and (new) concerted compositions by Bach himself. (At its extreme such imprecision happily admits, as a supposed emblem of Bach's church forces for concerted music, an engraving of men and boys grouped around a lectern and singing monophonic chant.)[8]

Since 2001 Andreas Glöckner has been the *de facto* spokesman on this disputed issue for the Bach-Archiv Leipzig, a powerful academic body that produces both the *Neue Bach-Ausgabe* and the *Bach-Jahrbuch*. Throughout the two preceding decades, however, this institution's

---

man unter einer gantzen Gesellschafft der Musicorum *etzliche/ und bevorab die besten und fürnembsten Gesellen heraus sucht/ daß sie* voce humana, *und mit allerley* Instrumenten ... *umbwechseln*); *Syntagma musicum* iii (Wolfenbüttel, 1619), 5.

[5] Rifkin's original 1981 essay on the subject ('Bach's Chorus') is reproduced in *EBC* as appendix 6 (pp. 189–208), with subsequent related writings listed in the bibliography (pp. 216–17). See also Joshua Rifkin, *Bach's Choral Ideal* (2002).

[6] Pierre-Jacques Fougeroux, in his account of an opera (*Tolomeo*) directed by Handel in London in 1728, writes that hunting-horns played in the final chorus, 'ce qui faisoit des merveilles', adding in a footnote that 'The chorus is composed of only four voices' (*Le Chorus est composé seulement de quatre voix*); Winton Dean, 'A French Traveller's View of Handel's Operas', *Music & Letters* 55 (1974), 178.

[7] See *EBC*, ch. 2 ('Bach as Cantor and *Director Musices* in Leipzig'), 7–16.

[8] Christoph Weigel, 'Der Cantor' (1698), reproduced in *Die Welt der Bach Kantaten* iii, ed. C. Wolff and T. Koopman (1999), 232.

unwritten policy seems to have been 'no comment', leaving it to others to dispute Rifkin's ideas in print,[9] while at the same time sending out a clear message that his 'theory' warranted no serious consideration. 'Still waiting for the book on the subject ... I have no intention of getting entangled in the long-running "dialogue over Bach's performing forces"', wrote Christoph Wolff (the Archiv's director) some 17 years after attending Rifkin's first presentation.[10] This prolonged silence did nothing to lessen the many misapprehensions that had been allowed to gather around the subject. In an attempt to dispel these I eventually drew together as much of the salient material as possible in *The Essential Bach Choir* (hereinafter *EBC*),[11] which – together with an updated summary[12] – is here cited frequently. No equivalent attempt to set out a contrary view has yet been made, so I shall preface my remarks on Glöckner's present contribution with a review of what can be gleaned of his senior colleagues' thinking.

A pair of letters to *Early Music* in 1998–9 constitutes Christoph Wolff's first and only published contribution specific to the 'debate'. After a memorable opening salvo[13] he proceeds to make 'just two points', the more immediately relevant of which concerns Bach's famous 1730 *Entwurff*,[14] a document which, as Wolff correctly says, nevertheless 'simply does not allow for a reconstruction of the composition of the actual vocal–instrumental ensemble'.[15] Wolff's thinking is that because 'three essential groups of musicians are not included' in the *Entwurff*'s tally – notably the Thomasschule's *externi* or day-boys – Bach may well have been able to draw on significantly more than the 12 or 16 singers mentioned.[16] (In

---

[9] Notably Günther Wagner (1986), Don Smithers (1997) and Ton Koopman (1998); see *EBC*, 210–11.

[10] Christoph Wolff, 'Bach's Chorus: Stomach Aches May Disappear!', *Early Music* 26/3 (1998), 540 [letter]. For Rifkin's 1981 paper ('Bach's Chorus') see *EBC*, app. 6 (pp. 189–208).

[11] See n. 2.

[12] See Andrew Parrott, 'Vocal Ripienists and J. S. Bach's Mass in B Minor', *Eighteenth-Century Music* 7/1 (2010), appendix (pp. 25–34); reprinted in this volume, Ch. 11.

[13] This consists of an attack on Rifkin's 'unyielding pursuit of an ageing and limping hypothesis' and includes unsubstantiated allegations of 'inaccuracies, inconsistencies and irrelevancies' and 'a general disregard for contextual matters and historical scholarship'; Wolff, 'Stomach Aches', 540–1, with Rifkin's reply at 541–2.

[14] '*Kurtzer, iedoch höchstnöthiger Entwurff einer wohlbestallten Kirchen* Music' ('Brief yet highly necessary outline of a properly constituted church musical establishment'); *EBC*, 163–70 (original and translation).

[15] Wolff's second point is a defence of his *NBA* edition of BWV23, pre-dating the discovery of ripieno parts (see below).

[16] University students (*studiosi*) are accounted for in the *Entwurff* (*EBC*, 165 and 168); on the dubious validity of invoking the two other categories see *EBC*, 104–5.

fact, the school's regulations appear to exclude *externi* specifically from Choir I,[17] and Wolff's sole supporting example, offered as a demonstration of 'the necessity of maintaining both accuracy and contextual perspectives', has turned out to be an unfortunate one.)[18]

Yet none of this helps answer our question: whether all, some, or only a select few were required to sing in Bach's concerted music (as opposed to all the other music which also formed part of Choir I's duties).[19] We may note in passing that at Hamburg C. P. E. Bach simply did not 'include the choirboys in choruses etc.'[20] With Rifkin's revised understanding of a key passage in the *Entwurff*, the question remains open: rather than revealing to us how many in Choir I might '*perform every chorus*' of his own music, as has long been believed, Bach is simply addressing the Town Council on an organizational matter concerning the staffing of Choirs I–III: 'it would be preferable to *set up* each choir with 16 persons'.[21] This revised understanding has now been tacitly adopted by Wolff.[22]

A rather more straightforward question of reasoning arises in connection with two 'Solo' indications in the Dresden set of performing parts of the *Missa*, BWV232¹. These isolated markings occur against the alto's 'Qui sedes' and the bass's 'Quoniam' (their only solo movements). In his 1994 edition of the complete Mass in B minor Christoph Wolff expresses the view, held since at least 1988 and repeated as recently as 2007, that not only do these markings imply a 'vocal tutti ensemble' elsewhere in the work (which of course they do), but also that the vocal tutti they imply *necessarily* comprises more than just the five concertists (why?), and that this is therefore 'a strong argument against Joshua Rifkin's view'.[23]

---

[17] *EBC*, 105; see also Parrott, 'Vocal Ripienists', 32 n. 107.

[18] G. E. Nietzsche joined the school's Choir III at the end of 1730, whereas Wolff had already placed him in Bach's Choir I, as an *externus*; 'Bach's Chorus: An Amplification', *Early Music* 27/1 (1999), 172 [letter], where Wolff also argues that 'this guy Nietzsche can hardly have represented an isolated single case'. For my response, see *EBC*, 105–6 n. 18. There is, in short, still no known example of an *externus* ever singing in the top choir, at least, not during Bach's lifetime.

[19] As Bach plainly tells us, several pupils took part in concerted music-making as string-players; *EBC*, 13–16.

[20] Parrott, 'Vocal Ripienists', 33.

[21] See *EBC*, 93–4.

[22] Cf. *The Bach Reader*, ed. H. T. David and A. Mendel (1945/R1966), 121; and *The New Bach Reader*, rev. and enlarged C. Wolff (1998), 146. In his *The Oxford History of Western Music* ii (2005), 362, Richard Taruskin inexplicably still uses the old mistranslation from the 1945 *Bach Reader*, with the usual consequences; see Parrott, 'Vocal Ripienists', 29.

[23] Quoted in a review by Rifkin of facsimile editions of the Mass in B minor in *Notes* 44 (1988), 797–8; see also Parrott, 'Vocal Ripienists', 12–13. This argument was reiterated by both Wolff and George Stauffer at the International Symposium on 'Understanding Bach's B-minor Mass' in Belfast

This is a very large logical jump indeed, resulting from an *a priori* rejection of a one-to-a-part 'tutti', and from two unproven (and questionable) assumptions – that each copy is intended to be read by more than one singer,[24] and that the word 'Solo' functions in effect as an *instruction* to these hypothetical extra singers *not to sing*. On the contrary, this is surely a simple piece of helpful information for the singer (to the effect that 'this is a solo as distinct from another ensemble movement'),[25] for otherwise one would have to wonder why a subsequent 'Tutti' indication is lacking in these two instances, why 'Christe eleison', for example, carries no equivalent warnings for extra singers *not to sing* with the duetting sopranos, and why comparably helpful solo/tutti indications are absent from a dozen equivalent spots in the carefully prepared set of vocal parts. In short, a vocal 'tutti' is formed simply when 'all' voices sing together, be they few or many, and in this case Bach's copies are designed clearly for five concertists, with no evidence whatsoever that additional singers were anticipated.[26]

'DU WAHRER GOTT UND DAVIDS SOHN', BWV 23

The same underlying preconception – that a vocal 'tutti' or choir is *necessarily* more numerous than a one-to-a-part ensemble – is also implicit in many editions of late baroque concerted music. This is certainly the case with Bach's Leipzig audition cantata 'Du wahrer Gott und Davids Sohn', BWV23, in the *Neue Bach-Ausgabe*. In this instance – quite unusually – the edition (by Christoph Wolff) adds conjectural solo/tutti markings to a chorus (the third movement), following the precedent of Carl Friedrich Zelter's annotations to the autograph score in the early 19th century.[27] (Zelter, who as Wolff notes was 'less distant from Bach's practices than we are today', also advocated the use of solo voices for the *St Matthew Passion*'s first choir.)[28] The first such editorial 'solo' indication appears at a duet section in bar 32, confirming the conventional understanding that the first vocal entry (at bar 9) is self-evidently intended for a four-part 'choir' of today's type (see Ex. 12.1).

With the re-emergence in 1999 of the *Alt-Bachische Archiv* and with it an unknown set of vocal ripieno parts to this work (which Rifkin had

    (November 2007), where it met with no discernible objections from their fellow panellists.

[24] See *EBC*, ch. 5.

[25] For a discussion of these and analogous markings in the instrumental parts see Rifkin, review in *Notes*, 797–8.

[26] For a full survey of implications for ripienists in the Mass in B minor, see Parrott, 'Vocal Ripienists'.

[27] Wolff, 'Bach's Chorus: Stomach Aches', 540.

[28] A. Glöckner, 'Zelter und Mendelssohn – Zur "Wiederentdeckung" der Matthäus-Passion im Jahre 1829', *Bach-Jahrbuch 2004*, 138.

Ex. 12.1 J. S. Bach, Cantata 'Du wahrer Gott und Davids Sohn', BWV 23, iii, bars 1–27

Ex. 12.1 *continued*

Ex. 12.1 *continued*

correctly postulated for its 1723 first performance)[29] a unique opportunity arose to test the accuracy of this conventional assumption.[30] And while these 'new' parts helpfully confirm the majority of Zelter's (and therefore Wolff's) markings, they also tell us something new about the opening of this chorus, namely that the ripienists *do not sing* at bar 9 but enter only at bar 24 where the voice parts are joined by the full instrumental forces. It emerges, then, not only that ripienists are employed in less than half of all the vocal writing (in recurring variants of a simple eight-bar phrase, always supported by the full instrumental ensemble), but also that the very opening vocal statement of the chorus is unquestionably intended for four concertists alone – for the one-to-a-part choir.

And this, as it happens, is precisely what I had earlier predicted, simply by using as a model Bach's own explicit practices in the handful of other works with indications or parts for ripienists (*EBC*, ch. 6):[31]

---

[29] Wolff had considered it 'not very likely' that the original set of parts for BWV23 included ripieno copies; *Bach: Essays on his Life and Music* (1991), 135. For the reasoning behind Rifkin's contrary view, see his *Bach's Choral Ideal*, 31.

[30] See Parrott, 'Vocal Ripienists', 15–16.

[31] See also Parrott, 'Vocal Ripienists', 13–14.

'my own impression ... is that any ripieno parts prepared under Bach's supervision would have begun later [than in Wolff's edition], with the instrumentally doubled repetition of this phrase at bar 24.'[32] Two principles are at play here. The first is Bach's use of a vocal ripieno to 'reinforce the full ensemble as it takes up musical ideas first introduced by concertists' (as in BWV21/6).[33] The second – not discussed in *EBC* – has far wider implications and may be addressed by looking again at bars 9–17 of Ex. 12.1 and then asking: what proven precedent is there for choral passages accompanied by continuo but *without instrumental ensemble* to be sung by ripienists as well as concertists? Put another way: do Bach's own works with ripieno parts contain comparably extended passages in which concertists and ripienists sing in unison but without orchestral support? The short answer to this last question appears to be 'no'. In half of the available relevant models such writing simply does not occur, and in another quarter its duration is negligible (less than three bars' worth), while at the opposite extreme the 16 consecutive bars that launch the *St Matthew Passion*'s 'Sind Blitze, sind Donner in Wolken verschwunden' prove utterly exceptional.[34]

In his report on the newly discovered material, Wolff neither draws attention to this one-to-a-part vocal opening nor hints at any discrepancy between his edition and the evidence of the parts.[35] Doubtless some will be tempted to dismiss the matter as an eight-bar wonder. Yet arguably these eight bars go to the very heart of the question: do we correctly understand how Bach chose to deploy singers in his own choral music? Certainly they demonstrate that the ever-present solo-voiced concertists' choir is easily overlooked, that the lessons of Bach's surviving ripieno parts are well worth learning, and that the default assumption, whereby all choral writing is taken to demand choirs of more than one singer per part, is at the very least questionable. We should also acknowledge that the sole cause of this particular inadvertent misrepresentation of Bach's intentions (albeit in just a single phrase) has been the continuing failure of Leipzig's senior Bach scholars to come to terms with Rifkin's findings.[36] And we must also conclude that, while Christoph Wolff's position is very clear, he is still far from setting out a case that might support it.

---

[32] *EBC*, 75 n. 13; strictly speaking, the voice parts are not so much 'doubled' as supported by the instrumental ensemble.

[33] *EBC*, 64–5, 74.

[34] See Parrott, 'Vocal Ripienists', 19–20 (inc. table 5).

[35] Christoph Wolff, 'Zurück in Berlin: Das Notenarchiv der Sing-Akademie. Bericht über eine erste Bestandaufnahme. Originale Ripienstimmen zu BWV23', *Bach-Jahrbuch 2002*, 167–9, 179. See also Joshua Rifkin, 'Bach's Chorus: Some New Parts, Some New Questions', *Early Music* 31/4 (2003), 573–80.

[36] The *NBA* volume containing BWV23 is dated 1992, a full decade after Rifkin first shared his thinking with other scholars.

Wolff's senior colleague Hans-Joachim Schulze, a former director of the Bach-Archiv, has never disguised his disdain for 'an altogether different view of historically "correct" performance practice' from his own,[37] and is in any case sceptical 'of recovering historical practice in its essential parameters and of drawing from it conclusions for how to proceed in the present and future'.[38] His withering review of the 2003 German edition of *EBC*, while failing to identify a single factual error, seeks instead to dismiss its entire thesis at a single stroke by discrediting the notion of any 'common practice in Lutheran Germany of Bach's time', on which I am supposed to have relied.[39] Yet, as far as the basic principles of concerted music are concerned, the wide range of evidence I have presented does indeed support such a notion, and it seems fairly clear that Schulze simply holds a *different* view of what that 'common practice' was. (I note that elsewhere Schulze himself draws freely on data from Berlin, Dresden, Gotha, Halle, Hamburg, Lübeck, Meiningen and Weissenfels in order better to understand Bach's own practices at Cöthen, Leipzig and Weimar,[40] while Glöckner has specifically acknowledged that 'circumstances in the Thomasschule choirs at Leipzig did not differ fundamentally from those in other mid-German municipal Cantoreyen'.)[41] These common principles by no means precluded local variation,[42] and of course good scholarship must always be alert to unexpected diversity and to all fundamental distinctions – city/court, town/village, Catholic/

---

[37] Hans-Joachim Schulze, 'Johann Sebastian Bach's Orchestra: Some UnansweredQuestions', *Early Music* 17/1 (1989), 14.

[38] '... die historische Praxis in ihren wesentlichen Parametern wiederzugewinnen und daraus Folgerungen für die gegenwärtige und künftige Verfahrensweise zu ziehen'; Hans-Joachim Schulze, *Bach stilgerecht aufführen: Wunschbild und Wirklichkeit* (1991), 28. This opinion is echoed by Glöckner in his introduction.

[39] Hans-Joachim Schulze, *Bach-Jahrbuch* 2003, 267–70. Schulze is undoubtedly irked at my book's having been 'highly praised' (p. 270), and perhaps also – if he has read my footnotes – by an illustration from his own work of the 'danger of holding preconceived ideas'; *EBC*, 131.

[40] Schulze, 'Johann Sebastian Bach's Orchestra', 3–15.

[41] '[... es wird übersehen,] daß sich die Verhältnisse am Leipziger Thomaskantorat nicht prinzipiell von denen in andern mitteldeutschen Stadtkantoreien unterschieden'; Andreas Glöckner, 'Bemerkungen zur vokalen und instrumentalen Besetzung von Bachs Leipziger Ensemblewerken', in *Vom Klang der Zeit: Besetzung, Bearbeitung und Aufführungspraxis bei Johann Sebastian Bach: Klaus Hofmann zum 65. Geburtstag*, ed. U. Bartels and U. Wolf (c. 2004), 86.

[42] Naturally enough, some establishments (buildings, composers, idioms) used a vocal ripieno more than others, but local differences are sometimes more apparent than real: organ pitch, for example, might vary from church to church (as Glöckner mentions), but vocal works were frequently transposed precisely in order to return the music to something like its original intended sounding pitch level.

Lutheran, north/south and so on. Indeed, in the present case it is precisely the repeated blurring of other critical distinctions – traditional motet/new concerted music, soloist-chorister/concertist-ripienist, institutional roster/performer line-up – that continues to cause so much confusion.

Issues of this sort recur in the present contribution from one of Schulze's protégés, Andreas Glöckner.[43] In his somewhat opaque introduction it is quality and quantity that are seemingly confused; certainly to link one-to-a-part singing in the concerted music of Bach's day to any simple 'deficit' or numerical 'inadequacy' of singers, as other scholars have done,[44] would be to perpetuate another fundamental misconception.[45] There is mention of 'technical problems in performing Bach's compositions' but not of how such problems might have been overcome (or caused?) by the numbers of singers proposed. As on earlier occasions, Glöckner's principal focus is 'Bach's own specifications' for the Thomasschule's four choirs, and here – yet again – he fails to draw critical distinctions: between concerted music and the traditional motet (with their different ways of deploying singers),[46] between the repertories of Choirs I and III (only one of which performed Bach's music), and between a simple institutional choir list and a vocal line-up for the single most demanding musical item within a lengthy church service (see above).[47]

---

[43] Glöckner is happy, for example, to project 'an old practice' from the mid-1860s, as recorded 50 or so years later, on to the first half of the 18th century; see his citing of Bernhard F. Richter, at p. 219.

[44] See Parrott, 'Vocal Ripienists', 30–2.

[45] See *EBC*, 114. On the other hand, the origins of concerted music were believed to have such a connection: according to Praetorius, Lodovico Viadana's innovative approach began 'when he saw that a motet for 5, 6, or more voices was often sung to the organ, but that there were seldom more than two or three singers or *cantores*, especially in monasteries, and that the symphony was thus deprived of much of its charm and elegance by the lack of the other parts' (*dieweil er gesehen/ daß offtmals eine Mutet von 5. 6. oder mehr Stimmen in die Orgel gesungen worden/ der Sänger oder* Cantorn *aber/ sonderlich in den Klöstern/ selten uber zwey oder drey gewesen/ und also aus mangel der andern Stimmen der* Symphony *an Lieblikeit und Zierde viel entzogen*); Praetorius, *Syntagma musicum* iii, 4, in a rather inaccurate paraphrase of the preface to Viadana's *Cento concerti ecclesiastici* (Venice, 1602).

[46] Aided by the misleadingly accommodating term *Figuralmusik* (figural music), Glöckner chooses not to discriminate between two very different genres of composition: on the one hand, elaborate newly composed concerted music involving instruments (Bach's famously 'intricate' works) and, on the other, the traditional motet repertoire (dating from the late 16th and early 17th centuries, vastly simpler than Bach's own motets, and left to prefects to direct). Each had its own performance requirements. The one is the supposed subject of Glöckner's essay, the other is not. See *EBC*, 17–27.

[47] In the space of a single sentence Glöckner manages to confuse Choir I with the Thomasschule's entire body of singers, concerted music with the

Thus, for example, Choir III rosters written on copies of the 200-year-old motet-style passion settings by Johann Walter can scarcely have any real bearing on Choir I's performances of Bach's concerted music. Similarly irrelevant is the report of 'unexpected' additional singers during Doles's tenure, which relates explicitly to 'the oft-performed motets'. Moreover, the Thomasschule regulations to which Glöckner gives particular weight (under his third heading) also concern the motet rather than 'the church cantata', as Rifkin explained as long ago as 1995;[48] consequently they cannot be held to substantiate any of Glöckner's subsequent claims about copy-sharing, vocal quartets, instruments, and Bach's own performance copies.

SINGER/INSTRUMENT RATIOS

A MARKED tendency to inflate singer numbers runs through Glöckner's work.[49] In briefly invoking 'students and other assistants' he picks up Wolff's earlier point about 'essential groups of musicians' not included in the *Entwurff* (see above).[50] What he does not trouble to do, however, is to enquire how many singers might have been among them and what their

---

full range of the choir's musical duties, and (by means of the slippery term *Figuralmusik*) concerted music with the old motet repertoire: 'And why would Leipzig city council have maintained 54 or 55 costly places in the *Alumnat* if as a rule only four *Alumnen* were needed to sing in the concerted music ...?'; p. 218.

[48] Joshua Rifkin, 'Bach's Chorus: Some Red Herrings', *Journal of Musicological Research* 14 (1995), 224–5, and more particularly the same author's 'Chorliste und Chorgröße bei Johann Sebastian Bach. Neue Überlegungen zu einem alten Thema', *Bach-Jahrbuch 2012*, 121–43.

[49] Three examples: (1) the assertion that Weimar's seven singers were 'supplemented with Bach's private students' is pure conjecture, and to add that 'we have no *further* information' about this is therefore doubly misleading as well as singularly uninformative; (2) there is no evidence for Glöckner's implication that Bach's 'larger cast' for a repeat performance of the Störmthal cantata BWV194 back in Leipzig would have included a 'larger' number of *singers*; (3) while Bach evidently had 'additional musicians ... at his disposal' from March 1729, only one of the 10 works listed in Glöckner's n. 43 – BWV110 – demonstrates the use of extra *singers*. Nowhere does Glöckner make any counterbalancing mention of Bach's explicit use of pupils as *players*; see n. 19 above.

[50] Glöckner's article unfortunately employs the term 'student' variously for pupils of the school and, as here, for students of the university (*studiosi*). When he writes of 'student helpers' there is potential for further confusion, in that Wolff's third category of additional musician consists of other 'helpers', whose inclusion is in any case scarcely justified by the single reference given; see Wolff, 'Bach's Chorus: Stomach Aches', 540–1; and *EBC*, 104.

Illus. 12.1 Fold-out illustration from Christian Siegismund Georgi, *Wittenbergische Jubel-Geschichte* (Wittenberg, 1756); London, British Library MS 9930, fol. 34(1)

role may have been. (Of the additional performers that are documented no more than two in any one year were singers.)[51]

In his final section ('Indications of the number of performers') Glöckner cites three well-known references to mixed ensembles of up to 40 or so persons[52] – and in so doing presents me with an opportunity to revisit the issue of singer/instrument ratios within large ensembles (*EBC*, ch. 9), a topic which appears to have attracted little or no comment elsewhere. The presumed relevance of Glöckner's references hangs on the assumption that forces of this sort would necessarily contain large numbers of singers, at least 12 and perhaps even 20 or more.[53] However, neither Gesner (1738), whose context is more rhetorical than documentary,[54] nor Trömer (1745), pithy in the extreme,[55] gives us any such details. In describing Hoffmann's Collegium Musicum, Stölzel (1740) proves decidedly more obliging,[56] though Glöckner's selective reporting of him turns out to be quite the opposite. First, the reader deserves to be informed that in this context 'A choir of such dimensions'[57] refers not to a *vocal* choir but – quite

---

[51] *EBC*, ch. 8, especially pp. 109–10. In most or perhaps all cases these supernumerary singers were basses.

[52] On the use of 40 as rhetorical topos, see Rifkin, 'Bach's Chorus: Some Red Herrings', 229. See also Parrott, 'Vocal Ripienists', 28 n. 77.

[53] Earlier, a whiff of red herring accompanies mention of one-to-a-part *instrumental* scoring (and recurs when BWV174 is cited): one-to-a-part vocal scoring carries with it no *necessary* implication of single strings.

[54] *EBC*, 174.

[55] 'There were more than 40 musicians in total'; *EBC*, 171.

[56] *EBC*, 136.

[57] More correctly, simply 'Such a choir', referring back to its membership of 'In all ... probably 40 persons'; *EBC*, 136.

unambiguously – to the mixed ensemble as a whole. Second, Glöckner (following Schulze's example)[58] has inexcusably withheld Stölzel's explicit information about its vocal component: not the anticipated dozen or more singers, but a four-person *Singechor* comprising one each of soprano, alto, tenor and bass[59] – a one-to-a-part choir at the head of an exceptionally large and illustrious musical body (founded by Telemann), right at the heart of Leipzig's musical life just a decade or so before Bach's arrival in the city.

As Trömer implies, a Lutheran university town mounting major outdoor celebrations for the Elector of Saxony regarded a mixed ensemble of around 40 musicians as suitably grand;[60] but is it possible to estimate the number of singers within such a group? Glöckner clearly wishes us to imagine 'choirs' of 16 and more singers, giving ratios of at least two of vocalists to every three instrumentalists (2:3). By contrast, my earlier analysis of relatively reliable documentary and iconographic sources from mid-18th-century Germany (*EBC*, ch. 9) shows singers being outnumbered by instrumentalists in significantly steeper ratios, ranging from roughly 2:5 to 1:7. In other words, in each of those particular examples there are well over twice as many instrumentalists as singers, and on occasion up to seven times as many[61] – statistics which fly in the face of today's common

---

[58] Schulze, *Bach stilgerecht aufführen*, 23.

[59] *EBC*, 136.

[60] Trömer's example relates to the outdoor performance in Leipzig of a Bach cantata on the occasion of the Elector's birthday in 1727; see *Bach-Dokumente* ii, ed. W. Neumann and H.-J. Schulze (1969), 164–7. See also Rifkin, 'Bach's Chorus: Some Red Herrings', 289.

[61] *EBC*, 128. Stölzel's 4 singers to ('probably') 36 instruments stretches this a little with its 1:9 ratio, reminding us perhaps that the numbers he gives are

Illus. 12.2 Detail from C. S. Georgi, *Wittenbergische Jubel-Geschichte*, showing the musical ensemble

expectation that a vocal choir should rarely be smaller than the orchestra that accompanies it, and may often be considerably larger.

A new and exceptionally detailed source makes it possible to test the reliability of these earlier statistics. While I have no pertinent information on how Leipzig marked the 1755 centennial anniversary of the Peace of Augsburg (1555),[62] little more than 40 miles away the university town of Wittenberg (now Lutherstadt Wittenberg) held elaborate celebrations, arranged 'at the most gracious command' of the Elector and all duly recorded in painstaking detail by the university's Professor of

---

of the *membership* of a Collegium Musicum and do not necessarily relate to any single performance. Even with 'just' 12 singers (to 28 instruments) those ratios would be stretched in the opposite direction (3:7).

[62] But see Michael Maul, 'Der 200. Jahrestag des Augsburger Religionsfriedens (1755) und die Leipziger Bach-Pflege in der zweiten Hälfte des 18. Jahrhunderts', *Bach-Jahrbuch* 2000, 101–18.

Theology for a handsome book published the following year.[63] A fold-out engraving included in the book shows a procession heading towards the Schloßkirche (where Luther posted his 95 theses in 1517); see Illus. 12.1. More or less in the middle of the procession comes a 41-strong musical ensemble; Illus. 12.2. With the engraving is the following caption:

Chorus Musicus, *bestehend*	Chorus Musicus, consisting
a) *aus 2 Hautboisten, mit Waldhörnern,*	a) of 2 oboists, with [2] horns,
b) *8 Violinen in zwey Reyhen,*	b) 8 violins in two rows,
c) *2 Hautboisten,*	c) 2 oboists,
d) *8 Violinen in zwey Reyhen,*	d) 8 violins in two rows,
e) *4 Fleut-Travers,*	e) 4 transverse flutes,
f) *8 Sänger, vier in einer Reyhe,*	f) 8 singers, four in a row,
g) *4 Violono Cello in zwey Reyhen,*	g) 4 violoncellos in two rows,[64]
h) *der grosse Violon, und 2 Fagotti zu beyden Seiten.*	h) the big violone, and 2 bassoons on either side.

The accompanying text explains:

> This choir alternated with the trumpets and kettledrums, and the singers were singing the following march ... 'Frohlocket mit Jubel-Gesangen, lobsinget ...'

> *Dieses Chor wechselte mit den Trompeten und Paucken ab, und sungen die Sänger folgenden March dabey ... Frohlocket mit Jubel-Gesangen, lobsinget ...*[65]

Though the 'March' being performed by this *Chorus Musicus* is lost and its composer unidentified,[66] what is remarkable here is that the picture and its accompanying text match in every detail and therefore afford us the rare opportunity of knowing the precise distribution of the musical forces involved in a specific performance.

Here then is a further example of a large mixed ensemble performing outdoors, like Trömer's, and numbering around 40. Its tally of 33 instrumentalists is undoubtedly exceptionally high, and with 21 strings and 10 woodwind instruments its numbers are effectively double those given by Bach in his 1730 *Entwurff*. Although the eight singers are not particularly likely to have functioned as distinct concertists and ripienists in a necessarily straightforward processional work for outdoor use, their two

---

[63] '... *auf allergnädigsten Befehl Sr. Königl. Maj. in Pohlen und Chur-Fürstl. Durchl. zu Sachsen, ec.*'; Christian Siegismund Georgi, *Wittenbergische Jubel-Geschichte* (Wittenberg, 1756), title-page.

[64] These portable 'violoncellos' are perhaps of the *da spalla* variety; see Marc Vanscheeuwijck, 'Recent Re-evaluations of the Baroque Cello and what they might mean for Performing the Music of J. S. Bach', *Early Music* 38/2 (2010), 181–92; and Charles Medlam, *Approaches to the Bach Cello Suites* (2013), 36–47.

[65] Georgi, *Wittenbergische Jubel-Geschichte*, 47.

[66] The two obvious candidates are Johann Philipp Wetzke and M. Jahn.

rows of four nevertheless suggest the traditional pairing of 4 concertists and (just) 4 ripienists called for in a handful of Bach's own works (see *EBC*, ch. 6). Moreover, this singer/instrument ratio of 8:33 (roughly 1:4) falls neatly in the middle of the range the earlier statistics would have predicted, while a ratio of, say, 16:25 (roughly 2:3) – implicit in everything Glöckner has written – falls well outside it. The evidence is reasonably clear: large instrumental forces do not imply comparably large vocal forces (nor do single voices necessarily imply single strings).[67]

CONCLUSION

MORE than a quarter of a century after Joshua Rifkin first opened up this whole subject for consideration, the updated Dutch edition of Christoph Wolff's major biography of Bach confidently declares:

> The normal composition of the vocal ensemble for church music given in Bach's 1730 *Entwurff* and called into question by Andrew Parrott – three singers of each voice range – is confirmed by two historical choir lists [for Choir I] respectively from 1729, with 12 singers ..., and 1744–5, with 17 singers ...[68]

By this account, what I have called into question – no mention of Rifkin in this scenario[69] – is nothing less than *Bach's own explicit data*, rather than a hand-me-down interpretation of it. And this alleged challenge is now supposed to have been dealt a fatal blow by a pair of choir lists. We are back where we started. In reality, what Bach says in the *Entwurff* has never been doubted: the institutional size of his Choir I has never been the issue. What is mystifying, and grows more so with each passing year, is why 'evidence' of this sort is still thought to provide a satisfactory response, when it does not even begin to address the point at hand.

While Wolff has chosen not to develop a case for his position, Schulze's stance has been to feign incredulity. If the single-voiced choir had been

---

[67] Recent corroboration of such ratios is also provided by details of an ensemble which was sent from Dresden in 1739 to perform under Zelenka's direction in the chapel at the Hubertusburg palace; it consisted of 5 singers (SAATB) and 14 instrumentalists (8 strings, 5 woodwind, organ), a singer/instrument ratio of almost 1:3. See Janice B. Stockigt, '"After six weeks": Music for the Churching Ceremonies of Maria Josepha, Electoral Princess of Saxony and Queen of Poland', in *Identity and Locality in Early European Music, 1028–1740*, ed. J. Stoessel (2009), 205.

[68] 'Die in Bachs Entwurff von 1730 geforderte, von Andrew Parrott in Zweifel gezogene Normalbesetzung des kirchenmusikalischen Vokalensembles von je drei Sängern pro Stimmlage wird durch zwei historische Chorlisten von 1729 mit 12 Sängern für den von Bach geleiteten Chor I bzw. 1744–45 mit 17 Sängern für Chor I bestätigt'; Christoph Wolff, *Johann Sebastian Bach* (Dutch edition, 2007), online preface.

[69] Rifkin's name is also consistently absent elsewhere in Wolff's biography.

part of common practice, he argues, then its '"discovery" would not have had to wait until the 21st century'. (Again, Rifkin's 20th-century achievements are pointedly ignored.) This is an astonishing statement to find from an historian; if taken as a general principle, it would imply that the passage of time can itself confer truth, since any deficiency in the orthodox belief would inevitably have been discovered earlier.[70] Yet a mind that is open rather than wedded to a particular theory would by now surely be exercised by the following questions. If the choir of 12 or more really was regarded as a fundamental requirement of concerted choral writing,

- why was a ripieno group so often explicitly regarded as optional? (*EBC*, ch. 4)
- how could ripienists possibly have read from the concertists' copies, given that they 'must be separately positioned in a place apart from the concertists'?[71] (*EBC*, ch. 5)
- why does Bach's (rare) ripieno writing almost always allow concertists pride of place? (*EBC*, ch. 6); and – not least –
- why does specific evidence for its use continue to be so elusive?

Meanwhile, it has fallen to Andreas Glöckner to maintain the party line, with a dedication that is (as recorded above) repeatedly heedless of flaws in logic, discrimination, and detail. (Here too Rifkin's name is duly suppressed.)[72] His technique for promoting the traditional image of Bach's choir is simple and (evidently) effective.[73] By omitting even to acknowledge inherent ambiguities in the familiar evidence – let alone any previous

---

[70] Schulze also writes that 'strictly speaking there should have been a trace of it', thereby magisterially dismissing each and every 'trace' that he wishes not to have to acknowledge in a wide range of musical, theoretical, documentary and iconographical sources (... *müßte sich genaugenommen irgendwo eine Spur davon finden lassen und dürfte die "Entdeckung" nicht dem 21. Jahrhundert vorbehalten geblieben sein*); Schulze, *Bach-Jahrbuch* 2003, 269.

[71] *EBC*, 38. Elsewhere Glöckner has misread the iconographical evidence of the well-known frontispiece to *Unfehlbare Engel-Freude* (Leipzig, 1710); Glöckner, 'Bemerkungen zur vokalen und instrumentalen Besetzung', 92; and see *EBC*, 54–5. How exactly would three separately positioned quartets of singers share a single set of SATB copies?

[72] We may also note that the *Bach-Jahrbuch* has not seen fit to review Rifkin's important monograph *Bach's Choral Ideal* (published in Dortmund), presumably on the grounds that, together with several relevant articles which appear to have been ignored, it is written in English.

[73] A paper by George B. Stauffer begins: 'Assuming that Andreas Glöckner's recent study of the choirs at the St Thomas School in Leipzig ... has finally demonstrated once and for all that Bach did indeed have a 'chorus' at his disposal for the performance of his sacred vocal works ...'; 'The *Symbolum Nicenum* of the B-minor Mass and Bach's Late Choral Ideal', presented at the International Symposium on 'Understanding Bach's B-minor Mass' (Belfast, 2007). See also Markus Rathey, book review in *Bach-Jahrbuch* 2006, 313.

discussion of them – he succeeds in reassuring those who share his preconceptions that there is really no need to explore the matter further. His chosen starting-point is therefore the confident if rather premature conclusion stated at the end of his introduction: 'we know ... how [Bach] wished to cast his instrumental and vocal forces'.[74]

And so the dance continues, as the scholarly response to Rifkin's unwelcome insights goes round in circles. When witnessing the Bach-Archiv Leipzig operating so far below its customary high ideals and standards, it is virtually impossible not to suspect that external factors have somehow overridden the straightforward desire to learn as much as possible about the workings of Bach's music. Future generations may develop a clearer view of how this has happened, but for the present what matters is that bright young Bach scholars, not least in Germany, should feel free to engage openly with the subject, whatever their elders may think of it.

POSTSCRIPT (2015)

For a further response to the article by Andreas Glöckner discussed above see Joshua Rifkin, 'Bach's Chorus: Against the Wall', *Early Music* 38/3 (2010), 437–9. The 'dance' continued the following year with Glöckner's '"The ripienists must also be at least eight, namely two for each part": The Leipzig Line of 1730 – Some Observations', *Early Music* 39/4 (2011), 575–86. This duly received a succinct reply from Rifkin: 'Bach's Chorus: More of the Same', *Early Music* 40/1 (2012), 165–6.

---

[74] The irony is that, while Bach's *Entwurff* in fact fails to tell us what we most want to know about the performance of his own music, it does strongly imply that *motets* could be sung one-on-a-part. These traditional motets, most of them in eight parts, are evidently a specific reason for his wanting at least three singers of each voice range assigned to each 'musical' choir: 'so that even if one person falls ill ... at least a two-choir motet can be sung'; see EBC, 20–7, 167.

13

J. S. Bach's *Trauer-Music* for Prince Leopold: Clarification and Reconstruction

There remained for him in Leipzig the melancholy satisfaction of providing the funeral music for his so dearly beloved Prince, and of performing it in person in Cöthen ...

(obituary of J. S. Bach)[1]

WITH the unexpected death of the 33-year-old Prince Leopold of Anhalt-Cöthen in November 1728 it fell to J. S. Bach as the Prince's honorary (or 'non-resident') *Capellmeister* and erstwhile employee to supply and supervise music for the ensuing funeral ceremonies. These were set for the following spring, doubtless to allow the fullest possible attendance from around the principality and further afield, while over the winter months the Prince's body (duly embalmed, one must presume) lay in Cöthen's small court chapel.[2] At the centre of elaborate funeral proceedings, painstakingly documented in court records,[3] were

- a Burial Service (*Beysetzung*), held late at night on 23 March (1729) and lasting until about two in the morning, and
- a Memorial Service (*Gedächtniß Predigt*), following just a few hours later on the morning of 24 March.

Both services were held in the town's Calvinist Jacobikirche, and each included 'Trauer *Musique*' (music of mourning).[4] No musical source survives, however, and the only real clue to Bach's music comes

First appeared in Early Music 34/4 (2011), 587–95.

[1] 'Er hatte noch das traurige Vergnügen, seinem so innig geliebten Fürsten, die Leichenmusic von Leipzig aus, zu verfertigen, und sie in Person in Cöthen aufzuführen'. Obituary by C. P. E. Bach and J. F. Agricola, in L. C. Mizler, *Musikalische Bibliothek* (Leipzig, 1754); *Bach-Dokumente* iii (1972), 84 (no. 666).

[2] The 'Balsamirung' of Margrave Carl Wilhelm is documented at Karlsruhe in 1738; see Klaus Häfner, *Der badische Hofkapellmeister Johann Melchior Molter (1696–1765) in seiner Zeit: Dokumente und Bilder zu Leben und Werk* (1996), 142.

[3] See Friedrich Smend, *Bach in Köthen* (1951), 80–1; see also English version, ed. and rev. S. Daw (1985), 97.

[4] A prompt payment was made on 25 March to the various musicians 'who helped perform music of mourning on the evening of 23 March at the Burial and on 24 March at the Memorial Service' ('*so den 23 Martij abends bey der*

Trauer=MUSIC,
bey der
Dem Weyland
Durchlauchtigsten Fürsten und Herrn,
HERRN
**Leopolden,**
Fürsten zu Anhalt,
Herzogen zu Sachsen, Engern und Westphalen, Grafen zu Ascanien, Herrn zu Bernburg und Zerbst ꝛc
in der Reformirten **Stadt=** und Cathedral - **Kirchen zu Cöthen**
am 24ten Martii 1729.
gehaltenen Gedächtnüß=Predigt
unterthänigst aufgeführet
Von
Sr. Hoch=seeligsten Durchlauchtigkeit
ehemahligen **Capell=Meister,**
Johann Sebastian Bach.

Cöthen, druckts Johann Christoph Schondorff.

Illus. 13.1 Title-page of the libretto [by Picander] of J. S. Bach's *Trauer-Music* for Prince Leopold [1729]

instead in the form of a libretto, headed in its earliest printed version 'Trauer-Music ... most humbly performed at the Memorial Service held on 24 March 1729'[5] (see Illus. 13.1). This may have been intended for use by those attending the ceremonies but is perhaps more likely to be a commemorative publication. Its text is known to be by 'Picander' (Christian Friedrich Henrici, the young Leipzig-based poet also responsible for the libretto of the *St Matthew Passion*) and is a substantial one in four parts (with a total of 24 movements), constituting the lost work catalogued today as *Klagt, Kinder, klagt es aller Welt*, BWV244a ('Let your lamentations, children, be heard by all the world').[6] No additional text is known, yet today's scholarly literature, taking its lead from Friedrich Smend (to whom we owe much of the documentation on which this article is based), tells of not one but 'two large-scale works' by Bach – one for each service.[7] Three claims are made in the present article: (1) that the notion of *two* lost Cöthen funeral compositions may now safely be rejected, (2) that the missing music may be more fully recoverable than has previously been believed, and (3) that the relationship of the *Trauer-Music* to the Memorial Service is not straightforward. These conclusions have led me to attempt a reconstructed setting (necessarily speculative) of the complete Cöthen *Trauer-Music* text, an enterprise which has benefited from the experience of performing the result first in concert (in 2004) and more recently on disc.[8]

My reasons for rejecting the idea of a second composition will emerge in due course, but it may be helpful at this stage to mention an earlier false trail. A *Trauer-Cantate* in three parts, intriguingly containing 'double choruses of uncommon splendour and most moving expression', is known to have been in the possession of Bach's early biographer J. N. Forkel, who believed it to be Bach's music for Prince Leopold's burial;[9] its subsequent disappearance, soon after Forkel's death in 1818, only perpetuated this

---

Beysetzung und am 24 Martij *bey der Leichen Predigt die Trauer* Musiquen ... *machen geholffen'*); *Bach-Dokumente* ii (1969), 190–1 (no. 259).

[5] '*Trauer-*MUSIC ... *am 24ten Martii 1729. gehaltenen Gedächtnüß-Predigt unterthänigst aufgeführet*'.

[6] There are three sources of the text: 1) the early printed libretto referred to above, 2) an earlier manuscript version, lacking Part IV (but with a heading for it), and 3) a later printed version, in Picander's *Ernst-Scherzhaffte und Satyrische Gedichte* iii (Leipzig, 1732). See Smend, *Bach in Köthen*, 205.

[7] Christoph Wolff, *Johann Sebastian Bach: The Learned Musician* (2000), 461. See Smend, *Bach in Köthen*, 86, 90–1, 169.

[8] The first performance of the reconstruction was given in New York in 2004 by the New York Collegium (dir. Andrew Parrott), and a recording made in 2010 by the Taverner Consort & Players (dir. Andrew Parrott) was issued by Avie Records in 2011: *J. S. Bach, Trauer-Music: Music to Mourn Prince Leopold*. An edition of the reconstruction is forthcoming.

[9] '... *bey der Begräbniss-Feyer seines geliebten Fürsten Leopold zu Cöthen ... aufgeführt*'; '*Doppelchöre von ungemeiner Pracht und vom rührendsten*

Table 13.1 Sources of arias and choruses

PART I		
1 *chorus*	Klagt, Kinder, klagt es aller Welt	
	Laß, Fürstin, laß noch einen Strahl (TO/1)	
3 *aria*	Weh und Ach kränckt die Seelen tausendfach	
	Buß und Reu knirscht das Sündenherz entzwei (MP/6)	
5 *aria*	Zage nur, du treues Land	
	Blute nur, du liebes Herz (MP/8)	
7 *chorus*	Komm wieder, teurer Fürstengeist	
	Doch, Königin! du stirbest nicht (TO/10)	
PART II		
3 *aria*	Erhalte mich <u>in der</u> Hälfte meiner Tage	
	Erbarme dich, <u>mein Gott, um</u> meiner Zähren willen (MP/39)	
5 *aria*	Mit Freuden sey die Welt verlassen	
	Aus Liebe will mein Heiland sterben (MP/49)	
PART III		
1 *aria*	Laß, Leopold, Dich nicht begraben	
	Komm, süßes Kreuz, so will ich sagen (MP/57)	
3 *aria*	Wird auch gleich nach tausend Zähren	
	Gerne will ich mich bequemen (MP/23)	
5 *aria/chorus*	Geh, Leopold, zu Deiner <u>Ruh</u>[e]	
	Ich will bei meinem Jesu <u>wachen</u> (MP/20)	
PART IV		
1 *aria*	Bleibet nun in eurer Ruh	
	Mache dich, mein Herze, rein (MP/65)	
3 *aria*	Hemme dein gequältes Kränken	
	Ich will dir mein Herze schenken (MP/13)	
5 *chorus*	Die Augen sehn nach Deiner Leiche	
	Wir setzen uns mit Tränen nieder (MP/68)	

MP = *St Matthew Passion*, TO = *Trauer Ode*

<u>Underlinings</u> draw attention to the occasional minor discrepancy of versification between model and parody texts

belief and eventually enshrined the work as a missing companion to *Klagt, Kinder*. In recent years, however, the music in question has been very convincingly identified as the *Zweychörige Trauermusik* (1724) for Duke Ernst Ludwig of Meiningen – composed not by Johann Sebastian but by his distant cousin Johann Ludwig Bach.[10]

Ausdruck'. Johann Nikolaus Forkel, *Über Joh. Seb. Bachs Leben, Kunst und Kunstwerke* (Leipzig, 1802), 56; Smend, *Bach in Köthen*, 90.

[10] Klaus Hofmann, 'Forkel und die Köthener Trauermusik von Johann Sebastian Bachs', *Bach-Jahrbuch 1983*, 115–18.

FROM the metrical patterns of Picander's verse it has long been recognized that all but one of the *Trauer-Music* choruses and arias are verse parodies of movements originally belonging to two of Bach's most exquisite compositions concerned with death: the *St Matthew Passion* and the *Trauer Ode* for the Electress of Saxony ('Laß, Fürstin, laß noch einen Strahl', BWV198).[11] (While the *Passion* was long thought to have been first heard less than a month after Leopold's funeral – on Good Friday 1729 – these two works are now both understood to date from 1727, a year and more *before* the Prince's death.)[12] The 12 parody movements found in *Klagt, Kinder* are listed with their models in Table 13.1. Picander's task on this occasion was to provide Bach with parallel texts of suitable character and content that could readily be substituted syllable by syllable for the originals. Thus, the alto *Passion* aria 'Buß und Reu' becomes 'Weh und Ach':

Buß und Reu *Weh und Ach*
Knirscht das Sündenherz entzwei, *Kränckt die Seelen tausendfach.*
Daß die Tropfen meiner Zähren *Und die Augen treuer Liebe*
Angenehme Spezerei, *Werden, wie ein heller Bach,*
Treuer Jesu, dir gebären. *Bey entstandnem Wetter trübe.*[13]

In only one case does Bach's music for a principal movement of the *Trauer-Music* resist clear identification – and for the simple reason that its words are not in verse but are non-metrical and taken from the Bible:

We have a God who comes to our aid and the Lord of Lords who saves us from death.

Wir haben einen Gott, der da hilfft und den Herrn, Herrn, der vom Tod errettet.[14]

(Psalm 68:21)

This was the chosen sermon text for Leopold's Memorial Service, and the function of Part II of the *Trauer-Music* was to reiterate and reinforce its message. The loss of Bach's setting has proved doubly unfortunate, for

---

[11] Parallels were first noted by Wilhelm Rust (*Bach Gesellschaft* xx/2 [1873], ix–xii), a process continued by Smend.

[12] Joshua Rifkin, 'The Chronology of Bach's St Matthew Passion', *The Musical Quarterly* 61/3 (1975), 360–87.

[13] Even with closely matching texts the process of substitution may not always prove entirely straightforward. Here for example, Bach's affecting repetition of 'treuer Jesu' (at bar 102) cannot be transferred directly to the grammatically incomplete 'bei entstandnem' at the corresponding point. Nevertheless, we may be sure that – in this instance, as in all others – Bach himself would instantly and effortlessly have produced a convincing alternative match of words and music.

[14] Smend gives 'einen Herrn', rather than 'den Herrn' as found in the Luther Bible; *Bach in Köthen*, 87, 212.

not only does it stand at the head of a seven-movement sequence, it also returns as its conclusion (*Repetatur Dictum*), thus seriously compromising any attempt at reconstruction. Generally agreed to have been a chorus (the heading is merely 'Psalm LXVIII v. 21'), it was in all probability fugal (or at least predominantly contrapuntal), the idiom most frequently employed by Bach for biblical passages of this sort.[15]

Smend argued that Bach would have been compelled to create a special setting: it 'could not have been a parody, that is, it had to be an original composition'.[16] And there the matter has rested. Yet, given that Bach was demonstrably relying (for whatever reason) on pre-existing works for all the other main movements, it seems unwise to rule out the possibility of another kind of parody, one where a *non*-metrical text might reasonably have been fitted to existing music of suitable proportion and character. The process is certainly not unknown in Bach's output: at least seven choruses were retexted in this way for the Mass in B minor. Any search for a suitable candidate naturally begins with the two 'parent' works, the *Trauer Ode* and the *St Matthew Passion*.

And perhaps one need look no further. While two *Trauer Ode* choruses are already put to work in *Klagt, Kinder*, a third remains unused: 'An dir, du Fürbild großer Frauen'. Obligingly the movement turns out to be not only fugal but also of suitable length and structure,[17] as well as (more predictably) entirely fitting in character, scoring and tonality. Indeed, Alfred Dürr (1992) very nearly made the same connection. Noting the absence of any recorded reuse of this one *Trauer Ode* chorus, he writes:

> It is quite conceivable, however, that it found a new place in a work that no longer survives, possibly as one of the biblical-text choruses in the *St Mark Passion*.[18]

If nothing else, Bach must have realized that setting the psalm text to the *Trauer Ode* chorus was perfectly practicable.[19] He may of course have chosen instead to compose a fresh movement, but in the circumstances there would seem to have been no obvious need to do so.

---

[15] See Smend, *Bach in Köthen*, 207.

[16] Smend, *Bach in Köthen*, 79; English version, p. 96. The *Bach-Werke-Verzeichnis* labels the movement 'Neukomposition'; *Kleine Ausgabe* (1998), 261.

[17] Bach's strategy with the *Trauer Ode* verse is to distribute its two halves in the ratio 3:1, allocating approximately 21 bars to the first and dispatching the second in a mere seven or so. The same strategy can be followed for the psalm text, which falls naturally into two almost equal if shorter halves.

[18] Alfred Dürr, *The Cantatas of J. S. Bach*, rev. and trans. R. D. P. Jones (2005), 867.

[19] I do not wish to imply that there is a single 'correct' way of retexting the chorus, rather that there appear to be various satisfactory ways.

Correct or not, this conjecture results in a plausibly and tantalizingly complete set of principal movements, all 14 of them of impeccable pedigree. What then of the missing recitatives, the music's connective tissue? It is of course impossible to recover Bach's own settings, given that none appears to have been a verse parody. But while the challenge of fashioning 10 modest *secco* recitatives for a practical reconstruction may not seem unduly daunting, something more seems to be demanded in most cases. The abundance of rich *accompagnato* recitatives in both the *St Matthew Passion* and the *Trauer Ode* tempts one to imagine that Bach may even have drawn on some of that material, too, rewriting voice parts as necessary.[20] (The remarkable evocation of funeral bells in the *Trauer Ode*'s 'Der Glokken bebendes Getön', for example, makes a strong case for its reuse.)

WITH the completion of a performable musical text (however conjectural), a further question looms large. How exactly did Bach's 'music of mourning' fit into the ceremonies it served?[21] Some two dozen Bach cantatas have two-part structures (to frame a sermon or marriage ceremony), but none falls into three parts, let alone Picander's four. Moreover the Cöthen *Trauer-Music* possesses neither the narrative of a Passion nor the liturgical framework of a Mass to help unify the whole. In order to understand the role it played in Leopold's obsequies, we must turn to the various court documents which set out the order of events in detail. For the two most informative of these, in which concerted music-making is succinctly indicated by the words '*Music*' or '*musiciret*',[22] see Table 13.2 (where those words are shown in bold). First comes a reminder of the disputed '*trauer Music*' heard at the Burial Service –

- following the arrival of the hearse at the Jacobikirche.

Then comes a surprise. At the Memorial Service, instead of the expected

---

[20] Detlev Gojowy, in arguing that the Cöthen *Trauer-Music* pre-dated the *St Matthew Passion*, went so far as to propose that nine *accompagnato* recitatives may have been related (with four of them involving transposition); 'Zur Frage der Köthener Trauermusik und der Matthäuspassion', *Bach-Jahrbuch 1965*, 122–34. Most of Gojowy's suggestions have been adopted by Alexander Grychtolik (2010) in what was mistakenly claimed as a first full reconstruction of the *Trauer-Music*. The various 'solutions' in my own reconstruction (2004) range from pure composition to the arguably 'bold' fashioning of new vocal lines against instrumental accompaniments imported wholesale not only from the Passion but also from the *Trauer Ode*.

[21] The question was brought into focus by the experience of performing the music under the very different conditions of a concert: while the larger-scale Parts I and II worked well together (in the first half), the more intimate Parts III and IV made a discernibly less successful pairing (in the second half).

[22] For specific uses of the German terms 'Music', 'musicalisch' and 'musicieren', see Andrew Parrott, *The Essential Bach Choir* (2000), 5, 19 etc.

Table 13.2 Court reports of the Burial and Memorial Services

Item	[Beysetzung]*	[Burial Service]
	Bey des durchl. Fürsten und Herrn, Herrn Leopolds, erblasseten Leichnahms Fürstl. Beysetzung ward	At the Burial of the Serene Prince Leopold's mortal remains
1	… mit allen Glocken geläutet	on the evening of Wednesday 23 March all the bells were rung.
2	Gegen x Uhr langete des hochseel. Fürsten verbl. Cörper mit ansehnl. gefolge auff dem trauer-wagen bey der Reformierten StattKirchen an	Around 10 o'clock the hearse bearing the body of the deceased Prince reached the Reformed [Calvinist] Town Church [the Jacobikirche] with an entourage of dignitaries
3	Hierauff ward die trauer **Music** eine ziehml. Zeit gehöret, biss alle Begleitende eingetreten und in der Kirche, welche schön illuminiret, aber mit trauer mehrentheils behängt war, in Ordnung gestellet war.	Thereupon the **music** of mourning was heard for a suitable length of time, until all those accompanying [the hearse] had entered and taken their places in the church, which was beautifully illuminated though draped almost entirely in funereal black.
4	Tratt der Fürstl. ConsistorialRath Christian Friedel zwischen den Tisch des Herrn und hochfürstl. Leiche und hielt ein auf diese höchst betrübte umbstände gerichtetes Gebeth.	The Prince's Church Councillor Christian Friedel took up position between the Lord's Table and the Serene Prince's body and delivered a Prayer concerning these most melancholy circumstances.
5	Ward gesungen: *Nun lasst uns den Leib begraben*, worunter man die Fürstl. Leiche ins Gewölbe brachte.	*Nun lasst uns den Leib begraben* (Now let us bury the body) was sung, during which the Prince's body was conveyed into the vault.
6	ward der Segen gesprochen und	the Blessing was pronounced and
7	mit Absingen den [sic] Liedes: *Hertzl. lieb hab ich dich o Herr* diese trauer Ceremonie ohngefehr umb 2 uhr beschlossen.	with the chanting of the chorale *Herzlich lieb hab ich dich, o Herr* (I hold you dear in my heart, O Lord) this ceremony of mourning was concluded at about 2 o'clock [in the morning].

* Aktenband, fol. 89r, transcribed in Smend, *Bach in Köthen*, 86–7.

Table 13.2 *continued*

Item	[Gedächtniß-Predigt]†	[Memorial Service]
	Den 24. Martij ward abermahl	Again on 24 March
1	mit allen Glocken gelautet, zu dreyen mahlen, nehml./ umb 7. 8. und 9. uhr.	all the bells were rung, three times, viz. at 7, 8 and 9 o'clock [in the morning].
2	gieng der Gottesdienst an und ward gesungen Ψ *XVI*. ...	the service began and Psalm 16 was sung ...
3	Ferner gesungen Ψ *XC* und noch unterschiedl. Sterbegesänge / biss die hochfl. Trauer verwandten sich eingestellet.	Psalm 90 and various other funeral hymns continued to be sung, until the arrival of mourners from the Prince's family.
4	**Musiciret.**	**Music** was performed.
5	gesungen *Freu dich sehr, o meine Seele*.	*Freu dich sehr, o meine Seele* (Rejoice greatly, O my soul) was sung.
6	gepredigt, und war der hochfl. gedächtnüss Text Ψ *LXVIII* v. 21 Wir haben einen Gott, der da hilft, und einen [*recte* den] Herrn Herrn, der vom Tode errettet.	the Sermon was preached, the text for the Prince's commemoration being Psalm 68 v. 21 We have a God who comes to our aid and the Lord of Lords who saves us from death.
7	nach Verhandelung und general Zueignung des Texts, auch Beschluß der Predigt darüber **Musizieret.**	after the explication of the text, treatment of its broader relevance, and the conclusion of the sermon, **music** on the same was also performed.
8	Die hochfürstl. Personalia verlesen und nach anleitung deren umbstände und des Textes die hohe Fürstl. Trauer verwandten und Bediente, auch alle Unterthanen getröstet	The account of the Life of His Serene Highness was read out, and, after guidance on certain particulars and on the Text, the Offering of Condolences was made to the mourners from the Prince's family, his servants, and also all his subjects
9	mit einem Kurtzen gebeth und dem Unser Vater beschlossen.	a short prayer and The Lord's Prayer marked the conclusion.
10	**Musiciret.**	**Music** was performed.
11	Der Segen gesprochen.	The Blessing was pronounced.
12	gesungen *Herr Jesu Christ wahr' mensch* und *Gott hertzlich thut mich verlangen* v. 9–11 worauff ein Jeglicher sich nach Hause begab.	*Herr Jesu Christ, wahr' Mensch und Gott* (Lord Jesus Christ, true man and God) [and] *Herzlich tut mich verlangen* (My heart yearns) vv. 9–11 were sung, whereupon everyone returned to their homes.

† Aktenband, fol. 89v, transcribed in Smend, *Bach in Köthen*, 87–8.

four musical interventions demanded by Picander's text, we read of just three –

- following the arrival of the principal mourners
- following the Sermon
- following the '*Personalia*' and Prayers.

On the basis of the libretto's title-page (see above and Illus. 13.1) Smend argued that there had to have been a fourth item of Bach's music in the service, 'even though it is not specifically mentioned' in the court records.[23] Given that these two sources of evidence are at variance in the matter, a decision must be taken about which – if either – to trust. While the purpose of the printed libretto remains uncertain, the function of the court records was purely and simply to record. Also in their favour is the fact that they comprise six documents (not just the pair reproduced in Table 13.2), which with a single exception (perhaps a simple oversight) yield entirely consistent information on the total number of musical components in the two ceremonies; nowhere is there any hint that as many as four were heard at the Memorial Service.[24]

Twin ceremonies calling for a *total* of four musical contributions, and a work of *Trauer-Music* made up of four parts – the arithmetic could scarcely be more suggestive. If, instead of being treated separately, the two services are viewed as a single entity (just as six services and a considerably longer time-span are encompassed by the *Christmas Oratorio*), a quite different picture emerges. I suggest that the four parts of Bach's *Trauer-Music*, each in effect a cantata, were designed to be heard over the course of the *combined* funeral ceremonies, within a period of not much more than 12 hours. (At Karlsruhe in 1738 Johann Melchior Molter's four-part *Trauer-Music* for Margrave Carl Wilhelm served a nocturnal *Actus* of two services spanning eight hours.)[25] An immediate and significant consequence of this suggested scenario is that the notion of a second lost work – an independent composition for the Burial Service – becomes redundant. Once again, Dürr appears close to reaching the same conclusion. In a footnote reporting Smend's belief in this other piece, 'of which not even the text survives', he comments:

> it is questionable whether Bach really had at his disposal in Cöthen the means of performing more than four sections of such onerous and demanding music in swift succession.[26]

---

[23] Smend, *Bach in Köthen*, 89, 167.

[24] The exception occurs in a very brief outline of the Memorial Service, drawn up in advance of the event, which (perhaps inadvertently) mentions just two musical items. See Smend, *Bach in Köthen*, 166.

[25] Häfner, *Hofkapellmeister Molter*, 142–3. The two services took place in different venues.

[26] Dürr, *The Cantatas*, 769–70.

While the arithmetic of my proposal may work impeccably, it also reminds us to look more closely at a problematic issue already apparent in Picander's libretto. This concerns the ritual functions of its four individual parts. The verse of Parts II and IV declares their purpose clearly, and their positions in the services seem certain: the one follows and reinforces the sermon, the other brings the whole proceedings to a close. Equally, Part I is surely intended to balance Part II and would therefore most naturally precede the sermon at the start of the Memorial Service,[27] where its general lamenting is arguably most appropriate. With all three available positions filled (by Parts I, II and IV in that order), the Memorial Service would therefore appear to have no room for Picander's Part III. And there are additional reasons for finding this Part III problematic. Its opening words 'Leopold, laß dich nicht begraben' ('Leopold, do not let yourself be buried') seem intentionally to anticipate the hymn 'Nun laßt uns den Leib begraben' ('Now let us bury the body'), sung as Leopold's body was taken down to the family vault towards the close of the Burial Service. A later verse, addressed to the Prince, evokes 'the spices/ With which we venerate your coffin' and the press of subjects around it who wish 'to pledge/ Their fealty to you even in death', also implying some point in the ceremonies before the coffin was finally removed from the congregation's sight. And in the closing verse the tenor sings

> Leopold, go to your rest ... You will dwell/ In the most beautiful heavenly peace/ As soon as your weary bones are buried.
>
> *Geh, Leopold, zu Deiner Ruh ... Nun lebst Du/ In der schönsten Himmels-Ruh,/ Wird gleich der müde Leib begraben.*

The music for these new words comes from the concluding 'burial' section of the *St Matthew Passion* ('Ich will bei meinem Jesu wachen').[28] In short, these are all indications that Picander's Part III would have been out of place in the Memorial Service but ideally suited, instead, to stand at the head of the Burial Service.

State funerals did not follow a single prescribed rite, and it is therefore easy to imagine how confusion about the order of events may have arisen. Perhaps an initial expectation, inadvertently perpetuated by the printed libretto, had been of a single service concluding with the burial and requiring no subsequent 'retiring' music. This common arrangement could explain not only the received sequence of Parts I–III but also the absence of Part IV from an early handwritten text.[29] Furthermore, if the libretto were purely a commemorative publication, any discrepancy would

---

[27] The model for the opening chorus of Part I is another opening movement – that of the *Trauer Ode*.

[28] For Picander's original wording of this passage, see Smend, *Bach in Köthen*, 83; English version, p. 99.

[29] See n. 6 above.

have been of little consequence; divorced from the ceremonies, the verse makes sense in either order. Be that as it may, the proposed (re)ordering of the four parts not only ties in with the court's detailed records but also produces – even reveals – a characteristically Bachian symmetry, in which the two longer parts frame the sermon (each in seven movements and in 'sharp' keys) and are themselves flanked by the two shorter ones (in five movements favouring 'flat' keys). Arranged thus, the four discrete parts may be said to form a more satisfyingly balanced whole (see Table 13.3).

MUCH of the attention the *Trauer-Music* has received in the past has focused on its relationship to the *St Matthew Passion*. Once it was acknowledged that the Cöthen music parodied the Passion, and not the reverse, this lost work, with its recycled and otherwise uncertain content, slipped quietly out of the spotlight. The question of priority or originality is, of course, something of a red herring; after all, the Mass in B Minor itself consists predominantly of recycled music. In the case of the *Trauer-Music* it might be argued that shortage of preparation time unduly influenced Bach's choices. But this, too, is questionable.[30] Both parent works had only ever been performed once, and very few, if any, of Cöthen's mourners will have attended those Leipzig performances. Bach undeniably had every reason to be proud of the chosen music, some of the finest he ever wrote, and Leopold's grand and solemn funeral gave him a perfect opportunity both to present it afresh to a large and distinguished assembly and to pay his last respects to a 'beloved Prince' in the way he knew best. Expectations of a self-sufficient monumental composition comparable to the *Passion* settings or to the Mass in B minor are clearly out of place. Perhaps best thought of as a skilfully constructed quartet of cantatas, Bach's homage to Prince Leopold surely ranks instead as a model of highly sophisticated occasional music. The more fully we understand the particular circumstances under which it was conceived and performed, the better we may therefore understand the music itself.

Although Bach had chosen to leave Cöthen almost five years earlier, it is clear that he retained great affection for the musical Prince, describing

[30] Smend's view that the funeral music was produced 'with all speed' appears to rest on a payment recorded on 27 November 1728, just eight days after Leopold's death: 'to *Musicus* Spiess for copying, engraving and producing musical materials ... 4.18 Thalers' (*Dem Musico Spießen vor Musicalien zu copiieren in Kupfer zu stechen und einzubringen ... 4.18 Thlr.*); Smend, *Bach in Köthen*, 77. Yet, while it may well have been possible for Bach to send material to Spiess at Cöthen within days of receiving a commission in Leipzig, it seems at least equally plausible that this payment relates instead to aborted preparations for the Prince's 34th birthday on 10 December. (Printing costs were regularly incurred in connection with the Prince's birthday; see Wolff, *J. S. Bach: The Learned Musician*, 200–1.) See also Rifkin, 'Chronology', 375 n. 50.

Table 13.3 The four parts of the *Trauer-Music* reordered

	arrival	pre-sermon	post-sermon	departure
Movements	5	7	7	5
Keys	d–c	b–b	(b–b)	B♭–c
Part	III	I	II	IV
Service	BURIAL	MEMORIAL	MEMORIAL	MEMORIAL

him warmly as one 'who both loved and knew music'.[31] Amongst the musicians from Halle, Merseburg, Zerbst and Güsten who travelled to Cöthen to perform at the funeral were the composer's 'wife and son from Leipzig'[32] – Anna Magdalena and (most probably) the 18-year-old Wilhelm Friedemann. Little more than seven years earlier Anna Magdalena's singing had earned her a position as the court's first full-time female musician, with a substantial salary second only to that of its *Capellmeister*. Yet the significance of her participation in the Cöthen *Trauer-Music* has received remarkably little comment. Not only did Bach assign to her all three *St Matthew Passion* soprano arias (one in each of Parts I, II and IV) – including the supremely expressive and demanding 'Aus Liebe'/'Mit Freude' – he also evidently felt at liberty to select a *female* singer to sing some of his very finest church music *in church* (and a Calvinist one at that).[33] Elsewhere other former Cöthen colleagues may have been given similar prominence; *Premier Cammer Musicus* Joseph Spiess in the violin obbligato to a retexted 'Erbarme dich', and the oboist J. L. Rose in the parody of 'Ich will bei meinem Jesu wachen'. Bach's viola da gamba player will surely have been Christian Ferdinand Abel, who is believed to have tutored Leopold on the instrument. The music-loving Prince certainly owned a viol, and he also 'sang a good bass'.[34] What better memorial could there have been for him than a bass aria with obbligato for viol? If my earlier conclusions are correct, the assembled mourners at the nocturnal Burial Service in the Jacobikirche ('beautifully illuminated though draped

---

[31] '... *einen gnädigen und Music so wohl liebenden als kennenden Fürsten*'; letter to Georg Erdmann, 28 October 1730, *Bach-Dokumente* i, 67 (no. 23). In the same letter Bach reports that Leopold's second wife, Friederica Henrietta, had struck him as an '*amusa*'.

[32] Smend, *Bach in Köthen*, 86.

[33] At Karlsruhe in 1738 three *Sängerinnen* are known to have taken part in the *Exequien*; see Häfner, *Hofkapellmeister Molter*, 145. See also Samantha Owens, 'Professional Women Musicians in Early 18th-Century Germany', *Music & Letters* 82 (2001), 32–50.

[34] Wolff, *J. S. Bach: The Learned Musician*, 192.

almost entirely in funereal black')[35] would have been greeted by the dolorous tones of Abel's viol in the *Passion* aria 'Komm, süßes Kreuz', poignantly transformed for the occasion into 'Laß, Leopold, dich nicht begraben' – 'Leopold, do not let yourself be buried'.

[35] See Table 13.2 (Burial Service, item 3).

14

Performing Machaut's Mass on Record

REVIEW

GIVEN the acknowledged historical significance of Guillaume de Machaut's *Messe de Nostre Dame*, it is remarkable that few performances appear to have been scheduled for the 600th anniversary of the composer's death. Clearly, several problems confront anyone attempting to present the work in concert: apart from the dubious box-office appeal of 14th-century church music and the uneasy relationship of liturgical music with the concert hall, this is demanding music, employing a vocal line-up quite different from today's predominant SATB formation and an idiom quite foreign to most of today's singers. Moreover, the Mass has frequently been assumed to require multiple exotic instruments. Ironically perhaps, a further reason why the work is so seldom programmed may be its very accessibility on gramophone records: with several recordings now available,[1] the considerable practical and musicological problems it poses may conveniently be bypassed.

The text-book fame of the *Messe de Nostre Dame* rests on the fact that it is the earliest complete polyphonic setting by a known composer. It also stands alone among surviving 14th-century settings in being in four parts throughout (rather than three). Although clearly an exceptional work, no special occasion is known for which it may have been written. Nor perhaps need there have been one, since the title 'de Nostre Dame', which appears in just one source, merely tells us that it is a mass 'of our Lady'; the plainsong it uses would qualify it for any of the more important Marian feasts in the Church calendar.

Interest in Machaut's mass in modern times goes back at least to a performance in Paris in 1918, but it was undoubtedly the 1956 recording by the Belgian group Pro Musica Antiqua under the direction of Safford Cape

First appeared in *Early Music* 5/4 (1977), 492–5; based on a broadcast for BBC Radio 3, April 1977.

[1] Safford Cape/Pro Musica Antiqua (Archiv), 1956; Alfred Deller/Deller Consort, members of Collegium Aureum (Harmonia Mundi), 1961; John McCarthy/Ambrosian Singers, Les Menestrels de Vienne (Belvédère/Centrocord), ?1966; Grayston Burgess/Purcell Choir (L'Oiseau-Lyre), 1968; August Wenzinger/soloists, members of the Schola Cantorum Basiliensis (Archiv), 1969; Konrad Ruhland/Capella Antiqua München (Telefunken), 1970; Charles Ravier/Ensemble Polyphonique de l'O. R. T. F. (Barclay), ?1971.

that first brought the work before the general musical public. Awarded a Grand Prix du Disque, the record remained unchallenged in the catalogues for over a decade, since when a further decade has produced a steady succession of at least six more versions. That a 14th-century mass should have been accorded so much attention is a clear sign of the fascination this astonishing music can still hold for musicians of today. However, not only did some of the recordings under consideration follow surprisingly closely on each other's heels, they also bear a greater similarity to each other than one might reasonably have expected, given how little is known about medieval performance practice. With one honourable exception, there are few obvious signs of new thinking, despite differences in surface detail. To what extent, then, does any one of these recordings represent the sort of performance the composer himself might have intended?

To answer this question we must consider some key issues facing the performer. The obvious first requirement is to establish a working text. But while good transcriptions may be readily available,[2] many textual issues necessarily remain open, not least the thorny matter of *musica ficta*. Suffice it to say that in no other 14th-century composition are such problems more acute, and that few of the recordings achieve even an internally consistent approach. Next, how is the Kyrie meant to work? Undoubtedly a ninefold Kyrie is required; in other words, each invocation should be heard three times, that is, 'Kyrie eleison' three times, 'Christe eleison' three times, and again 'Kyrie eleison' three times (a symbolic 3 × 3). But Machaut has provided only one setting of the first Kyrie, one of the Christe and two of the final Kyrie. So, either his polyphonic settings must be repeated accordingly (and this is what happens in three of the recordings) or they should be heard in alternation with plainsong (as in three others). This latter scheme, although arguably ignoring the rubrics *ter* and *bis* which occur in some of the sources, has the advantage of setting Machaut's music in relief and of mitigating what in purely musical terms might otherwise seem an undue repetitiveness. An interesting third approach is adopted in the Purcell Choir's recording under Grayston Burgess, for which Frank Ll. Harrison acted as Artistic Director. Here Machaut's music (based on a plainsong Kyrie) alternates with an organ elaboration of the same plainsong. Now, even though this alternation of organ polyphony and vocal polyphony may well be justified in principle, it seems to me that in this instance it does not work too well, probably because the organ music is of Italian provenance rather than French (the Faenza Codex), and also from a later generation.

Whatever method of performance Machaut may have had in mind for the Kyrie, he certainly could never have intended all these items of the Ordinary to be sung one after another, as they are on all but one of the recordings. In a liturgical context the component parts of the Ordinary of

---

[2] See David Fallows, 'Guillaume de Machaut and his Mass', *The Musical Times* 118/4 (1977), 288–91.

the Mass would have been separated, sometimes widely, by the chanting of the Proper, the texts specific to the occasion on which the Mass was being celebrated. As mentioned earlier, Machaut's mass 'de Notre Dame' may well have been intended for one or other of the major Marian feasts, and in the recording by the Ambrosian Singers under John McCarthy it is duly performed complete with Propers for the feast of the Assumption of the Blessed Virgin Mary. (This recording, incidentally, was made in Reims Cathedral, where Machaut himself was a canon.)

Any mass setting designed for liturgical use, if presented without proportionate space or musical contrast between movements, risks undue compromise in performance. A succession of five or six substantial blocks of polyphony (usually in similar style) may leave performers and listeners alike hankering after a variety in the music which is not necessarily there, simply because it did not need to be. There is, of course, no easier way of achieving such variety than by introducing colourful instrumentation. Between them, the seven recordings reviewed here offer the listener sundry instruments both from Machaut's own time and from the following 200 years or so: recorders, flutes, shawms, crumhorns, dulcians, cornetts, sackbuts, fiddles, violins, rebecs, lutes, psalterys, harps, organs, regals and bells. To be fair, the performance by Munich Capella Antiqua under Konrad Ruhland uses a single discreet instrumentation throughout; in other recordings, two or three combinations are heard in turn, while in yet others it is hard to discern any coherent principle at play. For example, in the only recording by compatriots of the composer (the French Radio Polyphonic Ensemble directed by Charles Ravier) the Credo is accompanied by two lutes. Or rather, two lutes are dimly present for the majority of the movement, but disappear without trace for the final Amen, presumably because as instruments of fixed pitch they are obliged to give up an unequal struggle with the singers, who by this point have sunk in pitch by almost a semitone.

Were instruments of this sort employed in the church of Machaut's time? And, if so, in what way? Indeed, were such instruments *ever* used in the medieval church? The organ's role is reasonably well attested, that of bells rather less so, but what reliable evidence is there for any other class of instrument? It has been widely assumed that the prominence of musical instruments in medieval religious art is in part a reflection of contemporary ecclesiastical practice. After all, the Psalms themselves are full of exhortations to praise God with manifold instruments, and corresponding illustrations abound in medieval psalters.

To understand the attitude of the medieval church towards musical instruments we must first look at the writings of the early Church Fathers.[3] To them, quite simply, instruments were evil:

---

[3] See James McKinnon, 'The Meaning of the Patristic Polemic against Musical Instruments', *Current Musicology* 1 (1965), 69–82.

> If an anagnost [cantor] learns to play the kithara, he shall confess this. If he does not return to it, his punishment shall be for seven weeks' duration. If he persists, he shall be dismissed and excluded from the church.
>
> (*Canones Basilii* 74)

The vehemence of this 4th-century Alexandrian law is shared by practically all early Christian writings on the subject, the prime reason being that the use of musical instruments was associated with sexual immorality. It can, of course, be argued that the need for legislation and for strong criticism of any abuse springs from the very occurrence of that abuse. True though this may be, condemnation of musical instruments is found only in relation to private recreation or to wedding festivities, plays and banquets – never to celebrations of the liturgy. Indeed, the music of the early Christian church was so dominated by the voice that the question of using wind or stringed instruments appears simply never to have arisen. Moreover, this way of thinking evidently persisted well into the Middle Ages.

The problem posed by the Psalms tended to be circumvented by interpreting their references to instruments in terms of allegory.[4] Thus when Psalm 97 tells us to 'Sing a psalm with the metal trumpet and the voice of the horn trumpet', an early medieval commentator explains that

> a fervent and intense study of evangelical preaching is understood by the metal trumpets; whereas kingly dignity is understood by the horn because kings are anointed from a horn. And not only that, but the proclamation of kingship is made by the horn.

(The organ evidently could stand apart from all this because of its ability to inspire allegorical thoughts in the listener, a line of argument which no medieval writer seems to have employed to justify the introduction into the church of other instruments.)

Clearly, medieval psalter illustrations and church carvings need to be interpreted with great caution;[5] the mere representation of instruments in such contexts speaks neither for nor against their use in church. From the 13th century, however, we find that illustrations of the Psalms routinely show the *a cappella* singing of monks grouped around an open book – surely a strong suggestion that the performance of vocal polyphony is unlikely to have required or attracted instrumental support.

The conservative nature of religious rites means that change rarely passes unnoticed. Thus Erasmus, more than a century after Machaut's death, criticizes instrumental music in much the same way as the

---

[4] See James McKinnon, 'Musical Instruments in Medieval Psalm Commentaries and Psalters', *Journal of the American Musicological Society* 21 (1968), 3–20.

[5] See Christopher Page, 'Biblical Instruments in Medieval Manuscript Illustration', *Early Music* 5/3 (1977), 299–309.

Fathers had done, but with the significant addition that it was now to be heard 'even in the holy temple, just as in the theatre'.[6] That this was a comparatively new development around 1500 is corroborated by other writings. For Machaut's time and earlier, however, there is no reason to doubt the clear words of a 13th-century Spanish Franciscan:

> For its various chants and sequences and hymns the Church uses only the organ; all other instruments have been banned because they were abused by play-actors.[7]

Of the seven recordings of the *Messe de Nostre Dame*, only one – by the Purcell Choir – dispenses with all instruments (apart from the organ, used independently for the Kyrie). While the performance may not be flawless, it admirably demonstrates that Machaut's music performed by voices alone can be every bit as exhilarating as when instruments are also pressed into service.

WHILE this issue of instrumental participation has received fairly close attention since at least 1957,[8] several similarly fundamental questions remain:

- Do we know whether solo voices or 'choir' or both were intended? The recordings represent each of these solutions, including a successful one by Capella Antiqua München, in which the top two parts are taken throughout by soloists, while the simpler lower two are each taken by two tenors (with instrumental doubling). It seems likely, however, that, even in the grandest cathedrals and monasteries of the Middle Ages, the number of singers capable of reading mensural notation (as opposed to plainsong) would generally have been very small – perhaps rarely more than three or four.
- What voice-types did Machaut have in mind? (It is highly unlikely that boys would have been expected to sing such elaborate polyphony.) This question necessarily hangs on another:
- What is known of the pitch standard Machaut's notation may imply? The short answer is 'next to nothing', which makes it all the more curious that only one director seems to have questioned the assumption that Machaut's music is best realized at or very

---

[6] Erasmus, *Desiderii Erasmi Opera Omnes* vi (Leiden, 1705), 731, quoted in McKinnon, 'Patristic Polemic', 78.

[7] Martin Gerbert, *Scriptores ecclesiastici* ii (St Blasien, 1784), 388.

[8] See Edmund A. Bowles, 'Were Musical Instruments used in the Liturgical Service during the Middle Ages?', *Galpin Society Journal* 10 (1957), 40–56; and Frank Ll. Harrison, 'Tradition and Innovation in Instrumental Usage, 1100–1450', *Aspects of Medieval and Renaissance Music*, ed. J. LaRue (1966), 319–35.

near (today's) $a' = 440$.[9] The main reason for this is perhaps that, at such a pitch, the two higher parts seem to lie well for our (falsettist) countertenors – which in turn raises one further question:

- On what basis do we assume that falsetto singing was cultivated in the Middle Ages?

As far as I know, none of these questions has yet received the serious scholarly attention it deserves. Some may well prove unanswerable, of course. Yet, after listening to these several recordings of Machaut's mass, I am left with the distinct impression that, more often than not, these vital questions may well not even have been asked.

PERFORMANCE NOTE (RECORDING, 1984)

LITURGICAL polyphony in the 14th century seems to have been the preserve of solo singers, not of 'choirs', and, apart from organ and bells, instruments had no place in liturgical music-making. (Depictions of instrumentalists in ecclesiastical contexts generally illustrate the angelic choirs of Psalm or Canticle.) Machaut's intricate music must surely have been conceived for four unaccompanied solo voices.

Very little can be ascertained about the work's intended sounding pitch. It is therefore strange that almost all recent performances have chosen today's $a' = 440$, presupposing both that falsetto singing was commonplace and that basses had no role. From Machaut's two-octave compass it seems preferable to infer a group of tenors and basses, and therefore a sounding pitch in the region of a 4th lower.

Machaut's extraordinary music makes much play with strong dissonances and their resolutions. The effect of these is the more forceful in the Pythagorean intonation in which 14th-century singers were schooled and which we have aimed to adopt: 4ths and 5ths are pure, major 2nds and 3rds very wide, and minor 2nds and 3rds very narrow.

Musica ficta presents exceptional problems in this work. In the 14th century, notes were not normally sharpened or flattened at the mere whim of singer or director; explicit notation was expected. Unfortunately, the surviving sources of this mass are all copies, which means that Machaut's exact intentions are often difficult to discern. In a manuscript prepared under the composer's direction, a sharp/flat sign might stay in force until the end of a line; copyists making line-breaks at different points might either follow the original notation slavishly (which would now give quite different results) or they might 'interpret' it, adding or cancelling the signs. Modern editors have tended to accept a high density of sharpened notes in

---

[9] Safford Cape, who performs the work one tone above $a' = 440$. For further discussion of these matters see Chapter 2 and, particularly, Chapter 3 of this volume.

Machaut's vocal lines and have therefore often been forced to inflect other voices to 'agree', thus compounding the errors of the medieval scribes. The present approach is deliberately very cautious.

The pronunciation of medieval Latin is not easily established, though in most places it was probably close to pronunciation of the vernacular. Educated guesswork is certainly involved in any attempt to recover how 14th-century French Latin may have sounded, but here at least the anachronism of Italianate pronunciation is avoided, which was imposed by Rome at a very much later date.

The chant is sung according to certain principles which are now generally accepted. The complex rhythms of 'pure' chant were lost in the later Middle Ages when large monastic and other choirs took over what had previously been confined to a small and virtuoso *schola*. The resultant 'equalist' practice may have been deplored by some theorists but was undoubtedly almost universal by the 14th century. In this recording tenors and basses sometimes sing the chant at different octaves, just as boys and men do when singing 'unison' chant; a comparable freedom may be still be heard in less self-conscious traditions of liturgical chant where the performers, like chant-singers of Machaut's time, work mostly from memory.

15

'Grett and solompne singing': Instruments in English Church Music before the Civil War

THE spirit of enquiry that characterizes current work on performance practices of the past appears as yet to have had little impact on the world of English church music. The principal reason for this may be the belief that Anglican choral singing has continued in an unbroken tradition from at least the Restoration up to the present day. Even the music of Tallis and Byrd has never entirely disappeared from its repertory, making it all too easy, when listening to such music sung by today's cathedral or college choirs, to imagine that one is hearing, as it were, the real thing. Here, I shall be concerned with just one of many issues: the use of instruments in the Anglican Church during the 16th and early 17th centuries. Were any instruments employed other than the organ? If so, which ones and under what circumstances?

Choral polyphony in England at the start of the 16th century was unquestionably the province of voices alone. But when we read of High Mass at St Paul's in 1514 being 'performed with great pomp and with vocal and instrumental music',[1] we may begin to wonder whether or not this 'instrumental music' was simply organ-playing. On the Continent something quite different might well have been expected by this time: at the wedding celebrations in Torgau of a future Elector of Saxony in 1500 two Masses had reportedly been sung 'with the help of' a cornett, 3 sackbuts, 4 crumhorns and organ.[2] In 1520 a moment of direct contact between the musicians of the English Chapel Royal and those of the French court occurred when, at the Field of the Cloth of Gold, Cardinal Wolsey celebrated Mass with both chapels taking part; according to an eye-witness account, the Credo was sung by the French singers with sackbuts and other wind instruments.[3] The occasion must have made a

---

First appeared in *Early Music* 6/2 (1978), 182–7; based on a broadcast for BBC Radio 3, October 1977, illustrated with anthems by Byrd, Gibbons, J. Mundy, Tomkins and Weelkes, performed by the Taverner Choir & Players.

---

[1] *Calendar of State Papers ... Venice II (1509–1519)*, ed. R. Brown (London, 1867), 178.

[2] Adolf Aber, *Die Pflege der Musik unter den Wettinern und wettinischen Ernestinern* (Bückeburg and Leipzig, 1921), 81; G. Reese in *Music in the Renaissance* (1954), 655.

[3] *Letters and Papers, Foreign and Domestic, of the reign of Henry = VIII* iii, pt I, ed. J. S. Brewer (London, 1867), 312. See also Michel Brenet, 'Notes sur l'introduction des instruments dans les églises de France',

strong impression on the English musicians present (Fayrfax and Cornysh amongst them) and indeed on Wolsey himself; only five years later we find Wolsey celebrating mass at St Paul's – in the presence of Henry VIII and various ambassadors – after which 'the quere sang *Te Deum*, and the mynstrelles plaied on every side'.[4] (Did the minstrels merely play *after* the singing?) Again in 1527 at St Paul's, 'Te Deum ... was solemnlie songen with the Kings trumpets and shalmes'.[5] Despite the presence of wind-players at court, their participation in its chapel services is not documented until the 1590s, though royal progresses seem to have invited the use of wind music: Queen Elizabeth was at Christ Church, Oxford, in August 1566, when

> with a canopy over her, carryed by four Senior Doctors, She entred into the church, and there abode while the quyer sang and play'd with Cornetts, *Te Deum*.[6]

Nine years later Worcester Cathedral greeted the Queen in similar style 'with grett and solompne singing and musick, with cornets and sackbutts'.[7] It should be emphasised, however, that none of these early accounts is clear enough to show exactly *how* voices and instruments may have interacted – in alternation or as a single body – or whether the instruments had a role entirely independent of the voices.

The last few years of Elizabeth's reign witnessed the beginnings of a revival in musical activity in the Anglican Church,[8] due in no small measure to the efforts of John Whitgift, Elizabeth's third and last Archbishop of Canterbury. The splendour of the service at Canterbury Cathedral in 1589 greatly impressed a visiting Italian, 'an Intelligencer from Rome, of good parts, & account' who had just arrived in England:

Riemann-Festschrift. Gesammelte Studien. Hugo Riemann zum sechzigsten Geburtstage überreicht von Freunden und Schülern, ed. Carl Mennicke (Leipzig, 1909), 282.

[4] Edward Hall, *Chronicle containing the History of England*... (London, 1809), 693.

[5] William Dugdale, *The History of Saint Paul's Cathedral* (London, 1818), 433. For a similar occasion in 1537 see John Milsom, 'Sacred Songs in the Chamber', in *English Choral Practice, 1400–1650*, ed. J. Morehen (1995), 161.

[6] Charles Plummer, *Elizabethan Oxford* (Oxford, 1887), 199.

[7] John Nichols, *The Progresses and Public Processions of Queen Elizabeth* i (London, 1823), 538.

[8] It has turned out to be erroneous to suggest that a statute for the permanent employment of 2 sackbutteers and 2 cornetteers at Canterbury may have been drawn up as early as 1532; Roger Bowers, 'Canterbury Cathedral: The Liturgy of the Cathedral and its Music, c. 1075–1642', in *A History of Canterbury Cathedral*, ed. P. Collinson, N. Ramsey and M. Sparks (1995), 440 n. 151.

> seeing him [the Archbishop] upon the next Sabaoth day after in the Cathedrall Church of Canterburie, attended upon by his Gentlemen, and servants ... also by the Deane, Prebendaries, and Preachers in their Surplesses, and scarlet Hoods, and heard the solemne Musicke with the voyces, and Organs, Cornets, and Sagbutts, hee was overtaken with admiration, and tolde an English Gentleman of very good qualitie (who then accompanied him) *That they were led in great blindnesse at Rome, by our owne Nation, who made the people there beleeve, that there was not in England, either Archbishop, or Bishop, or Cathedrall, or any Church or Ecclesiasticall governement; but that all was pulled downe to the ground, and that the people heard their Ministers in Woods, and Fields, amongst Trees, and bruite beasts; But, for his owne part, he protested, that (unlesse it were in the Popes Chappell) hee never saw a more solemne sight, or heard a more heavenly sound.*[9]

Elsewhere special payments to musicians are recorded for special church occasions. The anniversary of the monarch's accession, for example, was widely observed, and at Westminster Abbey in 1599 Edmund Hooper, Master of the Children, received 13s. 4d. 'for the cornets and sackbuts upon the queen's day'.[10] The same instruments were again in evidence for celebrations of St George's Day at Whitehall:

> there was short service, the clergy all being in their rich copes, with princely music of voices, organs, and cornets and sackbuts, with other ceremonies and music.[11]

From the turn of the century, similar references to wind instruments become increasingly frequent: they were heard at the christening of Princess Mary at Greenwich in 1605,[12] the visit of King James to Oxford in the same year,[13] the funeral of Prince Henry in 1612,[14] and that of James himself in 1625.[15] When Edward Kellie, Master of the Chapel Royal in Scotland, visited London in 1632, he 'carryed home an organist and two men for playing on cornets and sackbuts ... most exquisite in their severall

---

[9] George Paule, *The Life of the Most Reverend and Religious Prelate John Whitgift Lord Archbishop of Canterbury* (London, 1612), 79.

[10] Westminster Abbey, Treasurer's accounts no. 33653, fol. 4.

[11] George B. Harrison, *The Elizabethan Journals: A Second Elizabethan Journal, 1595–8* (London, 1938), 184.

[12] Edward F. Rimbault, *The Old Cheque-Book, or Book of Remembrance of the Chapel Royal from 1561 to 1744* (London, 1872), 168.

[13] Nan Cooke Carpenter, *Music in the Medieval and Renaissance Universities* (1958), 176.

[14] Thomas Birch, *The Life of Henry Prince of Wales* (London, 1760), 362.

[15] *The King's Musick*, ed. H. C. de Lafontaine (London, 1909), 58.

Illus. 15.1 '... two men for playing on cornets and sackbuts ... most exquisite in their severall faculties'; details from the case of a chamber organ by Christianus Smith (1643)

faculties',[16] and at the Chapel Royal in Whitehall in the 1630s there were rotas 'to be observed throughout the year by his Majesty's musitions for the wind instruments for waiting in the Chappell and at his Majesty's table'.[17] By this time cathedrals up and down the country show records of at least occasionally using wind instruments in their services: at York, Norwich, Exeter, Winchester, Worcester, Salisbury and Durham, amongst others.

The early 17th century was, of course, a period of considerable religious uncertainty in England, and one in which the role of church music in general was much debated. The organ was naturally at the centre of this debate, just as it had been under Edward VI, nearly a century before the Puritans came to power, when the Lower House of Convocation listed organ-playing among the '84 Faults and Abuses of Religion'.[18] And early in Elizabeth's reign a motion calling for the abolition of church organs had failed by just one vote.[19] The Puritan element within the Anglican Church was firmly against what it believed to be musical excess; as Sir Edward Dering put it,

> one single groan in the Spirit, is worth the Diapason of all the Church-Musick in the world. Organs, Sackbuts, Recorders, Cornets,

[16] William Dauney, *Ancient Scotish Melodies* (Edinburgh, 1838), 365.
[17] *The King's Musick*, ed. de Lafontaine, 87 (see also 72, 90, 97).
[18] Henry Davey, *A History of English Music* (London, 1921), 107.
[19] John Strype, *Annals of the Reformation* (London, 1709), 298–9.

&c. and voices are mingled together, as if we would catch God Almighty with the fine ayre of an Anthem, whilst few present do or can understand.[20]

Equally graphic is the sermon preached by the Puritan Peter Smart, senior prebendary at Durham Cathedral, on 7 July 1628:

This makes me call to remembrance, a strange speech little better than blasphemy, uttered lately by a young man, in the presence of his Lord, and many learned men: '*I had rather goe forty miles to a good service, then two miles to a Sermon.*' (Os durum.) And what meant he by a good service? his meaning was manifest; where goodly Babylonish robes were worn, imbroydered with images. Where he might heare a delicate noise of singers, with Shakebuts, and Cornets, and Organs, and if it were possible, all kinde of Musicke, used at the dedication of *Nabuchodonosors* golden Image. ... For if religion consist in Altar-ducking, Cope-wearing, Organ-playing, piping and singing ... If I say religion consist in these and such like superstitious vanities, ceremoniall fooleries, apish toyes, and popish trinckets, we had never more Religion then now.[21]

Biblical precedent was sought equally by those defending the use of instruments in churches:

Wherein doth our practice of singing and playing with instruments in his Majesty's chapel and our cathedral churches differ from the practice of David, the priests, and Levites? Do we not make one sign in praising and thanking God with voices and instruments of all sorts ?[22]

Going further, it was natural to question the exact function of instruments in worship. An anonymous writer defines it as keeping 'all the voices in tyme and in tune together, so that by listening to the Organ, every of the singers may correct his owne error, either for ill tuninge of the songe or for ill timinge'.[23] But not even all High Churchmen could convince themselves that instruments were really justifiable as a support for singing: Jeremy Taylor, one-time chaplain to Charles I, called them 'but a friend's friend to religion', and considered that singers in his own time needed less assistance than their biblical counterparts.[24]

---

[20] Edward Dering, *A Declaration* ... (London, 1644), 10.

[21] Peter Smart, *A Sermon Preached in the Cathedrall Church of Durham, July, 7. 1628* (London, 1640), 22–4.

[22] Henry Peacham, *The Compleat Gentleman* (1622); O. Strunk, *Source Readings in Music History* (1950), 332.

[23] London, British Library, MS Royal.18, B.19 (*The reasonable satisfaction* ...), fol. 12r.

[24] Percy A. Scholes, *The Puritans and Music* (1962), 218.

A more significant objection was that instruments tended to obscure the singers' words:

> though it be not in Latin, yet by reason of the confusedness of voices of so many singers, with a multitude of melodious instruments ... the greatest part of the service is no better understood, then if it weare in Hebrue or Irish.
>
> ('Articles ... to be exhibited by his Majestie's Heigh Commissioners, against Mr. John Cosin', 1629.)[25]

As a young prebendary at Durham, Cosin – an extreme High Churchman – came into sharp conflict with Peter Smart. The literature surrounding this confrontation and the resultant lawsuit provides a vivid picture of services at Durham around 1630. According to Smart,

> our *Durhamers* have been so eager upon piping and singing, that in stead of the Morning Prayer at 6. of the clock, which was wont to be read distinctly and plainly, for Schollers, and Artificers before they began their work, they brought in a solemne Service, with singing and Organs, Sackbuts and Cornets, little whereof could be understood of the people, neither would they suffer the Sacrament to be administred without a continuall noise of Musick, both instrumentall and vocal, to the great disturbance of these holy actions.[26]

Puritan revulsion at the various trappings of High Church practice is again set out by Smart in *A Short Treatise of Altars, Altar-furniture, Altar-cringing and Musick of all the Quire, Singing-men and Choristers* (1629):

> Why then are set before us so many objects of vanity, so many allurements of our outward senses, our eyes & eares, & consequently our minds from the meditation of Christs death & passion, and our sins which were the only cause of all our miseries & his lamentable sufferings. Can such paltry toyes bring to our memory Christ and his blood-shedding? Crosses, Crucifixes, Tapers, Candlesticks, gilded Angels, painted Images, golden copes, gorgious Altars, sumptuous Organs, with Sackbuts & Cornets piping so loud at the Communion table, that they may be heard halfe a mile from the Church? *Bernard* saith, no. *Orantium in se retorquent aspectum, impedunt affectum*: Such glorious spectacles, draw away from God the minds of them that pray, they further not, but hinder entire affections, and godly meditations.[27]

---

[25] *The Correspondence of John Cosin, D. D.*, pt 1, ed. G. Ornsby, Surtees Society 52 (London, 1869), 166.

[26] Peter Smart, *A Catalogue of Superstitious Innovations* (London, 1642), 9.

[27] Peter Smart, *A Short Treatise of Altars, Altar-furniture, Altar-cringing and Musick of all the Quire, Singing-men and Choristers* (London, 1643), 19.

THUS far no mention has been made of stringed instruments – nor indeed of verse anthems, for which viols are commonly believed to have been the natural (or ideal) means of accompaniment. On the face of it, it might seem curious that such a popular instrument found no regular place in church music, especially since it was common for choristers to be taught the viol as part of their musical education. But I am aware of only two contemporary references to the use of stringed instruments in conjunction with church choirs. Dr William Bedell, Lord Bishop of Kilmore in Ireland from 1629, was said by his biographer and son-in-law, Alexander Clogie, to have been

> made dissatisfied with the pompous service of Christ Church in Dublin, which was attended and celebrated with all manner of instrumental music, as organs, sackbuts, cornets, viols &c, as if it had been at the dedication of Nebuchadnezzar's golden image in the plain of Dura.[28]

This passage should be interpreted with caution, not only because it is a second-hand report (dating from c. 1675) but also because it is likely to have been more concerned to evoke the atmosphere of Daniel 3:5 than to give a precise description of earlier events at Dublin. In any case, it makes no specific reference either to verse music or to a whole consort of viols; no more does Lieutenant Hammond's 'relation' of music-making at Exeter in 1635, where he noted

> a delicate, rich & lofty Organ ... which wth their Vialls, & other sweet Instruments, the tunable Voyces, and the rare Organist, togeather, makes a melodious, & heavenly Harmony, able to ravish the Hearers Eares.[29]

If indeed viols were employed at Exeter at this time, one can assume neither that the practice was long established nor that it was widespread. Various practical objections to their use could be made, but the only contemporary one known to me is found in Charles Butler's *The Principles of Musik* (1636):

> becaus *Entata* [stringed instruments] ar often out of tun; (which soomtime happeneth in the mids of the Musik, when it is neither good to continue, nor to correct the fault) therefore, to avoid all offence (where the least shoolde not bee givn) in our

---

[28] Alexander Clogie, *Memoir of the Life and Episcopate of Dr William Bedell*, ed. W. Walter Wilkins (London, 1862), 140–1. At Christ Church, Dublin, 'the cathedral proctor was still paying wages in 1636 to two cornettists and two sackbutters, for their attendance in choir'; Thurston Dart, 'Henry Loosemore's Organ Book', *Transactions of the Cambridge Bibliographical Society* III/2 (1960), 150 (no source given).

[29] Hammond, *A Relation of a Short Survey of the Western Counties ... 1635*, ed. L. G. W. Legg, *Camden Society Miscellany* 16 (London, 1936), 74.

Chyrch-solemnities onely the Winde-instruments (whose Notes ar constant) bee in use.[30]

The unequivocal point here is that, for good practical reasons, stringed instruments played no part in church performance. In domestic settings, however, viol consorts were in their element, and here, with a handful of singers (rather than a full Anglican choir), the verse anthem evidently flourished as a form of intimate chamber music.

How then were the same verse anthems performed in church? Undoubtedly the usual way was the one most familiar to us, that is, with (church) organ accompaniment. After all, individual instrumental parts are found only in secular sources. But does the fact that no such parts survive in church sources prove that none ever existed? It can be argued that a number of organ accompaniments show signs of being reductions for keyboard of four- or five-part writing. Could those original parts have been played by wind instruments? Here we enter the realm of speculation, though it seems not unreasonable to imagine that where wind players were available they should occasionally have been given independent parts to play. Intriguingly, the Chapel Royal repertory included an anthem by William Lawes 'with verses for Cornetts and Sagbutts'; its text appears in Charles I's anthem-book, but unfortunately no music survives. This was most probably a work which, exceptionally, included instrumental interludes, though it is also at least possible that the verses in question were the usual solo sections, but designed in this instance to be accompanied by wind instruments (with or without organ).

It is certainly tempting to match at least one known verse anthem to a contemporary description of a performance involving wind: 'Know you not that a great prince is fallen?' by Thomas Tomkins was composed on the occasion of the death in 1612 of Henry, Prince of Wales. Before being taken to Westminster Abbey, the Prince's coffin stood in the chapel of St James's Palace, where

> the Gentlemen of the Kings Chappell, with the children thereof, sung divers excellent Anthems, together with the Organs, and other winde instruments.[31]

---

[30] Charles Butler, *The Principles of Musik* (London, 1636), 103. The statement comes in an annotation to the following passage: 'the moste solemn Musik, and ful Harmoni of Voices and loud Instruments in Consort, is moste fit for the moste solemn Congregations, at solemn Times, & and in solemn Places; when, upon soom extraordinari occasion, the Chyrch is assembled to prais and pray God for his goodness'; (p. 99).

[31] *The Funerals of the high and mighty Prince Henry, &c.* (London, 1613), sig. A4r.

WHETHER or not verse anthems were ever performed in the manner I have proposed, the presence of wind instruments with choirs is attested by far more documentary evidence than it has been possible to present here.[32] Nevertheless it would be unfortunate to leave the impression that their use was commonplace. For general purposes, the only musical instrument routinely employed in the Anglican Church before the Civil War was the organ – surely the natural and expected medium of accompaniment for verse anthems whenever they were performed by choirs and in church. Wind instruments were very much the preserve of the Chapels Royal and of the larger cathedral and collegiate choirs, where they were usually heard only on those special occasions when 'a grett and solompne singing' was called for. The different possible ways in which they were employed surely deserve further exploration.

---

[32] Roger Bowers has since argued that at Canterbury in the 1590s and early 1600s 'the band can have had no contribution to make to the accompaniment of the choir's sung polyphony. Until the early 1620s, almost all the players were not merely uneducated, but barely literate, unable even to sign their names in receipt of their pay. Probably they were members of the corps of city waits, in attendance merely to sound suitable pieces from their unwritten repertory at appropriate moments of the festal services – flourishes perhaps, at the entry and departure of the clergy'; Bowers, 'Canterbury Cathedral', in *English Church Polyphony: Singers and Sources from the 14th to the 17th Century* (1999), 441. Similarly, of the situation at Lincoln Cathedral in 1637 Bowers writes: 'It is unlikely that the waits could have substituted for, or complemented, the organ in the accompaniment of vocal polyphony; more likely perhaps is a contribution of fanfares and interludes at appropriate points in the services'; Roger Bowers, 'Lincoln Cathedral: Music and Worship to 1640', in *English Church Polyphony*, 74. The capabilities of the best municipal waits should not be underestimated, however: Edward and Orlando Gibbons grew up as the sons of a Cambridge and Oxford wait, Thomas Morley regarded the City of London's waits as 'excellent and expert Musitians' (*The First Booke of Consort Lessons* (London, 1599), dedication), while of the Norwich waits it was said that 'besides their excellency in wind instruments ... theyr voices be admirable, everie one of them able to serve in any Cathedrall Church in Christendoome for Quiristers' (William Kemp, *Kemps nine daies wonder* (London, 1600), [24]).

POSTSCRIPT (2014)

And are the said organs and other instrumentall musicke used att time of divine service as it out to be.

(Question 7 from Archbishop George Abbot's visitation of Chichester Cathedral, 1615)[33]

IN March 2013 a conference at the University of Cambridge[34] prompted me to revisit the material sketched out above (some 35 years earlier) and to test its central if understated conclusion: that the viol consort played no part in the performance of verse anthems by Anglican choirs. In recent years it has been noticeable that, despite the continuing absence of supporting evidence, the practice of matching a consort of viols to a college or cathedral choir in this repertory has regained some of the currency it enjoyed a few decades ago. Yet surely neither the Puritan 'proto-martyr' Peter Smart nor Sir Edward Dering (see above) would have missed an opportunity to condemn the use of stringed instruments in church had they ever encountered them. Nor in addressing both 'Cathedral Musick' and 'The Generous Viol' does the conservative Thomas Mace (1676) hint at any former connection between the two.[35] Rather, the environment in which viols clearly did engage with the verse anthem was essentially a private one – and one in which institutional choirs (as opposed to individual singers) had no natural place.[36] It thus seems

---

[33] Kenneth Fincham, 'Contemporary Opinions of Thomas Weelkes', *Music & Letters* 62/3–4 (1981), 352.

[34] 'Chains of Gold: Rhetoric and Performance in the Verse Anthem', University of Cambridge, 1–2 March, 2013. For an earlier valuable contribution to subject see Ian Payne, *The Provision and Practice of Sacred Music at Cambridge Colleges and Selected Cathedrals, c. 1547–c. 1646* (1993), ch. 8 ('The Provision and Use of Instruments by the Church, c. 1526–1646').

[35] Thomas Mace, *Musick's Monument* (London, 1676), 21–31, 231–4, 245–7. In 1635 the young Mace had been appointed 'Singing man' at Trinity College, Cambridge.

[36] Although music-making of this sort is of its very nature rarely documented, Lieutenant Hammond records an illuminating instance from 1634. After attending 'morning prayers' at Chester Cathedral, 'we all marcht to Mr. Organists Pallace, and their heard his domesticke Organs, Vyalls, with the voyces of this civill merry Company sweetly consorted'; Hammond, *A Relation of a Short Survey of Twenty-Six Counties*, 47. (A Parliamentary Survey of 1649 describes the choristers' singing school at Ely Cathedral as containing a 'roome with a place taken out of it for a place to play upon the vyall in'; Ian Payne, 'The Provision of Teaching on the Viols at some English Cathedral Churches, c. 1594–c. 1645: Archival Evidence', *Chelys* 19 (1990), 7.) George Herbert, whose 'chiefest recreation was Musick', frequented what may have been similar gatherings in Salisbury in the early 1630s: 'though he was a lover of retiredness, yet his love to *Musick* was such, that he went usually twice every week on certain appointed dayes, to the *Cathedral*

eminently reasonable to accept the clear testimony of the septuagenarian Charles Butler in 1636: that stringed instruments had no place in pre-Restoration church music-making (see above).[37]

Just one year previously, however, Lieutenant Hammond had heard 'Vialls, and other sweet Instruments' at Exeter Cathedral (see above). Significant though this account may be, does it really relate to the otherwise elusive viol consort? First, the notion of a 'whole' consort is called into question by the presence of 'other sweet Instruments', most probably the more common and therefore less noteworthy cornett and sackbut (both well documented at the cathedral).[38] Second, until well into the 17th century the term 'viol' did not necessarily refer specifically to the viola da gamba family and could still embrace any bowed stringed instrument. Thus the 'treble viols' seen and heard by Thomas Coryat in Venice in 1608 were undoubtedly violins,[39] and, more than half a century later, even that keen musical amateur Samuel Pepys could refer to the royal violin band in these terms:

> this is the first day of having Vialls and other Instruments to play a Symphony between every verse of the Anthem ... ('Lords day' 14 Sept. 1662)[40]

Might the instrumental group at Exeter (perhaps under the joint supervision of Edward Gibbons and John Lugge) therefore have comprised, say, two violins together with the more familiar wind instruments?[41]

> Church ... But before his return thence to Bemerton [his home just outside the city], he would usually sing and play his part, at an appointed private Musick meeting'; Izaak Walton, *The Life of Mr. George Herbert* (London, 1670), 87–8. Herbert played both lute and viol.

[37] Butler (c. 1560–1647) was a chorister at Magdalen Hall, Oxford, from 1579 to 1585, took his degrees there (BA in 1583; MA in 1587), and moved from Oxford only in 1593.

[38] See Payne, *The Provision and Practice*, 145.

[39] 'Of those treble viols I heard three severall there, whereof each was so good, especially one that I observed above the rest, that I never heard the like before'; Thomas Coryat, *Coryat's Crudities* i (Glasgow, 1905), 390.

[40] *The Diary of Samuel Pepys* iii, ed. R. Latham and W. Matthews (1971), 197 (14 September 1662).

[41] In September 1608 the chapter decreed 'that Peter Chambers do teache the Choristers under Mr Gibbons yf he be found fitte', and then the following April that he 'shalbe considered for his instrumentes, viz. one doble Sackbutte and one single Sackbutte as shalbe in reason thoughte fitte'; Payne, *The Provision and Practice*, 146. Later on, annual payments for repairs to the instruments abound, and in 1637 the chapter required 'two new Shagbutts and two new Cornetts to be provided for the service of the Quire with all convenient speed'; ibid., 146. Cf. ibid., 144, where 'a sett of vyolls' ordered on the same occasion is (wrongly?) assumed also to have been 'for the service of

An intriguing connection with musical activity elsewhere provides a hint that 'new' instrumental combinations of this sort might not have been entirely unknown at Exeter. Before moving to the city, where for more than 40 years he held the post of 'teacher of the choristers' at the cathedral, Edward Gibbons had been master of the choristers at King's College in his native Cambridge. Henry Loosemore, whose middle brother John was later commissioned to build a new organ for Exeter Cathedral, moved in the opposite direction; born into a Devonshire family he became organist at King's College in 1627 when barely 20.[42] In his early years at Cambridge, Henry compiled an organbook (*US-NYpl* Drexel 5469, evidently complete by the mid-1630s) which includes a 'A Verse for ye Organ, A Sagbut, Cornute & Violin' of his own composition. A likely performance context for such a work is strongly suggested (albeit some two decades later) in a poem published by a Cambridge student in 1653.[43] Praising the 'good *Musick* and Musicians' of the town, 'the Lusemores' are named 'For Organists', (John) Browne for sackbut and (?William) Saunders for violin;

> Then on his *Cornet* brave thanksgiving *Mun*,
> Playes in King's Chappell after Sermon's done[44]

This example may merely illustrate how instrumental music could function as an adjunct to worship, but it seems at least plausible that a new type of instrumental scoring – sometimes including the violin – may have begun to appear in verse anthems composed in the last decade or so before the Commonwealth.[45]

Be this as it may, wind instruments were undeniably a conspicuous part of church musical performance on several major occasions in late 16th- and early 17th-century England. Ten instances in which their role (and not merely their presence) is at least hinted at are listed here in concise form:

- 1598, Whitehall (St George's day): '2 psalmes and two antems songe with great melodie, organs, voices, shakbuts and other instruments.'
- 1599, St George's, Windsor: 'Then we heard some glorious music in the church at English vespers, choir with organ, cornet and fife accompaniment.' (Thomas Platter the younger)

---

the Quire'; for the full quotation see Andrew Freeman, 'The Organs of Exeter Cathedral', *The Organ* 6/22 (1926), 101.

[42] The youngest Loosemore brother, George, followed Henry to Cambridge and became organist at Jesus College in 1635.

[43] 'To Mr. Lilly, Musick-Master in Cambridge'; Nicholas Hookes, *Amanda, a sacrifice to an unknown goddesse* (London, 1653).

[44] It was quite usual for the Sermon to follow the Office, and for the Sermon in turn to be followed by music.

[45] Cf. Payne, *The Provision and Practice*, 151–5.

- 1601, Whitehall (Epiphany): the Russian envoy Grigorii Mikulin reports that 'they began to play on the organ, and on wind instruments, with much other music and song. The officers said, "They are singing the Psalms of David"'.[46]
- 1604, St Paul's Cathedral (the coronation of King James I): from the lower battlements 'an Antheme was sung, by the Quiristers of the Church to the Musicke of loud instruments'.
- 1605, Greenwich (the christening of Princess Mary): 'then begane an Antheme … (the Chorus whereof was filled with the help of musicall instrumentes).' Later, 'the Chappell and the Musitions joyned together, makinge excellent hermony with full Anthemes'.
- 1612, St James's Palace (prior to the funeral of Prince Henry): the Chapel Royal choir 'sung divers excellent Anthems, together with the Organs and other wind Instruments'.
- 1625, Westminster Abbey (funeral of James I): '2 Shagbutts and 2 Cornitors' are listed among the 'Singing men of Westminster'.
- 1629, Peter Smart: comprehensibilty is undermined by 'the confusedness of voices of so many singers, with a multitude of melodious instruments'. ('Articles … against Mr. John Cosin')
- 1634, Canterbury Cathedral: on the payroll are 'two corniters & two sackbutters, whome we do most willingly maintaine for the decorum of our quire'. (Answers in response to Laud's visitation articles)
- ?1635, Chapel Royal: *Before the mountains were brought forth* set by William Lawes [but not extant] is described as 'An Anthem with verses for Cornetts and Sagbutts'. (King Charles's anthem book)

---

[46] It may be relevant to note that 'the earliest known festal psalm in verse-form', Byrd's *Teach me, O Lord, the way of thy statutes*, has an Epiphany Sunday text.

16

Monteverdi's *L'Orfeo*

NOTE TO A RECORDING

INHABITING as it does a very different place from that of 'Opera' today, the world's earliest operatic masterpiece richly repays the attempt to understand it on its own terms. With a libretto entirely in verse and a setting which eschews verbal repetition, *L'Orfeo* relies predominantly on a form of recitative designed to enable each character 'almost to speak in music' (as Caccini put it) and to be intelligible at all times. As a consequence, high vocal extremes are absent and ranges modest (Orpheus himself barely exceeds a 12-note compass); pure vocal display is reserved for just two key moments; and nothing demands unnaturally big voices, not least because there is no 'orchestral' accompaniment for the solo singers to ride.

Monteverdi's stated aim (as voiced by his brother) was 'to make the word mistress of the music and not its servant', and the present performance treats his and Striggio's telling of the Orpheus myth as essentially poetic (rather than theatrical), as a refined courtly creation and, not least, as being of an intimacy utterly foreign to later 'grand' opera and to almost any large public arena. The *sala* in which *L'Orfeo* was first presented – probably with what we might regard as minimal staging – is estimated to have had a floor area of less than 30 × 40 feet. The two dozen or more instrumentalists may well have all been hidden from the audience (as for *L'Arianna* in 1608), with one half of the string body constituting an offstage band (playing 'within') and continuo instruments stationed in left and right corners of the stage, in close contact with the singers.

Those who embark on performing *L'Orfeo* are immediately confronted with an exceptional range of practical issues, some of them common to most early Italian music of the period (such as those of continuo style, ornamentation and rhythmic fluidity), others specific to this extraordinary composition. What follows can only hint at a few of these.

Pitch Several differing pitch standards were in use around Italy in the early 17th century, often within a single city and even within a single church.[1] Today's $a' = 440$, adopted for this recording, falls somewhere in the middle of the known possibilities and is a very plausible 'Florentine' pitch (between high Venetian and low Roman). Besides perhaps reflecting

---

First appeared as performance notes in the CD booklet for Claudio Monteverdi, *L'Orfeo: Favola in musica*, Taverner Consort & Players, dir. Andrew Parrott (2013).

the Mantuan court's strong cultural ties with Florence, it has the particular advantage of helping to anchor the solo vocal writing to the natural speech range of a singer's voice.

Transposition Independently of pitch standard, the question of transposition arises with the Underworld choruses and wind *sinfonie* at the ends of Acts III and IV. Here the high-clef notation is taken to have its conventional implication for downward transposition (in this case, by a 5th), producing fittingly sepulchral sonorities.[2]

Voices To cast a 'countertenor' as La Musica may appear fashionably sensationalist. Though soon to be totally eclipsed by the castrato, the adult male falsettist was in fact still reasonably common in Italy in the early 1600s (as Thomas Coryat discovered in Venice in 1608). Nor was it anything new for such a singer to take a female role, whether on stage or in church. What is less widely understood is that throughout the previous century the falsettist had ranked as a *soprano* (though that term now evokes a distinctly higher voice) and that his new position as an alto had barely begun. Monteverdi's alto writing (for the 'top' Shepherd) is in turn given to a high tenor, the expected 'alto' of the day.[3]

Stringed instruments The two 'little violins *alla francese*' that put in a brief appearance in Act II (albeit offstage) are taken to be *pochettes* or kits (here of rebec-style construction),[4] while the two 'bass viols' specified for the Underworld choruses are interpreted in line with earlier terminology to be midway in size and tuning between today's bass viols and the *contrabasso* instrument. More controversially perhaps, a tenor instrument tuned between viola and bass violin has been included in the violin band. All are set up to reflect what is understood of early 17th-century practice (as opposed to that of the mid-18th century).

Trumpets Ambiguities surrounding the opening Toccata have offered the opportunity of presenting it in three different fashions: played by trumpets, by muted trumpets, and by (almost) 'all the instruments' used in

---

[1] See Bruce Haynes, *A History of Performing Pitch* (2002). For several reasons, however, it would be unsafe to identify the pitch of the 1565 organ in S. Barbara as 'the pitch of the Mantuan court *cappella*' that performed *L'Orfeo* in 1607.

[2] See Andrew Parrott, 'Transposition in Monteverdi's Vespers of 1610: An 'Aberration' Defended', *Early Music* 12/4 (1984), 490–516; repr. in *Monteverdi*, ed. R. Wistreich (2012), 449–74 (also reprinted in this volume, Ch. 5).

[3] See Andrew Parrott, 'A Brief Anatomy of Choirs', in *The Cambridge Companion to Choral Music*, ed. A. de Quadros (2012), 7–26 (reprinted in this volume, Ch. 2).

[4] See David D. Boyden, 'Monteverdi's *Violini piccoli alla francese* and *Viole da brazzo*', *Annales musicologiques* 6 (1958–63); and Philip Pickett, *Behind the Mask: Monteverdi's Orfeo* (1992).

the *favola* proper (strings, cornetts and trombones, continuo). One point is explicit in Monteverdi's score: that the expected effect of muting these natural trumpets was to raise their pitch by a whole tone. It should also be noted that the clarino part, as well as the others, is played here without the now almost ubiquitous recourse to vent-holes. (The three statements of the toccata are performed as though first to announce from a distance the imminent arrival of a member of the nobility – Duke Vincenzo himself attended the first performance – then to accompany his entry into the *sala*, and finally to signal the commencement of the performance itself.)

Scores and libretto Quite apart from the variant endings to the opera, discrepancies abound between the libretto (1607) and the two versions of the score (1609 and 1615), and each has errors of one sort or another. Even the list of instruments at the head of the scores proves inconsistent with subsequent indications, while further ambiguity is caused by several of the performance rubrics – and also by their absence at other points. These various issues have necessarily all been looked at afresh. In addition, half a dozen or so rhythmic emendations have been made to familiar readings of the 1609 score, in places where Monteverdi's otherwise regular barring appears to have gone awry, and where the 1615 score itself seems to have aimed to correct the earlier version.

Balletto The Act I choral *balletto* ('Lasciate i monti') falls into three sections forming a conventional sequence or suite of dances – an opening duple-time movement (designed for the entry of the dancers), followed by what are clearly a galliard and a saltarello. A problematic feature of this is that the middle section ('Qui miri il Sole') has two sets of words but no musical repeat sign, and that a repetition either of the complete *balletto* (*abc abc*) or of just its last two parts (*abc bc*) 'has no justification in the dance treatises and, indeed, it contradicts the very nature of the dance suite'.[5] To repeat only this middle section (*abbc*) would seem, however, to disturb what is otherwise a musically well-balanced tripartite structure. No such problem arises with the reprise of the whole *balletto* a little later in the same Act – now with just a single text for the middle section (the first of the two stanzas again). Although libretto and score reveal no hint of disagreement in the matter, the solution adopted here is one that boldly presumes a shared misunderstanding on the part of the two publications: each appearance of the *balletto* is performed without any repetition (*abc*) and with the second text transferred to the reprise, where it now directly picks up on the two lovers' declarations of happiness.

A further much-discussed issue concerns the tempo relationships of the *balletto*'s three sections. Here they are performed 'proportionally', though not with the proportions their notation would necessarily have implied

---

[5] See Virginia C. Lamothe, 'Dancing at a Wedding: Some Thoughts on Performance Issues in Monteverdi's "Lasciate i monti" (*Orfeo*, 1607)', *Early Music* 36/4 (2008), 533–45.

ORNAMENTATION

From a letter to 'Opera' (October 2013)

SETTING aside the tricky question of whether a performance designed for repeated listening can support the same degree of added decoration as a live performance, two general points may be made. First, in this opera it is clearly necessary that for dramatic reasons no singer appears to vie with Orpheus (and Apollo) for supremacy in the art of vocal ornamentation. Second, as the overwhelming majority of the solo vocal writing is recitative (however far removed from later, more formulaic recitative), text is always paramount and sheer vocal display rarely apt. (In the same composer's *Combattimento* the narrator is expressly instructed not to add *gorghe* and *trilli* anywhere other than in one particular stanza.)

But I suspect it is primarily something else that has caught the reviewer's attention:[7] the sparsity of vocal embellishment at principal cadences where today's performances, presuming the grammatical requirement of an added ornament immediately before the 'resolution' is reached, routinely offer a prominent melodic flourish (often, it must be said, of dubious pedigree). I am indebted to my colleague Gawain Glenton for the important specific observation that in the music of Giulio Caccini – pre-eminent exponent of the new art of florid singing and teacher of Monteverdi's chosen Orpheus (Francesco Rasi) – perfect cadences with the voice part falling a tone to the tonic are almost never given more than the simplest single-pitch *trillo*. (His *Nuove musiche* of 1602 has 100 or so such cadences.) Rather than loading a penultimate syllable of text with musical significance, whether merited or not, this principle has the beneficial effect of lightening the ends of musical phrases and thus helping to maintain forward momentum.

There is, of course, much more to be learnt about this old 'new' manner of 'speaking in music', but any attempt to understand intricacies of this sort may represent at least a small step in the right direction.

---

[6] See Lamothe, 'Dancing at a Wedding'.

[7] An interesting caveat in the magazine's generally appreciative review (August 2013) of my recording of *L'Orfeo* concerns the evidently unexpected treatment of embellishment – 'or lack of it'.

17

Purcell's *Dido and Aeneas* on Record

ALMOST 90 years ago George Bernard Shaw was asked to review an amateur Purcell–Handel concert at Bow in London's East End. '... entirely unacquainted with these outlandish localities and their barbarous minstrelsy', he nevertheless set off (with a revolver as a precaution for his hazardous journey), determined not to leave Purcell's great music to the mercy his paper's other music critic. Although the 'Bowegians' evidently did not do Purcell full justice, GBS was delighted with the music. 'Dido and Eneas', he declared, 'is 200 years old, and not a bit the worse for wear'.

For all the professionalism of the most recent of recordings, I wonder, nevertheless, whether 90 years later we are any closer to understanding how best to bring Purcell's wonderful little opera to life. The six currently available recordings, in chronological order and with the conductor's name first, are these:

> Geraint Jones, with Kirsten Flagstad as Dido (World Records)
>
> Anthony Lewis, with Janet Baker (Oiseau-Lyre)
>
> Alfred Deller, with Mary Thomas (Harmonia Mundi)
>
> Raymond Leppard, with Tatiana Troyanos (Erato)
>
> Steuart Bedford, with Janet Baker (Decca)
>
> Sir John Barbirolli, with Victoria de los Angeles (HMV)

Dido and Aeneas is said to have been first heard in 1689, not on the public stage but at Mr Josias Priest's boarding-school at Chelsea, performed by young gentle-women.[1] Priest was a dancing master, and no doubt one of his main aims in commissioning this work from Purcell was to show off his young ladies in a series of dances. A small string orchestra and the necessary male voices for the chorus and the part of Aeneas must have been imported especially for the occasion. Nahum Tate's libretto has often been ridiculed: such lines as 'Our plot has took,/ The Queen forsook' and 'Thus on the fatal banks of Nile/ Weeps the deceitful crocodile' do not fall well on modern ears, but the plot is laid out with skill and economy.

First broadcast in *Building a Library: Record Review*, BBC Radio 3, 1978; subsequently published in *Building a Library: A Listener's Guide to Record Collecting*, ed. J. Lade (1979), 11–15.

---

[1] More recently it has been suggested that *Dido and Aeneas* is likely to have been written some years earlier for an undocumented court production; see Peter Holman, *Henry Purcell* (1994), 194–5.

Purcell's music matches this concision perfectly; the whole thing lasts little more than an hour, which means that in performance every detail has to be carefully judged and exactly in place – and that all the music will, conveniently enough, just squeeze onto one record.

There are four scenes. Act I is set in Dido's palace at Carthage, and we are plunged straight into the middle of the story. Belinda is trying to console the dejected Queen Dido, who has already fallen in love with Aeneas following his recent arrival from ruined Troy *en route* to Italy. Belinda, the queen's serving-maid (or perhaps her sister), has four dance-songs as well as the recitatives, and hers is a straightforward role, to comfort and support Dido. 'Shake the cloud from off your brow,/ Fate your wishes does allow', she sings. Elisabeth Schwarzkopf is the surprising choice as Belinda on Geraint Jones's 1953 recording, which has the great Wagnerian soprano Kirsten Flagstad as Dido. Apparently Flagstad, well into her fifties, struck up a warm friendship with the theatre director Bernard Miles after hearing his one-man send-up of *Tristan and Isolde* and their 'love-lotion'. The result was that 1951 saw the opening of London's small Mermaid Theatre with Flagstad singing Dido twice nightly in return for a bottle of stout per performance. The subsequent recording wears its 25 years pretty well. It has the feel of a mature performance, rather than of one assembled in a recording studio, and, even when tempos are perhaps too slow, Geraint Jones keeps a firm grip on the proceedings.

I do have some reservations, though. Schwarzkopf apparently was not in the original production, and despite some good singing she remains slightly detached from the rest of the performance. Moreover, it is somewhat confusing to the listener that she also sings the Spirit's music, and some of the Second Woman's. Still more distracting is her far from faultless English. All the other Belindas fortunately are English-speakers: perhaps the most winning of them is the bright-voiced Norma Burrowes in the most recent of the recordings, under Steuart Bedford. In the opera, words and music are supremely well balanced, as the poet Dryden recognized when he wrote that

> Musick ... has since arriv'd to a greater Perfection in *England*, than ever formerly: especially passing through the Artful Hands of Mr. *Purcel*, who has Compos'd it with so great a Genius, that he has nothing to fear but an ignorant, ill-judging Audience.[2]

To this we might add, 'and certain singers'. Fortunately, Flagstad's sung English is really very good, yet I imagine that reactions to her singing will be very mixed. The expressive scoops, for example, can become rather irritating, and there is an unfortunate dearth of conventional trills. But without doubt, this is very fine singing of its kind and Flagstad's beautifully

---

[2] John Dryden, 'Epistle Dedicatory', in *King Arthur* (London, 1691).

poised performance paints a very noble Dido. I found it interesting that almost all the singing on this 1953 recording seems to belong to quite a different tradition from that of the more recent ones. In particular, Schwarzkopf, Flagstad and their colleagues use discernibly less vibrato; they also cultivate freer, easier top notes (which need not lack dramatic tension), and in both respects I think they have the edge over the more pressurized voices we take for granted today.

An American mezzo-soprano, Tatiana Troyanos, takes the role of Dido in Raymond Leppard's recording for Erato. She has an exciting and colourful voice and her Dido certainly has distinction; but her performance is not completely even, and in particular is marred by some unclear diction which made me question whether she is indeed a native English-speaker. Dido has only two set numbers in the opera, and in recitative English-speaking singers should have a natural advantage – not that any of the recordings is as speech-like as I myself might have wished.

On Alfred Deller's recording it is sheer presence that Mary Thomas lacks by comparison with Flagstad and Troyanos. Also, Deller's performance suffers from a poor edition of Purcell's music. His concern to characterize each little detail seems somehow to undermine the opera's continuity, and this is emphasized by an unfortunate patchiness in the quality of the sound recording. The choice of a Dido can of course make or break a performance. The only British singer so far to offer both real authority and impeccable singing is Janet Baker, who made such an impression with her 1962 recording for Anthony Lewis on Oiseau-Lyre, and who has since returned to the opera in Steuart Bedford's Decca version.

With Act II the scene shifts from Dido's palace to The Cave, where a Sorceress holds court attended by two solo witches and a chorus of witches. These are the clear descendants of the witches in *Macbeth*, beloved of the Restoration theatre, and Purcell accordingly gives them some splendidly theatrical music. On Geraint Jones's recording, Arda Mandikian makes a suitably hysterical Sorceress (even if the chorus is a little too nice), pouring out sheer hatred for Dido. Such scenes are so far removed from modern theatre that there is a strong temptation to ham them up; I think it very difficult to get the balance exactly right. Deller shows two approaches side by side, with Helen Watts a straight but quite effective Sorceress and an over-enthusiastic coven of witches, who inevitably end up as comic figures.

This brings me to the role of the chorus, which elsewhere is less obviously dramatic. Especially at the opera's conclusion the chorus acts more as a commentator on the events, but is still by no means of peripheral importance. The standard of choral singing is highest on the two most recent versions, Leppard's and Bedford's, though Leppard's choir seems over-large for such an intimate work, and both sound somewhat anonymous.

As for the orchestra, much of its work is in accompanying the dances that punctuate the opera. Again, the two most recent versions have crisp, streamlined, modern string playing, yet none of the orchestras achieves the true lightness of touch that would have come naturally with baroque instruments. Some of the best playing can be heard in the Echo Dance for 'Enchanteresses and Fairees' at the end of the Cave scene, played by the Aldeburgh Festival Strings under Bedford; it is clean and efficient, if lacking a real will-o-the-wisp quality.

From The Cave the scene changes to The Grove outside Carthage, where Dido and Aeneas are relaxing after a boar hunt. Dido's attendants entertain them in song and dance with the tale of Diana and Actaeon. 'Oft she visits this lone mountain', sings the Second Woman, her one song in the opera; it is most pleasingly performed by Eileen Poulter (for Lewis) and by Felicity Lott (for Bedford). Then, as a storm conjured up by the witches sends the hunting party scurrying back to court, a false Spirit 'in form of Mercury himself' appears to Aeneas and commands him to leave at once for 'Italian ground'. Leppard introduces an organ at this point to support the voice, a simple enough touch, but one which is somehow at odds with Purcell's brilliant economy of means. Normally sung by a soprano or mezzo, the part of the Spirit is given by Deller to a tenor, which in an opera dominated by women's voices proves quite effective. It seems slightly perverse, though, to assign the role to a boy, as Bedford does – the opera is after all supposed to have been written for a girl's school – and moreover the boy sings in a completely dead-pan way, as though (to quote Shaw again) singing were merely 'a habit caught in church'.

Aeneas is nevertheless duly tricked, and left to ponder the consequences. 'All brawn and no brain' is how many view the Trojan prince in Purcell's opera. Certainly, the role is not a grateful one, as there is very little to sing and consequently hardly any time in which to build a character; it is very much Dido's opera. Maurice Bevan sings the part intelligently for Deller; despite a more noble voice, Thomas Hemsley on Jones's recording is not so successful because of flatness. Richard Stilwell paces the part quite well for Leppard, but to me his voice seems quite out of place in Purcell's music, while for Lewis, Raymond Herincx clearly opts for the 'cardboard cut-out' approach. The only tenor to tackle the part of Aeneas is Peter Pears, singing opposite Janet Baker in Bedford's recording – and a remarkable performance it is, too. Pears manages to create both a real character and a sympathetic one. The main reservation must be that his voice is now hardly that of a young warrior prince.

Aeneas's soliloquy appears to mark the end of the second act. No further music survives, yet the 1689 libretto has six more lines of text, suggesting a witches' chorus and a concluding dance. For this purpose two of the recordings successfully adapt music from other works by Purcell, though Jones does not end in the right key and the Britten–Imogen Holst edition used by Bedford has a chorus in the major key, which feels wrong between two short movements in the minor.

Act III opens on the quay-side, where Aeneas's sailors are preparing for departure: 'Come away, fellow sailors, come away'. Shaw was particularly fond of this music and described it as 'that salt sea air that makes you wonder how anyone has ever had the face to compose another sailor's song after it'. The opera ends with Aeneas's departure and Dido's self-destruction. This of course provides the musical climax of Purcell's compact masterpiece, in the form of the celebrated lament, and this in turn produces outstanding singing from Kirsten Flagstad and, twice, from Janet Baker.

Before summing up, I must mention the reissue of Sir John Barbirolli's 1966 version with the Ambrosian Singers and the English Chamber Orchestra. It has no pretensions to historical fidelity but compensates with an unfailing musicality, even when the tempos are excessively slow. Heather Harper's Belinda is pleasingly direct and consistently well sung, but Peter Glossop's Aeneas, though dramatically quite good, is to my ears vocally out of place. As Dido, Victoria de los Angeles is predictably more at ease in the set numbers than in the recitative, where her English diction does not do full justice to Purcell's music: it is not enough to have a well-known singer with a beautiful voice in the role of Dido. All the same, the performance is a memorable one and the real hero is Barbirolli.

The differences between Janet Baker's two performances as Dido, recorded 16 years apart, are remarkably few. In the interim her tone has become slightly less individual and, surprisingly, her diction a little less compelling. All the same, her singing of the lament in some respects is possibly even better than before. Ultimately it must probably be the singing of a Dido that dictates which performance of the opera as a whole is most to be recommended, and though I do not wish to underestimate the value of Kirsten Flagstad's historic recording, Janet Baker's combination of a truly distinguished voice and a native English tongue makes her her own strongest rival as the best Dido currently available on record. At this point it would be convenient to be able to say that Bedford's recording supersedes Lewis's older one, but both have their weak points of casting and of musical detail. It is disappointing that the new recording seems to offer merely a handful of theatrical tricks in place of any new interpretational insight. What I am saying is not that Bedford's version is inferior to Lewis's, but simply that it ought to have been superior. I suspect that a definitive *Dido and Aeneas* (whatever that may be) is still several years away. In the meantime, however, we have Janet Baker's two performances to enjoy.

RECORDINGS DISCUSSED

Flagstad, Hemsley, Schwarzkopf/Mermaid Singers and Orchestra/Jones (World Records)
Baker, Herincx, Clark/English Chamber Orchestra/Lewis (Oiseau-Lyre)
Thomas, Bevan, Sheppard/Oriana Concert Choir and Orchestra/Deller (Vanguard)

Troyanos, Stilwell, Palmer/English Chamber Orchestra/Leppard (Erato)
Baker, Pears, Burrowes/Aldeburgh Festival Strings/Bedford (Decca)
de los Angeles, Glossop, Harper/Ambrosian Singers/English Chamber Orchestra/ Barbirolli (HMV)

18

'Hail! Bright Cecilia' – Purcell at 350

IN November 1692 it was once again Henry Purcell's turn to provide music for his fellow 'Masters and Lovers of Musick' as they honoured their 'great Patroness' St Cecilia with a feast that evidently ranked as 'one of the genteelest in the world'. And the 33-year-old composer certainly excelled himself: *Hail! bright Cecilia*, an ode 'admirably set to Music by Mr. *Henry Purcell*', evidently went down so well with the musical assembly that it was performed twice 'with universal applause'.

It is indisputably an exceptionally fine composition, a shining example of a distinctively English genre – the choral and orchestral ode. But what also draws me to it is the very particular way in which this one work seems to open a window on Purcell's musical world – the environment which shaped him as a composer, and which he in turn helped to shape. The distinctive nature of the St Cecilia's Day celebrations, combined with specific clues found in the composer's autograph score, can, I believe, take us to very the heart of Restoration London's vibrant musical life, to the closely knit musical community which Purcell inhabited and which in many ways he dominated. Moreover, this can all feed into the way we perform the music and, ultimately, bring it more vividly to life.

ST CECILIA'S DAY ODES

THE first time we hear of the St Cecilia's Day meetings in London is in 1683, when Purcell produced his *Welcome to all the pleasures* for 'the Gentlemen of the Musical Society'. That was possibly the first time a new work had been specially commissioned for the occasion. Four stewards for the ensuing year are named: two gentlemen amateurs and two professional musicians, one of them the violinist and composer Dr Nicholas Staggins, Master of the King's Musick. This interesting social mix is also mentioned in the new monthly *The Gentleman's Journal*, which notes that of those who attend 'many are persons of the first Rank' but also that 'there are no formalities nor gatherings' as at other feasts. The occasion brought together not only professionals and amateurs but also court musicians and freelances, singers from church and theatre, virtuoso performers and musical tradesmen, Englishmen and foreigners, Protestants and Catholics – in short, a unique cross-section of musical London, gathered together solely 'to propagate the advancement of that divine Science'.

First broadcast in *The Essay: Purcell at 350*, BBC Radio 3, 2009.

As on most previous occasions, the St Cecilia's Day feast on 22 November 1692 was held right in the heart of the City of London, at Stationers' Hall – one of the few ancient Livery Halls still remaining, and within a stone's throw from where Christopher Wren's new St Paul's Cathedral was inching towards completion. Besides sundry court musicians and the musical luminaries of the day, such as Dr John Blow and Giovanni Battista Draghi (both of whom also composed St Cecilia's Day odes), a musical event of this nature would doubtless have attracted the likes of the Moravian composer and viol-player Godfrey Finger, Purcell's publisher Henry Playford, the German organ-builder 'Father' Smith (Bernard Smith), the Rev. John Gostling (Sub-dean of St Paul's, 'stupendious' bass singer and keen amateur viol-player), Dr William Holder (mathematician, clergyman and amateur composer), and perhaps, too, that incorrigible musical amateur Samuel Pepys, whose personal diary might have told us so much about *Hail! bright Cecilia*'s first performance, had he not chosen to abandon writing it when Purcell was not even 10 years old.

JOHN BLOW

As it is, we do have a report in *The Gentleman's Journal*, but, because it had carried a lengthy account of the previous year's meeting, this one is now purposely brief:

> to avoid repetitions, I shall onely tell you that the last was no ways inferior to the former.

This brings us to Dr Blow, the chosen composer in 1691. John Blow, the Amphion Anglicus to Henry Purcell's Orpheus Britannicus, was Purcell's senior by 10 years and most probably his one-time teacher. Over a period of some 20 years the intriguing musical relationship of these two composers involved a constant trading back and forth of musical ideas, a mutual indebtedness. Blow's *Venus and Adonis*, for example, was duly answered by Purcell's *Dido and Aeneas*, and parallel styles, forms, techniques, even harmonies, rhythms and melodies, can be found in dozens of works, sometimes composed only a matter of weeks apart. Initially Blow tended to be the innovator, but by the early 1690s it was the younger man who generally led the way. And remarkably enough, all this seems to have gone on without any hint of undue personal rivalry. (Thomas Tudway sums up this side of Purcell's personality: 'I knew him perfectly well. He had a most commendable ambition of exceeding every one of his time, and he succeeded in it without contradiction.')

'HAIL! BRIGHT CECILIA'

Perhaps the most striking thing about Blow's 1691 St Cecilia's Day ode is its grand scale, yet Purcell's *Hail! bright Cecilia* manages to be half as long again (lasting a good three quarters of an hour), even more splendid in its array of instrumental and vocal scorings, and more tightly organized – as well as being of unfailingly high musical invention. With an imposing 10-minute 'Symphony' (or overture, as we might call it), we are introduced to an orchestra that almost for the first time ressembles the orchestra we now know. Oboes (a French import) have joined the strings, and so too have a pair trumpets and kettledrums, though double basses have not yet been introduced, and bass violins (forerunners of the smaller cello) supply the bass line. Almost certainly the presence of the new French oboes (both players and instruments) dictated a new pitch for whole band, a 'low' French pitch, lower still than today's all-purpose 'baroque' pitch – something which has important implications for how we understand Purcell's vocal writing.

Generating the whole structure of Purcell's composition is, of course, the evocative text he was given to set. Officially anonymous, the ode was by a fashionable Irish clergyman and occasional playwright who had recently settled in London as a Royal Chaplain, Dr Nicholas Brady. Put briefly, music is represented in turn as magical in origin, as a force capable of stirring and soothing the passions, as the sister of number and ultimately as divine. In due course 'The noble organ', St Cecilia's emblematic instrument, is extolled as a paragon which no other instrument can quite match, whether the 'warbling' lute, the 'airy' violin, the 'lofty' viol, the 'am'rous' flute and 'soft' guitar, or the fife 'and all the harmony of war'. Brady's verse has often been disparaged, but I suspect that Purcell saw it as an absolute gift. Brady was certainly no Dryden, but as Dryden had observed,

> the Numbers of Poetry and Vocal Musick are sometimes so contrary, that in many places I have been oblig'd to cramp my Verses, and make them rugged to the Reader, that they may be harmonious to the Hearer: Of which I have no Reason to repent me ...[1]

In any case Brady's 'Hail! bright Cecilia' affords Purcell opportunity after opportunity to exercise what Henry Playford aptly describes as his 'peculiar Genius to express the Energy of *English* Words', a skill only partly explained by Purcell's 'weighing' of each syllable – something Handel, for all his admiration of Purcell, unfortunately never quite mastered in the English language.

PERFORMERS

JUST as Brady's lines proved an ideal vehicle for the composer, so too must Purcell's music have seemed a perfect offering to the assembled musical company, not least to his performing colleagues. And this is where Purcell's autograph score comes in. Carefully preserved in the

---

[1] John Dryden, 'Epistle Dedicatory', in *King Arthur* (London, 1691).

Bodleian Library at Oxford, it is in all probability the very copy used by the composer at the work's first airing on St Cecilia's Day 1692 (as well as subsequently) – and it is not merely a musical text; it gives us all sorts of hints about the nature of the performance. Particularly informative are the names of various singers. In performances nowadays we might expect to hear a line-up of soloists consisting of one soprano, one countertenor, one tenor and one bass (with an extra singer added for the bass duet). But this is evidently not at all what Purcell had in mind. Instead, the various solos and duets, together with a trio and a quartet, are carefully allocated to more than a dozen named singers, most of them associated with the Chapel Royal in one way or another, creating the distinct impression that much of the solo writing was tailor-made for these individuals, whose voices the composer will have known intimately. And in all likelihood these solo singers also constituted the choir, perhaps with a few additional men's voices and presumably with Chapel Royal boys supplying the treble line.

Immediately one name stands out: that of Mrs Ayliff, who is given the deceptively simple air, 'Thou tun'dst this world below'. Ayliff was a theatre singer, and had sung for Purcell in *The Fairy-Queen* earlier in the year. Yet it seems likely that in 1692 she was no more than 18 years old and called 'Mrs' Ayliff purely as an indication of her marriageable age. It is also quite possible that she was the first female singer to have sung at one of these otherwise all-male events.

Nevertheless, as solo voices, it is countertenors and basses that steal the limelight in *Hail! bright Cecilia*. Amongst the five basses one might well have expected to find the Rev. John Gostling, but perhaps his clerical status prevented him from singing at a public event, even a 'genteel' one such as this. John Bowman, singer-actor and member of the King's Private Musick, *is* there – he was certainly one of Purcell's favourite singers – but it was another member of the Private Musick, Leonard Woodson, who landed both the imposing opening invocation to St Cecilia and also the only complete solo movement for bass, 'Wondrous machine'.

THE COUNTERTENOR

BY contrast, the tenor voice, for reasons that may become clear, scarcely gets a look in, beyond taking the lower part in the sensuous duet 'In vain the am'rous flute'. Perhaps not unexpectedly it is the countertenor voice that Purcell seems to call on with greatest relish. 'The airy violin' is allocated to the French-born Alexander Damascene, himself a song composer, while Josiah Boucher is given 'The fife and all the harmony of war', with its accompaniment of trumpets and kettledrums and its arrestingly high top note on the word 'Alarm'. As for "Tis Nature's voice', in many ways the intimate heart of the piece, scored simply for voice and continuo, and boasting by far the most fluid and florid vocal writing in the entire work – well, according to *The Gentleman's Journal*, the stanza was 'sung with incredible Graces by Mr. *Purcell* himself'. Some punctuation might have helped us ascertain whether this means it was actually '*sung* ... by Mr. Purcell', or just with 'incredible Graces' *written* by Purcell. A print of the song, issued by Thomas Cross probably within a few months, is unambiguous: 'A Song Sung by himself at St Caecilia's Feast'. Even if Cross was not present at Stationers Hall and got his facts wrong, he clearly believed the composer (whom he knew) quite capable of singing demanding music in front of a discerning audience – not, I suspect, something many of today's eminent composers would care to do.

But this does little to help us answer another, and rather more important question: do we really understand what a Purcellian 'countertenor' was? Conventional wisdom is that the singing of alto parts exclusively or predominantly in falsetto is central to a British tradition of church singing stretching back through Byrd, Tallis and well beyond. However, I have not be able to find any serious evidence whatsoever to support this; and I really have looked. Part of the admittedly rather complex business of separating fact from fiction has to do with pitch: in the case of Purcell's music, the solos I have singled out can give quite a misleading impression on the written page, both if we are accustomed only to today's international pitch standard (almost a whole step higher than the 'low' French pitch mentioned earlier), and if we see them transcribed for modern convenience into the treble clef, with notes hanging low on the stave.

To cut a long story short, my own view is that the 1680s and 90s mark a mid-way point in the evolution of the countertenor, in which the falsettist countertenor we now know begins to emerge (especially in choral singing) but in which an earlier tradition is still predominant (especially in solo singing, and not least in Purcell's writing). In *Hail! bright Cecilia* the newer type appears in the duet 'Hark, each Tree its silence breaks', where the part lies significantly higher than others, is notated in an unusually high clef, and is explicitly labelled by Purcell 'High Contra tenor for Mr Howel'. Meanwhile, in the earlier tradition the countertenor is to all intents and purposes what we now call a tenor (and sometimes quite a high tenor). In other words, the modern tenor voice-type has been there all along, but music over the centuries has changed its habits and ended up calling the voice by a different name. This 'low' countertenor (our tenor) is the type Purcell predominantly uses in his solo writing, both in the 1692 ode and elsewhere. As for Purcell's tenor, we might best think of it today as a 'second' tenor to the countertenor's 'first' tenor. Thus, in *Hail! bright Cecilia* the young John Pate is given both a brief tenor solo in the opening chorus and a countertenor part later on. (Incidentally, Pate also seems to have taken over ''Tis Nature's voice' from the composer in at least one subsequent performance.)

Does any of this matter in performance? Purcell stands as arguably England's greatest composer, and the countertenor voice as emblematic of the vocal music that accounts for the largest part of his output. It therefore seems to me that, if we intend to do full justice to Purcell's incomparable vocal art, there can be little excuse for not trying to get the point straight. The falsettist countertenor has long characterized Purcellian performance, and has not infrequently disfigured it. The current abundance of skilled falsettists is surely insufficient reason to risk subverting Purcell's finely calibrated vocal writing. And plenty of tenors these days seem happy to rise to the challenge.

A BRIEF coda. In November 1695 it fell once more to John Blow to set to music the commissioned Cecilian ode (*Great Quire of Heaven*). For the service that traditionally preceded the feast he had also produced a *Te Deum & Jubilate*, with – true to form – clear echoes of and responses to Purcell's own magnificent setting. Given that most of the assembled company will have known Purcell well, and many will have been his life-long friends and professional colleagues, we can only imagine the atmosphere that must have hung over that year's proceedings, when news spread that the 36-year-old composer, their Orpheus Britannicus, had died just a few hours earlier, the eve of St Cecilia's Day.

Selected Recordings

All recordings made by The Taverner Choir, Consort and Players. For full details see <taverner.org>.

J. S. Bach, *Mass in B minor*, BWV232 (1985)

J. S. Bach, *Trauer Ode* for the Electress of Saxony, BWV198 (1998)

J. S. Bach, *Trauer-Music: Music to Mourn Prince Leopold*, BWV244a (2011)

Carlo Gesualdo, *Tenebrae Responses for Good Friday* (1997)

Josquin des Prez, *Mass 'Ave maris stella', Motets, Chansons* (1993)

Guillaume de Machaut, *Messe de Nostre Dame* (1984)

Claudio Monteverdi, *Vespers (1610)* (1984)

Claudio Monteverdi, *L'Orfeo: Favola in musica* (2013)

Henry Purcell, *Dido & Aeneas* (1981; 1995) [two recordings]

Henry Purcell, *'Hail! bright Cecilia'* (1986)

Henry Purcell, *The Pocket Purcell: A Tercentenary Tribute* (1995) [miscellaneous works]

Thomas Tallis, *Latin Church Music* (1988) [2 CDs, inc. 'Spem in alium' and Lamentations I & II]

John Taverner, *Mass 'Gloria tibi trinitas'* (1987)

John Taverner, John Browne, Robert Carver, *Masterworks from Late-Medieval England and Scotland* (1988)

Further Writings

'A Tale of Five Cities Revisited', *Early Music* 9/3 (1981), 342–3 [clefs and scoring in Striggio's *Ecce beatam lucem* (a40)]

'Performance Practice', in *The New Oxford Companion to Music*, ed. D. Arnold (1983) ii, 1407–12

'Signifying Nothing', *The Musical Times* 136/6 (1995), 267 [letter responding to Denis Stevens on Monteverdi]

'Bach's Chorus: A "brief yet highly necessary" Reappraisal', *Early Music* 24/4 (1996), 551–80 [a plea for serious exploration of Joshua Rifkin's proposal, after 15 years of disregard]

'Bach's Chorus: Who Cares?', *Early Music* 25/2 (1997), 297–300 [in reaction to an article by Ton Koopman]

'Bach's Chorus: Beyond Reasonable Doubt', *Early Music* 26/4 (1998), 637–58 [a response to Ton Koopman]

The Essential Bach Choir (2000)

Jeffrey Sandborg, *English Ways: Conversations with English Choral Conductors* (2001), 159–65 [interview]

Review of Karl Hochreither, *Performance Practice of the Instrumental-Vocal Works of Johann Sebastian Bach*, trans. M. Unger (2002), *Music & Letters* 85/4 (2004), 629–31

Bachs Chor: Zum neuen Verständnis (2003) [German translation of *The Essential Bach Choir*, with an additional appendix illustrating 'Three German Standpoints, c. 2000', as represented by Klaus Eidam, Christoph Wolff and Martin Geck]

'J. S. Bach's *Actus tragicus*: "Gottes Zeit ist die allerbeste Zeit" (BWV106)', in *From Renaissance to Baroque*, ed. J. Wainwright and P. Holman (2005), 269–70 [report on a workshop at York, 1999]

'Bach's Chorus: No Change', *The Musical Times* 151/4 (2010), 4–6 [in reaction to an article by Robert Marshall]

Index

A page reference followed by an asterisk indicates an illustration.

Aaron, Pietro, 23, 73–4, 77, 114
Abel, Christian Ferdinand, 359–60
Abell, John, 249–50, 275, 278, 282
Adam von Fulda, 66
Adriaenssen, Emanuel, 160
Agazzari, Agostino, 117, 153, 210
Agricola, Johann Friedrich, 109, 270, 347
Ailred of Rievaulx, 97
Albrici, Bartolomeo, 243
Allegri, Gregorio, 34
Anchieta, Juan de, 104
Anerio, Giovanni Francesco, 26, 161, 167, 170, 213, 216, 225, 229
Angleria, Camillo, 229
Antegnati, Graziadio, 223, 231
Antico, Andrea, 113*
Antwerp, 17
Archilei, Vittoria, 41
Arnold, John, 31
Ascham, Roger, 80, 89
Assandra, Caterina, 225
Aubrey, John, 78
Avignon, 106
Avison, Charles, 11, 14
Ayliff, [Mrs], 281, 394

Babán, Gracián, 54
Bach, Anna Magdalena, 359
Bach, Carl Philipp Emanuel, 3–4, 290, 303–4, 312–13, 325–6, 331
Bach, Johann Ludwig, 350
Bach, Johann Sebastian, xi–xii, 16, 37–8, 108, 109, 287–360, 397, 398
  Du wahrer Gott (BWV23), xii, 298, 299, 306–7, 318, 330, 332–6
  Entwurff, 38, 295, 320–2, 326–7, 330–1, 339, 343–6
  Gott ist mein König (BWV71), 37, 294, 297, 305–7, 310, 312, 315
  Mass in B minor (BWV232), 199, 290–313, 331, 352, 358, 397
  St Matthew Passion (BWV244), 292, 300, 305–6, 308, 319, 332, 336, 349–53, 357–9
  Trauer-Music for Prince Leopold (BWV244a), 347–60*, 397
  Trauer Ode (BWV198), 350–3, 357, 397
Bach, Wilhelm Friedemann, 295, 322, 359
Bacilly, Bénigne de, 38, 108, 142–3, 284
Bacon, Roger, 55, 57, 96
Banchieri, Adriano, 17–18, 26, 38, 108, 117, 158, 195–6, 213, 218–19, 229, 233, 242
Basel, Council of, 52
bass stringed instruments, 38, 185–6, 188, 238, 242, 247–8, 251–2, 255–61, 333, 343, 359–60, 377–8, 382, 393
bass voices, 30, 87–8, 89, 120, 174–7, 218–19, 221–2, 233, 273–4
basso continuo, xi, 117, 247–62, 381
Battre, H., 23, 69–73*, 76–7, 110
Bauldeweyn, Noel, 73
Beatis, Antonio de, 22
Beauvais Office, 58
Bêche, Marc-François, 141
Bédos de Celles, [Dom] François, 126
Beer, Johann, 36, 52, 108, 321, 324
Benda, Franz, 325
Bérard, Jean-Antoine, 131, 134
Bergamo, 83
Bermudo, Juan, 151, 169
Bernard of Clairvaux, 57, 97–8
Besard, Jean-Baptiste, 182
Biber, Heinrich Ignaz Franz von, 14
Birnbaum, Johann Abraham, 6
Bismantova, Bartolomeo, 155, 187, 242
Blankenburg, Quirinus van, 156–7
Blazey, David, 203
Blow, John, 108, 239–40, 245, 248, 253, 257, 260, 266, 277, 279, 284, 392, 396
Bodenschatz, see *Florilegium Portense*
Boen, Johannes, 58

Boethius, 97
Bologna, 110, 225, 232*
Boni, Giovanni Battista, 231
Bonifacio, Bartolomeo, 34
Bononcini, Giovanni Maria, 8
Bonta, Stephen, 195–7, 201, 203
Bontempi, Giovanni Andrea, 200
Bordoni, Faustina, 8–9
Bourgois, 23, 73, 76, 110–12
Boutelou, Antoine, 126
Bowen, Jemmy, 281, 284
Bowers, Roger, xi, 29, 34, 47–50, 56–7, 60–61, 81–2, 86–90, 92, 95, 205–27, 228–36, 376
boys' voices, 20–3*, 28–9, 36, 38, 42, 45, 47–50, 54, 59–60, 63–6*, 67–8, 69–77*, 78–9, 84–6, 88–90, 104–19*, 189, 197, 220, 234, 284, 325–6
Bracegirdle, [Mrs] Anne, 280–1
Brady, Nicholas, 393
Bressan, P(eter), 268–70
Brett, Philip, 201–2
Brossard, Sébastien de, 34
Brosses, Charles de, 39, 123–4
Browne, John, 397
Bruges, 22, 68, 72, 102, 105
Brumel, Antoine, 21, 119
Buonamente, Giovanni Battista, 190–1
Burgos, 23, 30
Burgundian court ordinances, 19, 62–3, 99–103
Burmeister, Joachim, 23, 119
Burney, Charles, 36, 39, 40, 42–3*, 53, 79, 250, 275–7
Burwell Lute Tutor, 11
Burzio, Nicolò, 19, 76, 100
Busnoys, Antoine, 19
Butler, Charles, 31, 52, 64, 79, 83, 86, 88, 89–90, 374–5, 378
Butler, [Mrs] Charlotte, 280–1, 286
Buxtehude, Dieterich, 27
Byrd, William, 6, 34–5, 41, 84, 368, 380, 395

Caccini, Francesca, 41
Caccini, Giulio, 78, 107, 114–15, 116–17, 131, 175, 283, 381, 384
Caffarelli, 44
Cambrai, 7, 20, 22–3, 51–2, 59–63, 65–7, 99, 103
Cambridge, 82, 85, 106, 158, 238, 240, 248, 269, 272, 376, 377, 379
Campion, Thomas, 77
Canterbury, 98, 271, 369–70, 376, 380
Cantone, Serafino, 226
cantus super librum, 17–19, 99–101
cappella, 36, 41, 44, 324–5
Carissimi, Giacomo, 18
Carver, Robert, 397
Casali, Lodovico, 118
Castaldi, Bellerofonte, 117–18
Castel, Louis Bernard, 5
Castello, Dario, 191
Castilhon, Jean-Louis, 138–9
castrato, 21, 23–4, 27–8, 36, 38, 40, 54, 67, 77–8, 92, 107, 114–16, 119, 124, 128, 134, 140–4, 173, 197, 219–20, 250, 281–2, 382
Cavalieri, Emilio de', 35
Cavalli, Francesco, 198–9
Cellini, Benvenuto, 106–7
Cererols, Joan, 54
Cerone, Pietro, 25, 52, 54, 117, 149, 152, 169
Cerreto, Scipione, 17, 117
Cesis, Sulpitia, 39, 185, 189, 225
chant, 16–19, 20, 48, 51–2, 56–7, 63, 75–6, 84, 95–6, 100–1, 150–1, 202, 224, 313–14, 318, 326, 328–9, 362–3, 365, 367
chant du livre (chant sur le livre), see *cantus super librum*
Charles the Bold, 62, 102
Charpentier, Marc-Antoine, 41, 52
Chaucer, Geoffrey, 79
Chester, 377
Cheverny, Dufort de, 133
chiavette, see clefs
Chichester, 34, 87–8, 377
chitarrone, see theorbo
choirs, x, xi–xii, 16–45*, 59–60, 62, 63–7*, 89, 104–5, 220, 234, 260, 284–5, 287–9, 290–346*, 365, 366, 394
Cima, Giovanni Paolo, 7–8, 38, 151, 210, 233

Cistercian Order, 55–6, 95
clefs, 24–7, 59–63, 147–8, 149, 154–5, 159–65, 166, 170, 180–1, 185, 192–3, 195, 206, 207–10, 212–13, 214–16, 225–7, 228–30, 398
Coclico, Adrianus Petit, 17
Cologne, 42
concertist, xii, 37, 287–8, 290–327, 328–9, 335–6, 338, 343–5
Conforti, Giovanni Luca, 115–6
Constance, 32
continuo, *see* basso continuo
contrapunto alla mente, 17–18, 100
Cooke, [Captain] Henry, 78
copies (copy-sharing), 33, 180, 259, 288, 290, 294, 299, 300, 303, 308, 311, 316, 317–20, 332, 335, 339, 345
Coppini, Aquilino, 225–6, 229
Corelli, Archangelo, 44
cornett, 14, 21*, 29–32, 38, 74, 78, 82, 146, 147, 165, 180, 181–3, 185–9, 192, 195, 197, 207–9*, 211, 224–5, 230, 235, 274, 363, 368–75*, 378–80, 383
Cornysh, William, 84, 369
coro favorito (*Favoritchor*), 33, 37, 287
Corrette, Michel, 126–7, 258
Corryat, Thomas, 79, 117, 378, 382
Cosin, John, 373, 380
Cöthen (Köthen), 298, 337, 347–60
countertenor, x, 23, 28–9, 46–121, 122–3, 140–4, 273–9, 382, 394–6
Couperin, François, 6, 9–10
Covarrubias, Sebastián de, 54
Cox, Richard, 103
Cramer, Carl Friedrich, 303
Croce, Giovanni, 164, 195–6, 209–10, 213, 226, 229
Cross, [Miss] Letitia, 281

Dallam (Dalham), Robert, 81, 239
Dammonis, Innocentius, 73
Darmstadt, 314
Decorus, Volupius, *see* Schonsleder
de la Rue, *see* La Rue
della Valle, Pietro, 116
Denis, Jean, 151
Dering, [Sir] Edward, 371–2, 377
Dijon, 102

Diruta, Girolamo, 150–51, 164, 166, 209–11, 232
Donati, Ignazio, 39, 316
Doni, Giovanni Battista, 158, 176, 219–21, 222, 229
Draghi, Giovanni Battista, 239, 243, 251, 279, 392
Dresden, 40, 108, 118, 290, 292, 295, 300–1, 312, 316, 323, 325, 327, 331, 337, 344
Dressler, Gallus, 52, 118
Dryden, John, 281, 386, 393
Duddyngton, Anthony, 81
Dufay (Du Fay), Guillaume, 16, 20, 23, 45, 51–2, 56, 59–67, 69, 103, 105
  Ave regina celorum, 20, 59–60, 65, 105
  Mass for St Anthony of Padua, 20, 60–63
Du Mont, Henry, 33–4
Duprez, Gilbert, 137
Durazzo, [Count] Giacomo, 145
Durham, 107–8, 371–3
Dürr, Alfred, 291, 352, 356

Early Music, ix, 1, 205, 330
effeminacy, 57, 95, 96–8
Ehmann, Wilhelm, 291, 315
Ekkehard V (of St Gall), see *Instituta Patrum*
Elford, Richard, 92
Ellis, Alexander J., 81, 272
Ely, 377
embellishment, *see* ornamentation
Encyclopédie, 124–5, 127, 136–8, 141–2
English court, *see* London
Erasmus, Desiderius, 30, 364–5
Eton Choirbook, 35, 84, 88
Evelyn, John, 78, 238, 249–51, 261–2, 273–5, 277–82
Exeter, 31, 270, 371, 374, 378–9

Fallows, David, 52, 57, 60–2, 69, 99, 101, 102–3, 110, 194, 200
falsetto, ix–x, 20, 23, 27–8, 46–94, 103, 109, 114–19, 120–1, 122–3, 127–32, 137–145, 219–20, 274–5, 277, 366, 395
Fattorini, Gabriele, 161, 229

fausset, 20, 51–5, 57–8, 128–131, 138–9, 140–3, 145
female voices, 23, 38–42, 45, 92, 116, 119, 123–4, 133, 135, 140–1, 143, 185, 220, 234, 275, 279–281, 359, 382, 394
Ferrara, 21, 24, 55, 65, 113
Finck, Hermann, 35, 52
Finger, Gottfried, 257, 258, 286, 392
fingering (keyboard), 242–3*
Florence, 22, 23, 30, 36, 67, 68, 104, 112, 114, 115, 158, 176, 225, 381–2
Florilegium Portense, 36
flute, 181, 189–90, 230, 269, 308, 323, 343
Fontana, Giovanni Battista, 187
Forkel, Johann Nicolaus, 349
Fougeroux, Pierre-Jacques, 44, 329
Framery, Nicolas Etienne, 124–5, 127, 136–8, 141–2, 144
Franc, Martin le, *see* Martin le Franc
Froissart (*Chroniques*), 53, 58
Frye, Walter, 103
Fuhrmann, Martin Heinrich, 37, 109, 315–16
Fux, Johann, 313

Gabrieli, Andrea, 152
Gabrieli, Giovanni, 32, 152, 164, 187–9, 191, 197, 212, 218, 224–5, 229, 235
Gagliano, Marco da, 177, 179
Galilei, Vincenzo, 30, 151, 152, 169
Gamble, John, 251
Ganassi dal Fontego, Sylvestro di, 180–1
Gardiner, John Eliot, 146, 194
Georgi, Christian Siegismund, 340–2*
Gerlach, Carl Gotthelf, 319, 322
Gesualdo, Carlo, 397
Ghent, 104
Gibbons, Edward, 376, 378–9
Gibbons, Orlando, 256–7, 368, 376
Gilbertine Order, 55–6, 95
Giustiniani, Vincenzo, 115–16
Glarean, Heinrich, 38, 90, 118
Glöckner, Andreas, 298, 328–30, 337–41, 344–6
Gluck, Christoph Willibald, 13–14, 125, 127
Gobert, Thomas, 33
Gonzaga, Scipione, 31, 115

Gostling, John, 250, 251, 253, 273, 278, 282, 392, 394
Goverts, Jan, 18–19
graces, *see* ornamentation
Greenwich, *see* London
Grimarest, Jean-Léonar le Gallois de, 128
Guidonian hand, 50*, 67
Guise, [Mademoiselle] de, 41
guitar, 250, 253, 393
Gyffard partbooks, 86

Hamburg, 37, 41, 44, 290, 298, 303–4, 312, 321, 324, 325–6, 331, 337
Hammond, [Lieutenant], 374, 377, 378
Handel, George Frideric, xi, 13, 16, 42–5*, 92–3, 237, 288–9, 321, 323, 329, 393
Handl, Jacobus, 36, 159
harpsichord, 13, 154, 156–8*, 166, 169, 179, 231, 238, 240–4*, 245–7, 248–55
Harris, Renatus, 239, 270–3
Harrison, Frank Ll., 88, 362
haute-contre, x, 27–8, 93, 122–45
Haydn, Joseph, 4, 11, 109
Haynes, Bruce, 223
Henrici, Christian Friedrich, *see* Picander
Herben, Matthaeus, 18
Herbert, George, 377–8
Hingeston, John, 241–2
Holder, William, 245, 392
Homilius, Gottfried August, 319
horn, 80, 323, 329, 343, 364
Horwood, William, 84
Hubertusburg, 327, 344
Humfrey, Pelham, 108, 284
Hunt, Arabella, 249, 251, 280

improvised vocal polyphony, 16–19, 48, 58, 75–6, 100–1, 103, 105
Innsbruck, 29, 83
Instituta Patrum, 55, 57, 95
instruments in church, 29–32, 36–8, 42–3, 56, 260, 288, 327, 363–5, 368–80
Isaac, Henricus, 23

Jacobs, René, 123, 127–8, 130–1, 139–40, 142, 144–5
Jacques de Liège, 98
Jacques (Jachetto) de Marville, 55, 104–5
Jambe de Fer, Philibert, 27, 93
Jélyotte, Pierre de, 125, 127, 133
John of Salisbury, 98
Jommelli, Niccolò, 42, 130
Josquin des Prez, 7, 24, 73, 159, 397

Kapelle, see *cappella*
Keller, Godfrey, 245, 253, 257, 266
Kellie, Edward, 370
Kemp, William, 376
Kenyon, Nicholas, 15
Keyte, Hugh, 203
King, Robert, 248
King, William, 248
Koopman, Ton, 316
Kuhnau, Johann, 109, 322

La Borde, Jean-Benjamin de, 126
Lalande, Jérôme de, 124–7, 130, 134, 136, 140–1, 144
Lalande, Michel-Richard de, 41
La Rue, Pierre de, 24
Lassus (Lasso), Orlande de, 21, 36, 92, 119, 159–60
Laud, [Archbishop] William, 89, 380
Lawes, William, 375, 380
Lebègue, Nicolas, 4
Le Cerf de la Viéville, Jean Laurent, 9, 44
Legros (Le Gros), Joseph, 125, 127, 136
Leinsdorf, Erich, 291
Leipzig, 6, 36, 37, 109, 158, 287–8, 292, 295, 297–9, 310–11, 313, 315, 319, 324–7, 328–46, 347, 349, 358–9
Le Jeune, Claude, 159
Lely, [Sir] Peter, 257
Lenton, John, 244, 260–1
Leoni, Leone, 229
Leopold of Anhalt-Cöthen, [Prince], xii, 347–60, 397
Liberati, Antimo, 27
Lincoln, 84, 376
liturgy, xi, 17–19, 29, 58, 63, 86, 194, 200–4, 224, 361–3, 366

Locke, Matthew, 31, 78, 243, 249, 252, 253, 274, 277–8
London, 44–5, 81, 83, 109–10, 238, 239–40, 247, 252, 269, 270, 272, 281–2, 286, 323, 329, 368–70, 376, 391–2, 395
　Westminster, 42–3*, 104, 239, 252, 260, 271, 285, 321, 370, 375, 380
　Whitehall, 239, 259–60, 270–1, 370–1, 379–80
Loosemore brothers (George, Henry, John), 379
Lübeck, 27, 337
Ludford, Nicholas, 84, 104
Lugge, John, 378
Lully, Jean-Baptiste, 4, 9, 122, 126, 128, 139
lute, 11, 22, 26, 31, 94, 154, 160–3, 165, 169, 179, 182, 228, 246–9, 254, 263, 286, 363, 378, 393
Luython, Carl, 158

Mace, Thomas, 238, 241, 248–9, 253, 260, 261, 263, 285, 377
Machaut, Guillaume de, 361–7, 397
Madin, Henri, 18
Maffei, Giovanni Camillo, 114
Malamini, Baldassare, 232*
Mancini, Giovanni Battista, 128, 130–1
Manlius, Johannes, 7
Mantua, 55, 146, 173, 175–7, 190–1, 200, 207, 222–3, 231, 382
Marie, Mathurin, 78
Marini, Biagio, 187, 189, 190
Marpurg, Friedrich Wilhelm, 12
Martini, [Padre] Giovanni Battista, 44, 171
Martini, Johannes, 68
Martin le Franc, 53
Matteis, Nicola, 250, 251, 253, 261, 262, 264
Mattheson, Johann, 2, 12, 13, 36–7, 38, 41, 108, 314, 315–17, 320, 321, 324
Maugars, André, 27
mean (*medius*) voice, 19, 28–9, 47, 49, 80, 84–7, 89, 101–2
Medici, Cosimo de', 107, 114
Mendel, Arthur, 148, 168
Mendelssohn, Felix, 287–8, 319

Merighi, Antonia Margherita, 92
Mermet, Louis Bolliou de, 135–6
Mersenne, Marin, 30, 38, 187, 191
Merula, Tarquinio, 191
Meude-Monpas, J. J. O. de, 131, 137
Milan, 36, 114, 226
Modena, 83, 185
Molter, Johann Melchior, 356
Monteverdi, Claudio, x–xi, 18, 35–6,
    78, 146–8, 164, 170–80, 185–93,
    194–203, 205–27, 228–36, 381–4,
    397, 398
  1610 Vespers, x, 35–6, 146–8, 170–9,
    185–93, 194–204, 205–27, 228–36,
    397
  Sonata sopra Sancta Maria, xi, 172,
    185–92, 194, 196, 200–4, 223–4
  L'Orfeo, 177–9, 185–7, 190, 197, 198,
    211, 224, 230, 234, 381–4, 397
Morley, Thomas, 3, 17, 24, 82–3, 84, 86,
    151, 155, 230–1, 376
Morsolino, Giovanni Battista, 26
Mozart, Wolfgang, 109, 110
Muffat, Georg, 4–5
Müller, Hans, 158
Müller, Hermann, 57
Munich, 21, 32, 92, 119
musica ficta, 53, 100, 362, 366
mutate voces, see *voces mutatae*

Namur, 31, 69
Nanino, Giovanni Maria, 161
Nemeitz, Johann Christian, 8–9
Neumann, Frederick, 14–15
North, Roger, 31, 40, 238, 243–6, 248–9,
    251–8, 260–4, 267, 280, 282, 284
Northumberland Household, 29, 85
Norwich, 83–4, 271–2, 371, 376

oboe, 45, 237, 266, 268–70, 273, 322–3,
    393
Obrecht, Jacob, 22, 23, 28, 68, 85, 105
Ockeghem, Jean de, 23, 28, 60, 61, 85
Oest, Johann Friedrich, 110
Oeÿnhausen, Heinrich Herrmann von,
    29, 40

organ, 21*, 166, 185, 223, 231–2*, 239–41,
    246, 248, 264, 269–72, 286, 364–5,
    371–4*, 382, 393 and *passim*
ornamentation, 7–10, 56, 100, 114, 130,
    242–6*, 263, 277, 282–4, 286, 381,
    384
Ornithoparcus, Andreas, 118
Osculati, Giulio, 225, 229
Ouseley, [Sir] Frederick A. Gore, 80–1,
    91
Oxford, 58, 66, 78, 79, 81–2, 256, 259,
    269, 270–1, 369, 370, 376, 378, 394

Padua, 32, 83
Paix, Jakob, 159–60
Palencia, 31
Palestrina, Giovanni Pierluigi da, 25–6,
    27–8, 36, 155, 159, 181, 213, 219, 220,
    227, 229
Palsgrave, John, 53
Paolucci, Giuseppe, 147, 155, 170
Pate, John, 277, 279, 282, 395
Peacham, Henry, 372
Penna, Lorenzo, 39, 50*, 155, 242
Pepusch, Johann Christoph, 315
Pepys, Samuel, 241, 249, 250, 282, 378,
    392
Pesaro, 21
Pesenti, Michele, 73
Pez, Johann Christoph, 325
Phillips, Peter, 90, 94, 120, 121
Picander (Christian Friedrich Henrici),
    348–9*, 351, 353, 356–7
Picchi, Giovanni, 187
Picerli, Silverio, 213, 229
pitch standard, x–xi, 14, 26–8, 45, 47, 49,
    60, 61–3, 77, 80–4, 90–1, 126, 136,
    146, 152, 158, 169, 171, 176, 179, 185,
    199–200, 222–3, 237, 269–73, 337,
    365–6, 381–2, 393
plainchant (plainsong), *see* chant
Player, John, 246
Playford, John and Henry, 78, 131, 238,
    248, 261, 263, 283–4, 392–3
Plummer, John, 103
Pordage, [Mr], 249, 251, 277, 282
Porta, Ercole, 222
Porter, Walter, 6, 78

Praetorius, Michael, 21, 26, 33–4, 37, 72, 77, 81, 90, 92–3, 119, 148–9, 154–5, 158, 167–70, 176, 179, 180, 181, 183–4, 187–9, 191, 197–8, 207, 212–3, 228, 231, 235, 287, 315, 317, 328
Prynne, William, 57, 97
Purcell, Henry, xi, 92–3, 108, 237–86*, 385–90, 391–6, 397
  Dido and Aeneas, 247, 250, 252, 268, 275, 279, 385–90, 392, 397
  'Hail! bright Cecilia', 247, 250, 256, 259, 266, 267, 274–7, 279, 281–3, 285, 391–6, 397

Quantz, Johann Joachim, 5, 8, 9, 11, 13, 93, 129–32, 138, 144, 270

Rameau, Jean-Philippe, 122, 125, 126, 139
Ramos de Pareia, Bartolomeo, 66–7
Rasi, Francesco, 177–9, 384
Razzi, Giacomo, 18
recorder ('flute'), 32, 181, 189–90, 230, 244–5, 250, 257, 264, 266–9, 323, 371, 393–4
Reggio, Pietro, 249, 250, 278, 281
Regis, Johannes, 23, 85
Rifkin, Joshua, 201, 289, 290–2, 295, 299–301, 303–4, 310, 316, 317–19, 321, 329–37, 344–6, 398
Rigatti, Giovanni Antonio, 180, 195, 207, 225, 229
ripieno (ripienist), xii, 33, 37, 41, 44, 287–8, 290–327, 329, 332–6, 343–5
Robert of Courson, 98
Roche, Jerome, 194, 200, 203
Rodio, Rocco, 152
Rogier, Philippe, 161, 229
Rognoni Taeggio, Francesco, 187
Rome, 17, 27, 31, 44, 54, 80, 106–7, 113–16, 158, 160, 176, 213, 222, 231, 249, 269, 270, 281–2, 369–70, 381
Rossi, Salamone, 161, 181, 190, 207, 235
Rossini, Gioachino, 137
Rotherham, 107
Rouen, 22, 101
Rousseau, Jean-Jacques, 13, 124, 126–7, 129, 130, 132, 134–7, 143
Rovetta, Giovanni, 233–4, 303
Ruckers family, 156–8*

sackbut, *see* trombone
Sagudino, Nicolo, 120
St Ambrose, 57, 96
Saint Gille, Jean de, 22
Salisbury, 29, 86, 89, 371, 377–8
Salmon, Thomas, 247
Salomo, Elias, 18, 52–3
Salzburg, 109
Samber, Johann Baptist, 155, 170
Savall, Jordi, 194, 198–9
Scarlatti, Alessandro, 36
Schadaeus, Abraham, 166
Scheibe, Johann Adolph, 1, 5, 12, 36, 41
Scheibel, Gottfried Ephraim, 40
Schein, Johann Hermann, 108
Schemelli, Christian Friedrich, 109
Schering, Arnold, 290–2, 296, 298, 299, 309, 315, 317–18, 319–20
Schlick, Arnolt, 21*, 76, 83, 104
Schmid, Bernhart, 159
Schonsleder, Wolfgang, 155, 192
Schubinger, Augustein, 29–30
Schulze, Hans-Joachim, 297–8, 337–8, 341, 344–5
Schütz, Heinrich, 3, 10–11, 27, 33, 37, 52, 164–5, 168–70, 175, 180, 189, 195, 207, 212, 229, 287
Scotland, 80, 120, 370, 397
Selle, Thomas, 314, 321
Sens Office, 58
Seville, 31
Shaw, George Bernard, 385, 388–9
Sheppard, John, 86
s'-Hertogenbosch, 83
Siena, 104
Siface (Giovanni Francesco Grossi), 250, 281
Simpson, Christopher, 238, 244, 256, 261, 263, 264
Smart, Peter, 372–3, 377, 380
Smend, Friedrich, 349, 351, 352, 356, 358
Smith (Schmidt), Bernard, 239–40, 246, 269, 270, 271–2, 273, 392
Smith, Christianus, 371*
Smith, Robert, 82, 269
Speer, Daniel, 187, 314
split keys, 84, 166, 231–2*, 246–7
Stadlmayr, Johann, 161–2, 229

Staggins, Nicholas, 250, 259, 260, 277, 284, 391
Stauffer, George, 296, 304, 311, 312, 331, 345
Stevens, Richard J. S., 110
Stoke next Clare, 107
Stölzel, Gottfried Heinrich, 340–1
Striggio, Alessandro [snr], 32, 202, 398
Stuttgart, 41, 188, 225
submissa voce, 20, 23, 51–2, 68

Talbot, James, 238, 249–50, 256–7, 258, 261, 266, 268–70, 272
Tallis, Thomas, 16, 32, 86, 90, 91, 94, 121, 368, 395, 397
Tansur, William, 270
Taruskin, Richard, 1, 93, 314, 320–1, 322–3, 331
Taverner Choir, Consort & Players, xii, 91, 146, 194, 250, 349, 368, 381, 397
Taverner, John, 85, 86, 120, 397
Telemann, Georg Philipp, 37, 319, 321, 341
temperament, xi, 14, 31, 84, 151, 166, 199, 231, 245–7, 271, 366
Testard, Robinet, 65*, 104
theorbo, 161, 245, 247–9, 251–3, 256–7, 324
Tinctoris, Johannes, 17, 46, 67, 100, 103
Tomeoni, Florido, 138–9
Tomkins, Nathaniel, 81
Tomkins, Thomas, 80, 368, 375
Torgau, 29, 368
Tosi, Pier Francesco, 128, 131, 246, 282
transposition, x–xi, 26–7, 38–9, 81–2, 84, 127, 146–93, 194–200, 205–16, 223–7, 228–36, 237, 269, 271, 337, 382
tremolo, 264–6
Trent codex, 69–73*, 76, 110–12
Tribou, Denis-François, 126
Troiano, Massimo, 119
trombone, 29–32, 149, 176, 180, 181, 183, 185, 188–90, 225, 230, 267, 368–75*, 378–80, 383
Trömer, Johann Christian, 340–1, 343
trumpet, 29, 32, 187, 257, 259, 262–4, 266–8, 286, 288, 294–5, 322–4, 343, 369, 382–3, 393–4

Tudway, Thomas, 260, 267, 392
tuning systems, *see* temperament
Turges, Edmund, 84
Turner, William (singer), 273, 277–8
Turner, William (antiquary), 241
Tye, Christopher, 104
Tyrol, 22, 105

Urbino, 105
Usper, Francesco, 33, 225, 229

Valencia, 54, 83
Valentini, Giovanni, 158, 222, 229
Vasari, Giorgio, 30
Vecchi, Orfeo, 225
Venice, 18, 22, 24, 26, 27, 33, 34, 39–40, 78, 79, 104, 106, 117, 164, 176, 182, 190, 207, 209, 212, 222, 233, 378, 381
Verona, 118
Verovio, Simone, 160–3*, 167
verse anthems, xii, 31, 94, 260, 374–80
Viadana, Lodovico, 32–4, 38, 117, 161, 165–6, 169–70, 180, 188–9, 195, 203–4, 207, 218–19, 229, 317, 338
vibrato, xi, 262–4, 387
Vicentino, Nicola, 24, 69, 74–5, 77, 85, 88
Victoria, Tomás Luis de, 16, 161, 165, 229
Vienna, 40, 109
Vincentius, Caspar, 166
viol, 31, 32, 181, 230, 238, 244, 246, 247–8, 251–2, 255–8, 260, 261, 263, 359–60, 374–5, 377–8, 382, 392–3
violin, 10, 31–2, 36, 38, 53, 147, 179–81, 183, 185–6, 189–91, 196–7, 211, 224, 235, 244, 258, 260–3, 286, 359, 378, 379, 382
Virgiliano, Aurelio, 180–1, 185, 188, 207–10*, 229–30
Visitatio sepulchri, 51
Vivaldi, Antonio, 39
voces mutatae (*voci mutate*), 69–77, 110
voices (categories, ranges and vocal scoring), x, 23–4, 27–9, 38–42, 45, 46–50, 59–60, 63–8, 69–77, 78–80, 84–94, 110–19, 122–7, 140–5, 170–9, 197–8, 211, 215–20, 221–3, 231, 233–5, 272–9, 365–6, 382, 394–6 and *passim*

Waelrant, Hubert, 160
Walgrave (Waldegrave), [Dr] William, 249
Walter, Johann, 339
Walther, Johann Gottfried, 35, 137, 296–7, 303, 321
Wells, 85, 89
Westminster, *see* London
Weston, William, 41
Whitehall, *see* London
Whythorne, Thomas, 107
Winchester, 79, 371
Windsor, 106, 239, 259, 379
Wittenberg, 340–3*
Wolff, Christoph, 295, 299, 318, 326, 330–1, 332, 335–6, 339, 344, 398
women's voices, *see* female voices
Worcester, 270, 369, 371

Wulstan, David, 28, 47, 80, 86, 89, 90, 92
Württemberg, 41, 316, 324–5
Würzburg, 41, 324

York, 371

Zacconi, Lodovico, 7, 90, 128, 182–3, 187–8, 191, 197, 200, 209–10, 229
Zahn, Johannes, 319
Zannetti, Gasparo, 189
Zarlino, Gioseffo, 26, 52, 148–9, 151, 152, 166, 169, 182, 200
Zaslaw, Neal, 122, 127, 128, 137
Zedler, Johann Heinrich, 296–7
Zelenka, Jan Dismas, 316, 327, 344
Zelter, Carl Friedrich, 332, 335
Zenobi, Luigi, 116

www.ingramcontent.com/pod-product-compliance
Lightning Source LLC
Chambersburg PA
CBHW050525300426
44113CB00012B/1961